Human Resource Development

Human Resource Development

Theory and Practice

2nd Edition

Edited by

Jeff Gold, Rick Holden, Jim Stewart, Paul Iles and Julie Beardwell

palgrave

macmillan

First edition 2010
Second edition 2013
Published by PALGRAVE MACMILLAN

Palgrave Macmillan in the UK is an imprint of Macmillan Publishers Limited, registered in England, company number 785998, of Houndmills, Basingstoke, Hampshire RG21 6XS.

Palgrave Macmillan in the US is a division of St Martin's Press LLC, 175 Fifth Avenue, New York, NY 10010.

Palgrave Macmillan is the global academic imprint of the above companies and has companies and representatives throughout the world.

Palgrave® and Macmillan® are registered trademarks in the United States, the United Kingdom, Europe and other countries

ISBN: 978–0–230–36715–9

This book is printed on paper suitable for recycling and made from fully managed and sustained forest sources. Logging, pulping and manufacturing processes are expected to conform to the environmental regulations of the country of origin.

A catalogue record for this book is available from the British Library.

A catalog record for this book is available from the Library of Congress.

Contents

List of Figures

List of Tables

Notes on Contributors

Editors

Jeff Gold is Professor of Organisation Learning at Leeds Business School, Leeds Metropolitan University and Leadership Fellow at Leeds University where he coordinates the Northern Leadership Academy. He has led a range of seminars and workshops on leadership with a particular emphasis on participation and distribution. He is the co-author of *Leadership and Management Development, Strategies for Action* (with Alan Mumford and Richard Thorpe, 2010), and the fifth edition of his *Human Resource Management* (with John Bratton) was published in 2012.

Rick Holden is Visiting Research Fellow at Liverpool John Moores University's business school. Prior to joining Liverpool, Rick held academic positions at Leeds Metropolitan University and Newcastle College of Arts & Technology. His research interests include reflective practice, workplace learning and the graduate labour market and he has published extensively in these areas. He was the editor of the Emerald journal *Education & Training* for twenty years and chaired the 2005 International Conference on HRD Research and Practice across Europe. He is Vice Chair of the University Forum for HRD Research Committee and the Forum's web manager. Prior to moving into academia, Rick was a training manager for the Confectionery Division of Cadburys.

Jim Stewart is Professor of HRD at Coventry Business School, where he leads the research for the Department of HRM. He has held professorial appointments at Nottingham Business School and Leeds Business School. Jim has authored, co-authored and co-edited over twenty books on HRD and numerous book chapters, journal articles and conference presentations. His research has included projects funded and commissioned by the EU, ESRC, UK government and employers in all sectors of the economy. Jim is Chief Examiner (Learning and Development) for the CIPD and Chair of the University Forum for HRD.

Paul Iles is Professor of HRD at Glasgow Caledonian University. He is a chartered psychologist and a Chartered Fellow of the CIPD. He has published and made presentations on a variety of HRD issues, including leadership and management development, team building and organizational learning, career development, coaching, mentoring, organizational change and development, international and comparative HRD and, recently, talent management.

Julie Beardwell is Head of Department, Corporate Development, at Leicester Business School and is responsible for overseeing executive education and consultancy work with a range of corporate clients. She has over twenty years' experience of designing, leading and delivering programmes in HRM. Julie is also Chief Moderator, Standards for the CIPD, and is Chartered Fellow of the Institute.

Contributors

Michelle Blackburn is Senior Lecturer in Human Resource Management and Organisational Behaviour at Sheffield Business School, Sheffield Hallam University. She is Chartered Fellow of the CIPD, Fellow of the Higher Education Academy and Member of the British Psychological Society. Michelle has taught in the UK, Africa and India and, prior to becoming an academic, she has had over twenty years of experience as a Human Resource Consultant supporting both private and public sector organizations.

Dave Chesley is Senior Lecturer in HRM at Leeds Business School. He teaches on a range of undergraduate, postgraduate and professional programmes in the HRM/OB and Employee Relations field, and he supervises dissertations and management research reports. He is Lead Tutor for the IoD's People Mean Business module run through Leeds Metropolitan University.

Julia Claxton is Principal Lecturer in Leadership and Organisational Development at Leeds Metropolitan University and Director of the MA HRM NHS Programme. She has held academic positions for twenty years. Previous to that she was the first female Asda food hall manager, a training manager for an SME and the area training manager for a large enterprise. She has also managed and owned an SME employing ten people and co-owned a learning and leadership consultancy. She has developed bespoke learning, leadership and leadership learning programmes for a number of organizations (including the local government, the British Council, SMEs and charities). She has designed and run action learning-led programmes and initiatives for three decades. She teaches, supervises and examines PhDs, DBAs and Master level research work. She has published on leadership and learning, most recently on employee engagement.

David Devins is Principal Research Fellow at the Policy Research Institute at Leeds Metropolitan University with more than twenty years of applied research experience associated with national human resource development policy. He undertakes policy research for organizations such as the Department for Work and Pensions, local authorities, the UK Commission for Employment and Skills and private sector employers. His PhD explored the connection between national skills policy and SMEs. He has published widely, contributing to books and articles in a variety of academic journals, and he has presented papers at conferences around the world. His research interests include the role of HRD policies and practices in supporting social mobility and the development and evaluation of coaching initiatives to support management and organizational development in both large and smaller organizations.

Catherine Glaister has been Senior Lecturer at Leeds Business School since 2003. She teaches learning and development, leadership and management dvelopment and skills development modules on a range of postgraduate, professional and undergraduate programmes. She is Fellow of the CIPD and Member of the British Psychological Society. Prior to joining the business school, Catherine worked for ten years for BT as an HR practitioner in a variety of roles including learning and development, strategic HR and generalist HR.

Vivienne Griggs is Course Leader for the postgraduate diploma at Leeds Business School. She teaches courses specializing in learning and development and business skills. Prior to moving to academia ten years ago, Vivienne was an HR manager. She maintains a strong business focus through research and as an Employment Tribunal panel member.

Victoria Harte is a part-time lecturer at Leeds Business School in the School of HRM/OB and a full-time doctoral student at the University of Sheffield, within the Management School. She was the Research Officer within the Leeds Metropolitan Institute for Enterprise and subsequently the Human Resource Development and Leadership Unit within Leeds Business School before deciding to take up her PhD full-time.

Niki Kyriakidou is Senior Lecturer in HRM/OB with a doctoral and master's degree in human resource management and a bachelor's degree in political sciences and public administration. Niki's research interests revolve around international human resource management, leadership and career development. She has published in the areas of leadership and management, learning theories and practice, workplace learning, cross-cultural HRD, graduate employment, and managing human resources in the Middle East and Mediterranean region. She has also contributed to numerous book reviews in professional and academic journals, and she acts as reviewer and referee for a number of publishers and academic journals. She chairs the Career Development and the International Human Resource Management research committees of the Euromed Institute of Business.

Nehal Mahtab is Senior Lecturer and Course Leader for the BA (Hons.) Business and HRM at Leeds Business School. He teaches reward management, strategic human resource management, people resourcing and talent planning, performance management, fundamentals of HRM and skills development modules on various undergraduate, postgraduate and professional programmes. Prior to joining the Leeds Business School, Nehal worked for ten years at the University of Dhaka, Bangladesh, as faculty member and prior to that he worked with Standard Chartered Bank, Bangladesh, in the Central HR department.

Patrick McCauley is an HR specialist and fellow of the CIPD. Patrick has combined management consultancy and training with a successful academic career, most recently as Senior Lecturer in Human Resource Management at Leeds Metropolitan University.

Chitra Meade is Senior Lecturer in Organisational Behaviour at Sheffield Hallam University. She has completed her PhD from Leeds Business School on distributed leadership in self-directed teams. She is an academic member of the CIPD and Fellow of HEA.

Shakiya Nisa is Senior Lecturer in Human Resource Management and Organisational Behaviour at Leeds Metropolitan University. Shakiya is Associate Member of the CIPD who joined Leeds Business School in 2010. She teaches on the MA in HRM and MBA graduate programmes and on related undergraduate courses. Her main area of expertise lies in the emotional experience of HR practitioners in the changing world of work, including the area of work–life balance. Shakiya's recent research interests include postgraduate employment prospects of south Asian graduates and international HRM in India. Shakiya previously worked as an HR practitioner in the retail, banking and public sectors.

Helen Rodgers is Senior Lecturer in Human Resource Management at Leeds Business School. She gained her PhD at Kent University and researches in aspects of gender at work and strategic learning. She is the course leader for MSc Leadership & Change Management, which is delivered across a range of countries in Africa.

Joanna Smith is Head of the School of Human Resource Management and Organisational Behaviour at Leeds Business School. Joanna's research interests focus around reward management, learning and development and the management of people in the education and voluntary sectors.

Crystal Ling Zhang is Senior Lecturer in HRM and OB in Leeds Business School. She received her doctoral and master's degrees in HRM and OB from Leeds University Business School. Crystal's research interests are international human resource management, cross-cultural learning, career development for ethnic minorities and talent management in China. She has published in the area of learning theories and practice, cross-cultural HRD, graduate employment, global leadership, and managing HR in India and China. She is co-editing a book on international and comparative HRM for the CIPD. She teaches at the executive level in the UK, China and Africa and has also delivered the management development programme for Sinopec in China and MA HRM for NHS in the UK.

Preface to the Second Edition

Our first edition was published in 2010. What may not be immediately obvious from this statement is that most of the content was written in 2009 and some at least of the research and thinking to inform that writing done in 2008. So, there will be a gap of around five years between that period and when this second edition was written. Much has changed and some, or most, is reflected in the revised chapters. What though are the general themes and trends that make a second edition necessary and of value?

One factor of relevance is the now completed rollout of the revised Chartered Institute of Personnel and Development (CIPD) qualification scheme. As Stewart and Sambrook (2012) argue, it is noteworthy that those qualifications make little use of the term HRD. More noteworthy is that the CIPD Profession Map, which provides the basis for the qualifications, makes no mention at all of HRD. But, satisfying the knowledge requirements of CIPD membership is still most effectively and most commonly achieved through acquiring academic qualifications. So, an up-to-date learning and teaching resource such as this second edition will have value in those settings. This is especially the case since the CIPD qualification scheme and membership again recognizes undergraduate awards.

Financial crises and recession formed part of the background of our first edition. In 2012, that background is more of a foreground. The crisis in the Euro zone and additional revelations of less than ethical practices in the UK banking sector, with associated consequences for recovering financial confidence and stability and economic growth, mean that employing organizations face greater pressure in maintaining viability and employees face greater risk to their employment and careers. HRD becomes more and not less significant in those circumstances, despite arguments and actions suggesting the contrary.

An additional factor is the irresistible and ongoing impact of technological developments. This factor will continue to influence and shape the life and work experiences of all citizens of developed countries and increasingly those in less-developed states. Technology is not only continuously opening up new ways of designing and accomplishing work (location independent customer service and location independent workers for example), it is also continuously opening up and potentially democratizing learning opportunities to location independent individuals. This is without the possibilities that have yet to be derived from Web3 and 4G technologies.

Not all of these factors have directly changed content in all of our chapters. Contributing authors have updated, revised and improved their chapters as they themselves deemed fit and each factor is of more or less relevance to different topics and chapters. But, all chapters have been updated and revised. We are confident that has produced a more relevant and valuable resource, and one which is responsive to meeting the challenges suggested by the changing conditions identified here.

Second editions can be compared to parenting a second child. The joy, wonder and fear are all a little less intense. But those emotions are nevertheless experienced. As with a child, we take satisfaction and some pride in the success of our first edition and we hope this second edition proves worthy of a similar reception.

Jeff Gold, Rick Holden, Paul Iles, Jim Stewart and Julie Beardwell

March 2013

Acknowledgements

Chapter 17 of this book considers the future of HRD. We collaborated with a number of colleagues from HRD practice and various Universities to produce it, so our thanks go to:

Elizabeth Bailey	Intraining Ltd
Michelle Blackburn	Sheffield Hallam University
Julia Calver	Leeds Metropolitan University
Julia Claxton	Leeds Metropolitan University
Peter Cureton	Liverpool John Moores University
Sue Davison	ETCBIZ
Shirley Gaston	Azesta
Jane Gaukroger	The Change Academy
Sean Gilligan	Webanywhere Ltd
Catherine Glaister	Leeds Metropolitan University
David Gray	Surrey University
Patricia Harrison	Liverpool John Moores University
Iestyn Hughes	Royal Bank of Scotland
Chris James	Self Employed
Vanessa King	The Change Space
Matthew Knight	Leeds University
Aileen Lawless	Liverpool John Moores University
David Preece	Teesside University
Clare Rigg	Tralee Institute
Mike Rix	Mike Rix Consulting
Sue Sherwin	Leeds Metropolitan University
Tim Spackman	Skipton Building Society
Jim Stewart	Leeds Metropolitan University
Paul Tosey	Surrey University
Carolyn Ward	Teesside University
Gennia Cuthbert	Sunderland University
Liz Window	Morrisons Plc
Simon Barraclough	Hallmark Cards Ltd

Sarah Kelsey	Leeds Metropolitan University
David Devins	Leeds Metropolitan University
Conor Gilligan	Webanywhere Ltd
Sudi Sharifi	Salford University
Sue Warburton	Worldplay
Dean Horsman	Leeds Metropolitan University

Permissions

The author and publishers would like to thank the following for permission to reproduce copyright material:

SAGE for Figure 2.2 from Gubbins, C. and Garavan, T. (2009) 'Understanding the HRD Role in MNCs: The Imperatives of Social Capital and Networking', *Human Resource Development Review*, 8: 245–275.

Palgrave Macmillan for Figure 2.4 from Pettinger, R. (2002) *Mastering Employee Development* (Palgrave Macmillan: Basingstoke).

Vivienne Griggs, Rick Holden and Anthony Hanlon for HRD in Practice 3.4 from Griggs, V., Holden, R. and Hanlon, A. (2008) *HRD Within Leeds Irish Health and Homes: Interview with Ant Hanlon* (Leeds Metropolitan University: Leeds).

Center for Applications of Psychological Type for Figure 5.1 from Thorne, G. and Gough, A. (1999) *Portraits of Type* (Center for Applications of Psychological Type: Gainsville).

Elaine Hall for Table 5.1 from Coffield, F., Moseley, D., Hall, E. and Eccleston, K. (2004) *Learning Styles and Pedagogy in Post-16 Learning: A Systematic and Critical Review* (Learning and Skills Research Centre: London).

Steve Armstrong for Figure 5.2 from Armstrong, S. (1999) *Cognitive Style and Dyadic Interaction: A Study of Supervisors and Subordinates Engaged in Working Relationships* (Unpublished PhD thesis, University of Leeds).

Taylor and Francis for Figure 5.3 from Kolb, D.A., Boyatzis, R.E. and Mainemelis, C. (2001) 'Experiential learning theory: previous research and new directions', in R.J. Sternberg and L.F. Zhang (eds) *Perspectives on Thinking, Learning, and Cognitive Styles* (pp 227–247) and Figure 10.2 from Marsick, V.J. and Watkins, K. (1999) 'Envisioning new organizations for learning', in D. Boud and J. Garrick (eds) *Understanding Learning at Work* (Routledge: London).

Pearson Education for Figure 5.4 from Honey, P. and Mumford, A. (2006) *The Learning Styles Questionnaire* (Peter Honey Publications: Maidenhead) and Figure 12.3 from Miller, D. (2011) *Brilliant Teams* (Pearson Education: Harlow).

Canadian Medical Association for Figure 5.5 from Curry, L. (1983) 'Learning Styles in Continuing Medical Education'. *Learning Style Theories*, 1981, p 118. (c) Canadian Medical Association. This work is protected by copyright and the making of this copy was with the permission of the Canadian Medical Association (www.cma.ca) and Access Copyright. Any alteration of its content or further copying in any form whatsoever is strictly prohibited unless otherwise permitted by law.

Wilson Learning for Figure 7.2 from Leimbach, M. (2010) 'Learning Transfer Model: A Research-Driven Approach to Enhancing Learning Effectiveness', *Industrial and Commercial Training*, 42(1): 81–86

Chartered Institute for Personnel and Development for Figure 7.3 from Marchington, M. and Wilkinson, A. (1996) *Core Personnel and Development* (CIPD: London) and Figures 8.6 and 8.7a from Anderson, V. (2007) *The Value of Learning: A New Model of Value and Evaluation* (CIPD: London).

Taylor and Francis and Allen and Unwin for Figure 8.1 from De Vaus, D. (1993) *Surveys in Social Research* (Routledge: London).

Vivienne Griggs, Michelle Blackburn and Joanna Smith for Figure 8.7b from Griggs, V., Blackburn, M. and Smith, J. (2012) *The Educational Scorecard: The Start of our Journey,* Conference paper.

Strategic Business Insights for Figures 9.2 and 9.6 from Tronsden, E. (2003) 'eLearning in Financial Services: A Case Based Analysis', *SRI Consulting Business Intelligence.*

ACAS for Figure 9.3.

Balance Learning for Figures 9.4 and 9.5.

Infinite Spaces for HRD in Practice 9.5 Figure.

Macmillan Cancer Support for HRD in Practice 9.7 Figure.

Chartered Management Institute for Figure 11.2 from Marsick Mabey, C. (2005) *Management Development That Works: The Evidence* (London: Chartered Management Institute).

Oak Tree Press for Figure 11.6 from Thorpe, R., Gold, J., Anderson, L., Burgoyne, J., Wilkinson, D. and Malby, R. (2009) *Towards Leaderful Communities in the North of England, 2nd Edition* (Oak Tree Press: Cork City).

Belbin for Table 12.1.

The Law Society for Table 15.1 from http://www.sra.org.uk/solicitors/cpd/solicitors.page, accessed 6 May 2012.

UCAS for Figure 16.1.

Higher Education Careers Service Unit for Table 16.1 from *What Do Graduates Do?* 2011.

Peter Elias and Kate Purcell for Table 16.2 from Elias, P. and Purcell, K (2004) *Researching Graduate Careers 7 Years On* (Higher Education Careers Service Unit).

Hallmark for Figure 16.2.

Eurobarometer for Figure 16.3 from http://ec.europa.eu/public_opinion/flash/fl_304_sum_en.pdf

Emerald Group Ltd. for HRD in Practice 16.4 from O'Donnell, H., Karallis, T., Sandelands, E., Cassin, J. and O'Neill, D. (2008) 'Case Study: Developing Graduate Engineers at Kentz Engineers and Constructors', *Education and Training*, 50(5): 439–542.

The Financial Times for 2 Roger Beale illustrations.

Figures 2.3, 3.1, 5.6, 8.2, 11.1, 11.3 and 17.1 are reproduced under terms of the Open Government Licence v1.0.

Every effort has been made to contact all copyright-holders, but if any have been inadvertently omitted the publishers will be pleased to make the necessary arrangements at the earliest opportunity.

Introduction

HRD? Starting your journey

Think back to the end of the 2012 Olympics and Paralympics. Much media time was expended on 'what can we learn from the Olympics?'. This ranged from learning about the limits of human endeavour to learning about how to move and manage huge numbers of people without riots! We note the testimony of some of the volunteers and how this impacted upon them and their lives:

> 'I've pushed myself and learnt more about myself, I've cried, I've laughed and more importantly, I've been part of a team that helped make London 2012 the best games ever!!'

> 'We had a very tight and intense bond with the people we worked with. We knew we were contributing to something very, very grand, much bigger than us.'

Our point is this. From whatever perspective you view the Olympics, whether it be acknowledgment of the level of training and preparation for the competitors, the organization development required to make the games a success or the impact upon the country as a whole in terms of how they react to disability, human resource development (or HRD) was at the heart of such processes. Strip away the glitz, ignore the politics and every aspect of the Olympics and Paralympics was about HRD.

So what is HRD about? At one level, HRD might be considered as a subject to study, consisting of a body of knowledge to master and perhaps some skills to practise, just like any other subject. You may well think it is connected to other subjects like Human Resource Management (HRM). Indeed it is, and so, if you like the idea of adding something on the learning and development of people to your repertoire, HRD could be a good option.

However, we think it is more than just another subject, because HRD is not just concerned with particular knowledge and skills but it is integral to our own personal and professional development. So much of our lives, now and in the future, is tied to how we cope with a wide range of factors to which we all have to respond. For example, learning about a subject and gaining skills to get a qualification and make yourself employable as a graduate (Chapter 16: Graduates and Graduate Employability) are some of the main reasons for going into higher education. But, before any engagement with higher education you are likely to have learned a bewildering array of things (Chapter 5: Learning Theories and Principles). This will probably have included dealing with the latest tablet and smart phone technologies, working in some capacity or other, and getting on with a new set of colleagues. Socially, you will have learned what you like to do in your spare time and how best to have a laugh with your friends. A lot of the time you will have learned these things without realizing it and some of these skills will last you for the rest of your life (Chapter 15: Lifelong Learning and Continuing Professional Development). But, on a very different level, gaining a higher level qualification is very much part of how countries, internationally, view the skills needed to compete in a turbulent and fast-changing world (Chapter 1: The Scope of HRD and National HRD Policies and Practice).

Most people pursuing a higher education qualification expect to get a job, or progress to a position, which matches their abilities. The uniqueness of an interest in, and understanding of, HRD is its potential value to whatever work or activity you do on completing your course. Of course, different organiza- tions view HRD differently; some organizations value their employees and are more encouraging about their development than others(Chapter 2: Strategic HRD and the Learning and Development Function). If you find yourself working in a smaller business or a charity, for example, they are likely to have a relatively informal approach to HRD (Chapter 3: Contrasting Contexts of HRD Practice), compared to larger organizations where HRD is likely to be more formal, planned and evaluated (Principles of HRD,Chapters 6, 7 and 8). But, whatever it is called and however it is organized, HRD is a feature of each and every organization. Wherever you work much learning and develop- ment occurs as you tackle work issues and solve problems. Sometimes you will be aware of this learning, but most of the time it will all be part of just fitting in and doing your job(Chapter 10: Workplace Learning and Knowledge Management).

Part of the attraction of working in a large organization may be their recogni- tion of the talent of their workforce (Chapter 13: Talent and Career Development) and, as someone with high potential, you might expect to move into a talent pool. Whether you fulfil your potential will partly depend on your efforts, but also on the support you receive from managers and leaders, and how far they have learned to take such responsibilities seriously (Chapter 11: Leadership and Management Development). Your team, or group, membership will be impor- tant (Chapter 12: Teams and Team Development), as will the approach to cross- cultural issues and diversity (Chapter 4: Cross-cultural HRD; Chapter 14: HRD and Diversity) within the organization.

Finally, just as you have to become familiar with the latest information and communication technologies, so do many organizations try to keep pace (Chapter 9: E-Learning). However, more important is how such developments impact on the future of work and learning (Chapter 17: The Future of HRD).

We subtitled this Introduction 'Starting your journey'. The interesting thing about journeys is that people approach and tackle them differently. Contrast how we have taken you through the book in this Introduction with the Contents pages. There is no one, best way to engage with the book. Your journey into HRD may follow the order of the chapters as we have presented them in this book. Alternatively, it might be a more idiosyncratic journey reflecting your particular interests and engagement with the world of work. Whichever your approach, we do hope that this book will help you shape the future of how you work and learn.

looking **out:**

macro considerations of HRD

In this section we begin the HRD journey firstly by setting out the scope of HRD, dealing with its history, emergence and debates about its definition. We also consider how HRD features in national policy areas such as skills and qualifications (Chapter 1: The Scope of HRD and National HRD Policies and Practice). We then take a look at how HRD may or may not feature in strategic decisions within organizations and the part played by specialized staff who focus on learning and development within organizations (Chapter 2: Strategic HRD and the Learning and Development Function). Not all organizations are the same, so we consider how HRD works in such contexts as the public and voluntary/community sectors and small- and medium-sized enterprises (SMEs) (Chapter 3: Contrasting Contexts of HRD Practice). Finally, globalization requires more attention to working within and across cultures and preparing people to do this (Chapter 4: Cross-cultural HRD).

The Scope of HRD and National HRD Policies and Practice

Jim Stewart, Julie Beardwell, Jeff Gold, Paul Iles and Rick Holden

Chapter learning outcomes

After studying this chapter, you should be able to:

- Define the scope of HRD
- Debate the meanings associated with HRD theory and practice
- Explain different models of National HRD (NHRD)
- Understand the key features of vocational and educational training systems (VET)
- Apply a range of concepts in critically assessing HRD practice

Chapter outline

Introduction
The scope of HRD
Academic disciplines
Contexts of practice
Models of NHRD
Vocational education and training
Key debates and emerging themes
Summary

Introduction

This book examines the idea of Human Resource Development (HRD). A general approach throughout the book is to focus on theoretical and conceptual understanding as well as the application of that understanding in practice. HRD is an area of professional practice as well as a subject of academic enquiry. This first chapter is to look at the foundations of both. In other words, we will discuss the results of academic theorizing and the results of research into professional practice. To achieve this purpose we will consider HRD from both a practitioner and an academic perspective; identify the academic disciplines that have been drawn on to develop associated concepts and theories utilized within HRD; discuss the various contexts in which HRD is argued to be practiced, with a particular

3

focus on the national context; and finally, examine the current debates and emerging themes in HRD research. Human Resource Development (HRD) as a term is more commonly used in academic contexts than it is in professional practice (Sambrook & Stewart, 2005). In professional contexts, the words training and development, are more common and are sometimes combined with learning, especially in job titles. In fact, the Chartered Institute of Personnel and Development (CIPD), the professional body in the UK, uses the words Learning and Talent Development rather than HRD in the title of its professional standards specifying the knowledge and skill requirements of professional practitioners (Stewart & Rigg, 2011). It also titles its web pages as Learning, Training and Development. So we can see here an immediate difference and distinction between HRD as a subject of academic enquiry and as an area of professional practice.

This simple difference also allows us to make a more important point. This is that HRD is a human construct and does not have a settled and accepted meaning. Different meanings are contested and subject to debate and argument (see Hamlin & Stewart, 2011 for an analysis) and there is no definitive basis for deciding between the various arguments and positions. So, personal judgement, based on the best available evidence and a critical evaluation of arguments built on that evidence, is the final determinant of a position on HRD.

activity

Visit the CIPD's website – **www.cipd.co.uk/subjects/lrnanddev/** – then contrast the CIPD's website with those of the University Forum for HRD – **www.ufhrd.co.uk/wordpress/** – and the Academy of HRD – **www.ahrd.org**

We want you to exercise your personal judgement throughout this chapter and indeed throughout the book. The Reflective questions below, as with others in the book, are designed to help you to achieve the objectives set for the chapter. These questions support the application and exercise of personal judgement. You will need to engage with others for this activity, who can be a group of colleagues or a seminar/tutorial group of students.

reflective question

1 What reasons can you think of for the greater use of HRD in academic contexts compared to professional practice contexts?

2 What implications other than ambiguity and uncertainty arise from HRD being a contested term?

3 What criteria might you use in judging the validity of evidence and the logic of arguments on the meaning of HRD?

The scope of HRD

As with its meaning, there is also debate over the scope of HRD, fuelled by differing views on the origins of the term and its relationship with other concepts. Some argue that the origins of HRD can be traced to what is known as Organization Development (OD), which began in the USA sometime in the

1940s (Blake, 1995). Others, including Blake, attribute the first specific formulation to the American writer Leonard Nadler (1970) who defined HRD as:

> *organized learning experiences provided by employers, within a specified period of time, to bring about the possibility of performance improvement and/or personal growth* (quoted in Nadler & Nadler, 1989, p.4)

This definition has shaped continuing debates and controversies. For example, there seem to be two purposes attached to HRD in the definition. One is the possibility of improving performance, the other is concerned with bringing about personal growth. These two possible purposes are, however, the focus of disagreement between those who adopt what is known as a performative focus for HRD and those who adopt what is known as a learning focus (Rigg et al., 2007). We do not need to examine these debates here but for now just note that the term HRD is American in origin and emerged in common usage there sometime in the 1970s.

Adoption of the term HRD came later to Europe and the UK, where it did not really prove popular until the late 1980s and more particularly the 1990s. Two early UK references were in Mumford (1986) and Stewart (1989). A simpler debate than that seen in the USA occurred in the UK between Oxtoby and Coster (1992), later contributed to by Stewart (1992), and published in the professional journal *Training and Development*. This debate centred on the values inherent in referring to employees, and thus people, as resources and so debated the validity and utility of the term HRD. Themes similar to those raised by Oxtoby and Coster are still subject to scrutiny (see, for example, Kuchinke & Han, 2005; Hamlin & Stewart, 2011). More sophisticated debates have since grown in the UK, including that of Lee (2004), who argues against any attempt to define HRD on the basis that, in uncertain and unpredictable times, this would give 'the appearance of being in control' and 'serve the political and social needs of the minute' (p.38).

An additional continuing theme in HRD debates is that of the relationship of the term to longer established concepts such as Human Resource Management (HRM). This is a theme addressed early on by Stewart and McGoldrick (1996) and in their later work with Watson (McGoldrick et al., 2004). The term HRM became prominent in the UK from the late 1980s as a particular approach to managing people, again after earlier work in the USA. HRM is argued to be more strategic in its outlook than personnel management as a necessary response to globalization and the internationalization of technology through gaining the commitment of workers as a source of competitive advantage and increasing productivity (Bratton & Gold, 2012). HRD could be seen as a subset of the HRM movement, although we will argue it has become increasingly a movement in its own right.

Another ongoing theme on both sides of the Atlantic is the relationship of HRD with education, training and development. Part of that theme is to define each of the concepts so that each can be distinguished from the others. Stewart (1999) is not alone in suggesting that it is a futile debate but it does continue to fascinate some. A final continuing theme is differentiating HRD from Strategic HRD (SHRD). This too might be argued to be futile, especially since some writers distinguish HRD from training on the basis that HRD is strategic while training is operational (Stewart & McGoldrick, 1996). Others insist on a difference between HRD and SHRD, for example Walton (1999).

Many of the debates referred to above concern, and are informed by, different views on the way HRD theory and practice draw on established academic disciplines, so we will examine those possibilities in the next section. Before moving on, the following Activity will be useful in furthering understanding of the debates that have led to current views on HRD.

activity

Access two articles from the journals below, which will help to answer the following questions:

1 What is meant by the notion of performative perspectives of HRD?
2 What is meant by the notion of learning perspectives of HRD?
3 What are the key differences between the two perspectives?
4 What in your view are the main arguments in for and against each perspective?

Human Resource Development International – http://www.tandfonline.com/toc/rhrd20/current

Human Resource Development Quarterly – www.josseybass.com/WileyCDA/WileyTitle/productCd-HRDQ.html

European Journal of Training and Development – www.emeraldinsight.com/journals.htm?issn=0309–0590

Academic disciplines

Part of the debate about HRD concerns which academic disciplines are the most significant and influential (see McGoldrick et al., 2004). HRD is concerned with human behaviour, so disciplines concerned with understanding and explaining that behaviour are of some potential relevance to HRD (Stewart, 2007). These disciplines are referred to as the social sciences and include economics, politics, geography, sociology, social psychology, psychology and anthropology. Each of these is argued to have informed and influenced the development of theory and understanding of HRD.

Psychology and its variants, such as social psychology, are also seen as central to the development of HRD. This is because the latter is focused on changing behaviour through learning, and psychology has been central in the development of learning theories. Chapter 5 recognizes this and it is rare to find a textbook on HRD that does not include some discussion of learning theory. However, human behaviour, while in some senses always a phenomenon of individuals, occurs in social contexts. This raises the possibility that learning is as much a social as an individual process. Thus, social sciences such as social psychology, sociology and anthropology are also drawn on because of their contributions to understanding human behaviour in the context of human collectives. A specific example of recent and current topicality is the application of the concept of culture in organization studies. This concept was originally developed in anthropology in the study of tribes, communities and societies (Stewart & McGoldrick, 1996). Its relevance and application within HRD is because of an interest in applying the concept of culture to the study of work organizations and the association of HRD with such organizations, as suggested by Nadler's definition, given above.

There are those who argue that HRD is primarily, if not exclusively, concerned with human behaviour in the context of work organization. This argument in part supports the view that economics, and to a lesser extent politics, are also essential disciplines informing HRD theory and practice (McLean, 2004). An example of the application of economic theory is the notion of human capital, which seeks to explain as well as justify an investment in education and training (see Becker, 1964). A related economic concept is that of return on investment, which is often argued to be the gold standard of evaluating HRD activity (and see also Chapter 8). Politics is argued to be of relevance because of its central concern with the notion of power and how it can be exercised in human groups. Power is a key concept in OD and, as we saw earlier, OD is held to be a component of HRD. This is not the only reason though, as it is an axiom of organizations that power is essential to influence decision-making, especially in relation to resource allocation, so HRD practitioners need to understand these processes if they are to secure resources to support their work (Stewart & Rigg, 2011). Geography may seem the least likely social science relevant to HRD, and it certainly has not been as significant as the other disciplines discussed. However, with the theme of globalization now prominent, along with the economic and social problems facing groups, communities, regions, cities and nations, it would seem that geography is bound to become another source of understanding for those in HRD in future years (Marquardt et al., 2004).

This brief summary of academic disciplines suggests that HRD is not itself subject to independent theorizing or theory development. This view is not necessarily widely shared (Mankin, 2001) but it does have some support (Stewart, 2007). The summary also suggests that only the social sciences are of interest to HRD. This view is also open to challenge, since at least some of the natural sciences also have useful and relevant contributions to understanding human behaviour. This is perhaps most obviously the case with the natural sciences concerned with the development and application of evolutionary theory, for example zoology, ethology and biology. Little use has been made to date of the natural sciences, or the newer hybrid disciplines, in developing HRD but they may become more significant in the future. Similarly, there are those who would wish to see a greater influence of the arts and humanities in HRD. This is part of a wider concern about the apparent failure of business schools to provide ideas relevant to actual business practice. There is a claim that the need to conform to rigorous models of scientific research loses the connection to the realities of practice (Ghoshal, 2005). Thus, research into the practice of HRD can reveal the very human processes of talk, persuasion, use of rhetoric and storytelling in bringing about HRD activities and the valuing of such activities (Gold & Smith, 2003; Lawless et al., 2011).

Contexts of practice

So far we have examined the origins and underlying academic disciplines of HRD and found that debates in these areas are not easily settled. The same is true when we look at the contexts of HRD practice. The definition given earlier from Nadler illustrates this quite clearly. It specifically mentions and focuses on employers. An alternative definition provides a different view and different possibilities:

> HRD is constituted by planned interventions in organizational and individual learning processes. (Stewart, 2007, p.66)

This definition allows for several additional contexts. First, the term organization is not limited to those who engage in an employment relationship with individuals. Therefore, according to this definition, HRD can be, and is, practised by more than employers. An example might be charitable organizations that rely on voluntary workers rather than employees. Another might be purely voluntary organizations such as interest or community groups. These might include groups such as the Scout movement or local youth clubs. Second, the focus on planned interventions in individual learning processes opens up a wide range of possibilities. It might also be said to cover what happens in schools during compulsory education. A more widely held view is that HRD encompasses further and higher education, since these two contexts have a firm focus on planned interventions in individual learning processes (see, for example, Stewart & Knowles, 2003; Stewart & Harte, 2008). Stewart and Harte (2012) for example clearly view higher education as HRD practice.

This brief discussion illustrates a number of important points. First, the definition of HRD that is adopted will influence and shape the contexts in which HRD is understood to be practised. Second, professional practice may be both helpful and legitimate as the defining feature determining contexts. Thus, where professionals with expertise in developing human resources work and practise determines the contexts of HRD practice. Adopting this suggestion as a guiding principle would allow for those contexts suggested in this section but it would not stop debate. For example, many who work in higher education, although their job and title includes the word lecturer, would not necessarily see themselves as HRD practitioners and so would argue against such a label.

A final point to arise from the discussion of contexts of practice is that HRD has historically and traditionally been associated with training in work organizations and as a tool of management in that context, but as it has developed as an academic subject, the contexts of practice have been broadened to encompass arenas not previously seen as legitimate. We can now say with confidence that HRD occurs in informal as well as formal organizations, at national and perhaps supranational as well as organizational levels and, with the rise of personal coaching for example, also at individual levels outside organizational contexts, especially since individuals are increasingly encouraged to become lifelong learners (see Chapter 15).

reflective question

1 How do the academic disciplines drawn on in researching and theorizing HRD influence the definition and meaning of the term?
2 Based on your understanding so far of the meaning of the term HRD, which academic disciplines have been and are most significant in shaping current definitions and meanings?
3 How does the definition of HRD influence contexts of practice? Which contexts of practice do you consider to be legitimate and why?
4 To what extent do you consider university lecturers to be HRD specialists? Justify your answer.

Models of NHRD

HRD, at a national level, is now a crucial emerging consideration with a focus on government interventions in pursuit of national economic and social agendas. National HRD (NHRD) can be described as an approach to how a country views the contribution of skills towards its economic and social life, reflected in the policies and practices of the state and its agents and organizations. NHRD is a relatively new term but interest in the importance of HRD and its contribution to a country's development has important roots in models and theories of development economics (Wang, 2008). For over fifty years, policymakers have employed the language of economics in seeking to develop manpower plans to match the demand and supply of skills for the economy (Bennison, 1980). In theory, using notions of supply and demand and the measurement of variables should enable movement towards equilibrium within the market. Of course, equilibrium may not produce the desired level of skills utilization; indeed, a consequence may well be a low demand for skills or skills of low quality. Left to itself, the market for skills may fail. This so-called market failure can take two forms. First, there may not be enough incentive for employers to attract those with skills to work for them, and second, employers may not be willing to bear the costs of training (Booth & Snower, 1996). In either situation or both, governments may wish to intervene to address the market failure. How much intervention will vary from country to country and be strongly connected to the cultural and historical factors that are manifest in the political stances taken.

We can make a general distinction between voluntarism, where a government sees its role as encouraging organizations to take responsibility for skills acquisition and HRD, and interventionism, where governments seek to influence decision-making on HRD in the interests of the economy as a whole (Stewart & McGuire, 2012). More likely, there is a mix of the two approaches with a preference towards one, as shown in Figure 1.1.

One way this contrast becomes manifest in policy terms is whether governments should impose a training levy on organizations to be returned as a fund to support training and development. In France for example, since the 1970s a training levy has been imposed on organizations annually as a proportion of payroll. If an organization provides HRD, it receives a grant. The question

Figure 1.1 Voluntarism vs. interventionism in HRD

is whether this intervention has increased the amount and quality of HRD in French organizations. Research suggests that there has been an increase in training expenditure in French organizations (Greenhalgh, 2001). However, the downside has been an expensive system for administering the levies and grants, with the main benefits going to already trained mobile workers and training providers who have a ready-made market. These are just the sorts of criticism that led to the decline of the UK's levy system in the 1980s, as part of a move by the government towards a more voluntarist approach, which put more faith in decision-makers in organizations to invest in HRD and skilled employees.

activity

Work with a partner. Each person answers the question and then compare your findings.

What are the pros and cons of a training levy/grant system from the perspective of:

• governments
• employers
• citizens
• employees
• trade unions?

The choices to be made between voluntarism and intervention at a national level are a reflection of a country's social and cultural traditions. In many European countries, for example, there is a tradition of support for vocational education following compulsory schooling. The state provides support in the form of the infrastructure for Vocational Education and Training (VET), its regulation and funding. Acceptance of the degree of intervention and support can become politically acknowledged by all parties, so that over time, consensus is achieved between the key players of government, employers and labour organizations.

There are, however, key debates on how much intervention is needed or how much should be left to employers (see UKCES, 2009b). Human capital theory is concerned with ideas relating to the value in investing in people as a form of capital against which returns can be measured and assessed (Garrick, 1999). This can result in a narrow interpretation of HRD based on what is tangible and easily measurable. That is, HRD needs to show a return like other expenditures and can be seen as a cost rather than an investment. There is little place for consideration of attitudes, feelings or the development of potential that cannot be measured against short-term targets. Thus HRD can easily become trapped by the constraints of measurement, especially in SMEs, where research has shown that there is little time for anything other than operational activities, controlled by narrow bottom-line performance measures (Garengo et al., 2005).

Financial pressures have also contributed to what has been seen as the low-skills equilibrium in the UK, whereby the economy has been trapped in a cycle of low value-added, low-skills and wages, coupled with high employment (Wilson & Hogarth, 2003). The key ideas here, first advanced by Finegold and Soskice (1988), are that, under pressure to keep costs down, products can be specified in low-skills terms, and 'other things being equal, the lower the specification, the lower the skill intensity of the production process... [and therefore] the lower demand for skill' (Wilson & Hogarth, 2003, p.viii). The apparent equilibrium is impervious to requests to increase skills levels, which provides a signal to the labour market of low-skills requirements, and simultaneously constrains a move in the direction of higher skills because there is a lack of a well-educated and trained labour force (Keep, 1999). Therefore, even when there are reported skills deficiencies or gaps, it is quite possible that there remain low skills. Bloom et al. (2004, p.12) talk about a 'latent skills gap', where organizations can accept and adjust to low-skill requirements, losing awareness of the restriction this imposes.

The challenge therefore is for organizations to break out of the low-skills equilibrium, and embrace high performance working in high-performing firms where skill development is focused on performance and learning is continuous and integrated into work (Sung & Ashton, 2005). High Performance Working (HPW) and its connection with high skills provides a link to the idea of developmental humanism, where managers become more concerned with empowering employees through learning and skill development – a strong contrast to human capital theory. In many organizations, it is recognized that the key ingredient in products, and especially in services, is the knowledge of the employees – the owners of intellectual capital acquired through their training and, more importantly, through their interaction with a network of customers, suppliers and each other. Recent evidence suggests that key HR practices such as training, sharing information and self-managed teams improve an organization's learning capability, which strongly influences the link between high performance work and overall organization performance (Camps & Luna-Arocas, 2012). In the UK, there has been strong interest in what are referred to as economically valuable skills which are associated with high skilled workers in areas such as the professions, management and professional roles (UKCES, 2010).

NHRD policy may be faced by extremes and polarization between high- and low-skill work practices. The crucial dilemma in NHRD between voluntarism and interventionism underpins some of the emerging models of NHRD identified by Cho and McLean (2004). One extreme form of interventionism would be a centralized model, imposed top down from central government, sometimes backed by a collectivist ideology as in China, or as a feature of centralized plans as in Mexico. The danger here is a squeezing out of private sector initiative and entrepreneurship, or the deadweight of administration and duplication as in France. The alternative decentralization, or free-market model, leaves decisions on HRD to market forces, perhaps with some stimulus and persuasion from the government. Between the extremes are various efforts to gain the benefits of voluntarism and interventionism. The UK, the USA and Australia all seek to provide an infrastructure for the supply of skills but, to varying degrees, expect the market for skills to be demand led from employers, where historical and cultural constraints may play a key role. European countries such as Austria, Germany and the Czech Republic take a more corporatist approach, seeking to generate agreement between the key stakeholders of government, employers and trade unions. Between, and perhaps above, the demand-led and corporatists models lie the tiger economies with a matchmaking model (Green et al., 1999), who seek to reconcile the dilemma of intervention and voluntarism by the intelligent use of forecasting data at government level to guide the supply infrastructure, and persuade and stimulate the demand for skills from organizations within the context of high growth and high skills aspirations. Thus, the matchmaking model is less to do with choosing between voluntarism and intervention or manpower planning, and more to do with a consistent approach in developing institutions to supply skills based on forecasts of global economic developments, and simultaneously to influence demand towards high performance production.

There is also another angle on centralization and decentralization, where responsibility for policies is shared between a central or federal government and regions, states or devolved authorities, for example in the USA, Australia and the UK. There are also efforts to move from one model towards another. For example, countries like the Czech Republic have sought transition from a centralized model towards a less interventionist corporatist model, as illustrated in HRD in Practice 1.1:

NHRD in the Czech Republic

HRD in Practice 1.1

NHRD in the Czech Republic is driven by the requirement to better align the vocational training system with labour market needs – particularly foreign-owned businesses – and increase the supply of skilled workers. The Czech economy relies heavily on immigrant labour, associated in part with high levels of Foreign Direct Investment (FDI), which requires higher level and different skills than those available in the local labour market:

Several reforms have been introduced to address this issue, modelled on lessons learned and policies adopted in other EU member states, particularly the UK:

- Vocational curriculum reform – focusing more on delivering skills and outcomes relevant to the labour market, including transferable skills
- Introduction of a National Qualification Framework (NQF) to specify standards of qualification and assessment, which involves partial as well as full qualifications

- Introduction of a national career framework, to indicate employers' skills needs across different job roles
- Sector councils established, involving employers and other organizations in the design of new curricula
- Introduction of approved assessors to separate training provision and assessment/verification of qualifications
- Establishment of HRD advisory councils in each region.

These reforms have been designed and implemented mainly through EU funding. There is little political will to commit state funds to education, with the Czech Republic allocating a relatively low proportion of its GDP to the education budget. EU funding is finite, so one of the critical factors is the extent to which a country will be prepared to sustain funding for reforms when EU investment comes to an end.

reflective question

1 Who do you think has most responsibility for ensuring a supply of skilled labour: government, employers or individuals?
2 What are the reasons for your answer?

Vocational education and training (VET)

As we can see from this analysis of NHRD, governments have a key role to play in establishing and supporting a vocational, education and training infrastructure composed of a variety of agencies, departments and processes working together as a system. Historically and culturally, it is crucial that the VET system is accepted as credible in terms of numbers and especially quality, indicated by the qualifications available and the standard of achievement. Qualifications often serve as a measurement by proxy of the supply of skills in an economy, and this process of equating skills with qualifications is referred to as credentialism. There are some doubts as to the validity of this process (Fuller & Unwin, 1999). Nevertheless, qualifications provide a currency for a VET system, with debates about the value of one qualification process against another and considerations about who has the credentials to practise in an occupational area. For example, in many areas of professional work, restrictions on those who can practise are set by professional bodies such as the Law Society. In the UK, there are more than 400 professional bodies, although not all of them can control entry to professional practice. In other areas of work practice, there have been restrictions in the UK since the Statute of Artificers (1563), which made it a requirement to gain an apprenticeship to work in various crafts.

reflective question

1 What are your credentials?
2 Do your qualifications, or those you are studying for, prove your ability to use certain skills?

The configuration of the VET system involving institutions, responsibilities and provision of resources will, of course, vary from country to country. In many countries, and nowhere more so than in the UK, it is something of a moving landscape, the exact profile regularly being changed and revised by the government of the day. This said, there are common features, as shown in Figure 1.2, and there is also evidence of attempts to bring consistency and compatibility between countries. For example, in the European Union (EU), under the Copenhagen Declaration (EC, 2003), the member states have begun a process to develop:

- A single framework for transparency of competencies and qualifications
- A system of credit transfer for VET
- Common criteria and principles for quality in VET
- Common principles for the validation of non-formal and informal learning
- Information for lifelong guidance.

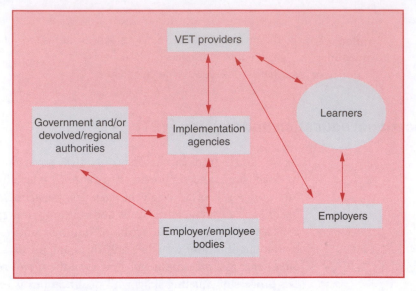

Figure 1.2 Configuration of VET systems

We suggest that the main outcomes of a VET system are an educated and trained workforce. This may be measured by qualifications, although much training at work does not lead to qualifications. We have already examined the possible NRHD models that inform policymaking at government and/or devolved authority and regional levels. Policies are implemented by agencies which may also provide funding for supporting and stimulating VET activities. Included among the agencies are those providing the framework and quality assurance for qualifications. Employer bodies attempt to give employers a voice to inform the working of the system and the standards required in qualifications. Employee bodies such as trade unions can also play a crucial role in ensuring that employees receive resources for HRD. While much HRD is provided by employers for learners in the crucial areas of youth development and adult learning, VET is supported and funded through providers. This includes institutions such as schools, universities and further education colleges, but also a large number of private providers. In the following section, we will consider the working of the VET system in the UK in more detail. As a final point here, it is worth noting that NHRD is another example of the debate and lack of consensus within the field of HRD. The term VET for example is preferred by many and Wang (2008) argues there is no need for the term NHRD as what it refers to is more accurately described as national policy on human development (HD), with HD being a longer established and more widely accepted concept.

activity You might like to learn more about the EC's VET approaches by going to http://ec.europa.eu/education/lifelong-learning-policy/vet_en.htm

The UK's VET system

The UK's VET system is informed by the demand-led model of NHRD. The role of government and its agents has been to improve the training infrastructure, providing support and funding where market failure is identified. While we will focus mainly on what are now seen as the policies of England, there are links to the policies of Wales, Scotland and Northern Ireland.

activity

For more details of skills strategy in Scotland, go to www.scotland.gov.uk/Topics/Education/skills-strategy/overview. The Welsh Assembly's Education and Skills page is wales.gov.uk/topics/educationandskills/?lang=en, and for Northern Ireland, go to www.delni.gov.uk/index/successthroughskills.htm.

A crucial feature of the infrastructure has been the development of a National Qualification Framework (NQF) based on vocational qualifications (VQs). Such qualifications are work related and can include National Vocational Qualifications (NVQs, or SVQs in Scotland) and awards such as Higher National Diplomas and Certificates (HND/C). In addition, so as to show the links between qualification levels and frameworks, a Qualifications and Credit Framework has been set up. This framework has nine levels, starting at Entry Level to Level 8. Learners can consider the demands that would be placed on them at each level. There is also a Framework for Higher Education Qualifications that shows the levels of degrees, doctorates and so on. However, the failure to link vocational qualifications to, and integrate them with, higher education and professional qualifications as well as to most schools is regarded as one of the weaknesses of the UK's framework which prevents responsiveness in innovation (Lester, 2011).

activity

Go to www.ofqual.gov.uk/qualifications-assessments/89-articles/145-explaining-the-qualifications-and-credit-framework for details of the Qualifications and Credit Framework.

How is it regulated? What is meant by Units as building blocks of qualifications?

NVQs cover most occupational areas and are work related by specifying the required outcomes expected in the performance of a task in a particular work role. Performance can be assessed against criteria or standards to achieve an NVQ. Skills and knowledge are reflected in the performance and achievement of an outcome. NVQs are organized into five levels of competence from 'competence that involves the application of knowledge in the performance of a range of varied work activities, most of which are routine and predictable' (level 1) to competences that involve the application of a range of fundamental principles across a wide and often unpredictable variety of contexts plus substantial personal autonomy and responsibility (level 5).

Each NVQ is based on the definition of National Occupational Standards (NOS) for occupational areas and purports to describe the performance of a competent person, including what is regarded as best practice. This requires some connection to what employers see as competent performance, which is achieved by the development and maintenance of NVQs by employer bodies. The number of NVQ certificates awarded provides an indicator of progress in the skill levels of the population. The Leitch report (2006) set targets for raising achievement in skill levels, aiming for 90 per cent of adults to have at least a level 2 qualification, a shift in balance towards level 3 intermediate skills, with 500,000 people a year in apprenticeships and 40 per cent of adults to have a level 4 or 5 qualification, equivalent to higher education.

While competence-based NVQs are now well established, criticism continues to be levelled at the meaning of competence used that emphasizes outcomes against standards. Many organizations in the UK now use NVQs as the basis of their skills training, as shown in HRD in Practice 1.2.

HRD in Practice 1.2

Morrisons announces its dedication to staff training

Supermarket chain Morrisons has announced that it is dedicated to developing workers and providing them with careers, not just jobs. The company revealed that it is taking steps to improve its NVQ training scheme. It claimed that it has always had a 'commitment to nurturing its people'.

However, it said a new initiative within the company would provide workers with a 'clear and direct path to progress' throughout the business. Under the new programme, workers will be able to increase their skills and gain qualifications such as NVQs. Through a 13-week course, members of staff can pick up a level 2 NVQ certificate in retail.

Skills training at a number of different levels will be available to employees with a clear five-step career ladder laid out for those looking to progress within the organization. This is based on the NVQ training and qualifications workers obtain, with the top rung of the ladder reserved for those who achieve an NVQ level 5, which is the equivalent of a foundation degree.

Source: Adapted from **www.learndirect.co.uk/businessinfo**

NVQs have not been without criticism. There have been persistent doubts that the NVQ framework has the support of employers (Raggatt & Williams, 1999) and it is claimed that qualifications give less attention to the importance of knowledge and understanding and providing support for developing skills (Grugulis, 2003). For example, the standard set for level 2 may simply be too disconnected from the requirements and values of employers who pursue improvement and growth (Gold & Thorpe, 2008). Wolf (2011) argued that low level NVQs have little use or value in the labour market but such qualifications are often taken by large numbers of 16–17 year olds.

One frequent criticism is that NVQs lack the rigour of academic qualifications such as GCSEs, A levels and degrees. This is a reflection of the cultural and historical tradition in the UK of separating thinking and doing; it has created what is usually termed the academic/vocational divide. Some attempt has been made to extend the NQF to show equivalence between academic and vocational qualifications. Thus an honours degree is equated with a level 6 NVQ and a Masters degree with a level 7 NVQ. In addition, following the Tomlinson report in 2004 and the *14–19 Education and Skills* White Paper in 2005 (DfES, 2005), the government set out to reform the school curriculum, including providing better vocational routes. This included the development of 14–19 diplomas in vocational areas which relate more closely to vocational skills and accommodate employment-based training through apprenticeships. While not always popular, such diplomas are being used in newly formed university technical schools, or UTS, which use industry backing from organizations such JCB and BT to focus the curriculum on specialized skills such as engineering. Further UTS are due to open in the next few years, so watch their progress at http://www.utcolleges.org/.

The development of 14–19 diplomas was seen as part of a broader concern with weaknesses in the UK supply of intermediate skills. Such skills have been traditionally related to craft skills acquired by serving an apprenticeship. In the 1980s, apprenticeships in the UK declined dramatically along with craft-based manufacturing. Rising unemployment among young people resulted in a youth training scheme but this was never seen as a replacement for apprenticeships and was regarded as a low standard qualification (Steedman et al., 1998). By contrast, countries such as Germany retained their apprenticeship systems, combining academic and technical skills with guidance from work experience, resulting in higher numbers of skilled workers (Grugulis, 2002).

The failure to provide sufficient numbers of apprentices in the UK is also a cause of the apparent skills gaps, filled in recent years by workers arriving from the EU. As a response, since the mid-1990s, and as part of the 14–19 reforms, there has been an attempt to recreate a golden pathway to intermediate skills from basic skills through level 2 to 3, by the introduction of a framework of work-based training that leads to apprenticeship status. Apprenticeships are delivered by a combination of work-based and off-site training, undertaken by work-based learning providers and further education colleges. In 2005, the Apprenticeships Task Force (2005) reported that apprenticeships do improve business performance and cost-effective training, along with better retention of staff. However, not all employers see the value of apprenticeships, with many preferring to upgrade the skills of existing employees (Lewis et al., 2008). There can also be a tension between learning theory (usually in a college) and doing the work, requiring apprentices to satisfy two different sets of expectations for success (Sligo et al., 2011). In addition, because what happens in the workplace is crucial in apprenticeships, there are bound to be variations in culture affecting the depth and breadth of opportunities for learning, including the chance to participate in skilled practices (Fuller & Unwin, 2003).

activity

Read more about apprenticeships at **www.apprenticeships.org.uk**/.

The VET policy in England is implemented through a range of institutions throughout the country. It is characterized by a lack of consistency, in that changes are fairly frequent and there are swings between the extent to which institutions operate at regional, sub-regional and local authority levels. Over recent years the responsibility for policy implementation has moved from the Learning and Skills Council (LSC) to the Skills Funding Agency and a National Apprentice Scheme.

Changes in the supply infrastructure are one thing, but for the VET system to work there has to be a response from employers and, in the UK, this response remains voluntary. There is a desire to make the UK a world leader in skills but this requires 'ambitious employers' (UKCES, 2009a) who provide work requiring 'economically valuable skills' (UKCES, 2010). This means that employers have a choice about how much they invest in HRD activity, and it seems that many choose to minimize costs. Even in organizations that take strategic management seriously, HRD can still remain a subsidiary issue (Coleman & Keep, 2001), with costs kept low despite recent evidence of the role of learning capabilities in high performance working (Camps & Luna-Arocas, 2012), This can leave a production process bound by a low product specification with an impact on the demand for skills (Green et al., 2003). How skills are understood and defined in an organization is a central concern in NHRD. Felstead et al. (2002), for example, point to the different uses of the word skill:

1 competence to carry out tasks successfully
2 the idea of hierarchical skill levels that are dependent on the complexities and discretions involved
3 the view that there are different types of skill, some generic and applicable in diverse work situations, and some specific and vocational and suitable for particular contexts.

The last point raises another key issue, regarding the extent to which skills can be regarded as generic and can therefore be provided as part of a VET system and preparation for work, or whether skills learned in the context of their use are more valued, in which case organizations need to take more responsibility. This remains a serious issue of contention in the UK (Payne, 2004). Recent surveys in England suggest that, in the midst of a recession, skills shortages are relatively small (Shury et al., 2010) but over a longer term, there could be significant demand for highly skilled work in areas such as the professions, technical roles, management and leadership, intermediate areas such as manufacturing and engineering and care work. Interestingly, there is also likely to be a persistence in low-skilled work (UKCES, 2010).

Trade unions could play a role within organizations to raise the profile of skills. Under the 2002 Employment Act, recognition can be granted to union learning representatives, who can promote the value of training and learning, including an analysis of training needs, advice to members and the arrangement of events for training and learning. They can also consult with employers on issues concerning members' training and learning, and are entitled to receive paid time off so they can be trained to carry out the role, attending courses with their union in order to acquire the skills to analyse needs and negotiate with employers (Lee & Cassell, 2004). Union Learn seeks to help unions to become learning organizations, to broker learning opportunities for their members and research union priorities on learning and skills. Research suggests that the Union Learning Fund (ULF) can help establish joint workplace training committees between unions and employers that improves trust during a recession (Stuart et al., 2010).

activity

Read more about Union Learn at **www.unionlearn.org.uk** and the Union Learning Fund at **http://www.unionlearningfund.org.uk/**. Examine the ULF toolkit and consider its use in managing learning projects.

Another source of possible stimulation, and one that certainly attempts to move skills and HRD into business plans, is the Investors in People (IiP) award, which has been operating since 1991. IiP provides a set of standards for training and development against which organizations can be assessed and reassessed on an agreed basis. It has survived with some revisions, the most recent being a more focused approach, using IiP criteria against business priorities chosen by the organization. It has been copied in countries such as Australia, Germany and France (Bell et al., 2004) and has now been extended to over 20 countries. Evidence suggests that using the IiP standard can help to provide a framework for HRD and HRM policy generally, increase investment in skills and can impact on performance and employee engagement (Tamkin et al., 2008; Bourne et al., 2008). IiP also enhances management capability which can improve performance (Bourne & Franco-Santos, 2010). The findings suggest that for IiP to work in terms of performance improvement, it is important to integrate HR policies so that key links are recognized, for example skills development with promotion and remuneration. One possibility, recognized for some time, is that those that do IiP are already performing well, so have least to gain by using it (Down & Smith, 1998). In addition, IiP could create a distinction between employee groups who are favoured in terms of training and those that are not, creating what Hoque (2008) refers to as 'training apartheid'.

activity

Form a group of three. Each person should visit the IiP home page – www.investorsinpeople.co.uk – allocate tasks as follows and report back on findings:

1 One person should examine 'How it works' and find examples of benefits
2 One person should explore 'Your Journey' and find out about assessment
3 One person should examine 'Tools and resources' and consider some of the case studies.

Awards such as IiP can play a significant role in providing a language to talk about HRD and this can lead to action. This is part of what Gold and Smith (2003) refer to as the 'learning movement', where positive talk about HRD and skills can become self-fulfilling. It also features the positive orientation of decision-makers about HRD and those who judge the results. However, central to the process were those who continued the positive talk as persuaders of others – this is not easy and requires stubbornness and good skills in nego-tiation and argument. Without these, and support from senior managers, HRD talk can easily be relegated behind other sorts of talk. Needless to say, there also needs to be a close examination of what kinds of products and services are being designed that require higher skills or lower skills.

Key debates and emerging themes

This chapter has shown that there are a number of areas of debate within HRD as both a field of academic enquiry and professional practice. These can be summa-rized as follows:

- Defining and attaching meaning to the term HRD
- The possibility of theorizing HRD
- The significance, role and impact of various established academic disciplines in HRD theorizing
- The responsibility of governments and employers to raise national skill levels.

Some of these debates have been engaged in since the emergence of the term HRD, for example defining and attaching meaning to the term. Some are more recent and are still, to some extent, emerging themes, for example the possibility of theorizing HRD, which has, in chronological terms, actually emerged after early attempts to produce theories of HRD (see Gold & Stewart, 2011 for a series of articles on this topic). This final section will identify a number of additional emerging themes in HRD debates.

The first theme is that of HRD in the development of small- and medium-sized enterprises (SMEs). Debates here centre on at least two factors. The first is the extent to which HRD is practised in SMEs and the extent to which HRD theorizing has taken enough account of the different and variable contexts of small organizations (see Stewart & Beaver, 2004). The second factor is that of SME development in the sense of supporting and facilitating the establishment of new businesses and social enterprises. The key question here is what, if any, role is there for HRD and HRD practitioners in that process, especially in light of the growing consensus that learning and development in SMEs are best considered as informal processes (CBI, 2003) and that SMEs are considered crucial for job creation in the future (Ellis & Tailor, 2011)?

A second emerging theme for debate is the value of adopting more precise foci for HRD research and practice, such as sector, function or method. Examples of the first of these include the public as opposed to the private sector, or even more specific sectors within that (see, for example, Sambrook & Stewart, 2007). An example of the second is Leadership Development which has in recent years attracted a good deal of research by HRD academics and specialization by HRD professionals. The third focus can be illustrated by a profusion of both research and practice interest in coaching for talent development as a method within HRD. All these varying foci and examples raise the question of whether HRD is different, and therefore worthy of special attention, in different sectors or functions or when particular methods are adopted. This is not a question to be addressed in this chapter, but it is one that a full reading of the book may at least help to answer.

The third emerging theme and area of debate is the relationship between HRD and other foci of academic research and professional practice. We have already mentioned the relationship with HRM but there are others such as Learning Organization, Organizational Learning and Knowledge Management. All these share similarities with HRD, in that they have emerged as terms used in academic contexts, have their own academic and professional journals and also are applied in practice with people holding jobs in work organizations with those or similar words used in their titles. The main issue is that the terms focus both academic enquiry and professional practice on the same social practices as does HRD (Stewart & McGuire, 2012). The questions that arise therefore concern the differences and similarities with HRD.

The final emerging theme and area of debate is the most recent and is referred to as critical HRD (CHRD). This focus has emerged partly in response to the rise of critical management studies, although some of the themes addressed in CHRD, such as ethics, have a longer history than critical management as an area of debate (see, for example, Stewart, 1998; McGoldrick et al.,

2004). CHRD questions the traditional and taken-for-granted assumptions of the purpose, nature, application and activities of HRD and raises issues to do with legitimacy, power, control and the economic and social context of HRD theory and practice. The term CHRD became established in several academic conferences of the late 1990s and early 2000s and has led to a number of special editions of journals (Trehan et al., 2004, 2006) as well as edited collections in books (Elliott & Turnbull, 2005; Rigg et al., 2007). CHRD does not represent a separate and particular strand in HRD research and practice, but provides alternative perspectives that can, and do, inform mainstream HRD theory and practice.

summary

○ HRD is a recent and abstract human construct and does not have a settled and accepted meaning. Different meanings are contested and subject to debate and argument.

○ There is a key debate among HRD professionals and academics between those who adopt a performative focus for HRD and those who adopt a learning focus.

○ HRD is concerned with human behaviour and so disciplines in the social sciences concerned with understanding and explaining that behaviour are of some potential relevance to HRD.

○ HRD is not restricted to work organizations and there has been growing interest in the practice of HRD in a range of contexts such as charities and voluntary contexts.

○ At a national level, HRD is now a crucial emerging consideration, with a focus on government interventions in pursuit of national economic and social agendas.

○ The approaches adopted to NHRD vary but with sufficient similarity and purpose that they can be classified on a continuum between voluntarism and interventionism.

○ The main outcomes of a VET system are an educated and trained workforce. This may be measured by qualifications, although much training at work does not lead to qualifications.

○ The UK's VET system is informed by the demand-led model of NHRD. The system is characterized by frequent changes with respect to the unit of implementation.

○ A crucial feature of the VET infrastructure has been the development of a National Qualification Framework (NQF) and a Qualifications and Credit Framework based on national vocational qualifications (NVQs, or SVQs in Scotland).

○ There have been attempts to create a pathway to intermediate skills from basic skills, by the introduction of a framework of work-based training that leads to apprenticeship status.

○ For the VET system to work, there has to be a response from employers, and in the UK, this response remains voluntary. There is a desire to make the UK a world leader in skills but this requires ambitious employers.

○ There are a number of emerging themes in HRD such as the development of small- and medium-sized enterprises (SMEs), the value of adopting more precise foci for HRD research and practice and the emergence of Critical HRD, which questions the traditional and taken-for-granted assumptions of the purpose, nature, application and activities of HRD.

discussion questions

1 What does the term HRD mean to you?

2 How would you differentiate HRD from training and development in work organizations? How does HRD relate to the term HRM?

3 How far should NHRD polices relate to economic and social wellbeing?

4 Is a high skilled, high productivity workforce possible?

5 What are the key features of a successful VET system?

6 Which of the emerging themes within HRD research are the most important and why?

further reading

references

Bosch, G. and Charest, J. (eds) (2010) *Vocational Training: International Perspectives*. London: Routledge.

Smith, A. (2006) Engagement or irrelevance? HRD and the world of policy and practice. *Human Resource Development Review*, **5**(4): 395–99.

Swanson, R.A. (2001) Human resource development and its underlying theory. *Human Resource Development International*, **4**(3): 299–312.

Wang, G. and Swanson, R. (2008) The idea of national HRD: an analysis based on economics and theory development methodology. *Human Resource Development Review*, **7**(1): 79–106.

Apprenticeships Task Force (2005) *Final Report*. London: Apprenticeships Task Force.

Becker, G.S. (1964) *Human Capital*. New York: National Bureau of Economic Research.

Bell, E., Taylor, R. and Hoque, K. (2004) *Workplace Training and the High Skills Vision: Where Does Investors in People Fit In?* Warwick: Centre for Skills, Knowledge and Organizational Performance (SKOPE).

Bennison, M. (1980) *The IMS Approach to Manpower Planning*. Brighton: Institute of Manpower Studies.

Blake, R. (1995) Memories of HRD. *Training and Development*, **49**(3): 22–8.

Bloom, N., Conway, N., Mole, K., Moslein, K., Neely, A. and Frost, C. (2004) *Solving the Skills Gap*. London: Advanced Institute of Management.

Booth, A.L. and Snower, D.J. (1996) Introduction: does the free market produce enough skills? In A.L. Booth & D.J. Snower (eds) *Acquiring Skills: Market Failures, Their Symptoms and Policy Responses*. Cambridge: Cambridge University Press.

Bourne, M., Franco-Santos, M., Pavlov, A., Lucianetti, L., Martinez, V. and Mura, M. (2008), *The Impact of Investors in People on People: Management Practices and Firm Performance.* Berkhamstead: Cranfield University.

Bourne, M. and Franco-Santos, M. (2010) *Investors in People, Managerial Capabilities and Performance.* Berkhamstead: Cranfield University.

Bratton, J. and Gold, J. (2012) *Human Resource Management: Theory and Practice.* Basingstoke: Palgrave Macmillan.

CBI (Confederation of British Industry) (2003) *Informality Works: A New Approach to Training for SMEs*. London: CBI.

Camps, J. and Luna-Arocas, R. (2012) A matter of learning: how human resources affect organizational performance. *British Journal of Management,* **23**(1): 1–21.

Cho, E. and McLean, G.N. (2004) What we discovered about NHRD and what it means for HRD. *Advances in Developing Human Resources*, **6**(3): 382–93.

Coleman, E. and Keep, E. (2001) Background literature review for PIU project on workforce development, research paper for the Performance and Innovation Unit. London: Cabinet Office.

DfES (2005) *14–19 Education and Skills*, White Paper. London: Department for Education and Skills.

Down, S. and Smith, S. (1998) It pays to be nice to people. *Personnel Review*, **27**(2): 143–55.

EC (2003) Enhanced Co-operation in Vocational Education and Training. Brussels: European Commission.

Elliott, C. and Turnbull, S. (eds) (2005) *Critical Thinking in Human Resource Development*. London: Routledge.

Ellis, C. and Tailor, D. (2011) The role of enterpreneurs and SMEs in driving the recovery. *BVCA Research Article*. Available at http://ssrn.com/abstract=1875764, accessed 25 June 2012.

Felstead, A., Gallie, D. and Green, F. (2002) *Work Skills in Britain 1986–2001*. London: Department for Education and Skills.

Finegold, D. and Soskice, D. (1988) The failure of training in Britain: analysis and prescription. *Oxford Review of Economic Policy*, **4**: 21–53.

Fuller, A. and Unwin, L. (1999) Credentialism, national targets, and the learning society: perspectives on educational attainment in the UK steel industry. *Journal of Education Policy*, **14**(6): 605–17.

Fuller, A. and Unwin, L. (2003) Learning as apprentices in the contemporary UK workplace: creating and managing expansive and restrictive participation. *Journal of Education and Work*, **16**(4): 407–26.

Garengo, P., Biazzo, S. and Bititci, U. (2005) Performance measurement systems in SMEs: a review for a research agenda. *International Journal of Management Reviews*, **7**(1): 25–47.

Garrick, J. (1999) The dominant discourse of learning at work. In D. Boud and J. Garrick (eds) *Understanding Learning at Work*. London: Routledge.

Ghoshal, S. (2005) Bad management theories are destroying good management practices. *Academy of Management Learning and Education*, **4**(1): 75–81.

Gold, J. and Smith, V. (2003) Advances towards a learning movement: translations at work. *Human Resource Development International*, **6**(2): 139–52.

Gold, J. and Stewart, J. (2011) Theorising in HRD: building bridges to practice. *Journal of European Industrial Training*, **35**(3)

Gold, J. and Thorpe, R. (2008) Training, it's a load of crap: the story of the hairdresser and his suit. *Human Resource Development International*, **11**(4): 385–99.

Green, F., Ashton, D., James, D. and Sung, J. (1999) The role of the state in skill formation: evidence from the Republic of Korea, Taiwan and Singapore. *Oxford Review of Economic Policy*, **15**(1): 82–96.

Green, F., Mayhew, K. and Molloy, E. (2003) *Employer Perspectives Survey*. Warwick: Centre on Skills, Knowledge and Organizational Performance.

Greenhalgh, C. (2001) Does an Employer Training Levy Work? The Incidence of and Returns to Adult Vocational Training in France and Britain, Research Paper 14. Oxford: Centre on Skills, Knowledge and Organisational Performance.

Grugulis, I. (2002) Skills and Qualifications: The Contribution of NVQs to Raising Skills Levels, Research Paper 36. Warwick: Centre on Skills, Knowledge and Organizational Performance.

Grugulis, I. (2003) The contribution of national vocational qualifications to the growth of skills in the UK. *British Journal of Industrial Relations*, **41**(3): 457–75.

Hamlin, R. and Stewart, J. (2011) What is HRD? A definitional review and synthesis of the HRD domain. *Journal of European Industrial Training*, **35**(3): 199–220.

Hoque, K. (2008) The impact of Investors in People on employer-provided training, the equality of training provision and the 'training apartheid' phenomenon. *Industrial Relations Journal*, **39**(1): 43–62.

Keep, E. (1999) Employer Attitudes Towards Adult Learning, Skills Task Force Research Paper 15. London: Department for Education and Employment.

Kuchinke, K.P. and Han, H.-Y. (2005) Should caring be viewed as a competence? (Re)opening the dialogue over the limitations of competency frameworks in HRD. *Human Resource Development International*, **8**(3): 385–89.

Lawless, A., Sambrook, S., Garavan, T. and Valentin,C. (2011) A discourse approach to theorising HRD: opening a discursive space. *Journal of European Industrial Training*, **35**(3): 264–75.

Lee, B. and Cassell, C. (2004) Electronic routes to change? a survey of website support for trade union learning representatives. *International Journal of Knowledge, Culture and Change Management*, **4**: 701–11.

Lee, M.M. (2004) A refusal to define HRD (pp.27–40). In M.M. Lee, J. Stewart & J. Woodall (eds) *New Frontiers in Human Resource Development*. London: Routledge.

Leitch, S. (2006) Prosperity for All in the Global Economy – World Class Skills. London: HM Treasury.

Lester, S. (2011) The UK qualifications and credit framework: a critique. *Journal of Vocational Education and Training*, **63**(2): 205–16.

Lewis, P., Ryan, P. and Gospel, H. (2008) A hard sell? The prospects for apprenticeship in British retailing. *Human Resource Management Journal*, **18**(1): 3–19.

Mankin, D. (2001) A model for human resource development. *Human Resource Development International*, **4**(1): 65–85.

Marquardt, M., Berger, N. and Loan, P. (2004) HRD in the Age of Globalization: A Practical Guide to Workplace Learning in the Third Millennium. New York: Basic Books.

McGoldrick, J., Stewart, J. and Watson, S. (eds) (2004) *Understanding Human Resource Development: A Research Based Approach*. London: Routledge.

McLean, G. (2004) National Human Resource Development: what in the world is it? *Advances in Developing Human Resources*, **6**(3): 269–75.

Mumford, A. (ed.) (1986) *Handbook of Management Development*. Aldershot: Gower.

Nadler, L. (1970) *Developing Human Resources*. Austin: Learning Concepts.

Nadler, L. and Nadler, Z. (1989) *Developing Human Resources*. San Francisco: Jossey-Bass.

Oxtoby, B. and Coster, P. (1992) HRD: a sticky label. *Training and Development*, **10**(9): 31–2.

Payne, J. (2004) *The Changing Meaning of Skill, Issues Paper 1*. Warwick: Centre on Skills, Knowledge and Organizational Performance.

Raggatt, P. and Williams, S. (1999) Government, Markets and Vocational Qualifications: An Anatomy of Policy. London: Falmer.

Rigg, C., Stewart, J. and Trehan, K. (2007) *Critical Human Resource Development: Beyond Orthodoxy*. Harlow: FT/Prentice Hall.

Sambrook, S. and Stewart, J. (2005) A critical review of researching human resource development: the case of a pan-European project (pp.67–84). In C. Elliott & S. Turnbull (eds) *Critical Thinking in Human Resource Development*. London: Routledge.

Sambrook, S. and Stewart, J. (2007) HRD in health and social care (pp.3–14). In S. Sambrook & J. Stewart (eds) *Human Resource Development in the Public Sector*. London: Routledge.

Shury J., Winterbotham M., Davies B., Oldfield K. and Constable S. (2010) *National Employer Skills Survey*. Wath-upon-Dearne, UK: Commission for Employment and Skills.

Sligo, F., Tilley, E.N. and Murray, N. (2011) Do apprentices' communities of practice block unwelcome knowledge? *Education + Training*, **53**(4): 297–309.

Steedman, H., Gospel, H. and Ryan, P. (1998) *Apprenticeship: A Strategy for Growth*. London: Centre for Economic Performance.

Stewart, J. (1989) Bringing about organisation change: a framework. *Journal of European Industrial Training*, **13**(6): 31–5.

Stewart, J. (1992) Towards a model of HRD. *Training and Development*, **10**(10): 26–9.

Stewart, J. (1998) Intervention and assessment: the ethics of HRD. *Human Resource Development International*, **1**(1): 16–22.

Stewart, J. (1999) *Employee Development Practice*. London:FT/Pitman.

Stewart, J. (2007) The ethics of HRD (pp.59–77). In C. Rigg, J. Stewart & K. Trehan (eds) *Critical Human Resource Development: Beyond Orthodoxy*. Harlow: Prentice Hall.

Stewart, J. and Beaver, G. (eds) (2004) *HRD in Small Organisations: Research and Practice*. London: Routledge.

Stewart, J. and Harte, V. (2008) Enterprise Education and Its Impact on Career Intentions, Paper Presented at the 9th International Conference on HRD Research and Practice Across Europe. Lille: IESEG School of Management, 21–23 May.

Stewart, J. and Harte, V. (2012) Evaluating enterprise education: issues in current practice. *Education + Training*, **54**: 259–339.

Stewart, J. and Knowles, V. (2003) Mentoring in undergraduate business management programmes. *Journal of European Industrial Training*, **27**(3): 147–59.

Stewart, J. and McGoldrick, J. (1996) Human Resource Development: Perspectives, Strategies and Practice. London: Pitman.

Stewart, J. and McGuire, S. (2012) Contemporary developments in Human Resource Development. In Stewart, J. and Rogers, K. (eds) *Developing People and Organisations*. London: Chartered Institute of Personnel and Development.

Stewart, J. and Rigg, C. (2011) *Learning and Talent Development*. London: Chartered Institute of Personnel and Development.

Stuart, M., Cook, H., Cutter, J. and Winterton, J. (2010) *Assessing the Impact of Union Learning and the Union Learning Fund: Union and Employer Perspectives*. Leeds: Centre for Employment Relations Innovation and Change, University of Leeds.

Sung, J. and Ashton, D. (2005) High Performance Work Practices: Linking Strategy and Skills to Performance Outcomes. London: DTI.

Tamkin, P., Cowling, M. and Hunt, W. (2008) *People and the Bottom Line*. Brighton: Institute of Employment Studies.

Trehan, K., Rigg, C. and Stewart, J. (2004) Special issue on Critical Human Resource Development. *Journal of European Industrial Training*, **28**(8/9): 611–24.

Trehan, K., Rigg, C. and Stewart, J. (2006) Special issue on Critical HRD. *International Journal of Training and Development*, **10**(1): 4–15.

UKCES (2009a) *Towards Ambition 2020: Skills, Jobs, Growth*. London: UK Commission for Employment and Skills.

UKCES (2009b) *Review of Employer Collective Measures*. London: UK Commission for Employment and Skills.

UKCES (2010) *Skills for Jobs: Today and Tomorrow*. London: UK Commission for Employment and Skills.

Walton. J. (1999) *Strategic Human Resource Development*. London: FT/Prentice Hall.

Wang, G. (2008) National HRD: new paradigm or reinvention of the wheel? *Journal of European Industrial Training*, **32**(4): 303–16.

Wilson, R. and Hogarth, T. (eds) (2003) Tackling the Low Skills Equilibrium: A Review of Issues and Some New Evidence. London: DTI.

Wolf, A. (2011) *Review of Vocational Education*. London: Department of Education.

chapter 2

Strategic HRD and the Learning and Development Function

Jim Stewart, Jeff Gold, Rick Holden and Helen Rodgers

Chapter learning outcomes

After studying this chapter, you should be able to:
- Explain the meaning of Strategic HRD (SHRD)
- Explain the key ideas informing an HRD strategy and policy
- Understand the link between change and HRD
- Assess the role of the learning and development (L&D) professional

Chapter outline

Introduction
SHRD and HRD strategy
HRD and change
The learning and development function
Summary

Introduction

Even before the recession, in a prescient view, the Leitch (2006) review of skills spoke of 'lingering decline' and a bleak future if we did not increase our skills. As the recession continued, the Chairman of the UK Commission for Employment and Skills, Charlie Mayfield (also Chairman of the John Lewis Partnership) highlighted the challenge for UK employers:

> Economic renewal in this decade will be a long haul, and to be sustainable must be powered by the skills and entrepreneurship of people up and down supply chains in different sectors of our economy. Developing skills is not a separate agenda, but an intrinsic part of securing growth and prosperity for the UK. It is central to the Commission's vision for a more dynamic demand led approach to skills as a source of competitive advantage for the UK economy. (UKCES, 2011, p.2)

We notice various aspects of this view. Firstly, and obviously, the linking of skills to economic renewal, but this is never a simple link. Secondly, skill development should not be considered as a separate issue but is vital for growth and prosperity for the country and competitive advantage for organizations. But then comes the crucial point; it requires a demand-led approach and this has to come from employers. Elsewhere the UK Commission makes similar linkages when it talks of the need to find 'ambitious employers' (UKCES, 2009) who provide work requiring 'economically valuable skills' (UKCES, 2010). In the meantime, however, recession did arrive and stayed and surveys suggested that training budgets were being reduced and the number of hours training received by staff were also being cut (CIPD, 2012).

The linking of skills to economic prosperity and competitive advantage suggests that HRD needs to be considered strategically by governments, organizations and individuals. Indeed, it is suggested that the move to make HRD more strategic provides a clear signal that learning and development are important. It has been shown to provide the crucial link between high-performance working, based on high-level skills and high discretion in work performance and decision-making (ILO, 2000) and organization performance (Camps & Luna-Arocas, 2012). Through learning by employees, organization strategy itself can be transformed. There are some important implications in making HRD more strategic (Bratton & Gold, 2012):

1 Staff are recruited for skilled work that will require learning and change
2 Staff are expected to relearn and retrain with attention to continuous learning
3 HRD emphasizes investment in people rather than training as a cost, allowing a longer term perspective on outcomes and value-added
4 Managers are involved and take responsibility for talent development (see Chapter 13)

In this chapter, we will seek to explore the connection between Strategic HRD (SHRD) and the HRD function.

SHRD and HRD strategy

Attaching the word strategy to organization functions is now so common that it is in danger of becoming meaningless. The word itself is associated with its own function of strategic management, which in these terms is seen to be a central part of general and senior management; for example a function of chief executives, managing directors, chief operating officers and other similar titles. It is also associated with the specialist and non-specialist contributions to organization management of top and senior functional managers, especially those with responsibility for finance, operations and perhaps marketing. The concern of top and senior managers with strategy follows from the history and development of the concept, which is mainly the application of economic theory to long-range planning and the long-term survival and prosperity in economic terms of business and commercial organizations. As with any and every other aspect and function of management, strategy has seen developments in theory and practice through academic research and academic and practitioner writing and publications.

In conventional terms, strategic management is concerned with ensuring the long-term survival of organizations. The key outcome of strategic management is a set of strategies that are themselves plans, programmes and activities and the resource allocations to support them. Strategies are based on an analysis of external and internal factors and a matching process to ensure that the organization continues to be successful, especially in relation to formulating and achieving appropriate organizational-level performance goals and objectives in the face of competition from other organizations operating in the same markets. While this is of some value, it is a limited perspective on the meaning of strategy. What emerges from it for HRD is a view that top managers set out a vision and mission for an organization and develop organization or corporate goals and strategy from which are derived business strategy and then functional strategy, including a strategy for HRD. This suggests a linear and static process, where fixed plans for HRD are formulated to contribute to the achievement of the business strategy, which in turn contributes to the achievement of the corporate strategy.

reflective question

1 Can there be a linear connection between organization strategy and HRD strategy and planning?
2 What are the reasons for your answer?

The logic of the orthodox understanding of strategic management and strategy is that HRD strategy is impossible in the absence of corporate and business strategy and that the purpose of HRD strategy is to support, or serve, business strategy. Stewart and McGoldrick (1996) adopted a different view of the strategic management process, which allows for a more proactive and processual contribution from HRD. In their nonlinear model of the strategy process, the focus is first on what they refer to as the strategic direction of a given organization. This suggests the possibility of differences between what actually happens in practice in relation to long-term survival and what was and is determined and planned by top and senior managers. Stewart and McGoldrick go on to argue that strategic direction is the result of the interplay of a number of internal factors, the most significant of which are culture, leadership, the commitment of employees, and the approaches and responses to changed and changing internal and external conditions. They further argued that HRD in theory and practice has a major influence on each of these factors:

- shaping organizational culture
- developing current and future leaders
- building commitment among organization members
- anticipating and managing responses to changed conditions.

Thus, HRD is a strategic function as it has a significant impact on long-term survival. This view has been supported by the work of Fredericks and Stewart (1996), who examined the connection between strategy and HRD from a processual rather than a functional perspective and argue that there are clear and mutually influencing relationships between organization structure (internally facing), organization strategy (externally facing), the actions and behaviours of organization members, management/leadership style and HRD policies and practices. So both pieces of work suggest that HRD is in and of itself strategic, since its practices have an impact on long-term survival.

SHRD

The previous points raise the question of whether there is any place for the concept of SHRD. If, as suggested above, HRD is by definition strategic, is there a need for and can there be any meaning attached to the concept of SHRD? Many would argue such a need and therefore a distinction between HRD and SHRD, prominent among them Garavan (1991, 2007), McCracken and Wallace (2000) and Walton (1999). Early work on SHRD by these authors adopted the conventional view of strategic management as being a long-term planning function in the hands (or perhaps brains) of top and senior managers. More recent work, summarized and applied by Garavan (2007), attempts to integrate both functional and processual perspectives on strategy to argue a meaning and space for SHRD. He defines SHRD as a 'coherent, vertically aligned and horizontally integrated set of learning and development activities which contribute to the achievement of strategic goals' (p.25). This view of SHRD suggests continuing responsiveness to organizational strategy and various components of it, including the strategies and goals of business units or departments, workforce plans and change programmes and problems and issues that require an HRD response such as compliance with regulations, waste and inefficiency and cost reductions (Mayo, 2004). Thus HRD proves it can create value by being business-led.

However, it also argued that such responsiveness in pursuit of strategic alignment makes HRD part of an agenda to achieve efficiency and outcomes and this is not easy to realize. Research by Anderson (2009) found that alignment required a great deal of iteration between managers and HRD practitioners requiring both formal and informal discussions. HRD practitioners need to involve themselves in 'dialogue and bartering' (p.275) but this also could enable an influence on strategic thinking. A related view of SHRD makes use of what is referred to as the resource-based view of strategy, which concerns how an organization's internal capabilities enable it to compete. Such capabilities can lead to superior performance and, crucially, are based on what people learn as part of their work and interactions with each other, customers and suppliers. Over time, these become core competencies. Clardy (2008) argues that HRD practitioners are in a good position to identify such competencies through their work with employees on skills, attitudes, knowledge and actions. As they do so, they can contribute more significantly to strategic plans. The idea that strategy can emerge from the interactions of employees fits nicely with Mintzberg et al.'s (1998) notion of a Learning School of strategy where 'real learning takes place at the interface of thought and action, as actors reflect on what they have done' (p.195).

activity

1 Go to Henry Mintzberg's home page at www.mintzberg.org
2 Explore his views on leadership, strategy and MBAs
3 How can students contribute to strategy in their colleges?

If SHRD can include emergent aspects of an HRD practitioner's work it provides significant opportunities. Viewing the organization as a site for work-place learning (see also Chapter 10), it is possible that new ideas for action can come from many sources. In particular, where work is knowledge-intensive, such as in professional firms, e.g. lawyers, learning from often complex and varied daily events can benefit the organization. However, as Watson and Harmel-Law (2010) found in a Scottish law firm, there is a need for support from managers and senior staff and contextual factors such as income generation targets need to considered as a possible constraint.

HRD strategies and plans

Despite the uncertainties over SHRD, it is nonetheless useful to apply the concept of strategy in relation to HRD practice. In common with Stewart (1999), we adopt here a meaning in common usage, that an HRD strategy is a course of action intended to have long-term rather than short-term impact on significant rather than marginal areas of performance at organizational rather than individual level. Intentions are formed and articulated through plans, which are necessary to justify budgets. As we know from recent surveys (CIPD, 2012), such budgets are under pressure and so plans need to relate clearly to adding value.

The particular course of action will also have been arrived at through a series of decisions resulting from analyses of external as well as internal factors and be intended to directly contribute to matching organizational capability to changed and changing market conditions in order to achieve competitive advantage. If the particular organization in question does not operate in a market and so does not have competitors, the purpose will be related to what-ever conditions affect long-term survival, for example satisfying funding and political stakeholders in the case of a public or quasi-public sector organization such as a university.

reflective question

1 For any organization in which you are currently located, what should be the purpose of HRD strategy?
2 What are the conditions that affect long-term survival?

So HRD strategies and plans appear as programmes and activities that make a contribution to long-term survival. Clearly in the last few years there have been many uncertainties for many organizations, including global competition and reduced spending by governments and consumers. While HRD budgets may also suffer, there are opportunities to plan and organize HRD strategies and integrate them into the organization (Tseng & McLean, 2008) so long as emergent learning can also be captured.

Cultural change programmes around, for example, developing high levels of customer service through attitudes and values as well as knowledge and skills are a clear example of an HRD strategy. Others commonly include leadership and/ or talent management programmes designed and intended to ensure a sufficient quantity and quality of future senior and top managers over a 5-, 10- or 20-year period. Here quality usually refers to a set of behavioural descriptors that reflect and express organizational values so as to ensure consistency and continuity in managerial and leadership style. Programmes to support the development of particular organizational forms, such as a learning organization (see Chapter 10), can also be described as HRD strategy. The use of the word support here is significant. HRD strategies are commonly components in a range of programmes and activities designed and intended to bring about the kinds of changes implicit in these examples. Other components will usually include related HR strategies in, for example, employer branding in support of recruitment and selection, job and work design, employee reward and performance management. These HRD and HR strategies will in turn be linked with business strategy. HRD in Practice 2.1 illustrates how the investment in learning and development by McDonald's shows a clear link between HRD and organizational goals and success.

McDonald's: learning and development award winner

HRD in Practice 2.1

According to its website learning is an integral part of the McDonald's culture. Winner of the HR Excellence Award for The Best L&D Strategy in 2009 and voted one of the UK's top employers for the last five years, strategic HRD is at the heart of McDonald's efforts to drive its business growth and enhance its image as an employer.

Commenting on the company's development of strategic HRD David Fairhurst, Senior Vice President and Chief People Officer, says the first step was to determine what staff qualities McDonald's needed in order to grow the business. Fairhurst calls these qualities the 3 Cs – Committed People, Competence, and Confidence. Next step was to ask their employees what they valued about working at McDonald's. The company calls these emerging values the 3 Fs – Family & Friends (everyone feels part of the team), Flexibility (work fits into lifestyle) and Future (growing and progressing by learning skills). The challenge, said Fairhurst, was to create a fusion between the 3 Cs and the 3 Fs.

McDonald's has an L&D strategy for each employee group: crew members; restaurant management teams and franchisees; and office staff and middle managers.

Training of crew members happens on the shop floor and in other settings. 94 per cent of McDonald's business managers begin their careers flipping burgers. For restaurant management teams and franchisees, the recent focus has been on flexible and field-based training. Other initiatives include a service leadership programme and an extended hours workshop. The former, designed to improve staff confidence, raised McDonald's mystery diner score by 2.5 per cent. The latter was developed to help managers prepare for a change to trading hours in certain restaurants.

The results for McDonald's have been dramatic. Increased staff engagement has halved crew turnover, from 80 per cent (2004) to 38 per cent (2010). Today McDonald's UK continues to grow at a tremendous rate, with 18 quarters of consecutive growth and 5,000 new jobs created over the past year. Judges at the 2009 Awards noted how the company's L&D was linked to the business plan ... business performance owing much to the success of this strategy.

Source: **www.hrmagazine.co.uk** and **www.britainstop employers.co.uk**

Designing and implementing programmes that meet the characteristics described here are not the only contribution of HRD practice. Other programmes and activities will need to be designed, implemented and conducted. They may not have long-term impact or be focused on significant aspirations and ambitions but they will nevertheless constitute an important contribution. We might signal the difference by the term plan rather than the word strategy. HRD plans will then be concerned with shorter time horizons, usually a year, and will cover a number and range of programmes and activities. The focus of these programmes and activities will be operational and intended to ensure that the day-to-day work of the organization can be accomplished. Examples might include:

- programmes to train new starters to replace staff losses as a result of labour turnover
- programmes to develop knowledge and skills associated with some new technology or system
- programmes to develop better team work
- programmes of supervisory or management development to prepare individuals for promotion in the immediate or short-term.

Another useful way of distinguishing between HRD strategies and plans is to apply the notions of maintenance and change. These have been applied to HRD practice for many years and one example is the work of Fredericks and Stewart (1996) referred to above. The basic idea is that HRD maintenance programmes and activities are intended to keep the organization as it is, and effective and efficient at what it currently does. This is achieved by HRD plans. In contrast to this, HRD change programmes are designed and intended to make the organization different and develop it to be able to do new and different things effectively and efficiently. This is achieved by HRD strategies. We will examine the application of this notion later in the chapter when we look at the connections between HRD and organizational change.

Perhaps another issue for consideration is whether HRD strategies have been too responsive to the taken-for-granted ideas and practices in organizations and may have contributed to difficulties during the global financial crisis of the late 2000s. If HRD plays a support role to business strategy, it can easily become distracted from long-term considerations, including impact on society and communities, in its formation of HRD strategies and programmes. It is argued therefore (MacKenzie et al., 2012) that HRD can seek to play a more proactive, strategic role by helping managers and leaders reflect more critically on assumptions that underpin the status quo in a process of strategic learning. It is important to focus on critique to avoid simply reinforcing assumptions that maintain the status quo (Starbuck et al., 2008).

HRD policy

HRD policy is different from both strategy and plans. As we have seen, these last two concepts are applied to programmes and activities: what HRD professionals do. Policy is a concept used to describe the framework within which decisions about programmes and activities are taken and which guides those decisions and their implementation. So policy is a set of principles that govern decisions and actions (Stewart, 1999). Such principles are not universal givens, however; they have to be determined and thus are a matter of human choice and decision. We will now describe a common process of determining policy as well as common features and content of HRD policy.

When looking at determining policy, it is as well to recognize that the process is not always, and does not have to be, a formal or deliberate process. Policy, like strategy, can emerge as the cumulative result of ad hoc processes and decisions. Whether the result of formal and planned processes or an emergent and evolving process, there will be a number of factors influencing the formulation and content of HRD policy. These include:

External factors:

- Government policies and programmes
- Technological developments
- Social conditions, for example demographics and norms
- Competitor and stakeholder actions.

Internal factors:

- Organizational history and traditions
- Structure and culture
- Levels of management support
- Current performance and expected future performance
- Other organizational policies, especially related HR policies.

This list is taken from Stewart (1999) and he makes the important point that the factors do not operate separately and independently of each other. They all interact with, and influence the impact of, each other in complex processes that are hard to identify. One consequence of this is that even when policymaking is planned and formalized, it will always be an iterative process. As well as being influenced by the factors identified above, policymaking will also be influenced by the preferences, interests and needs of a variety of different groups involved in determining policy. These commonly include:

- Senior managers
- HRD professionals
- Trade unions representatives if present
- Other professional staff, especially HR and financial officers.

The specific content of any HRD policy will reflect the particular influence of the factors and groups identified here and how they interact.

Another set of factors is concerned with the range of opportunities that are available in an organization for learning, both formal and informal which form what is referred to as a learning pattern (Govaerts & Baert, 2011) or learning system. Such patterns are related to the culture, history, structure and design of work in an organization and can become accepted and embedded over time. For example, some staff in a professional firm of architects may come to expect opportunities for their Continuing Professional Development or CPD (see also Chapter 15). Other staff, such as receptionists in the same firm may expect fewer formal opportunities, although they may well share informal opportunities. What is important is how an understanding of learning patterns can underpin the HRD policy that is formed. Further, in many organizations such as small and medium-sized enterprises (SMEs), HRD policy is likely to be less formal and less in evidence and learning patterns are strongly related to everyday working (see also Chapter 3).

Formal HRD policies will commonly comprise a written statement of principles informing and shaping decisions in relation to a range of HRD applications. These will normally include the following:

- A statement of purpose and objectives
- A statement of priorities
- Roles and responsibilities of various groups and parties, for example senior managers, line managers, HRD professionals and individual employees
- Cost allocation policy and process
- Place of and access to records
- Application of policy to various different categories of employees
- Application of policy to various different approaches to and types of HRD practice, for example educational programmes and other forms of external development versus internal programmes.

It will be clear that there are connections between the concepts discussed so far. There is a need for some level of consistency and congruence between strategy, plans and policy. But this is not always the case in practice, since practice is not a matter of the simple application of theory or logic, organizations are much messier than that.

activity

1 Go to www.stobartgroup.co.uk/careers/the-academy/group-learning-and-development-policy where you will find the Group Learning and Development Policy for the Stobart Group.

2 How does the policy relate to the various learning patterns that are likely to exist in this company?

HRD and change

The formation of strategies in organizations of whatever kind have an inevitable link to change. Strategies are often a response to perceived change in the environment but they also set in motion desired changes within the organization. We know that the rate of change is never constant (Tushman et al., 1986) and that the effects of change can be studied over different timescales and at different levels – individual, group or team, department, whole organization, societal, national and international. In recent years, we can see how the turbulence in the world has forced change of some kind at all levels. Some of the change could be understood as part of a long-term trend, such as the need for carbon reduction, but others have been surprises, raising the need for what Micic (2010) calls Future Management.

In organizations, change is not always seen as an HRD issue, and whether change links to HRD depends on the various ways in which those who make strategy see learning as a key response. Gold and Smith (2003) found that some managers saw the need for change in terms of HRD as a principal component. In addition, it becomes possible for HRD specialists to have a role as facilitators or change agents in ensuring that change can be managed and provide learning opportunities for others (McCracken & Wallace, 2000).

Types of change

It is not unusual to suggest that change and learning are the same thing. Certainly there seems to be a connection but we feel it is important to maintain some separation. We can think of some examples where change occurs but no one learns in terms of developing new skills or gaining knowledge, for example the installation of new equipment or a new procedure. We can also find examples of people finding new possibilities for change that emerge from their learning at work. The latter possibility has been increasingly recognized as a source of new knowledge gained by individuals and shared with others, which can be captured for change in the whole organization, but which can so easily be missed by managers (Bartlett & Ghoshal, 1997).

One thing that is clear – not all change is the same. Here we can make use of a distinction suggested by Hayes (2010) between incremental and transformational change. We present this as a dimension, as shown in Figure 2.1.

Incremental change occurs over a period of time but on a regular and continuous basis. However, such changes may hardly be noticed except that people are 'doing things better' through a process of 'tinkering, adaptation and modification' (Hayes 2010, p.24). There is a link between change and continuous improvement and this is sometimes formalized in continuous improvement teams (CITs) and the Japanese Total Quality Management (TQM) principle of Kaizen. This approach to change is connected to Toyota's lean manufacturing system, where changes for kaizanimprovement are identified and implemented quickly by those closest to the work (Wall, 2005). As small changes accumulate over time, it might be possible to identify some kind of transformation.

activity

Kaizen is a development from TQM and you might like to explore some of the tools available to help people learn about improvement at work. Go to **http://uk.kaizen.com/ kaizen-tools.html**. Which of these tools could be used in your work?

One of the features of incremental change is that there is less difficulty, or hassle, in making the changes identified (Buchanan & Boddy, 1992), whereas transformational change is considered to be a disturbance to the present and the creation of new dynamics that requires a break with the past. Rather than doing

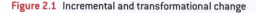

Figure 2.1 Incremental and transformational change

things better, the key question is: what can be done differently? For example, a manufacturing engineering company that shifts its purpose towards a design company because of the cost of manufacturing clearly makes a choice to change the path of its future development rather than remain in manufacturing.

How people in organizations understand the need for change also provides a close connection to the forms of learning suggested by Argyris and Schön (1978). First, single-loop learning is concerned with detecting errors and correcting them. There is no opportunity to challenge how things are done but incremental changes become possible. By contrast, there is double-loop learning, which challenges accepted practices based on particular assumptions that can be reconsidered. This can lead to new ideas and new practices. Bartunek and Moch (1987) use similar terms to describe frameworks of understanding for change. First-order change is concerned with incremental change that matches the shared understanding of those involved, while second-order change modifies how understanding occurs. They also add third-order change, which is concerned with developing the capacity to understand events as they occur, transcending single or particular ways of understanding to consider a variety of possibilities.

Hayes (2010) also considers how some organizations anticipate the need for change. They are proactive in seeking opportunities for change, which they can initiate, as well as understanding threats, for which they can prepare. By contrast, and this is probably more common, organizations might only change when they have to – such organizations are reactive. In recent years, many organizations have found out just what this means.

reflective question What is your orientation towards change? Are you proactive or reactive?

Change agents, skills and interventions

Different types of change and different approaches to implementing change require a variety of skills and knowledge of tools and techniques by those expected to lead and manage change. During the 1980s, this role was closely associated with transformational leaders who were expected to become 'change masters' (Kanter, 1985), relying on their charisma and vision to act as change champions and leaders of change. More recently, Kotter (2008) reasserts the importance of leaders to establish a sense of urgency as the first stage of his model. During the 1990s and 2000s, this role was expected to become part of the work both of managers throughout the organization and also of functional specialists such as HRD practitioners as change agents. In addition, experts in change could also be employed from consultancies outside the organization. Whoever undertakes such a role, there are some key questions to consider:

- How do individuals behave in times of change?
- Does theory inform our understanding of human change processes?

- What interventions are needed in the change process?
- What are the keys to successful and sustainable change?

If you look at any organization behaviour textbook in relation to change, you will see that, from a personal perspective, change is often difficult, largely influenced by emotions and can require an involved process of individual readjustment and reframing of a person's work context and orientation. Individual reactions to change are many and varied depending on a complex interaction of history, context, situation and individual orientation to change and work. People frequently experience a complicated mix of both positive and negative responses to change. In addition, the flow of responses may fluctuate and intensify over time and may be connected to the way in which change is presented by managers and colleagues at work (Balogun et al., 2008). The responses to change at any given point in time include:

- resentment
- frustration
- anxiety
- dissatisfaction
- fear
- insecurity.

This list is not exhaustive but does show the range of responses to a situation of change and the potential for 'disaffection' (Kanter, 1985) or indeed resistance to a change process. Such resistance is often seen as negative although, as Ford et al. (2008) put it, resistance to change could be used positively as a 'contribution to effective change management' (p.362).

The potential and real difficulties in change at work have been recognized for many years. As a consequence, a wide range of intervention tools and techniques have been developed for change agents during the 1950s and 60s, as part of what is called organization/organizational development or OD. This takes a whole organization approach to planned change. In OD, change agents seek to diagnose problems and find interventions based on behavioural science principles that are appropriate to assist the 'change effort' (Beckhard 1969, p.101). Diagnosis will involve collecting data, possibly through surveys and interviews, before developing plans for intervention to improve the situation. The aim is to find a degree of consensus between different groups and individuals, finding and building common ground where conflict and disagreement exists. In recent years, OD has become more integrated into HR and HRD, with some organizations using the job title OD Manager, often in the public sector and also at senior levels (Gillon, 2011). The main thrust of OD activity is to ensure effective change management and organization improvement.

Schein (1969) saw the change agent as a process consultant who facilitates interventions in an unbiased and positive way. We can see how such a view informs the way HRD and other initiatives that seek to promote learning at work are now implemented, which will be considered throughout this book, for example team work and team building, Investors in People, leadership and management development and so on. Among those who work in the field of

HRD, the roles of change agent and facilitator are seen as the most important (Nijhof & de Rijk, 1997). As facilitators of change, there has been considerable attention given to the skills that need to be learned and practice. For example, Buchanan and Boddy (1992) provide a list of competencies for effective change agents, which include:

- clarity of specifying goals
- team-building activities
- communication skills
- negotiation skills
- influencing skills to gain commitment to goals.

Facilitators need to understand the distinction between task and process as a group operates to achieve its objectives. They need to listen to the language being used within group interactions. Task language is concerned with *what* the group is doing whereas process language is concerned with *how* the group performs or will complete a task. Crucially, process words enable facilitators to find tools and techniques for completing tasks (Mann, 2006). For example, a group that say, 'We need to understand why our customer service is poor', indicates the need for a problem analysis tool.

Many organizations also specify facilitating change as a skill for managers. For example, a large UK financial services organization identifies 'driving change' as one of the competencies managers require. Facilitation however is seldom a neutral process and access to tools and techniques can also have a political impact (Kirk & Broussine, 2000).

activity

Try an online OD toolkit at www.zenska-mreza.hr/prirucnik/en/en_manual.htm. Use the toolkit with a group of others to diagnose a problem and consider possible interventions for change. What tool can you find to help a group analyse why customer service is poor?

Facilitation is not just about managers solving problems or driving change; it also involves helping staff identify and benefit from learning opportunities. This is a key theme within this book, especially in Section 3 when we consider HRD at work. Suffice to say that there has been significant interest in recent years in managers as coaches and mentors (CIPD, 2011). However, such learning-oriented roles by managers can also be constrained by contextual factors that hinder learning (see Ellinger & Cseh, 2007), a theme we also consider in more detail in this book.

The learning and development function (LDF)

We noted above that while a degree of conceptual ambiguity exists as regards HRD and SHRD, it is nonetheless useful to think about the concept of strategy in relation to HRD practice. A degree of consensus exists among leading practitioners and academics that HRD can, and should, operate strategically within an organization. However, exactly what such practice should look like, how the function should be positioned and managed in terms of such a responsibility, remains problematic. You will also notice that for this section of the chapter we have used the title Learning and Development Function (LDF) which is more recognized, and used by practitioners, than HRD.

Over the last decade, there have been signs that the LDF has shifted in significance. In 2005, Sloman talked about a shift from training to learning. Since then, survey data (e.g. CIPD, 2012) suggest that with continuing pressure on reducing costs, the LDF is expected to be more organization- and business-focused. As we have indicated above, this brings change management and OD into more prominence as a skill set for the function. The LDF has always had to operate with respect to forces both within and external to the organization (see, for example, Hendry et al., 1988; Gold & Smith, 2003) but it becomes crucial whether the LDF can, during turbulent and difficult times, enhance its position in the organization as a strategic player. One approach is based on the idea of HRD as a business partner.

Business partner

In abstract, the idea of a business partner is simple. In order to engage appropriately with the strategic development of the organization, the LDF operates as a partner alongside the various business units and as an agent to facilitate change in the organization. The word partner is crucial, implying that HRD has an equal, credible and legitimate role to play in relation to the most important business decisions taken by the organization. The LDF becomes responsible for aligning HRD with the business strategy and ensuring that HRD can add value at any level within the organization. In this model, HRD has a key leadership role, working in collaboration with other senior figures to help determine the vision and direction of the organization (Ulrich, 1997). Gubbins and Garavan (2009) add the word strategic and position the Strategic Business Partner model on the right-hand side of a chart (Figure 2.2), which seeks to map the changing nature of HRD professional roles from the traditional role – training intervention focused – to one of transformational strategic partner. This is not exactly a neat, linear continuum but it does usefully capture the point that the journey away from this traditional role may well involve a range of different pathways and configurations. Recently Ulrich et al. (2009) outlined the opportunity for business partners in HRM more generally to take an active role in business-focused transformation. (See Analoui [1994] for further discussion of the more traditional and transactional roles, and Gilley & Maycunich Gilley [2003] for the more transformational roles.)

It is important to note that the business partner model may well seek to integrate a number of sub-functions. Three such sub-functions might be:

• *Shared services:* routine transactional services across organizations, for example standard training programmes

- *Centres of excellence:* small teams of experts with specialist knowledge of cutting-edge HRD solutions, for example electronic knowledge management, mentoring
- *Strategic partners:* HR professionals working closely with business leaders influencing strategy and steering its implementation.

The essence of the business partner model is captured in Figure 2.3, which forms the basis for how the civil service, drawing on the work of Ulrich (1997), seeks to put the business partner model into practice within HR generally.

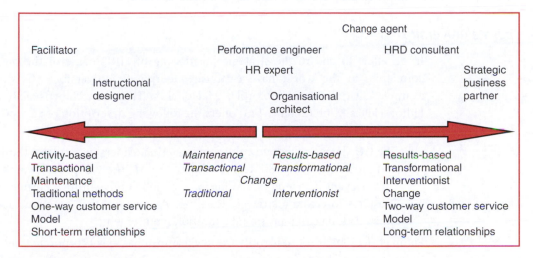

Figure 2.2 Shifting roles of the HRD professional

Source: Gubbins and Garavan (2009)

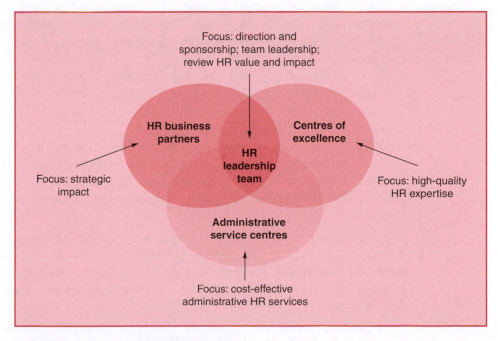

Figure 2.3 The business partner model in the UK civil service

Source: Cabinet Office (2005, p.11)

This partnering model has not been without criticism. Firstly, it is argued that if most focus is given to business issues, this can lead to a neglect of staff issues (Francis & Keegan, 2006). Secondly, research suggests that the model can result in divisions among HR staff and a loss of trust by employees. In addition, HR managers, and this would include the LDF, may not have the right skills for business nor to make the HR strategy-business strategy linkage (Griffen et al., 2009; Caldwell, 2010). There could be a tendency for HR practitioners to exaggerate the effectiveness of their partnering abilities, which would not enhance their position against other organization functions.

The corporate university

In an effort to ensure the strategic positioning of HRD some of the biggest companies in the world have established corporate universities (CUs); for example BAE Systems, Motorola, McDonald's, Heineken, Lloyds TSB and Hilton Hotels. Gibb (2008, p.143) offers the following description of a corporate university:

> The CU shapes corporate culture by fostering leadership, creative thinking and problem solving. Strategic is the key word. The CU provides strategically relevant (learning) solutions for each job family within a corporation. It aspires to create a strategic learning organization that functions as the umbrella for a company's total education requirements.

Paton et al. (2007) seek to identify the key features that make corporate universities distinctive. Three are suggested:

1 *Corporate-level initiatives in large, highly complex and differentiated settings:* CUs will have a presence on the board. They may be distinct from the HRD function within large business units. They aim to deliver a specific corporate contribution, avoiding replication or duplication with what is managed or delivered at a local level.

2 *The pursuit of continuing corporate alignment:* The CU is seen as a vehicle by which control of HRD activities, broadly interpreted, can most effectively be aligned with strategic priorities, such as post-merger integration, customer loyalty, developing leadership.

3 *The raising of standards, expectations and impact:* For Paton et al. (2007), it is the CU that can really reflect the strategic priority afforded to learning. Issues might be: ensuring the highest quality of provision including harnessing the best available technology to create a virtual learning platform across global sites.

A fourth feature of the model, of course, is the use of the term university. Advocates of CUs claim this provides the critical symbolic factor. It raises the status of organizational learning (Chapter 10) to its very highest level. For example, Motorola – one of the pioneer corporate universities – defended its decision arguing:

> Motorola management has always tried to use words in ways that force people to rethink their assumptions. The term university will arouse curiosity and, we hope, raise the expectations of our workforce and our training

and education staff. We could have called it an educational resource facility but who would that have electrified? (Wiggenhorn, 1990)

HRD in Practice 2.2 provides an example of a corporate university established in 2010 where the relationship between the initiative and strategic HRD is pre-eminent.

HRD in Practice 2.2

Westinghouse University: aligning a corporate university to meet the needs of business objectives

Westinghouse Electric Company operates in the nuclear power industry. Over 50 per cent of the world's nuclear plant is based on Westinghouse technology. It has over 14,000 employees world-wide. Westinghouse University was launched in the spring of 2010 to meet three critical, long-term needs: 1) to support both a rapidly expanding global workforce and select customers, partners and suppliers; 2) to transfer knowledge from experienced employees to new recruits; and 3) to enable the company to deal with the evolving market demands in the nuclear industry. Breaking from the tradition of in-person training, Westinghouse University is 100 per cent based on a virtual learning environment.

A key feature of the Westinghouse University is that learning is delivered via seven colleges which strive to fulfil the collective mission: 'To implement the learning strategy and related processes required to meet the enterprise-wide learning demands of our growing business'. The college structure is designed to enable learning to be delivered in an integrated way across the business as a whole rather than individually to separate business units. Each college is led by a Dean who provides leadership, acquires and maintains resources, manages curriculum development, and oversees personnel.

A Learning Management System underpins the university in order to administer and co-ordinate training provision worldwide.

Source: Corporate University Xchange (2012)

Critics of CUs (see, for example, Walton, 2005) have been concerned that most are simply rebadged training departments. This is an important point. It is easy to give the HRD function a new name but if its actual practice is little different, then the role has not changed. Others consider that many CUs are too close to traditional universities in their curriculum and direction and, as a result, fail to manage effectively the tensions between organizational HRD needs on the one hand and those of individuals within the organization on the other (see also Gibb, 2011).

LDF positioning and management

With this in mind, if we now try and translate this conceptual thinking into the implications for the positioning and day-to-day management of the LDF, two important sets of questions arise: first in terms of a centralizing–decentralizing tension and second in relation to the capabilities of those aspiring to purportedly new HRD roles. Hirsh and Tamkin's (2005) research sought to ascertain how, in practice, organizations align their HRD activity with business needs. Their findings uncover some underlying dilemmas. For example, they note that business needs can be both corporate and local, but which of these should influence what happens in terms of HRD practice at ground level? If line managers are taking greater responsibility for the training and development of their teams, this will act as a force towards devolvement, including devolved budgets. A desire for just in time training and tailored learning closer to the job reinforces such pressures. However, Hirsh and Tamkin's research shows that, for large organizations in particular, a perceived need to measure and control spend 'and to focus on corporate priorities' creates a powerful 'centralizing effect' (p.33). Shared service initiatives, operating a call centre-type role, further reinforce centralizing tendencies and plans.

Hirsh and Tamkin (2005) report the case of Diageo, one of the world's leading drinks businesses. Diageo provides an interesting example of how a company has sought to deal with the corporate–local tension. Their corporate policy is to devolve and embed training and learning throughout the business. However, Diageo differentiates between resources for strategic, company-wide priorities and those for more local and operational needs. A process called the organization and people review aims to join and integrate the top-down view with the bottom-up view. HRD operates with local managers to identify capability issues. This information is then amalgamated upwards and a corporate perspective added at group level. This might be conceived of as an example of what Gibb (2008, p.158) calls a hub and spoke model.

Various questions of capability flow from the different ways of thinking about how HRD might be positioned. Two of some significance are noted below; one external to the function and the other much closer to home.

One of the anticipated challenges noted by advocates of the business partner model concerns line management. If, as part of an intimate engagement with strategy, an implication is that line management take on board a much greater responsibility for the day-to-day, week-by-week development of their staff (the devolvement of responsibility discussed above), have they the capability to fulfil such a responsibility effectively? A recurrent concern flagged by the CIPD as a result of its annual learning and development survey work has been this very theme. For example, while coaching has become a crucial HRD activity in organizations, usually enacted by line managers, it is seldom evaluated so it is difficult to show if this activity is adding value (CIPD, 2012) (see also Chapter 8).

In addition, to play any kind of leadership role at the strategic centre of the organization clearly has implications for the capabilities of senior HRD professionals. Two are considered critical; first, power and influence, and second, learning expertise. Stewart and McGoldrick (1996) argue that 'a strategy for augmenting influence is virtually imperative if the HRD department is to survive' and the reader will note that we have been discussing a role that is much more than mere survival. However, as Caldwell (2010) found, some organizations appoint managers without HR expertise or credentials to senior HR roles, because those with credentials cannot make the link to business strategy.

The following extract, drawn from research undertaken with HRD practitioners about the politics of their role (Holden & Griggs, 2011), illustrates the lived experience of one HRD manager who works for a large UK car dealership as she seeks to develop a strategic presence within the organization:

> I do go to Board meetings but I'm not a director ... I mean I influence as much as I can but it's hard work, it really wears you down. I've tried to make HRD a lever of change and I have driven a lot through but it's a battle, it's a real struggle ... you've got to be permanently selling it and by nature HR people are not salespeople. It's the art of balancing what we need operationally, today, now, with what's best for the business in the longer term ... And one of the problems here is that if you're not an accountant you don't fit ... they're so insular they won't look outside the motor trade and so I can't say 'Look, it works here' ... they just won't see it ... and of course we're women ... I'm sorry but that's the case and all the other directors are men.

Reflecting on the factors that may enhance and detract from a high level of power and influence within an organization, the issue of gendered power relations in HRD raises some important questions (Hanscome & Cervero, 2003). The majority of HRD professionals in the UK are female.

In relation to learning, the necessary expertise goes beyond a technical proficiency in identifying and managing learning needs and provision. The strategic HRD role requires an understanding of knowledge management and organizational learning (Chapter 10) and, increasingly, an appreciation of how technology may be utilized as a strategic learning tool.

Pettinger (2002) combines the two factors of influence and expertise in a simple matrix, shown in Figure 2.4.

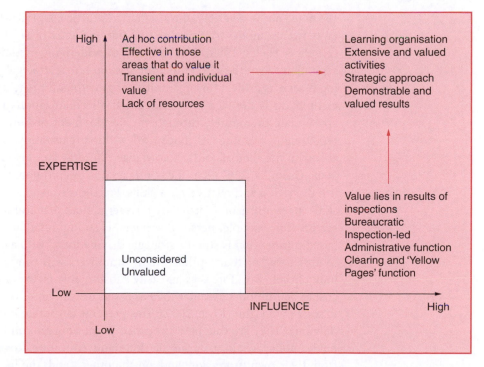

Figure 2.4 The balance of expertise and influence

Source: Pettinger (2002)

Before we conclude this chapter, two important additional considerations need to be addressed.

Outsourcing

Over recent years there has been a growing trend for various training tasks to be undertaken by external organizations (Braun et al., 2011). This might mean the use of external provider for training programmes, for which the term out-tasking might be more appropriate (Richman & Trondsen 2004).

Alternatively, comprehensive outsourcing may see an external contractor take complete control of an organization's HRD function. Simmonds and Gibson (2008) identify the impetus for outsourcing as cost, competence and capacity. They cite the example of Unilever, which has taken transactional activities and delivery outside, with transformational and strategic activities remaining in Unilever's remit. While the authors identify a set of problems with any outsourcing of HRD, they suggest that the administrative, operational and transactional-type activities can be overcome, but less so the strategic. More recently, however, research within the context of SMEs provides some support for successful outsourcing going beyond the transactional and engaging in organizational change (Rippon, 2012). An important research need is to explore further those organizations that have taken, or are taking, this step and to assess the particular significance in terms of HRD.

Competing on costs not skills

We noted above a variety of ways that, in practice, an HRD function may move away from a model based on ad hoc training activity or planned maintenance (Fonda & Hayes, 1988). Nonetheless, an underlying assumption has been the aspiration to see the HRD function develop into a strategic player where learning is seen as critical for organizational growth and prosperity. The flaw in this assumption is the lack of evidence that all organizations necessarily see it as appropriate to compete through the development of human capital. As Keep (2009) rightly reminds us, much work within organizations does not sit comfortably with the rhetoric of the knowledge economy (see also Bolton & Houlihan, 2008; Grugulis, 2007). On the contrary, it is often highly routinized, involving low discretion and relatively low skills. For some organizations, in some sectors, skills are a third or fourth order issue; almost a marginal concern. In such sectors (for example, personal services, cleaning, retail and wholesaling) cost-based competition is still the strategic driving force, with a consequent pressure to deskill rather than upskill. 'Many employers will continue to view the vast bulk of their workforces as an easily substitutable factor of production, or as a cost to be minimized, rather than as assets or sources of competitive advantage in their own right' (Keep, 2009). This presents corporate HRD managers with a dilemma. They are caught at the pinch point between, on the one hand, wider public policy goals in terms of skills and education, together with rhetoric from their own profession, and, on the other hand, the hard business realities and competitive pressures of the sector and market in which they operate. Of course, it could still be argued that the function is engaging strategically with the business goals of the organization when it refuses demands for training and opportunities for skill enhancement, but clearly the enhanced status given to learning within, say, the corporate university model is inappropriate. It follows, therefore, that if we equate best practice HRD with the kinds of models and developments discussed above, this is likely to remain, as Keep (2005) eloquently puts it, a 'minority sport'.

summary

○ Conventional views on strategy are based on top managers setting out a vision and mission for an organization and developing organization or corporate goals and strategy from which are derived business strategy and then functional strategy, including a strategy for HRD.

○ An alternative view is that HRD can have a key role to play in shaping organizational culture, developing current and future leaders, building commitment among organization members and anticipating and managing responses to changed conditions to ensure long-term survival.

○ HRD strategy is a course of action that is intended to have a long-term, rather than a short-term impact on significant rather than marginal areas of performance at organizational rather than individual level.

○ HRD plans are concerned with shorter time horizons, usually a year, and will cover a number and range of programmes and activities. The focus of these programmes and activities will be operational and intended to ensure that the day-to-day work of the organization can be accomplished.

○ HRD policy describes the framework within which decisions about programmes and activities are taken and which guides those decisions and their implementation.

○ Organization strategies imply change but are not always linked to HRD.

○ Types of change can vary between incremental and transformational. Organizations can be proactive or reactive in anticipating the need for change.

○ Various models of change inform the skills needed to manage and implement change at work.

○ Change agents need to use ideas and tools for intervention in change projects and facilitate intervention in an unbiased and positive way.

○ HRD practitioners can operate as a business partner to align HRD with business strategy.

○ Many large organizations have developed corporate universities to raise the status of learning.

○ The HRD role in organizations must manage key dilemmas relating to centralizing and decentralizing HRD activities and the balance between expertise and influence.

○ Recent years have seen a trend toward outsourcing HRD activities such as training.

discussion questions

1 Can HRD ever be considered strategic?
2 Investment or cost? How important is this litmus test for HRD and why?

3 Does all change lead to learning?
4 What are the key skills of a change agent?
5 What value is the business partner model for HRD in practice?

further reading

references

Chia, R. (2002) 'Rhizomic' model of organizational change and transformation: perspective from a metaphysics of change. *British Journal of Management*, **10**(3): 209–27.

Govaerts, N. and Baert, H. (2011) Learning patterns in organizations: towards a typology of workplace-learning configurations. *Human Resource Development International*, **14**(5): 545–59.

Horwitz, F.M. (1999) The emergence of strategic training and development: the current state of play. *Journal of European Industrial Training*, **23**(4/5): 180–90.

Watson, S., Maxwell, G.A. and Farquharson, L. (2007) Line managers' views on adopting human resource roles: the case of Hilton (UK) hotels. *Employee Relations*, **29**(1): 30–49.

Analoui, F. (1994) Training and development: the role of trainers. *Journal of Management Development*, **13**(9): 61–72.

Anderson, V. (2009) Desperately seeking alignment: reflections of senior line managers and HRD executives. *Human Resource Development International*, **12**(3): 263–77.

Argyris, C. and Schön, D. (1978) *Organizational Learning: A Theory of Action Perspective*. Reading, MA: Addison Wesley.

Balogun, J., Hope Hailey, V. and Johnson, G. (2008) *Exploring Strategic Change*. London: Pearson Education.

Bartlett, C. and Ghoshal, S. (1997) The myth of the generic manager: new personal competencies for new management roles. *California Management Review*, **40**(1): 92–116.

Bartunek, J.M. and Moch, M.K. (1987) First-order, second-order, and third-order change and organization development interventions: a cognitive approach. *Journal of Applied Behavioral Science*, **23**(4): 483–500.

Beckhard, R. (1969) *Organizational Development: Strategies and Models*. Reading, MA: Addison.

Bolton: S.C. and Houlihan, M. (2008) *Work Matters: Critical Reflections on Contemporary Work*. Basingstoke: Palgrave Macmillan.

Bratton, J. and Gold, J. (2012) *Human Resource Management: Theory and Practice*, 5th edn. Basingstoke: Palgrave Macmillan.

Braun, I., Pull, K., Alewell, D., Stomer, S. and Thommes, K. (2011) HR outsourcing and service quality: theoretical framework and empirical evidence. *Personnel Review*, **40**(3): 364–82.

Buchanan, D. and Boddy, D. (1992) *The Expertise of the Change Agent: Public Performance and Backstage Activity*. London: Prentice Hall.

Cabinet Office (2005) *Professional Skills for Government (PSG): HR Professional Standards Workbook*. London: Cabinet Office.

Caldwell, R. (2010) Are HR business partner competency models effective? *Applied HRM Research*, **12**(1): 40–58.

Camps, J. and Luna-Arocas, R. (2012) A matter of learning: how human resources affect organizational performance. *British Journal of Management*, **23**(1): 1–21.

CIPD (2011) *The Coaching Climate.* London: Chartered Institute of Personnel and Development.

CIPD (2012) *Learning and Talent Development*. London: Chartered Institute of Personnel and Development.

Clardy, A. (2008) Human resource development and the resource-based model of core competencies: methods for diagnosis and assessment. *Human Resource Development Review*, **7**(4):387–88.

Ellinger, A. and Cseh, M. (2007) Contextual factors influencing the facilitation of others' learning through everyday work experiences. *Journal of Workplace Learning*, **19**(7): 435–52.

Fonda, N. and Hayes, C. (1988) Education, training and business performance. *Oxford Review of Economic Policy*, **4**(3): 108–119..

Ford, J.D., Ford, L.W. and D'Amelio, A. (2008) Resistance to change: the rest of the story. *Academy of Management Review*, **33**(2): 362–77.

Francis, H. and Keegan, A. (2006), The changing face of HRM: in search of balance. *Human Resource Management Journal*, **16**(3): 231–49.

Fredericks, J. and Stewart, J. (1996) The strategy-HRD connection. In J. Stewart and J. McGoldrick (eds) *Human Resource Development: Perspectives, Strategies and Practice*. London: Pitman.

Garavan, T. (1991) Strategic human resource development. *Journal of European Industrial Training*, **15**(1): 17–31.

Garavan, T. (2007) A strategic perspective on human resource development. *Advances in Developing Human Resources*, **9**(1): 11–30.

Gibb, S. (2008) *Human Resource Development: Process, Practices and Perspectives*, 2nd edn. Basingstoke: Palgrave Macmillan.

Gibb, S. (2011) *Human Resource Development: Foundations, Processes, Contexts*. Basingstoke: Palgrave Macmillan.

Gilley, J.W. and Maycunich Gilley, A. (2003) *Strategically Integrated HRD: Six Transformational Roles in Creating Results-driven Programmes*, 2nd edn. Cambridge: Perseus.

Gillon, A. C. (2011) Does OD practice within the HR profession in the UK reflect the academic rhetoric? *Leadership & Organization Development Journal*, **32**(2): 150–69.

Gold, J. and Smith, V. (2003) Advances towards a learning movement: translations at work. *Human Resource Development International*, **6**(2): 139–52.

Griffin, E., Finney, L., Hennessy, J. and Boury, D. (2009) *Maximising the Value of HR Business Partnering*. Horsham: Roffey Park.

Grugulis, I. (2007) *Skills, Training and Human Resource Development*. Basingstoke: Palgrave Macmillan.

Gubbins, C. and Garavan, T.N. (2009) Understanding the HRD role in MNCs: the imperatives of social capital and networking. *Human Resource Development Review*, **8**(2): 245–75.

Hanscome, L. and Cervero, R. (2003) The impact of gendered power relations in HRD. *Human Resource Development International*, **6**(4): 509–25.

Hayes, J. (2010) *The Theory and Practice of Change Management*. Basingstoke: Palgrave Macmillan.

Hendry, C., Pettigrew, A. and Sparrow, P.R. (1988) The forces that trigger training. *Personnel Management*, **20**(12): 28–32.

Hirsh, W. and Tamkin, P. (2005) *Planning Training for your Business*, report no. 422. Brighton: Institute of Employment Studies.

Holden, R. and Griggs, V. (2011) Teaching the politics of HRD: a journey in critical curriculum development. *International Journal of Management Education*, **9**(2) 71–82.

ILO (International Labour Office) (2000) *High Performance Work Research: Project Case Studies*. Geneva: ILO.

Kanter, R.M. (1985) *The Change Masters: Corporate Entrepreneurs at Work*. London: Taylor and Francis.

Keep, E. (2005). *The Firm, Society and Social Inclusion; Addressing the Societal Value of HRD*. Paper presented at the 6th European Conference of HRD, Leeds.

Keep, E. (2009) Labour market structures and trends, the future of work and the implications for initial E&T, Beyond Current Horizons, Kirk, P. and Broussine, M. (2000) The politics of facilitation. *Journal of Workplace Learning*, **12**(1): 13–22.

Kirk, P. and Broussine, M. (2000) The politics of facilitation, *Journal of Workplace Learning*, **2**(1): 13–22.

Kotter, J.P. (2008) *A Sense of Urgency*. Boston, MA: Harvard Business Press.

Leitch, S. (2006) *Prosperity for All in the Global Economy: World Class Skills*. London: HM Treasury.

Mackenzie, C., Garavan, T. and Carbery, R. (2012) Through the looking glass: challenges for human resource development (HRD) post the global financial crisis – business as usual? *Human Resource Development International*, **15**(3): 353–64.

Mann, T. (2006) Tools for action. *Training Journal,* May: 39–42.

Mayo, A. (2004) *Creating a Learning and Development Strategy*. London: Chartered Institute of Personnel and Development.

McCracken, M. and Wallace, M. (2000) Towards a redefinition of strategic HRD. *Journal of European Industrial Training*, **24**(5): 281–90.

Micic, P. (2010) *The Five Futures Glasses, How to See and Understand More of the Future with the Eltville Model*. Basingstoke: Palgrave.

Mintzberg, H., Ahlstrand, B. and Ampel, J. (1998) *Strategy Safari*. London: Prentice-Hall.

Nijhof, W.J. and de Rijk, R.N. (1997) Roles, competences and outputs of HRD practitioners: a comparative study in four European countries. *Journal of European Industrial Training*, **21**(6/7): 247–55.

Paton, R., Peters, G., Storey, J. and Taylor, S. (2007) *Handbook of Corporate University Development*. London: Gower.

Pettigrew, R. (2002) *Mastering Employee Development*. Basingstoke: Palgrave Macmillan.

Richman, H. and Trondsen, E. (2004) Outsourcing: what can it do to your job? *Training and Development*, **58**(10): 68–73.

Rippon, L (2012) *Managing Change Through Corporate Re-structuring: A Case Study Evaluation of the Outsourced HR Role*, unpublished Postgraduate Diploma in HRM Dissertation, Leeds Metropolitan University.

Schein, E. (1969) *Process Consultation: Its Role in Organization Development*. Reading, MA: Addison-Wesley.

Simmonds, D. and Gibson, R. (2008) A model for outsourcing HRD. *Journal of European Industrial Training*, **32**(1): 4–18.

Sloman, M. (2005) *Training to Learning: Change Agenda*. London: CIPD.

Starbuck, W., Barnett, M. and Baumard, P. (2008) Payoffs and pitfalls of strategic learning. *Journal of Economic Behavior & Organization,* **66**(1): 7–21.

Stewart J. (1999) *Employee Development Practice.* London: FT/Pitman.

Stewart, J. and McGoldrick, J.A. (1996) *Human Resource Development: Perspectives, Strategies and Practice*. London: Pitman.

Tseng, C-C. and McLean, G.N. (2008) Strategic HRD practices as key factors in organizational learning. *Journal of European Industrial Training*, **32**(6): 418–32.

Tushman, M.L., Newman, W.H. and Romanelli, E. (1986) Convergence and upheaval: managing the unsteady pace of organizational evolution. *California Management Review*, **29**: 22–39.

UKCES (2009) *Towards Ambition 2020: Skills, Jobs, Growth*. London: UK Commission for Employment and Skills.

UKCES (2010) *Skills for Jobs: Today and Tomorrow*. London: UK Commission for Employment and Skills.

UKCES (2011) *Employer Ownership of Skills*. London: UK Commission for Employment and Skills.

Ulrich, D. (1997) *Human Resource Champions: The Next Agenda for Adding Value and Delivering Results*. Boston: Harvard Business School Press.

Ulrich, D., Alenn, J., Brockbank, W., Younger, J. and Nyman, M. (2009) *HR Transformation: Building Human Resources From the Outside In*. New York: McGraw-Hill.

Wain, D. (2007) *Lies, Damned Lies and a Few Home Truths: Reflections on the 2007 Learning and Development Survey*. London: CIPD.

Wall, S.J. (2005) The protean organization: learning to love change. *Organizational Dynamics*, **34**(1): 37–46.

Walton, J. (1999) *Strategic HRD*. London: Financial times/Prentice Hall.

Walton, J. (2005) Would the real corporate university please stand up. *Journal of European Industrial Training*, **29**(1): 7–20.

Watson, S. and Harmel-Law, A. (2010) Exploring the contribution of workplace learning to an HRD strategy in the Scottish legal profession. *Journal of European Industrial Training,* **34**(1): 7–22.

Wiggenhorn, W. (1990) Motorola U: when training becomes an education. *Harvard Business Review*, **68**(4): 71–83.

Woodall, J., Gourlay, S. and Short, D. (2002) Trends in outsourcing HRD in the UK: the implications for strategic HRD. *International Journal of Human Resource Development and Management*, **2**(1/2): 50–63.

Contrasting Contexts of HRD Practice

chapter 3

Vivienne Griggs and Rick Holden

Chapter learning outcomes

After reading this chapter, you should be able to:
- Understand the nature and characteristics of the public sector, voluntary/community sector and the small business sector within the UK economy
- Explore the critical features of these sectors in relation to HRD
- Reflect on key issues affecting a more strategic, planned and focused approach to HRD within these organizational contexts

Chapter outline

Introduction
The public sector
The voluntary, community and faith sector
The small business sector
Summary

Introduction

> The most valued knowledge for HR management (HRM) is likely to come from learning to apply HRM theories and techniques in particular organizational contexts. (Tyson, 1999, p.51)

Much research on HRD has focused on large private sector organizations. To what extent can this be applied to organizations operating in different organizational contexts? What impact do the size, sector and ownership of a business have on its learning and development (L&D) strategy? The range of contexts is considerable and it is beyond the scope of one chapter to address all potential contextual factors. Our focus is: the public sector, the voluntary and community sector, and small businesses. These are under-represented in the literature and present a challenging and distinctive context for HRD. Through attention to these contexts, we aim to highlight that important differences do exist and to provide detailed, critical illustrations in order that the implications for a 'contingency' approach to HRD practice are identified and captured.

reflective question

1 If you were to observe the management of people in a large retail store, a hospital, an environmental charity and a small plumbing firm, what similarities and differences would you expect to see?
2 How might these impact on HRD in each of these organizations?

The public sector

In most countries of the world the public sector is a significant feature of the organizational landscape. The public sector comprises central government, local government and public corporations. In the UK central government includes the civil service, the armed forces and the NHS; whilst local government includes, for example the police, education and the range of functions managed and delivered by local authorities. Examples of public corporations in the UK are the Royal Mail and London Underground. Unsurprisingly, given the range of functions and services undertaken by public sector bodies, they are a major employer. In the UK in excess of 20 per cent of people in employment work in the public sector (http://www.ons.gov.uk/ons/search/index.html?newquery= public+sector+employment)

A key feature of public sector organizations is that they are owned and controlled by government (or local government) and principally funded by taxation. Their overarching purpose is to serve the common good; a central element of which is the provision of public goods and services. In the recessionary times of the late 2000s/early 2010s many countries of the world are taking steps to reduce the size of the public sector with consequential political controversy. Much of the industrial unrest witnessed in countries like Spain, Greece, France and the UK in the early part of the 2010's has been in reaction to attempts to reduce the size of the public sector. Their funding arrangements mean they are held accountable to the public and the very nature of services such as health and education mean they are inevitably thrust more into the public eye. For example, the deaths of two children whilst in the care of social services (Victoria Climbie in 2001 and Baby P in 2007), resulted in a public outcry. Subsequent investigation into how social services managed such cases led to the acknowledgement of the need for much stronger training to help safeguard children in care.

In the next section we highlight some of the current challenges for learning and development in the public sector. They are not unique to this sector, however these issues do create a picture of the current climate for public sector organizations and a sense of the issues facing HR and learning and development professionals.

Challenges for learning and development in the public sector

The last 20–30 years has seen public sector organizations, internationally, come under increasing pressure to cut costs and improve efficiency and performance. In the UK, and led by the Coalition Government of 2011, the pace of this change has been intensified in response to a perceived need for 'austerity' measures. A key feature of the 'modernisation of the public sector' agenda (Webb et al., 2008) has been the comparison with private sector management practices. This has highlighted weaknesses, inefficiencies and an inability to shed the image that public sector organizations are sluggish bureaucracies with little interest in the 'customer'. Beevers (2006), for example, compares the experience of shopping in the morning in Marks & Spencer with queuing outside the local housing offices in the afternoon to highlight what he calls the 'business case' for public sector organizations to adopt 'customer service excellence' practice (p.3). Truss (2008) suggests that the values underpinning HR (or personnel/people management as it was in the 1980s) included paternalism, standardization, job security, collectivism and the aspiration to be a model employer. Reforms since the late 1980s are characterized by market solutions, deregulation, agencification and structural devolution. Two examples are those of Best Value (local government) and Agenda for Change (NHS) introduced in the UK in 1999 and 2004 respectively. The aim of Best Value was to improve local services in terms of both costs and quality. The Agenda for Change introduced annual development reviews for all NHS staff in the context of a Knowledge and Skills Framework, a generic competency framework (see also HRD in Practice 3.2).

Pressure for reform is ongoing. As part of the 'Building productive public sector workplaces' series the CIPD (2010) report low levels of trust and confidence in senior management among public sector employees. Management of change and people management capabilities were particular areas of criticism. The report recommended line manager and leadership development as part of its plans for improvement. This requirement for leadership development was also supported by Stephen Moir speaking at the CIPD Centres Conference, 2012. He highlighted that the current climate of austerity is outside the experience of most public sector leaders whose careers have been developed in times of growth and that therefore the current climate presents a new set of challenges (Moir, 2012).

Partnership working

A further consequence of public sector reform has been the increased use of the voluntary and private sectors in the delivery of public services in the UK. Inter-organizational work is now part of their core business for many public service organizations. This requires the organizations to constantly engage with the hierarchies of other organizations at different levels to deliver services that meet service users' complex needs (Pratt et al., 2007).

Morris and Farrell (2007), in a review of ten public sector organizations, found there had been considerable moves to concentration on core activities via outsourcing. This extends the role of partnership working to enable the public sector to meet its objectives. In her research in a UK local authority Thursfield (2008) suggests that public management initiatives, such as 'Public Private Partnership' and 'Best Value', prevent collaboration between managers and departments. Her conclusion was that this political context was an impediment to collective learning.

Nature of the workforce

Motivation: It is suggested that public sector workers may be driven by a different motivation to workers in the private sector, focusing on the social worth of work rather than economic gain (Coyle-Shapiro & Kessler, 2003). Georgellis et al.'s (2011) research suggests individuals are attracted to the public sector by intrinsic rather than extrinsic rewards. A study by Harris (2008) considering the changing nature of HR in UK local government found that the changes may have hidden costs regarding employee commitment. Public sector trade unions across Europe fear that sustained pressure to weaken terms and conditions may fundamentally affect the longer term psychological contract for such workers. Whilst this remains speculative it is useful to note CIPD (2012) findings that public sector workers view their talent management activities less favourably and are more pessimistic in relation to future learning and development opportunities than their private sector counterparts.

Managing Professionals: Professional work is a predominant part of service delivery for some public sector organizations. Areas such as education, health and local government involve professional working in managed contexts. Gold et al. (2010) suggest that the nature of professional expertise requires individuals to act with independence and discretion and therefore presents a particular challenge for the management and leadership of these workers. Pratt et al. (2007) highlight multiple hierarchies as a distinctive characteristic of public service organizations, where professional hierarchies exist as distinct features within the overall organization. One example of this would be in higher education where academics have their own formal hierarchies. These run in parallel to the management structure, so a lecturer could progress to a reader and then professor, or through a management route to Head of School and Dean.

Learning and development for professionals is often governed by professional bodies and achieved through a focus on continuous professional development (CPD). In this context professional bodies in the UK have increasingly adopted the rhetoric of reflective learning (Holden & Griggs, 2011). This can make it difficult for organizational HRD to ensure commonality of provision between different types of professionals. The result is often a tension between organizational ownership and management of learning and development and that pursued by the professional body.

Trade union: Labour Force Survey data suggest trade union presence in 2011 was significantly higher for public sector employees, at over 87 per cent, compared with the private sector (less than 30 per cent). In terms of collective bargaining the difference is equally pronounced; over 67 per cent of public sector employees had their pay determined by collective agreement, whilst the figure was less than 17 per cent for private sector employees (https://www.gov.uk/government/publications/trade-union-membership-2011). These stark differences in union activity suggest a different employment relations climate that raises important considerations for HR practitioners.

We have outlined above a number of important contextual factors for contemporary public sector organizations. The characteristics of HRD in the public sector are largely un-researched. This said, in what follows we seek to illustrate, both from research and practical examples, three key themes: strategic HRD; leadership and professional development; and L&D practices. These provide some insight into the emerging HRD profile within the public sector and how it is seeking to address the challenges it faces. We stress, though, that it is intended to show examples of practice rather than a definitive picture of a complex and diverse set of organizations.

HRD in the public sector

To what extent does evidence suggest that public sector organizations have adopted a more strategic approach to HRD as a way of tackling the relentless process of change? The CIPD (2012) report that, whilst private and non-profit sectors appear to be taking a more integrated approach to both learning and development and performance and organizational development, this trend was not seen as significant in the public sector. In contrast, Truss's (2008) in-depth research with six public sector organizations provides clear evidence of a more strategic role for HR and HRD. Initiatives in the areas of induction, management and career development, and performance development, for example, are part of a strategic response to becoming high-performing public sector bodies. But, strategic HRD has not necessarily replaced traditional, administratively focused, approaches; rather it has been 'grafted on' (p.1083). As a result the authors argue that those in senior HR roles face more intense and complex tensions and ambiguities than those in the private sector.

Positive testimonies are evident from those public organizations which have been accredited as Investors in People (IiP). Proportionately there are more medium- to large-sized organizations with IiP in the public than in the private sector. Whilst there remains some controversy surrounding the impact of IiP, research has suggested that nearly 90 per cent of public sector organizations with IiP agree that it has played an important part in managing change and the integration of a new organizational culture (PACEC, 2006).

Our research similarly indicates a degree of progress in some public organizations which have sought to link L&D at a strategic level to major change programmes. Leeds City Council provides such an example.

Leeds City Council

HRD in Practice 3.1

Leeds City Council has a stated aspiration to be 'the best city council in the UK'. Learning and development has a key role to play in delivering the required culture change to meet this aim. The chief executive is keen to ensure that the HRD strategy directly supports organizational aims and, as part of this drive, the leadership team has recently approved a coaching scheme. Previously a limited amount of executive coaching had been used for the most senior officers in the council but the focus here is on new cross-council coaching.

The council's approach is based upon the GROW model (Whitmore, 2009) and CLEAR (Hawkins, 2011).

To achieve the chief executive's aim of transformational change the council should aim for the process to challenge underlying assumptions that may otherwise hamper development.

The scheme is intended to offer cost effectiveness because it builds in-house coaching expertise. It allows the council to set guidelines which align with business objectives and respond to changing business needs. There is a safe and monitored learning environment to enable coaches to develop their skills whilst applying them to real work issues.

Source: Nicholls (2012)

Leadership and professional development

As noted above the professional workforce is highly significant in some public sector organizations. In the NHS, for example, HRD is seen as incorporating professional education and continuous professional development, distinct from some private organizations with a focus on L&D to meet specific workplace needs. This creates a tension between professional capabilities and the ability to work within and across organizations. The Healthcare Commission inquiry (2009) (http://webarchive.nationalarchives.gov.uk/20130107105354/http://www.dh.gov.uk/en/Publicationsandstatistics/Publications/PublicationsPolicyAndGuidance/DH_098660) into high mortality rates at the Mid-Staffs NHS Trust in 2009 highlighted the need for the medical profession to incorporate people management training as part of the professional development of their members at all levels. In response to the high profile deaths of a number of small children in care advocacy of more effective multi-agency working is high on the agenda. Professionals from across education, health, social work, criminal justice and voluntary sectors are required to overcome traditional professional and agency boundaries to reconfigure their practice (Black, 2012). Training for multi-agency work has become a requirement.

Many of the large public sector bodies in the UK have created Leadership Units (for example, The National College for Leadership of Schools and Children's Services and The Leadership Centre for Local Government) designed to shape future leadership by providing development and support. Public Service Leadership is a forum of 11 of such bodies. They have developed the Public Sector Leadership Community of Practice whose website 'showcases leadership learning, joint research and innovative practice across the public sector'.

Web Links

Go to **http://www.publicserviceleadership.org.uk/** and **www.education.gov.uk/nationalcollege/** for more information

Interestingly, Leslie and Camwell (2010), based on research with civil servants and local government officers, argue that, whilst leadership is central to the delivery of the deficit reduction agenda of European Governments, the need is not for the recruitment or development of more leaders 'it is about exercising more leadership at all levels (p.304)'.

Learning and development practices

In an attempt to address the research deficit of HRD in non-profit (public and voluntary sectors) Birdi et al. (2007) compared employee development activities in a large sample of both types of organization. Their findings suggest that non-profit organizations had greater engagement in individual learning practices (on the job training, formal off job courses, e-learning, personal development reviews) than their profit-making counterparts. Furthermore, the study suggested that greater proportions of both management and non-management employees took part in these learning practices in the non-profit sectors compared with the profit-making sectors. The authors point to the nature of work that non-profit organizations do to explainin the difference. They are more dependent upon the qualities of their personnel as opposed to the private sector where technology may play a more significant role in achieving organizational objectives. A further reason suggested is the greater legislative and government pressure to maintain and update employee skills in public sector organizations.

Support for this analysis is provided by the fact that public sector organizations, such as Local Authorities and NHS Trusts, are invariably major employers in their locality and are committed to, and active in, the pursuit of equality of opportunity. In Newham Borough Council, for example, home of the 2012 Olympics, a key training effort has been in soft skills training to enable staff to deliver quality customer service. Neighbouring Southwark has turned to e-learning to train staff in customer care. Their programme includes a strong ethos of equality and diversity to better serve the local population, which comprises the largest ethnic minority community in the UK. The UK police force has possibly invested more than any other public sector body in diversity training following an inquiry finding that the Metropolitan Police were 'institutionally racist' (MacPherson, 1999). A new model of race and diversity training was introduced and evidence to an enquiry in 2012 (Benetto, 2012) suggested trainees appreciated the more realistic role-play that involved real victims and witnesses and training in the community.

Anecdotal evidence suggests that public sector organizations may be more likely to extend L&D opportunities beyond the perceived needs of the job, particularly for young people. Many local authorities, for example, seeking to develop their role as 'exemplar employers' have responded to the challenge to take on more apprenticeships. The British Army places a lot of emphasis on education for their employees, in part to help people obtain careers when they leave the forces.

reflective question Do public sector organizations have a broader responsibility to educate their employees beyond the specific job-related training of their role? Does this responsibility differ to that of private sector organizations?

Go to www.apprenticeships.org.uk/LAToolkit/Identify-solutions-to-get-there/Employers/Public-sector-1.aspx and www.army.mod.uk/training_education/education/14541.aspx

Access to learning opportunities for traditionally disenfranchised employees has been a particular focus of trade union activity within the public sector. A report published by the OECD (2012) highlights the UnionLearn model as an example of good practice and notes its importance in equality of access to training. Research into the impact of UnionLearn representatives (ULRs) indicates activity is increasing year on year with a positive impact upon workplace learning (Saundry et al., 2011). Given that the bulk of ULRs are to be found in public sector organizations their impact on the private sector is an important feature of the public sector HRD landscape.

Finally, in terms of the way L&D practices are managed and delivered in the workplace, we note research from the CIPD (2010, 2011). Greater responsibility being devolved to learners and line managers is seen as the most significant organizational change that will affect L&D in the public sector in coming years. The CIPD argue that the public sector has lagged behind private sector practices in this respect. Also, as part of austerity measures in the early 2010s, public sector bodies face declining L&D budgets and are reducing the use of outside contractors and moving to in-house learning.

The preceding discussion has incorporated illustrations of L&D in the public sector. To conclude this section we provide an integrated example of how one organization is seeking to address all these challenges (HRD in Practice 3.2).

The UK National Health Service

HRD in Practice 3.2

Strategic HRD

The NHS is described by Dean Royles, Director NHS Employers, as an industry rather than an organization. So how can HRD Strategy respond to this complexity? There is a tension between the needs of individual trusts and programmes across the whole of the NHS. This is addressed through an approach to devolve responsibility to trusts but offer centralized resources for key programmes and managing change. The vision for the NHS is set by politicians but the translation of this into organizational strategies is determined by individual trusts. The Coalition government (2011–)aims to introduce a new NHS Commissioning Board which will provide clear national standards and accountability. The trusts and clinical commissioning groups will then determine the approach they will take to HRD strategy depending on their local priorities. In essence, a top-down vision is supported by bottom-up initiatives and shared services, as appropriate.

One example is the development of the Knowledge and Skills Framework (KSF) developed as part of the Agenda for Change. Northumberland Care Trust use a learning and development catalogue to embed KSF. The catalogue represents the formal learning and development offered by the trust and partner organizations. Each event is linked to the KSF to support performance development reviews (see also: **www.nhsemployers. org/SharedLearning/Pages/UsingtheLearningand DevelopmentCataloguetoEmbedtheKSF.aspx** and Institute of Employment Studies, 2010, for an independent review of the KSF). A further example is IiP, which is achieved at trust level. Calderdale and Huddersfield NHS Foundation Trust used IiP to help them merge two hospitals. The IiP framework was used to overcome organizational cultural differences and improve its strategies in people management and development (Goddard & Palmer, 2010).

Leadership and professional development

The NHS Leadership Academy's (**www.leadershipacademy.nhs.uk**) principal purpose is to develop outstanding leadership in health, with a continual focus on improving patients' experiences and health outcomes. It seeks to support equality of access to opportunities for developing leadership skills – putting nurses, doctors and other frontline leaders on an equal footing with non-frontline managers. One of the core elements of the NHS Leadership Academy's support to chairs, chief executives and executive directors, for example, is executive coaching.

Managing professionals is a particular challenge within the NHS with multi-professional groups working together, so a hospital may contain a range of distinct professional groups, such as engineers, clinicians, finance etc. This has resulted in a clear focus on self-directed learning within a broader agenda for talent and leadership development. An innovative local initiative is provided by Salford Royal NHS Foundation Trust as part of their organizational development strategy. The Trust have introduced a Clinical Leaders' Development Programme, to develop outstanding clinical leadership across professional boundaries. As part of the development programme each participant undertakes a quality improvement project of their choosing in order to apply theory to practice; for example the improvement of patient care in intensive care (Perry, 2011).

Another aspect of leadership development is the NHS graduate training programme. The Scheme recruits between 150 and 200 trainees a year onto its two-year programme, which offers a fast track, blended learning experience to trainees consisting of rotational work experiences, professional academic qualifications, personal learning and development, and exposure to high-level NHS stakeholders. An interesting glimpse of the content is provided by one of the participants on the HR 'stream' of the graduate programme:

I carried out a 12 month placement at St Helen's and Knowsley Teaching Hospitals NHS Trust as part of my development on the NHS Graduate Management Training Scheme. During my placement the HR Department implemented a peer to peer coaching initiative in the form of Action Learning Sets to share learning as a team and to put that learning into action. Continuous professional development was a strong aspect of the departmental culture. Deborah Smith, NHS HR Graduate Management Trainee

L&D practices

In a move away from bureaucratic practices of the past, current provision has a strong focus on individual development plans and provides a flexible, cost conscious offering. Use of e-learning helps here. The NHS have a Learning Management System (LMS) which provides e-learning for statutory training. It contains a national catalogue of e-learning courses which cover a wide number of subjects (**www.connectingforhealth. nhs.uk/systemsandservices/icd/informspec/etd**), and learning is also playing a broader role in communication and knowledge-sharing. For example, the chief executive of the Heart of England Trust posts regular updates on Twitter. This is representative of a desired culture of knowledge-sharing in the NHS to encourage collaboration between local trusts and points to the increasing role of social media in L&D.

In relation to equality and diversity training NHS Employers have named 17 NHS trusts to act as partners to share good practice and learning. Lancashire Care NHS Foundation Trust, for example, have developed a City and Guilds accredited course to raise staff awareness of issues around sexual orientation and to support lesbian, gay, bisexual and transgender employees. The UnionLearn website contains many positive cases of the unions working in partnership with the NHS to improve learning and development access to employees. For example, the Mersey Care NHS Trust and the Prison Officers Association (POA) is creating a range of learning opportunities for employees, their families, service users and carers and the wider community through the Union Learning Zone, based at Mersey Care's e-café (**www.unionlearningfund.org.uk/ case-studies/theunionlearningzone.cfm**).

Acknowledgement: Dean Royles, Director, NHS Employers (2012).

This case illustrates the complexity and diversity of the NHS. We should stress that the intention of HRD in Practice 3.2 is to provide examples of practice not to generalize what happens throughout the NHS.

We look now to the second of our 'contexts': the voluntary sector.

The voluntary, community and faith sector

The voluntary sector within the UK describes businesses that are not owned by the government or by private individuals in order to make a profit. Terms such as the 'charity sector', the 'not-for-profit sector' and the 'third sector' are often used interchangeably. The sector includes organizations registered with the Charity Commission, as well as a wide variety of others, including housing associations, places of worship, trade unions, sports and recreation clubs, and small voluntary groups. Definitions have been widely discussed (Billis & Glennerster, 1998; Myers & Sacks, 2001; Parry et al., 2005) and yet there is still a lack of consensus (Blackmore, 2004). Kendall and Knapp (1995) described it as a 'loose and baggy monster', reflecting the diversity and difficulty of categorization.

The Conservative/Liberal Democratic Coalition Government renamed the previous Office of the Third Sector as the Office for Civil Society. This reflects a change in terminology, replacing 'third sector' in Government usage by the term Civil Society or Big Society. While acknowledging this complexity and the imprecise boundaries, there are particular features of organizations in this sector that warrant examination.

The National Council for Voluntary Organizations (NCVO) claims that in 2010 there were 765,000 people employed in the UK's voluntary sector. However, recent cuts to public sector funding are also impacting on the voluntary sector. The NCVO suggests that charities are facing nearly £3 billion in cuts over the spending review period (2011–2015) which is anticipated to have an impact on both the number and distribution of employees (data.ncvo-vol.org.uk/almanac/voluntary-sector/work/what-impact-has-the-recession-had-on-employment-in-the-voluntary-sector/).

Prior to the current funding cuts, the voluntary sector had seen ten years of growth. This was partly attributable to changes in government strategy. Kendall (2003) suggests that it is linked to almost 20 years of public sector delivery being contracted out by local and central government. Consequently, voluntary organizations are competing with public and private sector companies for funding. Government funding is targeted in particular areas to support the political agenda. Public service agreements set out the government's priorities, funding for projects will be targeted at these and therefore changes in the government's priorities will influence the funding available for different voluntary sector organizations or projects. In the same way public sector organizations are shaped by the political agenda, the altered approach to the provision of funding to voluntary organizations means that they are also subject to greater political influence.

Challenges for learning and development in the voluntary sector

Clearly, some management issues will be common across all types of organization, whether they are in the public, private or voluntary sector. Parry et al. (2005) suggest that HRM in the voluntary sector may have similarities to the public sector because of the lack of profit motive and the employees' commitment to the organization's aims. Some studies have started to look at HRM in the sector but few have specifically examined HRD. From the literature, we have identified some characteristics that are relevant to the learning climate of an organization:

- *A mixed workforce:* One of the defining characteristics of the sector is the large number of volunteers working alongside the paid workforce. The majority of voluntary sector organizations continue to rely heavily on volunteers, which has a fundamental impact on the nature of management. In terms of learning and development, surveys show a mixed approach to the voluntary workforce, with some organizations concentrating their efforts solely on paid employees. Walton (1996) highlights a gap in HRD literature to the learning needs of non-employees.
- *Culture:* It is claimed that the sector has a distinctive culture due to the participative forms of decision-making and the values linked to the particular cause or mission of the organization (Cunningham, 2001). If staff choose to work in these organizations because they believe in their aims, intrinsic motivation may be more of a driver than extrinsic rewards. This potentially has a significant impact on the psychological contract of employees.
- *Complexity of stakeholders:* Billis and Glennerster (1998) discuss multiple stakeholders as a dominant characteristic, and stakeholder ambiguity as a key distinguishing feature, of voluntary agencies. In an organization with a profit motive, a clear exchange process is often evident. Good performance may be linked to increases in pay, and organizational objectives may be achieved through a range of financial incentives. Employees therefore have a clear understanding of the traditional management relationship and are accountable to the shareholders/owners of the business. In voluntary organizations there is often accountability to a number of different groups, further exacerbated by the public sector relationship outlined above. This is supported by the experience of Tony Lee, the ex-operations director for NatWest and subsequently chief officer for the Muscular Dystrophy Campaign, who claims that the contrast between the sectors is that the commercial world is much simpler as there are far fewer stakeholders (Hill, cited in Myers & Sacks, 2001).
- *Management processes:* Kellock Hay et al. (2001) note the unique sectoral characteristics that can 'complicate the management process'. The highly individualistic characteristics and the value-led nature may influence the way people are managed. This is likely to provide a wide diversity of approaches and impact on learning and development processes in these organizations.

- *Resources:* By their very nature, these operations are lean in terms of overheads; budgets are tight and spending needs to be clearly justified. Although employee costs can total up to 70 per cent of a voluntary organization's budget, people management in the sector has traditionally taken a back seat to the more pressing concerns of fundraising and delivery (Zacharias, 2003). The range of financial sources also tends to be greater than in other sectors and funding streams may be irregular and unpredictable, making long-term planning difficult (Armstrong, quoted in Parry et al., 2005).

reflective question What impact do you think the distinctive characteristics discussed above are likely to have on learning and development in such organizations?

Evidently, some of these distinctive features create a challenge for HRD. In their investigation of change management in the voluntary sector, Kellock Hay et al. (2001) identified the lack of time and resources for training as a barrier to change. Parry et al. (2005) found that finding money for training can be problematic in the voluntary sector as it cannot be budgeted for in service contracts. The timescale for the payback of learning and development may be an issue linked to the nature of funding. If contracts are short-term, investment in longer term learning and development initiatives may be difficult to justify. One consequence of budgetary constraints is that training is often supply-driven rather than demand-led. Organizations will undertake training when grants or subsidies are offered, but this opportunistic approach to training makes a strategic approach difficult to achieve.

Research shows that over two-thirds of voluntary sector SMEs do not have a dedicated HR specialist (Newsome & Cunningham, 2003). A strong commitment from trustees and managers to learning and development may overcome this lack of specialist skills, but in some organizations, there is a lack of recognition of the value of training and development. This may be an indication that the training and HR needs of these employees are not being met.

The complexity of stakeholders and workforce diversity are clearly significant for HRD. Training needs will be at three levels: the trustees, the paid workforce and the volunteers. HRD in Practice 3.3 outlines one particular charity facing a number of obstacles to the development of a more strategic approach to training and development

HRD in Practice 3.3

Learning and development at a mental health charity

A mental health charity provides support for vulnerable adults in a UK city. There are approximately 60 paid employees and a similar number of volunteers. Volunteers are mainly counsellors and are required to have a counselling qualification. Training and development for paid employees is inconsistent across the organization, since some managers have been proactive in this area, whereas others have had little involvement. In the past, staff have applied for 'whatever took their fancy'. Consequently, a small number who showed an interest have done lots of training – whether it was relevant or not – and other people have chosen not to do any at all. Evaluation of training has been based on comment sheets completed at the end of the event.

The barriers to learning and development noted by the personnel officer include:

- The range of stakeholders: the clients, the staff, the executive committee, the local healthcare professionals, the funders (government and private bodies) and other partnership organizations (other charities and healthcare providers).
- The role of the personnel officer is process and procedurally driven. There is no specific learning and development function.
- There is no senior support for HR, the personnel officer feels she is often ignored. The strategy is dominated by the chief executive who has a strong focus on service delivery but does not recognize the importance of learning and development.

- There is a strong counselling culture, in line with the services provided. This manifests itself in a strong people orientation, treating everyone as individuals. One symptom of this is a reluctance to adopt any generic HR policy which has hampered a strategic approach to HRD.

Three drivers for change have begun to impact on the receptiveness of the organization to an HRD strategy:

- A staff satisfaction survey highlighted that people felt they weren't getting enough of the right sort of training.
- The appointment of a new senior director who had previously worked in a larger social care charity with a strong training ethos.
- The government's introduction of competitive tendering processes for allocating funds to charity organizations. It is believed that staff skills, qualifications and experience will be considered as part of the selection criteria.

Source: Griggs and Holden (2008)

activity What steps would you take to improve the effectiveness of learning and development in the case of this mental health charity?

Learning and development in the voluntary sector

Despite a number of potential barriers and constraints for learning and development in the voluntary sector, there is considerable evidence of good practice. For example, Zacharias (2003) highlights a charity for the homeless in London called Broadway, which overcame recruitment difficulties by developing an 'intensive programme of core skills and on the job training'. Similarly, Hill and Stewart (2000) identify a range of good practice in a youth and community work charity, where the very nature of the charity and its strong people focus appear to have a positive effect on HRD.

In fact, the distinctive qualities of the sector may themselves facilitate a learning culture. Beattie (2006) claims that there is greater evidence of caring behaviour in the voluntary sector, where these person-centred values may generate a more receptive learning climate. Studies of knowledge management projects show how vital culture and social relations are. Consequently, high levels of staff engagement could mark a commitment to continuous learning.

The diverse working relationships may present clear opportunities for the development of staff. In private organizations, individual performance is often rewarded despite attempts to encourage teamwork. Where the workers share a common goal linked to strong personal values, the approach to good performance is likely to be less individualistic. Collaboration in working practices could therefore lead to greater knowledge-sharing and creation of ideas. The level of empowerment and commitment could indicate that self-directed learning is appropriate for trustees and other voluntary roles.

Partnership working between public and private sector organizations provides opportunities for learning networks and communities of practice. Public sector organizations working within the same domain, for example housing or child services, are likely to have common goals that should encourage collaborative working. Similarly, local charities are sometimes affiliated to a national charity and can therefore share best practice and learning.

Volunteers are sometimes people who have been out of the workforce for a variety of reasons and the provision of work experience through volunteering may be a path into paid employment. This can be enhanced through training and qualifications. Opportunities for employees may also be attractive as part of an employment package that cannot compete with salaries in the private sector. Courtney (1994) states that voluntary organizations are a major employer of paid and unpaid people with low academic attainment and suggests that the development of NVQs could provide accreditation and hence recognition of their extensive skills and experience. It could be argued therefore that learning and development have a particular focus in this sector. Similarly, the importance of workplace learning (see also Chapter 10), rather than a reliance on formal training provision, may be a key feature for organizations without the budget for expensive training courses.

To end this section on a positive note HRD in Practice 3.4 describes a voluntary organization where a very strong ethos results in the creation of a learning culture as a pathway towards achieving its organizational objectives. Many of the features of a strategic approach to HRD are present in theis case, including a commitment to learning from senior managers, environmental scanning to respond to external changes, and a flexible and supportive approach to learning and development.

HRD in Practice 3.4

Leeds Irish Health and Homes (LIHH)

LIHH is a charitable organization offering a variety of services and support not just to the Irish, but to the wider community in Leeds. It was established in 1992 when a steering committee of concerned Irish community representatives was convened in response to empirical and anecdotal evidence highlighting several areas of concern to health and social care professionals in Leeds. The organization's primary purpose is to enable people to live as independent a life as possible within their ethos of Care, Culture and Community, **www.lihh. org**. This is done through a combination of supported housing and outreach services. It ranges from one-to-one support and home visits to activities that help people overcome social isolation such as days out and luncheon groups.

There is a strong focus on learning and development in LIHH. The chief executive (CE) has a social work background and recognizes the value of creating opportunities to reflect on and review practice, thus integrating learning with day to day work. This commitment is shared by the Board who appreciate that staff need to be properly trained. One demonstration of this is the agreed annual budget for training; it is the same for each member of staff, so the lowest paid worker receives the same budget as the CE. The charity has Investor in People's 'gold' status.

The focus on development is about meeting individual and organizational needs. The culture of the charity is that people have a say in what happens and this extends to training, so the approach is both flexible and specific in relation to existing skills and current issues. Line managers review development needs with staff through appraisal and supervision. This is a two way dialogue rather than a prescriptive or standardized approach. At an organizational level, changes in strategy drive consideration of training and development requirements; for example the desire to develop services around dementia in response to an ageing client profile.

Looking for cost effective means of raising skill levels extends to the use of government funded online training. This is where local authority e-learning packages are made available to voluntary organizations. One such initiative enabled the CE to access group learning exercises, such as equality and diversity and induction, which could be delivered as training sessions.

A strong focus on learning is also evident in the regular training sessions and team meetings. These engage all staff in reviewing business plans and policies and provide an opportunity for sharing practice. This is augmented for new staff by a mentoring programme which draws on the experience of those with longer service (it is perhaps testament to the culture of the organization that turnover is very low). In order to respond to opportunities and challenges in the external environment in an appropriate way, a community development worker looks at government policies in areas such as health and social care.

L&D is also seen as key for senior managers in developing their strategic knowledge and planning skills. This occurs through encouragement to involve themselves in strategic groups, networking and direct training/mentoring opportunities. This helps the organization in political, environmental and economic terms. Through learning and development LIHH ensure they are prepared to meet the challenges of turbulent economic times.

Source: Hanlon et al. (2008)

activity

From the HRD practice evident within Leeds Irish Health and Homes, draw out some illustrative examples of the issues discussed so far in this chapter.

We have identified some unique features of the voluntary sector that impact on HRD, providing both opportunities and potential barriers. However, the start of our discussion was the initial difficulty over defining the sector, due in part to a diversity of organizations and we must be careful therefore not to over-generalize the characteristics. Interestingly, Clutterbuck and Dearlove (1996) suggest that size may be a more important determinant than sector, so a small computer training company will have more in common with a small charity than with a computer giant such as IBM. The influence of the size of business and the implications for HRD in the small business sector is the focus of the final part of this chapter.

The small business sector

Much of the literature on which our prevailing understanding about HRM and HRD is based reflects policy and practice in large organizations. However, over 99 per cent of European businesses are small, accounting for two-thirds of the working population (EC, 2012). Figure 3.1 shows that in the UK small businesses (0–49 employees) account for 46 per cent of employment and 35 per cent of turnover.

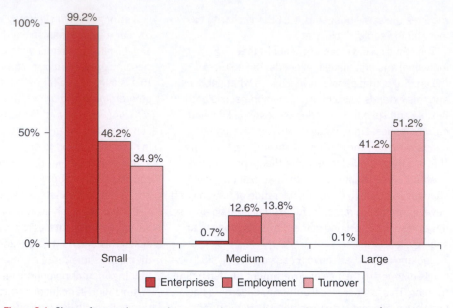

Figure 3.1 Share of enterprises, employment and turnover by size of business, 2011 (Department for Business Innovation and Skills)

Given the size and significance of the small business sector it is unsurprising that is seen by government as the sector to drive renewed economic growth and competitiveness (www.bis.gov.uk). However, whilst small businesses may create more jobs than their large firm counterparts, high rates of business failure among small firms mean that more of their jobs are lost. This suggests that the net picture of job creation hides an underlying picture of substantial 'job churn'. The potential role of L&D in providing support to reduce the high rates of business failure remains an interesting but largely un-researched question. Indeed, there is considerable Government interest in the extent to which L&D support for small business can both help reduce business failure and encourage growth. However, herein lies a key problem.

There is evidence (see for example PIU, 2001; Leitch, 2006) that the small business sector reflects recurrent weaknesses in terms of training. Using conventional measures of activity small firms are less likely to provide training than their large firm counterparts. CIPD data (2005) suggests that nearly 50 per cent of organizations employing less than 19 employees provide no training. Data from the *National Employers Survey 2007* (LSC, 2008), indicates that establishments with 25 or more staff are much more likely to provide training, both on and off the job, than smaller establishments. Similarly, the smaller organization is less likely to have a training plan and training budget.

It is particularly interesting to look at how many small businesses have been accredited with IiP. Its objective is to assist organizations to improve business performance through enhanced HRD practice. However, as noted by Smith and Collins (2007), there would appear to be considerable doubts as to its value to the vast majority of small businesses. In 2012 whilst 44 per cent of organizations with 250 employees or more are IiP accredited, less than 1 per cent of small businesses have this standard (UKCES, 2012). A key conclusion drawn by Smith and Collins is that small firms 'are not standard' and there are real difficulties in matching IiP requirements with the individual requirements of small businesses.

Interestingly, while there are compelling data to suggest a lack of formal training provision, small businesses appear highly positive about the value and potential benefits of training. Something of a training paradox can be identified. Survey evidence suggests that small business owners and managers hold a generally very positive attitude towards training. Yet over 85 per cent admit to not having provided their workforce with any training over the previous 12 months (Matlay, 2004). Exploration of this paradox is revealing and offers insights into the challenges facing small businesses in terms of L&D activity.

Challenges for learning and development in the small business sector

It is important to recognize that a small business is not a small large business and that it is a mistake to apply large firm solutions to small enterprises. Small businesses 'are not scaled down versions of large enterprises' (Johnson & Devins, 2008, p.9). Managing in a small business is likely to be highly individualized and difficult to relate to any 'textbook' formula of the management of training and development (Table 3.1).

Table 3.1 Characteristics of large vs. small firms

Large	Small
Long-term orientation	Short-term orientation
Predictive and planned business activity	Reactive and unplanned business activity
Annual budgetary planning	Weekly cash flow
Control and governance via board of directors	Dominance of owner/manager
Bureaucratic, hierarchical	Flatter, employees closer to 'boss'
Professional managers	Business people
Likely to have HR specialists	Unlikely to have HR specialist
More likely to have a trade union	Less likely to have a trade union

activity

Think about any of your work experience. Has this involved work in a small organization? What distinctive features can you recall?

While acknowledging the danger of an overly simplistic generalization we might suggest that the context in which L&D operates within a small business is one of a more flexible labour force, more individualized employment relationships, a clearer and shared perception of the primary goal and a greater awareness of the need for change.

Raising demand

The Leitch Report (2006) on workforce development in the UK called for much greater demand-led training from within the small business sector. However, the 'structural' barriers identified above create difficulties for small businesses to make full use of the training market. A number of perceptions about available training make matters worse. These include concerns about:

- the cost of training
- the availability of directly relevant training
- uncertainty and ignorance about products such as IiP and vocational qualifications.

In response to such difficulties, there has been no shortage of publicly funded initiatives that have sought to help small businesses to access and engage in a greater level of training and development activity. However, the track record of such initiatives is not good. The case below provides some illustration of the problems encountered.

HRD in Practice 3.5

'Business as usual': the case of the learning broker

The Human Resource Development and Leadership Unit at Leeds Metropolitan University was commissioned to do an evaluation of an initiative to stimulate demand for workplace learning among small businesses within the metal engineering sector in south Yorkshire. Monies had been made available to business for training via an 'expert' training intermediary: a learning broker. A number of interrelated problems combined to undermine the impact of the initiative:

- Many organizations brought forward training they were planning to do anyway. Companies appeared happy to chase a grant to assist with training needs already identified rather than engage in a more fundamental review of how training could play a role in medium-to-long-term business development.
- A tension existed between pressures on the broker to meet short-term targets (i.e get some visible training underway) and longer term organizational training and development needs. There were missed opportunities for a broker-initiated consideration of systems of production and the adoption of newer technologies.
- The broker was an employee of the employers' body representing the businesses in this sector and thus freedom of action to provide objective advice was compromised by his own position in the network of vested interests.

The researchers concluded that the relationship between small firms and an expert training intermediary held potential but not without significant shifts in thinking in terms of levels, use and conditions attached to public monies allocated to enhance demand for skills within the small business sector.

(See also Holden et al., 2006)

Re-visiting the paradox

In response to the apparent paucity of training activity within small businesses recent research has begun to raise the issue of whether this is correctly identified as a lack of training or is more a problem of definition. In other words, learning activity may well be taking place but be of a character and nature that does not sit comfortably with any commonly understood definition of formal training (i.e. mainly off job and/or provided by external sources). In a seminal article on this issue Hill and Stewart (2000) argue the need for alternative ways of understanding HRD in small businesses. They examined HRD policies and practice in three small organizations using a model of HRD that typically underpins IiP policy and practice as a benchmark. In the main this confirmed the sort of analysis highlighted earlier, i.e. a lack of formal training together with few formal systems to identify, access and evaluate training activity. However, Hill and Stewart suggest that closer scrutiny of actual practice revealed a different picture. One technical manager interviewed noted that workforce training and development activities were ad hoc, 'with a reliance on the *informal sharing of expertise* on the shop floor' (emphases added). The same manager suggested that mistakes were treated as 'learning opportunities' and employees were encouraged to make suggestions for improved working practice on the basis that 'they are the experts'. Hill and Stewart conclude that the nature of training and development in small firms mirrors the characteristics of the businesses themselves – both are essentially informal, reactive and short-term in outlook.

Learning and development in practice

As a result of the growing body of research exploring HRD in the small business sector Gold and Thorpe (2008) suggest there is now recognition that 'informal learning should be given the acknowledgement and prominence it warrants'. Three key facets of this informal learning landscape are highlighted below. Together they provide a more realistic and accurate portrayal of learning and development activity and the extent to which this can play a role in helping a small business achieve organizational effectiveness.

Workplace job instruction and coaching

Much L&D activity in small businesses can be described as direct supervision and corrective coaching by an experienced manager or employee. Johnson and Devins (2008) argue that this informal training and assessment, based on personal observation and task specific coaching, suits the purposes of many small organizations. Of some importance are the relationships that are established. In their research with 80 tourism and hospitality small businesses Kyriakidou and Maroudas (2010) highlight that owner-managers readily acknowledged the significance of their role in developing well-trained, competent staff. The majority pointed to the establishment of a 'trusting relationship' where they believed they were perceived 'less like a boss and more like a coach or supporter' (p.40).

In recent years the potential of coaching within small organizations has been recognized by Government. A £200m initiative was announced by the Business Innovation and Skills Department in 2012 focusing attention on potential high-growth small businesses. (See also http://www.bis.gov.uk/policies/economic-development/leps/lep-toolbox/helping-smes/coaching)

Networks

The significance of networks is recognized in the small business literature (see, for example, Blundel & Smith, 2001). However, it is only relatively recently that researchers have begun to focus on this point in the context of learning. Taylor and Thorpe (2000) for example, challenge the view of the small organization MD's learning being akin to operating as an 'intellectual Robinson Crusoe', identifying the importance of a extensive social dimension to their management decision-making. Theodorakopoulos and Wyer (2001) highlight how networking is an integral part of small business learning; learning is 'built' through relationships. This includes interface with key 'others' as diverse as customers, suppliers, the bank and the accountant. Closer to home, key relationships are those with staff, and an owner/manager's friends and family. While some effective learning may result from 'fleeting interfaces', significant areas of understanding and insight often require the build-up of a longer term, trusting relationship. Jones et al. (2010) argue that it is a small organization's limited managerial resources which means they are dependent upon knowledge from external sources, including feedback from customers and suppliers. This knowledge, though, is critical to improving organizational performance. A number of researchers in the field refer to this as the acquisition and development of social capital (see, for example, Hynes, 2009). Networks, formal and informal, are the key to developing this social capital. Jack et al. (2008) highlight the need for social skills in building and sustaining bridging (external links) and bonding (internal ties) networks.

Organizational culture

Not all small businesses have the sort of organizational culture which provides a context for informal learning to flourish. Ahlgren et al. (2007) identify three types of organizational learning culture, strongly influenced by the attitudes and modus operandi of the owner manager. These are expansive, restrictive and passive restricted. Companies in which the manager held an expansive attitude to learning were characterized by opportunities for all employees to develop, an emphasis on team work and social and informal learning and where managers were facilitators of employee learning. Interestingly the research suggests that small businesses in the care sector were the most likely to have embraced an expansive learning culture (see also Rainbird et al., 2009). Research elsewhere supports the same argument. Kyriakidou and Maroudas (2010) talk of 'the development of a learning culture by allowing people to gain from each other by sharing experience, skills and knowledge' in their study of small hospitality businesses. Importantly, a strategic dimension is also evident in this portrayal of L&D; the authors point to the link between a strong learning culture and the achievement of longer term goals through the retention of good staff.

Other parts of the book develop ideas about knowledge management in greater depth (see Chapter 10). However the importance of an organizational culture in providing a context for the development and dissemination of knowledge within a small organization is important to note. Higgins and Mirza (2012) highlight that in many small businesses knowledge is gained through practice as opposed to formal instruction. They argue that in terms of the most effective policy and practice to support small organizations there is a need to recognize that 'learning through practice with its focus on real world issues and lived experiences and which are contextually embedded in the owner-manager's environment, offers the best prospects for small business learning' (p.1).

In HRD in Practice 3.6 two case studies are drawn from very different sectors. However, in both, key aspects of L&D practice can be seen to reflect the essential characteristics of 'informal learning' highlighted above.

HRD **in Practice** **3.6**	## Small business learning

Case A operates in the pharmaceutical sector developing hygiene products for onward sale to mainstream 'household name' companies. It has a Managing Director, a Finance Director and ten R&D employees. Organizational success is dependent on the products being 'frontline' and 'leading edge'. Work is flexible, 'everybody doing everything'. Although the MD and FD officially take the formal decisions these are usually preceded by discussions with the staff. There is no formal training policy and recessionary times have meant that little formal training takes place. However, knowledge is constantly developing within the organization.

Learning is informal, mirroring the organization of work within the business. It is driven by concrete problems originating from customers and collaborators in research projects. Extensive use is made of Facebook, both internally and with many of the organization's external links. When resources permit, staff attend research seminars and trade events. These activities generate useful discussion back at work and help extend their external networks of contacts. The MD and FD run quarterly coaching-oriented, development sessions with all staff.

Case B is an inner city bar, initially owned by three partners and run by a full-time manager together with 12–15 part-time employees, mostly local students. Following two years of losses a business re-think resulted in one of the partners being bought out. The remaining partners, James and Tom, adopted different roles. James began to address certain strategic issues and Tom thought carefully about the week-by-week work. James had informal discussions with their accountant and bank. He also had a chat with his brother, himself an accountant. Tom sought to tap his network of reps, suppliers and ex-tutors from college. An experienced restaurateur ,for whom Tom had worked previously, highlighted a number of 'tricks of the trade'. One-to-one instruction, followed by coaching in quiet periods, was introduced in the 'art' of operating the hand pumps in order to reduce wastage. A weekly staff meeting introduced by Tom was revelatory. Staff took on different responsibilities in terms of live music, a limited snack menu, the graphic art and design for promotions. It became noticeable that the staff were a close bunch, reliable, hard-working and sharing a strong identification with the bar's ethos. Most of them helped out with a major refurbishment for nothing. Financially, turnover began to increase and a year later the business generated a small profit.

Sources: Wihak and Hall (2011) and Holden and Walmsley (2008).

In this section we have sought to discuss HRD practice in small businesses. The significance of the small business sector to the skills policy agenda within the UK is not in doubt, given their relative importance as employers and potential sources of increased productivity, innovation and competitiveness. While conventional wisdom portrays a picture of weak, demand-limited training activity we have sought to question this interpretation. Increasingly, research suggests that this paints an unnecessarily negative picture; one that does not take sufficient account of the informal, flexible nature of much workforce development that takes place in small organizations. Of course, informal learning and development is not the preserve of the small business. It is evident in all organizations. However, on any continuum (see also Wihak & Hall, 2011) an organization's size is likely to show a strong relationship with the level and significance of informal learning. The nature of work in a small organization is often messy, untidy and fraught with difficulties. Much the same can be said for L&D. This said, in the best of cases this learning can lead to effective strategic developments which support organizational objectives. While it is important to recognize the nature and character of small business learning, this is not to cede that there remains a strong case for enhancing further the demand for, and application of, skills within the small business workplace. Government rhetoric is well intentioned. However, it is practice that engages with, responds to and is directly relevant to small businesses that is likely to increase organizational demand for skills. If the market in which such practice is deployed is less driven by targets and more accommodating, supportive and understanding of the small business world, HRD practice and the learning it generates can add real strategic capability to the small business.

summary

⦿ The HRD challenges facing organizations in these three sectors have been explored. They include:
– the need to 'modernize' (public sector)
– the nature of the work and the workforce (all three sectors)
– the complexity of stakeholders (the voluntary and community sector)
– the absence of any specialist HRD position/function (the voluntary sector and small businesses)
– the short-term orientation (small businesses).
⦿ In relation to the different contexts, distinctive characteristics of the HRD landscape have been identified and illustrated. For example:
– Public Sector: leadership and professional development, equality of access to learning
– Voluntary Sector: collaborative learning; the integration of work and learning
– Small Businesses: the power of informal learning.

⦿ Critically, in terms of HRD practice, there is no neat formula which can be easily transferred from the large private firm into a charity or a small business. Similarly, the leadership challenge facing many public sector organizations is largely unique to the sector. Of course, to say that no aspects of good practice are transferable would be a nonsense. Rather, this chapter has argued for sensitivity to context and how managers and employees face subtly different demands, are accustomed to different cultures and face business pressures which are mediated differently because of the context.
⦿ Ultimately, HRD practice needs to be contingent on the situation if it is to be most effective in supporting the development of both individuals who work within such contexts and the organization as a whole. Examples in this chapter clearly indicate that this is not just rhetoric, demonstrating how their approach to HRD practice can achieve the contribution to which all protagonists of HRD aspire.

discussion questions

1 Identify three differences between a large private sector firm and an organization in one of the other sectors addressed.

2 The Metropolitan Police being labelled institutionally racist and the death, in care, of 'Baby P' are examples of how public sector organizations face very distinctive pressures. What are the implications for HRD?

3 Why is the complexity of stakeholders, referred to in the voluntary and community sector of particular relevance for HRD?

4 Why did we question the 'prevailing' evidence about the level of training and development undertaken by small businesses?

5 Recall an example from each of the sectors where HRD is linked to strategic change. What do you feel is the particular contribution L&D can make?

further reading

Beattie, R. and Waterhouse, J. (2012) *Human Resource Management in Public Service Organizations*. London: Routledge.

Venter, K. and Sung, J. (2011) *Do Skills Matter? A Literature Review on Skills and Workforce Development in the Third Sector*. Available from http://www.skills-thirdsector.org.uk/documents/complete-report-literature-review.pdf, accessed 26 July 2012.

references

Ahlgren, L. Riddell, S. and Weedon, E. (2007) *Experiences of Workplace Learning in SMEs*. Edinburgh: Centre for Research in Education Inclusion and Diversity.

Beattie, R.S. (2006) Line managers and workplace learning: learning from the voluntary sector. *Human Resource Development International*, **9**(1): 100–19.

Beevers, R. (2006) *Customer Service Excellence in Public Services*. Sunderland: Northern Housing Consortium.

Benetto, J. (2012) *Police and Racism: what Has Been Achieved Ten Years After the Stephen Lawrence Inquiry?* London: Equality and Human Rights Commission.

Billis, D. and Glennerster, H. (1998) Human services and the voluntary sector: towards a theory of comparative advantage. *Journal of Social Policy*, **27**(1): 79–98.

Birdi, K.S., Patterson, M.G. and Wood, S.J. (2007) Learning to perform? A comparison of learning practices and organizational performance in profit and non-profit-making sectors in the UK. *International Journal of Training and Development*, **11**(4): 265–81.

Black, K. (2012) *Building New Knowledge? The Case of Multi-Agency Working with Children's Services in England, 13th International Conference on HRD Research and Practice Across Europe, 25–27 May*. Universidade Lusiada de Vila Nova de Famalicao.

Blackmore, A. (2004) *Standing Apart, Working Together: A Study of the Myths and Realities of Voluntary and Community Sector Independence*. London: NCVO.

Blundel, R.K. and Smith, D. (2001) *Business Networking: SMEs and Inter-Firm Collaboration: A Review of the Literature*. Sheffield: DTI/Small Business Service.

CIPD (2005) *Who Learns at Work?* London: CIPD.

CIPD (2010) Delivering more with less: the people management challenge. *Building Productive Public Services Workplaces Series*. London: CIPD.

CIPD (2012). *Learning and Talent Development: Annual Survey Report 2012*. London: Chartered Institute of Personnel and Development.

Clutterbuck, D. and Dearlove, D. (1996) *The Charity as a Business: Managing in the Public Sector, Learning from the Private Sector*. London: Directory of Social Change.

Courtney, R. (1994) Directions in voluntary sector management. *Management Development Review*, **7**(3): 33–6.

Coyle-Shapiro, J. and Kessler, I (2003) The employment relationship in the U.K. public sector: a psychological contract perspective. *Journal of Public Administration Research and Theory*, **13**(2): 213–230.

Cunningham, I. (2001) Sweet charity! Managing employee commitment in the UK voluntary sector. *Employee Relations*, **23**(3): 192–206.

European Commission (2012) *European Small Business Portal*, http://ec.europa.eu/small-business/index_en.htm

Georgellis, Y., Iossa, E., Tabvuma, V. (2011) Crowding out intrinsic motivation in the public sector. *Journal of Public Administration Research and Theory*, **21**(3): 473–93.

Goddard, S. and Palmer, A. (2010) An evaluation of the effects of a National Health Service Trust merger on the learning and development of staff. *Human Resource Development International*, **13**(5): 557–73.

Gold, J., Thorpe, R. and Mumford, A (2010) *Leadership and Management Development*, 5th edn. London: CIPD.

Gold, J. and Thorpe, R. (2008) Training, it's a load of crap: the story of the hairdresser and his suit. *Human Resource Development International*, **11**(4): 385–99.

Griggs, V. and Holden, R.J. (2008) *Interview with Mental Health Charity Personnel Officer*. Leeds: Leeds Metropolitan University.

Hanlon, A., Griggs, V. and Holden, R.J. (2008) *HRD within Leeds Irish Health and Homes: Interview with Ant Hanlon*. Leeds: Leeds Metropolitan University.

Hawkins, P (2011) *Leadership Team Coaching: Developing Collective Transformational Leadership*. London: Kogan Page.

Harris, L (2008) The changing nature of the HR function in UK local government and its role as 'employee champion'. *Employee Relations*, **30**(1), 34–47.

Higgins, D. and Mirza, M. (2012) A Contemporary Theoretical Position towards Social Learning in the Small Firm, *Irish Journal of Management,* **32**(2): 1–17

Hill, R. and Stewart, J. (2000) Human resource development in small organizations. *Journal of European Industrial Training*, **24**(2/3/4): 105–17.

Holden, B.T. and Walmsley, A. (2007) *The Dr Wu's Story: Interview with Ben Holden*. Leeds: Leeds Metropolitan University.

Holden and Griggs (2011) Not more learning logs! A research based perspective on teaching reflective learning within HR professional education. *Human Resource Development International*, **14**(4): 483–91.

Holden, R.J., Nabi, G., Gold, J. and Robertson, M. (2006) Building capability in small businesses: tales from the training front. *Journal of European Industrial Training*, **30**(6): 424–40.

Hynes, B. (2009) Growing the social enterprise: issues and challenges. *Social Enterprise Journal*, **5**(2): 114–25.

Institute of Employment Studies (2010) *Review of the NHS Knowledge and Skills Framework by* Brown, D., Mercer, M., Buchan, J., Miller, L., Chubb, C., Cox, A., Robinson, D.NHS Employers, April 2010.

Jack, S., Dodd, S.A. and Anderson, A. (2008) Change and the development of entrepreneurial networks over time. *Entrepreneurship & Regional Development*, **20**(2): 125–59.

Johnson, S. and Devins, D. (2008) Training and workforce development in SMEs: myth and reality. *Sector Skills Development Agency, SSDA Catalyst*, **7**.

Jones, O., Macpherson, A. and Thorpe, R. (2010) Learning in owner-managed small firms. *Entrepreneurship & Regional Development*, **22**: 7–8, 649–73.

Kellock Hay, G., Beattie, R., Livingstone, R. and Munro, P. (2001) Change, HRM and the voluntary sector. *Employee Relations*, **23**(3): 240–55.

Kendall, J. (2003) *The Voluntary Sector: Comparative Perspectives in the UK*. London: Routledge.

Kendall, J. and Knapp, M. (1995) A loose and baggy monster: boundaries, definitions and typologies In J. Davis-Smith, C. Rochester and R. Hedley (eds) *An Introduction to the Voluntary Sector*. London: Routledge.

Kyriakidou, O. and Maroudas, L. (2010) Training and development in British hospitality, tourism and leisure SMEs. *Managing Leisure,* **15**: 32–47.

Leitch, S. (2006) *Prosperity for All in the Global Economy: World Class Skills*. London: HM Treasury.

Leslie, K. and Camwell, A. (2010) Leadership at all levels: leading public sector organizations in an age of austerity. *European Management Journal*, **28**(4): 297–305.

LSC (Learning and Skills Council) (2008) *National Employers Survey 2007: Key Findings*. Coventry: LSC.

Macpherson, Sir W. (1999) *The Stephen Lawrence Inquiry*. London: HMSO.

Matlay, H. (2004) Contemporary training initiatives in Britain: a small business perspective. *Journal of Small Business and Enterprise Development*, **11**(4): 504–13.

Moir (2012) *HR in Times of Austerity: A Public Sector Perspective*. London: CIPD Centres Conference.

Morris, J. and Farrell, C. (2007) The 'post-bureaucratic' public sector organization: New organizational forms and HRM in ten UK public sector organizations. *International Journal of Human Resource Management*, **18**(9): 1575–88.

Myers, J. and Sacks, R. (2001) Harnessing the talents of a loose and baggy monster. *Journal of European Industrial Training*, **25**(9): 454–64.

NCVO (National Council for Voluntary Organizations) (2006) *The UK Voluntary Sector Almanac 2006: The State of the Sector*. London: NCVO.

Newsome, K. and Cunningham, I. (2003) *More Than Just a Wing and a Prayer: Identifying Human Resource Capacity Among Small and Medium Sized Organizations in the Voluntary Sector*. Department of Human Resource Management: University of Strathclyde.

Nicholls, A. (2012) *Learning and Development within Leeds City Council*, Unpublished Postgraduate Diploma in HRM Dissertation. Leeds: Leeds Metropolitan University.

OECD (2012) *Better Skills, Better Jobs, Better Lives: A Strategic Approach to Skills Policies*. OECD Publishing, http://dx.doi.org/10.1787/9789264177338-en.

PACEC (2006) *The Impact of IiP in the Public Sector*. Cambridge: Public and Corporate Economic Consultants.

Parry, E., Kelliher, C., Mills, T. and Tyson, S. (2005) Comparing HRM in the voluntary and public sectors. *Personnel Review*, **34**(5): 588–602.

Perry, S. (2011) *Case Study: Clinical Leaders' Development Programme*. Salford Royal NHS Foundation Trust.

PIU (Performance and Innovation Unit) (2001) *In Demand: Adult Skills in the 21st Century*. PIU: Cabinet Office.

Pratt, J., Plamping, D. and Gordon, P. (2007) *Distinctive Characteristics of Public Sector Organizations and Implications for Leadership*. Leeds: Centre for Innovation in Health Management.

Rainbird, H., Leeson, E. and Munro, A. (2009) *Skill Development in the Social Care Sector*. Birmingham and Edinburgh: University of Birmingham and Edinburgh Napier University.

Saundry, R., Hollinrake, A. and Antcliff, V. (2011) *Research Paper 12*. Institute for Research into Organizations, Work and Employment: University of Central Lancashire.

Smith, A.J. and Collins, L.A. (2007) How does IiP deliver the lifelong learning agenda to SMEs? *Education and Training*, **49**(8/9): 720–31.

Taylor, D. and Thorpe, R. (2000) *The Owner Manager – No Isolated Monad: Learning As a Process of Co-Participation*. Paper presented at 23rd ISBA Conference, Aberdeen.

Theodorakopoulos, N. and Wyer, P. (2000) *Small Business Growth and the Use of Networks*. Proceedings of 23rd ISBA Conference, Aberdeen.

Thursfield, D. (2008) Managers' Learning in a UK Local Authority: The Political Context of an In-house MBA. *Management Learning*, July, **39**(3): 295–309.

Truss, C., (2008) Continuity and Change: the role of the HR function in the modern public sector. *Public Administration*, **86**(4): 1071–88.

Tyson, S. (1999) How HR knowledge contributes to organizational performance. *Human Resource Management Journal*, **9**(3): 42–52.

UKCES (2012) *Research To Support The Evaluation Of Investors In People: Employer Survey*. London, UK Commission for Employment and Skills.

Walton, J. (1996) The provision of learning support for non-employees. In J. Stewart and J. McGoldrick (eds) *Human Resource Development: Perspectives, Strategies and Practice*. London: Pitman.

Webb, S., Casanegra, M., Evans, A., Fjeldstad, O.-H., Isaksen, J., Funke, I., Webb, R. and Wescott, C. (2008) *Public Sector Reform: What Works and Why?* Washington DC: World Bank.

Wihak, C. and Hall, G. (2011) *Work Related Informal Learning*. Ottawa: Centre for Workplace Skills.

Whitmore, J. (2009) *Coaching for Performance: Growing Human Potential and Purpose. The Principles and Practice of Coaching and Leadership*, 4th edn. London: Nicholas Brealey Publishing.

Zacharias, L. (2003) Small change. *People Management*, **1**: 24–7.

Niki Kyriakidou, Crystal Ling Zhang, Paul Iles and Nehal Mahtab

chapter 4

Cross-Cultural HRD

Chapter learning outcomes

After studying this chapter, you should be able to:

- Consider different positions in comparative HRD
- Define the concept of culture
- Analyse some key theoretical perspectives on culture
- Analyse the role and importance of HRD in international enterprises
- Critically analyse intercultural and cross-cultural training (CCT)
- Consider HRD in international organizations with particular reference to China and the Middle East

Chapter outline

Introduction
Comparative HRD: the nationality thesis
Institutionalist approaches and national business systems
What is culture?
The concept of culture and HRD
HRD in international enterprises
Cross-cultural/intercultural training
International knowledge transfer and HRD
Summary

Introduction

With increasing globalization, issues of culture and cultural awareness have become more important. However, national differences in values and practices persist, and various models have been developed to analyse cultural differences, linked to differences in behaviour. This chapter explores the importance of institutionalist and culturalist explanations of national differences in institutions, values and behaviours. The development of international managers and other staff has become imperative, and cross-cultural training (CCT) in particular has grown in importance. This chapter discusses different types of global or international staff, especially the kinds of competences and skills needed to perform effectively in the light of cross-cultural adjustment problems. It analyses the kinds of training and development strategies necessary for effective performance, using various case studies to illustrate effective practice. Finally, the chapter explores the role of HRD in joint ventures and knowledge transfer, especially the role expatriates can play in coaching and mentoring locals, with particular reference to China and the Middle East.

Comparative HRD: the nationality thesis

The nationality thesis argues that globalization does not necessarily force countries, sectors and firms towards a convergence in their structure, culture, patterns of behaviour and HRD policies and practices. Institutional and cultural legacies continue to exert an influence, for example US firms differ from German firms in the strategic role played by HRD, the role of the unions and their commitment to training and development. Different frameworks have been developed to analyse and examine this issue; the most significant contributions to the debates so far have come from culturalist and institutionalist approaches (Vo, 2009).

Institutionalists argue for the importance of different national institutions or business systems in explaining comparative differences in HRD. Culturalists argue for the continuing importance of national culture to explain such differences, explaining organizational structure and practice as a collective enactment of beliefs and values or shared cognitive structures, ideas and understandings (for example Hofstede, 2001). We shall explore culture in more detail below. The claim here is that organizational patterns and processes, and managerial beliefs and behaviours, are driven by shared understandings and ideas. In contrast, institutionalists argue that this approach fails to consider cultural patterns as dynamic and emerging characteristics linked to historical development, with close relationships to specific institutions and social groups.

HRD in particular is performed differently in different countries and HRD policy and practice remains diverse. Globalization is often overstated; most trade is not global but uneven, mostly regional and conducted between relatively distinct national economies. Most international enterprises are not genuinely transnationals, but national companies with international business operations; their income, employment, strategic decisions, board composition and share ownership are still mainly rooted in their home country, and nation states remain significant global players, with distinctive laws and regulations.

Institutional theorists claim that organizations are socially constituted, rooted in institutional settings. They analyse national institutions and their interactions with business and management as national business systems. Usually the state, the financial and educational/HRD systems, the industrial relations system, and the network of business associations such as chambers of commerce are seen as key institutions affecting business and management. They all impact on enterprises' HRD processes, such as how firms go about training and development.

For example, Germany and Japan may be seen as collaborative business environments, in contrast to the more competitive Anglo-Saxon US/UK models.

Institutionalist approaches and national business systems

Institutional perspectives therefore see national institutional arrangements as relatively robust, demonstrating significant inertia in the face of pressures for change. They focus on macro-level societal institutions, in particular those that govern 'access to critical resources, especially labour and capital' (Whitley, 1999, p.47), and look to differences in the organization and the activities of the state, the capital, labour and financial systems, and the route taken by different countries to industrialization and modernization. Systematic analysis of the major national institutions and the interactions between institutional arrangements is termed the 'national industrial order' by Lane (1992) in her analysis of British financial- versus German production-oriented capitalism, and 'national business systems' by Whitley (1999) in his analysis of divergent capitalisms and the different paths taken by nations. This is the term we will use here.

Whitley (1999) distinguishes three ideal types of national business systems:

1 *Particularistic:* lacking trust in formal institutions, with a weak or predatory state, weak collective intermediaries and norms governing transactions, and paternalistic authority relationships, for example China. This leads to flexibility and opportunistic hierarchies. Opportunistic hierarchies rarely develop complex and stable organizational capabilities, owner control is typically direct and personal, coordination is highly personal and non-routinized, and flexibility is the response to the unpredictable environment.

2 *Collaborative*: interlocking institutions encouraging cooperative behaviour such as Japan, Germany, Austria and Sweden. This leads to cooperative hierarchies and corporatist/interventionist approaches (see also Chapter 2). Owners and managers share authority with employees and partners, and skilled manual workers are typically integrated into the organization as core members and social partners.

3 *Arm's-length*: flexible entry and exit within an institutionalized formal system, with competitive capital markets. The state acts as a regulator, and training is seen more as a matter for individual firm investment than a matter for coordinated collaboration between the state, employers and unions, for example the USA, and California in particular. This leads to isolated hierarchies, where independence between collective actors is low, formal procedures govern interrelationships, and owners tend to be remote from managers. Firms are reluctant to share authority, and organizational competences and competitive capabilities are highly firm specific.

However, there is a danger of overgeneralization. Whitley (1999), for example, claims that Japan and Germany are examples of collaborative business environments generating cooperative hierarchies, but there are significant differences between the Japanese and German education and training systems, such as the development of the internal labour market in large Japanese firms, as opposed to the great support German firms receive from the system of education and technical/vocational training, which focuses on skill development that is responsive to economic needs (Lane, 1995). German firms are strong in professional specialization and career advancement within functional hierarchies, in contrast to the rotation of generalist managers often practised in Japan.

The institutional perspective is criticized as being over-determined by national stereotypes, and neglecting the potential for human agency. It is also difficult to apply in transitional periods. In his study of retail practices in China, Gamble (2003) argues that it is difficult to assess what exactly constitutes the contemporary Chinese national business system, and thus what the distinctive Chinese approach to HRD actually is. So we also need to explore culturalist perspectives.

What is culture?

Although there is no standard definition of culture, the concept of culture is deeply rooted in human history. Culture usually refers to the shared attitudes, beliefs and behaviours that individuals learn from the family and society in which they live – a dynamic process, impacting on everything that people do and think. We learn culture through interaction, observation and imitation in order to participate as members of a social group.

activity

In groups of four or five, discuss the differences in national cultures. List some components of your own national culture. Write down your definition of culture in no more than 20 words.

Culture is typically defined as:

> the system of shared beliefs, values, customs, behaviours, and artefacts that the members of society use to cope with their world and with one another, and that are transmitted from generation to generation through learning. (Bates & Plog, 1990, p.7).

Culture is therefore often seen as the set of commonly held and relatively stable beliefs, attitudes and values that exist within an organization (organizational or corporate culture) or society (national or societal culture). It influences the way organizations and managers undertake and implement decision-making and resolve problems (Hall, 1984). Culture is embodied in symbols, rituals and heroes, and reflected in organizational communication, such as manners, dress codes, social rules and norms and role models.

Cultural dimensions

According to Kluckhohn and Strodbeck (1961), there are six fundamental dimensions for cultural analysis:

- Who are we, and how does society conceive of people's qualities, for example good, bad, lazy, capable of being changed?

- How do we relate to the world – existence?
- What do we do? In some countries, this question refers to what someone does, in others to what someone is.
- How do we relate to each other? For example, do we think of ourselves as individuals or members of a social/professional group?
- How do we think about time? According to Harris et al. (2004), western societies see time as a commodity to be managed effectively. Other societies, for example Mediterranean countries and many Asian countries, have looser relationships with time.
- How do we think about space, for example room size, physical space between two people when they are talking to each other? Northern European and Japanese people often desire more distant relationships than many African or southern European peoples.

Perhaps the most influential cultural theorist has been Hofstede (2001), whose typology of cultural dimension is widely used in cross-cultural research. In a survey of IBM employees, Hosftede found:

- National differences in behaviour and attitudes
- Such differences did not change much over time
- National cultural values were more significant than work-related values, such as those related to profession/age/gender/position in the organization
- People bring their ethnicity and culture to the workplace.

Hosftede's cultural dimensions are as follows (adapted from http://geert-hofstede.com/dimensions.html):

- *Power distance* (PD) focuses on the degree of equality, or inequality, between people in the society. A high power distance ranking indicates that inequalities of power and wealth have been allowed to grow and are generally accepted. In organizational terms, PD relates to the centralization of power and degree of autocratic leadership (Harris et al., 2004).
- *Individualism* (IDV) focuses on the degree to which the society reinforces individual or collective achievement and interpersonal relationships. High IDV indicates a larger number of looser relationships, and low IDV typifies societies of a more collectivist nature.
- *Masculinity* (MAS) focuses on the degree the society reinforces the traditional masculine work role model of male achievement, control and power. High MAS indicates that the country experiences a high degree of gender differentiation, while low MAS indicates low levels of differentiation and discrimination between genders, with females treated relatively equally to males.
- *Uncertainty avoidance* (UA) focuses on levels of tolerance for uncertainty and ambiguity within the society. High UA indicates rule-oriented societies that develop laws, rules, regulations and controls in order to reduce uncertainty. Low UA indicates a society that is less rule-oriented, more readily accepting of change and more risk-oriented.
- *Long-term orientation* (LTO) focuses on the extent to which a society exhibits a pragmatic, future-oriented perspective rather than a conventional historic or short-term point of view. Countries scoring high on this dimension have a

long-term perspective, easily accept change and emphasize thrift and investment, for example China. Cultures scoring low on this dimension, for example many West African societies, believe in absolute truth, are traditional and have a short-term perspective.

• *Indulgence versus Restraint* (IVR) focuses on the extent that a society allows or suppresses gratification of basic and natural human drives in relation to enjoying life and having fun. This dimension is about the subject of happiness and relates to the importance of leisure, of controlling your own destiny and of freedom of expression. For example, countries scoring low in Indulgence and high in Restraint dimensions will not think free expression of thoughts important.

In organizational settings, taking the two dimensions of UA and PD together, you can see differences in the way employees think about organizational structure and operations, as shown in Table 4.1.

For example, in societies with high UA and high PD, such as Japan and France, the key element is the standardization of work processes by specifying work contents (Harris et al., 2004). Employees in high UA and low PD societies, such as Israel and Germany, tend to work in organizations where roles and procedures are clearly specified and coordination and control are achieved through qualifications and skills acquisition.

Schwarz (1990) developed his classifications because of difficulties with Hofstede's; collectivism/individualism have some values in common, and the dichotomy implies a polar distinction in which individual and collective goals cannot be coincident (Gouveia & Ros, 2002). Schwarz (1990) included seven dimensions of analysis:

1 conservatism
2 hierarchy
3 mastery
4 affective autonomy
5 intellectual autonomy
6 egalitarian commitment
7 harmony.

Steenkamp (2001) argues that Schwartz's classification is superior in its theoretical grounding, but has not been empirically tested.

Another well-known approach is based on the work of Trompenaars (1997), who defines culture as an instrument to solve three universally shared problem

Table 4.1 Thinking about organizational structure and operations

Dimensions	Structure and operations	Countries
Low UA, high PD	Personal bureaucracy	Hong Kong, India
High UA, high PD	Full bureaucracy	Japan, France
Low UA, low PD	Marketplace bureaucracy	UK, Scandinavia
High UA, low PD	Workflow bureaucracy	Israel, Germany

Source: Based on Brooks (2003)

areas: human relationships, time and nature. Trompenaars and Hampden-Turner (1997) consequently identify seven bipolar dimensions:

- Universalism versus particularism
- Communitarianism versus individualism
- Neutral versus emotional
- Diffuse versus specific cultures
- Achievement versus ascription
- Human–time relationship
- Human–nature relationship.

Each dimension represents a dilemma for acting and deciding. People are often forced to choose. For example, in the UK, we would tend to favour universal in terms of preferences for rules for everyone to follow, whereas in Spain, there might be a preference to work out rules based on the particulars of a situation. If people are unaware of these preferences, this is likely to result in misunderstandings and difficulties.

reflective question   How aware are you of your cultural preferences?

Go to **http://www.thtconsulting.com/Website/OurTools/CCOL.asp**, for further explanation of the dimensions.

Hofstede's work has received sustained criticism, particularly in terms of methodology, especially since the publication of the second edition of the original book (Hofstede, 2001). McSweeney (2001, 2002) finds national culture implausible as a systematically causal factor of behaviour, arguing that both functionalist and other paradigms are needed for future research and for understanding social behaviour in different national cultures.

The concept of culture and HRD

The increasing drive of most international corporations to standardize managerial practices across nations has been influenced by national cultural values as companies search for effective international practices. Little research has been conducted on the impact of culture in the area of HRD (McGuire et al., 2001). As Ardichvili and Kuchinke (2002, p.145) report:

> International and comparative research is one of the fastest growing areas of scholarly inquiry in HRD. All international HRD studies, regardless of specific topics of investigation, sooner or later refer to culture. Therefore, the treatment of culture in international HRD research is a matter of central importance.

Culture and perceived cultural distance have been shown to affect entry modes of international enterprises, such as acquisition, greenfield site or joint venture (JV) (Holliman et al., 2008). Interventionist models of HRD tend to be more commonly found in societies showing lower IDV and LTO, but lower UA than countries showing voluntarist models, as Chapter 1 has shown.

National culture may particularly impact HRD; some Asian or Latin employees may expect training styles to be formal, deferential and directive (high PD), resisting group work that mixes hierarchical levels or involves direct, open criticism or feedback. Scandinavians may expect HRD to be informal and participative, and see direct feedback as welcome. People from high UA cultures, for example Japan, may be unhappy with experiential training, for example action learning and outdoor development, which involve some risk and uncertainty, preferring more structure. Learning styles may vary also with culture (see Zhang et al., 2006; Zhang & Iles, 2008; and HRD in Practice 4.1).

HRD in Practice 4.1

Kellogg, Brown and Root

Kellogg, Brown and Root (KBR) was formed in 2001 when Halliburton, the US firm, brought three business units dealing with defence and civil infrastructure, oil and gas projects, and petrochemical projects into one subsidiary. KBR has global revenues of nearly $6bn and operates in over 100 countries. It has a workforce of 45,000, of which 12,000 are located in the UK.

The attraction and retention of managerial talent was seen as vital to the formation of effective teams appropriate for the different projects. However, a previous attempt to export a competency framework developed at the Houston headquarters of Halliburton had been unsuccessful. During 2002 and 2003, KBR drove through a massive project to create a global competency framework. This was achieved by the creation of global steering groups clustered around over 100 job families. The outcome was a series of definitions of the core skills of individual jobs. These job-specific competencies were supplemented by 39 transferable managerial behaviours applicable to most KBR managers, whatever their country of location. The system is supported by an online database, and forms the basis of performance management and career planning by enabling senior management across the whole company to search for talent in other countries. The link to the corporate intranet assists younger managers to plan their careers by accessing information on the skills needed for their current job or any post anywhere in the company.

Source: Carrington (2003, in Edwards & Rees, 2006, p.182)

activity

Taking Hosftede and Trompenaars' cultural dimensions into consideration, try to identify and critically analyse the difficulties a management development scheme like that developed in KBR might encounter in practice, in terms of definitions of the core skills of individual jobs.

Discuss your answers with your group members, supporting your arguments from your experience and what you have read so far in this chapter.

For Redding (1994), most research has been positivist and descriptive; more interpretative and ethnographic methods using semi-structured interviews or observation studies could be employed (Mallory et al., 2008). Many researchers, however, continue to rely on Hofstede (2001), even in studies of China, which was not included in the original study (Hong Kong, Singapore and Taiwan, which were, show different profiles). We can illustrate these problems with regard to Chinese culture.

Chinese culture and HRD

Hofstede (2001) appears to assume that national territory corresponds to cultural homogeneity, but China is not homogeneous, instead it displays strong regional differences and many minority ethnic/religious subcultures. The words individualism and collectivism appear to differ in meaning in different countries (Mead, 1994). Japanese employees may be more loyal to their organizations, while Chinese employees may well be more loyal to their families. However, both adopt the principle of collectivism, not western individualism.

The fifth Hofstede variable, LTO or Confucian dynamism – the capacity to adapt traditions to new situations, a willingness to save, a thrifty approach to scarce resources, a willingness to persevere over the long-term and subordinate one's own interests to achieve a purpose, and a concern with virtue (Hofstede & Bond, 1988; Hofstede, 1991) – did not appear in his original work, but was identified by Chinese scholars as important among Chinese employees.

Other studies have taken different approaches. Using Confucian ideas more directly, they show significant generational diversity in cultural values. Liu (2003) has used interview and survey studies in two factories in northeast China, where recent organizational reforms (performance-based reward, less job security and so on) have led to differences in assumptions, beliefs and values between first generation, pre-reform employees and second generation, younger employees, hired post-reform. Confucianism influences the way employees perceive the organization as a symbolic family, amplified by an earlier Maoist-era ideology emphasizing group rewards. Younger workers expressed unhappiness with regard to harmony at the expense of poor performance, and differed in their interpretation of bureaucracy, security, stability and loyalty. They saw these factors in less relational, more conditional, contractual and calculative ways, more like many young westerners.

Li and Nimon (2008) have also shown generational differences among Chinese workers, distinguishing between the social reform, Cultural Revolution, consolidation, and pre-liberation generational cohorts. The Cultural Revolution cohort, born in the 1940s and 50s, was least satisfied with recent economic reforms and their current position; and was more likely to work in state-owned enterprises, especially when compared to the younger social reform cohort. These two studies illustrate that culture can change and is not static; we need to take generational diversity into account when considering culture. Gamble (2003) also warns us that cultures should be considered not as a static monolith but a shifting and changeable repertoire with diverse strands.

Cultural arguments linking Chinese economic performance to Confucian values therefore neglect the ways in which cultures change, interacting with and influencing each other. Confucian culture stresses practical realism and pragmatism. China has always flourished more when open to other cultures (for example the Tang Dynasty, 618–907) than when culturally closed. Ideas have been introduced from outside, indigenous elements reinterpreted, links built with foreign ideas, and cultural elements refocused, for example education redirected to science and technology rather than the humanities. An about-turn on Confucian values may also occur, with li (profit) put ahead of yi (justice), and outdated values, for example gender inequality, may be rejected.

There are, however, attributes of Chinese culture not found in the west, such as *guanxi* (interpersonal relations), which remains of key importance for conducting business. Authority may be based on interpersonal relations rather than legal rationality. *Guanxi* is essential if approval is to be granted in order to access resources, generating personal obligations in response to requests for assistance by someone in the network.

Another distinctive cultural attribute is the concern for loss of face. The Chinese do not usually attempt to convince others that they know best; dialogue and encouragement are more important than linear communications or persuasion.

reflective question   What do you think the consequences of these Chinese cultural values might be on HRD policies and practice?

Culture and HRD in the Middle East

The Middle East is often neglected in Western HRD textbooks, although some books and journal issues specifically addressing HR issues in the Middle East have recently appeared (for example Budhwar & Mellahi, 2006).

One issue is what territories actually constitute the Middle East. Some definitions include, for example, Cyprus and Turkey, while others restrict the term to the Levant; but, however defined, it is very diverse in terms of language, religion, governance and economic development – some countries are major importers of labour, and others rely heavily on the remittances of migrant labour. Literacy and education levels also vary widely. However, across the region, some common issues for HRD include:

- the influence of national and international politics
- the impact of religion, ethnicity and culture
- the influence of Western multinationals
- the significance of gender.

In much of the region, gendered inequality in career paths is widespread, especially for rural and poor women, although in some countries, upper-class women are afforded better career opportunities than in many Western countries; reported discrimination in Turkey, for example, is lower than the EU average, and women play an increasingly active economic role, including at senior levels. In Iran, gender segregation in employment has also opened up other career opportunities for women, who have made great advances in university education.

Management styles in the Arab world, especially the Gulf States, may be seen as distinctive, constituting a 'fourth paradigm' (Weir, 2000, 2003), although Budhwar and Mellahi (2006, p.296) claim that there is no Middle Eastern model. This style is held to consist of:

- family businesses
- autocratic but consultative ownership

- a rhetoric of consultative decision-making within an essentially hierarchical structure; joint decision-making may be seen as a weakness, and one-to-one consultation is preferred (Muna, 1980).

From the perspective of Hofstede (2001), Arab cultures are seen as high in masculinity, relatively high in long-term orientation, and middling on individualism, uncertainty avoidance and power distance. Some researchers have noted that HRD often reflects Islamic values (Tayeb, 1997) and that an Islamic work ethic can be identified, influencing a range of attitudes towards organizational change and commitment. In particular, the family is the cornerstone of social life, with social identity and loyalty oriented to the wider extended family, despite the diminution in size of the typical household and the tendency of younger generations to have a more independent life (Suliman, 2006). In much of North Africa, as we saw in China, more individualized work values have also emerged, especially among younger generations educated abroad and with access to western media (Budhwar & Mellahi, 2006; Yahiaoui & Zoubir, 2006).

A distinctive feature of Arab HRM is the role of networks; like Chinese *guanxi*, interpersonal connections are rooted in family and kinship ties but extend into business and organizational life. This phenomenon is often termed *wasta* in the Gulf States or *piston* (pull, clout or connections) in French-influenced North Africa. Although the importance of networks is evident elsewhere – such as the role of military and university connections in Israel – *wasta* in the Arab world is often professionalized, with mediators interceding on behalf of clients to obtain advantages in jobs, documents, tax breaks, training and university admissions. Such practices may help to humanize the workplace, but Arab critics often condemn such intercessionary *wasta* as illegal or unethical – unlike *guanxi* in China, the phenomenon is less publicly acknowledged. However, they often continue to seek and provide *wasta* benefits for themselves, their relatives and their friends. Nepotism is also common in Iran, especially for senior managerial positions, and favouritism also remains an issue in Turkey (Hutchings & Weir, 2006).

In many Middle East countries, the public sector remains dominant, although some countries, such as Jordan and Turkey, have embarked on structural adjustment and privatization programmes to reduce government expenditures and turn around unprofitable state-owned businesses (Budhwar & Mellahi, 2006). These are often accompanied by changes in HRD policies, moving away from centralized civil service models towards the expansion of training and performance management/talent management initiatives. Generally, international enterprises apply more strategic HRD and better pay and training than local organizations, although with greater pressures on performance (Budhwar & Mellahi, 2006). However, in the Gulf States, training and development programmes are far more extensive in the public sector (Suliman, 2006).

HRD in international enterprises

Internationalization and the effective use of international HR located outside the home/parent country are major issues affecting firms in an increasingly global economy. Key questions include: why and how do enterprises adopt different

HRD policies and practices in areas such as training, talent management and career development? One framework developed by Budhwar and Mellahi (2006) draws attention to the influence of:

- national-level factors – culture and the national business system
- contingent factors – organizational size, structure, ownership, stage of internationalization, life cycle stage
- organizational-level corporate and HRD strategies.

Here we will view an international enterprise's HRD policies and practices as the product of an interaction between three factors (Shen, 2005):

1 *Home (parent) country factors:* such as domestic, cultural, legal, political and economic factors. Multinationals often remain deeply rooted in the national business systems of their country of origin, rather than being global, rootless, footloose entities (see Ohmae, 1990).
2 *Host country (local) factors:* such as cultural context, as reflected in local regulations and practices, for example the Chinese and Arab contexts explored earlier.
3 *Firm-specific factors:* for example senior management's attitudes towards internationalization and the international strategy, structure, and corporate culture of the firm.

Perlmutter (1969, p.11) argued that the international enterprise can choose four generic orientations to HRD, depending on its orientation to foreign people, ideas and resources:

1 *Ethnocentric:* here the international enterprise takes an international approach, exporting the home system and making strategic decisions at headquarters, with mother–daughter relationships with subsidiaries. Key positions like CEO and finance director are filled with parent country nationals (PCNs), that is, expatriates; for example, a Japanese bank in Thailand may be run mostly by Japanese. This approach is more common in some sectors, for example banking and finance, and in some countries, especially those high in uncertainty avoidance, for example Germany and Japan. It has the advantage of maximizing global efficiency and standardization, but minimizes local responsiveness – local managers who may know their local labour and product markets well are marginalized – and worldwide learning – all strategic ideas and initiatives tend to come from the home country headquarters. For example, a French manager in a Chinese–French JV producing handicrafts for the French market may employ the HRD practices of the French parent company (Mallory et al., 2008).
2 *Polycentric:* here the enterprise adopts a multinational, or multidomestic, approach, adapting its HRD policies to the local system, for example the role of *guanxi* in China, and *wasta* in the Middle East. Local subsidiaries enjoy much autonomy as 'sisters', and host country nationals (HCNs) occupy important positions. This strategy is more common in some sectors, for example advertising and food, where local responsiveness is important and in enterprises from some countries, for example European countries.

In addition, some positions, for example HRD director, are also most likely to be filled by locals, as cultural differences in motivation and reward may be seen as important. However, the strategy minimizes standardization, as each subsidiary can go its own way. Worldwide learning is inhibited, as ideas and innovations in one subsidiary tend to stay there. One reason for this is that HCNs are unlikely to be promoted to positions in other countries, or to headquarters.

3 *Geocentric:* here the enterprise takes a global approach to operations. Through global sourcing of talent and global training programmes, it promotes employees to positions and subsidiaries regardless of nationality. It is likely to employ many transcountry/third country nationals (TCNs) to maximize global standardization as well as worldwide learning – using similar HRD vehicles to spread learning – and local responsiveness – by using HCNs or cosmopolitan TCNs rather than ethnocentric PCNs. This strategy is characteristic of transnational companies seeking to maximize global efficiency, national responsiveness and worldwide learning. Firms may thus create new HRD systems, different from home and local systems.

4 *Regiocentric:* here the enterprise uses a regional approach, with managers from a particular region, for example Europe, East Asia, North America, enjoying regional (but not global) autonomy. Common HRD policies are developed across the region (but not globally), for example within Europe, there may be regional sourcing of talent and pan-European mobility, but this may not extend to Asia or North America.

Cultural distance between countries is also seen as an issue. Where subsidiaries are located in distant countries, enterprises seem to prefer to deploy PCNs, although they may be less willing to go in these situations. In addition, the age of the subsidiary affects choice: the longer a subsidiary has been in operation, the fewer PCNs may be used, as the need for control may be diminished in long-standing, presumably successful, affiliates.

Enterprises may have several motives for using international transfers:

- to fill positions with technically qualified staff
- to facilitate management development
- to facilitate organization development through knowledge transfer and the development of common corporate structures, culture and policies.

However, expatriates may experience problems, resulting in various degrees of failure, such as early return and underperformance – often judged more likely for US than European expatriates. They may struggle to adapt to the local culture, language, laws and customs. Their families (spouses and children) may also struggle since both parties may be operating outside their comfort zone. This is often described in terms of culture shock and problems of cultural adaptation, or the degree of psychological comfort with the host country. This involves work, interaction and general adjustment (Waxin & Panaccio, 2005). HRD has a key role to play here since job satisfaction and organizational socialization have been found to play important roles in the adjustment of Taiwanese expatriates in the USA by Liu and Lee (2008).

reflective question   Why do expatriates/PCNs often find it hard to adapt to different cultures?

Expatriation often demands a high degree of interaction between members of different cultures. Western expatriates from individualist cultures are likely to value independence and self-sufficiency, whereas collectivists may value social relationships, gift giving and reciprocity (Tan et al., 2005). Expatriates behaving in a masculine manner, asserting themselves and engaging in competitive behaviour, may not be well received in more collectivist/feminine cultures. Self-presentation and saving face may be more evident here, and the expatriate may need to 'give face, save face and above all avoid causing loss of face' (Hutchings & Murray, 2002, p.37).

These adjustment/adaptation problems may be reduced if careful attention is paid to systematic HRD. Often the PCN may be recruited in an informal way – approached over a vacancy at a coffee break or by the water cooler – using general or purely technical selection criteria – loyalty, commitment, professional competence – to meet immediate organizational needs. Rarely is the nature of the assignment taken into account. Is it to:

- fill a position?
- open a new branch or process?
- operate in a JV?
- transfer knowledge to locals?
- or is it a mixture of all these?

Rarely is the subsidiary company's requirements taken into account; however, doing so may build trust between the parent company and its subsidiary. The person's motives for going are also not often considered. Is it to:

- travel?
- enjoy an adventure?
- escape a job, a career, a personal difficulty?
- pursue an interest in international issues?
- pursue an interest in the specific country or culture?
- advance a career?

Whether these expectations are aligned with company expectations or in conflict with them is also not often considered.

If the assignment is to be a long-term one, with significant degrees of interaction with locals, for example a CEO or HR director position for three years, rather than a technical troubleshooting assignment expected to last three days, then it is worth investing in more systematic HRD processes. The candidate's interest and experience, qualifications, linguistic abilities, and cross-cultural competences may all be taken into account. For example, does the candidate:

- have experience of residence or education abroad?
- speak more than one language?
- demonstrate openness to new experiences, empathy, respect and a lack of ethnocentrism?

- show good communication skills, including nonverbal communication?
- show an interest in an international career, or the specific job, company, and/ or culture?
- show a tendency to avoid narrow stereotyping?
- show adaptability, flexibility and a tolerance of ambiguity?

In addition, the company will need to take diversity issues into account:

- childcare issues and dual career issues may mean a reluctance to travel
- partners may find visas, work permits and jobs commensurate with their skills and experience hard to get
- companies may falsely assume that customers or partners overseas will not accept women in senior positions, and so be reluctant to hire them.

National laws on equal opportunity need to be taken into account, for example many Japanese companies in the UK and USA have often run into problems by discriminating against women or non-Japanese employees.

Alternative forms of international working are being used by international enterprises in response to a dual career couple and work–life balance issues, as well as the desire to reduce expatriation costs and respond to localization pressures from governments. Such international work forms include short-term assignments, international commuting and frequent flying. Sparrow (1999) includes among 'international' staff: home-based managers focusing on different global markets, internationally mobile managers, technical professionals and transitional managers. These roles all have implications for the type of HRD required and the skills that need to be developed.

In addition, using HCNs (locals) more widely carries distinct advantages. They are often cheaper to employ, not just in terms of salaries but in terms of travel, accommodation and family costs, and they are familiar with the local laws, culture, government officials and local languages. They may also allow the company to present a local face, and demonstrate that it is a good corporate citizen by offering opportunities to locals, enhancing its reputation with key stakeholders such as government and customers.

However, the company may doubt the loyalty or commitment of locals to act in the interests of corporate control, locals may find communication with corporate headquarters difficult, not knowing the language fluently or the people well, and they may be blocking developmental, international opportunities for talented, promising, high-potential PCNs.

Another alternative is to use TCNs; they may be cheaper than PCNs, and are often cosmopolitan career internationals, with substantial international experience and probably good linguistic skills. However, there may be local resentment, TCNs may be seen as blocking HCNs' opportunities, or they may come from politically sensitive countries.

Other alternatives may be to practise inpatriation, bringing subsidiary staff, whether TCNs or HCNs, to the headquarters to transfer knowledge, test suitability, socialize into company culture, and build multicultural teams. Virtual assignments through international collaboration on projects by videoconferencing, email and telephone rather than physical travel are becoming more common. The use of a greater variety of shorter assignments – troubleshooting, contractual assignments, rotational assignments, knowledge transfer activities, training, personal development, short-term commuters, frequent flyers – is also increasing.

All such initiatives can be assisted by cross-cultural training (CCT), to which we now turn.

reflective question

1 Why do expatriates often report adjustment/adaptation problems on repatriation to their home country?
2 Why do you think alternatives to expatriation have grown in popularity?

Cross-cultural/intercultural training

It is common to assess cross-cultural/intercultural competences through interviews, assessment centres and personality tests, sometimes created specifically for international working. CCT may also be offered before departure and in-country, as well as before and after repatriation, which may be even more of a culture shock than expatriation. Failures to cope may be expensive for the employee, for example loss of self-confidence and reputation, stress and, for the company, loss of business opportunities and damage to the brand. These costs may be reduced by better preparation. Personality dimensions, in particular openness, may be related to CCT performance, as are adaptability, teamwork and communication, as measured by a group discussion exercise (Lievens et al., 2003). This suggests that attention must be paid to recruitment and selection, including selection for CCT. However, selection is still often haphazard and unsystematic, based on job knowledge and technical competence.

CCT is defined by Brislin and Yoshida (1994, p.2) *as*:

> formal efforts to prepare people for more effective interpersonal relationships and for job success when they interact extensively with individuals from cultures other than their own.

Tarique and Caliguri (2004, p.284) see it as any:

> planned intervention designed to increase the knowledge of expatriates to live and work effectively and achieve general life satisfaction in an unfamiliar host culture.

CCT is often proposed as an anticipatory mechanism to enhance cultural adjustment, and Black and Mendenhall's (1990) review showed that it had a strong positive impact on self-confidence, interpersonal relationships with locals, perceptions of host culture, and expatriate adjustment and performance. A meta-analysis by Deshpande and Viswesvaran (1992) also showed positive results, especially on expatriate job performance.

Several CCT models have been put forward. Black and Mendenhall (1990) distinguish three kinds of training:

1 *factual training:* for example presentation of cultural knowledge through lectures, handouts, DVDs and so on
2 *analytical training:* for example courses presenting analytical models such as those of Hofstede or Trompenaars

3 *experiential training:* for example action learning, outdoor training, multi-cultural team-building activities involving direct experience of working with people from other cultures.

They argue that such types vary according to the rigour of the training process and the degree to which modelling processes are used. As one moves from factual to analytical to experiential training, more rigour is introduced, and a greater variety of modelling processes employed. Which models are most appropriate depends on:

- *Degree of cultural novelty:* the more culturally distant the country is, for example China vs. France for a British person, the more experiential methods may be necessary
- *Degree of interaction with HCNs:* the more interaction is anticipated for the PCN, for example long vs. short stay, job as HR director or CEO rather than technician, the more experiential the method required.

Gudykunst and Hammer (1983) differentiate training methods based on two criteria:

1 *process or method of delivery,* for example didactic (cognitive) vs. experiential (emotional/behavioural)
2 *content,* for example culturally general vs. culturally specific. One example is the culture assimilator, which presents collections of critical incidents to which people have to respond with their best explanation – these can be either culturally specific or general.

Such training can be work or private life oriented, or both. In addition, it can occur in a classroom or training room, at work, or in virtual environments. Four categories of CCT can therefore be distinguished, as shown in Figure 4.1.

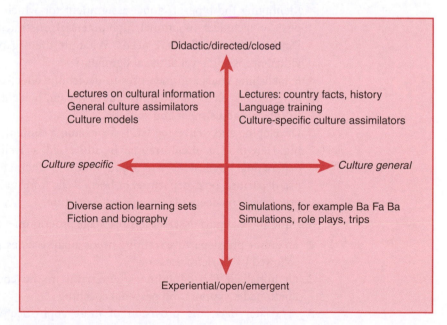

Figure 4.1 Models of cross-cultural training

In a meta-analysis on the effectiveness of CCT, Mendenhall et al. (2004) found that lectures, presentations, culture assimilators and discussions were the most frequently used methods. These didactic methods were useful for knowledge transfer, but less effective in changing behaviour and attitudes and enhancing adjustment and performance. However, many findings were non-significant, suggesting that other factors, like the type of assignment being prepared for, affected the impact of didactic training. Pre-departure training, especially imparting basic information, seems to positively affect the accuracy of prior expectations and subsequent adjustment (Caliguri et al., 2001). Waxin and Panaccio (2005) found that CCT accelerated the adjustment of expatriates, but that this was moderated by prior international experience – that is, it had its largest impact on those managers with little prior international experience – and cultural distance, where it tended to have most effect. The type of CCT employed also had an effect; experiential methods were generally more effective, especially if culturally specific.

One example of the use of experiential methods in CCT is given by Lewis (2005), who highlights the use of dramas and other simulations as a more rigorous method in, for example, exploring decisions to invest. Another is blended action learning (combining face-to-face action learning sets in five European partner countries and an e-learning platform called the Cultural Fluency Club) to develop cross-cultural skills and cultural awareness of SME leaders (Stewart, 2008). The executive training programme for European companies in Japan also mixes language training, seminars, company visits and in-house training in a hybrid blend of experiential and analytical methods in small groups (Lievens et al., 2003).

According to Tarique and Caliguri (2004, p.285), designing effective CCT involves:

- Identifying the type of global assignment for which CCT is needed. Is the position technical, functional, high potential, or strategic/executive?
- Determining specific CCT needs. What are the organizational context, individual needs and level of the assignment?
- Establishing goals and measures to determine effectiveness in the short- and long-term, such as the cognitive, affective and behavioural changes necessary to enhance adjustment and success.
- Developing and delivering CCT, for example content, methods and sequencing. Here models of culture may be addressed, as well as mixing didactic and experiential methods seen as appropriate and whether these are best delivered pre-departure, post-departure, or both. Basic information may be appropriate pre-departure, deeper learning post-departure.

Tarique and Caliguri describe a three-stage programme, comprising:

1 an online pre-departure training needs analysis assessing development needs, followed by a briefing session
2 an initial CCT programme after arrival in the country, accompanied by continued e-support and personal coaching
3 at a later date, the provision of more sophisticated training, again with e-support.

Other factors to be considered are:

- Intranet-based training, multimedia and distance/blended learning may all be useful here.
- Evaluating the programme's success against stated goals. Adjustment may be measured by interviews, surveys and appraisal records that balance CCT with other HR practices, especially recruitment, selection, reward, appraisal and career/talent management.
- Considering the training needs of HCNs and TCNs, not just PCNs, as in JVs (discussed below).

According to Briscoe and Schuler (2004), other issues in CCT include:

- Who delivers CCT?
- What are the effects of language differences?
- Who takes responsibility?
- Should CCT be exported, or employees brought to regional or centralized training centres?
- Should each subsidiary/JV develop its own CCT?
- Should CCT be localized, or integrated?

In the HRD processes of multinational enterprises, both transfer (of home HRD practices to affiliates) and adaptation (of HRD to local practices) processes occur. These transfer processes often involve knowledge transfer, whether of technology or HRD processes such as better training or career/talent management policies and practices (Collings & Scullion, 2007).

International knowledge transfer and HRD

In an international context knowledge transfer is of the utmost importance. How is this process best described ? Jankowicz (1999) uses metaphors of 'export sales' and 'new product development' to discuss knowledge transfer across cultural and linguistic boundaries. In the first case, the assumption is made that both parties share the same conceptual background and assumptions, whereas in the second case, the two parties are seen as equal collaborators. Every language encodes phenomena differently, so the meaning encoded by one party may be subtly different from that encoded by the other. Jankowicz (1999, p.319) argues that instead of knowledge transfer, the term 'mutual knowledge creation' is preferable, as it refers to the negotiation of new understanding; Iles and Yolles (2003, p.301) prefer the term 'knowledge migration'.

A number of factors have been found to affect such knowledge migration: a knowledge-sharing environment, ICTs, and organizational structure.

Knowledge migration may flow from a knowledge source, that is, the knowledge base, often in the 'west', such as the corporate HQ of an international enterprise, to a knowledge destination or sink, often in the 'south' or 'east', such as an affiliate or JV in China or the Middle East (Figure 4.2) (See Iles & Yolles, 2002, 2003). The process may be facilitated by a knowledge intermediary such as a consultant or academic, a project team, or expatriates.

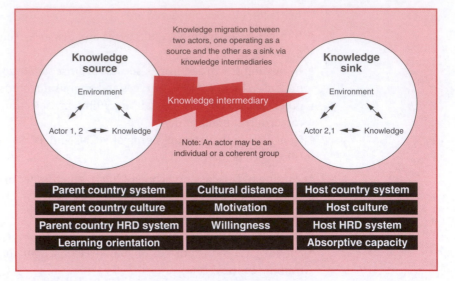

Figure 4.2 Knowledge migration in international enterprises and JVs

The process of transfer is often seen as covering several stages, from 'identifying the knowledge to the actual process of transferring the knowledge to its final utilization by the receiving unit' (Minbaeva et al., 2003, p.587). A firm's HRD processes may constitute a significant source of competitive advantage over local, indigenous firms, and may be critical to the firm's successful operations. Therefore transferring such processes, and using HRD processes to help transfer other processes, is crucial to effectiveness. Grant et al. (2000, pp.115–16) argue that 'the movement of knowledge between different geographical locations is central' to the process of adding value in international enterprises.

In addition to concerns over whether knowledge of Western HRD practices can be unproblematically transferred in the way suggested, a further question arises as to whether it is appropriate to attempt to transfer Western HRD practices to other contexts, as the public services of developing countries face different problems and in different contexts. Within JVs, one-way transplant programmes are often less successful than more collaborative, process-oriented approaches that make use of local expertise as to what is needed and how it may be delivered in ways that suit local conditions and circumstances.

Expatriate managers may be given the job of transferring knowledge through training, coaching or mentoring, as in the Anglo-Chinese retail store studied by Gamble (2003). The effectiveness of this depends on the manager's willingness and ability, which in turn depends, as Figure 4.2 shows, on the learning orientation of the source and its strategic objectives. Effectiveness of transfer is also affected by parent and host country characteristics, such as the national culture and institutional/business systems, as well as the cultural distance between source and sink. In addition, the learning, or absorptive capacity, of the sink affects how well transfer occurs.

The ability and willingness of local personnel to learn will also determine how well they acquire HRD knowledge. Effective communication is vital for the transfer of knowledge. The importance of motivation and willingness in the transfer of knowledge has also been widely recognized. Valuing different cultures, building relationships, listening and observing, coping with ambiguity, managing others, translating complex ideas, and taking action are all necessary, and can be enhanced by HRD as shown in HRD in Practice 4.2.

Trust vital to cross-cultural working

HRD in Practice 4.2

Establishing effective cross-cultural working (HRD 2007 – conference report)

The basis of effective cross-cultural working is trust and transparency – and the first step to building that trust is fair and effective recruitment, delegates to HRD 2007 were told by Roland Dubois, CEO of the Industrial and Vocational Training Board of Mauritius.

'It starts there,' Dubois said. 'In Mauritius, people used to be recruited based on their skin colour. But globalization means you now cannot afford not to recruit the best candidate whatever their background.'

In talking about how organizations can promote effective multicultural working, Dubois drew on lessons learned from Mauritius's hybrid population: the 1.2 million inhabitants include Indians, Chinese, Europeans, Africans, Sri Lankans and Bangladeshis.

Mauritius wants to keep attracting more international companies and foreign workers. 'The trend for migration is universal; like it or not people will continue to migrate,' Dubois said, noting that diversity brings challenges. 'The story of Richard Gere and Shilpa Shetty this week caused anger in India,' he said, referring to the much publicised kiss giving by the American actor to the Big Brother winner. 'It was an example of a lack of cultural awareness.'

In Mauritius, at a national level the government has worked hard to promote diversity and multiculturalism. For example, children are taught many languages in schools so they can learn about each other's cultures. A Ministry of Arts and Culture promotes multicultural activities and every religion has public holidays for religious events.

A similar commitment was also needed at organizational level, Dubois said. If companies wished to build a high-performance but diverse team they need to improve communication, emphasise teamwork, ensure equity in recruitment and promote an agreed vision and set of values.

Source: Rima Evans, 17 April 2007 (People Management)

International JVs and HRD

Many international enterprises have entered into a variety of strategic partnerships, mergers and acquisitions, JVs and other more limited projects. The term alliances refers to generic forms of cooperation, and equity JVs are a special case, cemented by ownership sharing through equity holdings. However, JVs, especially international JVs, often fail, associated with differences in culture, HRD practices and management style (Iles & Yolles, 2002, p.3).

JVs constitute entities with particularly complex sets of HRD practices due to the high levels of interaction between employees of different corporate and national backgrounds with collaborating partners (see, for example, Schuler et al., 1993; Dowling et al., 1994). JVs also need to use HRD and career management practices to reduce psychic distance and encourage identification, therefore HRD plays a significant role in affecting JV success. Particularly important issues are:

- the appropriate selection of JV personnel
- the use of experienced PCNs
- CCT
- the joint training of HCNs and PCNs
- building a unique JV culture through HRD, taking elements of host and home culture as well as new elements not found in either.

Clearly alliances involve sharing people and HRD practices, and HRD issues, especially orientation to the JV and issues of corporate and national culture, will be key. JVs provide significant opportunities for organizational learning, especially the transfer of culturally embedded knowledge if trust is developed and substantial non-contractual inputs invested (Fitzgerald, 2000). Benefits are likely to be appropriated asymmetrically, according to the organizational learning capacity of the partners (Pucik, 1988). A vital part of a learning infrastructure includes HRD policies supporting the protection of competitive advantage, especially the transfer and accumulation of knowledge, enabling partners to learn more about each other, more from each other, and more from the alliance itself – learning that can also be useful for other units and alliances. Some partners may emphasize learning, others may not, and 'the behaviours and styles of managers in organizations have a significant impact on the ability and willingness of a firm to learn' (Schuler, 2001, p.317). HRD policies and practices may support or inhibit knowledge flows, sharing and development, and establishing mechanisms to enhance trust may benefit the relationship between alliance partners (Schuler, 2001).

Universal attributes and different cultural values: The Globe leadership study

The behaviour and the universal attributes for global leaders were examined by a multicultural team of researchers who led the Global Leadership and Organizational Behavior Effectiveness (GLOBE) research project. GLOBE is the name of a cross-cultural research effort that exceeds all others (including Geert Hofstede's landmark 1980 study) in scope, depth, duration, and sophistication. It examines the relationship between the culture and successful management and leadership behaviour/strategies in 26 countries worldwide. According to the GLOBE project, leadership is seen as an integral part of a manager's responsibilities and is defined as

> ... the ability of an individual to influence, motivate, and enable others to contribute toward the effectiveness and success of the organizations of which they are members [p.15].

Their initial research led them to propose the nine GLOBE cultural dimensions as per House et al.'s (1994) findings:

Power distance: Degree to which people expect power to be distributed equally.

Uncertainty avoidance: Extent to which people rely on norms, rules, and procedures to reduce the unpredictability of future events.

Humane orientation: Extent to which people reward fairness, altruism and generosity.

Institutional collectivism: Extent to which society encourages collective distribution of resources and collective action.

In group collectivism: Extent to which individuals express pride, loyalty, and cohesiveness in their organizations and families.

Assertiveness: Degree to which people are assertive, confrontational and aggressive in relationships with others.

Gender egalitarianism: Degree to which gender differences are minimized.

Future orientations: Extent to which people engage in future-oriented behaviours such as planning, investing, and delayed gratification.

Performance orientation: Degree to which high-performance is encouraged and rewarded.

Based on the above dimensions, the GLOBE project then identified twenty-two leadership attributes that were widely seen as universally applicable across cultures (e.g. encouraging, motivational, dynamic, decisive, having foresight) and eight leadership dimensions that were seen to be universally undesirable (e.g uncooperative, ruthless, dictatorial, irritable). But several other attributes were found to be culturally contingent; that is, their desirability or undesirability was tied to cultural differences. These included characteristics likes ambitious and elitist. (Steers et al., 2010, p. 254).

activity

In groups, can you please identify traits in leaders of your culture that people in other cultures rejected?

Moreover, the GLOBE project grouped their findings into six distinct leadership dimensions (Table 4.2):

Table 4.2 GLOBE project leadership dimensions

GLOBE leadership dimensions	Characteristics of dimensions	Regions where leadership dimensions are widely endorsed
Autonomous leadership	Individualistic, independent, unique.	Endorsed in Eastern European and Germanic clusters: weaker endorsement in Latin American cluster.
Charismatic/value-based leadership	Visionary, inspirational, self-sacrificing, decisive, performance-oriented.	Endorsed in all regions, but particularly in Anglo, Asian, and Latin American clusters; weaker endorsement in Arab cluster.
Humane leadership	Modest, tolerant, sensitive, concerned about humanity.	Endorsed particularly in Anglo, Asian and Sub-Saharan African clusters; less so elsewhere.
Participative leadership	Active listening, non-autocratic, flexible.	Wide variations in endorsements across all regions, but less so in Arab and Latin American clusters.
Self protective leadership	Self-centred, procedural, status-conscious, face-saving.	Wide variations in endorsements across all regional clusters.
Team-oriented leadership	Collaborative, integrating, diplomatic.	Endorsed in all regions, but particularly in Anglo, Asian, and Latin American clusters; less so in Arab cluster.

Source: Based on House et al. (1994), Culture, Leadership and Organizations.

Substantial Western leadership models have tried to identify the qualities of Asian leaders. The GLOBE study of leadership compares individual Asian countries with other counterparts on various leadership dimensions.

For example, the success of the Asian economy in the past decade, has encouraged academic researchers and practitioners to analyse what constitutes a successful leader and his/her qualities in the context of Asian cooperations. Unlike the task-oriented Western leadership theories, Asian leadership is rooted in Confucian philosophy which concentrates on trust, harmony and justice in a long-term orientation (Byosiere & Luethge, 2009; Hosftede & Bond, 1988). Therefore, Western leadership theories originating in more individualist values may not be applicable in more collectivistic/paternalistic Asian cultures.

Harmony and relationship (*guanxi, inhwa and wa*) are essential components of Asian businesses and leadership styles.

activity

For more information and current research conducted on leadership in Asian countries, please go to:
- Asian leadership institute: **www.asianleadership.com/index.php**
- Asian women in business: **www.awib.org**
- Asian strategy and leadership institute: **www.asli.com.my**
- Asian business council: **www.asiabusinesscouncil.org/mission.html**

It is important to note, however, that Hofstede (2006, p.883) presented seven differences between the GLOBE Project led by House et al. (2004) and his own work. These differences are: 1) new data versus existing data; 2) team versus single researcher; 3) managers versus employees; 4) theory-driven versus action-driven; 5) US inspired versus decentred; 6) organizational culture as similar or different in nature to/from societal culture; 7) national wealth as a part, or as an antecedent, of culture. He questions the validity of the questionnaire employed in the GLOBE research and contests that the prevalence of the desirable items versus the desired items in the questionnaire design may convey hidden meanings not intended or understood by the GLOBE team.

summary

○ Despite the claims of some that globalization will lead to a convergence of management practices, including HRD, national differences persist.

○ To understand comparative and cross-cultural HRD, it is necessary to take both an institutionalist and culturalist perspective, but also to see that countries and organizations can, within parameters, make different strategic choices.

○ It is difficult to describe, for example the contemporary Chinese business system consists of a mixture of models. In addition, Arab culture and Chinese culture seem to be undergoing rapid change, with the emergence of more individualistic values.

○ The influence of family and networks (in Arab culture, *wasta*, in China, *guanxi*) remains powerful, and exerts a great influence on HRD, such as who is selected to provide training, or who is selected for training and development initiatives.

○ HRD is important for international enterprises, especially in preparing international staff not just long-term expatriates.

○ CCT, especially experiential training, is particularly important in enhancing adjustment and effectiveness.

○ HRD also plays a key role in transferring or migrating knowledge across borders, between the enterprise and its subsidiaries, expatriates and locals, and between parties in JVs in particular.

discussion questions

1 Are organizational or individual differences in culture likely to be more or less strong than national cultural differences? Give examples for your answer.

2 Think about the strengths/weaknesses of cultural dimensions. How will these impact in business, especially in HRD? Why might they be of interest to managers?

3 Why should CCT programmes vary depending on the type of global assignment under consideration?

4 What factors would you need to take into account in designing and evaluating an e-CCT programme? When would this be preferable as a CCT method?

5 You are a British consultant working in a multinational company, developing an induction programme for expatriate assignees in South Africa. Identify and analyse the cultural and HRD factors that might affect this. How will you overcome any barriers?

further reading

Adekola, A. and Sergi, B. (2007) *Global Business Management: A Cross-cultural Perspective*. Aldershot: Ashgate.

Brewster, C. (2007) HRM: the comparative dimension. In J. Storey (ed.) *Human Resource Management: A Critical Text*, 3rd edn. London: Thomson Learning.

Fang, T. (2003) A critique of Hofstede's fifth national culture dimension. *International Journal of Cross Cultural Management*, **3**(3): 347–68.

Lee, L.-Y. and Croker, R. (2006) A contingency model to promote the effectiveness of expatriate training. *Industrial Management & Data Systems*, **106**(8): 1187–205.

references

Ardichvili, A. and Kuchinke, P. (2002) The concept of culture in international and comparative HRD research: methodological problems and possible solutions. *Human Resource Development Review*, **1**(2): 145–66.

Bates, D.G. and Plog, F. (1990) *Cultural Anthropology*. New York: McGraw-Hill.

Black, J.S. and Mendenhall, M. (1990) Cross-cultural training effectiveness: a review and a theoretical framework for future research. *Academy of Management Review*, **15**: 113–36.

Byosiere, P. and Luethge, D.J. (2009) Asian leadership. In H. Hasegawa and C. Noronha (eds) *Asian Business & Management: Theory, Practice and Perspectives*. New York, NY, U.S.: Palgrave Macmillan, pp. 125–45.

Briscoe, D.R. and Schuler, R.S. (eds) (2004) *International Human Resource Management*, 2nd edn. London: Routledge.

Brislin, R. and Yoshida, T. (1994) *Intercultural Communication Training: An Introduction*. New York: Sage.

Brooks, I. (2003) *Organisational Behaviour: Individuals, Groups and Organisation*, 2nd edn. London: Prentice Hall.

Budhwar, P.S. and Mellahi, K. (eds) (2006) *Managing Human Resources in the Middle East*. London: Routledge.

Caliguri, P.M., Philips, J., Lazarova, M. Tarique, I. and Bürgi, P. (2001) Expectations produced in cross-cultural training programs as a predictor of expatriate adjustment. *International Journal of Human Resource Management*, **12**(3): 357–72.

Carrington, L. (2003) Nine day wonder. *People Management*, 12 June: 42–3.

Collings, D.G. and Scullion, H. (2007) Global staffing and the multinational enterprise. In J. Storey (ed.) *Human Resource Management: A Critical Text*. London: Thomson.

Deshpande, S.P. and Viswesvaran, C. (1992) Is cross-cultural training of expatriate managers effective? A meta-analysis. *International Journal of Intercultural Relations*, **16**: 295–310.

Dowling, P.J., Schuler, R.S. and Welch, D.E. (1994) *International Dimensions of Human Resource Management*, 2nd edn. Belmont, CA: Wadsworth.

Edwards, T. and Rees, C. (2006) *International Human Resource Management: Globalisation, National Systems and Multinational Companies*. Harlow: FT/Prentice Hall.

Fitzgerald, S.P. (2000) *Building Personal and Procedural Trust Through Sino-American Joint Ventures: The Transfer of Culturally Embedded Knowledge*. Paper presented to the 7th International Conference on Advances in Management, Colorado Springs, July.

Gamble, J. (2003) Transferring human resource practices from the United Kingdom to China: the limits and potential for convergence. *International Journal of Human Resource Management*, **14**(3): 369–87.

Gouveia, V.V. and Ros, M. (2002) The Hofstede and Schwarz models for classifying individualism at the cultural level: their relation to macro-social and macro-economic variables. *Psicothema*, **12**(Suppl.): 25–33.

Grant, R.M., Almeida, P. and Song, J. (2000) Knowledge and the multi-national enterprise. In C. Millar, R. Grant and C. Choi (eds) *International Business: Emerging Issues and Emerging Markets*. Basingstoke: Macmillan (now Palgrave Macmillan).

Gudykunst, W.B. and Hammer, M.R. (1983) Basic training design: approaches to intercultural training. In D. Landis and R.W. Brislin (eds) *Handbook of Intercultural Training: Issues in Theory and Design*, vol. 1. Elmsford, NY: Pergamon.

Hall, E.T. (1984) *The Dance of Life: The Other Dimension of Time*. Garden City, NY: Anchor.

Harris, H., Brewster, C. and Sparrow, P. (2004) *International Human Resource Management*. London: CIPD.

Hofstede, G. (1980). *Culture's Consequences: International Differences in Work-Related Values*. LA, Beverly Hills, USA: SAGE Publications.

Hofstede, G. (1991) *Cultures and Organizations: Software of the Mind*. London: McGraw-Hill.

Hofstede, G. (2001) *Culture's Consequences: Comparing Values, Behaviors, Institutions, and Organizations across Nations*, 2nd edn. Thousand Oaks, CA: Sage.

Hofstede, G. (2006) What did GLOBE really measure? Researchers' minds versus respondents' minds. *Journal of International Business Studies*, **37**: 882–96.

Hofstede, G. and Bond, M.H. (1988) The Confucius connection: from cultural roots to economic growth. *Organizational Dynamics*, **16**(4): 5–21.

Holliman, D.M., Mallory, G.R. and Viney, H.P. (2008) *What Role Does Managerial Perceptions of Cultural Difference Play in the Selection of Foreign Markets and Appropriate Entry Strategy?*. Paper presented to British Academy of Management, Harrogate, September.

House, R. J., Hanges, P. J., Javidan, M., Dorfman, P. W. and Gupta, V. (eds) (2004) *Culture, Leadership and Organizations: The GLOBE Study of 62 Societies*. Thousand Oaks, CA.: Sage.

House, R. J. et al. (1994) *Culture, Leadership, and Organizations: The GLOBE Study of 62 Societies*. Thousand Oaks, CA: Sage Publications.

Hutchings, K. and Murray, G. (2002) Australian expatriates' experiences in working behind the bamboo curtain: an examination of guanxi in post-communist China. *Asian Business and Management*, **1**: 373–93.

Hutchings, K. and Weir, D. (2006) Understanding networking in China and the Arab world: lessons for international managers. *Journal of European Industrial Training*, **30**: 272–90.

Iles, P.A. and Yolles, M. (2002) International joint ventures, HRM and viable knowledge migration. *International Journal of Human Resource Management*, **13**: 624–41.

Iles, P.A. and Yolles, M. (2003) International HRD alliances in viable knowledge migration and development: the Czech academic link project. *Human Resource Development International*, **6**(3): 301–24.

Jankowicz, D. (1999) *Towards a meaningful HRD function in the post-communist economies of Central and Eastern Europe*. Proceedings from the Academy of Human Resource Development Annual Conference, Baton Rouge, pp.318–26.

Kluckhohn, F. and Strodbeck, F. (1961) *Variations in Value Orientations*. Evanston, IL: Row Peterson.

Lane, C. (1992) European business systems: Britain and Germany compared. In R. Whitley (ed.) *European Business Systems, Firms and Markets in their National Contexts*. London: Sage.

Lane, C. (1995) *Industry and Society in Europe*. Aldershot: Edward Elgar.

Lewis, M.M. (2005) The drama of international business: why cross-cultural training simulations work. *Journal of European Industrial Training*, **29**(7): 593–98.

Li, J. and Nimon, K. (2008) The importance of recognising generational differences in HRD policy and practices: a study of workers in Qinhuangdao, China. *Human Resource Development International*, **11**(2): 167–82.

Lievens, F., van Keer, E., Harris, M. and Bisqueret, C. (2003) Predicting cross-cultural training performance: the validity of personality, cognitive ability and dimensions measured by an assessment centre and a behavior description interview. *Journal of Applied Psychology*, **88**(3): 476–89.

Liu, C. and Lee, H. (2008) A proposed model of expatriates in multinational corporations. *Cross Cultural Management*, **15**(2): 176–93.

Liu, S. (2003) Cultures within culture: unity and diversity of two generations of employees in state-owned enterprises. *Human Relations*, **56**(4): 387–41.

McGuire, D., O'Donnell, D., Garavan, T.N., O'Donnell, D. and Murphy, C. (2001) The cultural boundedness of theory and practice in HRD? *Cross Cultural Management: An International Journal*, **9**(2): 25–44.

McSweeney, B. (2001) The essentials of scholarship: a reply to Geert Hofstede. *Human Relations*, **55**(11): 1363–72.

McSweeney, B. (2002) Hofstede's model of national cultural differences and their consequences: a triumph of faith – a failure of analysis. *Human Relations*, **55**(1): 89–118, www.it.murdoch.edu.au/ffsudweeks/b329/readings/mcsweeney.doc.

Mallory, G., Yu Yang, G. and Ray, T. (2008) *I Did It My Way: The Impact of National Culture on Operational Decision Making by Managers Working Overseas*. Paper presented to British Academy of Management, Harrogate, September.

Mead, R. (1994) *International Management: Cross-cultural Dimensions*. Oxford, Blackwell.

Mendenhall, M., Stahl, G., Ehnert, I., Oddou, G., Osland, J. and Kuhlmann, T. (2004) Evaluation studies of cross-cultural training programs: a review of the literature from 1988–2000. In D. Landis and J. Bennett (eds) *The Handbook of Intercultural Training*. Thousand Oaks, CA: Sage.

Minbaeva, D.B., Pedersen, T. Bjorkman, I., Fey, C. F. and Park H.J. (2003) MNC knowledge transfer, subsidiary absorptive capacity, and HRM. *Journal of International Business Studies*, **34**(6): 586–99.

Muna, F. (1980) *The Arab Executive*. London: Macmillan.

Ohmae, K. (1990) *The Borderless World*. London: Collins.

Perlmutter, H.V. (1969) The tortuous evolution of the multi-national company. *Columbia Journal of World Business*, **4**: 9–18.

Pucik, V. (1998) Strategic alliances, organizational learning, and competitive advantage: the HRM agenda. *Human Resource Management*, **27**(1): 77–93.

Redding, S.G. (1994) Comparative management: jungle, zoo or fossil bed? *Organization Studies*, **15**(3): 323–59.

Schuler, R. (2001) HR issues in international joint ventures and alliances. In J. Storey (ed.) *Human Resource Management: A Critical Text*, 2nd edn. London: Thomson Learning.

Schuler, R., Dowling, P.J. and de Cieri, H. (1993) An integrative framework of strategic international human resource management. *Journal of Management*, **19**(2): 419–59.

Schwartz, S. (1990) Individualism-collectivism: critique and proposed refinements. *Journal of Cross Cultural Psychology*, **21**(2): 139–57.

Shen, J. (2005) Towards a generic international human resource management model. *Journal of Organizational Transformation and Social Change*, **2**(2): 83–102.

Sparrow, P. (1999) International recruitment, selection and assessment. In P. Joynt and R. Marlin (eds) *The Global HR Manager: Creating the Seamless Organization*. London: CIPD.

Steenkamp, J.B. (2001) The role of national culture in international marketing research. *International Marketing Review*, **18**: 30–44.

Steers, R.M., Sanchez-Runde, C.J and Nardon, L. *(2010) Management Across Cultures: Challenges and Strategies*. Cambridge University Press.

Stewart, J.A. (2008) *A Blended Action Learning Programme to Develop Cross-Cultural Skills for SME Leaders* Paper presented to British Academy of Management, Harrogate, September.

Suliman, A. (2006) Human resource management in the Arab Emirates. In P.S. Budhwar and K. Mellahi (eds) *Managing Human Resources in the Middle East*. London: Routledge.

Tan, J., Hartel, C., Panipucci, D. and Strybosch, V. (2005) The effect of emotions in cross-cultural expatriate experiences. *Cross Cultural Management*, **12**(2): 4–15.

Tarique, I. and Caligiuri, P. (2004) Training and development of international staff. In A. Harzing and J. van Ruysseveldt (eds) *International Human Resource Management*. London: Sage.

Tayeb, M. (1997) Islamic revival in Asia and human resource management. *Employee Relations*, **19**: 352–64.

Trompenaars, F. (1997) *Riding the Waves of Culture: Understanding Diversity in Global Business*. New York: McGraw-Hill.

Trompenaars, F. and Hampden-Turner, C. (1997) *Riding the Waves of Culture: Understanding Cultural Diversity in Business*, 2nd edn. London: Nicholas Brealey.

Vo, A.D. (2009) *Transformation in the Management of Human Resources and Labour Relations in Vietnam*. Abington: Woodhead.

Waxin, M.F. and Panaccio, A. (2005) Cross-cultural training to facilitate expatriate adjustment: it works! *Personnel Review*, **3**(1): 51–67.

Weir, D. (2000) Management in the Arab world: a fourth paradigm? In A. Al-Shamali and J. Denton (eds) *Arab Business: The Globalisation Imperative*. Kuwait: Arab Research Centre.

Weir, D. (2003) Human resource development in the Middle East: a fourth paradigm. In M. Lee (ed.) *HRD in a Complex World*. London: Routledge.

Whitley, R. (1999) *Divergent Capitalisms: The Social Structuring and Change of Business Systems*. Oxford: Oxford University Press.

Yahiaoui, D. and Zoubir, Y.H. (2006) Human resource management in Tunisia. In P.S. Budhwar and K. Mellahi (eds) *Managing Human Resources in the Middle East*. London: Routledge.

Zhang, L.C. and Iles, P. (2008) *Do We Turn into Pumpkins? The Experience of British-Educated Returnees to China*, British Council conference, Going Global 3, London, 3–5 December.

Zhang, L.C., Allinson, C.W. and Hayes, J. (2006). *Acculturation through British Higher Education: A Qualitative Exploration in the Malleability of Cognitive Style and Acculturation Process in Chinese Students Following Cross-Cultural Experience*. 18th Congress of the International Association for Cross-Cultural Psychology, Athens.

SCCL Engineering

Introduction

SCCL Engineering is a trading division of SCCL Ltd, a family owned and managed business which has been operating since 1895. Based on the production of components for steam engines in shipping and railways, since the 1930s the company has established itself as a leading producer of investment casting and composite curing technology, with 80 per cent sales for export. The current owners are the Rodgers family, and two brothers, Martyn and Malcolm continue to work in the business, and form the Board with their father, mother and sister. In the last year, SCCL Engineering was established as a separate division along with SCCL Design. Martyn became the manager of Engineering while Malcolm became MD of Design and the business as a whole.

Engineering is mostly reliant on Design for its work but part of the reason for separation was to allow more freedom to pursue other work in a very uncertain global situation. In particular, Martyn hoped to prove to the family his capability as a leader.

He set the following statements of strategic intent

- Quickly establish the need for project-based working and build on the strengths of a well renowned and respected company and workforce
- Develop key strategic partnerships with suppliers and customers
- Develop a workforce capable of achieving flexibility and ownership of the finished product.

Strategic HRD?

Since its foundation the business had always valued its employees. There are 45 staff in Engineering who are generally highly skilled, which inevitably leads to concerns when they approach the age of retirement. This is not uncommon in precision engineering but it may not be easy to replace these people with a ready-made equivalent. There have been no apprentices for five years.

There are four managers who were all appointed from within the business, although with little previous experience of management. Martyn saw a strong need to move towards project-based production with project managers, which would enable a move towards more team work and even self-organising teams around projects. He saw such restructuring as a step towards increased awareness of market movements and changes.

Martyn wanted to initiate a process of customer learning with the aim of allowing a sharing of knowledge about customers. Shared by focusing on critical interactions with customers and reviewing findings to produce outcomes that improve the customer relationship and inform the development of products.

He knew that learning and development would be necessary to move Engineering in the right direction. He wanted to identify the main skills domains for working in project teams and learning from customers, which he knew would be challenging for the existing workforce. He hoped to develop a personal training and development plan for everyone, as part of a commitment to learning (and accreditation, such as Investors in People?). Most importantly, he wanted to prove his leadership capability to the rest of the family.

Questions

1 Is there a place for an HRD strategy in this business? What would be the key features of such a strategy for SCCL Engineering?
2 What are the implications of project-based working and customer learning? What skills are needed for staff and managers?
3 Is there value in obtaining external accreditation?
4 How can Martyn establish his credentials as a leader of learning?

section 2

looking **in:**
principles of HRD

In this section, we deal with some of the key ideas and theories that play a part in the practice of HRD. HRD is concerned with learning at work, so theories of learning must inform practice. There are a variety of theories of learning (Chapter 5: Learning Theories and Principles). In many organizations training is still the common discourse for much HRD activity and Chapter 6 addresses a first key step in the training process. In many organizations training the organization (Chapter 6: The Practice of Training: the Identification of Training Needs). If needs can be identified clearly, such information can be used to design and deliver training (Chapter 7: The Practice of Training: the Design and Delivery of Training) and then, importantly, show that it adds value, although there are different views on how this can be measured (Chapter 8: Evaluation of Human Resource Development).

chapter

5

Learning Theories and Principles

Crystal Ling Zhang, Niki Kyriakidou and David Chesley

Chapter learning outcomes

After studying this chapter, you should be able to:
- Analyse the nature of learning and its importance in the context of an organization
- Define learning and explain the learning theories
- Evaluate various models of learning styles and their complexity
- Apply learning theories in the organization

Chapter outline

Introduction
What is learning?
Learning theories
Learning principles
Summary

Introduction

Learning is a human phenomenon, essential to growth and development, and occurring throughout life. We not only learn to be better (at whatever), but have the opportunity to learn how to learn better or faster. The effectiveness of learning can itself be manipulated. HRD is concerned with the provision of learning and the development of opportunities that support the achievement of business strategies and the improvement of organizational, team and individual performance (Armstrong & Baron, 2002). An understanding of learning is therefore crucial for anyone involved in HRD: trainers, consultants and facilitators, assessors of qualifications and, especially, managers and leaders. As Sadler-Smith (2006, p.2) points out, 'learning is at the heart of *organization*'. However, there is also a connection between views about how work should occur and ideas about learning. Such ideas will inform a manager's understanding of behaviour at work, and the motivation and skills required.

What is learning?

Before defining learning, we can distinguish between education, training and learning. According to Mayo and Lank (1994):

- *Education* is the exposure to new knowledge, concepts and ideas in a relatively programmed way. It is normally aimed at increasing knowledge, or modifying attitudes and beliefs.
- *Training* includes those solutions to a learning need that involve being taught or shown a way of doing things. It is essentially skill oriented.
- *Learning* is employee need centred and starts with the individual as a beneficiary.

In this context, it can be argued that learning is a knowledge-creating process through transforming experience (Kolb, 1984), but it is also a knowledge-skills-insight process because people can do something different and/or become more aware of what they know and can do when they learn. According to Honey and Mumford (1996):

> Learning has happened when people can demonstrate that they know something that they did not know before (insights and realizations, as well as facts) and/or when they can do something they could not do before (skills).

Important aspects of learning are:

- *knowledge* – what someone knows
- *skills* – what someone can do
- *employee attitudes* – the beliefs that shape how they do things
- *experience* – what someone actually does.

For the first three elements, learning can be demonstrated as an end result or outcome (Gold et al., 2010). For the last element, there needs to be a process through which people achieve outcomes. In the process, people do things actively and passively, which may result in outcomes, and this is also a part of learning. So, learning is both a process and the outcomes achieved.

Another distinction can be made between learning and development. Learning refers to the acquisition of knowledge, skills and experience for fulfilling current needs, whereas development refers to enhancing an existing skill or qualification for future needs and career prospects. According to Gold et al. (2010), development embraces all the activities through which people learn.

activity

Form a group of four. Each person should identify the factors influencing their learning and development process. Share your findings with each other and produce a list of factors. Use this list throughout the chapter to identify if there are theories and models to support your ideas.

Learning theories

Learning theories are crucial, but one important point needs to be made at the outset: human beings learn throughout their lives but much of this learning is hardly recognized because it happens informally without conscious awareness.

Michael Eraut (2000) refers to this as 'non-formal learning'. Theories are used to explain how learning occurs and this is made more explicit in more formal events, although growing attention is being given to the value of informal and implicit learning (see Chapter 10). In this chapter we will provide a broad overview of the range of learning theories and consider their use in HRD. Learning theories can be loosely divided into four categories:

- *Behavioural theories* – explanations of learning that emphasize observable changes in behaviour.
- *Cognitive theories* – explanations of learning that focus on mental processes.
- *Experiential theories* – explanations of learning that focus on the way experience is made meaningful through reflection and consideration of future actions.
- *Social and sociocultural learning theories* – explanations of learning that stress the importance of learning new behaviours by observing and adopting the behaviours, attitudes and emotional reactions of others.

In general, there has been an evident shift away from behaviourist experiments with animals (Pavlov, 1927; Skinner, 1953) and explanations addressing a child's learning, towards theories which focus more on adult learning. The distinction between dependent learning in the first two cases and self-directed learning in the last group is of considerable significance (Knowles, 1973). The adult learner's accumulated experience is also acknowledged as one of the resources for learning. Furthermore, their increasing readiness, the internalized motivation and the problem-centred orientation to learning were all characteristics for the premise of andragogy (Greek word meaning man-leading, that is, for adult learners), compared with pedagogy (child-leading, that is, for child learners) (Knowles, 1984). Due to the complexity and richness of the field, this chapter can only provide an introduction; further reading will enhance understanding. To an extent the explanations found in the different theories of learning are contested; certainly no one theory provides a perfect description of learning processes in work settings.

activity

Go to www.infed.org/thinkers/et-knowl.htm and read about the ideas and life of Malcolm Knowles. In pairs, discuss the differences between adult learners and children learners.

Behavioural approach to learning

Much of the early research into learning observed the learning process through animals. Deeply rooted in the positivistic tradition, this school of psychologists sought laws of learning. The best-known representatives of this school are Russian scientist Ivan Pavlov (1849–1936) and American psychologist Burrhus Skinner (1904–90). They argued that learning is a result of reinforcement from an individual's experience. Researchers from this school of thought – behaviourism – were interested in behaviours that could be observed, measured and controlled. Any internal cognitive and mental activities in people's minds were excluded due to their inaccessibility.

Pavlov's (1927) research is considered important to learning in organizations and demonstrated how internal mental activities could be measured and observed. He argued that all learning could be explained by the phenomenon of classical, or Pavlovian, conditioning. Pavlov started the experiment by training dogs to salivate in response to food:

- In Stage 1, no learning is involved since dogs have an automatic and instinctive salivation response to the sight of food.
- In Stage 2, Pavlov combined the food with a new stimulus – the sound of the bell – where the dogs in the experiment would salivate to the new stimulus, if it were repeatedly associated with food.
- In Stage 3, after successful conditioning, Pavlov found dogs could be conditioned to salivate to the sound of a variety of stimuli (bells, tones, buzzers), even when no food appeared.

These experiments demonstrated how physiological reflexes could be conditioned to respond to a new situation and a new stimulus. Stage 2 demonstrates a state of learning, whereas in Stage 3, learning has taken place when the stimulus–response has been bonded.

Skinner (1953) advanced the ideas of Pavlov and developed a theory called operant conditioning from his research on the impact of reward and punishment on animal learning. He observed how rats learned to obtain food by pulling a lever, showing that subjects learn to operate on the environment to achieve a certain goal. This kind of learning refers to a response that has some effect on the situation or environment. Skinner noted that learning could be enhanced not only through reward (a positive reinforcer), but also when the subject associated the behavioural response to a punishment (a negative reinforcer). Positive reinforcement in work settings could be a form of reward, such as money, promotion, recognition or praise from a manager, whereas negative reinforcement refers to unpleasant stimuli, such as a threat or criticism. Behaviour could be shaped by reinforcement, while established behaviours could be maintained by intermittent reinforcement (Nye, 2000).

Behaviourism does seem to underpin how a lot of work is designed, where tasks are broken down into specific actions that must be performed against a specified standard. Practice will make perfect through reinforcement and feedback, but then the behaviour can be repeated over time, so long as the conditions of the task do not change. For those involved in helping staff to learn the required behaviours, objectives can be set, which state what a person can do against a set of criteria after the learning has occurred. Objectives can be specified as outcomes (as at the start of each chapter in this book). It could be argued that such specification will help people to learn and enable the setting of goals and the seeking of feedback on performance, although not everyone seeks feedback (VandeWalle & Cummings, 1997).

activity

Go to **www.learningandteaching.info/learning/behaviour.htm** for more details on behaviourist theories.

In pairs:

– Consider the extent to which you feel reinforcement has been a feature of learning at college.

– How would this behaviourist view of learning help you to write a booklet of instructions on how to use a mobile phone?

Cognitive learning theory

The behaviourist approach has been criticized for ignoring an individuals internal mental activity. In the 1920s and 1930s, psychologists Wolfgang Köhler (1887–1967) and Jean Piaget (1896–1980) demonstrated the limitations of behaviourist research, maintaining that learning is actually more complicated than stimulus–response development. Köhler observed the learning processes of chimpanzees using a stick as a tool to reach fruit and bring it into the cage, and argued that the animal's problem-solving skills developed through insight rather than a simple stimulus–response association. By observing the way children adjust to their environment, Piaget also concluded that the simple behaviourist school could not explain children's learning. He believed learning occurs as a sequence, in which information is processed in different distinct stages: the stimulus perception stage, the sense-making stage and finally the restructuring and storage phrase.

These critiques of behaviourism resulted in a field of psychology known as cognitivism, which gives greater attention to what behaviourists tend to ignore: how people process information by thinking, using the resources of memory. The analogy of a computer seems relevant. People register inputs from the environment through their senses and these are processed into memory or rejected. Learning is concerned with acquiring new information that connects to what is already stored but makes an adjustment accordingly. The idea of a schema is used to explain how information is organized into knowledge patterns that can be called upon when needed. Schemas can also affect those situationally activated preconceptions that are likely to be called on when interpretating a specific event and organizing individual's memory objects (Derry, 1996). Cognitive learning in HRD helps people to build meaningful patterns that can lead to new insights, discover new ways of understanding through seeing relationships, or even challenge existing patterns to produce new ways of seeing and understanding.

activity

Go to www.learningandteaching.info/learning/cognitive.htm to explore various cognitive learning theories. Discover the meanings of constructivism and multiple intelligences. How do cognitive theories help other people to learn?

Cognitive styles

As people choose what to attend to, according to existing patterns of cognition, this can also affect what is ignored. People establish particular ways of thinking and understanding, which will affect what they are prepared to try and do. Patterns of thinking can settle into styles and this has been a key interest among cognitive theorists for many years. For example, Swiss psychoanalyst Carl Jung (1875–1961) formulated a model of cognitive styles or personality types: the introverted and the extroverted; and further subdivided them into four function types: thinking, feeling, sensation and intuition (Jung, 1923). Thinking and feeling were associated with a rational way of information processing, while sensation and intuition were associated with an irrational manner. Jung's work and theory have had a great impact on later researchers, for example Isabel Myers (1897–1980) and David Kolb (1939–).

Based on Jung's early work, and to make the work more accessible, Myers (1962) developed a way to measure the cognitive styles called the Myers-Briggs Type Indicator (MBTI). The MBTI extended and redefined the Jungian concepts of rational and irrational and referred to them as judgement and perception respectively. The indicator has a series of questions associated with four bipolar discontinuous scales: extraversion and introversion, sensing and intuition, thinking and feeling, and judging and perceiving, as shown as Figure 5.1.

Myers also proposed the possible mixing of the different function types from Jung (1923), so that the possible matching of various types results in Myers' 16 distinct personality types (Figure 5.1). There are three versions of the MBTI, which vary according to the length of the questionnaire: the abbreviated form of 50 items; the standard 93-item Form M; and the long 126-item Form G (Myers & McCaulley, 1985). Each is designed to produce one of the 16 combinations of preferences, in terms of cognitive, behavioural, affective and perceptual perspectives. Thorne and Gough (1999) summarized the ten most common MBTI types, based on their positive and negative traits, as shown in Table 5.1.

Following Jung's proposal, Myers' theory shares the idea that style is one part of the observable expression of a relatively stable personality type. Even though some researchers (for example Bayne, 1994) stress the versatility of individuals to move beyond their dominant function to exploit or develop auxiliary preferences, both Jung and Myers believed that the personality type would become dominant by adulthood and this versatility would be restricted by the individual's strong and habituated preferences (Coffield et al., 2004). Myers promoted her theory from a purely academic context to a wider audience in organizations, high schools, and in the field of counselling and marital relations. As such, the MBTI has been widely accepted as a research instrument and is one of most popular personality measures, having been translated into a number of languages (Furnham & Stringfield, 1993).

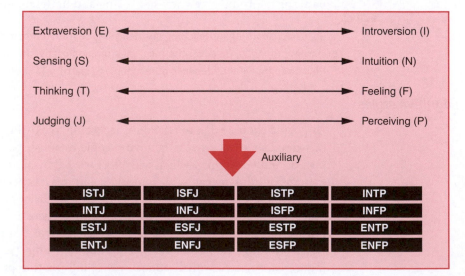

Figure 5.1 Myers-Briggs Type Indicator (MBTI)
Source: Coffield et al. (2004, p.48)

Table 5.1 Thorne and Gough's (1999) summary of the MBTI types

Type	Positive traits	Negative traits
INFP	Artistic, reflective, sensitive	Careless, lazy
INFJ	Sincere, sympathetic, unassuming	Submissive, weak
INTP	Candid, ingenious, shrewd	Complicated, rebellious
INTJ	Discreet, industrious, logical	Deliberate, methodical
ISTJ	Calm, stable, steady	Cautious, conventional
ENFP	Enthusiastic, outgoing, spontaneous	Changeable, impulsive
ENFJ	Active, pleasant, sociable	Demanding, impatient
ENTP	Enterprising, friendly, resourceful	Headstrong, self-centred
ENTJ	Ambitious, forceful, optimistic	Aggressive, egotistical
ESTJ	Contented, energetic, practical	Prejudiced, self-satisfied

Source: Coffield et al. (2004, p.48)

activity

Visit the Myers & Briggs Foundation – **www.myersbriggs.org**

Find out about the use of this instrument in everyday life and consider how to develop a career as a professional MBTI consultant via training.

There has been, and continues to be, much interest in cognition with the development of a range of tests to understand how people process information and identify their cognitive style. In the 1960s, Wallach (1962), Gardner (1962) and Hudson (1968) developed definitions of cognitive styles and linked the concepts of individual style, thinking and behaviour. From the 1970s, the emphasis of the research was further developed and applied in pedagogical settings (Sternberg & Grigorenko, 2001). Cognitive style has been widely recognized by researchers as the individual's consistent differences in information processing (Kogan, 1971; Messick, 1976; Allinson & Hayes, 1994; Riding & Rayner, 1998). Witkin and Goodenough (1981) pointed out that cognitive style relates more to how information is processed rather than the content of the information that is processed, that is, the individual differences in how people perceive, think, solve problems, learn and relate to others.

The Cognitive Style Index (CSI), developed by Chris Allinson and John Hayes (1994), is one of the most well-known and reliable tests used in organizational settings. Working with a split brain metaphor, Allinson and Hayes (1996) suggested that:

> Intuition, characteristic of right-brain orientation, refers to immediate judgment based on feeling and the adoption of a global perspective. Analysis, characteristic of left-brain orientation, refers to judgment based on mental reasoning and a focus on detail (p.122).

The resulting theory of the intuitive–analytical dimensions of cognitive style is captured by the CSI. It has a self-reporting format, with 38 statements requiring a choice between true, uncertain and false options. The score for the CSI ranges

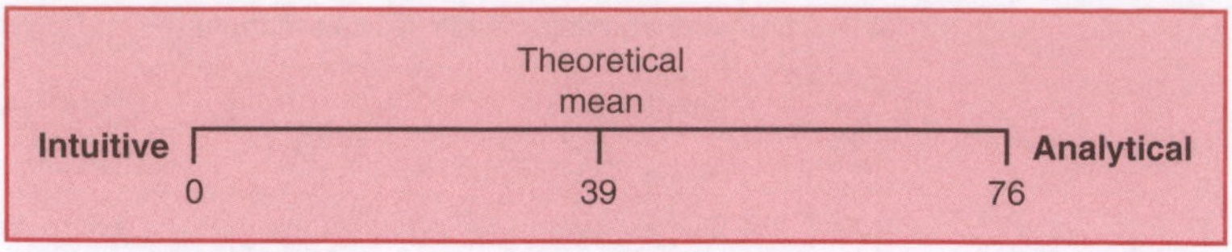

Figure 5.2 Cognitive style index scale

Source: Armstrong (1999, p.74)

from 0 to 76, with a theoretical mean of 39; the closer the score is to 76, the more analytical the respondent is deemed to be, while the nearer the score is to 0, the more intuitive the respondent is, as shown in Figure 5.2.

The CSI has been widely used as a tool on a national and international basis. It has been translated into several languages (Lofstrom, 2002) and used for cross-cultural studies. Coffield et al. (2004, p.138) argue that 'the CSI has the best psychometric credentials' out of 71 learning styles models that they reviewed and assessed.

Although the CSI has a reputation of being the most reliable instrument for organizational settings, there have been challenges from other scholars on its degree of simplification of the individual's information processing (Sadler-Smith, 2006; Hodgkinson & Clarke, 2007). They argue that there is interaction and interdependence between the different styles, that is, intuition and analysis are not contrasting opposites, but are two dimensions, each ranging from high to low on, which can be combined to generate four quadrants, such as high intuition and high analytic or high intuition and low analytic.

Neurocognitive theory

The cognitive theories discussed so far have attempted to explain the process of learning from a psychological framework. However, in recent years, there has been interest in studies of the working of the brain and central nervous system, or neuroscience and learning. For example, advances in neuroscience research have demonstrated that learning involves the physical formation of neuronal contacts (Toni et al., 1999). A landmark study of taxi drivers in London has shown that their brains have a larger frontal hippocampus than matched control volunteers (Maguire et al., 2000), but no changes were observed as a result of driving.

There have been growing attempts to bring neuroscience together with cognitive psychology and philosophy of human reasoning and this is referred to as neurocognitive theory. Neurocognitive theory is proposed as a unifying concept for understanding learning from the physical and biological structures (the brain), and the psychological and cognitive processes (Anderson, 2009). Importantly, differences in the brain structures between male and female could explain differences in learning and cognition (Baron-Cohen et al., 2005; Perrin et al., 2009). During neurological disorders such as Alzeihmer's, Parkinson's or autism, the neuronal connections in the brain are altered and have been shown to have profound effects on the normal mental functions of information acquisition, processing and recalling. Interestingly, a recent study of Alzheimer's patients showed that bilingual sufferers retained cognitive function for four more years than monolingual sufferers, even though both had similar damage to the brain (Craik et al., 2010). Neuroscience has uncovered many of the functions of each part of the brain, however the processing of information and experience and the ability to use these to view the self and the world are still a mystery. Nevertheless, future multidisciplinary approaches to theory building in this area can open up new avenues for inquiry (Anderson, 2009). In particular, there is a trend toward viewing cognition as a result of an integration of networks from different areas of the brain (Meehan & Bressler, 2012).

Experiential learning

Both behavioural and cognitive learning theories are considered to be part of the 'standard paradigm of learning' (Beckett & Hager, 2002, p.98). Behaviourism is mainly concerned with stimulation from the outside that elicits a response, and cognitivism is concerned with how information is processed under the influence of existing knowledge, stored in the brain as schema. Over the past 30 years, while research in both theories has continued, there has been strong interest in the interaction between a person and their environment. Both the person and the environment, whether it is other people or physical things like books, working or just living, can provide experiences that can become a source of learning.

The use of experience in learning has it roots in the work of John Dewey and Kurt Lewin, but the most well-known experiential learning theory was developed by Kolb (1976). His experiential learning model is based on a learning cycle and his main contribution has been to re-evaluate the conventional definition of cognitive style. He refers to learning style as a 'differential preference for learning, which changes slightly from situation to situation. At the same time, there is some long-term stability in learning style' (Kolb, 2000, p.8). The stages in Kolb's learning cycle are concrete experience (CE), reflective observation (RO), abstract conceptualization (AC) and active experimentation (AE), shown in Figure 5.3. Ideally learners can:

- involve themselves in new experiences openly and without bias (CE)
- reflect on the new experience and observe it objectively from many angles (RO)
- formulate and generalize the observation into a logical concept (AC)
- test the concept in a new situation (AE).

The tension in the abstract–concrete dimension is between relying on conceptual interpretation or on immediate experience in order to grasp hold of experience, while the tension in the active–reflective dimension is between relying on internal reflection or external manipulation in order to transform experience (Coffield et al., 2004). To help individuals to assess their approach to learning, Kolb (1976) developed the Learning Style Inventory (LSI), which provides information about the individual's relative emphasis on the four abilities in the learning cycle.

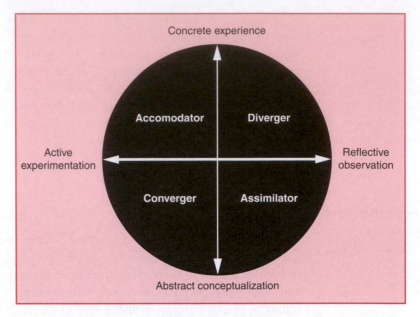

Figure 5.3 Kolb's experiential learning cycle and basic learning styles

Source: Kolb et al. (2001, p.229)

activity

Go to **www.learningandteaching.info/learning/experience.htm** for more information on experiential learning.

If you want to learn more about Dewey, go to **http://dewey.pragmatism.org/**

For more on Lewin, try **www.infed.org/thinkers/et-lewin.htm**

Kolb's experiential learning theory has been popularized in management development and education from the 1980s, however, there are a number of critics of its conceptual assumptions and practical inconsistencies in complex organizational settings (e.g. Holman et al., 1997; Kayes, 2002; Reynolds & Vince, 2004, 2007; Seaman, 2008; Reynolds, 2009; Yeo & Gold, 2011). Based on Vygotsky's (1978) social and sociocultural learning theory, and Bakhtin's (1981) philosophy of language, Yeo and Gold (2011) argue that Kolb's version of experiential learning theory neglected the depth and integration among individuals' self-action, interaction and transaction. They claim that the experiential learning should have an integrated nature and be underpinned by socio-psychological meta-theories that seek to question 'where we are? (social context) and 'who we are?' (cognition) in relation to 'what we learn?' (action).

While there are disagreements regarding Kolb's theory and his LSI, his work has attracted considerable interest since the 1970s and has influenced the development of other models of learning style. Peter Honey and Alan Mumford (2006) believe that each learning style in the learning cycle, shown in Figure 5.4, has its own characteristics, each with its own unique strengths and weaknesses. Honey and Mumford (2006, p.43) emphasize that 'no single style has an overwhelming advantage over any other. Each has strengths and weaknesses but the strengths may be especially important in one situation, but not in another instance.' Learning styles are identified by completing the Honey and Mumford

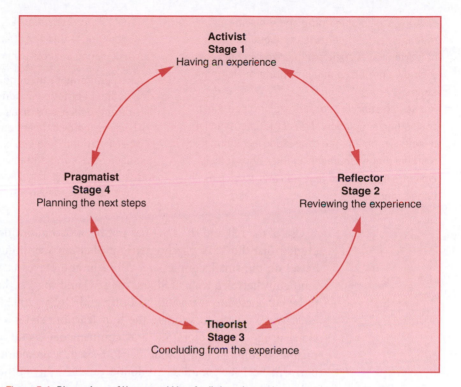

Figure 5.4 Dimensions of Honey and Mumford's learning cycle

Source: Honey and Mumford (2006)

Learning Styles Questionnaire (LSQ), designed specifically for managers and professionals. It asks questions about general behavioural tendencies rather than just learning, as is the case with Kolb's LSI. The LSQ consists of questions with simple agree or disagree answers, which probe the preferences for the four learning styles. As a detailed practical manual with simple language for management people, Honey and Mumford try to make people aware of their strengths in the four types of learning styles.

Experiential learning cycles have enabled some interesting developments in helping students to become more self-directed, as shown in HRD in Practice 5.1.

Problem-based learning

HRD in Practice 5.1

Tutors at Leeds Metropolitan University have sought to help students become more self-directed in the study of change in international contexts. The module emphasizes that individual experience is an important learning resource that individuals draw on when facing difficult and ambiguous situations. This reservoir of experience is consciously used as a rich resource for learning. This is based on the principle that as adult learners, students attach a great deal of meaning to learning gained through experience. Further, and following Kolb's learning cycle, through review, reflection on and analysis of experience, greater depth can be provided to learning.

The module lasts one semester and covers three phases:

- *Phase 1: familiarization.* Learners are introduced to the processes and methodology that highlight the distinctive inter- and multidisciplinary nature of the module. Each student is able to identify existing styles of learning and problem management. Students learn about the idea of learning as a cycle as theorized by Kolb and their own preferred and less preferred learning styles.

- *Phase 2: research*. Learners are provided with a case study simulation of an actual international business problem. The case study incorporates material that encourages an inter- and multidisciplinary approach to research and developing understanding.

- *Phase 3: dramatization*. Learners are formed into negotiating teams and are required to prepare for participation in a role-playing exercise.

A key outcome of the module was the use of knowledge in practice in addition to becoming more self-directed as learners. As one student recorded:

I became more confident during the role play when I was able to put theory into practice. I learned how to persuade others and express my own opinions. We were able to test the use of knowledge in the role play. We were no longer passive students.

Use of the LSI and the LSQ has not been without criticism. Sugarman (1985) argued that the LSI's psychometric evaluation was limited and low in quality, based on the small sample size. Allinson and Hayes (1990) also point out the ambiguity between Kolb's LSI and the LSQ and suggest that more research needs to be conducted to test validity. Duffy and Duffy (2002, cited in Coffield et al., 2004) were unable to validate the four learning styles and two bipolar dimensions using both exploratory and confirmatory factor analysis and were also unable to employ such psychometric tests as a predictor of students' academic performance. Such studies cast doubts on the utility of the LSQ.

Research on learning styles has continued. One of the most interesting models has been developed by Lynn Curry (1983, 1987) and is referred to as Curry's 'onion' model of learning styles. She reviewed the psychometric qualities of different learning style instruments and categorized them according to the three-layered 'onion' model, shown in Figure 5.5.

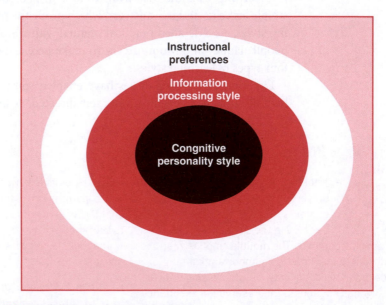

Figure 5.5 Curry's 'onion' model of learning styles
Source: Curry (1983, 1987)

The categories are instructional preferences, information-processing style and cognitive personality style. In Curry's model, the inner layer (cognitive personality style) is more stable and significant in complex learning, while the outer layer of instructional preferences is easier to modify and influence, but less important in learning.

reflective question How would you develop training based on the different learning styles?

Learning style or cognitive style?

There has been some confusion over the concepts of learning style and cognitive style for many years. Four different arguments have been attempted to contribute to the nature of individual style:

1 Some researchers (Entwistle, 1981; Campbell, 1991; Riding & Cheema, 1991; Coffield et al., 2004) argue that these terms are used loosely and interchangeably. Riding and Cheema (1991) argue that: The terms cognitive style and learning style have been much used by theorists, but what they mean still remains very much up to its author.

2 It is argued that cognitive style is different from learning style and can only be considered as a subcomponent of learning style (Dunn & Dunn, 1993). With the argument that learning style is a biological and developmental set of personality characteristics, Dunn and Dunn (1993, p.2) remarked that: learning style is more than merely whether a child remembers new and difficult information most easily by hearing, seeing, reading, writing, illustrating, verbalizing, or actively experiencing; perceptual or modality strength is only one part of learning style. It also is more than whether a person processes information sequentially, analytically, or in a left-brain mode rather than in a holistic, simultaneous, global, right-brain fashion; that, too, is only one important component of learning style. It is more than how someone responds to the environment in which learning must occur or whether information is absorbed concretely or abstractly; those variables contribute to style but, again, are only part of the total construct.

3 Another school acknowledges that learning style has a more rigid meaning and it mainly focuses on the information-processing style in a learning environment and learning activities (Claxton & Ralston, 1978; Riding & Rayner, 2002). Claxton and Ralston (1978) define learning style as a student's consistent way of responding to and using stimuli in the context of learning. As the precursor of learning style, cognitive style has a wider concern about how information can be processed in a wider variety of settings, rather than just the learning context. Riding and Rayner (2002, p.51) went on to argue that: learning style is an individual set of differences that include not only a stated personal preference for instruction or an association with a particular form of learning activity but also individual differences found in intellectual or personal psychology. While the two terms – learning style and learning strategy – are used interchangeably by some (Cronbach & Snow, 1977), Sternberg and Grigorenko (2001) and Riding and Rayner (2002) distinguish

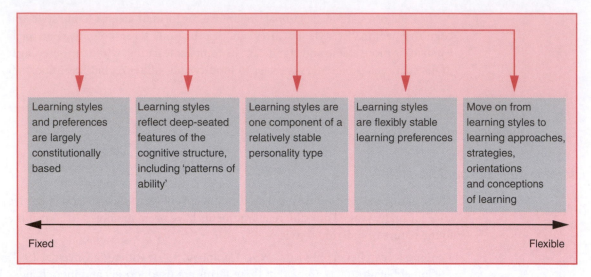

Figure 5.6 Coffield et al.'s families of learning styles

Source: Coffield et al. (2004, p.9)

between learning style and learning strategy – the former referring to an individual's fixed trait, while the latter is generally used for more task- and context-dependent situations.

4 Some researchers attempt to make sense of the confusing field and review the origin and development of cognitive style and learning style (Curry, 1983; Riding & Rayner, 2002; Coffield et al., 2004). Coffield et al. (2004) summarized a continuum of learning styles, claiming that it is based on the extent to which the developers of learning style models and instruments appear to believe that learning styles are fixed, as shown in Figure 5.6.

At the left end of the continuum, researchers strongly believe in the influence of genetics on fixed, inherited traits, and the interaction of personality and cognition. At the right end of the continuum, theorists place more emphasis on personal factors such as motivation, environmental factors, and the effects of the environment on the individual's cognitive style.

Social and sociocultural learning theories

As approaches to measuring preferences for learning or problem solving, both cognitive styles and learning styles have been criticized for their focus on individuals and their distortion of the contextual factors that affect how a person learns and works (Reynolds, 1997). Being identified with a particular kind of style can also lead to stereotyping. For example, if you are classified as an activist under the LSQ framework, this can create expectations of how you will or will not learn. Holman et al. (1997) also critique learning styles for their emphasis on the individual and suggest giving more importance to social conditions and interactions with others.

For example, social learning theorist Albert Bandura (1977) argues that learning is a dynamic interplay between the person, the environment and behaviour. He emphasizes how the environment explicitly affects learners (Gold et al.,

2009). Learning occurs through indirect observation and modelling, for example a child observes their mother, remembers the observed behaviour and practises those learned behaviours. The social learning approach involves four interrelated processes: attention, memory, motor and motivation (Bandura, 1977).

activity

Go to **http://tip.psychology.org/bandura.html** for more information about Bandura's work.

The Virtual Faculty at Massey University has a project devoted to the work of Vygotsky at **http://www.massey.ac.nz/ffalock/virtual/project2.htm**

Another theory that considers the effect of social factors is based on the work of Russian social psychologist, Lev Vygotsky, who in the 1920s and early 1930s developed a sociocultural activity approach to learning. This approach to learning gives more attention to the importance of social interaction in the learning process. Learning is more than just what happens internally, it is also the fruit of interactions between the social to the individual. Two crucial contributions from Vygotsky are the mediating tools between subject and goal in the learning action, and the idea of a zone of proximal development (ZPD). By mediating tools, Vygotsky (1982) meant the obvious physical tools needed to complete an action such as a table, a chair and so on, and the psychological tools such as writing, language and so on. All these tools mediate how individuals think, feel and behave.

For consideration of ZPD, Vygotsky's theory gives importance to identifying the learner's lower and upper limits of ability, that is, the learner's optimal performance level or the ZPD. According to Vygotsky, learning occurs by the introduction of new mediating tools, physical or psychological or both. These tools could potentially enable individuals to perform better but also cause disturbance to existing ways of understanding and behaving. Such a learning process is achievable only with support, or scaffolding. In this approach, learning is the consideration of existing capacity and the skill to find solutions to problems that an individual is facing and moving towards more advanced learning that is relative to the existing capacity. An example of sociocultural learning is shown in HRD in Practice 5.2.

James faces a dilemma

HRD in Practice 5.2

James is a senior manager and ex-MD of a business he had helped establish but was then forced out of by other managers during a restructuring. Working with six other managers in a learning group, he sought help to work out what he could do next. As the subject in the action, his stated goal was 'help me sort out the mess I am in ... I need to make a decision'. Others in the group were quite aware of James' difficulties because the story had featured in previous meetings, when they had heard that he

seemed to be heading towards a victory in his battle with the business he had helped establish. A lawyer had advised that a settlement had been offered and should be accepted, although James tended to favour a fight to the finish.

James was facing a dilemma between two sets of mediating tools. Firstly, the choosing to fight approach, which was James' preference for most business situations. As a mature business manager, who had set up and developed two other businesses, he took pride in his ability to take a principled stand and stay firm when faced with difficulty. He linked this to his mother's influence. This mediating tool can also be seen in terms of reverse action, where the tool acts to define the subjectivity of James. It has enabled James in the past both in business and in personal terms. James' principled stand was also the source of a feeling of being stuck and unable to move on because he was holding out for what he thought he was entitled to.

Secondly, taking advice provided an acceptance that he could settle for less and get on with setting up a new business. It would avoid the wait and was supported by two others whom he felt compelled to listen to, his lawyer and his wife. Up to this point, this tool, based on an interaction with others, had been secondary.

Having heard the story from James, the challenge from other managers served to reinforce this second tool, which now became equal in strength to the first, and hence a disturbance to James in whom unlearning became possible. A supportive challenge was offered to James: how close to acceptable was the settlement offer? James quickly responded with quite close interpreted by others as acceptable. Other questions related to the assumptions James was making about the apparent poor performance by other managers at the tribunal, and James own views about backing down as a negation of his identity. Unlearning became relearning through the acceptability of the settlement and the loss of time and opportunity in waiting for a reconvened tribunal. Finally, the dilemma was resolved by a new tool for action and reverse action, referred to by James as 'taking my own advice'. With the goal achieved, James could then move into new actions with new goals. This involved other tools of mediation, including his mobile phone with which he could instruct his legal advisers and his wife within minutes of the meeting ending. Further, his pride could be retained but now enhanced with a new tool that allowed advice to become accepted and translated as 'taking my own advice'.

A further development of the social approach to learning is found in the work of Lave and Wenger (1991), who used the term situated learning to emphasize the development of knowledge and expertise through activity and practice in work situations. This is a form of natural learning that highlights the context and culture in which learning occurs. In contrast to the classic psychologically-driven theories of learning, developed mainly in laboratory or classroom settings, situated learning theories occur in workplace settings. It is argued that learning is about participation in a community of practice. For example, a community of practice occurs in the system of apprenticeships in carpentry, and the legal and medical professions. This system is developed through instances of formal and informal learning in various work activities. The term 'legitimate peripheral participation' was developed by Lave and Wenger (1991) to refer to the learning process from apprentice to expert.

Learning principles

All activities in HRD imply a view of how learning occurs, whether this is made explicit or not. As we have suggested, for much of the last century, the very process of organizing tended to imply a particular approach to learning based on behaviourism and mechanistic assumptions about humans. The contrasting theories of cognitive learning and experiential learning gained more favour towards the last quarter of the 20th century, along with a recognition of the difference between pedagogical and andragogical notions of learning (Knowles, 1973) and the move towards knowledge-based organizations. There is also far more interest in everyday learning now, which is socially and culturally enabled and constrained, but which can be harnessed as a source of competitive advantage. All these theories have some value and it is the task of those involved to derive key principles for good practice. We will attempt to do this in the following sections.

Application of behavioural theories

Behaviourism deals with cause and effect, and learning practices based on behavioural theories predominantly use external stimuli to arouse a behavioural response. These theories explain how training effectiveness is improved by understanding the following:

- People respond to reinforcement (such as rewards) within training
- Reinforcement is a motivator to participate in training
- Responses to stimuli are dependent on the individual, so the instruction needs to be oriented to the individual
- Effectiveness of rewards must be individually determined, that is, different strokes for different folks
- HRD programmes should progress from the simple to the complex
- HRD programmes should include sensitization, practice and feedback to managers and employees – potentially through the growing use of coaches and mentors at work.

However, behaviourism has gained a notorious reputation, with its association with the ruthless efficiency of industrial organizations and rigid systems of bureaucracies (Gold et al., 2009), and ignores the emotions, preferences or motivations of learners who process information differently.

Application of cognitive theories

Cognitive theories focus on mental processes such as memory, aptitude, intelligence and lateral thinking. Adult learners ought to be given the opportunity to build on prior experience rather than starting anew. The learning practice should take into account the social, cultural and environmental contexts and must recognize the dynamic nature of change and the role of previous experience. It must also acknowledge the different ways people give meaning to, and make sense of, their experiences. Implementing cognitive and learning style theories requires the following:

- Learner understanding should be a central feature of any design
- Learners are active and will learn more if they have some control over the learning process
- Information should be organized to facilitate, rather than control, learning
- Learners progress from the simple to the complex (not complicated, but holistic and complex)
- Informed by neurocognitive theory, learning is related to patterns or networks of brain activity and the central nervous system
- Learners need to learn how to learn, by understanding and testing out learning or cognitive styles or trying new ones.

The last point about learning to learn has become a particularly strong feature in debates about learning in recent years. There has been an emphasis on people taking more responsibility for learning and this has government backing as part of a policy of lifelong learning. Similarly, professionals are frequently required to undergo continuing professional development (see Chapter 15). A number of commentators, such as Brookfield (1986), call for more self-direction in learning and part of this encouragement requires individuals to develop learning skills and understand their learning preferences.

activity

Form a group of three. Each person lists their learning skills, that is, those skills that enable you to learn. Compare your responses. How can you enhance your learning skills?

Go to http://www.niace.org.uk/lifelonglearninginquiry/docs/WEL0002i.pdf, and read the Declaration on Learning from the Learning Declaration Group. Discuss the Challenge.

Application of social and sociocultural learning theories

Social and sociocultural learning theories stress the importance of learning new behaviours through observing and adopting the behaviours, attitudes and emotional reactions of others. Organizations can take advantage of our understanding of these theories by facilitating the appropriate informal and formal communication processes. A key aspect involves setting up apprenticeship or mentoring schemes – partnering a trainee with a tradesperson or mentor. Guidelines for a learning practice should include the following:

- Learning occurs through exposure to others, both formally and informally
- Interaction with others in the course of everyday practice is a source of learning
- Learning can also be inhibited by exposure to others as well as individual feelings about their abilities
- Learners acquire new skills and knowledge when they see these as relevant to what they do in practice
- Culture and history play a role in what people learn, which may be positive or otherwise
- Learners may need help to be able to cope with new tasks or solve problems.

A positive work climate will aid the application of learning about work, and that climate should include positive and genuine feedback about their efforts. A supportive environment enhances positive outcomes when individuals attempt to utilize their new learning in the workplace. Learners can be stretched to try new actions with appropriate support and this can occur every day by watching others, doing work and talking about it, especially through sharing stories about problems (Brown & Duiguid, 1991).

However, is learning always positive and why do some of us aspire to continual learning whilst others have an instrumental appreciation of the relative merits of their learning and the context in which they find themselves? In the now seminal work by Paul Willis (1977), *Learning to Labour*, we see an ethnographical study utilizing a number of research methods to get a clear understanding of 'the lads' motivations towards schooling. Willis noted that 'the lads' were happy settling for a basic career which would lead them into industry. Average grades were not a failure; they simply secured a factory job. Once inside the factory it was then up to 'the lads' to determine how far they wanted to venture on a potential management pathway. However, the key is that they had worked out what they needed to attain to get in! They understood the amount of learning it took. The high-performance work cultures of today would struggle with individualistic and instrumental approaches to self-development which may not be well-received by management! Yet commentators such as Bowles and Gintis (1976) believed that an unintentional purpose of education and schooling was to allow individuals to locate their place in society. As such, by rejecting their schooling and settling for average grades, 'the lads' had inadvertently placed themselves in a working class niche. In this study, schoolchildren become resigned to their fate where the education system becomes a conveyor belt for working class reproduction. If, as managers in global organizations we are truly committed to learning and continuing self-development for the benefit of individuals and organizations a whole, is it now time to reflect on how learning and development can enable employees to rise, for talent to be spotted and to come through the ranks and for any learning to be both agreeable to the individual and the organization? Is it not time to realign the conveyer belt from the start of schooling, even before potential employees enter the building?

summary

⭕ Learning is a lifelong process and HRD is concerned with providing learning opportunities for the work context. There has been a growing interest in implementing good learning practices in organizations.

⭕ Learning is concerned with the acquisition of knowledge, skills and attitudes through experiences. Learning is both the process of acquisition and the outcomes achieved.

⭕ Learning theories have been evolved through several stages in history, from the observation of animal behaviour to the development of learning in children and adults.

⭕ Globalization and technological change have implications for what skills and knowledge are needed and how learning occurs.

⭕ Learning occurs both informally and formally at work, and differs between children and adults.

⭕ Behaviourist theories start with Pavlovian conditioning and the importance of reinforcement in the learning process. Behaviourist ideas on learning have a close connection with mechanistic assumptions on work design and organization.

⭕ Cognitive approaches to learning emphasize that individuals perceive stimulus, evaluate feedback, store and use information. Research on cognitive and learning styles enables the measurement and diagnosis of preferences, although there are concerns about the validity of such measures.

⭕ Neurocognitive theory based on recent advances in understanding of how the brain works are influencing ideas on learning.

⭕ Social and sociocultural learning theories suggest that individuals learn and develop through observation and modelling. They stress the importance of the community of practice and the hands-on experience of learning in the workplace rather than in a classroom or laboratory environment.

discussion questions

1 Why is learning important in the workplace?

2 What are the main differences between the behavioural and cognitive approaches to learning? Identify the key players in each respective school of thinking and explain their work.

3 What do you understand by the concepts of punishment and the learning cycle? Illustrate with examples from work or college.

4 What is the difference between learning style and cognitive style? Why is the concept of learning style important for managers and employees?

5 How does culture affect learning? What cultures influence how your class learns?

further reading

references

Billett, S. (ed.) (2010) *Learning through Practice*. Springer: Dordrecht, The Netherlands.

Coffield, F., Moseley, D., Hall, E. and Ecclestone, K. (2004) *Learning Styles and Pedagogy in Post-16 Learning: A Systematic and Critical Review*. London: Learning and Skills Research Centre.

Engeström, Y. and Sannino, A. (2012) Whatever happened to process theories of learning? *Learning, Culture and Social Interaction,* **1**(1): 45–56.

Wenger, E. (1999) *Communities of Practice: Learning, Meaning and Identity*. Cambridge: Cambridge University Press.

Allinson, C.W. and Hayes, J. (1990) Validity of the learning styles questionnaire. *Psychological Reports*, **67**: 859–66.

Allinson, C.W. and Hayes, J. (1994) Cognitive style and its relevance for management practice. *British Journal of Management*, **5**(1): 53–72.

Allinson, C.W. and Hayes, J. (1996) The cognitive style index: a measure of intuition-analysis for organizational research. *Journal of Management Studies*, **33**(1): 119–35.

Anderson A.R. (2009). Neurocognitive theory and Constructivism in science education: A review of neurobiological, cognitive and cultural perspectives. *Brunei International Journal of Science and Maths Education,* **1**(1), 1–32.

Armstrong, S. (1999) *Cognitive Style and Dyadic Interaction: A Study of Supervisors and Subordinates Engaged in Working Relationships*, unpublished PhD thesis, Leeds, UK: University of Leeds.

Armstrong, M. and Baron, A. (2002) *Strategic HRM: The Key to Improved Business Performance*. London: CIPD.

Bakhtin, M.M. (1981) *The Dialogic Imagination: Four Essays by M. M. Bakhtin*, M. Holquist (ed.). Austin: University of Texas Press.

Bandura, A. (1977) *Social Learning Theory*. Englewood Cliffs, NJ: Prentice Hall.

Baron-Cohen, S., Knickmeyer, R.C., Belmonte, M.K. (2005). Sex differences in the brain: implictions for explaining autism. *Science*, **310**: 819–23.

Bayne, R. (1994) The 'big five' versus the Myers-Briggs. *Psychologist*, **7**(1): 14–16.

Beckett, D. and Hager, P. (2002) *Life, Work and Learning: Practice in Postmodernity*. London: Routledge.

Bowles, S. and Gintis, H. (1976) *Schooling In Capitalist America: Educational Reform and Contradictions Of Economic Life*. New York: Basic Books.

Brookfield, S. (1986) *Understanding and Facilitating Adult Learning*. Milton Keynes: Open University Press.

Brown, J.S. and Duguid, P. (1991) Organizational learning and communities of practice: toward a unified view of working, learning, and innovation. *Organization Science*, **2**(1): 40–57.

Campbell, B.J. (1991) Planning for a student learning style. *Journal of Education for Business*, **66**(6): 356–58.

Claxton, C.S. and Ralston, Y. (1978) (eds) *Learning Styles: Their Impact on Teaching and Administration*. Washington, DC: American Association for Higher Education.

Coffield, F., Moseley, D., Hall, E. and Ecclestone, K. (2004) *Learning Styles and Pedagogy in Post-16 Learning: A Systematic and Critical Review*. London: Learning and Skills Research Centre.

Craik, F.I.M., Bialystok, E., and Freedman, M. (2010). Delaying the onset of Alzheimer's disease: Bilingualism as a form of cognitive reserve. *Neurology*, **75**: 1726–29.

Cronbach, L.J. and Snow, R.E. (1977) *Aptitudes and Instructional Methods*. New York: Wiley.

Curry, L. (1983) *Learning Styles in Continuing Medical Education*. Ottawa: Canadian Medical Association.

Curry, L. (1987) *Integrating Concepts of Cognitive Learning Styles: A Review with Attention to Psychometric Standards*. Ottawa: Canadian College of Health Services Executives.

Derry, S. (1996) Cognitive schema theory in the constructivist debate. *Educational Psychologist*, **31**(3/4): 163–74.

Duffy, A. and Duffy, T. (2002) Psychometric properties of Honey and Mumford's Learning Styles Questionnaire (LSQ). *Personality and Individual Differences*, **33**: 147–63.

Dunn, R. and Dunn, K. (1993) *Teaching Secondary Students through their Individual Learning Styles: Practical Approaches for Grades 7–12*. Boston: Allyn & Bacon.

Entwistle, N. (1981) *Styles of Learning and Teaching*. Chichester: Wiley.

Eraut, M. (2000) Non-formal learning, implicit learning and tacit knowledge in professional work (pp.113–36). In F. Coffield (ed.) *The Necessity of Informal Learning*. Bristol: Policy Press.

Furnham, A. and Stringfield, P. (1993) Personality and occupational behaviour: Myers-Briggs Type Indicator correlates of managerial practices in two cultures. *Human Relations*, **46**(7): 827–40.

Gardner, R.W. (1962) Cognitive controls in adaptation: research and measurement (pp.118–48). In S. Messick and J. Ross (ed.) *Measurement in Personality and Cognition*. New York: Wiley.

Gold, J., Thorpe, R. and Mumford, A. (2009) How leaders and managers learn (pp.261–78). In J. Gold, R. Thorpe and A. Mumford (eds) *Handbook of Management and Leadership Development*. Aldershot: Gower Press.

Gold, J., Thorpe, R. and Mumford A. (2010) *Leadership and Management Development: Strategies for Action*. London: Chartered Institute of Personnel and Development.

Hodgkinson, G.P. and Clarke, I. (2007) Exploring the cognitive significance of organizational strategizing: a dual-process framework and research agenda. *Human Relations*, **60**: 243–55.

Holman, D., Pavlica, K. and Thorpe, R. (1997) Rethinking Kolb's theory of experiential learning in management education. *Management Learning*, **28**(2): 135–48.

Honey, P. and Mumford, A. (1996) *Managing the Learning Environment*. Maidenhead: P. Honey.

Honey, P. and Mumford, A. (2006) *The Learning Styles Questionnaire: 80 Item Version*. Maidenhead: P. Honey.

Hudson, L. (1968) *Frames of Mind: Ability, Perception and Self-Perception in the Arts and Science*. London: Methuen.

Jung, C. (1923) *Psychological Types*. London: Pantheon Books.

Kayes, D. C. (2002) Experiential learning and its critics: preserving the role of experience in management learning and education. *Academy of Management Learning & Education*, **1**(2): 137–49.

Knowles, M. (1973) *Adult Learner: A Neglected Species*. Houston: Gulf Publishing.

Knowles, M.S. (1984) *Andragogy in Action: Applying Modern Principles of Adult Education*. San Francisco: Jossey-Bass.

Kogan, N. (1971) Educational implications of cognitive styles (pp.242–92). In G.S. Lesser (ed.) *Psychology and Educational Practice*. Glenview, IL: Scott Foresman.

Kolb, D.A. (1976) Management and the learning process. *California Management Review*, **18**(3): 21–31.

Kolb, D.A. (1984) *Experiential Learning: Experience as the Source of Learning and Development*. Englewood Cliffs, NJ: Prentice Hall.

Kolb, D.A. (2000) *Facilitators Guide to Learning*. Boston: Hay/McBer.

Kolb, D.A., Boyatzis, R.E. and Mainemelis, C. (2001) Experiential learning theory: previous research and new directions (pp.227–47). In R.J. Sternberg and L.F. Zhang (eds) *Perspectives on Thinking, Learning, and Cognitive Styles*. Mahwah, NJ: Lawrence Erlbaum.

Lave, J. and Wenger, E. (1991) *Situated Learning: Legitimate Peripheral Participation*. Cambridge: Cambridge University Press.

Lofstrom, E. (2002) Person-situation interactions in SMEs: a study of cognitive style and sources of job satisfaction. In M. Valcke and D. Gombeir (eds) *Learning Styles: Reliability and Validity,* proceedings of the 7th Annual European Learning Styles Information Network Conference, 26–28 June, University of Ghent.

Maguire E.A., Gadian D.G., Johnsrude I.S., Good C.D., Ashburner J., Frackowiak R.S. and Frith C.D. (2000) Navigation-related structural change in the hippocampi of taxi drivers. *Proceedings of the National Academy of Science USA,* **97**(8): 4398–403.

Mayo, A. and Lank, E. (1994) *The Power of Learning.* London: Institute of Personnel Management.

Meehan, T. P. and Bressler, S.L. (2012) *Neurocognitive Networks: Findings, Models, and Theory, Neuroscience & Biobehavioral Reviews,* available from http://dx.doi.org/10.1016/j.neubiorev.2012.08.002.

Messick, S. (1976) Personality consistencies in cognition and creativity (pp.4–22). In S. Messick (ed.) *Individuality in Learning*. San Francisco, CA: Jossey-Bass.

Myers, I.B. (1962) *Manual: The Myers Briggs Type Indicator.* Palo Alto, CA: Consulting Psychologists Press.

Myers, I.B. and McCaulley, M.H. (1985) *Manual: A Guide to the Development and Use of the Myers-Briggs Type Indicator*. Palo Alto, CA: Consulting Psychologists Press.

Nye, R.D. (2000) B.F. Skinner and radical behaviourism (pp.7–46). In R.D. Nye (ed.) *Three Psychologies: Perspectives from Freud, Skinner, and Rogers*, 6th edn. Belmont, CA: Wadsworth.

Pavlov, I.P. (1927) *Conditioned Reflexes: An Investigation of the Physiological Activity of the Cerebral Cortex,* transl. and ed. G. Anrep. London: Oxford University Press.

Perrin, J., Leonard, G., Perron, M., Pike, G.B., Pitiot, A., Richer, L., Veillette, S., Pausova, Z. and Paus, T. (2009) Sex differences in the growth of white matter during adolescence. *Neuroimage,* **45**(4): 1055–66.

Reynolds, M. (1997) Learning styles: a critique. *Management Learning,* **28**(2): 115–33.

Reyolds, M. (2009) Wild frontiers – reflections on experiential learning. *Management Learning,* **40**(4): 387–92.

Reynolds, M. and Vince, R. (2004) Critical management education and action-based learning: synergies and contradictions. *Academy of Management Learning and Education,* **3**(4): 442–56.

Reynolds, M. and Vince, R. (eds) (2007) *The Handbook of Experiential Learning and Management Education.* Oxford: Oxford University Press.

Riding, R. and Cheema, I. (1991) Cognitive styles: an overview and integration. *Educational Psychology,* **11**(3/4): 193–215.

Riding, R. and Rayner, S. (1998) *Cognitive Styles and Learning Strategies: Understanding Style Differences in Learning and Behaviour*. London: David Fulton.

Riding, R. and Rayner, S. (2002) *Cognitive Styles and Learning Strategies: Understanding Style Differences in Learning and Behaviour*, 5th edn. London: David Fulton.

Sadler-Smith, E. (2006) *Learning and Development for Managers*. Oxford: Blackwell.

Seaman, J. (2008) Experience, reflect, critique: the end of the 'learning cycles' era. *Journal of Experiential Education,* **31**(1): 3–18.

Skinner, B.F. (1953) *Science and Human Behavior*. New York: Macmillan.

Sternberg, R.J. and Grigorenko, E.L. (2001) A capsule history of theory and research on styles (pp.227–47). In R.J. Sternberg and L.F. Zhang (eds) *Perspectives on Thinking, Learning and Cognitive Styles*. Mahwah, NJ: Lawrence Erlbaum.

Sugarman, L. (1985) Kolb's model of experiential learning: touchstone for trainers, students, counselors and clients. *Journal of Counseling and Development,* **64**(40): 264–68.

Thorne, A. and Gough, H. (1999) *Portraits of Type: An MBTI Research Compendium,* 2nd edn. Gainesville, FL: Center for Applications of Psychological Type.

Toni N., Buchs P.A., Nikonenko I., Bron C.R. ands Muller D. (1999). LTP promotes formation of multiple spine synapses between a single axon terminal and a dendrite. *Nature,* **402**(6760): 421–25.

VandeWalle, D. and Cummings, L.L. (1997) An empirical test of goal orientation as a predictor of feedback-seeking behavior. *Journal of Applied Psychology,* **82**: 390–400.

Vygotsky, L. S. (1978) *Mind in Society. The Development of Higher Psychological Process,* M. John-Steiner, S. Scribner, & E. Souberman (eds). Cambridge, MA: Harvard University Press.

Vygotsky, L.S. (1982) *Collected Works*. Moscow: Pedagogica.

Wallach, M.A. (1962) Commentary: active-analytical vs. passive-global cognitive functioning (pp.199–215). In S. Messick and J. Ross (eds) *Measurement in Personality and Cognition*. New York: Wiley.

Willis, P. E. (1977) *Learning To Labour: How Working Class Kids Get Working Class Jobs*. Aldershot: Ashgate Publishing Group.

Witkin, H.A. and Goodenough, D.R. (1981) *Cognitive Style: Essence and Origins*. New York: International Universities Press.

Yeo, R. K. and Gold, J. (2011) *(Re-) Interpreting Experiential Learning Theory for Management Development: A Critical Inquiry*, paper presented at Academy of Management Conference, August.

Vivienne Griggs, Catherine Glaister, Michelle Blackburn, Patrick McCauley and Rick Holden

chapter
6

The Practice of Training: The Identification of Training Needs

Chapter learning outcomes

After studying this chapter, you should be able to:

- Explain the meaning of training need
- Understand types of training need in relation to knowledge, skills and attitudes
- Understand inward and outward approaches to, and closed and open perspectives of, training problems
- Distinguish between different levels of training need
- Understand a systematic process for the identification of training needs

Chapter outline

Introduction
The meaning of training need
Types of training need
Indicators of training needs
The identification and assessment of training needs
Problems with the identification of training needs
Summary

Introduction

The government constantly urges employers to carry out more training since it is perceived as crucial to our success as a nation and points out that the UK's record for investing in training compares unfavourably with our economic competitors. The UK Commission for Employment and Skills (UKCES) highlight the need to raise 'employer ambition and demand for skills to a level akin to our international competitors' (UKCES, 2011, p.3). They point out that the UK's poor record on training is leading to permanent skills gaps, especially prevalent in skilled trades (e.g chefs, electricians, plumbers). The Commission argue we need to understand why over 60 per cent of UK organizations appear to carry out little or no training.

But what is training and does it differ from learning or indeed development? The terms training, learning and development are often used interchangeably. While understandable, this can mask important distinctions. The CIPD defines training as 'an instructor-led, content-based intervention, leading to desired changes in behaviour' (Sloman, 2005). Learning is defined by Wilson (2005) as a 'relatively permanent change of knowledge, attitude or behaviour occurring as a result of formal education or training, or as a result of informal experiences'. According to Gold et al. (2010) development embraces all the activities through which people learn.

We would argue that the lines between training, learning and development cannot be firmly drawn, and there must, and should, be interchange between the terms. For the purposes of clarity, however, in this chapter we will use the term training needs analysis. This is conventional discourse in many organizations. We would argue, however, that once a gap has been identified in terms of knowledge, skills or attitude, a range of options are open in terms of how to address this gap; some of these would be what the CIPD would define as training, others as learning.

The meaning of training need

Originating with the Industrial Training Boards (ITBs) (see Reid et al., 2004, for a useful positioning of the ITBs within the evolution of HRD), the use of a structured approach to the identification, planning, delivery and evaluation of training has long been advocated. This four-stage process, shown in Figure 6.1, has been widely adopted. It is systematic and emphasizes 'logical and sequential planning and action' (Buckley and Caple, 2007, p.24).

The model matches conventional wisdom of the need for rationality and efficiency with an emphasis on cost-effectiveness. However, the process is not so neat, ordered and predictable in real organizations. Although often criticized for its inflexibility, simplicity and lack of consideration of contextual issues, we would argue that the systematic model still provides a practical tool to analyse and manage these processes within organizations today. It is only a model, but its simplicity can be seen as its strength, and it can be applied widely and usefully across a range of organizations, with consideration of organizational context being built in at each stage. The model is reflected in how Chapters 6, 7 and 8 unfold. In this chapter, our focus is on the first stage in the model, while

Figure 6.1 A four-stage training model

Chapter 7 addresses stages two and three, and Chapter 8 deals with evaluation. We move now to a consideration of training needs.

It is axiomatic that any expression of a training need must be justified in terms of improving how people are working and, by implication, how the organization is performing. This requires an identification of what is not working so well, where it is not working and how significant this is. Without this, expenditure on training or any HRD activity is difficult to justify, according to conventional views (Moore & Dutton, 1978). According to Bratton and Gold (2007, p.329), 'assessing and analysis of training needs is concerned with identifying gaps between work performance and standards of work or performance criteria that have a training solution'. This gap is categorized in terms of the knowledge, skills and attitudes that are required for the job and how these can be learned. It could be added that this apparent training need only really exists when clearly identified training helps to address organizational problems or exploit organizational opportunities. There must be a purposeful problem-solving approach if training is to make a worthwhile contribution to the health and prosperity of the organization. Many organizations' training activities come unstuck at this first hurdle. One of the most persistent findings is that training needs are often not identified (Boydell & Leary, 1996). This is discussed by Kearns and Miller (1997), who question why so few organizations have any clear idea of the value-added they achieve from their training investment. They offer some incisive suggestions:

- It is generally assumed that training per se is a 'good thing'
- Senior management may support whatever training activities are being arranged, presumably because they sanctioned them in the first place
- Vague assumptions are made about vague improvements in vague measures of performance, for example management skills, communication, organizational culture, and these improvements are (predictably and appropriately) vaguely attributable to allegedly related training events
- Trainers are notoriously defensive about the value of their role, and often hide behind notions of how esoteric and ephemeral their contributions are, and how philistine it is to try to impose crude measures of cost-effectiveness.

Another challenge to value-added is the tendency to initiate training activities in the face of an organizational crisis or period of great change, so as to be seen to be doing something. We will be discussing the identification of training needs as a positive and proactive attempt to engage with the real strategic and operational problems and opportunities of the organization. Clearly, there can be different perceptions of training needs from different points of view.

activity

Consider the following scenario:

A university designs and delivers an MSc programme in employee relations. It is intended as a training and developmental programme for practising and aspiring HR managers wishing to specialize in this field. One of the postgraduate students is an area officer for a national trade union, seconded to the programme on full pay for a year by his employer.

How might the actual training needs of the trade unionist compare to and contrast with the training needs of the HR managers on the programme? How could this possible set of conflicts be resolved?

Types of training need

We look now to different types of training need that can exist within an organization. To shape the discussion in this section, a broad distinction is made between:

- knowledge
- skills
- attitude

This distinction is one that is part of training and education's conventional wisdom and is derived from the work of an American educational expert, Dr Benjamin Bloom (1956), who sought to develop a taxonomy, or classification, of learning behaviours that could be used in the design and assessment of learning. Bloom's taxonomy consists of three domains of learning: cognitive, psychomotor and affective. These broadly cover the distinction we have made: knowledge connects to the cognitive domain; skill connects to the psychomotor domain; and attitude connects to the affective domain. Each domain has been elaborated to provide a useful way of considering learning and development needs, objectives of processes and assessment (see Chapter 7 for more on this taxonomy).

reflective question

Go to www.learningandteaching.info/learning/bloomtax.htm
Do you think objectives are necessary for learning? Think about this question in relation to different scenarios and settings.

Knowledge

It is evident that knowledge, its creation, management and use are key ingredients of products and services. Many organizations are now knowledge based (OECD, 1996), and as knowledge workers, many employees provide the source of an organization's intellectual capital (Edvinsson & Malone, 1997).

All staff will need to know what to do in order fulfil their particular roles. Thus, many staff need a sound knowledge of their professional or technical specialisms. This is probably easiest to identify if one takes a steady-state perception of the specialism. However, it has become increasingly important to update knowledge through continuing professional development (CPD) and lifelong learning (see also Chapter 15). In addition, there is a need to know about the particular environment within which their specialism operates and the organization's policies and procedures. For example, HR managers will need a broad knowledge of the technology of the industry within which they work and lawyers specializing in unfair dismissal need a knowledge of personnel practice.

Knowledge is strongly connected to Bloom's (1956) cognitive domain and has been further elaborated to included comprehension, application, analysis, synthesis and evaluation. You may recognize such words from the objectives or outcomes specified in formal training courses and college modules. More recently, Anderson and Krathwohl (2001) modified the cognitive domain to indicate the importance of creating knowledge as a higher order form of knowing;

it is one that clearly chimes with the growing interest in knowledge production and management (see also Chapter 10).

Skill

Knowledge in itself is rarely sufficient to ensure satisfactory performance; it almost invariably needs to be combined with the development of the necessary skills. Imagine the damage that could be caused by a plumber, a car mechanic or even a brain surgeon with impressive theoretical knowledge but no task-related skills. There are debates, however, on the meaning of the term skill. For example, and as we saw in Chapter 1, Felstead et al. (2002), suggested that skill can mean:

- competence to carry out tasks successfully
- the idea of hierarchical skill levels that are dependent on the complexities and discretions involved
- the view that there are different types of skills, some generic and applicable in diverse work situations and some specific and vocational and suitable for particular contexts.

The current trend is to emphasize competence and/or competency. The subtle difference in spelling is not insignificant. Competence refers to abilities to perform within an occupational area to a standard required in employment. A person is competent if the output of their work meets written standards as specified by performance criteria and evidence required. In the UK, such standards form the basis of National Vocational Qualifications (NVQs, SVQs in Scotland), which are set within the Qualifications and Credit Framework (QCF) and are a crucial feature of the vocational education and training system (see also Chapter 1).

Competency, on the other hand, is concerned with behaviour. Perhaps the best-known view of competency is from Boyatzis (1982), who was concerned with a manager's characteristics or abilities (see also Chapter 11) that allow them to achieve effective or superior performance. The CIPD's (2008, p.1) definition is:

> the behaviours that employees must have, or must acquire, to input into a situation in order to achieve high levels of performance.

Armstrong (2002) suggests three key aspects of competence:

- *Input:* knowledge, skills and personal attributes
- *Process:* the behaviour required to convert the input into outputs
- *Output:* the outcomes achieved.

Thus, competence or competency are concerned not only with the inputs and processes of behaviour but also with the outcomes of people's behaviours.

Whichever stance is taken, competences or competencies allow a specification of the skills someone needs to have and use at work and therefore allows training needs to be assessed. For example, here is how a large financial services organization in the UK sets out its competencies:

- self-control
- self-development
- personal organization
- positive approach

- delivering results
- providing solutions
- systemic thinking
- attention to detail
- creating customer service
- delivering customer service
- continuous improvement
- developing people
- working with others
- influencing
- leading
- delivering the vision
- change and creativity.

For each competency, there is a definition and description, with indicators that enable assessment and measurement. For example, the competency of creating customer service is indicated by:

- anticipating emerging customer needs and planning accordingly
- identifying the customers who will be of value to the company
- recommending changes to current ways of working that will improve customer service
- arranging the collection of customer satisfaction data and acting on them.

Competency frameworks such as these provide a statement of the skills (as behaviours) needed at work and provide the benchmark against which employees can be assessed for training needs. These descriptions may be applied differently to different roles or levels in the organization, so the expectations for a call centre advisor would be different to those for a senior manager.

activity

A Woman's Touch is a building and domestic repairs business. It employs exclusively female craftspeople. This exploits an obvious niche market of women who need repairs and home improvements but feel more comfortable admitting another woman into their homes. It was soon found that there was a secondary market of practically incompetent and technophobic men who were happier to admit their limitations to a woman.

The business has grown hugely – and even has a branch in Spain serving British ex-pats. The chief executive now wishes to create a specialist training college for her staff, with the main task being induction of new recruits. What are your suggestions for a competencies framework for the employees of A Woman's Touch?

Many organizations, particularly in the public sector, publish their competency frameworks online. It is worth examining some of these frameworks to familiarise yourself with their structure and content.

Attitudes

An attitude is usually understood as a particular mental state of a person, which can be positive or negative, affecting judgements, decision-making and motivation. Attitudes concern people, including oneself, and situations past, present and future. Attitudes are a key aspect of what Gibb (2011) calls the third dimension of needs, alongside emotional intelligence, 'the awareness and management of emotions in order to act effectively in social situations' (p.129). Krathwohl et al. (1964) referred to attitudes as part of the affective domain of learning. This includes not just attitudes but also emotions, values, feelings, motivation, beliefs and interests. As you might imagine, such terms are highly connected to each other and we will use attitudes as a general term to cover them all.

Attitudes will affect how work is carried out; therefore an organization might seek to employ people who show the right 'attitudinal commitment' (Guest, 1989, p.49), and this attention to attitudes is one of the distinguishing features of HRM (Bratton & Gold, 2007). There are some attitudes universally appropriate for all jobs, such as enthusiasm and conscientiousness. However, there can be specific attitudes necessary for particular jobs. This may involve particular attitudes on flexibility, customer care, cost control, quality and so on. Organizations are becoming increasingly aware of the importance of identifying attitudes during recruitment as a requirement for skill development. A recent policy statement at ASDA, for example, stated: 'Recruit for attitude, train for skill.'

One difficulty with attitudes is that we are talking about someone's mental state, which we cannot directly perceive. What we perceive are their behaviours; we then construct assumptions about the nature of the attitudes that have motivated or driven the behaviours. This is a well-known feature of social psychology called attribution theory. One view argued by those who work with behavioural theories of learning is that attitudes, because they cannot be seen directly, cannot be learned; only the behaviour can be changed through the right stimulus and reinforcement. However, an alternative view would highlight attitudes as crucial to performance and training. For example, Noe (1986, p.737) presented a formula for what he terms trainability: trainability = f (a function of ability, motivation, and perceptions of the work environment).

In this formula, motivation indicates that learners need to have a degree of enthusiasm, or a positive attitude towards training, as well as abilities relating to knowledge or skill acquisition. The third part of the formula, work environment perceptions, is one that will have an impact on attitudes, especially feelings about whether new ideas or new skills learned through training can be used and applied at work and whether others, such as managers, will support their use and application. This is a feature of what is often referred to as an organization's learning climate (see also Chapter 10).

reflective question   Can attitudes be changed? Are attitude-change programmes possible at work? Consider health and safety, discrimination and ethical awareness.

It has been necessary to look at knowledge, skills and attitudes separately for the purpose of explaining them. However, most training needs will involve a combination of all three. The case study at the end of Chapter 8 addresses training for lunchtime supervisors in schools in Hull. One issue is the extent to which the training needs identified in this case provide a challenging mix of knowledge, skills and attitudes.

Indicators of training needs

A systematic approach to training, as indicated by Figure 6.1, suggests something more than guesswork or intuition in identifying training needs (McGehee & Thayer, 1961). There needs to be an objective and rigorous process of data collection followed by analysis to allow informed decision-making about whether a training solution is required or not. There are key questions relating to what sort of information within an organization may suggest the need for training intervention and how best this information might be analysed and made sense of in terms of the most effective actions to take.

Before we search for these indicators, we need to focus on the purpose of the training. One view is that we need to be clear about the organizational objectives the training is intended to achieve. This is what Chiu et al. (1999) refer to as a business-oriented approach, with an emphasis on business outcomes. Most training is oriented towards intermediate objectives, such as improving supervisory skills, and it is merely assumed that, ultimately, this will have a beneficial impact on the effectiveness of the organization. Instead, the focus should be on designing the training to meet the ultimate business objective. For instance, instead of the bland aim of improving supervisory skills, data could be collected on the real problems facing the business, for example production costs, absenteeism and so on. We could then examine how these indicators can be influenced (for good or ill) by the supervisor's ability to perform their role. That way the direct link to organizational and job effectiveness is identified immediately and measures of success can be built into the exercise upfront. With this approach in mind, these are some of the possible indicators of training needs:

- *Output:* Where output is below established standards, there may well be a training problem. The possible reasons for poor output are varied: poor technical skills, poor information flow, limited supervision and so on.
- *Varying standards:* Where standards of performance vary significantly between broadly similar groups of employees, there is likely to be a training need. The reasons for the differences must be ascertained and good practice identified and disseminated.
- *Time:* If standard times are not being met, there may be a training need. Also, there is a need to identify unproductive time use and train staff to use time more effectively.
- *Turnover and absenteeism:* 'People join organizations but they leave managers.' High turnover may well indicate unsatisfactory treatment or conditions. It may also indicate poor induction and/or occupational or line manager training.
- *Delays:* Bottlenecks in operational processes may be due to limited knowledge or skills. Improved managerial or technical performance (brought about by better training) may address the problem.

- *Complaints:* Complaints from customers (especially influential ones) are often the impetus required to ensure that relevant training needs are met.

In reality, of course, there may well be a complex mix of factors that highlight a need for training. Consider HRD in Practice 6.1, which looks at difficulties the BBC has experienced.

BBC trains to meet technology challenges

HRD in Practice 6.1

In 2008, the BBC was fined a record £400,000 by Ofcom for faking winners and misleading audiences in a series of competitions on TV and radio. The watchdog criticized the BBC for serious breaches of its editorial standards. When the breaches were revealed, the BBC responded by putting more than 19,000 staff through a series of Safeguarding Trust training workshops led by senior programme makers and based around real-life editorial scenarios.

At the same time, however, the BBC sought to deflect any suggestion that the problems had arisen because of reductions in training spend. Caroline Prendergast, the corporation's training and development director, said the BBC had not cut its training budget and that training remained a high priority, pointing to the fact that the BBC's learning board was chaired by the deputy director general.

Prendergast identified changes in technology and audience tastes as the biggest learning and development challenges facing the industry: 'Technology is changing all the time and for us that means having to train people to produce programmes that will work across different platforms, such as MP3 players and mobile phones.' Prendergast also pointed to an increasingly mobile workforce, which was forcing the corporation to review and revise its delivery of training: 'We have to look at tailoring things to different situations.' Thus, online learning is playing an increasingly important role, alongside more traditional methods.

Source: Phillips (2008)

HRD in Practice 6.1 illustrates that while the specific stimulus for the Safeguarding Trust training was the critical Ofcom report, the organization's training effort is not purely reactive. The biggest training challenges it faces are driven by change: technological, workforce and changes in audience tastes. Importantly, it also highlights that in practice there may well be an uneasy relationship between training and aspects of change within an organization.

One of the most crucial indicators for considering training, learning and development needs more widely is change at work. Of course, change can vary in scope, depth and duration; however, it is recognized there is often a connection between change and identifying needs for training and learning, or at least there ought to be. Research by Reed and Vakola (2006) suggests that, traditionally, training needs are not sufficiently connected to change or cultural issues.

In contrast to the business-oriented approach, Chiu et al. (1999) also refer to the trainee-centred approach. This gives more emphasis to individuals working out their own needs through self-assessment and using feedback from others, and which we consider below.

activity

With a group of three or four, consider an organization you know well – perhaps a university or an organization where you have some work experience – think about some of the main challenges you consider to be affecting the organization. Identify three challenges and describe their main indicators. Consider the extent to which there may be training needs present.

The identification and assessment of training needs

Having considered certain indicators of training need, we will now examine the various processes available for their systematic identification. A systematic needs assessment can guide the subsequent stages of design, delivery and evaluation; indeed, it can be used to specify a number of key features for the implementation and evaluation of the training (see also Chapters 7 and 8). It is primarily conducted to determine where training is needed, what needs to be taught and who needs to be trained (Goldstein, 1993).

Levels of training need

It is useful to think of training needs existing at three levels. This was first suggested by McGehee and Thayer (1961) and has subsequently been advocated by others such as Boydell and Leary (1996) in the UK. These levels are organization, job and individual.

At the organizational level, the concern is with the whole organization, starting with strategy and objectives, key measurements and indicators, change projects, and more ephemeral features such as organizational climate and culture. At job level the concern is with the range of tasks and responsibilities involved in a specific job role or group of jobs in a section or department. Systematic processes are used to collect data and analyse how work should be done against a standard. Skills, knowledge and attitudes can be specified. The third level is that of the individual. The task here is to assess performance against the measurement standards for the job. It is assumed that each person has a responsibility to perform against the standard and receive training if they cannot meet that standard.

At each of these levels, there are a range of methods available and we shall discuss each level separately. However, training problems are often a complex mix of needs at all three levels. Consider the example of Prudential plc, winner of the best learning and development strategy at the HR Excellence Awards in 2010. As part of a significant organizational re-focusing programme, driven by a need to address its market position and because of complex new regulatory frameworks in the financial products industry, a new learning and development strategy was formulated in 2009. Training needs were identified at all three levels:

- Organizational: training was needed to help the Pru achieve its strategic goal of moving the corporate culture towards behaviours consistent with a high-performing organization in the retirement industry. The company argued that all levels of staff had to commit and engage with an updated set of values and attitudes.
- Job: as part of this culture change senior managers used a series of business forums with managers to identify their needs and how to meet them; training needs for the sales force were identified in relation to the quality of product and compliance issues and this resulted in a highly successful series of Selling to Succeed programmes
- Individual: challenging commercial aspirations within a new financial regulatory framework meant all staff faced training needs wherever they worked in

the business. A redesign of its learning management system (on the company intranet) enabled individuals to identify certain learning needs themselves and record these in an individual learning account.

It has long been recognized that there needs to be some consideration for integrating the three levels (Moore & Dutton, 1978), taking a more holistic view of the connections between the vertical, horizontal and lateral aspects. This has been a view advocated by organization development practitioners who take a more systemic or activity-based view of organizations (see also Chapter 2).

Organization-level needs

The first level of analysis may be at the level of the whole organization, assessing what skills the organization has now and what it requires now and in the future. It focuses on the congruence between training objectives with such factors as the organizational strategy, the available resources, constraints and support for the transfer of learning to the workplace (Salas & Cannon-Bowers, 2001). Depending on the size of the organization, it may also be necessary to conduct this analysis at the levels of division, department and team. We must not underestimate the importance of training in facilitating the pursuit of corporate goals. Lack of training may even make the goals unattainable. For example, in March 2008, Terminal 5 opened at Heathrow Airport and very soon descended into chaos, with many delayed and cancelled flights and thousands of bags misdirected or even lost. In a report to the House of Commons Transport Committee (House of Commons, 2008), British Airways admitted that a failure to adequately address training needs to operate the new systems contributed to the Terminal 5 fiasco.

A clear understanding of an organization's strategy is a prerequisite to a consideration of needs. For organizations that choose to compete on the basis of quality, highly skilled workers are essential; for those that compete on cost, they are an unjustifiable extravagance (Redman & Wilkinson, 2006), and large sections of the British economy still compete on cost, particularly in the current economic climate. Identifying organization-level needs is concerned with considering which of the organization's goals can be achieved through training and whether any particular areas of the organization require investment in training, but this has to fit with the competitive strategy of the organization. A logistics company in the north of England delivering a low-cost, high-volume service focuses the identification of needs on those that are essential to delivering each order, while a successful building society in the same locality adopts a longer-term strategy, considering skill requirements to enable growth and competitive advantage in the future. This level of review may be appropriate for corporate and HR planning processes. In addition, Hackett (2003) identifies new products, new technology, work processes or systems and new legislation as specific drivers of learning needs.

The type of needs you might identify in this kind of analysis could be needs that apply to the whole of the organization, such as a new computer system, or a new strategic focus following a merger or organizational change. Reid et al. (2004) identify four types of organization-level review: global; competence and performance management; critical incident; learner centred.

We now consider some of the strategies and procedures available when identifying training needs at the organizational level:

- *Analysis of the culture of the organization:* Obviously this is vital when trying to engineer a change in culture. However, in any situation, understanding an organization's values and desired outcomes allows consideration of acceptability and receptiveness to change implied by any training or learning intervention. For example, research on the success of many Asian firms shows that it has been built on their collectivist cultural orientation to developing and sharing learning in teams (Lucas et al., 2006). In this way, cultural indicators will have a distinct influence on the identification process.

- *Skills audit:* This is a process to identify the relevant skills or competences required by the organization and then assess whether these are present. It is necessary to consult widely with management, service departments, line managers, team leaders, prospective trainees, who may all be fertile sources of information.

- *Standards of performance and competency framework:* After establishing the standards, an assessment must be made of the shortfall between the required standards and the actual ones being achieved. Gibb (2011) stresses that the observation and assessment of learning and development needs should take place within a context of performance management in the organization, so that the needs will relate to business development.

- *HR plan:* This describes – quantitatively and qualitatively – the capabilities of the current workforce and the anticipated future requirements in terms of skills and performance levels. It can help to develop an understanding of training needs, in the sense that identified shortfalls, or gaps, can be met, in part, with training. Thus an HR plan is likely to include training proposals designed to address changing skill needs and performance deficiencies.

- *Analysis and synthesis of appraisal records:* Training needs will have been identified for specific individuals through the appraisal/performance review discussions. These may well build up over the whole organization to indicate a wider, more general pattern of training needs.

- *Critical incidents:* This involves the collection of data from a wide range of activities where the work makes a significant contribution. It can be argued that this covers all activities, or should do. However, it is increasingly recognized that interactions with clients and customers are important sources of understanding in knowledge-based and professional work (Gold & Thorpe, 2009). Incidents can be positive or negative but, crucially, provide a story about what happened, what people did and why it was significant. This is a long-established technique first presented by Flanagan (1954) and can be used for different purposes, but collating such data from significant incidents can reveal key patterns that indicate training needs.

- *Useful sources of written information available within the organization:* This may include corporate plans, personnel records, and reports from training, joint consultative or safety committees. All are increasingly available on management information systems.

- *External research:* Government reports, national and local employment statistics and so on can all prove useful.

The analysis at this level could be conducted by the management team, the HR department or an outside consultant. In addition to these methods, there are other approaches that allow a whole-organization diagnosis of needs. For example, in the 1980s and 1990s, Total Quality Management (TQM) provided tools for engendering a culture of continuous improvement. The European Foundation for Quality Management (www.efqm.org) provides an excellence model, which allows an organization to be assessed against nine criteria, including leadership, customer results and people results. The assessment is based on data from across the organization and reveals possibilities for improvement including training, learning and development needs. Similarly, the balanced scorecard provides a framework against which long-term performance can be evaluated. It identifies four perspectives: financial, customers, internal business, learning and growth (Kaplan & Norton, 1996). The UK government's Investors in People (IiP) standard also promotes and enables training needs analysis. Organizations committed to gaining IiP recognition are provided with tools to show them exactly how good they are and what areas they can focus on to enable further improvements and productivity gains (see also Chapter 1).

Job-level training needs

Following the more generic training needs of the organization, the next stage is to consider the particular requirements of each job. This considers what someone must learn to do in order to do a job effectively. A range of methods is outlined below:

- *Job analysis or job training analysis:* This is the process of examining a job in order to identify its component parts. With relation to the responsibilities of the job holder, what knowledge, skills and attitudes are required to perform the role effectively? A job analysis will usually consist of three components:
  - *The job description:* an outline of the purpose and responsibilities of the job – the obvious starting point for the analysis
  - *The personnel (or person) specification:* a description of the qualities required of an employee in order to be able to discharge those responsibilities adequately – this details the organization's criteria for selection, but prior training may be an element, as may be future trainability. Perhaps most important of all, the personnel specification may prevent the problem of recruiting unsuitable staff and then trying to train away the problem
  - *The job specification:* perhaps better called the training specification a description of the knowledge, skills and attitudes required of the job holder.
- *Problem-centred analysis:* Similar to a job analysis but the focus will be on areas of performance where problems generally occur.
- *Key task analysis:* Again, similar to job analysis but prioritizing the elements within the job that have the greatest impact on performance. Each key task is analysed to see what knowledge, skills and attitude are required. Bee and Bee (2003) assert that this will be the six to eight most important tasks or functions performed in the job.
- *Competency analysis:* Uses a competency framework to consider which competencies are required in a job or work area.

reflective question

Think about these two scenarios:

1 A job, for example a contact centre adviser, that is closely defined and prescriptive and where new starters are frequent.
2 A job, for example a health and safety executive, where legislation determines necessary changes to some requirements of the role but others remain unchanged.

What type of job-level analysis do you consider might be appropriate in each scenario?

Job-level analysis can also include more generic role or occupational analysis. For example, National Occupational Standards (NOS) describe what a person needs to do, know and understand in their job to carry out their role in a consistent and competent way. They are developed for employers by employers through the relevant Sector Skills Councils or standard setting organizations. NOS can be used to inform the content of training since they specify in detail what constitutes good practice.

Identifying job-level training needs is often an important part of the planned maintenance of an organization and a necessary response to changing conditions and new problems.

Individual-level training needs

Consider this, probably apocryphal, reflection on behalf of a senior manager, following a major organizational restructure and relocation:

> We've designed the organization structure very rationally; we've set up all the necessary control mechanisms; we've designed all the jobs intelligently. The problem is that the jobs all have to be done by idiosyncratic, temperamental and sometimes downright hostile people.

Obviously, considering the training needs of a particular job does not signify that everyone starting the job will require training in all those areas. A new starter may already have had training or experience that matches the requirements of the job. Consequently, this stage concentrates on which individuals require training and what their particular needs are. It is essentially matching the skills of the person to the skills of the job and ascertaining where gaps exist. We can point to a variety of approaches and, mostly, this level of analysis is completed as part of a performance management process.

A CIPD (2009) survey found that 75 per cent of respondents used performance management activities to set objectives or targets and 62.7 per cent assessed progress against targets. Just over 50 per cent of respondents suggested that review meetings discussed development opportunities, while career development was discussed by around a quarter of the organizations surveyed. It is clear therefore that performance management had both a control purpose and a development purpose, which can create tensions and difficulties. This is partly to do with judgements about a person's performance and the decisions that can be made as a consequence. Such decisions are seen by employees as feedback, with a variety of responses, as shown in Figure 6.2.

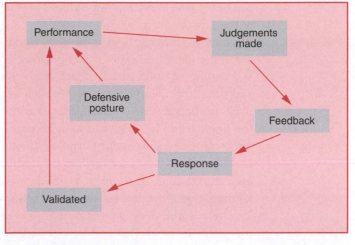

Figure 6.2 Responses to feedback

The crucial variable is 'validated'. If feedback is positive or negative, and the response is accepted, this can lead to improved performance, perhaps by undertaking training if gaps are identified. However, if the response is a defensive posture, the identification of needs might not be accepted and this could lead to a negative impact on performance. DeNisi and Kluger (2000) suggest that feedback can help someone to focus on what to do or learn and this will improve performance, but it can also affect a person's view of self and the response can be emotional and detrimental to performance. VandeWalle and Cummings (1997) suggest a key factor is learning goal orientation, where people have a willingness to develop new skills and master new situations. Such people are proactive in seeking feedback and making good use of it. Bearing in mind, these considerations on feedback, we now consider some of the methods for identifying individual level needs:

- *Performance standards:* Where there are clear performance standards in place, these can be used as an indication of gaps in performance and potential learning needs; for example a sales executive who regularly misses their sales target of completing 20 sales per day.
- *Comparative methods:* Where there is a clear framework of performance standards and a comprehensive system of training records in place, it is then possible to try to discover the sort of competencies that correlate with good performance. For example, it may be that the most effective team leaders have excellent planning skills, while the poorer ones are noticeably weak in this area.
- *Direct observation:* There is a long history of observation at work for assessing training needs. Traditionally, this has been connected to time and motion studies producing quantitative data (See Note 1). In more recent years, the value of qualitative data has been recognized, which is more suitable for discussion with employees.
- *Individual appraisal:* Many organizations use performance appraisal to review individual performance and this is often linked to a development review and the production of a personal development plan. This may or may not be competency based (see above). Together with other forms of appraisal, this

can be valuable in identifying barriers to effective performance, including lack of training (Hackett, 2003).

- *Multisource feedback:* A wider range of feedback sources may also be appropriate in the identification of training needs. For example, 360 degree appraisal is a system of collecting feedback from managers, peers and subordinates, and could include other viewpoints such as from customers and suppliers. It may also be valuable to seek feedback from mentors and coaches. However, this approach to feedback can soon become counterproductive if mainly used for control and judgement purposes. (Fletcher, 2001). Smither et al. (2005) looked at multisource feedback in 24 studies but found that much depended on factors such as reactions to feedback, orientation, beliefs about change and taking action if the process was to lead to improved performance.

- *Assessment and development centres:* These are most likely to be used for managers or graduates and would include a range of exercises designed to assess performance and encourage reflection on personal development. The focus is often skills rather than knowledge based. A key issue is whether the purpose is assessment, as for selection, or development that results in an accepted personal development plan for participants. The two purposes can become confused and as Woodruffe (2000, p.32) warns: 'Assessment centres masquerading as development centres are wolves in sheep's clothing.'

activity

SHL are one of the main providers of psychometric questionnaires and are very active in the provision of development centre support. They can be found at **www.shldirect.com**

Examine the different methods they offer and consider which you feel you would be happy/unhappy to take.

- *Self-assessment:* In recent years, much greater attention has been paid to on self-assessment, encouraging individuals to take greater responsibility for the identification of their own needs. Reflection and self-assessment are key elements of many professional courses and in such a context an individual should be able to identify areas where they require development. This is also useful in addressing needs that are not apparent to observers, who may focus on results rather than behaviours and attitudes. For example, a manager may deliver a presentation that is well received by the audience but may lack confidence in their own performance and therefore have spent longer than necessary in preparation. Training to address this need may be beneficial to future performance but would not have been identified by an outside observer. The use of technology may also play a role in self-assessment. One tool, for example, might be an online test and, increasingly, organizations request employees to complete initial appraisal assessments online. However, there is a danger that self-reported needs could be a wish list of courses, which may not tie in with the organization's objectives. Campbell and Lee (1988, p.307) argued that self-appraisal is an 'important developmental and motivation tool for individuals', but there are likely to be differences between a person's self-appraisal and an appraisal by their superior.

reflective question Think about any employment you are doing or have recently undertaken. To what extent can you identify your own individual training needs? How have you benchmarked/validated what you have identified as training needs?

Problems with the identification of training needs

The identification of training needs forms a fundamental and critical component in the training process and, more broadly, in HRD. However, it is important to acknowledge some potential issues. In practice, identification of needs is often ad hoc rather than systematic, and organizations undertaking a systematic approach do not always complete all three levels of analysis. Political and pragmatic considerations may influence an organization to be highly targeted in its training needs analysis; for example, individuals in the public eye, new starters, or high-potential individuals. Complex scenarios may be interpreted incorrectly initially and result in misleading training need assessments (see HRD in Practice 6.2).

HRD in Practice 6.2

Sales training

In a large call centre organization, customer services and telesales were structured as separate departments. As part of the launch of a new product, the telesales centre was asked to promote and capture sales. Telesales agents were recruited through an agency and given training in the product, sales and customer service techniques. The initial results showed that sales were high, agents were motivated in their work and targets were being met. However, the customer service department received a high volume of complaints. The substance of the complaints was that telesales staff were sometimes rude to customers, hung up the phone in an abrupt manner if it became clear that the customer was not going to purchase, and even put through sales that were not sanctioned by the customer.

Customer service managers questioned the quality of training undertaken by the telesales agents. However, it came to light that the agents were paid commission for the level of sales they achieved. Customer service targets were measured but not rewarded and no sanctions were applied for orders that were subsequently cancelled.

There are a number of important issues and questions that emanate from an uncritical adoption of a systematic approach to training needs identification and assessment. These include, first, the issue of whether reliance on formal needs assessment results in a narrow focus on training rather than encouraging a more creative process and a culture of learning. Consider, for example, the case of companies offering a training allowance for individuals to spend as they choose, as part of an employee-led development scheme (Hamblett & Holden, 2000). The aim of such schemes is to generate greater enthusiasm for learning and stimulate new opportunities. Pettinger (2002) presents an interesting illustration of a greeting cards company that insists its staff do 30 days of training per year and, as long as one event is directly work related, they can do whatever they want.

Secondly, a focus on the current requirements may ignore changes in the working environment, thus developing skills for today rather than tomorrow (or, even worse, for yesterday). It has been suggested for some time now that instead of regarding training needs analysis as a one-off process, it should become continuous (Moore & Dutton, 1978). We have seen that organizations can produce a vast amount of data relating to their performance and operations at different levels. Such data can help to identify needs and allow employees to recognize opportunities from work. However, this does require a positive learning climate with support from line managers and others, with the roles of coaching and mentoring seen as particularly important (see also Chapter 12). Increasingly, the skill of developing others has appeared in competency frameworks for managers (IRS, 2001). A key difficulty comes from failing to secure senior management commitment. Many training and learning programmes fail to reach their goals because of organizational constraints and conflicts (Salas & Cannon-Bowers, 2001). These should be identified upfront and senior managers engaged to ensure they can be overcome.

Thirdly, identifying the wrong need, or where the need is only partially related to training, will hamper the success of the training if it is not targeting the real performance problem. One problem involves distinguishing training needs and training wants. This may be a particular problem in the context of the self-assessment of training needs. Further, identifying a gap between actual and desired performance does not necessarily indicate a training need. A wider review of performance issues and HR practices is required to ensure that the need can, or should, be met through training. HR departments themselves may be a constraint because they may have a vested interest in delivering particular sorts of training and development. This relates to a wider debate about the role of HR. In a traditional training environment, there may be a preference for formal training delivery at the expense of other more work-based methods. Further, HR may develop approaches it considers good for its employees, which reflect the wants and desires of HR departments and their senior managers, rather than a proper analysis of the requirements of work activity. This is a reflection of the inherent tension between the business-oriented approach and the trainee-centred approach referred to by Chiu et al. (1999). The HR-driven top-down approach is certainly more prevalent in larger organizations but would be less suited to smaller organizations and other contexts (see also Chapter 3).

Fourthly, training needs analysis involves the collection of data, but how can we ensure the data are reliable and valid? For example, where performance appraisal is used as a means of identifying needs, factors such as the frequency of appraisal and whether it is linked to performance-related pay may influence the validity of the data received. Is an employee likely to be honest about identifying their weak points if the discussion links to a reward for their performance?

Finally, the stakeholders at each level of analysis may have conflicting priorities. Initiatives can easily become a wish list for managers who make assumptions for others about what they are required to learn (Hicks & Hennessy, 1997). This is often connected to management views of how change occurs in organizations. Apart from the failure to see training needs as an essential aspect of change (Reed & Vakola, 2006), there are also failures to understand the cultural and historical influences that affect responsiveness to communication for change and readiness to change (Bernerth, 2004). Once again, we can highlight the importance of the roles of managers in supporting learning and being aware of the continuous developmental requirements in their interactions with employees.

activity

With a group of three or four, consider what steps could be taken to overcome each of the potential barriers mentioned above.

summary

A training need is defined as the gap between the knowledge, skills and attitude possessed by the target individual or group and those needed to perform required occupational roles.

Training needs will often involve a combination of knowledge, skills and attitudes, which provides a challenge for effective intervention.

A range of potential indicators of training needs exists in all organizations. These include data on organizational performance, signs and indications of organizational problems (for example complaints, turnover) and needs related to organizational change.

If effective training is to be implemented, training needs must be carefully analysed and assessed. A useful framework involves analysis and assessment at three levels: the organization, the job or occupation and the individual.

At each level, techniques are available to the trainer to generate a specification of what is required to meet identified needs.

The identification and assessment of training needs is not necessarily straightforward. Pursued mechanistically, a focus on current requirements may ignore changes on the horizon.

Gathering the appropriate data may be difficult, particularly in politically sensitive areas within the organization. Stakeholders at different levels in the organization may have different, if not conflicting priorities, thus making it difficult to achieve a consensus on training need specifications.

discussion questions

1 What are the three main levels at which training needs are assessed and **who** could assist in the identification of needs at each of these levels?

2 Consider any job you have held. What were the main responsibilities you had to discharge? What were the main qualities the organization demanded from applicants for the job (for example qualification, experience, communication ability, motivation)? What did they miss? What are the knowledge, skills and attitudes needed to perform the job adequately? Have you been objective in your analysis?

3 What are three potential problems with the use of appraisals to identify training needs?

4 Should all training be business oriented? Discuss this with reference to identifying training needs.

5 Consider how this chapter links with the earlier chapters in the book. Can you identify any synergies or possible tensions?

note

1 Time and motion study, also known as work study or industrial engineering, has its roots in Taylorism. Taylorism saw benefits in the extensive streamlining of the processes involved in work tasks. The link to training and development is that the time and motion study would break down tasks into the various physical movements required and then determine an appropriate time to fulfil each movement effectively. See, for example, Benyon (1973) for a lively account of some of the difficulties caused by such practice within the Ford Motor Company.

further reading

references

Ballantyne, I. and Povah, N. (2004) *Assessment and Development Centres*. London: Gower.

Bowman, J. and Wilson, J. (2008) Different roles, different perspectives: perceptions about the purpose of training needs analysis. *Industrial and Commercial Training*, **40**(1): 38–41.

Gibb, S. (2011) *Human Resource Development: Foundations, Processes, Contexts*. Basingstoke: Palgrave Macmillan.

Gould, D., Kelly, D., White, I. and Chidgey, J. (2004) Training needs analysis: a literature review and reappraisal. *International Journal of Nursing Studies*, **41**(5): 471–86.

Anderson, L.W. and Krathwohl, D.R. (eds) (2001) *A Taxonomy for Learning, Teaching, and Assessing: A Revision of Bloom's Taxonomy of Educational Objectives*. New York: Longman.

Armstrong, M. (2002) *Employee Reward*, 3rd edn. London: CIPD.

Bee, R. and Bee, F. (2003) *Learning Needs Analysis and Evaluation*. London: CIPD.

Benyon, H. (1973) *Working for Ford*. Harmondsworth: Penguin.

Bernerth, J. (2004) Expanding our understanding of the change message. *Human Resource Development Review*, **3**(1): 36–52.

Bloom, B.S. (ed.) (1956) *Taxonomy of Educational Objectives: The Classification of Educational Goals, Handbook I, Cognitive Domain*. New York: McKay.

Boyatzis, R.E. (1982) *The Competent Manager: A Model for Effective Performance*. London: Wiley.

Boydell, T. and Leary, M. (1996) *The Identification of Training Needs*. London: CIPD.

Bratton, J. and Gold, J. (2007) *Human Resource Management: Theory and Practice*. Basingstoke: Palgrave Macmillan.

Buckley, R. and Caple, J. (2007) *The Theory and Practice of Training*, 5th edn. London: Kogan Page.

Campbell, D.J. and Lee, C. (1988) Self-appraisal in performance evaluation: development versus evaluation. *Academy of Management Review*, **13**(2): 302–14.

Chiu, W., Thompson, D., Mak, W. and Lo, K. (1999) Re-thinking training needs analysis: a proposed framework for literature review. *Personnel Review*, **28**(1/2): 77–90.

CIPD (Chartered Institute of Personnel and Development) (2008) Competency and competency frameworks factsheet, www.cipd.co.uk/subjects/perfmangmt/competnces/comptfrmwk.htm

CIPD (2009) *Performance Management In Action: Current Trends And Practice - Hot Topic*. London: Chartered Institute of Personnel and Development.

DeNisi, A.S. and Kluger, A.N. (2000) Feedback effectiveness: can 360-degree feedback be improved? *Academy of Management Executive*, **14**(1): 129–39.

Edvinsson, L. and Malone, M.S. (1997) *Intellectual Capital*. New York: Harper.

Felstead, A., Gallie, D. and Green, F. (2002) *Work Skills in Britain 1986–2001*. London: DfES.

Flanagan, J.C. (1954) The critical incident technique. *Psychological Bulletin*, **51**(4): 327–58.

Fletcher, C. (2001) Performance appraisal and management: the developing research agenda. *Journal of Occupational and Organizational Psychology*, **74**(4): 473–87.

Gibb, S. (2011) *Human Resource Development: Foundations, Processes, Contexts*. Basingstoke: Palgrave Macmillan.

Gold, J. and Thorpe, R. (2009) Collective CPD professional learning in a law firm (pp.30–46). In D. Jemielniak and J. Kociatkiewicz (eds) *Handbook of Research on Knowledge-Intensive Organizations*. Hershey, PA: IGI Global.

Gold, J., Thorpe, R. and Mumford, A. (2010) *Leadership and Management Development*. London: Chartered Institute of Personnel and Development.

Goldstein, L. (1993) *Training in Organizations*. Pacific Grove, CA: Brooks/Cole.

Guest, D. (1989) HRM: implications for industrial relations. In J. Storey (ed.) *New Perspectives on Human Resource Management*. London: Routledge.

Hackett, P. (2003) *Training Practice*. London: CIPD.

Hamblett, J. and Holden, R. (2000) Employee-led development: another piece of left luggage? *Personnel Review*, **29**(4): 509–20.

Hicks, C. and Hennessy, D. (1997) Identifying training objectives: the role of negotiation. *Journal of Nursing Management*, **5**(5): 263–65.

House of Commons (2008) *The Opening of Heathrow Terminal 5, House of Commons Transport Committee, HC 543*. London: TSO.

IRS (Industrial Relations Services) (2001) *Competency Frameworks in UK Organizations*. London: IRS.

Kaplan, R.S. and Norton, D.P. (1996) *The Balanced Scorecard – Translating Strategy into Action,* Boston, MA: Harvard Business School Press.

Kearns, P. and Miller, T. (1997) *Measuring the Impact of Training and Development on the Bottom Line*. London: FT Pitman.

Krathwohl, D.R., Bloom, B.S. and Masia, B.B. (1964) *Taxonomy of Educational Objectives: The Classification of Educational Goals*, Handbook II, Affective Domain. New York: David McKay.

Lucas, R., Lupton, B. and Mathieson, H. (2006) *Human Resource Management in an International Context*. London: CIPD.

McGehee, W. and Thayer, P.W. (1961) *Training in Business and Industry*. New York: John Wiley.

Moore, M. and Dutton, P. (1978) Training needs analysis: a review and critique. *Academy of Management Review*, **3**(3): 532–45.

Noe, R.A. (1986) Trainees' attributes and attitudes: neglected influences on training effectiveness. *Academy of Management Review*, **11**(4): 736–49.

OECD (Organization for Economic Co-operation and Development) (1996) *The Knowledge-Based Economy*. Paris: OECD.

Pettinger, R. (2002) *Mastering Employee Development*. Basingstoke: Palgrave (now Palgrave Macmillan).

Phillips, L. (2008) BBC trains to meet technology change. *People Management*, **14**(19): 8.

Redman, T. and Wilkinson, A. (2006) *Contemporary Human Resource Management: Text and Cases*. London: Pearson.

Reed, J. and Vakola, M. (2006) What role can a training needs analysis play in organizational change? *Journal of Organizational Change Management*, **19**(3): 393–407.

Reid, M.A., Barrington, H. and Brown, M. (2004) *Human Resource Development: Beyond Training Interventions*. London: CIPD.

Salas, E. and Cannon-Bowers, J.A. (2001) The science of training: a decade of progress. *Annual Review of Psychology*, **52**: 471–99.

Smither, J., London, M. and Reilly, R.R. (2005) Does performance improve following multisource feedback? A theoretical model, meta-analysis and review of empirical findings. *Personnel Psychology*, **58**(1): 33–66.

Sloman, M. (2005) *Training to Learning: Change Agenda*. London: CIPD.

UK Commission for Employment and Skills (UKCES) (2011) *UK Employer Skills Survey 2011: First Findings Briefing Paper*, December 2011, Adjusted 22 December. http://www.ukces.org.uk/assets/bispartners/ukces/docs/publications/uk-ess-first-findings-2011-amended-22-dec.pdf

VandeWalle, D. and Cummings, L.L. (1997) A test of the influence of goal orientation on the feedback-seeking process. *Journal of Applied Psychology*, **82**(3): 390–400.

Wilson, J. P. (2005) *Human resource development: learning & training for individuals & organizations*, 2nd edn. London: Kogan Page

Woodruffe, C. (2000) *Development and Assessment Centres: Identifying and Developing Competence*. London: CIPD.

chapter 7

The Practice of Training: The Design and Delivery of Training

Catherine Glaister, Rick Holden, Vivienne Griggs, Patrick McCauley and Michelle Blackburn

Chapter learning outcomes

After studying this chapter, you should be able to:

- Understand the relationship between the identification of training needs and the design and delivery of training and learning
- Identify and explain the range of factors that will influence decisions about training and learning strategies and methods
- Identify a wide range of training and learning methods available to meet identified needs and explain the relative strengths and weaknesses of these approaches
- Understand the decisions necessary to determine fit for purpose training and learning solutions

Chapter outline

Introduction
Designing training
Training and learning methods
Trends and issues
Summary

Introduction

What is going on in Roger Beale's cartoon below? Clearly it is some sort of training or learning event, perhaps addressing interpersonal relationships at work. A waste of money? We might speculate that the focal figure (the boss?) thinks so. However, the trainer might be firmly of the view that the methods being employed are entirely fit for purpose. This captures the essence of this chapter. It is about the design and delivery of effective training and learning. The observant reader will have noticed we have complemented the term training with that of learning. Recall that at the start of Chapter 6, we noted the issue of a potentially confusing terminology. We noted our position that a training method was not necessarily the same as a learning method. Our position in this

©Roger Beale

chapter is that if we only consider possible training solutions, we are potentially ignoring a range of interventions that are more appropriately labelled learning. Thus, in this chapter, the terms are deliberately used interchangeably to convey that a broad range of solutions may need to be part of decision-making. For a fuller discussion on this issue, see the CIPD publication *Training to Learning* (Sloman, 2005).

In Chapter 6, we examined the importance of carefully identifying training needs before committing resources to meet those needs. An analysis of the job, or task, provides the cornerstone for progressing towards interventions, which will, in time, meet and remove any training gap. Building on this framework, this chapter explores a range of factors to address in the design of training and learning – such as the characteristics of the trainees, and how best to utilize our understanding of what we know about how individuals and groups learn most effectively. Inevitably, issues of cost and available resources are also part of these design considerations.

The second half of the chapter looks at how these various design considerations can be translated into practice. What alternative methods of delivery might be possible? Can a skill need be effectively delivered using e-learning, and what implications does a preferred method of delivery have in terms of trainer capabilities?

While the chapter unfolds in this way, there is clearly an inextricable relationship between design and delivery. The choice of a particular method, or combination of methods, needs to be fit for purpose. A particular strategy might appear highly appropriate in terms of its ability to meet the main objectives, but is unrealistic in terms of costs or because it requires considerable time away from work, which may be opposed and resisted by those involved. Many a training intervention has floundered because those responsible for its design and delivery had not thought carefully enough about the cultural context in which the programme was being implemented.

HRD in Practice 7.1 provides an interesting example of the how one large UK retailer seeks to put training into practice. The reader might usefully reflect back to this case throughout our more detailed discussion of design and delivery practice issues as they unfold in the remainder of the chapter.

Learning and development at Harvey Nichols

HRD in Practice 7.1

According to its website Harvey Nichols consider their success is the result of 'the valuable contribution of our members of staff, through their attitude, their skills, their knowledge and their expertise'. Its programme Vision and Values incorporates training in the workplace. It seeks to embed clear brand values into everyday performance and behaviours and is seen as key to business success. The three brand values (and associated behaviours) are:

- **Fashion leadership**

Informed on current trends in fashion and food
Stylish and showing passion for fashion
Being well presented and well groomed
Inspirational to external and internal customers

- **Exclusive but accessible**

Show pride in the Harvey Nichols experience
Personalise all aspects of the customer journey
Invest time in the customer
Share product knowledge eagerly

- **Provide a feel good experience**

Welcoming, using eye contact and positive body language

Eager to help customers and willing to go the extra mile
Taking steps to delight the customer
Finding a way to say yes

A creative approach to learning and development plays a key role in making the people values and behaviours a reality within the business. Critically, departmental managers are equipped with train the trainer skills thus ensuring that they can train their staff on a day-to-day, week-by-week basis, using discussions, role plays of desirable and undesirable behaviours, and other workplace-based training exercises. In this way Harvey Nichols has moved away from generic training courses for all sales assistants. Traditional training has been replaced with methods that allow for immediate feedback, ongoing support, and flexibility, recognizing the difficulty of precisely defining the skills involved in reading the customer. Transfer of training problems and barriers are thus minimized.

Source: Adapted from Sloman (2005) and http://careers.harveynichols.com/Home.aspx

Designing training

Training provision is big business in the UK. According to the *National Employers Skills Survey 2009*, the UK spent over £39.2bn on training activity in 2008 (UKCES, **2010a**). While economic recession undoubtedly has had an impact on resources available, there is no sign that spend on training will not remain a significant part of many organization's expenditure. Indeed, there is a body of opinion that argues economies should seek to train their way out of recession (see, for example, UKCES, **2010b**). Importantly, though, whatever the level of total spend, there are nagging doubts as to whether the money allocated to training is always well spent. Estimates suggest that only between 15–20 per cent of the learning investments organizations make actually result in work performance changes (Liembach, 2010). Of course, one of the difficulties here is that we lack sound ways and means to ascertain value for money. This is a theme addressed in the next chapter. Other concerns are a failure to identify needs effectively and a failure to design appropriate training to meet the identified training needs. It is the latter issue that we will address in this chapter. Reference to the model of training activity noted in **Chapter 6** suggests that it is but a simple step from the identification of training to the implementation and delivery of some form of training event or programme. In practice, it is more complex than this.

activity

Consider the following scenario:

Thornlea is a family-controlled, medium-sized, high-spec engineering company specializing in components for the defence industry. Although profitable, recent market pressures have resulted in a new business plan, which has seen a layer of the organizational hierarchy removed. The eight supervisors are now known as team leaders, but have received no guidance as to whether they should be doing anything differently. When the suppliers of new computer-controlled machinery were delivering on-the-job training, there were few problems, but since they have gone the supervisors, or rather the team leaders, complain that they aren't equipped to handle the problems.

What are you first thoughts as to how such training needs may best be met?

While the broad thrust of the required training at Thornlea is reasonably clear, how best to meet this need raises various questions. Should the training be completed away from work? This is not a big company, is there someone within the organization (a senior manager?) capable of leading such a training effort, or will external help be needed? Is the nature of the training need focused more on skills or knowledge? Among the eight supervisors, might there be differences (age, experience, personality) that need to be taken on board in any training provision? What efforts were made to embed the learning done by the suppliers? Thus, there is a mix of issues and questions facing whoever assumes the responsibility for some sort of training effort to meet this need.

In Figure 7.1, a range of design issues are summarized. Careful analysis of these is important, both in terms of choosing an appropriate training strategy and then planning and designing it. We would argue that this is the case for formal training events as well as less traditional options, including workplace learning. An initial distinction is useful. The spheres labelled 1, 2 and 3 are what we would describe as design principles. Spheres 4, 5 and 6 are a number of (potentially) complicating factors. At the heart of the design principles are issues about purpose (for example, what we hope to achieve) and harnessing our understanding of the learning process. The pressure on many organizations today means that they may well start with the complicating factors. A trainer might ask: 'How much can I spend on this?' and then work backwards. However, acknowledging a consensus among professional bodies such as the CIPD and the Institute of Training and

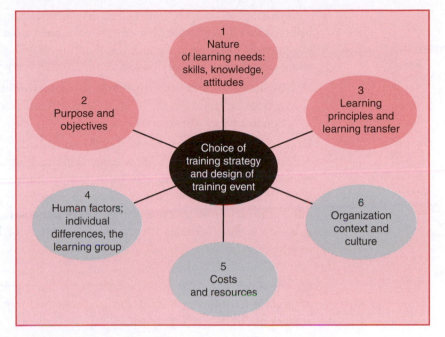

Figure 7.1 A training design framework

Occupational Learning, good practice suggests that organizations should begin with the design principles and then address the complicating factors. This is the path we will follow. Having considered the identification of training needs in **Chapter 6**, we begin with purpose and objectives.

Purpose and objectives

A well-prepared statement of intent (The purpose of this training is to...), together with a set of unambiguous objectives, is important for three reasons:

1 It provides the link between the training needs analysis and the design and delivery of training, enabling the trainer/manager to consider which path to follow in order to achieve the end goal.
2 It reduces uncertainty and doubt on behalf of prospective trainees.
3 It offers a basis upon which evaluation can subsequently be undertaken (see also Chapter 8).

The acronym SMART offers a highly practical tool to help determine the appropriate objectives. The acronym has various guises, which more or less say the same thing, but most commonly it stands for:

- Specific – objectives should specify what they want to achieve
- Measurable – the extent to which objectives have been met
- Achievable – are the objectives achievable and attainable?
- Realistic – are the objectives realistically achievable with the available resources?
- Time – within what time frame are objectives to be achieved?

SMART objectives are not the preserve of the training world. The example below shows how the SMART criteria have been used to formulate a training objective in the area of financial accounting, helping the trainer/manager to address design and delivery issues.

> By the end of a two-hour workshop, trainees will be able to create a profit and loss spreadsheet using Excel 2010 and utilize summation and subtraction formulae with complete accuracy.

Drawing on the work of Bloom (1956) and his development of taxonomies of learning in the areas of knowledge, skills and attitudes, it is important to acknowledge that while it may be relatively straightforward to construct a SMART objective for a basic skill or knowledge need, this becomes more difficult for attitudes and more complex combinations of knowledge and skill. A good example is the construction of objectives for leadership training and development.

activity

Working with a partner, visit the website of the training provider, Fenman, and look particularly at the section devoted to training objectives: **http://www.fenman.co.uk/cat/ product_info/training_objectives.pdf**

Consider the following questions:

1 What sort of words are best suited to objectives and what words are best avoided?
2 What may make the setting of SMART objectives difficult? Think, for example, about a scenario requiring leadership training for senior managers.
3 Write a SMART objective for a student about to go on a three-month placement as part of their degree.

Learning principles and transfer of learning

The subject of learning is vast and complex with a huge literature. Consider for a moment the amount of learning achieved by a three-year old child, without any engagement in the processes so favoured by the institutions established as the guardians and gatekeepers of learning: schools, universities, training centres and so on.

Chapter 5 provides fuller treatment of learning theories. In this chapter, our approach to the bewildering array of avenues one could take in pursuit of understanding learning is characterized by two key criteria:

- learning is central to effective training
- pragmatism.

Thus, with a brief acknowledgement of the body of knowledge about learning, we move on to identify a set of learning principles, a set of rules or guidelines that can usefully guide the design of learning events at a practical and workable level. Two illustrations help us make this point. Skinner (1950) is known for his work with rats and pigeons. Through the judicious provision of food to reward appropriate behaviour, Skinner, in effect, trained pigeons to dance and play ping pong. For our purposes here, it is the principle that learning is likely to be more effective when it is reinforced through appropriate reward. Our second illustration draws on research into individual differences. One such difference might be that we learn in different ways, with different styles (Kolb, 1984; Honey & Mumford, 1992; see Coffield et al., 2004, for a critical review). The learning principle here is that learning is likely to be more effective when it is geared to the individual.

Thus, the psychology and sociology of learning have yielded a number of general principles that apply to most learning situations. These principles are that learning is likely to be more effective when:

- clear goals and targets are established
- it is carefully and thoughtfully sequenced and structured
- learners receive relevant feedback
- it is appropriately rewarded and reinforced
- the learner is actively involved
- it engages understanding
- it is meaningful to the individual/group in terms of their job responsibilities.

One observation on these principles might be that they are little more than common sense, or, more critically, that they are too obvious. However, our experience of teaching trainers over the past 20 years suggests that whatever the level of common sense and however obvious they may appear to be at first sight, they have had a rather disappointing impact on the average trainer or manager in industry. There is a further point. Considered on its own the provision of feedback may be obvious. But when taken in combination with other principles, some complexity results which benefits from careful consideration.

If training has taken place away from work, how learning will be transferred back to a work situation is a further important consideration impacting on design, and should not be left to chance. Some estimates of transfer suggest that as little as 5 per cent to 20 per cent of what is learnt finds its way back into the workplace (Liembach, 2010; Grossman & Salas, 2011). Transfer might be especially difficult for what Blume et al. (2010) refer to as open skills or far transfer tasks, where the application of new skills needs to be adapted to a variety of situations and in different ways, such as management and leadership skills or team skills.

It could be argued that effective transfer of learning is most likely when the learning principles are satisfied, but this may not suffice. Drawing on the learning transfer activities used in over 30 studies Leimbach (2010) identifies three categories of factors, shown in Figure 7.2.

The model suggests that learning needs to focus on the learner, the training and learning intervention and ultimately organizational support. Without taking these factors into account it is suggested that transfer of learning, and any consequent return on investment for both the learner and organization, will be adversely affected.

reflective question Imagine you work in a busy city-centre restaurant three nights each week. The manager has arranged for you to attend a food hygiene training course.

1 What principles of learning do you hope will be reflected in the training?
2 How might the transfer of learning be enhanced?

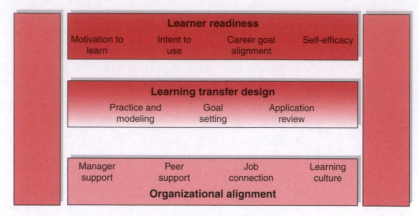

Figure 7.2 A model of the transfer of training

Source: Leimbach (2010, p.83)

We move now to the first of our complicating factors, a range of human, or people, issues.

Human factors

It is perhaps a little unfair to regard people as a complicating factor but consider the following short case, which demonstrates why we have taken this stance.

activity

The reluctant learner

Reflecting on the first of a two-day, in-house effective communication course, the two trainers consider that it has been a successful day. They felt the objectives had largely been met – apart, that is, from Joanna. From the outset, Joanna had been 'troublesome'. She arrived a little late. She interrupted proceedings several times, only to make comments about the poor communication skills of certain managers in the organization. For the first group exercise after lunch, she seemed to be on another planet and was clearly all packed up and ready to leave half an hour before the scheduled finish time. The trainers resolve to have a quiet word with Joanna first thing the next morning. After some hesitancy, Joanna opens up. She feels she has been sent on the course unnecessarily. She acknowledges a clash with her boss but feels that it is him, not her, that needs training. No consultation about the course was undertaken, she simply received an email on Monday saying, 'Attend on Wednesday'. To cap it all, Wednesday was Joanna's birthday.

1 What do you consider to be the main problems here?
2 Why should this have an impact on the learning process?
3 What principles of learning are involved?

The case of the reluctant learner illustrates how individual differences, due to their circumstances and characteristics, can cause difficulties. Knowles' work on adult learning (see, for example, Knowles et al., **2011**) indicates that individual differences, in terms of motivation to learn and the extent to which individuals are self-directed and ready to learn, are likely to be particularly relevant in relation to achieving success in any training intervention. Thinking back to **Chapter 6**, the way in which training needs are identified may also be an important influence in terms of motivation and readiness to learn. For example, an ambitious high performer, who has been identified as having potential for promotion and has been sent on a programme to help them achieve their aims, would arguably have a different mindset to an individual with problematic performance issues (Joanna perhaps?), who has been sent on a programme in order to address them.

There is a range of other factors, including learning styles, which we have already noted as an example of an important principle of learning. The phrase 'I'm too old to learn' is still commonly heard and reflects two further, potentially important, differences. First, research evidence suggests that cognitive capabilities such as short-term memory and information processing do decline with age (Stammers & Patrick, **1975**). Second, and possibly more important, is the individual's perception that they are too old to learn, which links back to our point about an individual's learning disposition. Previous experiences of learning, positive or negative, in terms of education more generally and learning at work in particular, add further complexity. Buckley and Caple (**2007**) also suggest the importance of background and emotional disposition (including culture and social class) as factors influencing learning.

Acknowledgment and recognition of individual differences are clearly important in any consideration of how best to meet an identified training need. If training is one-to-one (discussed later in this chapter), there may be some real prospect of this being taken on board. But, much training takes place in a group context.

reflective question

1 What particular challenges might a lecturer face when teaching groups of students?
2 Are these similar for a trainer working within, for example, a chain of hotels or for a large car dealership?

Clearly a group is simply a collection of individuals and hence the differences and issues discussed above may be compounded. While there is much truth in the phrase know your audience, there are likely to be practical issues in terms of the amount of information available to the trainer/manager in terms of design and, critically, the extent to which individual differences can be catered for in a group situation. That said, some training needs can only really be tackled through groupwork (see also **Chapter 12**). Furthermore, many trainers would argue that groups can be fun to work with. If the dynamics of a group situation can be effectively harnessed by the trainer, a richer learning experience may well result.

Thus far we have considered the trainee, both in a group and individual context, but what about the trainer? Just as a group of trainees may reflect a complicated mix of individual differences, so might any group of trainers. These will include levels and nature of competence, nature of skills (stand up delivery versus facilitation, skills to assess and so on), motivation and orientation. Honey (**2007**), in an extension to his work on learning styles, notes that trainers also have styles and suggests that there may be a tendency to use them as an excuse: 'I'm an activist so I work best with learners who are also activist. That's just the way I am.' Trainers who are best equipped to help diverse learners are those who:

- know their own strengths and how this translates into their approach and style
- are alert to differences among their participants
- adjust their approach style to cater for a range of different learning style preferences.

Costs and resources

We have heard of stories where huge amounts of money appear to have been spent on training provision or seemingly bizarre events organized in the name of good training. Kellaway (**2000**), for example, describes what she terms the 'ultimate nightmare in training programmes'. For a full week, a group of managers are transported to a training centre where they must relinquish every aspect of their ordinary lives and set up their own micro-society. Some are stripped of their belongings and labelled immigrants. Others are chosen to form the elite and enjoy a lavish lifestyle. The rest are designated middles and are threatened by the underclass and harassed by the elite. After several days of bitter warfare, the game comes to an end and the remaining days are spent analysing what has transpired.

reflective question

Kellaway called this, 'The Course from Hell'.

1 Why do you think she has concerns about such a programme?
2 What might have been the rationale of the course designers?

Kellaway despairs at the expense of such provision, when the clues to improved managerial performance 'are not in simplified models of societies' but 'right under our noses'. Such an example suggests an almost unlimited training budget. In reality, most organizations are not like this. Resources for training and learning are scarce and must be negotiated. It is not uncommon to hear of organizations cutting their budget when times are tough. This is why we refer to costs and resources as a complicating factor. Contrast the situation facing the trainer in two organizations with which the authors have close links: the Skipton Building Society, the fourth largest society in the UK; and Elite Packaging, a relatively small company that packages and distributes items to contract. The Skipton head office has a suite of comfortable, well-equipped training rooms, with state-of-the-art connections to web-based learning. In contrast, Elite Packaging, although it takes training seriously, has no dedicated training resources and must use the canteen for any group-based training sessions. So, while there may be sound reasons, in terms of learning principles, group size, learning environment and so on, to develop an intensive three-day team-building programme, with group sizes of no more than 12, some of these aspirations may have to be sacrificed in the face of budgetary and working constraints – it can be virtually impossible to release 12 people at any one point in time in a small company.

A key factor affecting the level of resources available to a training department will be the maturity and status of the function within the organization (see also Chapter 2).

Economic realities will also have a direct impact on the amount of resources available, not just in terms of budgets but also resources and headcount. The CIPD Learning and Talent Development Survey (2012) found a direct relationship between economic circumstances and learning, commenting that 'organizations that reported a worsening economic situation over the past twelve months were more likely to report reduced resources for learning and talent development, decreased funds and reduced headcount in the department'.

Organizational context

Our final issue concerns the organizational context into which any training intervention is to be introduced, and the level of harmony and integration between learning and key aspects of organizational context, which will either help or hinder progress. This will include, crucially, the level of vertical integration between organizational strategy and HR strategy, and the extent to which HR strategies and approaches are themselves horizontally integrated and aligned to support and reinforce each other. Beardwell and Claydon (2010) provide a useful discussion of these concepts. As highlighted in Chapter 6, the role of performance management processes, and the relationship between these and learning interventions, is worthy of particular consideration. It can be argued that one outcome of a performance management system should be to ensure continuous learning and development, as well as being a tool to assist in the identification of training needs. In other words, there is the potential for a performance management process to be a development tool in its own right. As discussed in **Chapter 6**, processes such as the provision of multisource feedback and appraisal can potentially add further value here. While the adoption of performance management by organizations is widespread, the nature of such systems varies significantly and may be a factor to consider in the selection of a particular development solution.

A further crucial aspect of context is organizational culture. Look back for a moment to the cartoon at the start of this chapter. Let's assume that the training need for some kind of teamwork is a legitimately identified need. The training implemented has clearly forced individuals to get upfront and personal with members of their work team. But the boss has a problem. He is worried how others will view these kinds of techniques. One could almost hear him saying: 'This isn't the sort of thing we do around here.' The practice may conflict with the values and beliefs that characterize the workplace or wider organization. However, this is not the place to discuss organizational culture in depth. It suffices to say that organizational culture can be the vital link between learners, the learning content and the transfer of learning into the workplace. Of course, there is a tension here. As noted by Swart et al. (2004), learning has a critical role to play in the development of organizational culture, yet organizational values, defence routines and taken-for-granted ways of working can provide real impediments and barriers to new learning. A paradox may result: 'Because of the way this organization learns, it cannot learn', (see also Chapter 10).

In summary, organizational context provides a crucial backdrop to the success of any training intervention. A critical analysis at an early stage, to identify barriers and enablers within the reality of the work situation (where the training ultimately needs to be applied), will be important in influencing choice and ultimately success. By identifying and harnessing enablers, such as senior management support or a motivated body of line managers, the chances of successful learning can be maximized. In contrast, the identification of problems and barriers at an early stage allows them to be acknowledged and mediated against. The discussion above presents a complex web of factors to be considered when deciding which particular learning intervention is best suited to addressing a particular learning need, and the subsequent planning and design. It is important to recognize that these factors will not all be of equal weight in any given situation, and that the specific context surrounding a learning need, and the priorities within it, will be of key importance. What is really driving investment in a particular training programme? In Chapter 10 we consider this issue further and consider how organizations may be able to identify the key barriers to transfer.

Training and learning methods

We turn now to how these various design issues can be acknowledged, addressed and utilized in the delivery of training and learning. We seek to provide an overview of the broad range of learning solutions, many of which can be creatively blended together to provide bespoke solutions to meet individual, team and organizational needs.

In providing an overview of the options available, it is worth noting that these have been categorized by many different authors according to different criteria. Marchington and Wilkinson (1996) aim to provide a framework to assist in the analysis of learning methods, and differentiate according to two main criteria:

1 the extent to which methods are individually, or group, based
2 the extent to which they are self-directed and participative (andragogical), or have high levels of control by tutors, trainers and other experts (pedagogical).

These are represented visually as two axes, shown in Figure 7.3, and you are invited to position methods within the diagram.

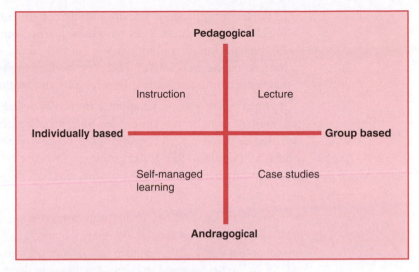

Figure 7.3 A framework of training and learning methods

Source: Adapted from Marchington and Wilkinson (1996)

Focusing on the issue of control, Hackett (2003) provides an analysis of the extent to which training methods are trainer- or learner-centred and concludes that three main categories exist:

1 *Training-centred methods,* such as the lecture, which has the obvious advantage of high levels of control by the trainer over content and pace of delivery.
2 *Learner-centred methods,* such as self-development questionnaires and learning logs, which hand over this control, to a greater or lesser extent, to the learner.
3 *Coaching,* which Hackett claims is the only method to allow a learning partnership to develop between trainer and learner.

No categorization of methods is perfect. Our approach draws on Mumford's (1997) review of methods in terms of their relationship to work. We suggest two broad categories of options, off-the-job and integrated, and consider each method in terms of how it is distinct from, or integrated with, the actual performance of work-related tasks:

• *Off-the-job learning options:* lectures, discussions, case studies, role plays, business games, group dynamics, e-learning and off-the-job skill instruction. These methods tend to be constructed purely for the purpose of learning, rather than to achieve a task or workplace activity. They may be delivered either internally or externally. They include methods that may be delivered as part of a larger programme or course, or as a stand-alone option. The focus tends to be trainer-centred rather than learner-centred. Table 7.1 has more details, including the strengths and weaknesses of each option.
• *Integrated learning methods:* on-the-job training, coaching, shadowing, mentoring, exercise/project work, action learning, job rotation and secondment. These methods combine a concern for learning with the performance of tasks/workplace activities. They tend to enlist the support of helpers to aid

in the learning process, and are heavily dependent on an appropriate learning climate for success. They tend to be learner-centred with the opportunity for recognition of individual needs, and based on experiential learning, harnessing the emotions and senses as well as cognitive capabilities. Table 7.2 has more details, including the strengths and weaknesses of each option.

As noted at the start of **Chapter 6**, the CIPD defines training as 'an instructor led, content based intervention, leading to desired changes in behaviour' and learning as 'a self directed, work-based process, leading to increased adaptive potential' (Sloman, **2005**). According to this, the off-the-job learning options would mostly be considered as training, and the integrated options as learning.

activity

It is likely that you will be familiar with at least some of the methods outlined in Tables 7.1 and 7.2. Think about the different methods you have experienced within your education and working life. Compare your evaluation with others. Do you rate some as more effective or less effective? Why? Discuss your findings.

Trends and issues

Traditional off job provision vs. integrated methods

As recently as 2007, responses to the CIPD annual surveys of learning and development still rated traditional off-the-job training courses as one of the most effective and one of the most frequently used methods of learning. Commenting on the adoption of particular methods in his critique of the survey, Wain (2007, p.23) notes that 'irrespective of claims to the contrary, formal and traditional approaches remain highly significant in learning and development practice'.

Table 7.1 Off-the-job methods

Method	Description	Benefits and strengths	Problems/points to watch
Lecture	A structured talk or presentation to convey required information, for example product knowledge, new policy/procedure	Suitable for large audiences. A cost-effective way of communicating key information. Sequence and structure can be carefully thought through. Trainer-centred, with high degree of control over content	Limited opportunity for participation, communication tends to be one way, although questions may be usefully integrated. Ability of participants to assimilate and understand material may not extend much beyond 30 minutes. Heavily dependent on the quality of the delivery
Discussion	Free exchange of information and ideas, but working to a clear brief provided by the trainer, for example a discussion of barriers to effective internal communications	Seeks involvement of the trainee. Suitable where subject matter involves opinion or grey areas, also when attitudes need to be addressed. Good for getting engagement as regards application of learning and feedback to trainer	Discussions often stray off the point. Superficial discussion may be unhelpful, vague and woolly. Control issues need careful thought by trainer. Some degree of prior knowledge may be required to make discussion useful rather than purely opinion-based

continued

Table 7.1 Continued

Method	Description	Benefits and strengths	Problems/points to watch
Case study	Presentation of scenario (real or fictitious) describing organizational practice and behaviour. Trainees are asked to analyse the documented problem and/or reflect on described practice, for example an unfair dismissal case, a financial problem, departmental reorganization	Seeks involvement of the trainee. Suitable where a careful look at the problem or set of circumstances (free from pressures of an actual event), is beneficial. Provides opportunities for exchange of ideas and encourages consideration of alternative solutions. Tests trainees' ability to apply theory to practice. Can provide examples of organizational good practice	Decisions taken in case study settings are removed from the reality of decision-making. Unrealistic scenarios may predominate. Quality of de-brief crucial for effectiveness. Overuse can result in trainees treating it as a mechanistic exercise
Role play	Trainees enact a role they may have to play at work, for example interviewing a customer or negotiating an agreement. Other trainees, or actors, may be employed to play the role of significant others to enhance credibility	Involves the trainee. Good for training where suitable behaviour needs practising. Trainee can practise, in a safe environment, and receive personal feedback. Role plays that are videoed offer a particularly valuable resource for reflection and managing feedback	Some trainees may be fearful/embarrassed. Unreal situations may encourage atypical behaviours unlikely to be seen in reality. Requires clear purpose, sound briefs and good facilitation on behalf of trainer. Can be time-consuming and resource-demanding
Business game	Trainees manage a range of organizational issues or problems on the basis of information given to them. Outcomes of decisions are fed back to trainees to influence subsequent decision-making. Sophisticated games may be computer assisted or even based in virtual reality	Involves trainees, practically, in dealing with management problems. Simulation of a real-life problem or scenario aids transfer of learning. Enables theory to be put into practice and consequences reflected upon	Limited or unreal outcomes from decisions made may undermine value of method. May result in trainee disengagement. Extent to which game reflects reality is critical
Group dynamics	Trainees are put into groups to carry out a simulated exercise and behaviour is examined, for example group decision-making, intergroup conflict, intragroup communication	Potentially powerful way to understand self and impact of self on others and vice versa. Increases insight and understanding of working with other people and getting work done through other people	Learning can be hurtful as well as helpful – the facilitator's role is critical in managing this. High levels of skills required on behalf of the facilitators. Danger of trainees treating exercises as just a bit of fun and/or opting out. Invariably time-consuming and resource-demanding
E-learning	Learning is delivered through the internet or an organization's intranet	Can effectively overcome time, place, pace issues and barriers. Good for material that can be broken down into distinct blocks and is not subject to interpretation or change. Sophisticated technological applications enable high risk training to be undertaken safely and effectively, for example flight simulation. Usefully used as part of blended solutions	Much e-learning is little more than electronic page turning. May not be fit for purpose. Can isolate trainees. To cope effectively with skills requires sophisticated applications that are expensive. Learner support should not be ignored
Off-the-job skill instruction	A skill is taught by explanation, demonstration and practice, for example how to operate a computer	Most suitable for a wide range of psychomotor skills. Particularly good where task analysis reveals potential difficulties or blocks to achieving mastery	Part or whole approach may cause trainer difficulty re. the most appropriate strategy. Trainee likely to experience difficulty if asked to absorb large chunks of information or procedures before opportunity for practice. A good employee does not necessarily make a good instructor

Table 7.2 Integrated methods

Method	Description	Benefits and strengths	Problems/points to watch
On-the-job training	Sometimes referred to as 'sitting by Nellie'. Training is undertaken at the workplace, often involving demonstration followed by supervised practice. Often used for semi-skilled jobs but potential for developing individual skills in all types of work	Can effectively integrate work and learning. Realistic and immediate. Transfer problems minimized	Potential to learn bad habits as well as good. Choice of 'Nellie' is critical. To do well requires planning and an understanding of trainee/learner
Coaching	An individual meets a coach on a one-to-one basis to work on a range of work-related issues, some of which may also include personal factors. Distinct from mentoring with its focus on specific behavioural change and/ or performance improvement, for example customer service telephone training, leadership development	Targets individual needs. Enables trainee to practise skills in real situations under supervision and monitoring. Good for situations where trainee may be experiencing difficulties or problems. Potentially good role for line manager to adopt. Cost-effective and promotes devolvement of learning responsibility. Facilitates learning transfer	Not a substitute for basic skills and knowledge. Can be time-consuming and resource-demanding. Frequently line managers require coaching skills, so further resources are required. Trainees can become overdependent on coach. An appropriate (open) work culture/learning climate will enhance likelihood of success
Shadowing	Trainees observe a skilled, experienced practitioner at work, and discuss their perceptions with the practitioner. Process should require shadow to reflect on experience	Integrates work and learning. Enables trainee to witness first hand real day-to-day jobs and tasks being performed. Promotes wider participation in learning effort beyond training specialists	Tends to be time-consuming and can slow down the person being shadowed. Real work can be mundane and boring, so the learning may be mundane and boring. Requires some structure, for example building in regular reflection and review
Mentoring	An identified mentor supports and encourages the trainee (referred to as a mentee) to manage their own personal development. The mentor, usually a senior professional or manager, helps the mentee find the right direction and developmental solutions to career and other issues	Develops the individual rather than training them. Particularly suitable for aspects of career development. Enables a person to question assumptions, shift mental context. Good for addressing attitudes and feelings as regards work problems, issues and so on. Can assist individual to address organizational politics	Not appropriate for helping to enhance specific skills re. performance. Time-consuming and resource-demanding. Best over a longish period. Good mentors are hard to find. Mentoring relationships can be difficult and uneasy. Important that a mentor understands self before they mentor others
Exercise/project	Trainees asked to undertake a particular work-related task leading to a required outcome, for example computerizing client records or setting up a staff absence control system	Suitable for any situation where trainee might benefit from practice following knowledge and theory input. Can be individual or group based. Much scope for the imaginative trainer to design appropriate and challenging exercises to test and further develop trainees' capabilities	Unrealistic projects/exercises risk disengagement. Should be challenging but attainable. Design critical to ensure sufficient focus on learning rather than just on task
Action learning	Individuals work in groups, addressing real organizational problems. Emphasizes the importance of critical questioning and reflection in learning. Can be project based	Integrates work and learning. Maximizes opportunities for experiential and social learning. Harnesses the power of critical reflection and learning as a force for individual and organizational change	If participants do not have a genuine organizational problem to focus on, initiatives may fail. Benefits from strong facilitation. Needs champions and sponsors within the organization for success

continued

Table 7.2 Continued

Method	Description	Benefits and strengths	Problems/points to watch
Job rotation	Moving around a number of jobs to build experience across job roles. Often a feature of graduate training programmes	Provides broad experience and awareness of aspects of a number of roles in a shorter period of time than via natural progression. Should broaden perspective and outlook. Chance to develop new skills, knowledge and networks	May prove frustrating, as potentially insufficient time to deliver in roles experienced. Resource hungry due to learning curves. Consistency of learning support via different line managers may vary
Secondment	Trainee spends a substantial period of time (typically 3–12 months) in a different job (sometimes in a different organization) or with different responsibilities from normal. No special arrangements. just normal work	Provides experience of a new role and environment. Opportunities to develop new knowledge, skills, outlook and networks	Potential problems may arise in identifying appropriate job or role. Responsibility for learning and critical reflection lie solely with individual. Tensions may arise on resumption of old role

Reports over the last four years however, (CIPD, 2009–2012) suggest that this conventional approach to employee development is now changing, with a shift in emphasis towards more integrated and work-based provision being at least partly driven by economic necessity. In-house development programmes, coaching by line managers and on-the-job training are now rated as most effective (CIPD, 2012) with only 19 per cent of respondents rating 'instructor-led training delivered off-the-job' as the most effective development practice. The public sector in particular was more likely than other sectors to make less use of classroom and trainer-led instruction and over a third of public sector organizations reported having reduced their use of external suppliers and moved to in-house provision (see also Chapter 3).

However, we should not under-estimate the continued popularity of training using traditional methods. There is clearly a tension here, illustrated by the rapid rise in the use of e-learning, but with most managers reporting that they believe e-learning methods are 'not a substitute for face-to-face or classroom learning' (CIPD, 2011).

Given this it is important to recognize that such traditional off-the-job training approaches do have value, and the way they are designed, adopted and applied can be specifically tailored to meet organizational needs. The fact that a learning solution is conducted away from the job itself can be a real advantage. This is well-illustrated in the case of role play, often used as a way of practising skills in a safe environment where it is important for the individual and the organization that mistakes are not made in reality. Activities such as union negotiations and interviewing can fall into this category, as can work involving more vulnerable groups. One corporate role play organization (www.corporateroleplay.co.uk) lists the Police Authorities, the NHS and MOD amongst its clients, providing role play simulations to cover a variety of situations where it would otherwise be very difficult to practice vital skills. Role play examples would include: vulnerable witness; suspect interview; patient simulation; customer relations; and aspects of Human Resource Practice.

Another explanation for the continuing use of traditional methods may be that organizations can find themselves in a position where they are required to meet immediate needs, such as the provision of health and safety training in response to a number of accidents, or customer care training in response to a number of complaints. Traditional training packages may provide quick, cheap, easy and accessible ways of demonstrating compliance with legislative requirements and evidence that such needs have been addressed. This last point reflects the pressure many organizations face to provide simple measures of their training effort. Annual reports regularly refer to an average number of training days received by employees. In unionized organizations this would usually be an issue of interest and perhaps negotiation for Trade Union Learning Representatives (TULRs).

Finally, we might note that in some organizations a lack of capability and imagination on the part of staff with training responsibilities may contribute to a failure to respond to complex skill needs with the most fit for purpose learning solutions.

activity

Visit the following website devoted to experiential learning: **www.learningandteaching. info/learning/experience.htm**

With others, critically assess how the experiential learning cycle might be used as a basis for reducing the reliance on traditional off-the-job training.

The rise of e-learning

While off-the-job courses remain popular, there has been a shift in exactly how such provision is delivered. The ability to harness IT as a delivery tool in training and learning has witnessed considerable growth in recent years. E-learning and web-based training materials have been extensively adopted by a wide range of organizations. Chapter 9 discusses this whole field in more depth. Here it is appropriate to note two key points.

First, some organizations have acted upon what they see as the enormous potential in such delivery. The example in HRD in Practice 7.2. indicates training provision underpinned by e-learning.

HRD in Practice 7.2

Hilton Hotels

According to Hilton Hotel's website the Hilton University is the company's 'award winning e-learning facility'. It is structured into five 'faculties' (see **www.hiltonworldwide.com/careers/ development/**) including the Hotel College (providing brand standards and compliance training to enable hotels to meet guest expectations), the Commercial College (providing sales, revenue and customer marketing training) and the Leadership College (providing executive and leadership development programmes for Hilton's worldwide senior leadership). According to Hilton Hotels its e-learning provision is a 'superb, varied range of learning opportunities to help you develop your skills and your career. There is a tremendous range of subjects on offer with an increasing number of them being available in different languages'.

Second, despite the purported benefits of e-learning, its overall effectiveness as a training method is far from proven. A key factor here may be the extent to which a lot of e-learning fails to address the basic principles of learning discussed earlier in this chapter. In other words, much e-learning can be little more than electronic page turning, neither interactive nor geared to the needs of the individual trainee or learner.

Flavour of the month: coaching and mentoring?

Traditionally viewed as a relatively directive way of improving performance of a work-related task, the field of coaching has expanded considerably and coaching by line managers is now rated as the second most effective learning and development practice (topped only by in-house development programmes) by participants in the CIPD Learning and Talent Development survey (CIPD, 2012). Defined by the CIPD (2011), 'coaching targets high performance and improvement at work and usually focuses on specific skills and goals although it may also have an impact on an individual's personal attributes. The process typically lasts for a relatively short period'. While most coaching is delivered by line managers (CIPD, 2012), alternative approaches include executive coaching, peer coaching and coaching pools, such as those used by the transport delivery company TNT. TNT have recently introduced a coaching pool of trained line managers that can be accessed by any employee when a development need is identified, (Wolf, 2012). A fuller discussion of coaching can be found in Chapter 13.

Coaching skills are also valuable within a mentoring relationship although the focus will be different, with the strength of mentoring being its long-term holistic approach. Making links with other developmental processes, Klasen and Clutterbuck (2002, p.16) believe that 'mentoring derives its immense effectiveness in employee learning and development from being an integrated method that flexibly combines elements of the four other one-to-one development approaches, coaching, counselling, networking/facilitation and guardianship'. The CIPD recognize the commonality with coaching in terms of models and skills used, but draws attention to the potential for mutual learning and longer-term individual and organizational development offered by mentoring, as well as organizational learning and maximizing potential and energy within the organization (CIPD, 2011). Traditionally, a mentoring relationship would be one in which 'a more experienced colleague uses his or her greater knowledge and understanding of the work or workplace to support the development of a more junior or inexperienced member of staff' (CIPD, 2011). One example would be the inclusion of mentoring as part of graduate development schemes such as that run by Hallmark Cards (see Chapter 16).

The best of both worlds: a blended approach?

Although loosely configured into a classification of off-the-job and integrated methods, this chapter has considered a wide range of potential training and learning methods. Of course, the most effective programmes tend to be those based on a sound analysis of learning needs and detailed consideration of the factors discussed earlier in the chapter. From this base, effective solutions may well creatively combine a number of methods as seen by the number of winners of national awards who have chosen to use some type of blended approach. The website www.nationaltrainingawards.com/ gives details of previous winners and the rationale underpinning the programmes. Two examples of such are illustrated in HRD in Practice 7.3.

The Bupa Personal Best programme

HRD in Practice

7.3

The BUPA programme, award winner in 2006, delivers learning in the care homes themselves, using a modular approach, which includes experiential learning, interviewing care home residents to develop a greater understanding and appreciation of their needs, and the development of individual action plans to specify actions to be taken in the future. One specific activity reported in *People Management* (Phillips, 2006) involved staff putting themselves in the place of residents, being lifted mechanically into bed and fed pureed food to learn for themselves what these experiences felt like. A series of customer service training modules has been developed to complement the Personal Best programme.

London Metropolitan Police Constable Foundation Training

An Award winner in 2009, the Met have adapted a computer assisted method of training previously only used by senior managers for critical decision-making. The training blends IT with traditional classroom techniques. Trainees work in small groups and view scenarios sourced by networked computers. They respond by recording real-time decisions and their rationale for the decisions taken as the scenarios unfold. Trainers control the information sent to the groups and record trainee responses using video. In a subsequent de-brief, decisions are discussed and analysed and learning points highlighted.

Source: People Management, 2009

Engaging hard to reach groups

It is generally acknowledged that some methods of learning potentially act as barriers to some disenfranchised groups, who may be put off by the use of methods they associate with previous negative experiences, (Leitch, 2006). The role of skills development in creating social mobility is acknowledged by both Government (Department for Business Innovation and Skills, 2010) and trade unions. According to UnionLearn (2011) since 1999 over 2600 TULRs have been recruited and trained, with one of their key priorities for the period April 2011–March 2014, being to reach disadvantaged learners in the workplace and the community.

There are also inspirational examples of best practice in this area such as the Safer Places Project. A winner of the National Training Awards 2010, Safer Places is a voluntary organization helping women who have suffered domestic violence, a consequence of which has been an inability for many to engage with learning and education. SureStart and JobCentre Plus developed a range of modular courses linked to employability with some offering City and Guilds accreditation. Timescales for completion are flexible allowing for women to complete the courses even if the nature of their personal lives means they are disrupted, and a support structure is put in place for up to 13 weeks after completion. Delivering individual and community benefits, outcomes are impressive in terms of student numbers, attrition and attainment. It has proved individually empowering, with many women noting enhanced self-confidence. 50 per cent of those completing the courses gained City and Guilds accreditation and 30 per cent entered employment or further education within 13 weeks.

summary

⭕ Effective and fit for purpose training and learning requires careful and thoughtful translation of identified needs into learning strategies.

⭕ This process is aided by the recognition of a range of factors, including the objectives of any training or learning, an understanding of how learning principles can maximize effective learning, the characteristics of the learners/trainees, and the constraints of limited resources and organization context.

⭕ Specific objectives, which can be clearly communicated and are measurable, avoid ambiguity and assist in designing fit for purpose training activity.

⭕ Learning principles that can usefully be considered in the design of training or learning include:
  – learning is likely to be more effective when relevant feedback is provided
  – learning is likely to be more effective when the learner is actively involved.

⭕ Training that is at odds with the culture of the organization will cause tension and requires careful management.

⭕ While resource constraints will influence what can be done in practice, a wide range of methods and solutions are available to the trainer.

⭕ A useful distinction is between off-the-job learning options and integrated learning methods.

⭕ There is rarely one best method. All methods have different strengths and weaknesses; the key is to match method(s) with needs.

⭕ While a majority of organizations continue to make use of off-the-job methods, recent years have seen methods such e-learning, coaching and mentoring gain in popularity.

⭕ Blended learning, involving appropriate combinations of methods, is increasingly seen as the way forward, enabling more of the critical design factors to be addressed. Imaginative use of blended learning may well offer opportunities to meet the challenges of engaging hard to reach, or disenfranchised, learners.

discussion questions

1 Why might setting SMART objectives for interpersonal skills training be more difficult than for a range of IT training (e.g. Excel)?

2 How can learning principles be integrated into the effective design of training?

3 How might the notion of the integration of work and learning be used to differentiate between different methods of training or learning?

4 Why are methods such as coaching and mentoring increasingly popular?

5 Identify a training need where a blended learning solution might be most appropriate.

further reading

references

Cunningham, I., Dawes, G. and Bennett, B. (2004) *The Handbook of Work Based Learning*. Aldershot: Gower Publishing Ltd.

Knowles, M. S., Holton III, E. F. and Swanson, R. A. (2011) *The Adult Learner: The Definitive Classic in Adult Education and Human Resource Development*. Oxford: Butterworth-Heinemann.

Sloman, M. (2005) *Training to Learning: Change Agenda*. London: CIPD.

Truelove, S. (2006) *Training in Practice*. London: Chartered Institute of Personnel and Development.

Beardwell, J. and Claydon, T. eds (2010) *Human Resource Management: A Contemporary Approach*, 6th edn. Harlow: Prentice Hall.

Bloom, B.S. (ed.) (1956) *Taxonomy of Educational Objectives: The Classification of Educational Goals, Handbook I, Cognitive Domain*. New York: McKay.

Blume, B.D., Ford, J.K., Baldwin, T.T. and Huang, J.L. (2010) Transfer of training: A meta-analytic review. *Journal of Management*, **36**(4): 1065–105.

Buckley, R. and Caple, J. (2007) *The Theory and Practice of Training*, 5th edn. London: Kogan Page.

CIPD (2009) *Learning and Talent Development Annual Survey Report 2009*. London: CIPD.

CIPD (2011) *Coaching and Mentoring: Factsheet*, available at: http://www.cipd.co.uk/hr-resources/factsheets/coaching-mentoring.aspx

CIPD (2012) *Learning and Talent Development Annual Survey Report 2012*. London: CIPD.

Coffield, F., Moseley, D., Hall, E. and Ecclestone, K. (2004) *Learning Styles and Pedagogy in Post-16 Learning: A Systematic and Critical Review*. London: Learning & Skills Research Centre.

Department for Business Innovation and Skills (2010) *Skills for Sustainable Business Strategy Document, Full Report*. London: Crown Publishing.

Grossman, R. and Salas, E. (2011) The transfer of training: what really matters. *International Journal of Training and Development*, **15**(2): 103–20.

Hackett, P. (2003) *Training Practice*. London: CIPD.

Honey, P. (2007) *The Trainer Styles Questionnaire*. Maidenhead: P. Honey.

Honey, P. and Mumford, A. (1992) *The Manual of Learning Styles*. Maidenhead: P. Honey.

Kellaway, L. (2000) *Sense and Nonsense in the Office*. London: FT/Prentice Hall.

Klasen, N. and Clutterbuck, D. (2002) *Implementing Mentoring Schemes*. Oxford: Butterworth Heinemann.

Knowles, M. S., Holton III, E. F. and Swanson, R. A. (2011) *The Adult Learner: The Definitive Classic in Adult Education and Human Resource Development*. Oxford: Butterworth-Heinemann.

Kolb, D.A. (1984) *Experiential Learning: Experience as the Source of Learning and Development*. Englewood Cliffs, NJ: Prentice Hall.

Leitch, S. (2006) *Prosperity for All in the Global Economy: World Class Skills*. London: HM Treasury.

Leimbach, M. (2010) Learning transfer model: a research-driven approach to enhancing learning effectiveness. *Industrial and Commercial Training*, **42**(1) 81–6.

Marchington, M. and Wilkinson, A. (1996) *Core Personnel and Development*. London: IPD.

Mumford, A. and Honey, P. (1997) *How to Choose the Right Development Method*. Maidenhead: Peter Honey Publications.

Phillips, L. (2006) BUPA stars. *People Management*, **12**(22): 30–3.

Skinner, B.F. (1950) Are theories of learning necessary? *Psychological Review*, **57**: 193–216.

Sloman, M. (2005) *Training to Learning: Change Agenda*. London: CIPD.

Stammers, R. and Patrick, J. (1975) *The Psychology of Training*. London: Methuen.

Swart, J., Mann, C., Brown, S. and Price, A. (2004) *Human Resource Development: Strategy and Tactics*. Oxford: Butterworth Heinemann.

UK Commission for Employment and Skills (UKCES) (2010a) *National Employer Skills Survey for England 2009: Key findings report, Evidence Report 13, March 2010,* available from http://www.ukces.org.uk/assets/bispartners/ukces/docs/publications/evidence-report-13-ness-key-findings-2009.pdf

UKCES (2010b) *Now Is the Time to Invest in Skills: An Open Letter to Employers*, available at http://www.unionlearn.org.uk/extrasUL/about/SkillsAdvert.pdf

UnionLearn (2011) *Working for Learners: A Handbook for Learners and Their Union Learning Representatives*. London: TUC

Wain, D. (2007) *Lies, Damned Lies and a Few Home Truths in Reflections on the 2002 Learning and Development Survey*. London: Chartered Institute of Personnel and Development.

Wolf, C. (2012) How to make a success of employee coaching: the 2012 Xpert HR Survey. *IRS Employment Review,* IRS.

chapter 8

Evaluation of HRD

David Devins and Joanna Smith

Chapter learning outcomes

After studying this chapter, you should be able to:

- Explain the importance of evaluation in HRD
- Understand the key ideas and perspectives relating to evaluation
- Explain how evaluation is connected to HRD policy
- Assess various methods of evaluating HRD
- Examine the future direction of HRD evaluation

Chapter outline

Introduction
Theoretical perspectives
Evaluation of NHRD
Evaluation of HRD in the workplace
Evaluation Models
Future direction of evaluation
Summary

Introduction

Evaluation is a relatively young discipline, which has its roots in the work of Campbell and Stanley (1963), who were responsible for popularizing the distinction between experimental and quasi-experimental design. Over the years, the discipline has evolved and developed, and it is applied to many policies and practices, organizations, teams and individuals. It forms the core of many strategic planning processes, organizational development, HRD and individual development practices. In fact, some people suggest that there is very little that cannot be evaluated. One guru, when describing the scope of what can be evaluated, declared: 'Everything. One can begin at the beginning of a dictionary and go through to the end, and every noun, common or proper, calls to mind a context in which evaluation would be appropriate' (Scriven, 1980, p.4). While cautioning against this all-embracing view, it is clear that evaluation of one form or another has a key role to play in the field of HRD at a range of levels – national, sectoral, organizational, divisional, team and individual – along with a wide range of strategic, tactical and operational activities.

A key question to ask is: Why do evaluation? Sometimes, it is because we have to, because there is a contractual obligation to undertake an evaluation. It is often the case that someone, somewhere, has provided some resources and they want to know what their money has been spent on, if it has made a difference, or if it could have been spent more wisely elsewhere. Demonstrating the impact of an HRD intervention is an important part of reinforcing its value and utility. Equally, evaluation may be done because there is a wish to learn from experience and improve the design of a programme, policy or practice. We may want to involve others in reflecting on the process or performance of an intervention to build capacity and share understanding. Clearly there are many reasons why we should evaluate; however, evaluation is often lacking, or may be done as an afterthought, and the gains to be had from a well-designed and implemented evaluation will not be realized.

reflective question

1 In your experience, what type of things do you evaluate?
2 Why do you do it?
3 How do you do it?

For further information about the evaluation community, see the UK's Evaluation Society – www.evaluation.org.uk – or the European Evaluation Society – www.europeanevaluation.org

Theoretical perspectives

There is no single, universally accepted definition of the term evaluation, as the following selected quotes from the burgeoning evaluation literature illustrate:

> The process of determining the merit, worth or value of something or the product of that process. (Scriven, 1991, p.139)

> Evaluation is the systematic application of social research procedures for assessing the conceptualization, design, implementation and utility of social intervention programmes. (Rossi & Freeman, 1993, p.5)

> Evaluation is the systematic assessment of the operation and/or outcomes of a programme or policy, compared to a set of explicit or implicit standards as a means of contributing to the improvement of social policy. (Weiss, 1998, p.4)

The definitions highlight some common themes associated with evaluation, emphasizing:

1 systematic approaches
2 some thing (process, project, programme or policy)
3 outcomes and impact
4 utility.

In this chapter, evaluation is used as a general term that encompasses these attributes, which, as we will see, can be applied to a variety of aspects of HRD.

It should be noted that there is a wide range of types of evaluation: ex ante, summative, formative, comprehensive, theory-driven, utilization focused and meta-evaluation, to name but a few. The following key terms highlight the focus of the different approaches:

- *Ex ante evaluation:* at the start of the project/programme (also known as formative)
- *Interim evaluation:* during the project/programme (formative and summative)
- *Ex post evaluation:* at the end of the programme (summative).

Adopting a particular approach to evaluation often means adopting a particular approach to research and a particular view of the world, which has, at its extremes, the notions of positivism underpinned by an experimental approach or relativism underpinned by a constructivist approach.

From its roots in positivism ...

Underpinning much evaluation in the early days was the logic of experimentation. For more than 30 years, policy trials and rigorous social experiments have been a primary method of evaluating potential new policies, particularly in the USA, in advance of widespread policy implementation. These approaches generally involve the random assignment of individuals to treatment and control groups so that the impact of a policy intervention may be assessed. This approach is widely acknowledged as the gold standard in terms of evaluation design. At its simplest, the logic of experimentation underpinning this approach involves a four-stage process:

1 Randomly assign research subjects to two or more matched groups
2 Apply a treatment (or in this case a policy instrument) to one group and not the other
3 Measure both groups before and after the treatment of one
4 Compare the changes in the treated and untreated groups.

The two groups are studied before and after the experimental treatment and at the same points in time, to allow comparisons and conclusions to be drawn about the effect of the intervention (see Figure 8.1). In this way, exogenous or confounding factors that might otherwise influence outcomes ought to be randomly distributed between the treatment and control group. As long as the samples in each group are large enough, differences in the outcomes of the two groups can be attributed to the treatment.

The core element of this approach is the theory of causation. It is argued that since the groups are randomly matched to begin with, the only difference between them is the application of the programme, and it is therefore only the treatment that can be responsible for the difference in outcomes. While one cannot observe causation, it has to be inferred from the repeated succession of one event by another. In a classic analysis, a causal relationship exists if:

- the cause preceded the effect
- the cause was related to the effect
- we can find no plausible alternative explanation for the effect other than the cause.

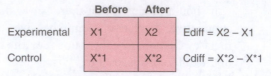

	Before	After	
Experimental	X1	X2	Ediff = X2 − X1
Control	X*1	X*2	Cdiff = X*2 − X*1

Effect of intervention = Difference between Ediff and Cdiff

Figure 8.1 Classic experimental design

Source: de Vaus (1993, p.35)

Perhaps importantly in the field of policy evaluation, experimental design does not explain why an effect takes place nor does it seek to understand why an intervention works or does not work (Pawson & Tilley, 1997). The unique strength of experimentation is in describing the consequences attributable to deliberately varying a treatment (that is, causal description). In contrast, experiments do less well in clarifying the mechanisms through which, and the conditions under which, causal relationships hold (that is, causal explanation). Causal explanation is an important route to the generalization of causal descriptions, because it identifies which features of the causal relationship are essential to transfer to other situations, an outcome of considerable interest to policy planners. What experiments do best is improve causal descriptions; they do less well at explaining causal relationships. The experimental method does not set out to explain why an intervention works, and the experimental paradigm has often struggled to deliver clear answers to the questions posed by policy planners and decision makers in terms of what works – the programmes, projects or actions taken to develop human capital. To understand why there is an inconsistency of outcomes, different questions need to be asked in terms of why, or how, the processes have affected behaviours.

activity

1 Why would you use a scientific approach?
2 Can you find a good example? (Google it.)
3 What value does it have in the HRD context?

... to constructivism

In the 1970s, many social science disciplines were gripped by the debate on positivism, and witnessed the rise of oppositional perspectives known variously as interpretative, phenomenological or hermeneutical, for example. This coincided with a move towards the usefulness of evaluation as a means of informing decisions or, most optimistically, enlightening decision makers and those involved in the development and implementation of policies and programmes (Weiss, 1980). Together, the oppositional perspectives and the pragmatic approach to evaluation led to an approach referred to as constructivism (or sometimes constructionism, see Note 1). The constructivist paradigm has its roots in anthropological traditions. Instead of focusing on explaining, this paradigm focuses on understanding the phenomenon being studied through ongoing and in-depth contact and relationships with those involved. Relying on qualitative data and rich descriptions, the constructivists' purpose is 'the collection of holistic world views, intact belief systems and complex inner psychic and interpersonal states' (Maxwell & Lincoln, 1990, p.508). In other words, who are the people involved in the programme and what do the experiences mean to them?

While there are a number of approaches to social constructivism (Gergen, 1985, 1994; Pearce, 1992; Shotter 1993; Burr 1995), the key features are as follows:

- The use of language, organized into conversations, discourses, narratives, and stories, provides the means by which we come to experience our world and construct a reality. Thus language, as a social resource, has a central role in the making of phenomena that may come to be accepted as real.

- Meanings are made through a relational process between people that become embedded into ongoing ways of talking, which in turn may become accepted versions of reality in a particular local context. The taken-for-granted view of the world provides a variety of truths and facts about a reality, which may be 'highly circumscribed by culture, history or social context' (Gergen, 1985, p.267). The extent to which meanings continue to be accepted depends not on empirical validity but the day-to-day workings of social processes in a particular time and place. What comes to be accepted as real serves a function within a particular historical and cultural context with no claim to truth beyond the context.

- By participating in different relationships in different contexts, we acquire various ways of talking, which can be used for the achievement of valued ends in different situations. Meanings are unlikely to remain constant since, as a consequence of our participation in different relationships, versions of reality are always open to further or revised specification, offering the possibility of new meanings to emerge via a social process leading to a new or revised version of reality.

The idea is that initiatives and programmes that go under the microscope cannot and should not be treated as independent variables. Rather, all policies and interventions are constituted in complex processes of human understanding and interaction. Proponents of the constructivist approach, such as Guba and Lincoln (1989), see evaluators as facilitating an exchange of meaning between stakeholders, where, through dialogue, stakeholders jointly construct a consensus about an intervention. Through this lens, programmes work through a process of reasoning, change, influence, negotiation, persuasion and choice. While traditional evaluation emphasizes outputs and outcomes, this form of evaluation emphasizes processes and particularly the myriad of stakeholders who may be involved in developing and implementing an intervention, strategy, programme or project.

activity

1 Why would you use a constructivist approach?
2 Can you find a good example? (Google it.)
3 What value does it have in the HRD context?

Somewhere between positivism and relativism

Throughout recent decades there have been heated exchanges between the proponents of positivist and constructionist approaches to evaluation. Between the extremes of positivism and constructivism lies a pluralist view of evaluation, which calls for both breadth and depth in programme evaluation (Cronbach, 1982).

This approach is taken further by Rossi and Freeman (1993), who highlight a threefold distinction of evaluation activities based on analysis related to the conceptualization and design of interventions, monitoring or programme implementation, and assessment of programme utility.

This has developed into theory-based evaluation on the premise that interventions are based on a theory – either implicit or explicit – which explains how and why it will work. The key to understanding what really matters about a programme is through identifying this theory (sometimes referred to as the programme logic model). By combining outcome data with an understanding of the process, a great deal can be learned about the programme's impact and its most influential factors (Weiss, 1995).

A more recent development has been the advent of realist evaluation (Pawson & Tilley, 1997), which seeks to position itself as a model of scientific explanation avoiding the traditional epistemological poles of positivism and relativism. Realism's key feature is its stress on the mechanics of explanation and its contribution to a progressive body of scientific knowledge.

reflective question

1 Are there any problems associated with combining outcome and process data?
2 What implications does this have for research methods?
3 Is this approach becoming more or less popular? Why/why not?

Evaluation of NHRD

Several models have been introduced to explore evaluation within the context of the organization and workplace training. However, much evaluation work today is conducted on national government programmes with government departments and quasi-government agencies. The concept of NHRD policies and practice was introduced in Chapter 1. While it may be difficult to define and varies from country to country, the general focus of NHRD has developed out of a government interest in workforce development as a strategic issue. In the UK in particular, NHRD is often focused on the development and utilization of skills in order to enhance competitiveness and alleviate social exclusion. The system remains fragmented, with a range of government departments and agencies responsible for various aspects of the system.

At the current time the government has founded its approach to NHRD policy (focused on adult learning and skills) upon three principles (BIS, 2010):

(i) Fairness – a belief that those without basic literacy and numeracy skills should be first in line for help.

(ii) Responsibility – empl oyers and citizens must take greater responsibility for ensuring that their own human capital needs are met (with an expectation that employers and learners will co-invest alongside government in meeting the costs of intermediate and higher level qualifications).

(iii) Freedom – for providers of post-compulsory education to serve the interests of individuals and communities. The stated objective is to deliver a system which is able to respond to the needs of individuals, communities and an increasingly dynamic economy.

One of the key debates surrounding public policy intervention is whether and how much public intervention is needed. Intervention will vary from country to country and be strongly connected to cultural and historical factors and the nature of the political economy in particular places. The Wolf Review of Vocational Education in England (DfE, 2011) is a prime example of the use of evidence drawing on a range of research and evaluation studies, often commissioned by government departments or quasi-government agencies to develop thinking and shape the agenda.

activity

Working with a partner, find out about aspects of NHRD in England. Go to the Department for Business Innovation and and Skills – **www.bis.gov.uk** – and the UK Commission for Employment and Skills – **www.ukces.org.uk**

For Scotland, go to **www.scotland.gov.uk/Topics/Education** for Wales, go to **http://new.wales.gov.uk/topics/educationandskills/?skip=1&lang=en** and for Northern Ireland, go to **www.delni.gov.uk/index**

Thinking about a policy or programme related to NHRD:

1 What was it seeking to achieve?

2 What actions were/are required to take it forward?

3 What factors are/were critical to its success?

Evaluation frameworks: the ROAMEF cycle

A framework is critical to the successful development and implementation of evaluation. There is a wide range of frameworks to be applied to appraise and evaluate policy and NHRD. An example of one endorsed by the government is provided in the *Green Book* (HM Treasury, 2003), which is a systematic approach used to guide national government appraisals and evaluation in the UK. It provides a useful overview to illustrate the key characteristics of evaluation throughout the policy process – important when considering evaluation within the context of NHRD – however, it is only one of a wide range of frameworks that may be used to evaluate public policy.

activity

Working in groups of three, each person checks one of the following frameworks for evaluation:

• **http://ec.europa.eu/dgs/secretariat_general/evaluation/index_en.htm** – the European Commission

• **www.esrc.ac.uk/funding-and-guidance/tools-and-resources/impact-evaluation/science-in-society.aspx** – *Evaluating Science and Society Initiatives*

- **www.wkkf.org/knowledge-center/resources/2010/w-k-kellogg-foundation-evaluation-handbook.aspx** – the *Kellogg Foundation Evaluation Handbook*.

Identify the key features of each framework and share your results.

The basic model of evaluation outlined in the *Green Book* is the ROAMEF (rationale, objectives, appraisal, monitoring, evaluation and feedback) cycle, shown in Figure 8.2 and used in the Evaluation Strategy produced by the Department for Business Innovation and Skills[1]. The underlying rationale for policy intervention is usually founded in market failure, as discussed in Chapter 1, or where there are clear government distributional objectives (societal equity) that need to be met. Market failure refers to where the market has not and cannot of itself be expected to deliver an efficient outcome and a publicly funded intervention will seek to address this (*Green Book*, p.11). The nature of intervention will vary from country to country and be strongly influenced by a variety of social, economic, cultural and political factors.

The *Green Book* outlines a circular process of evaluation, where the first step is based on a process or systems approach through an appraisal of the proposed intervention (ex ante evaluation). Towards the end of the process, an outcomes-oriented evaluation (ex post evaluation) is prescribed to determine whether the intervention has worked and to what extent.

Rationale

Various reviews (e.g. DfE, 2011; UKCES 2010)) marshal both research and evaluation evidence to highlight that a skilled workforce has positive impacts on high-level economic aims such as productivity and GDP growth. At the same time, it provides evidence of a major skills deficit, which is reflected in

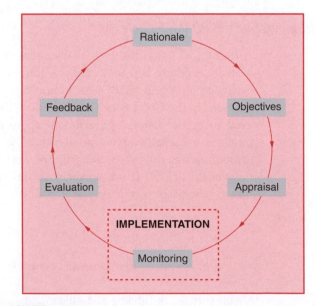

Figure 8.2 The ROAMEF cycle

Source: HM Treasury (2003, p.3)

skills at various levels when international comparisons are made. There is some evidence of different forms of market failure exerting an influence on policy, including:

- *Externalities:* leading to an underinvestment in training by employers where employers are concerned that, once trained, an employee will leave the firm before the firm has recouped its investment
- *Imperfect information:* leading to employees being unable to judge the quality of their training or appreciate the benefits
- *Credit market imperfections:* where low-paid employees in particular are likely to be credit constrained or unable to pay for training.

These market failures mean that the level of training provided by the market is likely to be inefficiently low from society's point of view. In the case of aspects of NHRD, it has been argued that the market in the UK is not failing per se, but simply that a low skill equilibrium has been reached which has particular negative consequences for industry, economy or society. The policy response is not always therefore about remedying a market failure but also about trying to change the equilibrium position (UKCES, 2010).Well-designed interventions, engaging employers and providing high-quality flexible approaches to skills development, may help to bridge gaps and improve NHRD.

Objectives

If an intervention is worthwhile, the objectives of the new policy, programme or project need to be clearly stated. Objectives may be expressed in general terms so that a range of options can be considered to meet them. There is usually a hierarchy of outcomes, outputs and targets that should be clearly set out. Objectives and their targets should be SMART:

- Specific
- Measurable
- Achievable
- Realistic
- Time bound.

An illustration of such an approach may propose an objective related to the development of skills, linked to an output in terms of number of training places and/or numbers completing training, which in turn may be linked to an outcome associated with the value of extra human capital or earnings capacity.

Appraisal

The purpose of appraisal is to help develop an intervention that meets the objectives of government action. Appraisal emphasizes consideration of the costs and benefits of different intervention models (including a do nothing model), with a view to identifying an approach that represents value for money. A key element of the appraisal is the treatment of uncertainty about the future, and techniques such as sensitivity and scenario analysis and methods may be used.

At the heart of appraisal lies the valuing of the costs and benefits of identi-fied options. This can be a far from straightforward process, as the relevant costs and benefits to government and society of all options should be valued and the net benefits or costs calculated. As suggested earlier, HRD-related intervention at the micro- and macro-level needs to show a return like other expenditures and is often viewed as a cost rather than an investment. Costs can be expressed in terms of relevant opportunity costs, fixed, variable, semi-variable and step costs, and inputs may come from accountants, economists and other specialists, depending on the type of appraisal. Benefits can be expressed in terms of taking into account the direct effects of interventions, as well as wider societal effects using real or estimated market prices, or the results of commissioned research to ascertain the benefits associated with an intervention. Various other adjustments to the value of costs and benefits may be made to take account of equity, inflation and discounting.

Some form of appraisal of risk should also be part of this stage of the evalua-tion process and account for the over-optimism that characterizes many project appraisers, as well as assessing uncertainties associated with the development and implementation of the intervention.

reflective question

1 What is the purpose of appraisal?
2 Who should undertake appraisal?
3 What are the weaknesses of the *Green Book* approach to appraisal?

Monitoring

All organizations keep records and notes and discuss what they are doing. This simple administration becomes monitoring when it encompasses the systematic collection of data, particularly relating to the financial management and outcomes of a policy, programme or project during implementation. It is a key element of performance management, which seeks to ensure the successful implementation of an HRD intervention. An effective monitoring system will:

- ensure that management information is measuring what is important in terms of inputs (such as costs), outputs, outcomes and impact
- put in place controls to ensure that the data are accurate
- provide regular financial and progress reports.

Monitoring will help to answer questions at various points in the life of a proj-ect, such as: How well are we doing? What difference are we making?

reflective question

1 Why should we monitor?
2 Who should monitor?
3 What is the difference between monitoring and evaluation?

Evaluation

The section below on evaluation in the workplace provides a more detailed intro-duction to various models of evaluation of HRD and provides an opportunity to explore further the nature of evaluation within the organization context. However, within the ROAMEF cycle, evaluation is identified as a discrete activity to be completed towards the end, or at the end, of a programme. The main aim of this stage is to examine what has happened against what was expected to happen. A key element of this is to establish what would have happened in the absence of the intervention (the counterfactual). Other important concepts to consider when analysing data as part of an evaluation are additionality, displacement and deadweight, (descriptions of these and many other concepts relevant to evaluation are available in the evaluation glossaries at www.oecd.org/dataoecd/29/21/2754804.pdf and www.un.org/Depts/oios/mecd/mecd_glossary/index.htm).

Feedback

Feedback is a critical part of the process since, without it, recognition of the value of an intervention, potential improvements to the process identified though the evaluation, and the value of the evaluation itself will not be recognized. For some time, the challenge of connecting the outcomes of research and evaluation processes with the inputs that professionals and politicians use to make judgements and take decisions has been recognized (Davies et al., 2000; Nutley et al., 2003) and forms an important dimension of the future of evaluation related to HRD intervention, which we will return to towards the end of this chapter.

Some observations on the ROAMEF approach

The ROAMEF framework, or variations of it, has become a central part of the approach to evaluation adopted by many organizations, especially those in the public sector, as a way of judging the success or otherwise of interventions. As well as being systematic and logical, the model is systemic as the feedback loop provides information about activities so that necessary improvements may be identified.

There are some obvious consequences of this model for the evaluation of NHRD. One of these is that evaluation appears as a distinct stage of the process and its placement towards the end of the process tends to mean that, in some instances, evaluation is something of an afterthought. In this case, evaluation tends to be completed towards the end of the programme, with a certain degree of pressure to undertake the activity quickly to reach a judgement on the success, or otherwise, of the programme. However, as outlined above, it can encourage reflection on various types of evaluation and appraisal activities throughout the policy-making process (similar to the CIRO model outlined below). Furthermore, by adopting an approach that takes account of the interests of various stakeholders, and cultural and contextual factors, as part of the evaluation process, a more responsive approach to evaluation can be adopted (Stake, 2004). This shifts the emphasis of evaluation away from proving towards feedback and learning.

Evaluation of HRD in the workplace

HRD is a collective process involving a range of people and activities. The purpose of evaluation will vary depending on the objectives of relevant stakeholders. Stakeholders may be both internal to the workplace and external providers or sponsors (Griggs et al., 2012). Good workplace evaluation will engage stakeholders at the ex ante, interim and ex post stages outlined above. Harrison (2005, p.144) argues for a participatory approach to evaluation 'that has been produced in collaboration with key partners'. However, the objectives of different stakeholders may vary. Any evaluation may need to adopt a range of methods and measures to evaluate the success in meeting such objectives. Examples of varying stakeholder objectives for training for middle managers are outlined in Table 8.1. We will return to these later.

It is important that HRD practitioners are aware of the philosophical constructs of the positivist and constructivist approaches to evaluation. However, Kenny et al. (1979) caution those involved with the practical aspects of evaluation to take a pragmatic approach. They argue that a rigorous scientific approach, however desirable, is not practicable in most workplace settings. However, if evaluation does not take place and/or is not subject to some rigour, the success or otherwise of training and development interventions undertaken by organizations remains unmeasured and unproven. It can be safely asserted that Kenny et al.'s writings are no less relevant today. There is access to greater quantities and (it is hoped) greater quality of data from which to evaluate. The need to justify and measure success has arguably never been more at the forefront of business and society's thinking. Edwards (2005) recognizes the current societal phenomenon of measuring performance and satisfaction, from the success of schools and the individual child's progress within them, to how happy we are with our hotel bed, bus or burger. She notes that this process of measurement is prevalent within the

Table 8.1 Stakeholder objectives for training middle managers

Stakeholder	Possible objectives
Individual	Obtain formal qualification to improve promotion prospects within or outside the organization
Line manager	Develop independence and confidence in role and reduce reliance on them as middle manager becomes more autonomous
HR department	Ensure consistency between managers and ensure all such managers are working within a common competency framework
External training provider/ sponsor (including colleges and universities)	Deliver/finance a well received training intervention which results in repeat business and/or positive publicity
Finance department	Provide positive financial return on investment
Senior management team	Improve overall organizational performance and meet strategic organizational objectives

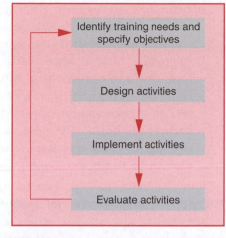

Figure 8.3 A four-stage training model

workplace via competence frameworks and staff appraisals. Phillips (1994a, 1994b) identifies the dangers of such a climate as being self-fulfilling, carrying out evaluation for evaluation's sake.

Evaluation fits within the four-stage training model, referred to in Chapters 6 and 7, and shown in Figure 8.3.

The potential danger here is to consider evaluation as the last activity of the cycle, that is, we evaluate at the end of a training and development intervention. The references made earlier to ex ante, interim and ex post should mean embedding evaluation as a continuing process throughout the cycle.

With the macro- and micro-contexts of evaluation of workplace training and development interventions in mind, it is appropriate to consider the purpose of evaluation and then critique some established models of evaluation in the workplace.

Purpose of evaluation

The evaluation of HRD activity at work involves the collection and interpretation of data. The results of this process can be used for a variety of purposes according to particular needs. For example, senior managers might need evidence that a programme of learning on customer service was having a measurable impact on performance.

Easterby-Smith (1994) identifies four distinct purposes of evaluation:

1 *Proving:* This shows that something happened. It may justify the costs of training, provide evidence for its ongoing delivery, and confirm it was the right thing to do (or, of course, the converse).

2 *Improving:* This identifies how the training intervention might be improved. The tendency is for this to be measured and acted on after the training has been completed. However, noting the need for ex ante and interim evaluation, this could be done at various stages of delivery.

3 *Learning:* Participants in HRD activities can review what they are learning and consider not only how to make changes in the context of the activity but also what might be used at work or in the future.

4 *Controlling:* This is often the focus of training departments. Evaluation results help to control the quality of training providers, the costs and the behaviour of the participants. Easterby-Smith (1994, p.19) notes the proliferation of such a purpose, particularly in large public sector organizations such as the police. The need to ensure consistency between central and regional (or in the case of education, individual local schools) is growing, as the tension to allow autonomy and yet ensure national standards increases.

In addition to these purposes, it is also suggested that because evaluation is concerned with the collection and interpretation of data, the results can be used to persuade and influence others of the value of HRD activities (Gold et al., 2010). It is a reminder that information can be used for a variety of purposes, as a representation of the facts or a version of events, told from a particular point of view (Clarke, 1999).

Evaluation models

Kirkpatrick's evaluation model

In 1959, Kirkpatrick published articles outlining techniques for evaluating training programmes. These articles described a four-level process for the evaluation of training. This process has been commonly referred to as the Kirkpatrick model. The four levels are shown in Figure 8.4.

This all seems quite logical and sensible but, as HRD in Practice 8.1 shows, it can be difficult to implement.

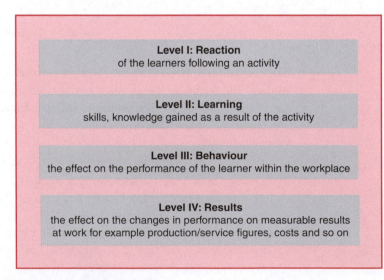

Figure 8.4 Levels of evaluation for training

Source: Adapted from Kirkpatrick (1998)

Evaluation is a tricky business

Rose spent three months evaluating evaluation activity and processes at National Westminster Bank. As a large organization with many operating divisions, the bank had around 12 different and separate HRD departments and functions. Rose found that most had the same simplistic approach: end of course questionnaires ruled, most were read by the HRD staff involved in the delivery and then filed. No analysis or reporting occurred, except in a few isolated examples. Rose also established the reasons for this:

1 No higher level evaluation occurred because it was considered too time and resource intensive to do so.
2 No information beyond learner satisfaction was ever asked for by senior or operational managers.
3 HRD staff had what they believed they needed to validate and improve their work and performance.

Because Rose investigated evaluation as part of the requirement of her professional qualification, she became an expert on the research and writing on evaluation and so reckoned the situation she found was untenable. She designed a corporate approach to evaluation for implementation across the bank and then spent the next nine months getting it accepted both corporately and in each of the bank's divisions. The approach didn't go into return on investment or anything overly sophisticated. But it did achieve the generation of data on changes in work behaviour and performance following learning and development events, and also the production of evaluation reports for every activity, which fed into quarterly and annual divisional and corporate reports on the value of investing in employee development. An improvement over what previously existed was achieved.

Basarab, cited in Kirkpatrick (1998), notes that the first two levels of the model refer to internal drivers for the training department to evaluate the effectiveness of its provision. The second two levels refer to external drivers, which evaluate the participants' contribution to business operations and overall organizational success.

Reaction

The first level measures the participants' reactions to the training and development intervention they have experienced. Typically, data are collected ex post, via happy sheets, or other forms of what Kirkpatrick (1998, p.20) refers to as measures of customer satisfaction. Figure 8.5 provides an example.

The reasons for measuring reactions are varied. It can help to measure what is learned by participants. It measures an emotional response, which, although not scientifically proven as accurate, does give relatively quick data from which to evaluate the effectiveness of the intervention. Both Kirkpatrick (1998) and Alliger et al. (1997) caution those interpreting data that positive reactions do not always equal a good training experience and negative reactions do not always equal a poor one. A baseline conclusion could be that positive reactions do not guarantee learning, but do make participants more amenable to further training and may encourage learning. Participants may also be more positive in their recounting of the experience to their manager and peers, thereby influencing future participants' expectations. Conversely, a negative reaction may disengage a participant from learning and future training activities. The bad publicity such reactions may produce in the wider workplace will not help the efforts of a training department to promote such interventions in the future.

Performance and Development Review Training

Please give your views and comments regarding your day						
Excellent 4	Very good 3	Satisfied 2	Not satisfied 1 (please give details)			
How did you rate the content of the programme?			4	3	2	1
Comments						
How did you rate the facilitator?			4	3	2	1
Comments						
How did you rate the quality of the handouts?			4	3	2	1
Comments						
How did you rate the venue?			4	3	2	1
Comments						
How was the quality of catering?			4	3	2	1
Comments						
Were your overall objectives met?			4	3	2	1
Your objectives were:						
Any other comments:						

Thank you for your feedback

Figure 8.5 Reaction-level evaluation sheet

Bramley (1999, p.367) suggests that some basic questions should be asked before reaction data are gathered. What information is needed? How can it be collected? It is suggested that happy sheets do not predict learning or changes to behaviour. These sheets are therefore limited to collecting data on only the first level of Kirkpatrick's model. Bramley (1999) also suggests that for repeat interventions to different groups of participants, the gauging of reactions only needs to be done a few times. Unless the intervention changes, the range of reactions is likely to be the same.

This critique of Kirkpatrick's first level supports the suggestion above that the evaluation made at this level is an internal driver for the training department. Positive reactions can justify the intervention and garner support and funding for its repetition. Negative reactions can improve the quality of the intervention, from redesigning training aspects to changing the sandwiches served at lunchtime. The quality of the intervention can be improved prior to delivery. Reactions can also be gathered from participants during the training intervention. This may be done via interim happy sheets or more qualitative focus groups. If there is a danger of negative reactions, such timely evaluation allows providers to amend and correct perceived shortcomings before the end of the event. This may result in more positive reactions later. Alliger et al. (1997) note that the 'usefulness' of learning is important for the application of training in the workplace. They urge designers to consider this at the planning stage. This relates to the need to engage relevant stakeholders from the outset in training intervention design. Workplace constraints and the perceptions of workers, when they return to their roles, are key to ensuring that these do not become blocks to effective learning and transfer of behaviour.

activity

Working with a partner, consider the following questions:
1 How important are emotional reactions as measures of a successful training intervention?
2 Do you agree with Bramley that such data need only be collected a few times for the same event?

Learning

Tests of learning are undertaken to achieve educational and professional qualifications via assessments. The evaluation of learning from training interventions can follow the same process; however, this is often not designed into such interventions. It may be undesirable from the participants' viewpoint, too costly to administrate, or the learning taking place may be deemed too difficult to measure. Some interventions require assessment. Training to drive a forklift truck or to be a workplace first aider needs certification via formal testing. Other interventions, for example coaching or diversity training, may have more subjective outcomes, which do not require testing and can be difficult, if not impossible, to assess. There is also an argument that what is tested is not necessarily what is actually learned as a result of an intervention. Bramley (1999, p.368) cautions that 'participation in an event does not equal learning'. A formula for measuring how much participants have learned can be expressed as the gain ratio:

$$\text{Gain ratio} \frac{\text{Post-test} - \text{Pre-test}}{\text{Possible} - \text{Pre-test}} \times 100$$

Bramley (1999, p.369) suggests that 'the average gain ratio across the group is a measure of the efficiency of the programme'. He argues that a group average of over 70 per cent is needed to be efficient. If the percentage is lower, Bramley suggests splitting the group into those with pre-knowledge and those without. The ratios may vary and show the intervention is appropriate for one group but not another. There is another danger with high pre-knowledge. The success of individual test results may be high, but this shows the extent of their prior learning, not the success of this specific training intervention. The importance of effective training needs analysis and a link to job analysis is critical here to the efficiency of the intervention (see Chapter 6).

Behaviour

Although evaluation of learning may evidence the extent to which something is learned, it will not predict the extent to which such learning will be used effectively in the workplace. The third element of Kirkpatrick's model seeks to address this. Bramley (1999) suggests a worker's performance is a combination of their ability and motivation and the opportunity to display such learning. He argues for the 'hardwiring' of learning when applied in the workplace. Rock (2006) provides extensive physiological evidence for the importance of using the hardwired brain as opposed to using working memory. The latter requires great physical and mental energy. For example, the first time someone drives a car, the levels of concentration and effort are significantly greater than for someone who has driven the same route for many years. So in the workplace, learning that can be regularly practised and reinforced is likely to result in changed behaviour.

This assumes that the worker has learned well from the training intervention, and that their ability to apply the learning to the workplace is within their mental and physical capacity. For example, an update on employment law may inform line managers of their legal rights and responsibilities to help them manage their staff more effectively, but it alone is unlikely to equip them to represent the work organization in legal proceedings. Workers may be more motivated to apply learning if they see an immediate benefit to themselves and, if they are turned into business objectives, to the overall success of the organization. If changed behaviour is likely to result in a pay increase or promotion, it too is likely to be more motivating and therefore more readily applied.

However, workers need opportunities to apply their learning. Recruitment and selection training may only be applied once or twice a year by some participants, as job vacancies to which they may apply come up infrequently. Opportunities may also be limited by an organization's culture. A training intervention that encourages creativity and enterprise may be stifled in the workplace by hierarchical organizational structures and an autocratic management style. Those having undertaken diversity training may be ridiculed in the workplace for perceived political correctness. Unless such participants are confident of the messages learned, they may suppress any application in order to retain the respect of immediate work colleagues.

In order to maximize the application of learning, Bramley (1999, p.370) recommends the use of practical performance tests, rather than written assessments, when evaluating at the learning level of Kirkpatrick's model. A study by Rouiller and Goldstein (1993, cited in Bramley 1999, p.374) identified seven scales to measure the transfer climate. The emphasis was on how line managers can influence the adoption of new behaviours after training. The scales focused on:

- goal setting
- the closeness of training behaviour to normal behaviour
- whether equipment was available in the workplace
- the autonomy of those trained to handle problems
- the degree of negative and positive feedback
- the impact of no feedback because line managers were too busy to provide it
- the degree of ridicule those trained received if they applied their learning.

From Rouiller and Goldstein's studies, the tests at the end of the training intervention only predicted 8 per cent of participants' behaviour transfer scores (that is, participants could score highly in the test but perform badly in the workplace). The transfer climate measure, described above, predicted 46 per cent (see Bramley 1999, p.374).

Results

This level of the Kirkpatrick model is the most obviously business focused. It evaluates the extent to which a training intervention has had a positive impact on overall organizational success. Bloom (1964, cited in Wilson, 2005, p.411) refers to the 'impact of learners' understanding, behaviour or attitudes'. The key here is to define what impact is sought from the training at its earliest development stage. Why has the intervention been commissioned? Who decided it should take place? What were the learning objectives? How do these objectives impact on organizational success? How will that success be measured?

Some outcomes of training interventions may be difficult if not impossible to measure (Edwards, 2005). Some interventions can give results that are relatively easy to measure numerically. Examples include the reduction in accidents following health and safety training, or an increase in sales after sales training. However, other interventions, such as leadership programmes, produce more subtle changes to behaviour and attitude, which may take years for statistical evidence of effectiveness to show.

reflective question   How would you measure the results of diversity training?

It may be helpful, given the complex nature of evaluating results, to establish how this level will be measured at the design stage of training. To be truly effective, the relevant stakeholders should decide on what measurements to make. Referring back to Table 8.1, the differing objectives of each stakeholder need different measurements of effectiveness. Table 8.2 suggests what these might be.

There is no end to the possible measures of effective results an organization could choose. However, to carry out all those suggested above would take significant time and expense. The key is to decide the measures at the planning stage and focus on them. The danger of this is that the measures chosen may not be the right ones. The cost of analysing data to provide evidence of results also needs to be factored in. One model for considering a range of measures of results is Kaplan and Norton's (1992) balanced scorecard. This combines financial and non-financial measures. Griggs et al. (2012) have developed an Educational Scorecard as an adaptation and this is discussed in more detail below

Table 8.2 Evaluation of development training for middle managers

Stakeholder	Possible objectives	Measurement of results
Individual	Obtain formal qualification to improve promotion prospects within or outside the organization	Awarded formal qualification; x% of participants obtain formal qualification
Line manager	Develop independence and confidence in role and reduce reliance on them as middle manager becomes more autonomous	Less line management time spent in support of middle managers No costs (financial or reputation) to the organization as a result of middle managers' autonomous decisions Financial savings to organization as line managers able to focus on own tasks
HR department	Ensure consistency between managers and that all such managers are working within a common competency framework	Fewer examples of middle managers operating outside organizational policies and processes; x% compliance with company rules, measure increase from baseline pre-training
External training provider/ sponsor (including colleges and universities)	Deliver/finance a well received training intervention which results in repeat business and/or positive publicity	Participant reacts positively via happy sheet evaluation. Workplace send more participants to similar events. Provider/sponsor has good news stories to publicise
Finance department	Provide positive financial return on investment	Financial benefits (more sales, profit, less wastage) outweigh cost of programme
Senior management team	Improve overall organizational performance and meet strategic organizational objectives	Improved business reputation, higher market share, better labour turnover, reduced absenteeism, organizational objectives met on time (or early)

activity

Working with a partner, go to the home page of Balanced Scorecard Institute –www. balancedscorecard.org

Explore how the process of the balanced scorecard might be used to measure results of HRD activity.

Another danger when trying to extract the direct cause and effect of HRD interventions is that extraneous factors may influence results. Improved market share may be due to better management training, but could be attributed to failings by an organization's competitors. Higher labour turnover after a training programme could evidence the unplanned result that managers have been trained for promotion, which they find sooner with other employers. The impact of government policies, the economic environment, and supplier and competitor behaviour are all examples of external factors that could influence results.

However, such limitations should not stop this level of evaluation from being attempted. It provides a direct link back to why the intervention was identified at the outset. It offers evidence for improvement or modification. It could provide justification to the training department and other stakeholders that the intervention is worthwhile and should be continued. Without such a business focus, any evaluation may miss the point and, as Phillips (1994a) states, become evaluation for evaluation's sake.

reflective question Think about some workplace training you have done or the course you are studying:

1 How would you evaluate its effectiveness?
2 How does your employer or course provider evaluate its effectiveness?
3 Does one aspect of Kirkpatrick's model apply more than any other?

The CIRO evaluation model

Harrison (2005, p.144) offers an overall critique of the Kirkpatrick model, cautioning its use in the workplace: 'All generic models must be tailored to fit specific needs, and even Kirkpatrick does not always suit context.' This omission is arguably overcome by the use of another evaluation model, the CIRO, which refers to:

- Context
- Inputs
- Reactions
- Outcomes.

The model was developed by Warr et al. (1970) and Hamblin (1994), originally for the evaluation of management training (see also Chapter 10). It supports the arguments made earlier in this chapter that evaluation activities should take place before, during and after the intervention.

Context

This is the ex ante aspect of evaluation. It aims to evaluate the context in which the training intervention took place. It will review the objectives and purpose of the training. Why was it commissioned? Who supported the intervention (and possibly, who did not)? It will evaluate how effective the preparation was for training. What briefings and support were put in place to ensure the training would meet its objectives? It should identify what worked and how the preparation and planning could be improved for future delivery. The context may also be wider in terms of the business climate in operation at the time of the intervention. If the training was delivered at a time of great success, would its outcomes be different at times of difficulty? Would managers be equally keen to release staff and engage in motivational activity to encourage behavioural change if the operating environment was less positive? Techniques for data collection would include interviews, questionnaires, briefings, written tests and feedback from others ahead of development.

Inputs

This evaluates the resources required to deliver the training intervention. There are tangible costs such as materials, external training consultant fees, room hire and subsistence. Harrison (2005, p.145) recommends accurate records are kept as these costs are incurred for review after the event. There should be a measure between the resources used and the extent to which they met the learning objectives set during the context stage above. It is important to account for hidden costs, such as staff time away from their job. The opportunity cost of not undertaking the training should be higher than the cost of taking staff out of the workplace for hours or days, in order to justify its efficiency and effectiveness. It could be argued that this is attempting to 'measure the unmeasurable' (Edwards, 2005, p.407). Measuring the cost of not doing something can be difficult to predict. Techniques for data collection would include session reviews, questionnaires, written or practical tests, feedback from others during events, and interviews.

Reactions

In many respects, this is similar in definition to the same term used in the Kirkpatrick model. It measures the emotional responses of participants to the training they have experienced. A broader range of reactions might be included here. For example, the reactions of the deliverers of the training and those of the managers, peers and subordinates to an individual's training will all inform the evaluation process. Harrison (2005, p.145) notes that there should not be 'an indiscriminate use of happy sheets', but that such data collection must be used and relate back to the objectives of the training. Techniques for data collection would include questionnaires and interviews.

Outcomes

This stage of the CIRO model initially sounds similar to the results level of the Kirkpatrick model. However, Hamblin (1994) developed a four-level structure of analysis for outcomes. These levels integrate the internal and external drivers identified by Basarab above. Indeed, Warr et al. referred to a continuum of immediate, intermediate and ultimate outcomes (see Harrison 2005, p.146). Hamblin's four levels are:

1 *The learner level:* measures what is learned by individuals, not unlike the learning level of Kirkpatrick's model.
2 *The workplace level:* measures changes in job behaviour (again not unlike the behaviour aspect of Kirkpatrick). Measurement may be in the form of appraisal, observation and from discussions with the individual, their peers and line manager.
3 *The team/departmental/unit level:* Hamblin includes within this level the operational measures (for example increases in production, reduced wastage) that can be attributed to a specific department.
4 *The organizational level:* these are the broader outcomes that may take time (years, possibly) to evaluate fully. It could include hard measures of increased share price or market share, or it could be softer outcomes of culture change, which, of course, could lead to hard measures.

Techniques for data collection would include questionnaires, interviews, debriefing meetings, feedback from others relating to behaviour and performance, measurements of performance and results achieved. HRD in Practice 8.2 shows the approach taken to data collection for a large programme of development for SME managers.

HRD in Practice 8.2

Senior Managers Coaching for Performance Programme at Morrisons

By December 2010 over 200 senior managers at the supermarket chain, Morrisons had undertaken a coaching programme using ideas from elite sports coaching and with the aim of developing managers From Shop Floor to Top Floor. The success of this was then evaluated as follows:

The aims of the evaluation were to evidence:

- the extent to which the programme had developed the coaching skills of participants
- the extent to which the programme led to improved personal or business performance
- whether the programme strengthened knowledge and action associated with Morrisons' core values
- how the programme might be improved.

The evaluation used the following framework:

- Reaction of participants
- Learning (skills and knowledge gained)
- Behaviour (the effect of performance in the workplace)
- Impact (the effect of changes in performance at work).

A third party, independent research organization was commissioned to undertake the evaluation, their responsibility being to design the evaluation, collect, analyse and report on findings.

The overall findings and implications for Morrisons were that the programme was valuable to participants and that the design of the programme was, on the whole, appropriate to the set objectives. Specific issues were identified for improvement which included organizational factors such as duration and location, along with strategic considerations relating to organizational culture. The evaluation exercise also identified further issues for deeper evaluation and the desirability for a longitudinal study of the participants evaluated.

Source: Devins and Clark (2011)

activity

Working in groups of three, consider how you would evaluate a training event on communication for ten participants in a management consultancy team. The task is to show that the three-hour event has had an impact on the participants and performance. For a site devoted to resources for evaluators go to **www.lancs.ac.uk/fss/projects/edres/ltsn-eval/**

These evaluation models provide a systematic route for gathering data relating to HRD activities, allowing the purpose of evaluation to be met. There are limitations, in that the models are stronger when activities are clearly identified and completed in a limited time frame, such as training courses. HRD involves a wider view of learning at work and beyond, however, and there is often a time-lag between learning events and use. For example, completion of a professional qualification, such as the Chartered Institute of Marketing, may not lead to an immediate impact at work.

A further difficulty arises from the range of variables that affect learning at work, where it becomes more precarious to attempt to link impact at the different levels implied by the models above. For example, reactions to an HRD event may be strong but participants find they are prevented from applying learning to their work, because of the opinions of their fellow workers, the requirements of their managers, or the way the work is defined. These are features of an organization's learning climate (see also Chapter 10).

Responsive models

The different purposes of evaluation and the difficulties of applying systematic models of evaluation have resulted in a number of approaches to evaluation which take more account of the interests of different stakeholders and their requirements. Such approaches are referred to as 'responsive evaluation' (Stake, 2004) and give more attention to cultural and context factors and providing feedback for ongoing learning.

One approach, presented by Patton (1997), focuses on utilization by those who have an interest in what is happening, so that they can make decisions based on evaluation information as it emerges. The role of the evaluator is to facilitate such judgements, 'rather than acting as a distant, independent judge'.

Another approach is concerned with making action possible, especially where learning is concerned with dealing with complex and difficult issues. This is referred to as 'action evaluation' (Rothman, 1997). Stakeholders can set goals, expressing values and motivations which can be shared with others in a project, and allowing for agreement on direction. Actions can be set and evaluated on a continuous basis.

activity

Go to **www.beyondintractability.org/bi-essay/action-evaluation** to find out more about action evaluation.

For more resources on helping learners to actively review HRD activities, go to **www. reviewing.co.uk**

Evaluation and organization change

Throughout this book, links have been made with the pressures on many organizations to change, leading to new definitions of what organizations do and how work is defined. For example, work is increasingly team based and requires interaction with others in different locations, physically and virtually, within and between organizations. Further, such work is frequently knowledge based and relies on the interactions of professionals and experts. Therefore organizations need to see change continuous with learning as a crucial capability to achieve this.

A number of approaches to supporting change through learning and evaluation have been presented. For example, Preskill and Torres (1999) present a model of evaluative enquiry based on key ideas relating to reflection, dialogue and the use of questions between change participants and stakeholders to surface assumptions and clarify values. The purpose of evaluation is to support learning and respond to the emerging patterns of information needs for decision-making. The process is ongoing and becomes part of work practices on a continuous basis. In a similar vein, Rix and Gold (2000) develop the idea of a reflective infrastructure to support change agents leading complex projects, where evaluation is completed throughout the project and data are interpreted and fed back to help improve the operation of the project, especially where difficulties occur.

Future direction of evaluation

Evaluation continues to develop and evolve as a discipline and a practice in response to new threats and challenges. Globalization will continue to influence organizations and evaluation practice, and the need to build evaluation capacity and to share experiences on an international scale, will require new competencies and set new ethical challenges at both the macro- and the micro-level. A recent CIPD report (2008) identified future changes in terms of, for example, the prevalence of coaching and e-learning as key learning and development practices, and employers' preferences for the development of skills such as interpersonal skills and communications skills. Evaluation models and methods will need to take account of these developments as they evolve. For some time, the challenge of connecting the outcomes of research and evaluation processes with the inputs that professionals and politicians use in making judgements and taking decisions has been recognized in the literature and, if evaluation is to have an impact on policy and practice, there remains a need to develop approaches that facilitate this. A key challenge will be to incorporate these developments into the future education and training of evaluators and those who plan to undertake evaluations of HRD activity at the macro- and micro-levels. There have been some calls for professionalizing evaluators and providing standards and/or competencies to underpin their learning and development (Russ-Eft, 2008).

In 2007, the CIPD published a report, *The Value of Learning: A New Model of Value and Evaluation* (Anderson, 2007). In many respects, the concerns of those evaluating learning in the workplace remain unchanged from those addressed by the models discussed earlier. However, the emphasis of Anderson's report is keenly focused on the external aspects of the evaluation of learning. The concept of return on investment is not new. Phillips and Phillips (2001) stressed the need in some work organizations for a positive business return on the investment made in training the workforce. Kearns (2005) sought to find a calculation process to measure the economic return of individual learning. In simple terms, such measurements could be seen as a more sophisticated version of cost–benefit analysis. The focus for the early 21st century is the externality of training's success. Any benefits to the individual learner or training department are viewed as relatively insignificant if the training does not benefit the whole organization.

As identified by Anderson (2007), the benefit is the extent to which training interventions are aligned with, and help achieve, the strategic objectives of the organization. She dismisses a 'one size fits all set of metrics' (p.2). Three key elements are identified for successful training and meaningful evaluation:

- the previously noted alignment
- the use of a number of evaluation methods
- working out which approaches are right for specific organizations.

What appears to frustrate many HRD professionals is the belief that training interventions in their organizations cannot be fully measured. In a CIPD survey (2006), 80 per cent believed that their training interventions delivered far more than they could prove. However, only 36 per cent of organizations surveyed specifically sought to evaluate training inputs against bottom line outputs. Detailed evaluation appears too time-consuming and of little interest to line managers. This appears contradictory to the earlier exhortations to involve line managers, as one of many stakeholders, in the evaluation process from the outset.

This is where the future of evaluation looks destined to change. Organizations are more concerned with investing in their 'human capital' (Anderson, 2007, p.3). One perpetual feature of people is their potential to be both an asset and a liability. This can depend on their personal behaviour, response to management and general attitude to work. The capital concept implies that human resources are investments. In order to improve the return on this expensive investment, it needs to be nurtured – only then can the asset be truly appreciated. If it is starved of investment (that is, development), it may well turn out to be a costly liability for the organization. This is a significant change from the historical view of training in many organizations. When times were hard, the training investment was often the first to be cut. Organizations have woken up to the dangers of this short-termism.

Anderson identifies two new models of evaluation that emphasize the importance of strategic alignment and the definition of value in different organizations. The first, the value and evaluation process, is a linear model noting three elements, shown in Figure 8.6.

The second model consolidates the concept of return on investment. It also affirms the position of graduate recruiters by introducing the concept of return on expectation. The model identifies four values and evaluation practices that organizations may use, shown in Figure 8.7a. These can be summarized as:

- Learning function measures, with senior management trust but short-term emphasis
- Return on investment measures, with a focus on metrics and a short-term emphasis
- Benchmark and capacity measures, focusing on metrics but with a longer-term emphasis
- Return on expectation measures with senior management trust and long-term emphasis (see Anderson, 2007, p.11)

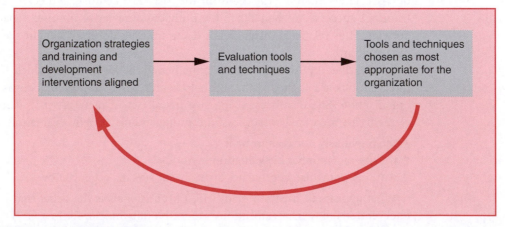

Figure 8.6 Value and evaluation process

Source: Adapted from Anderson (2007, p.5)

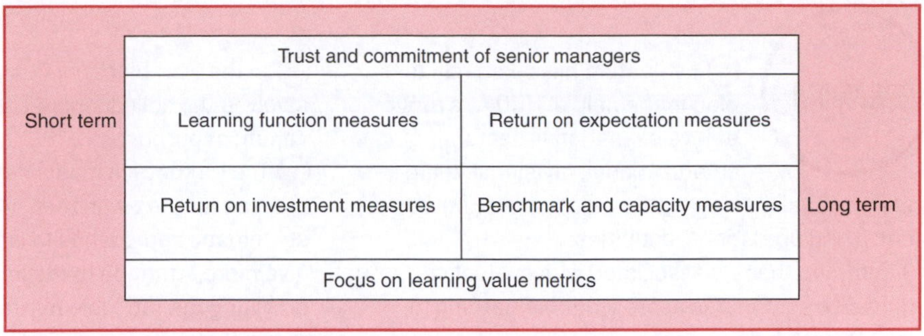

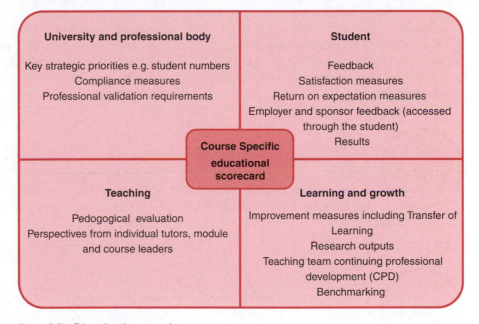

Figure 8.7a Measures of returns model

Source: Adapted from Anderson (2007, p.11)

Figure 8.7b Educational scorecard

Source: Griggs et al. (2012)

Griggs et al. (2012) have critiqued the concept of return on expectation as still focusing on one or two stakeholders, rather than viewing evaluation more holistically. Their Educational Scorecard has been specifically developed from an Educational Training Provider perspective, but endeavours to encapsulate all stakeholder needs within a single model (Figure 8.7b).

The term training intervention could be substituted for the term course if this model were to be adapted for the workplace.

Each approach to evaluation could be used exclusively or in conjunction with other approaches, subject to the needs of the organization, its strategic objectives, and the way training and development interventions are then aligned. Each approach identifies a different emphasis in the business; from short-term to long-term measures, and from learning metrics to senior management commitment to evidence organizational strategic success.

summary

○ Evaluation has a key role to play in the field of HRD at a range of levels – national, sectoral, organizational, divisional, team and individual – along with a wide range of strategic, tactical and operational activities.

○ Common themes associated with evaluation emphasize systematic approaches, something to evaluate such as processes, projects, programmes or policies, outcomes, impact and utility.

○ The logic of experimentation underpins much evaluation theory but recent years have seen a shift towards a more pragmatic approach and a more pluralist view of evaluation.

○ Evaluation of NHRD programmes is guided by a systematic approach referred to as the ROAMEF (rationale, objectives, appraisal, monitoring, evaluation and feedback) cycle.

○ In the workplace, evaluation of HRD activity at work involves the collection and interpretation of data for a variety of purposes.

○ The Kirkpatrick model describes a four-level process for the evaluation of training that underpins systematic approaches to evaluation. Other models give more attention to the importance of context in providing the rationale for training and the support that may or may not be provided.

○ Different purposes of evaluation and the difficulties of applying systematic models of evaluation have resulted in a number of approaches to evaluation that take more account of the interests of different stakeholders and their requirements.

○ Evaluation can be a vital part of change projects.

○ Future approaches to evaluation need to ensure that HRD activities are aligned with, and help to achieve, strategic objectives.

discussion questions

1 Can the value of HRD activity be proven?

2 Can evaluation ensure that public funds are spent efficiently and for the benefit of society?

3 How can different interests in HRD activity be satisfied in the workplace?

4 Should evaluation become a profession?

5 What is the value of evaluation in change projects at work?

note

1 There are important differences between constructivism and constructionism. However, we do not intend to explore these differences here. See Patton (2002) for a fuller explanation. http://www.berr.gov.uk/assets/biscore/economics-and-statistics/docs/e/10-1098-evaluation-strategy-evidence-based-decision-making.pdf

further reading

Hale, R. (2003) How training can add real value to the business, part 1. *Industrial and Commercial Training*, **35**(1): 29–32.

Holton, E. and Naquin, S. (2005) A critical analysis of HRD evaluation models from a decision-making perspective. *Human Resource Development Quarterly*, **16**(2): 257–80.

Russ-Eft, D. and Preskill, H. (2005) In search of the holy grail: return on investment evaluation in human resource development. *Advances in Developing Human Resources*, **7**(1): 71–85.

Tamkin, P., Yarnell, J. and Kerrin, M. (2002) *Kirkpatrick and Beyond: A Review of Models of Training Evaluation*. Brighton: Institute of Employment Studies.

references

Alliger, G.M., Tannenbaum, S.I., Bennett, W., Jr., Traver, H. and Shotland, A. (1997) A meta-analysis of the relations among training criteria. *Personnel Psychology*, **50**: 341–58.

Anderson, V. (2007) *The Value of Learning: A New Model of Value and Evaluation. London:* CIPD.

BIS (2010) *Skills for Sustainable Growth*. Strategy Document [online] http://www.bis.gov.uk/assets/biscore/further-education-skills/docs/s/10–1274-skills-for-sustainable-growth-strategy.pdf

Bramley, P. (1999) Evaluating training and development. In A. Landale (ed.) *Gower Handbook of Training and Development*, 3rd edn. Aldershot: Gower.

Burr, V. (1995) *Introduction to Social Constructionism*. London: Routledge.

Campbell, D.T. and Stanley, J.C. (1963) *Experimental and Quasi-Experimental Designs for Research*. Chicago: Rand McNally.

CIPD (Chartered Institute of Personnel and Development) (2006) *The Changing Role of the Trainer: Building a Learning Culture in your Organization*. London: CIPD.

CIPD (Chartered Institute of Personnel and Development) (2008) *Learning and Development: Annual Survey Report 2008*. London: CIPD.

Clarke, A. (1999) *Evaluation Research*. London: Sage.

Cronbach, L. (1982) *Designing Evaluations of Educational and Social Programs*. San Francisco, CA: Jossey-Bass.

Davies, H., Laycock, G., Nutley, S., Sebba, J. and Sheldon, T. (2000) A strategic approach to research and development. In H. Davies (ed.) *What Works?* Bristol: Policy Press.

de Vaus (1993) *Surveys in Social Research*, 3rd edn. London: University College London.

Devins, D. and Clark, J. (2011) *Evaluation of the Coaching for Performance Programme at Morrisons: Survey Results*. Leeds: Policy Research Institute, Leeds Metropolitan University.

DfE (2011) *Review of Vocational Education*. The Wolf Report. [Online] https://www.education.gov.uk/publications/standard/publicationDetail/Page1/DFE-00031–2011

Easterby-Smith, M. (1994) *Evaluating Management Development, Training and Education*, 2nd edn. Aldershot: Gower.

Edwards, Z.C. (2005) Evaluation and assessment. In J. Wilson (ed.) *Human Resource Development*, 2nd edn. London: Kogan Page.

Gergen, K.J. (1985) Social constructionist inquiry: context and implications. In K.J. Gergen and K. Davis (eds) *The Social Construction of the Person*. New York: Springer Verlag.

Gergen, K.J. (1994) *Relationships and Realities*. Cambridge, MA: Harvard University Press.

Gold, J., Thorpe, R. and Mumford, A. (2010) *Leadership and Management Development: Strategies for Action*. London: CIPD

Griggs, V., Blackburn, M. and Smith, J. (2012) *The Educational Scorecard: a More Appropriate Evaluation?* Proceedings of the 11th European Conference on Research Methods, University of Bolton, UK, 28–29 June 2012.

Guba, E.G. and Lincoln Y.S. (1989) *Fourth Generation Evaluation*. Newbury Park, CA: Sage.

Hamblin, A.C. (1994) *Evaluation and Control of Training*. Maidenhead: McGraw-Hill.

Harrison, R. (2005) *Learning and Development*, 4th edn. London: CIPD.

HM Treasury (2003) *The Green Book: Appraisal and Evaluation in Central Government*. London: TSO.

Kaplan, R.S. and Norton, D.P. (1992) The balanced scorecard: measures that drive performance. *Harvard Business Review*, **70**(1): 71–9.

Kearns, P. (2005) *Evaluating the ROI from Learning: How to Develop Value-based Training*. London: CIPD.

Kenny, J. Donnelly, E. and Reid, M. (1979) *Manpower Training and Development*, 2nd edn. London: IPM.

Kirkpatrick, D.L. (1998) *Evaluating Training Programs*, 2nd edn. San Francisco, CA: Berrett-Koehler.

LSC (Learning and Skills Council) (2006) *Impact Evaluation of the National Phase of the Leadership and Management Development Programme*. Coventry: LSC National Office.

Maxwell, J.A. and Lincoln, Y.S. (1990) Methodology and epistemology for social science. *Harvard Educational Review*, **60**(4): 497–512.

Nutley, S., Percy-Smith, J. and Solesbury, W. (2003) *Models of Research Impact: A Cross Sector Review of Literature and Practice*. London: Learning and Skills Development Agency.

Patton, M. (1997) *Utilization-focused Evaluation*, 3rd edn. Thousand Oaks, CA: Sage.

Patton, M.Q. (2002) *Qualitative Evaluation and Research Methods*, 2nd edn. Thousand Oaks, CA: Sage.

Pawson, R. and Tilley, N. (1997) *Realistic Evaluation*. London: Sage.

Pearce, W.B. (1992) A 'camper's guide' to constructionisms. *Human Systems*, **3**: 136–61.

Phillips, J.J. (1994a) *Measuring Return on Investment*, vol. 1. Alexandria, VA: American Society for Training and Development.

Phillips, J.J. (1994b) *Measuring Return on Investment*, vol. 2. Alexandria, VA: American Society for Training and Development.

Phillips, P.P. and Phillips, J.J. (2001) *Measuring Return on Investment,* vol. 3. Alexandria, VA: American Society of Training and Development.

Preskill, H.S. and Torres, R.T. (1999) *Evaluative Inquiry for Learning in Organizations*. Thousand Oaks, CA: Sage.

Rix, M. and Gold, J. (2000) With a little help from my academic friend: mentoring change agents. *Mentoring and Tutoring*, **8**(1): 47–62.

Rock, D. (2006) *Quiet Leadership: Six Steps to Transforming Performance at Work*. London: HarperCollins.

Rossi, P.H. and Freeman H.E. (1993) *Evaluation: A Systematic Approach*. London: Sage.

Rothman, J. (1997) *Resolving Identity-based Conflict in Nations, Organizations, and Communities*. San Francisco: Jossey-Bass.

Russ-Eft, D. (2008) *Expanding Scope of Evaluation in Today's Organizations*, paper presented at the International HRD Conference, Lille.

Scriven, M. (1980) *The Logic of Evaluation*. Inverness, CA: Edgepress.

Scriven, M. (1991) *Evaluation Thesaurus*, 4th edn. Thousand Oaks, CA: Sage.

Shotter, J. (1993) *Conversational Realities*. London: Sage.

Stake, R.E. (2004) *Standards Based and Responsive Evaluation*. Thousand Oaks, CA: Sage.

UKCES (2010) *Ambition 2020. World Class Skills and Jobs for the UK*. UK Commission for Employment and Skills. [online] http://www.ukces.org.uk/assets/ukces/docs/publications/ambition-2020-the-2010-report.pdf

Warr, P.B., Bird, M.W. and Rackham, N. (1970) *Evaluation of Management Training*. Aldershot: Gower.

Weiss, C.H. (1980) Knowledge creep and decision accretion, *Knowledge: Creation, Diffusion, Utilisation*, **1**: 381–404.

Weiss, C.H. (1995) Nothing as practical as good theory: exploring theory-based evaluation for comprehensive community initiatives for children and families. In J. Connell, A.C. Kubisch, L.B. Schorr and C.H. Weiss (eds) *New Approaches to Evaluating Community Initiatives: Concepts, Methods and Contexts*. Washington D.C.: Aspen Institute.

Weiss, C.H. (1998) Have we learned anything new about evaluation? *American Journal of Evaluation*, **19**(1): 21–33.

Wilson, J. (ed.) (2005) *Human Resource Development*, 2nd edn. London: Kogan Page.

Investigating a training and learning problem: school lunchtime supervisors

Most people can remember school dinners! In recent years Jamie Oliver has campaigned widely to change attitudes and behaviour in relation to healthy food in Britain's schools. The impact of Jamie Oliver's campaigning encouraged Hull City Council to launch a free school dinner programme, offering free school meals to all primary school children. As part of the monitoring of the project, it was highlighted that there was a lack of training for lunchtime supervisors. Lunchtime supervisors, as distinct from the catering staff who prepare and serve the food, provide supervision for children during the lunch break. Existing training was ad hoc with uncertain impact on performance. In order to investigate the perceived lack of training, Hull City Council commissioned the University of Hull to undertake a study of the training needs of lunchtime supervisors in 71 Hull primary schools.

All 71 schools were sent a survey to hand out to their lunchtime supervisors, asking questions about their role, their likes and dislikes, what they found challenging and the support they received. Six schools were selected to take part in a more in-depth study; chosen to vary in size, location and economic prosperity of the area. A representative from Hull University interviewed both the head teachers and the lunchtime supervisors over a period of several months. She spent a week working as a lunchtime supervisor and spoke to lunchtime supervisors, in groups and one-to-one, to understand what was required in the role and how the role was managed. A number of needs were identified:

- Head teachers wanted supervisors to be trained in encouraging and managing playground activities
- The lunchtime supervisors themselves identified managing behaviour and resolving conflict as a key requirement
- The project manager highlighted developing confidence, understanding the role and understanding children's needs as critical requirements.

Additionally, as part of the investigation, a number of other important contextual factors were highlighted:

- The government, in the form of Ofsted, measures the quality of lunchtime supervision as one factor in its assessment of school performance
- Hull City Council had reported difficulties in recruiting lunchtime supervisors with the right skills. The work is low paid and confined to the lunchtime period
- Many of the existing supervisors had left school without qualifications. Few had undertaken any sort of formal learning since leaving school
- The role of lunchtime supervisors appeared to be undervalued by head teachers, teachers, children and even the employees themselves
- There was a lack of integration of the supervisors with the wider school team, highlighting the need to address their role and perceptions of their role
- Some existing staff had been in the role for over 20 years, believed their experience was sufficient and questioned the need for training
- A number of existing staff had other part-time jobs, thus limiting their availability for training.

Although the project identified a number of training needs the case highlighted some broader issues. Schools are managed as businesses and have to control tight budgets. A training initiative for lunchtime supervisors would have to compete with other priorities. On what basis would such a decision be taken? And what about the supervisors themselves? The job is almost exclusively held by women who are trapped in a low-skill cycle. Due to poor education, they can obtain only low-skilled work. In these low-skilled roles, they do not receive training or development to enhance their skills and have little potential to move out of these low-skilled, low-paid jobs.

Source: Stead, F., Griggs, V. and Holden, R.J. (2007) The Case of the Hull Dinner Ladies: Interview with Faye Stead, Leeds Metropolitan University

Questions

1 Why do you feel it was important to undertake a training needs analysis in respect of this group of employees?
2 From the findings of the investigation what are the main decisions that would need to be taken in moving forward?
3 Identify other employee groups trapped in low-skill cycles. Consider different economic sectors. Is it more likely to be a problem in some sectors than others? Should an organization be responsible for offering HRD opportunities to all its employees? Should HRD professionals engage in this debate, or should they focus on the effect of HRD on business goals?

Activities

1 Develop an outline proposal to meet the training needs identified. Include in the proposal:
  - the method(s) to be used
  - how the proposed training will reflect important ideas about learning and key principles of learning
  - consideration of the characteristics of this particular group of trainees
  - where the training might take place and when
  - a consideration of resources and costs in relation to the proposed training.

2 Consider the evaluation of the proposed training. As in 1, develop an outline proposal, which addresses:
  - an appropriate framework for the approach to be adopted for the evaluation
  - how evaluation data might best be collected
  - the value of the training activity to different stakeholders
  - the extent to which the process of evaluation employed might further assist the learning of the lunchtime supervisors

looking **at:**
HRD at work

Beyond the basics of HRD practice, there are many exciting developments and areas of application. None more so than the combination of technology and human beings (Chapter 9: E-Learning). We also know that learning at work varies across different organizations and even within the same organization and this raises issues about what we call learning climates. We also know this is connected to whether knowledge is created and shared (Chapter 10: Workplace Learning and Knowledge Management). Leaders and managers have a role to play in this and for many years there has been concern about how to develop good leaders and managers (Chapter 11: Leadership and Management Development). Most of us work in groups or teams so there has been a lot of interest in how to help groups become teams and how to help them develop (Chapter 12: Team Development). There has also been a lot of interest in recent years in identifying and developing people of talent, although there are debates about what talent actually means and different ways of developing talented staff. We do know that coaching and mentoring are often used (Chapter 13: Talent and Career Development). In some cases, learning and potential might be inhibited by stereotypes about ethnicity, colour, religion, sex, disability or sexual orientation; although in many organizations, there is a promotion of the value of diversity. The law is quite clear about discrimination but attitudes play a role too (Chapter 14: HRD and Diversity).

Finally, two topics that we feel are very relevant for your future journey. Firstly, after you qualify as a professional you are likely to be required to show continuing professional development (CPD). However, given the rate of change in the world, everyone will need to become a lifelong learner to some degree (Chapter 15: Continuing Professional Development and Lifelong Learning). Secondly, you might have expectations about your own learning once you graduate and how far your skills have made you employable (Chapter 16: Graduates and Graduate Employability).

E-Learning

Rick Holden and Jim Stewart

Chapter learning outcomes

After studying this chapter, you should be able to:

- Explain the meaning of e-learning
- Position e-learning within developments in open and distance learning and technology-based learning
- Consider different configurations of e-learning within HRD practice
- Understand key issues in the management of an e-learning resource
- Critically assess the contribution of e-learning within HRD practice

Chapter outline

Introduction

If we were to surmise that our sailor is engaged in some form of learning activity what might this be? There are a range of possibilities. Through his laptop he might be engaged in a network discussion, accessing a learning module from his company's intranet, reflecting on his personal development through an online diagnostic, accessing a free-standing tutorial guide on effective sailing! The point is that the power of today's technology can take us a long way from traditional ways of training and learning. This chapter seeks to explore how HRD practice is being influenced by what is termed e-learning. We view e-learning as a method of, or approach to, training and learning vis-à-vis other possibilities, including lectures, coaching and one-to-one instruction (see Chapter 7); one option amongst many in terms of how training and learning needs can be addressed. The first section of the chapter seeks to locate e-learning within a broader set of developments in terms of how we approach learning and development (L&D).

E-learning: revolution or evolution?

E-learning has been hailed by some as reflecting a revolution in learning (Galagan, 2000; Badran, 2007). If our sailor is indeed engaged in learning of some sort this might be testimony to this revolution in practice. However, we prefer to think of it as more evolutionary. To help explain this point it is first useful to consider two definitions of e-learning:

> E-learning refers to the use of a collection of learning materials using digital technologies, which enable, distribute and enhance learning
>
> Fee (2009)

> E-Learning is instructional content or learning experiences delivered or enabled by electronic technologies, including the internet, Web 2.0, intranets and extranets
>
> Bondarouk and Ruel (2010)

Advanced, new technology is at the heart of both definitions. But does the harnessing of information and communication technology (ICT) constitute a revolution? Technology has been used throughout history to deliver and support learning. Looking back we might identify the slate, chalk and blackboards, radio and television, as all significant in their time. Is learning via a laptop or a mobile phone really any different?

Open and distance learning and machine-based learning

We can usefully locate this evolutionary development in broader developments in how we approach and seek to manage learning and development. Whilst there is an important distinction between distance education and open learning (see, for example, Hodgson et al., 1987) the term open and distance learning (ODL) refers to that practice which has sought to increase access to learning, enhance choice and give learners a greater sense of autonomy and responsibility for learning (Calvert, 2006). Whereas in the early days of ODL the delivery mechanism incorporated technologies such as print based media, cassettes and videos, today ODL is often taken to be synonymous with e-learning (http://edutechwiki.unige.ch/en/Open_and_distance_learning) using the latest computer and web-based technologies.

An even more direct line can be drawn between e-learning as practiced today and machine-based learning. Teaching machines can be traced back to the 1920s although the work of Skinner in the 1950s and 1960s (Hills, 2003) is more significant. Skinner is perhaps most famous for his work with pigeons and rats in terms of a behaviourist understanding of learning (see also Chapter 5). However, he was enormously influential in the development of machine-based learning.

activity

Watch the clip of Skinner explaining and advocating machine-based learning on You Tube at www.youtube.com/watch?v=EXR9Ft8rzhk

The pedagogy underpinning Skinner's advocacy of machine-based learning is of programmed learning. Programmed learning has three elements: it delivers information in small bites, it is self-paced by the learner, and it provides immediate feedback, both positive and negative, to the learner (Ravenscroft, 2001). Early teaching machines provided a linear sequence of prescribed materials or content. With the development of branching programmes (see also Aldrich, 2005), we can see the origin of many of today's e-learning packages. Branching programmes introduced alternative sequences or pathways related to a learner's response. Figure 9.1 illustrates a Bristol Tutor teaching machine. The content (for example, How to Write a Technical Report) is loaded onto the machine via a reel of specially constructed paper. The learner views the material through the window or screen and navigates their way through the material via the push buttons on the lower part of the console. These buttons interact with the content and control what is visible to the learner. At various points questions are asked to test understanding and enable progression or the presentation of remedial material where incorrect responses are made.

reflective question

Think about any sort of learning you have accessed via your lap top. Whilst a little heavy to take on the bus, do you feel the Bristol Tutor (Figure 9.1) operates significantly differently in terms of some of the fundamental aspects of the process of learning?

Our point is that whilst on the face of it there is a world of difference between the Bristol Tutor teaching machine and today's iPads and mobile phones nonetheless technology is being harnessed to deliver and support learning. There are examples of e-learning on the market today which, in terms of how learning content is designed and presented, are not substantively different from that delivered via the Bristol Tutor. The evolutionary nature of e-learning and

Figure 9.1 A teaching machine: the 'Bristol Tutor'

its antecedents are hopefully more apparent using this illustration. The comparison also begins to raise some important questions about the characteristics of e-learning in the 2010s; for example in relation to access, flexibility, learner control and interactivity. We will return to these issues as the chapter progresses. First we look to the different contexts and configurations that we can identify in current e-learning practice and which enables an important theoretical positioning of e-learning.

Perspectives on e-learning practice

Contexts and applications

Researchers and practitioners agree that e-learning is growing rapidly and that such growth will continue. One estimate indicates the global market for e-learning will reach $107.3 billion by the year 2015 (www.prweb.com/ releases/elearning/corporate_elearning/prweb4531974.htm) an increase of 300 per cent from the position in 2009. This global market includes three distinct contexts.

First is formal education. The rise in the use of e-learning in this context is also associated with government policy. Chapter 16 demonstrates the global expansion of higher education, much of which is being supported by the use of e-learning. In many countries e-learning has moved rapidly from the margins to being a predominant form of post-secondary education. Data from the USA, for example, indicates that a quarter of all students in post-secondary education were taking fully online courses in 2008 (Allen & Seaman, 2008) and a report by Ambient Insight Research suggests that in 2009 almost half of post-secondary students in the USA were taking some or all of their courses online. It is projected that this figure will rise to 81 per cent by 2014. E-learning is playing a significant part in what appears to be a major restructuring of higher education (Garrett et al., 2005) as demand increases exponentially in the developing economies of the world where e-learning facilitates provision across widely dispersed populations. Guodong and Zhongjiao (2010) provide an interesting commentary of the case in China.

The second major context is at work. Whilst the United States and Europe dominate the e-learning market with more than a 70 per cent share of the revenues, Asia-Pacific represents the fastest growing market for e-learning, with revenues projected to grow at a compounded annual rate of more than 20 per cent in 2012–2015 (http://www.prweb.com/releases/elearning/corporate_elearning/prweb4531974.htm). In the UK CIPD (2011a) data indicates that over three-quarters of organizations use e-learning and project continued growth.

Third, and extending outside the formal institutions of work and education, is society and communities. E-learning is seen by governments as a way of increasing the amount of learning as well as extending the range of people involved. The UK's **learndirect** initiative was launched in 2000. It was given a remit to use new technology to transform the delivery of learning and skills across England, Wales and Northern Ireland. **learndirect** has become the UK's leading e-learning provider, reaching into local communities, the workplace and people's homes with flexible, accessible and supported online learning. According to its website (www.learndirect.co.uk) 10,000 people log on and learn with **learndirect** every day; more than 3.5m people have improved their skills since 2000 and more than 500,000 Skills for Life test passes have been achieved with them.

There are a number of significant factors that explain the rise in the popularity and use of e-learning (for a fuller discussion see also Pollard and Hillage, 2001; Fee, 2009). A clear link can be identified between the points raised above about the positioning of e-learning within broader developments in open/distance learning and machine-based learning and the following factors:

Reduced costs: a key factor in many decisions to adopt e-learning is its potential to deliver to large numbers of learners (and who may be geographically dispersed), at a at lower costs than more traditional interventions;

Access: e-learning can be used anywhere and is accessible 24/7 provided the necessary hardware and connectivity are available;

Technological capability: speed and quality of ICT facilitates access and current technology (internet, Web 2.0, Skype etc.) supports a wide variety of learning activity. Also, the sophistication of today's e-learning design technologies ensure material can be easily and quickly updated to meet changing requirements;

Immediacy: organizations using e-learning for workforce development claim that the just-in-time benefits of e-learning are of real value;

Standardization and consistency: carefully designed learning materials and resources delivered via e-learning ensure that each and every participant gets the same content delivered in the same way, such as in training for standards (financial products, compliance etc.).

Consideration of HRD in Practice 9.1 clearly indicates the importance of the first two points above in the rationale for two organizations to deploy e-learning.

HRD
in Practice
9.1

E-learning for widely dispersed staff

The communications company Siemens utilizes e-learning to deliver training to staff dispersed across the globe. For example, a team of six or seven engineers working on a project in Africa need training but it is not cost-effective to bring them back to Europe for a short training session. Their project has a limited life and so it is also not cost-effective to set up a training infrastructure at their worksite.

E-learning was the answer that impressed a training manager from Royal and Caribbean Cruise Lines, who has a similar problem of widely dispersed and mobile staff. He was also impressed with the apparent facility of web-based training to deliver a common standard of training, wherever staff happen to be.

Source: Based on Brockett (2008)

Inextricably interlinked with a number of the points highlighted above, though, is what Njenga and Fourie (2010) refer to as a techno-positivist ideology; 'compulsory enthusiasm about technology that is being created, propagated and channelled repeatedly by the people who stand to gain either economically, socially, politically or otherwise' (p.200). The figures for the projected increase in the global market for e-learning are clear testimony to the fact that those already selling technology-based education and training products have a vested interest in promoting the use and purported benefits of e-learning. Respondents to a CIPD survey on e-learning (2004) were clear that those companies selling products related to e-learning were a major factor in driving adoption and increased use.

An additional factor explaining the use of and growth in e-learning has been in part the outcome of public policy support and funding and other government-led initiatives for its promotion. Sambrook (2003) identifies a focus by national governments and their agencies on, for example, lifelong learning and work-based learning as part of their policy initiatives.

At this point we should emphasize that the case for e-learning in relation to some of the factors highlighted above is far from proven. We will have more to say about issues such as the effectiveness of learning, for example, later in this chapter. We look now to a consideration of different types of e-learning.

Types of e-learning

activity Consider these three learning and development scenarios:

1) A group of customer service advisors are directed to some pre-course learning materials on understanding other people located on the company's intranet, prior to a workshop on effective interpersonal skills.

2) A trainee helicopter pilot spends four hours each day for three weeks in the company's flight simulator.

3) Five students form a learning set as part of a UK Business School's MBA programme. But they are located in Manchester, Tokyo, Birmingham, Lahore and Delhi. They are working together on a joint project using Blackboard, the university's virtual learning platform.

Think about the learning processes that will be taking place in each of these scenarios.

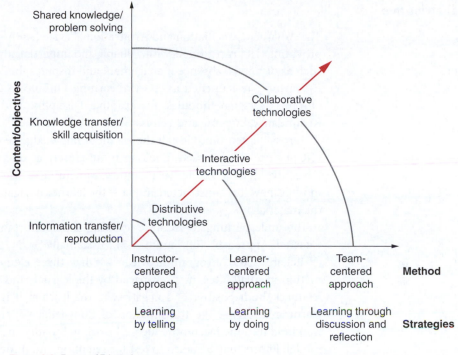

Figure 9.2 Types of E-learning

Source: Tronsden, 2003, p. 6

All are examples of e-learning sitting comfortably with one or other of our definitions cited above. But clearly they are different in terms of what actually happens. The model highlighted in Figure 9.2 helps us make sense of the range of e-learning practices. It also serves as a useful device to begin to raise important questions aboiut e-learning, the pedagogy involved and its likely effectiveness as a way of meeting learning and development needs.

It is important to highlight the two axes on which the model is built. Firstly, the vertical axis is about the content of the e-learning; the purpose to which it is being put. Chapter 7 identifies the importance of the construction of objectives as a basis for effective learning. The vertical axis in the model seeks to distinguish between three types of objectives: those relating to information, those relating to skills and the transfer of knowledge, and those relating to problem-solving scenarios.

Secondly, the horizontal axis relates to a fundamental aspect of learning: the approach or teaching/learning strategy that might be adopted. Again three distinctions are made, effectively captured by the descriptors: learning by telling, learning by doing and learning by reflection and discussion. The basis is thus established for three ideal types of e-learning: distributive, interactive and collaborative. It is useful to explore each of these in terms of what they may look like in practice.

Distributive

The Advisory Conciliation and Arbitration Service (ACAS) have a reputation for providing HR practitioners with valuable and impartial advice on a range of areas such as dismissal, absence management and disputes. In 2007 it launched ACAS E-Learning; re-launched as ACAS Learning OnLine in 2013. ACAS Learning OnLine offers ten modules, for example Discipline and Grievance, Handling Redundancy, Bullying and Harassment.

Across the ten modules all the essential knowledge required to inform good HR practice is addressed. Looking more closely at one module, Equality and Diversity, Figures 9.3 and 9.4 capture something of the look and feel of the module, how it is constructed and how the learner navigates his/her way through the material.

The underpinning to ACAS e-learning sits comfortably with an 'Instructor Centred Approach' (cf Figure 9.2). Essentially it is programmed learning (Pritchard 2009). Programmed learning has three elements: it delivers information in small bites, it is self-paced by the learner, and it provides immediate feedback, both positive and negative, to the learner. It is primarily a model of learning involving the transmission of knowledge. There is minimal interaction built into the learning. Much e-learning, broadly speaking, is based on this model. Efforts may be taken to test for retention and understanding through use of questions and tests etc. but essentially it is a didactic process: from instructor/trainer (author of the content) to the learner/trainee.

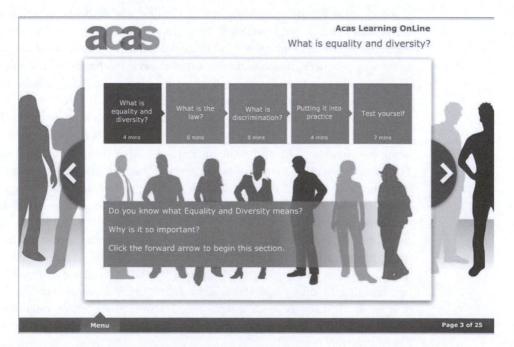

Figure 9.3 Extract from Equality & Diversity module (ACAS Learning OnLine)

Source: Reproduced by permission of ACAS Learning OnLine.

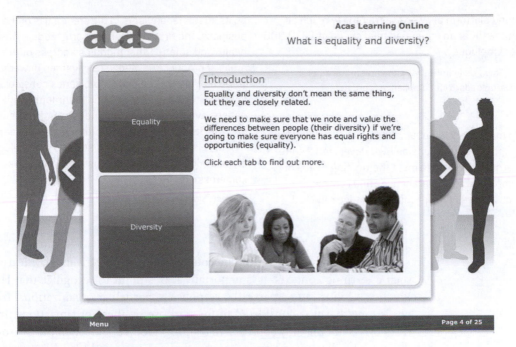

Figure 9.4 Extract from Equality & Diversity module (ACAS Learning OnLine)

Source: Reproduced by permission of ACAS Learning OnLine.

activity

Register at the ACAS e-learning site:

https://elearning.acas.org.uk/

Explore a module you have some interest in and think carefully about the approach and techniques ACAS use to deliver the e-learning.

The underpinning to ACAS E-Learning sits comfortably with an instructor centred approach (see Figure 9.2). Essentially it is programmed learning (Pritchard, 2009), which has three elements: it delivers information in small bites, it is self-paced by the learner, and it provides immediate feedback, both positive and negative, to the learner. It is a primarily a model of learning involving the transmission of knowledge. There is minimal interaction built into the learning. Much e-learning, broadly speaking, is based on this model. Efforts may be taken to test for retention and understanding through the use of questions and tests, but essentially it is a didactic process: from instructor/trainer (author of the content) to the learner/trainee.

The two examples below illustrate such e-learning in HRD in Practice 9.2.

Clydesdale and Yorkshire Banks

HRD in Practice 9.2

The National Australia Group, Europe, of which the Clydesdale and Yorkshire Banks are a part, has introduced a Learning Campus containing more than 30 modules of e-learning material covering the areas of legislative and compliance training. It estimated an approximate cost of £10.7m per year to deliver the material via workshops, but delivery via the e-learning platform allowed the training to reach all staff in the UK at an estimated total spend of £230,000 (£2 per employee).

Source: Towards Maturity www.towardsmaturity.org/elements/uploads/NAG_Compliance_Story.pdf

B&Q

To help meet the additional training needs caused by strong growth and expansion B&Q developed a suite of e-learning modules to meet the training needs of staff employed at its warehouses and centres. The modules address the specific knowledge required by its customer advisers in different parts of the business. The first, and compulsory, module was health and safety. Other modules address different areas of product knowledge (e.g. garden power tools). Three modules in the Showroom series consider issues involved in selling kitchens and bathrooms, with options available to meet the needs of typical customers. The development of the initial series of e-learning modules is regarded as a first stage in the deployment of e-learning to achieve low cost delivery and learning compression.

Source: Sloman, 2005

We will have more to say in due course about the effectiveness of learning in such e-learning contexts. It is important at this point to recognize that HRD in Practice 9.2 illustrates a particular response to particular organizational training needs; one that was considered fit for purpose by these organizations. In both cases this is not the only approach to training adopted, indeed in the case of B&Q the modules illustrated have subsequently been extended beyond a stand-alone package to link up with other strategies, for example coaching.

Interactive

Whilst knowledge is a key component of many training needs (see also Chapter 6) organizations also highlight different skills and behavioural competencies they wish to encourage within their workforce. Consider, for example, Harvey Nichol's desire to train their shop floor staff in behaviours linked to their main brand values (such as welcoming by using eye contact and positive body language) as noted in Chapter 7. The interactive type of e-learning purports to be a way of harnessing technology to assist in this process. Reference back to Figure 9.2 indicates a teaching and learning strategy of learning by doing. A move away from a model of programmed learning and towards experiential learning (see also Chapter 4) is evident.

A leading player in the design and development of interactive e-learning is Engage in Learning. The company has a range of management and soft skills titles, for example, leadership, customer service, performance coaching and influencing skills. In the constraints of this chapter we can only seek to highlight one key component of what their e-learning tries to do. In Figures 9.5 and 9.6 two screen shots from two different online courses illustrate how content is used imaginatively to illustrate real practice and from which any trainee can endeavour to learn appropriate behaviours and skills. There is an element of 'what would you do now?' in the context of an unfolding scenario. In the example it is an angry customer. Dependent upon choice appropriate feedback is provided.

HRD in Practice 9.3 provides a case study of how one organization has used an Engage in Learning title to meet a particular set of identified needs.

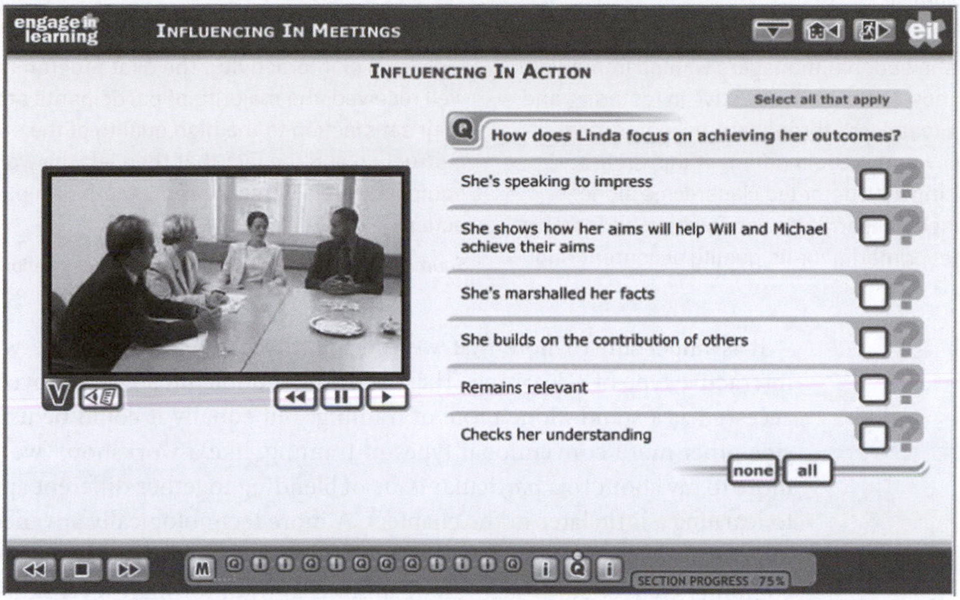

INFLUENCING IN ACTION

Select all that apply

Q How does Linda focus on achieving her outcomes?

She's speaking to impress

She shows how her aims will help Will and Michael achieve their aims

She's marshalled her facts

She builds on the contribution of others

Remains relevant

Checks her understanding

none   all

SECTION PROGRESS 75%

Figure 9.5 Extract from influencing skills (engage in learning)

Source: Reproduced by permission of Balance Learning.

THE ANGRY CUSTOMER

ACKNOWLEDGING THE PROBLEM

Q What would you say next?

"I'm sorry that you've had such a difficult time. I don't have you listed for today. Do you have the appointment card with you?"

"I'm so sorry. I'll see if I can find someone to help you"

"I don't blame you for being angry. We are in complete chaos. I don't know how anybody ever keeps any appointments straight around here"

section progress 0 5 4 %

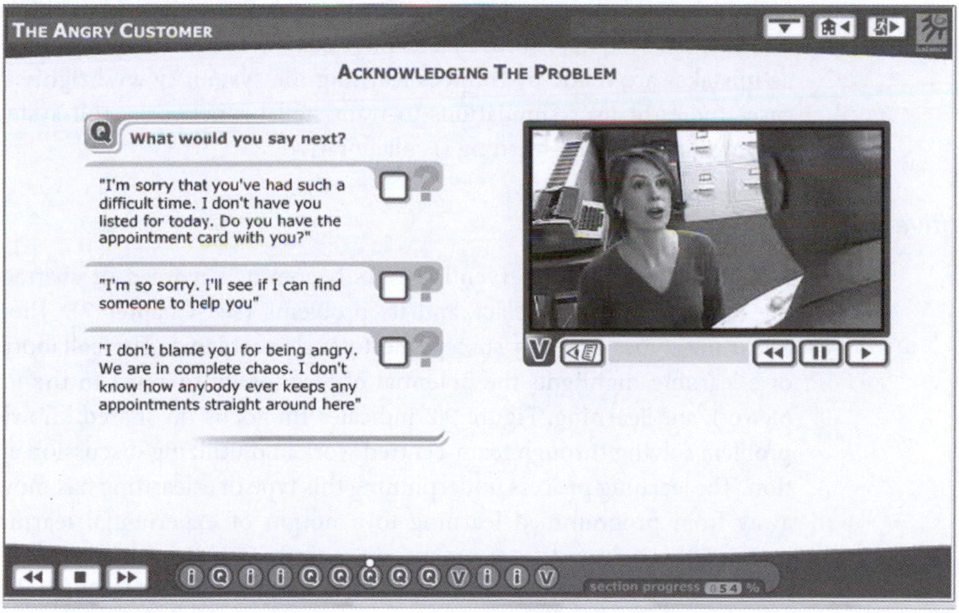

Figure 9.6 Extract from handling complaints and angry customers (engage in learning)

Source: Reproduced by permission of Balance Learning.

Urgent need for leadership training

HRD in Practice 9.3

Brooks Automation Inc. develops and produces hardware and software for semiconductor and other complex manufacturing industries. Faced with an increasingly competitive business environment, Brooks decided to invest more resources in leadership training for managers. Feedback from a series of internal focus group meetings showed that managers wanted immediate training in how to be more effective in fostering and developing teamwork throughout the enterprise. Brooks knew that it could not meet this urgent demand using instructor-led classrooms alone. It chose Engage in Learning's Leadership and Teamwork programme, primarily for its quality of content and high level of interactivity. The pilot programme was well received; the majority of participants attributing their satisfaction to the high quality of the e-learning instruction and the fact that they left the workshop equipped with a personalized, step-by-step plan of action.

Source: **www.balancelearning.co.uk/t-bcase.aspx**

It is important to note that we can identify a range of practice within the interactive type of e-learning. The e-learning module illustrated above might be accessed as a stand-alone piece of training. But equally it could be used alongside other more conventional types of training, like a workshop, (we will have more to say about this particular issue of blending together different approaches to learning a little later in the chapter). A more technologically advanced use of interactive e-learning involves the use of sophisticated simulation equipment, computer controlled, which can be utilized to train for high-level skills. Several industries dependent upon high-tech equipment (military, health service, transport) use simulators which provide trainees with feedback as they learn and practice the requisite skill. BT use simulators to train staff in detecting and fixing faults across its extensive network. The benefit of training and practicing within a simulation system ensures that its huge customer base are not suddenly cut off as mistakes are made by trainees learning the system (www.brightwave.co.uk/case-studies/bt-uses-simulations-to-train-staff-on-network-fault-system).

Our third type of e-learning is collaborative.

Collaborative

Any formal learning intervention risks becoming divorced or abstracted from the reality of the workplace and its problems (see Chapter 7). The first two e-learning types are also susceptible to such problems. The collaborative type of e-learning highlights the potential of technology to assist in the integration of work and learning. Figure 9.2 indicates the focus on shared knowledge and problem solving through team-centred work and utilizing discussion and reflection. The learning process underpinning this type of e-learning has moved firmly away from programmed learning to a notion of experiential learning where learning through and from practice is central. Thus, in this form of e-learning there is much less formal content or curriculum. E-learning is being deployed to facilitate a range of practices, including discussion, networking, communities of practice, mentoring and group-based project work.

It has become popular to see such activities as forming an important part of how organizations seek to manage information and knowledge. The Bank of Montreal call their knowledge management system the kCafé, for knowledge café (Tronsden, 2003; see also Figure 9.6). This captures the essence of collaborative e-learning, ensuring that the social element is at the heart of knowledge management processes.

Thus, collaborative e-learning sits very comfortably alongside knowledge sharing systems. HRD in Practice 9.4 illustrates how BAE Systems (formerly

British Aerospace) have developed a virtual knowledge management system which drives and supports collaborative learning throughout the organization.

BAE Systems

BAE Systems designs and manufactures a range of defence products, employing 130,000 people across 5 continents and 110 sites. Through a partnership with Autonomy, a Hewlett Packard company specializing in the design of software to manage information, the company has developed a knowledge management solution to its high-tech, rapidly changing business environment. Critically, it wanted a technology that would help build a self-sustaining culture of learning and continuous improvement across the company, incorporating education, training and research. The developed system, called the BAE University aggregates content from many sources in many different formats, structured and unstructured. This content is then automatically categorized without the need for any manual intervention, and hyperlinks are inserted to related content. This allows employees to navigate easily through the site to access pertinent content.

According to Richard West, Head of Organizational Development and E-learning: 'We discovered engineers working in different parts of the country on precisely the same problem – a wing construction issue – but in very different areas, a military aircraft and an airbus. Tools like Autonomy ensure that this sharing of best practice is more likely, particularly in a global organization.' E-learning through the knowledge management system effectively brings people together, helping ensure that the problems of not knowing what a person is doing on the other side of the factory or office, let alone the other side of the world, are minimized. This collaborative feature of the system is highlighted by Richard West arguing that e-learning is not just about editorial content 'the virtual university offers access to people ... what better way of learning than from someone else's experience in the business?'

Autonomy (2012)

Of fundamental importance to the development of this collaborative type of e-learning is the capability provided by Web 2.0. Web 2.0 is different from its predecessor 'because it is a read-write web providing a democratic architecture for participation, encouraging people to share ideas, promoting discussion and fosters a greater sense of community' (Martin et al., 2008). The social networking sites Facebook and Twitter are two of the most well known applications utilizing Web 2.0 technology.

1. Blogs, wikis and podcasts are all dependent upon Web 2.0 technology. How might these be used in the context of HRD?
2. Consider Roger Beale's cartoon below. What issues does this raise ?

Web 2.0 has also enabled the development of virtual worlds and virtual communities. A number of organizations, recognizing the need for more innovative and engaging e-learning have been experimenting with the use of virtual worlds. The rationale is that the virtual world provides environments that allow unique forms of experimentation and exploration. Second Life is possibly the best known virtual world. Users join a community, become residents and are able to interact with each other through avatars. Residents can explore the world (known as the grid), meet other residents, socialize, participate in individual and group activities, and create and trade virtual property and services with one another.

HRD in Practice 9.5 best illustrates the interest and potential for the virtual world in the context of L&D.

<table>
<tr><td>HRD
in Practice
9.5</td><td>## Crossing the Virtual Border: CBSA and Loyalist College in Second Life</td></tr>
</table>

Source: Reproduced by permission of Infinite Spaces.

Traditionally, Canadian Border and Service Agency trainees spent several weeks shadowing professional border guards. In a post 9/11 environment such training methods were no longer deemed suitable. Trainees reverted to classroom settings for role-play but the exercises were felt to be unrealistic and ineffective. With the aid of Loyalist College, a Canadian post-secondary community college, a virtual border crossing simulation was created in Second Life which offers trainees realistic hands-on experience. Some trainees practice riding across the border as civilians, while others play the role of border guards. A Second Life script generates information from the virtual license plates on the cars passing through and replicates the information in the guard booth. Relevant issues are programmed to appear in the guard station – just as they might in reality – such as problem driving records, stolen car warnings. Trainees playing the role of civilian border crossers can load contraband items to see if the trainee guards will discover these and learn how to react. The simulation requires all trainees to improvise, think on their feet and negotiate a tense and difficult interpersonal encounter. The training offered through Second Life is considered to improve the performance of trainees in subsequent assessments, prior to working in such contexts for real.

Source: Jarman (2009)

Martin et al. (2008) make an important distinction between Web 2.0 and Enterprise 2.0. The latter seeks to utilize Web 2.0 capability but within a single organization. Applications can then be made to suit the particular needs of the organization and be protected by their firewalls and security. For example, Phizer, the world's largest pharmaceutical company developed Phizerpedia (based on Wikepedia) and made it available to all employees. The UK Government's Department for Work and Pensions have an online Staffroom forum and T-Mobile have created a company specific Facebook site to assist in the recruitment and subsequent induction of its graduate recruits (Martin et al., 2008).

Thus far we have established a conceptual basis in order to understand, position and illustrate a range of e-learning practice. Relatively little attention has been paid to questions about the effectiveness and management of such a resource. It is to this agenda that we now turn in order to address a number of critical issues in the deployment of e-learning in practice.

E-learning: issues and questions

Effectiveness

We have noted a number of factors which provide, on the face of it, a strong rationale for the deployment of e-learning, including access, availability, safe environment, just-in-time learning, integration of work and learning. JISC, an influential body that supports UK institutions of higher education to develop new technologies, defines e-learning as enhanced learning. However, for all the hype and rhetoric surrounding its growth some uncertainty remains about its effectiveness as an approach to, or method of, learning. We lack robust, large-scale research data on effectiveness, in particular data on cost benefit and return on investment. This is a difficulty which bedevils any sort of L&D intervention (see also Chapter 8). The newness of technological developments which are very evident in e-learning also contributes to this lack of evaluative data.

An exception, within the context of higher education, is a meta-analysis of research undertaken by the US Department of Education (Means et al., 2009). This study explored the relative efficacy of online versus face-to-face instruction. Findings included:

- students who took all or part of their classes online performed better, on average, than those taking the same course through traditional means
- the effectiveness of online learning approaches appeared across a broad range of content and learner types

Elsewhere, though, research in the context of HE suggests minimal or no significant differences (Russell, 1999; Baudoin, 2010).

Within the corporate world a similar, somewhat uncertain, picture is evident. Organizations who have invested heavily in e-learning are anxious to promote a return on their investment. Dixons Retail, for example, report a 25 per cent improvement in customer service metrics whilst Sky reckon to have saved £700,000 annually as a result of their pre-induction e-learning programmes (www.towardsmaturity.org). Over and above the perceived impact of e-learning in specific cases such as these we lack robust research on the difference e-learning can make compared to more traditional methods. Data from the CIPD's annual learning and development survey is interesting; while it reports a significant rise in the popularity of e-learning, the respondents remain somewhat equivocal about its effectiveness. In 2008 only 8 per cent rated e-learning as very effective (Taylor, 2008) and Newton and Doonga (2007) echo these findings. In the context of a rising market for e-learning the authors indicate a significant ambiguity amongst training managers about the potential benefits.

There is no simple answer to the question, does e-learning work? What exactly are we trying to measure? The number of learners accessing a particular e-learning programme provides us with one measure but tells us little about the impact upon changed behaviour. Definitive outcomes in terms of enhanced learning require very complex controlled experiments. A more useful line of enquiry is to assess what factors assist learners to engage with and benefit from e-learning in order to improve the deployment and management of e-learning.

E-learning: fitness for purpose

A large portion of the e-learning market is occupied by what is called generic material (courseware which is written for an unspecified audience). Whilst generic e-learning offers a relatively cheap solution to certain needs, more ambitious programmes of in-house provision require a much higher front end investment. The advantages that many organizations see in more bespoke material are those of relevance, engagement and transfer. Inevitably, a tension becomes evident: the difficulty of reconciling what is fit for purpose within budget constraints.

E-learning might work for one particular need with fit for purpose e-learning materials but not for other needs. There is considerable anecdotal data that suggests e-learning makes particular sense in the context of addressing IT training and learning needs. Microsoft, for example, made extensive use of e-learning at the launch of its tablet PC; the challenge being to create an interactive experience that was to be delivered on the tablet itself (see Case Studies on www.brightwave.co.uk). In all Microsoft Office applications there is in-built e-learning. Accessed via the Help icon this is essentially Type 1 e-learning that can provide timely and fit for purpose learning when the user hits a problem or difficulty.

A key issue is the extent to which practice is led by either the 'e' or the learning of e-learning. We noted earlier that many professionals believe the growth in the use of e-learning has been driven in part by vendors, they suggest that technology rather than learning principles have led the development of e-learning. Critics of e-learning have pointed out that it can be simply electronic page-turning or e-reading (Masie, 2001) with minimal or no interactive elements. If the purpose is skill enhancement then it remains highly doubtful if e-learning of this sort offers any added value. A key principle of learning (see also Chapter 7) is that it will be more effective when the learner is active, so an important issue becomes the level of interactivity which can be built into e-learning.

Drawing on Laurillard (2008), there is a strong argument that e-learning should start with the educational or training problem and use this analysis to target the solution we should be demanding from technology. Similarly, Njenga and Fourie (2010) argue that effectiveness is inextricably linked to how e-learning is deployed. Effectiveness flows from well-designed materials and a clarity about whether the main purpose is one of knowledge transmission, knowledge creation or skill enhancement (see Figure 9.2). Towards Maturity (www.towardsmaturity.org), a website devoted to raising standards in the use of e-learning in the workplace, identifies six key strands of activity: defining need, learner context, work context, building capability, ensuring engagement, and demonstrating value. Decisions about the use and integration of e-learning are assisted by use of this model and help ensure a degree of fitness for purpose. Readers familiar with Chapter 7 and Figure 7.1 will note considerable similarity between some of the fundamental issues about the design of L&D and the model developed by Towards Maturity.

reflective question

Think about any e-learning you have experienced.

Reflect on the extent to which you feel your experience of e-learning suggests it was fit for purpose.

The use of virtual worlds for L&D provides a good example of this fitness for purpose controversy. Cross et al. (2007), for example, in the context of the use of virtual worlds as a learning and development tool, question whether virtual worlds are a solution looking for a problem. 'Virtual worlds can provide a platform for collaboration, community and commerce but so can a sofa'. Clark (2009) argues that 'the key to anything online is to get a broad reach of people ... the learning curve required for Second Life prevents many general users from returning regularly ... mobile is the future of any activity online. This is something that Second Life will struggle to penetrate.' Similarly, generating a familiarity with the technology, for example controlling the avatar, is identified as a problem with the use of the virtual world for training and learning.

However, on the basis of the use of Second Life with HRD students at the University of Edinburgh in the context of performance appraisal, Morse (2011) identifies some real potential in terms of skills practice. In effect it is role-play with a difference (see also Aldrich, 2005). It allows 'the experimental self to engage in a wide variety of roles ... generating an opportunity to be very different from the normal physical representations of self by modifying gender, race, age or ability/disability' (Morse, 2011, p.857). This complements earlier experimental work using the virtual in education/training contexts. In a US study high school students could choose avatars of a different gender to explore perceptions and reactions to courtesy, flirtation, discrimination and so on. 'This identity adoption process trains students to solve problems from the point of view of the roles they are assuming, opening them up to new perspectives and challenging them to think in new ways' (Lee & Hoadley, 2007). We should also note that the virtual world offers the possibility of the enhanced role play discussed above to operate with participants who might be located in different locations around the globe; another perspective on the fitness for purpose question.

Integration: blended learning?

In an effort to explain the somewhat contradictory CIPD data noted above Taylor (2008) argues that we need to move away from a notion of e-learning as a stand-alone alternative to more conventional methods of training and learning and to view it as simply part of the learning mix. He argues that those polled for the survey are likely to have taken an inclusive interpretation of e-learning to include 'from LMS-delivered courses to electronic performance support systems to the use of social networks and Google to support informal learning' (p.13). He highlights a key statistic: '65 per cent of respondents strongly agree it is more effective when used with other forms of learning' (p.14). Thus, we have a scenario where e-learning is integrated with other methods of training and learning.

Jochems et al. (2004) define integrated e-learning as involving a media mix, 'that is to say a mix of methods each having certain characteristics in terms of costs, availability, effectiveness, efficiency, appeal and so forth on the one hand, but a coherent one in the sense that the specific combination of methods is the result of a systematic design procedure on the other' (p.5). In the corporate world 'blended learning' (Wain, 2008) has become the commonly used term to describe this particular application of e-learning.

Blended learning in practice

HRD in Practice 9.6

Accenture has implemented a blended learning program for senior executives that includes a high-fidelity simulation of senior executive experience. According to the L&D manager, 'To be successful, our most senior executives need to bring together a variety of skills both people skills to negotiate with clients and manage others, as well as business skills ... the blended learning solution combines face-to-face role-plays of client meetings with an online business simulation that models a large client engagement. Our senior executives have a chance to practice the most difficult parts of their job and get candid and rich feedback on their performance.'

Source: Chief Learning Officer (2012)

BT Openreach used blended learning to meet a major diversity training initiative. A blend of classroom training alongside an online, interactive Diversity Awareness Programme was created for over 30,000 employees. The DAP introduces the training, contains interactive video sequences and briefing guides. It is managed by 200 Diversity Ambassadors who provide offline workshops, facilitation and support.

Source: www.brightwave.co.uk

Leeds Metropolitan University integrates traditional face-to-face teaching with online group discussions on its Masters in Leadership and Change Management course delivered in countries such as Malawi and Swaziland. For example, a 3-day workshop, delivered in-country, introduces students to research methods. It is followed by a series of synchronous and asynchronous group discussions (with tutor input as appropriate) using the university's virtual learning platform and which assists students manage their work-based research project.

Source: Leeds Metropolitan University, 2012

To understand how blended learning may answer several of the questions related to fitness for purpose it is important to recognize the complexity of learning in many workplace and education settings. Learning needs are often combinations of knowledge and skill. Jochems et al. (2004) discuss e-learning in the context of its role in assisting strategies which are not directed at discrete skills, knowledge elements and attitudes, 'but at a combination of them in integrated learning goals or competences' (p.3).

Clearly, in the context of a blended learning or integrated e-learning scenario, the initial issue we raised as regards e-learning effectiveness becomes subservient to the more general question of the evaluation of the teaching and learning strategy adopted (see also Chapter 7).

Managing an e-learning resource

This issue raises a number of questions in relation to the role of the HRD professional. Earlier in the book (Chapter 2 for example) we noted a shift in emphasis in recent years from training to learning and that the role of the HRD professional has, and is, changing accordingly (Sloman, 2005). It is claimed that less emphasis on direct and face-to-face instruction, or training delivery, is a feature of the change. Use of e-learning certainly demands less direct training delivery. The corporate leadership and development team at the City of Edinburgh Council, as a result of a major investment in e-learning, argue that it has 'freed up valuable time enabling the corporate learning team to move to a more consultancy led, bespoke service' (www.brightwave.co.uk). Another claim is that responsibility for initiating and managing learning is increasingly being passed to individual employees in work organizations. This too is enabled and supported by e-learning. A requirement for changed attitudes towards training and learning on the part of HRD professionals and employee learners is highlighted as critical to the success of e-learning by over 90 per cent of respondents in the CIPD (2008) survey.

Some commentators argue that there is a distinctiveness about e-learning which requires a new set of capabilities and competencies in terms of how the resource is managed. We are unconvinced by such arguments. A professional approach to managing an e-learning resource is simply part of the evolutionary process of utilizing whatever is available to ensure an appropriate and effective functional capability. This said, there are a number of aspects of e-learning that any HRD professional must acknowledge and build into their repertoire of capability. To a large extent the issues are inter-related and link also to our discussion on the relationship of e-learning with Strategic HRD (see below). Two such issues are highlighted here:

Learner control: As intimated above, e-learning involves a greater level of responsibility being taken by the learner him/herself. This will vary depending upon the type of e-learning undertaken (see Figure 9.2). Nonetheless, underpinning the purported advantages of e-learning in terms of ease of access, flexibility and so on is the suggestion that greater learner control enhances and improves the learning effort. However, in a review of evidence Granger and Levine (2010) cast doubt on this. They point out that there is long-standing research evidence that trainees often make poor decisions about their own learning and that the availability of e-learning may actually serve to exacerbate this problem. Furthermore, the authors point out that in relation to factors such as perceptions and attitudes to learning, learner satisfaction and the capability of e-learning to address individual differences the evidence is conflicting and ambiguous. Importantly, results from their own research indicate that the issue of an appropriate level of learner control is especially problematic when the training content is complex in nature. The implications of Granger and Levine's review are of some importance for the management of an e-learning resource. Appropriate support systems are critical.

Support systems: The implication of the research highlighted above is that of support infrastructure. This might incorporate anything from support in the careful identification of need in the first place, through to assistance in transfer of learning. Ellis et al. (2009), on the basis of research with students in the UK, argue that a management imperative is to address student perceptions about what the e-learning experience involves if 'we wish to improve the quality of the student experience on line' (p.316). Raj (2011) explores possible gender differences and finds that female students are more active in engaging with e-learning tools. Student evaluation data in respect of their virtual learning environments highlight ease of navigation and technological reliability (i.e. minimum downtime). Within the corporate world Joo et al. (2011), for example, suggest that a 'positive organizational climate in the enrolment of e-learning as well as application of learned knowledge and skills to the job task are critical to learning transfer' (p.982). Similarly, but with a focus upon issues of access and use e-learning, Ramayah et al. (2012) highlight the importance 'of both management and organizational support in ensuring effectiveness', arguing that 'the ease of use of the system is often taken for granted' (p.135). In a review of the difficulties faced by the UK's Department for Environment, Food and Rural Affairs (DEFRA) in introducing a major e-learning initiative, Clarkson et al. (2006) highlight a failure to view the change strategically. Poor take-up and completion of available e-learning provision was explained by a somewhat simplistic approach to the initiative. No attempt was made, for example, to involve line management to act as an appropriate interface between the available e-learning and the workforce.

Above all, research suggests that a face-to-face or social support capability, whether from tutors, first line supervisors or indeed from a learner's own community of practice, is a vital HRD management consideration. Such support needs to be part of the integrated e-learning or blended learning design from the outset (see also Jochems et al., 2004; Pachler & Daly, 2011). This leads nicely to our final issue, the relationship between e-learning and strategic HRD.

Strategic HRD

A key issue in the rise in popularity of e-learning is its relationship with strategic HRD. The technological capability and power which is now available to organizations is also a key factor here. As we have seen, many higher education institutions have taken strategic decisions to place a virtual learning system at the heart of their provision. In the corporate world organizations such as BAE Systems and Westinghouse (see also Chapter 2) have taken the decision to make major investments in technology in order to deliver and manage the bulk of their L&D effort via e-learning. This is not to say that those organizations who have taken a decision to limit the use of e-learning to a highly specific need – perhaps for sales training where its representatives are geographically dispersed – are not acting strategically. But it is the significant shift to e-learning which raises some interesting questions about whether e-learning offers a very real potential to assist an organization in developing its strategic HRD presence and positioning. HRD in Practice 9.7 illustrates the apparent success of the way Macmillan Cancer Research have sought to harness and deploy e-learning to assist the organization in meeting its changing organizational goals.

Macmillan Cancer Research

HRD in Practice 9.7

Learn Zone provides free and easy access to a wide variety of learning resources, online courses and professional development tools from Macmillan Cancer Support.

Macmillan's Learn Zone provides an extensive range of resources to a wide audience. This is significant in helping Macmillan achieve its strategic objectives. The charity is a source of support for people living with cancer and a force for improving cancer care. Macmillan directly employs only a relatively small number of staff. However, over 4000 professionals working in primary care trusts are funded by and badged as Macmillan. Also, Macmillan wanted to build and enhance the education and development opportunities beyond the professional staff and extend them to people affected by cancer. An over-arching learning and development strategy was implemented to meet such aspirations. The strategy made it clear that Macmillan wanted to go further than just offering e-learning courses, its objective was to make full use of learning technology to develop, deliver, support and manage learning both face-to-face and virtually. Thus, the Learn Zone is at the heart of this strategy with a number of entry points for professionals, members of the public, staff and volunteers. A wealth of learning resources are thus made available, together with the ability to connect with others through online spaces that have been created to share good practice.

Source: Macmillan (2012)

A further set of examples are provided by some leading international corporate universities, which notion we introduced in Chapter 2; a vehicle used to create strategic learning organizations. They use the word university (a seat of learning) to help ensure that learning is at the heart of the organization's efforts to achieve its goals. What is important to note here, as regards the relationship between e-learning and the corporate university, is the deployment by such organizations of the full potential of technology. The organization's whole approach to L&D is mediated by technology, from needs analysis, through delivery and into evaluation. This is not to say that e-learning necessarily prevails as a delivery mechanism (see above on blended learning), but that it is the platform through which L&D is organized and managed. The senior director responsible for the Hilton University regards it as an invaluable tool for learning and development, 'often indistinguishable from the L&D function itself' (CIPD, 2011b). The centrality, inclusivity and power of the system helps ensure that L&D effectively underpins and helps lead the HRD effort of the whole organization. The Bank of Montreal's positioning of their Knowledge Café (Figure 9.7) usefully illustrates how this

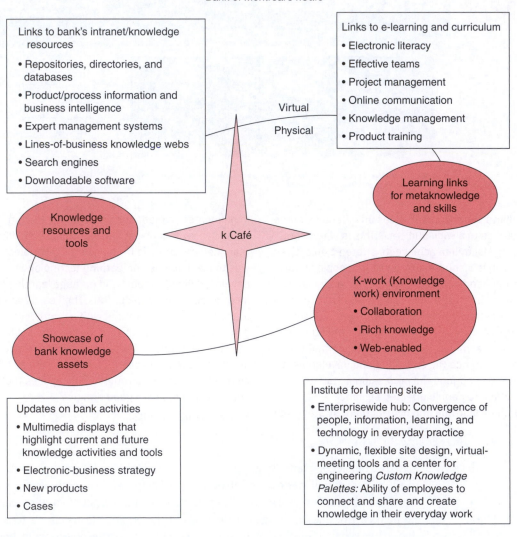

Figure 9.7 The knowledge Café

Source: Bank of Montreal in Trondsen (2003)

e-learning facility sits at the heart of the company's approach to, and management of, learning. Of note in Figure 9.6 is how the kCafé can integrate e-learning with more traditional learning, both formal and informal, and embed knowledge work and learning in everyday practice.

Ongoing developments in e-learning

Heraclitus' saying that 'nothing endures but change' might have been written with e-learning in mind! The pace of change over the last 10 to 15 years has been rapid and significant in terms of what is now regarded as normal in the worlds of education and training. Yet it remains difficult to see exactly how things will develop over the next 10 to 15 years. Two radically different points are highlighted below, but juxtaposed in this way they reflect a key tension which, in our view, is likely to characterize developments over the next decade and beyond.

Mobile technology

It is not our purpose here to chart the latest products in digital hardware and software. However, the developments that have taken place in terms of mobile technology (like iPads, smartphones and apps) are significant to our final thoughts on e-learning. Mobile social networking, for example, is the fastest-growing, consumer mobile app category. Social network platforms are sucking in increasing amounts of network traffic. They are becoming portals and storage for increasing amounts of messaging and e-mail traffic, videos, photos, games and commerce.

reflective question

Consider the words of Terry Anderson in his preface to a book on Mobile Learning:

With easily available software add-ons my phone can become a piano, a guitar, a drum machine, a level, a bookshelf, a camera, a fake zippo lighter, a database, a web browser, an e-mail client, a game machine, a TV (for watching You Tube), a voice recorder, a weather forecaster, and a GPS

Anderson, in Ally (2009)

Think about what you learnt yesterday or last week. To what extent did your mobile phone figure in this learning?

Reflect on the extent to which you feel learning how to use iPads, smartphones and so on can be effective.

Within Ally's book (2009) are powerful testimonies to the power and efficacy of mobile learning. Gregson and Jordan (p.215), for example, argue that those who will receive the most benefits from mobile learning are individuals who live in developing countries and in remote locations since they can access learning materials from anywhere and at anytime. Kenny et al. (p.75) report on the growing use of mobile technology to enhance the quality of nursing practice education. It is considered fit for purpose because of the nature of the work of healthcare workers; on the move most of the time and needing to access information for just-in-time application.

Potentially, its greatest strength in terms of fitness for purpose in an education/training context is the access it provides to collaborative learning (Clough et al., p.99). It is no great leap to see a shared conversation about the activities of a recent night out becoming a reflective learning conversation with a university tutorial group or a work-based action learning set. The key to its potential, and the principal reasoning for its inclusion in this look ahead,, is its ubiquity. Use of the mobile is predicted to increase globally, in all aspects of life. Use in education and training will be no exception. The key is in the word mobile. If we think back to a number of the applications of e-learning discussed in this chapter, wherever they sit on the configurations model (Figure 9.2) the potential for the future is not so much a change in content as the way that learning is accessed and managed.

No techno-utopia

After reading the words of Anderson, above, we could be forgiven for becoming fully signed up members of the techno-positivists (Njenga & Fourie, 2010). The arguments about ease and equality of access form a powerful discourse. However, it is one that must not go unchallenged. Increasingly, HRD professionals must resist being sidetracked by the technology.

Two fundamental counterarguments to the prospect of techno-utopia can be raised. The first relates to access and the second requires us to revisit the central theme of effective learning (see also Clegg et al., 2003; Kirkwood, 2009). Accessibility to PCs, the internet and mobile phones is strongly correlated with wealth. We dismiss at our peril problems such as access, connectivity and broadband width. Acknowledgement of such factors must increasingly permeate into strategic decisions about e-learning.

The second point takes us back to the debate about the extent to which e-learning (however it is configured) is fit for purpose. We have warned above of the dangers of HRD professionals being sidetracked by the technology. We re-assert Cross's (2007) question as regards the virtual world: to what extent is e-learning a solution to a problem? Callahan (2011) provides a highly pertinent critical view of online learning; all the more interesting in the context of this book in that it focuses on the education and training of HRD professionals. She acknowledges the pressure for HRD to seek innovative means to improve the education and training of professionals. However, the fundamental concern raised by Callahan is that 'we often fail to reflect on the implications of technology for our practice ... HRD may lose the potential to help people when its professionals become de-personalized cogs facelessly delivering pre-packaged online services' (p.837). Such an assessment cannot be divorced from any interpretation of what HRD is about and the nature of its practice. Callahan echoes the views of the editors of this book when she says HRD stands for dialogue, interaction and relationships. 'While learning through interaction and dialogue can certainly be accomplished in online environments it is a pale shadow of what could be achieved through substantive face-face interaction' (p.873).

Such arguments are not a Luddite reaction to all things new. Rather, they sound a note of caution, that we must balance the arguments about the purported benefits of new digital and web-based tools with our understanding of the learning process and learning efficacy. In sum, we anticipate the next ten years will be ones in which, despite the relentless advance of technology, HRD professionals will increasingly take fit for purpose decisions about the deployment and management of e-learning resources.

summary

◯ Whilst e-learning utilizes new technologies it is not a revolutionary approach to L&D. Its growth in both higher education and the corporate world has been exponential.

◯ Three types of e-learning can be identified – distributive, interactive and collaborative – which relate to the content/objectives of the e-learning and to underpinning pedagogic strategies.

◯ E-learning offers a number of potential benefits (e.g. accessibility, just-in-time learning, integration of work and learning). However, robust evaluative data is somewhat lacking.

◯ Some of the most advanced applications of e-learning purport to enhance collaborative learning (e.g. using Web 2.0). However, the effective use of any e-learning requires the application of sound learning principles that are relevant to all forms of HRD practice.

◯ Practice based research suggests that e-learning is increasingly combined with other methods through blended learning.

◯ E-learning is a resource which must be managed effectively; implications for support systems, for example, cannot be ignored.

◯ A number of organizations have sought to deploy e-learning in such a way as to enhance the strategic positioning of the L&D function.

◯ Developments in mobile technology strengthen the arguments of the techno-positivists. It is the responsibility of HRD professionals to mediate some of the rhetoric associated with e-learning and ensure that the deployment of e-learning is fit for purpose.

discussion questions

1 How should we think about e-learning in the context of established ideas and theories about learning?

2 Identify and consider examples of how the three types of e-learning may offer fit for purpose solutions to different training and learning needs.

3 What are some of the key issues in the management of e-learning?

4 How might an HRD professional look to use e-learning as part of strategic HRD?

5 Why do we imply that e-learning does not reflect some sort of techno-utopia?

further reading

references

Conole, G. and Oliver, M. (2007) *Contemporary Perspectives in E-Learning Research: Themes, Methods and Impact on Practice*, Part of the Open and Distance Learning Series, F. Lockwood (ed.). London: RoutledgeFalmer.

Fee, K. (2009) *Delivering E-Learning*. London: Kogan Page.

Pachler, N. and Daly, C. (2011) *Key Issues in E-Learning*. London: Continuum www.towardsmaturity.org

Aldrich, C. (2005) *Learning by Doing*. San Francisco: Pfeiffer.

Allen, I. E. and Seaman, J. (2008) *Staying the Course: Online Education in the United States*. Needham MA: Sloan Consortium.

Ally, M. (ed.) (2009) *Mobile Learning: Transforming the Delivery of Education and Training*. Edmonton: AU Press.

Ambient Insight Research (2009) *US Self-Paced E-Learning Market*. Monroe, WA: Ambient Insight Research.

Autonomy (2012) *BAE SYSTEMS – The Right Information to the Right People in Real Time; Case Study*. San Francisco: Autonomy Inc.

Baudoin, E. (2010) Exploring diversity of learning outcomes in e-learning courses. *International Journal of Training and Development*, **14**(3): 223–38.

Badran, A. (2007) *e-Learning: A Global Revolution*. MIT LINC Conference, Dubai, November 2, available at http://linc.mit.edu/conference/presentations/Badran.ppt

Bondarouk, T. and Ruel, H. (2010) Dynamics of e-learning: theoretical and practical perspectives. *International Journal of Training and Development*, **14**(3): 149–54.

Brockett, J. (2008) Cruise firm 'raids' Siemens for ideas. *People Management*, September, p. 11.

Callahan, J. (2011) The online oxymoron: teaching HRD through an impersonal medium. *Journal of European Industrial Training*, **34**(8/9): 869–74.

Calvert, J. (2006) *Achieving Development Goals – Foundations: Open and Distance Learning, Lessons and Issues*. Retrieved 6 June 2006 from http://pcf4.dec.uwi.edu/overview.php

Chief Learning Officer (2012) *Five Innovative Examples of Blended Learning*, http://clomedia.com/articles/view/five_innovative_examples_of_blended_learning/2

CIPD (2004) *E-Learning Survey Results*. London: CIPD.

CIPD (2008) *Learning and Development: Annual Survey*. London: CIPD.

CIPD (2011a) *Focus on E-Learning, Survey Report*. London: CIPD.

CIPD (2011b) *Corporate University Case Study: On Hilton University*, HR-inform, http://hr-inform.cipd.co.uk/Policies-and-documents/case-studies/learning-and-development-strategy/Index.aspx

Clark, J. (2009) Mobile Dilemma. In Hansen, L. (d.) What happened to Second Life, *BBC News Magazine,* 20 November.

Clarkson, D., Griggs, V. and Holden, R. (2006) *The Introduction of E-Learning into DEFRA: Interview with Dan Clarkson*. Leeds: Leeds Metropolitan University.

Clegg, S., Hudson, A. and Steel, J. (2003) The emperor's new clothes: globalization and e-learning in higher education. *British Journal of Sociology of Education*, **24**(1): 39–53.

Clough, G., Jones, A.C., McAndrew, P. and Scanlon, E. (2009) Informal learning evidence in online communities of mobile device enthusiasts. In Ally, M. (ed.) *Mobile Learning: Transforming the Delivery of Education and Training*. Edmonton: AU Press.

Cross, J., O'Driscoll, T. and Tronsden, E. (2007) Another life: virtual worlds as tools for learning. *E-Learning Magazine*, Issue 3.

Ellis, R.A., Ginns, P. and Piggott, L. (2009) E-Learning in higher education: some key aspects and their relationship to approaches to study. *Higher Education Research and Development*, **28**(3): 303–18.

Fee, K. (2009) *Delivering E-Learning*. London: Kogan Page.

Galagan, P.A. (2000) The E-Learning Revolution. *Training and Development*, **12**: 25–30.

Garrett, R., Matkin, G.W. and Kumar, V. (2005) *Regulation, E-learning, and the Changing Structures of Higher Education,* A White Paper to Guide Discussion for the International Seminar: Regulation of E-Learning: New National and International Policy Perspectives.

Granger, B.P. and Levine, E.W.L. (2010) The perplexing role of learner control in learning: will learning and transfer benefit or suffer? *International Journal of Training and Development*, **14**(3): 180–97.

Gregson, J. and Jordaan, D. (2009) Exploring the challenges and opportunities of M-learning within an international distance education programme. In Ally, M. (ed.) *Mobile Learning: Transforming the Delivery of Education and Training*. Edmonton: AU Press.

Guodong, Z. and Zhongjiao, J. (2010) From e-campus to e-learning: an overview of ICT applications to Chinese higher education *British Journal of Educational Technology*, **41**(4): 574–81.

Hills, H. (2003) *Individual Preferences in E-Learning*. Aldershot: Gower.

Hodgson, V.E., Mann, S.J. and Snell, R.S. (1987) *Beyond Distance Teaching, Towards Open Learning*. Milton Keynes: Open University Press.

Jarman, L. (2009) Pedagogy, education and innovation in 3-D virtual worlds. *Journal of Virtual Worlds Research*, **2**: 1.

Jochems, W., van Merriënboer, J. and Koper, R. (2004) *Integrated E-Learning: Implications for Pedagogy, Technology and Organization*. London: RoutledgeFalmer.

Joo, Y.J., Lim, K.Y. and Park S.J. (2011) Investigating the structural relationships among organizational support, learning flow, learners' satisfaction and learning transfer in corporate e-learning. *British Journal of Educational Technology*, **42**(6): 973–84.

Kenny, R., Park, C., Burton, P. and Meiers, J. (2009) Using mobile learning to enhance the quality of nursing practice education. In Ally, M. (ed.) *Mobile Learning: Transforming the Delivery of Education and Training*. Edmonton: AU Press.

Kirkwood, A.(2009) E-learning: you don't always get what you hope for. *Technology, Pedagogy and Education*, **18**(2): 107–21.

Laurillard, D. (2008) The teacher as action researcher: using technology to capture pedagogic form. *Studies in Higher Education*, **3**(2): 139–54.

Lee, J.J. and Hoadley, C.M. (2007) Leveraging identity to make learning fun. *Innovate,* **3**:6.

Macmillan (2012) *Celebrating Innovative L&D at Macmillan Cancer Support in the Charity's 100th Year*. Available at http://www.towardsmaturity.org/elements/uploads/

Towards_Maturity_Macmillan_Case_study_July_2011.pdf, accessed 4 March 2013.

Martin, G., Reddington, M. and Kneafsey, M.B. (2008) *WEB 2.0 and HR: a Discussion Paper*. London: CIPD.

Masie, E. (2001) No More Digital Page-Turning. *E-Learning Magazine*, 1 November.

Means, B., Toyama, Y., Murphy, R., Bakai, M. and Jones, K. (2009) *Evaluation of Evidence Based Practices in Online Learning: A Meta-Analysis and Review of Online Learning Studies*. Washington DC: US Department of Education.

Morse, S. (2011) Utilising a virtual world to teach performance appraisal: an exploratory study. *Journal of European Industrial Training*, **34**(8/9): 852–68.

Newton, R. and Doonga, N. (2007) Corporate e-learning: justification for implementation and evaluation of benefits: a study examining the views of training managers and training providers. *Education for Information*, **25**: 111–30.

Njenga, J.K. and Fourie, L.C.H. (2010) The myths about e-learning in higher education. *British Journal of Educational Technology*, **41**(2): 199–212.

Pachler, N. and Daly, C. (2011) *Key Issues in E-learning: Research and Practice*. London: Continuum.

Pollard, E. and Hillage, J. (2001) *Exploring E-Learning*, Report 376. Brighton: Institute of Employment Studies.

Pritchard, A. (2009) *Ways of Learning: Learning Theories and Learning Styles in the Classroom*. London: David Fulton.

Raj, R. (2011) Evaluating the innovation of online learning systems in higher education. *International Journal of Management Cases*, **13**(4): 12–23.

Ramayah, T., Ahmad, N.H. and Hong, T.S. (2012) An assessment of E-training effectiveness in multinational companies in Malaysia. *Educational Technology and Society*, **15**(2): 125–37.

Ravenscroft, A. (2001) Designing E-learning Interactions in the 21st century: revisiting and rethinking the role of theory. *European Journal of Education*, **36**(2): 133–56.

Russell, T.L. (1999) *The No Significant Difference Phenomenon*. North Carolina State University.

Sambrook, S. (2003) E-learning in small organizations. *Education and Training*, **45**(8/9): 506–16.

Sloman, M. (2005) *Training to Learning*. London: CIPD.

Taylor, D.H. (2008) *The Role of E-Learning in the Mix: Reflections on the 2008 Learning and Development Survey*. London: CIPD.

Tronsden, E. (2003) *E-Learning in Financial Services: A Case Based Analysis*. Menlo Park, CA: SRI Consulting Business Intelligence.

Wain, D. (2008) Why the end of the blend is not in sight. *People Management*, 12 June, p. 21.

Workplace Learning and Knowledge Management

Jeff Gold

Chapter learning outcomes

After studying this chapter, you should be able to:

- Explain the meaning of workplace learning, Organizational Learning (OL) and Knowledge Management (KM)
- Understand key ideas relating to workplace learning
- Explain how knowledge is produced at work
- Understand how knowledge can be managed at work

Chapter outline

Introduction
The organization as a learning system
Organizational learning
Knowledge creation and management
Summary

Introduction

Crisis, recession, financial uncertainty and ongoing change and flux. Do not be surprised when you enter an organization in the next few years to be greeted with such terms and find that the need for what Prahalad and Hamel (1990) called a collective core competence of learning is given more emphasis. While HRD might often be understood in relatively narrow terms of skills, competences, courses and training, there has been a shift in emphasis to how learning is occurring throughout an organization. As Sloman (2003) suggested, we are in the age of the learner and learning and with this notion comes an image of more knowledge-based work (OECD, 1996), requiring people to interact with human and technological networks that can be globally distributed (Hardt & Negri, 2008). From the start of the 2000s, the importance of knowledge, its creation and management have focused attention on employees as knowledge workers who are a vital source for an organization's intellectual capital (Edvinsson & Malone, 1997). However, between the individual and the collective idea of a workplace or organization, there are the opportunities and situational factors, such as work autonomy, that contribute to or prevent people from learning (van Ruysseveldt & van Dijke, 2011). That is, to a greater or lesser extent a workplace provides space, an environment and a climate for learning, where most people gain and apply skills and knowledge every day of their working lives (Billett, 2006). In this chapter, we will consider how this move to a more collective organizational view of learning at work provides new possibilities for HRD.

The organization as a learning system

A long-standing conundrum that has bedevilled many HRD practitioners is that, despite their efforts to deliver training efficiently, learning might not result in sustained changes in skills, behaviour and attitudes. Mayo (2005, p.19), for example, suggested that a 'frightening amount of training' does not result in learning for two reasons. First, training can be divorced from the workplace and so become irrelevant to those attending. Second, the training might not be supported by the context and environment of the workplace. Does this seem familiar?

reflective question

1 How effective are you in using training to change what you normally do?
2 What helps and what hinders you?

Taylor (1991) argued against the narrow focus on training through simple systematic models, which are only suitable in stable environments. In recent years there has been growing interest in considering the contextual issues that affect learning at work, such as the motivation and interests of learners, but also factors like history and the response of others, such as managers, leaders and fellow workers. These elements together constitute a learning culture at work. To consider the various factors requires a more systemic approach to HRD (Chiaburu & Tekleab, 2005) and an understanding of the organization as a learning system, or what is usually referred to as workplace learning.

Workplace learning encompasses a broad view of HRD where individuals who learn always undertake such learning in a context, which may be more or less supportive, and where such learning may more or less balance the needs of individuals with organizational requirements (Jacobs & Park, 2009). This can be quite a challenge because of the lack of awareness of taken-for-granted assumptions that dominate life in organizations. For example, Morgan's *Images of Organization* (2006) highlights the role of metaphor in explaining complex phenomena such as the workplace by combining images and language. Thus, an organization can be seen as a machine and this image can inform any decisions then made in reality. However, we must remember that metaphors are a way of talking and understanding and are not the reality – organizations are not machines but it can be useful to consider them as such. The danger arises, as Mintzberg (1990, p.19) argued, when the idea of the organization structure as machine bureaucracy is accepted as the *only* way to structure an organization. In HRD, Marsick and Watkins (1999) have suggested that the machine metaphor lies behind the way learning is based on a deficit model of identifying gaps against a hard standard, with little room for considering attitudes, apart from how they can be manipulated to reinforce desired performance. One consequence is the way that accounting procedures reinforce the dominance of the machine metaphor by requiring a measurement of the cause and effect links of HRD to the bottom line.

Workplace learning requires the machine metaphor to be challenged and attempts to employ alternative ways of understanding. Jacob and Park (2011) suggest looking at workplace learning using three factors, each of which can be considered in different ways. Firstly, there is the location, which can be on-the-job or off-the-job (away from the work setting). Secondly, there is the degree of planning, with a variation between a structured approach and an unstructured approach. Thirdly, there is the HRD specialist as facilitator, who can play an active and direct role in the learning process, or a more passive limited role, perhaps requiring a systemic understanding of learning in an organization. Based on these factors, a number of different combinations can be considered in workplace learning, such as on-the-job/unstructured/passive where the work itself provides opportunities for learning, but cannot be planned for; where HRD specialists are not present but others, such as peers and managers, can affect whether there is a response to the opportunities.

reflective question

1 What kind of opportunities for learning can be considered with the combination off-the-job/unstructured/active?
2 What would help learning in this situation and what would prevent it?

While the idea of workplace learning is hardly a new phenomenon, like many other aspects of what Gold and Smith (2003) have called the 'learning movement', there is often a link to how learning is a source of competitive advantage, especially in a knowledge-based economy (Harrison & Kessels, 2004) where strategies for knowledge need to be linked to overall business strategy (Scarso & Bolisani, 2010); clearly, the implication is that learning is a good thing. One way of seeing the organization as a system for learning is by highlighting the interdependence between strategy, the role of managers and teams and knowledge transfer (Hirsh & Tamkin, 2005). Competency frameworks are often seen as a way of making such links manifest through performance management systems that declare development requirements that reflect business needs. However, research on the use of competencies suggests that the way they are used and the support that follows in learning is vital (Strebler et al., 1997), this highlights the working of what is referred to as the learning climate or environment. For example, based on research on apprentices, Fuller and Unwin (2003) suggest that a learning environment can be considered as more or less expansive or restrictive on a continuum. Expansive environments are characterized by access to learning and qualifications, career progression, the valuing of skills and knowledge and, crucially, managers as facilitators. It is not too difficult to work out the nature of a restrictive environment.

The transfer of learning

At the centre of an expansive learning environment lies the relationship between line managers and their staff and, typically, it is front-line managers who make up the majority of an organization's management group, interacting with 80 per cent of staff (Hassan, 2011).

Recent research has explored the importance of this relationship for learning and development (Hutchinson & Purcell, 2007). While it is often formal training programmes that are identified, it is managers who provide the structure and support that sets the climate for learning, which also affects what happens after training has been completed. This highlights again the difficulty of transferring learning from HRD events to behaviour and performance at work, which was first considered in Chapter 7.

One way to begin tackling this difficult issue in HRD is to diagnose the factors that affect or prevent transfer. Holton et al. (2007) have developed a Learning Transfer System Inventory (LTSI) which relates to:

a Motivation factors relating to the expectations people have in applying new skills

b Secondary influences concerning the degree of preparedness of learners and their belief or conviction in their ability to use new skills

c Environmental elements such as manager support or sanctions and peer support

d Ability elements relating to the opportunity to apply new skills, the energy and workload of learners and the way in which training is designed to link to work performance.

While a variety of factors can be revealed, it is often found that managers and leaders are not sufficiently accountable for a transfer of learning. Burke and Saks (2009) suggest that there are three components of accountability: the pre-training expectations of trainees so that they have clear goals and expectations for attendance and what they will learn; that trainees have control over their learning and its application in the workplace; and that they have a strong sense of personal obligation to attend and apply learning and are clear what they must do when they return to work to begin to use newly acquired skills and knowledge. Of course, this does assume that managers at all levels are able and willing to accept accountability. As a result, there is growing interest in selecting managers responsible for supporting staff development and this includes allocating them the role of coach or mentor (see also Chapters 11 and 13). Thus, the interdependent systemic view of workplace learning also seeks to engender a coaching culture where, according to Clutterbuck and Megginson (2005, p.44), coaching becomes the 'predominant style of managing and working together'. This view brings us closer to the performance of work and how this provides opportunities for learning (see below). Recent survey evidence suggests that coaching and mentoring are being used mostly to improve performance but also to enhance employee engagement (CIPD, 2011). In addition, leaders and managers at all levels are symbolic role models for others with an impact on knowledge creation (Von Krogh et al., 2012).

The transfer of learning issue has been long recognized as a difficult one in HRD and, importantly, can prevent the achievement of a return on investment (ROI) from HRD events. The nature of the difficulty, and its importance to the future status of HRD professionals, would suggest the need for a more creative approach. Recently, Mooney and Brinkerhoff (2008) have shown how an improvement in the ROI can be shown through collaboration between organizations. In the UK, Colwill et al. (2012) sought to work collaboratively on this issue where problems and solutions are jointly developed and become part of a learning process that progressively improves actions. HRD in Practice 10.1 shows how one HRD manager is working on this process.

HRD in Practice 10.1

Transfer of learning for a first line manager programme at BUPA Care Homes

BUPA Care Homes is a major provider of care provision for the elderly, with over 300 homes each managed by a Home Manager. The difficulty with enabling transfer of learning focused on the relationship between first line managers (FLMs) and their managers. First line managers report to the Home Manager and, while there had been support for the programme from the FLMs, Home Managers are struggling to see what is in it for them. Home Managers were very much concerned with compliance and had a 'what gets measured gets done' mentality. There was also little clarity about the Home Manager role in this training. I saw the need to build an appropriate performance measure into the front line management programme so that Home Managers could link their accountability for performance to it.

Following the first meeting, and reporting back at the review meetings, I could report how I sought to increase Home Manager accountability for FLM performance after attending their programme. Firstly, I ensured that a robust learning review (which considered their learning and, more importantly, their actions as a result of their learning) was built into the design of the programme by introducing the concept of action challenges – a method of transferring learning into real workplace actions. Secondly, I supported this by the introduction of a new performance management process which provided the HM's with the tools to make the development of their FLM's seem more core and hence more sustainable. Finally, I also needed to re-align the objectives and expectations of the HM with those of our senior leaders in order to reinforce the level of importance being placed on FLM development.

Moving towards a more systemic understanding of the workplace as a space for learning also requires a consideration of how there are different interpretations of the various activities and processes of work. It is within such activities and processes that people learn what they are allowed to do and what they should not do. For example, changes in processes advocated by management as part of a lean production development usually require learning but employees may be reluctant to engage, seeing it as a threat to their skills and their relationships with others (Bratton, 2001). There is a significant degree of uncertainty in how learning can be brought about in the workplace and Gold and Smith (2003) provide an image of the contested possibilities, shown in Figure 10.1.

This image begins to bring into play some of the less considered features of workplace learning. There is still a place for formality in the HRD system where

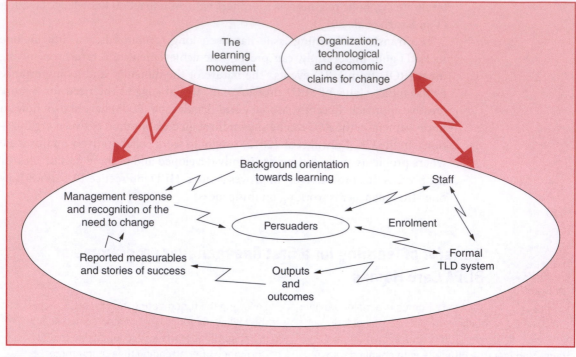

Figure 10.1 Contested possibilities in HRD

Source: Adapted from Gold and Smith (2003)

training and other more recognized learning events are delivered. Outside the organization, in addition to the key considerations of pressures to change, there is also the learning movement, a part of the environment where recommendations, ideas and exhortations relating to learning and development are made, but managers may or may not respond to these. It is suggested that some managers are more favourably disposed towards learning and development but this does not immediately become delivered learning. The jagged arrows indicate possible contests and the need for persuasion. Here there are key roles for managers as well as others who speak positively about learning, but there are also those who may not. Even if people complete activities, there is no certainty that learning follows (Antonacopoulou, 2001), nor that a precise cause and effect value can be shown – the spread of something good, or otherwise, by word-of-mouth story-telling is more likely.

reflective question Does this image come close to the way ideas about learning are spread in your organization, or any organization you know?

The informal system

A systemic view of workplace learning extends understanding to consider any learning that takes place in the context of the workplace, and this has to include much of what occurs as a response to work issues, including mistakes, accidents, problems or just simple incidental conversations; indeed, anything that occurs at work which instigates and sustains a change in knowledge, skills and attitudes. However, when this occurs, learning may not be the word used by those involved. Some of it remains implicit and tacit (Reber, 2003), with little or no conscious awareness that it has happened or is being used. Alternatively, there might be some incidental but just-about recognized reaction to events, or a more deliberate use of events for the purpose of learning. These three possibilities are presented as a typology of informal or, as preferred by Eraut (2000a), 'non-formal learning'. Whatever changes have been made can remain local and protected by those involved so that the benefits or otherwise do not move to other parts of the organization. The important contrast to formal HRD is the way that skills development takes place naturally (Stuart, 1984), in a non-contrived manner, in response to the issues that occur almost every day at work, mainly resulting from the work itself, especially through interactions with others, such as customers and fellow workers. This calls for an embellishment of the systemic metaphor with the idea of what Felstead et al. (2005) call 'learning as participation'. There is now much interest in the everyday processes of learning, much of it informal, through participation in work practice. The influence of the work of Russian psychologist Vygotsky (1978) and the sociocultural theory of human development is noticeable. The theory highlights how learning occurs through participation in action and interaction with others who can provide support to learn new skills. This process focuses on how mediation occurs through the use of tools such as language, social signs and symbols to create new understanding in individuals. The linking of individual learners to their social and cultural context is part of what Beckett and Hager (2002) see as an 'emerging paradigm' of learning, which is:

- organic and holistic
- contextual
- activity and experience based
- found in situations where learning is not the main aim
- activated by individual learners rather than by trainers or teachers
- often collaborative or collegial.

reflective question

1 Do you often learn when the main aim is not learning?
2 How influential are others in what you learn?

Fenwick (2008) has examined some of the key research in workplace learning over the past few years. The focus has been on the relationship between individual learning and the collective idea of the workplace. She found the idea of context to be particularly evident but with two contrasting possibilities of how the idea is understood. First, there is a view that context is a 'container' in which 'the individual moves' (p.237). Within the container are the social and physical factors that make up an environment and this includes people and technology. It might also include the ways of talking and the various practices present. Second, there is the view of context as a 'web of relations', where individuals become inseparable from actions carried out jointly with others or a set of norms and

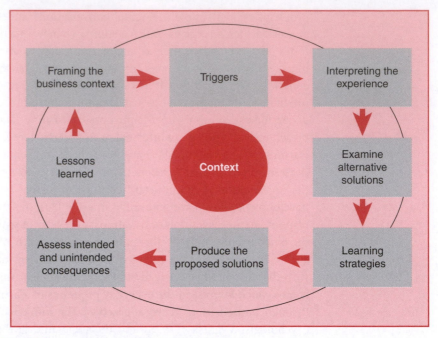

Figure 10.2 A model for informal and incidental learning

Source: Marsick and Watkins (2001, p.29)

values that are socially formed. This view is particularly pertinent to research on what are referred to as communities of practice and a cultural view of organizing (see below). A key aspect of context relevant to both views is how power is analysed (Hager, 2004), although there is less research devoted to this.

However it is viewed, context is considered an essential component of models to take advantage of informal learning. For example, Marsick and Watkins (2001) provide a model for using informal and incidental learning, shown in Figure 10.2.

The model shows how context provides everyday possibilities for learning, which begins with some kind of trigger. This may take the form of a challenge or a problem, perhaps even a surprise. Crucially, the learner is placed in an action such as watching others, asking questions or solving a problem. The learning lies in the action of working (Sambrook, 2005) rather than as part of a formal process of planned learning. Such moments create sufficient dissatisfaction to require some kind of further examination and assessment and the interpretation is affected by context, which can promote or even inhibit the examination. Marsick and Watkins (2001, p.29) point out that while the model suggests progression, making sense is more likely to proceed as an ebb and flow rather than as a sequence. For example, lack of time and space can inhibit the move from interpretation to alternatives. Context includes history, which influences the choice of alternatives, and implementation may require new skills or special permissions, perhaps redefining roles and responsibilities. There may also be variations in providing resources for ambiguous projects. However, if action can be taken, outcomes can be assessed and lessons learned for future actions. If sustained, these can also feed into the context for further learning in the future. In this way, informal learning becomes more explicit and is available as actionable knowledge for organizations (Yang, 2012), a theme we will explore below.

Billett (2006) also seeks to make the learning as participation metaphor in workplace learning more explicit, arguing for a workplace curriculum. He argues that 'individuals themselves will ultimately determine how they participate in and learn through what is afforded them' (p.33). A key point is that all organizations require employees to learn, and that it is 'erroneous' (p.9) to refer to workplaces as informal learning environments, since by necessity an organization provides workers with affordances to engage with learning at work, so that they can fulfil their role as defined by the division of labour. This also engenders various contests about the composition of the curriculum reflecting differing interests and goals. One issue might be how the requirements of the work are related to learning opportunities. Van Ruysseveldt and van Dijke (2011) suggest an inverse U-shaped relationship between workload and learning opportunities where lower workload increases a person's experience of learning opportunities but eventually, at higher levels of workload, there is a decrease in such experience. The work drives out the learning. However, this process was affected to some degree by the amount of task autonomy available. When autonomy was high, survey results suggested that a relatively high workload still provided experiences of learning opportunities, and decline came relatively later. Another issue might be how more experienced workers might limit participation in workplace learning if they perceive a threat from new workers. There may also be cultural and historical norms that prevent access to participation, for example the so-called glass ceiling for women managers (see Davidson & Burke, 2011).

A key feature of support will how relationships work (Marsick, 2009). Peers and colleagues will have an impact on learning experiences, depending on the impact on their interests. Managers can play a key role in supporting staff to engage with opportunities through providing feedback, providing opportunities for acquiring knowledge and new skills and coaching (Kyndt et al., 2009).

Organizational Learning

The learning as participation metaphor as an elaboration of the systemic metaphor connects with ideas that organizations are learning on a continuous basis in a variety of ways. Indeed, learning is so embedded in what people do, how they work and the systems that connect the parts together, it becomes possible to consider Organizational Learning (OL) as the source of life at work (Gibb, 2002). There is a great deal of attraction in considering OL as crucial to securing competitive advantage and change. A key idea is that if current ways of working – the organization's routines that accumulate through the experience of everyday working and responding to problems – are less likely to secure competitive advantage or, in more recent circumstances, organizational sustainability (Smith, 2012), then new ways must be found and learned (Antonacopoulou et al., 2005). However, this is not easy and one of the most useful contributions in OL has been made by Argyris (1999) and Argyris and

Schön (1996). Where current ways of working are accepted, change only occurs in response to errors or problems that need to be corrected to bring things back to normal. This is referred to as single-loop learning and is the most common form of OL. There is no challenge to accepted routines and ways of working based on embedded assumptions accepted by everyone. A commonly used analogy to understand this is the use of a thermostat in maintaining the temperature of a room. By contrast, if ways of working are insufficient in the face of more difficult problems, such as changes in markets or technology, single-loop learning will not be enough because the embedded assumptions remain in place. What is required is a challenge to these assumptions and principles of working, a process referred to as double-loop learning. An example would be an engineering company that focused on manufacturing, which increasingly found itself outcompeted on cost by overseas competition. The challenge to assumptions resulted in a new focus on design engineering, using the knowledge of its workers, allowing manufacturing to switch to lower-cost producers as necessary. As we will see below, there is link between OL and finding or creating and then using knowledge as the source of competitive advantage and/or sustainability.

OL is broadly a field of study of 'the learning processes of and within organizations' (Easterby-Smith & Lyles, 2003, p.9), and while it has certainly been important in recent years, as Mirvis (1996) has indicated, the foundation of OL lies in the development of systems ideas dating back to the 16th century. However, it wasn't until the 1950s that systems ideas began to be used in considering organizations as, for example, social systems and processors of information. These alternatives to the dominant machine metaphor of organizations are now themselves taken-for-granted. The idea that organizations learn, like humans, is embedded, and yet organizations are not humans, but the idea of learning is transposed to organizations as if they were. For example, Dixon (1994) adapts Kolb's learning cycle (see Chapter 5) to form an organizational learning cycle based on the generation of information, its dissemination, integration and interpretation before its use in action. However, there are barriers to moving from individual learning to other levels such as groups and teams and, of course, organizations (Schilling & Kluge, 2009). Fiol and Lyles (1985) argued that there was a lack of a clear definition of learning at levels beyond individuals and confusion with other terms such as adaptation and change.

One model of OL that attempts to link individual, group and organizational levels of analysis has been presented by Crossan et al. (1999). They argue that OL begins with learning at the individual level, then the group level before reaching the organizational level. There are four processes, working bidirectionally to create and apply knowledge, which form the 4Is model and they are:

- *Intuiting*: individuals see patterns in their experience that provide new insights, which they translate into metaphors for possible communication to others
- *Interpreting*: individuals explain their insights to themselves and then others, through talk, which then become possible ideas for application
- *Integrating*: the group shares in the understanding and takes action as a consequence

- *Institutionalizing:* the learning at individual and group levels becomes organizational through 'systems, structures, procedures and strategy' (p.525) with which others can work.

Crossan et al. (1999) acknowledge that these processes, while forming a learning loop, are unlikely to flow without difficulty. For example, as outlined by Lawrence et al. (2005), power and politics are likely to play a role. Thus, in the stages from intuition to interpretation, new ideas can be considered but take place against a background of what is and is not rewarded. Any group will have a history of accepting or rejecting new ideas based on their interests. It is suggested that influence becomes crucial, requiring the control of resources, particular expertise that is seen as relevant and social skills that are in tune with the culture. The working of power can create a feeling of repression and a suppression of, sometimes critical, views and opinions which can help an organization learn (Blackman & Sadler-Smith, 2009).

Another well-known OL model is Nonaka and Takeuchi's (1995) knowledge-creating model, as modified by Nonaka et al. (2000). The model is presented as a spiral of knowing-that passes through conversion modes and make up the SECI model:

- *Socialization:* tacit knowledge of individuals shared with others
- *Externalization:* conversion of tacit knowledge into explicit metaphors, analogies, concepts and models
- *Combination:* new knowledge is combined with existing knowledge
- *Internalization:* whatever emerges from combination is enacted and becomes part of behaviour and accepted and so the process begins again.

Nonaka et al. (2000) also identify the importance of context, which can enable or inhibit the conversions. They conceptualize a context of shared space for knowledge creation, which they refer to as Ba. This can be physical, such as an office, or virtual, such as email or wiki, or mental, such as shared experiences. The nature of Ba varies with different phases, but it originates at the socialization phase, where face-to-face experiences are vital for the transfer of tacit knowledge.

activity

Read more about Argyris at **www.infed.org/thinkers/argyris.htm** and Schön at **www.infed.org/thinkers/et-schon.htm**

Find out more about Nonaka's spiral and Ba at **www.polia-consulting.com/A-Japanese-approach-of-KM-the-Ba.html**

These various OL models all imply or require some consideration of tacit knowledge, which, as we will consider below, is far from easy. There are other difficulties with OL models. For example, Weick and Westley (1996) suggest that the words organization learning are an oxymoron, and are thus in contradiction. Preferring instead to consider the more active processes of learning and organizing, since organization cannot be directly perceived, they also suggest using a cultural view of organizing to consider the dynamic of exploring and exploitation. This begins to tackle the assumption that organizations are single, unified entities. Yanow (2000) adopts a cultural view, for example, to consider the practice of groups and the values, beliefs and norms that are shared through talk, rituals, myths and stories. What we normally refer to as organizations are composed of a variety of groups, practising (or organizing) according to the local meanings and understanding created within the group. OL in this way becomes more concerned with the process of organizing, and learning at this local level can be as much about preserving what is valued and sustaining the life of the group as it is about change and innovation.

Communities of practice

The cultural view of OL connects with the importance of work practice as the source of knowing and the creation of knowledge, leading to the need for a practice-based understanding of how this occurs (Nicolini et al., 2003). For example, one of the most important contributions is the work on communities of practice (CoPs), where learning is mostly informal and improvisational, situated in the practice of the work in a local context (Lave & Wenger, 1991). Learning occurs by becoming a participant in practice. Brown and Duguid (1991) used the idea of CoPs to show how practice-based learning among technicians can be at variance to what others, such as managers outside the practice, consider to be the correct, or espoused, way of doing things. It is practice in context that is learned, including the sharing of stories about practice and what is effective. This local knowledge can be very different to the abstract knowledge contained in work manuals or the talk of more senior managers. Yanow (2004, p.12) highlights how local knowledge is frequently underprivileged in organizations at the expense of more theory-based and abstract knowledge, which is usually considered as expert. However, it is argued that local knowledge can also be expert since salespersons and those working in the field are likely to learn about their practice of communicating with customers through their interactions, often in great detail. They learn about the lives and identities of those whom others might measure as numbers. Both ways of understanding stem from different cultures that need to be considered in OL.

In recent years, CoPs have been recognized as a source of creativity and there has been an effort to formally recognize their value. In spite of the apparent informal and self-organizing quality around the demands of the situation, it is argued that they can be directed by managers and become more oriented towards 'their companies' success' (Wenger & Snyder, 2000, p.145). There is widespread application of the idea of CoPs in the private and the public sector, often as part of knowledge management techniques and toolkits.

However, there has also been criticism of the way CoPs have been commandeered by managers and consultants with too much focus on the formation of CoPs rather than on the context of situated learning and the practice that occurs (Roberts, 2006). There is also a downplaying of the tensions, disagreements, contradictions and power issues in the way CoPs negotiate meanings (Marshall & Rollinson, 2004) and the different kinds of knowledge that can occur in practice between virtual communities and those more closely located (Amin & Roberts, 2008). Research and debate continue about CoPs, with wide variety of meanings and uses are attached to the terms (Li et al., 2009), but a crucial point remains concerning the importance of everyday practice that makes the life of any group at work, which is not always amenable to management control.

The learning organization

Operationalizing CoPs has been one of the moves by managers in organizations to create learning organizations or learning companies. Thus while OL is a field of study, the learning organization (LO) is an attempt to make some of the ideas manifest in the workplace. In response, a range of models and formulas have been presented to provide guidance and even prescription. For example, Pedler et al. (1991, p.1) defined their version of the learning company as an 'organization which facilitates the learning of all its members and continuously transforms itself'. They included suggestions for the dimensions of a learning company, which provided differentiation from a non-learning company, including:

● A learning approach to strategy
● Participative policymaking
● The use of ICT to inform and empower people
● Reward flexibility
● Self-development for all.

Of course, given the comments made earlier, it could be rather difficult to classify any organization as non-learning. Nevertheless, these dimensions give a flavour of the kinds of activities that could be pursued. Others, such as Peter Senge (1990a), suggested that learning organizations could be built on the basis of five disciplines:

● Personal mastery
● Shared vision
● Team learning
● Mental models
● Systems thinking.

Senge (1990b) was also keen to highlight the role of leaders as designers, teachers and stewards, whose job it was to challenge current mental models and support systemic thinking. In particular, leaders needed to work the idea of creative tension by developing a gap between current realities and feasible future possibilities. Thus the organization could engage with a generative learning process to create a new future, in contrast with adaptive learning, where the organization simply coped with the present.

From the late 1990s, the idea of the LO remained popular and even appeared in government policy documents, along with other learning entities such as 'learning regions' or 'learning cities' (Longworth, 2006). The metaphor became one of a journey, possibly never completed but there is a retention of the persuasive appeal of the LO. Örtenblad (2004) suggested that the vagueness of the idea can be a source of creativity, although this is unlikely in bureaucratic structures. Digital organizations with a knowledge-based workforce may be most suited to the idea of a LO (Cabanero-Johnson and Berge, 2009).

To help the journey of LOs, there are various diagnostic tools. For example, the Dimensions of the Learning Organization Questionnaire (DLOQ) is based on

Watkins and Marsick's (1993) model, suggesting that the LO needs to consider dimensions at the people and the systems levels (Yang et al., 2004). People-level dimensions include:

- Create continuous learning opportunities
- Promote enquiry and dialogue
- Encourage collaboration and team learning
- Empower people towards a collective vision

and the structural dimensions are:

- Connect the organization to its environment
- Establish systems to capture and share learning
- Provide strategic leadership for learning.

There are also outcome variables, such as the:

- Gain of organizational knowledge
- Increase of organization financial performance.

Another tool is provided by Garvin et al. (2008), who present three building blocks for measuring:

1 a supportive learning environment
2 concrete learning processes and practices
3 leadership behaviour that reinforces learning.

To some extent, the development of these tools is making the idea of the LO more meaningful, despite the scepticism among more critical observers (Sambrook & Stewart, 2002). However, there is evidence to suggest that an organization that develops its learning capabilities will benefit from improved performance, both financially and non-financially in terms of job satisfaction, innovation and efficiency (Goh et al., 2012).

activity

Go to www.partnersforlearning.com/instructions.html where you can find an online version of the DLOQ.

Knowledge creation and management

Since the late 1980s, when writers such as Drucker (1988) identified the need to change from the mechanistic command and control organization towards an information-based organization, knowledge and its creation and management have been considered as the source of lasting competitive advantage. The emphasis on knowledge has spawned a plethora of terms, such as knowledge workers, knowledge-intensive organizations, the knowledge-based view of the firm, knowledge societies and so on. Knowledge has been seen as the key ingredient of products and services (OECD, 1996) and innovation (Gardner et al., 2007), and those who make, manipulate and apply it are part of an organization's intellectual capital (Edvinsson & Mallone, 1997) and a reason for investing in HRD as part of an organization's human capital accumulation (Garavan et al., 2001).

Information as knowledge

As indicated in other chapters (for example Chapter 9), advances made in the application of ICT, especially over the internet, allow the digitization, storage, retrieval, analysis and communication of information. In addition, there has been a convergence around microtechnologies, computing, telecommunications, broadcasting and optical electronics to make what Castells (2000) has seen as the new age of information, with revolutionary consequences. Part of this revolution is the way that information-processing devices incorporate feedback that allows the accumulation and transfer of information, something that companies such as Google and Facebook might readily exploit before your eyes on a daily basis.

reflective question What assumptions are being made about the connection between information and knowledge?

It would seem that much of what is considered in KM is indistinguishable from information. For example, Mayo (1998, p.36) defined KM as:

> the management of information, knowledge and experiences available to an organization – its creation, capture, storage, availability and utilization – in order that organizational activities build on what is already known and extend it further.

The information as knowledge equation is clearly prevalent in KM systems and more widely in a range of tools and devices. Even if the starting point is people, who learn something new, through codification and recording this can be made available for searching by others anywhere in the world. This view of knowledge is clearly an option in deciding a strategy for managing knowledge (Hansen et al., 1999). Thus many organizations see KM as the installation of networked software and the allocation of roles to knowledge officers, company librarians, webmasters and information consultants. Capture and storage mean the resource can be counted as intellectual capital, even though there are many reasons why people in organizations may not use the KM tools available (Lubit, 2001). However, 'knowledge ... has several meanings' (Machlup 1980, p.27). Scarbrough and Swan (2001, p.8) suggest that the systems and technologies of KM tend to 'gloss over the complex and intangible aspects of human behaviour', including learning in the workplace, where, we argue, much of what really counts for knowledge is created and used in practice. It becomes difficult to separate knowledge from those who know or the 'knowing subject' (Tsoukas, 2000) who always exists in some place of action, embedded in some collective way of life.

Knowing-that and knowing-how

While any discussion on knowing and knowledge is fraught with difficulty, it is common to use a distinction first made by Ryle ([1949]1984) between knowing-that and knowing-how. The former is concerned with concepts and abstractions that can be made explicit and communicable, based on facts and explanations. For individuals, it is their embrained knowledge (that is, knowledge dependent on their conceptual skills and cognitive abilities), as suggested by Blackler (1995). This form of knowledge is highly valued in our society and can become public, available in a codified form, and easily stored and transferred, for example in books, journals and papers from internet databases. It is what you are reading now or have to read for your assessments. As suggested above, this is barely distinguishable from information.

By contrast, knowing-how is personal, based on knowing what to do according to the requirements of the situation. According to Blackler (1995), this is 'embodied knowledge', and is related to doing and practice that can also become collective knowing-how, as embedded knowledge in organization routines and norms. Eraut (2000b, p.128) suggests that dealing with new or unexpected events 'cannot be accomplished by procedural knowledge alone or by following a manual'. This kind of knowing is tacit and it is generally accepted that without consideration of the tacit dimension in knowledge creation and management, there is little benefit from the accumulation of codified knowledge generated by advances in ICT. As identified earlier, it is also the source and potentially the outcome of OL models, such as that of Nonaka et al. (2000) or that which is passed on to others in a CoP. According to Polanyi (1967), tacit knowing, the key source of this idea, is not easy to put into words. For example, we can usually pick out a face we know from a large crowd but it would be difficult to say how we do this. As Polanyi states: 'this knowledge cannot be put into words' (p.6). This makes some of the claims relating to tacit knowledge and its role in KM problematic, or, as Beckett and Hager (2002, p.120) point out, there is a 'multiply ambiguous' nature of tacit knowledge with a variety of meanings. Thus Collins (2001), who is concerned with the transferability of tacit knowledge in science, provides the following classification:

1 *Concealed knowledge:* the tricks of the trade, deliberately concealed and not passed on to others, or not included in journals with insufficient space for such details.
2 *Mismatched salience:* there are an indefinite number of potentially important variables in a new and difficult experiment and the two parties focus on different ones.
3 *Ostensive knowledge:* words, diagrams, or photographs cannot convey information that can be understood by direct pointing, demonstrating or feeling.
4 *Unrecognized knowledge:* work performed in a certain way without realizing the importance of this – others pick up the same habit during a visit, and neither party realizes that anything important has been passed on.
5 *Uncognized/uncognizable knowledge:* humans do things such as speak acceptably formed phrases in their native language without knowing-how they do it.

Gourlay (2006, p.67) seeks to remove some of the ambiguity by suggesting that we use the term tacit knowledge in those situations where there is evidence of action or behaviour 'of which the actors could not give an account', which is closer to Polanyi's view considered above. He argues that managers can create the conditions for experiences to influence tacit knowledge but this can also 'be in a negative direction' (p.67), as defensive routines. This view also has the potential to bring KM closer to learning and, as argued by Spender (2008), helps to move theory towards the creation of knowledge. Spender suggests that 'knowledge-as-practice' is best placed to deal with uncertainties, failures, 'not-knowing or knowledge-absence' (p.166) which can then become the source of creativity. However, such creativity might also be constrained. Knowing, however creative, may not flow and since OL models such as Crossan et al.'s (1999) referred to above, suggest a flow of ideas from 'the individual to the group to the organizational level' (p.532), this flow might not be continuous, resulting in blockages. As shown by Berends and Lammers' (2010) study of a KM project in a bank, the flow of the project was frequently interrupted and sometimes abandoned, partly as result of the range of different interpretations of the project, leading to political struggles between different groups.

activity

Work with a partner. How much tacit knowing is there in reading this question? Share your comments.

Try the following link to resources and publications on KM – www.kmresource.com/

Go to http://www.innovation.at/wp-content/uploads/2011/02/An_Illustrated_Guide_to_Knowledge_Management.pdf to examine a KM guide.

Increasingly, it would seem that the opportunities for learning and knowledge creation in response to failures and knowledge gaps are becoming more evident, requiring new ways of organizing as a response. For example, project-based organizing enables a response to customer demand that expects differentiated goods and services in sectors such as fashion, the arts, software, digital and multimedia (Sydow et al., 2004). Such products and services need to be customized through negotiation rather than standardized for a mass market, and therein lies the space for not-knowing and creativity. To take advantage of these possibilities so that learning can be shared requires devices such as project reviews, critical incident logs and informal sharing of ideas (Brady & Davies, 2004). Projects allow the tension between exploring new possibilities and exploiting the reality of those possibilities to be accommodated. In this way, an organization can become what O'Reilly and Tushman (2004) call ambidextrous. Such organizations have a more versatile structure and configuration, allowing innovation, new products and services to be developed but within an accountable framework.

It is not just within projects that knowledge can be created. As suggested by Newell et al. (2004), a team may not have all the relevant knowledge for its work and needs to network with others. This process draws on what Nahapiet and Ghoshal (1998, p.243) call social capital, defined as the 'sum of the actual and potential resources, available through, and derived from, the network of relationships possessed by an individual or social unit'. The use of social capital depends on trust and reciprocity. For sharing knowledge that feeds relationships to build social capital, there need to be opportunities to share knowledge, a degree of empathy, help and trust and a belief that the knowledge is accurate and reliable (von Krogh, 2003).

Learning from both exploitation and exploration adds to an organization's ability to work with new information, especially from external sources such as customers, suppliers, regulatory agencies and others, and this can then be used to innovate by adapting and making changes to products and services. This ongoing learning process between organizations, and especially from customers, leads to a type of working referred to by Victor and Boynton (1998, p.195) as co-configuration. Such work 'brings the value of an intelligent and "adapting" product'. Co-configuration is synonymous with knowledge creation and knowledge sharing. It is oriented to both individuals and groups and has the potential to link learning at the individual level to that of the organization. Daniels (2004) identifies two features of learning for successful co-configuration. First, learning for co-configuration where different departments representing different specialisms find a mechanism for dialogue to negotiate their practices. Second, through interaction with customers and others, learning is articulated so that knowledge can be shared. Both processes become interdependent in a dialogue around customer and practice.

The ability of an organization to recognize the importance and value of new information from customers or suppliers, accept it for possible use and then actually apply it, is referred to as absorptive capacity (Cohen & Levinthal, 1990) and is seen as a key feature of OL (Sun & Anderson, 2010). It is suggested that in rapidly changing environments or even turbulent times, some organizations need dynamic capabilities (Teece et al., 1997) to recognize the need to change strategy and reconsider its core capabilities (Wang & Ahmed, 2007). Both require learning about the use of resources in new routines and developing new configurations for practice, which in turn are connected to knowledge creation and management (Easterby-Smith & Prieto, 2008).

summary

- Difficulties in implementing systematic models of training have led to an interest in understanding the contextual issues that affect learning at work.
- Understanding the organization as a learning system is referred to as workplace learning.
- Workplace learning requires the use of different ways of understanding organizations and contrasts with the dominant image of organizations as machines.
- Informal learning at work includes much of what occurs as a response to work issues, including mistakes, accidents, problems or just simple incidental conversations, although changes that occur often remain protected by those who made them.
- There is growing interest in how organizations can take advantage of informal learning by emphasizing participation to make learning more explicit.
- OL is concerned with the routines of working that accumulate through experience of working and dealing with problems and finding new ways of working where required. It requires a consideration of learning at different levels of the organization.
- A cultural view of OL can lead to a consideration of communities of practice, where learning is informal and situated in practice.
- The LO and action learning are ways managers and others have tried to stimulate and take advantage of OL.
- Knowledge, its creation and management have been considered as the source of lasting competitive advantage. There are different ideas relating to the meaning of knowledge, such as the distinction between knowing-that and knowing-how.
- Tacit knowledge is considered important to models of KM but difficult to capture or even put into words.
- New ways of organizing, working, sharing knowledge and learning in an ongoing process with customers, suppliers and others are emerging.

discussion questions

1 Should line managers take responsibility for HRD?

2 How can informal learning be considered in organizations?

3 Do organizations learn? Can such learning be used for competitive advantage or sustainability?

4 Is the learning organization achievable?

5 What is the link between absorptive capacity and organization learning?

further reading

Davies, L. (2008) *Informal Learning*. Aldershot: Gower.

Duguid, P. (2005) 'The art of knowing': social and tacit dimensions of knowledge and the limits of the community of practice. *Information Society*, **21**(2): 109–18.

Hsu, L-C. and Wang, C-H. (2012) Clarifying the effect of intellectual capital on performance: the mediating role of dynamic capability. *British Journal of Management*, **23**(20): 179–205.

Raelin, J. (2010) Work-based learning: valuing practice as an educational event. *New Directions for Teaching and Learning*, **124**(Winter): 39–46.

references

Amin, A. and Roberts, J. (2008) Knowing in action: beyond communities of practice. *Research Policy*, **37**(2): 353–69.

Antonacopoulou, E.P. (2001) The paradoxical nature of the relationship between training and learning. *Journal of Management Studies*, **38**(3): 327–50.

Antonacopoulou, E.P., Ferdinand, J., Graca, M. and Easterby-Smith, M. (2005) *Dynamic Capabilities and Organizational Learning: Socio-Political Tensions in Organizational Renewal*. London: Advanced Institute of Management.

Argyris, C. (1999) *On Organizational Learning*. Oxford: Blackwell.

Argyris, C. and Schön, D.A. (1996) *Organizational Learning II*. Reading, MA: Addison-Wesley.

Beckett, D. and Hager, P. (2002) *Life, Work and Learning: Practice in Postmodernity*. London: Routledge.

Berends, H. and Lammers, I. (2010) Explaining discontinuity in organizational learning: a process analysis. *Organization Studies,* **31**(08): 1045–68.

Billett, S. (2006) Constituting the workplace curriculum. *Journal of Curriculum Studies*, **38**(1): 31–48.

Blackler, F. (1995) Knowledge, knowledge work and organizations: an overview and interpretation. *Organization Studies*, **16**(6): 1021–46.

Blackman, D. and Sadler-Smith, E. (2009) The silent and the silenced in organizational knowing and learning. *Management Learning,* **40**(5): 569–85.

Brady, T. and Davies, A. (2004) Building project capabilities: from exploratory to exploitative learning. *Organization Studies*, **25**(9): 1601–21.

Bratton, J. (2001) Why workers are reluctant learners: the case of the Canadian pulp and paper industry. *Journal of Workplace Learning*, **13**(7/8): 333–44.

Brown, J.S. and Duguid, P. (1991) Organizational learning and communities-of-practice: toward a unified view of working, learning, and innovation. *Organization Science*, **2**(1): 40–57.

Burke, L.A. and Saks, A.M. (2009) Accountability in training transfer: adapting Schlenker's model of responsibility to a persistent but solvable problem. *Human Resource Development Review,* **8**(3): 382–402.

Cabanero-Johnson, P. and Berge, Z. (2009) Digital natives: back to the future of microworlds in a corporate learning organization. *The Learning Organization,* **16**(4): 290–97.

Castells, M. (2000) *The Rise of Network Society.* Malden, MA: Blackwell.

Chiaburu, D. and Tekleab, A.G. (2005) Individual and contextual influences on multiple dimensions of training effectiveness. *Journal of European Industrial Training,* **29**: 604–23.

CIPD (2011) *The Coaching Climate.* London: Chartered Institute of Personnel and Development.

Cohen, W. and Levinthal, D. (1990) Absorptive capacity: a new perspective on learning and innovation. *Administrative Science Quarterly,* **35**: 128–52.

Clutterbuck, D. and Megginson, D. (2005) *Making Coaching Work.* London: CIPD.

Collins, H.M. (2001) Tacit knowledge, trust, and the Q of sapphire. *Social Studies of Science,* **31**(1): 71–85.

Colwill, M., Johnson, N., Kelsey, S., Shire, J., Clegg, J., Jones, O., Rix, M. and Gold, J. (2012) *Working Towards Increasing ROI from Learning: A Transfer of Learning Project,* paper presented to European HRD Conference, Portugal.

Crossan, M., Lane, H. and White, R. (1999) An organizational learning framework: from intuition to institution. *Academy of Management Review,* **24**: 522–37.

Daniels, H. (2004) Cultural historical activity theory and professional learning. *International Journal of Disability, Development and Education,* **51**(2): 185–200.

Davidson, M. and Burke, R. (2011) *Women in Management Worldwide: Progress and Prospects.* Aldershot: Gower Publishing.

Dixon, N. (1994) *The Organizational Learning Cycle: How We Can Learn Collectively.* Maidenhead: McGraw-Hill.

Drucker, P. (1988) The coming of the new organization. *Harvard Business Review,* **66**(1): 45–53.

Easterby-Smith, M. and Lyles, M.A. (2003) Introduction: watersheds of organizational learning and knowledge management. In M. Easterby-Smith and M.A. Lyles (eds) *The Blackwell Handbook of Organizational Learning and Knowledge Management.* Oxford: Blackwell.

Easterby-Smith, M. and Prieto, I. (2008) Dynamic capabilities and knowledge management: an integrative role for learning? *British Journal of Management,* **19**(3): 235–49.

Edvinsson, L. and Malone, M.S. (1997) *Intellectual Capital.* New York: Harper Business.

Eraut, M. (2000a) Non-formal learning, implicit learning and tacit knowledge in professional work. In F. Coffield (ed.) *The Necessity of Informal Learning.* Bristol: Policy Press.

Eraut, M. (2000b) Non-formal learning and tacit knowledge in professional work. *British Journal of Educational Psychology,* **70**: 113–36.

Felstead, A., Fuller, A., Unwin, L., Ashton, D., Butler, P. and Lee, L. (2005) Surveying the scene: learning metaphors, survey design and the workplace context. *Journal of Education and Work,* **18**(4): 359–83.

Fenwick, T. (2008) Understanding relations of individual collective learning in work: a review of research. *Management Learning,* **39**(3): 227–43.

Fiol, C.M. and Lyles, M.A (1985) Organizational learning. *Academy of Management Review,* **10**(4): 803–13.

Fuller, A. and Unwin, L. (2003) Learning as apprentices in the contemporary UK workplace: creating and managing expansive and restrictive participation. *Journal of Education and Work,* **16**(4): 407–26.

Gardner, H.K., Anand, N. and Morris, T. (2007) Knowledge-based innovation: emergence and embedding of new practice areas in management consulting firms. *Academy of Management Journal,* **50**(2): 406–28.

Garavan, T.N., Morley, M., Gunnigle, P. and Collins, E. (2001) Human capital accumulation: the role of human resource development. *Journal of European Industrial Training,* **25**(2/3/4): 48–68.

Garvin, D., Edmondson, A. and Gino, F. (2008) Is yours a learning organization? *Harvard Business Review,* **86**(3): 109–16.

Gibb, S. (2002) *Learning and Development: Processes, Practices and Perspectives at Work.* Basingstoke: Palgrave Macmillan.

Goh, S.C., Elliott, C. and Quon, T. (2012) The relationship between learning capability and organizational performance: A meta-analytic examination *The Learning Organization,* **19**(2): 92–108.

Gold, J. and Smith, V. (2003) Advances towards a learning movement: translations at work *Human Resource Development International,* **6**(2): 139–52.

Gourlay, S. (2006) Towards conceptual clarity for 'tacit knowledge': a review of empirical studies *Knowledge Management Research & Practice,* **4**(1): 60–9.

Hansen, M.T., Nohria, N. and Tierney, T. (1999) What's your strategy for managing knowledge? *Harvard Business Review,* **77**(2): 106–16.

Hardt, M. and Negri, A. (2008) *Multitude.* London: Penguin.

Harrison, R. and Kessels, J. (2004) *Human Resource Development in a Knowledge Economy.* Basingstoke: Palgrave Macmillan.

Hager, P. (2004) Lifelong learning in the workplace? Challenges and issues. *Journal of Workplace Learning,* **16**(1/2): 22–32.

Hassan, F. (2011) The frontline advantage. *Harvard Business Review,* **May**: 106–14.

Hirsh, W. and Tamkin, P. (2005) *Planning Training for your Business.* Brighton: Institute of Employment Studies.

Holton, E.F., Bates, R.A., Bookter, A.I. and Yamkovenko, V.B. (2007) Convergent and divergent validity of the learning transfer system inventory. *Human Resource Development Quarterly*, **18**(3): 385–419.

Hutchinson, S. and Purcell, J. (2007) *Learning and the Line: The Role of Line Managers in Training, Learning and Development*. London: CIPD.

Jacobs, R. and Park, Y. (2009) A proposed conceptual framework of workplace learning: Implications for theory development and research in human resource development, *Human Resource Development Review*, **8**(2): 133–50.

Kyndt, E., Dochy, F. and Nijs, H. (2009) Learning conditions for non-formal and informal workplace learning. *Journal of Workplace Learning*, **21**(5): 369–83.

Lave, J. and Wenger, E. (1991) *Situated Learning: Legitimate Peripheral Participation*. Cambridge: Cambridge University Press.

Lawrence, T.B., Mauws, M.K., Dyck, B. and Kleysen, R.F. (2005) The politics of organizational learning: integrating power into the 4I framework. *Academy of Management Review*, **30**(1): 180–91.

Li, L.C., Grimshaw, J.C., Nielsen, C., Judd, M., Coyte, P.C. and Graham, I. (2009) *Use of Communities of Practice in Business and Health Care Sectors: A Systematic Review*. Implementation Science. Available from http://www.implementationscience.com/content/pdf/1748–5908–4–27.pdf, accessed 24 May 2012.

Longworth, N. (2006) *Learning Cities, Learning Regions, Learning Communities*. London: Routledge.

Lubit, R. (2001) The keys to sustainable competitive advantage: tacit knowledge and knowledge management, *Organizational Dynamics*, **29**(3): 164–78.

Machlup, F. (1980) *Knowledge: Its Creation, Distribution, and Economic Significance*, vol. 1, *Knowledge and Knowledge Production*. Princeton, NJ: Princeton University Press.

Marshall, N. and Rollinson, J. (2004) Maybe Bacon had a point: the politics of interpretation in collective sensemaking. *British Journal of Management*, **15**(Special 1): 71–86.

Marsick, V.J. and Watkins, K. (1999) Envisioning new organizations for learning. In D. Boud and J. Garrick (eds) *Understanding Learning at Work*. London: Routledge.

Marsick, V.J. and Watkins, K. (2001) Informal and incidental learning. *New Directions for Adult and Continuing Education*, **89**: 25–34.

Marsick, V. J. (2009) Towards a unifying framework to support informal learning theory, research and practice. *Journal of Workplace Learning*, **21**(4): 265–75.

Mayo, A. (1998) Memory bankers. *People Management*, **22** January: 34–8.

Mayo, A. (2005) What are the latest trends in training and development? in CIPD *Latest Trends in Learning, Training and Development*. London: CIPD.

Mintzberg, H. (1990) The design school: reconsidering the basic premises of strategic management. *Strategic Management Journal*, **11**(3): 171–95.

Mirvis, P.H. (1996) Historical foundations of organization learning. *Journal of Organizational Change Management*, **9**(1): 13–31.

Mooney, T. and Brinkerhoff, R.O. (2008) *Courageous Training*. San Francisco: Berrett-Koehler.

Morgan, G. (2006) *Images of Organization*. London: Sage.

Nahapiet, J. and Ghoshal, S. (1998) Social capital, intellectual capital and the organizational advantage. *Academy of Management Review*, **23**(2): 242–66.

Newell, S., Tansley, C. and Huang, J. (2004) Social capital and knowledge integration in an ERP project team: the importance of bridging and bonding. *British Journal of Management*, **14**: S43–57.

Nicolini, D., Gherardi, S. and Yanow, D. (eds) (2003) *Knowing in Organizations: A Practice-based Approach*. New York: Armonk.

Nonaka, I. and Takeuchi, H. (1995) *The Knowledge-creating Company*. New York: Oxford University Press.

Nonaka, I., Toyama, R. and Konno, N. (2000) SECI, Ba and leadership: a unified model of dynamic knowledge creation. *Long Range Planning*, **33**: 5–34.

OECD (Organization for Economic Co-operation and Development) (1996) *The Knowledge-based Economy*. Paris: OECD.

Örtenblad, A. (2004) The learning organization: towards an integrated model. *Learning Organization*, **11**(2): 129–44.

O'Reilly, C. and Tushman, M. (2004) The ambidextrous organization. *Harvard Business Review*, April: 74–81.

Park, Y. and Jacobs, R. (2011) The influence of investment in workplace learning on learning outcomes and organizational performance. *Human Resource Development Quarterly*, **22**(4): 437–58.

Pedler, M., Burgoyne, J.G. and Boydell, T. (1991) *The Learning Company: A Strategy for Sustainable Development*. Cambridge: McGraw-Hill.

Polanyi, M. (1967) *The Tacit Dimension*. Garden City, NY: Doubleday.

Prahalad, C.K. and Hamel, G. (1990) The core competence of the corporation. *Harvard Business Review*, **68**: 79–91.

Reber, A.S. (2003) Implicit learning and tacit knowledge. In B.J. Baars (ed.) *Essential Sources in the Scientific Study of Consciousness*. Boston: MIT Press.

Roberts, J. (2006) Limits to communities of practice. *Journal of Management Studies*, **43**(3): 623–39.

Ryle, G. ([1949]1984) *The Concept of Mind*. Chicago: University of Chicago Press.

Sambrook, S. (2005) Factors influencing the context and process of work-related learning: Synthesizing findings from two research projects. *Human Resource Development International*, **8**(1):101–19.

Sambrook, S. and Stewart, J. (2002) Reflections and discussion. In S. Tjepkema, J. Stewart, S. Sambrook et al. (eds) *HRD and Learning Organizations in Europe*. London: Routledge.

Scarbrough, H. and Swan, J. (2001) Explaining the diffusion of knowledge management: the role of fashion. *British Journal of Management*, **12**(1): 3–12.

Scarso, E. and Bolisani, E. (2010) Knowledge-based strategies for knowledge intensive business services: a multiple case-study of computer service companies. *Electronic Journal of Knowledge Management*, **8**(1): 151–60, available online at www.ejkm com.

Schilling, J. and Kluge, A. (2009) Barriers to organizational learning: An integration of theory and research. *International Journal of Management Reviews*, **11**: 337–60.

Senge, P.M. (1990a) *The Fifth Discipline: The Art and Practice of the Learning Organization*. New York: Currency Doubleday.

Senge, P.M. (1990b) The leader's new work: building learning organizations. *Sloan Management Review*, **32**(1): 7–23.

Sloman, M. (2003) *Training in the Age of the Learner*. London: CIPD.

Smith, P.A.C. (2012) The importance of organizational learning for organizational sustainability. *The Learning Organization*, **19**(1): 4–10.

Spender, J.-C. (2008) Organizational learning and knowledge management: whence and whither? *Management Learning*, **39**(2): 159–76.

Strebler, M., Robinson, D. and Heron, P. (1997) *Getting the Best out of your Competencies*. Brighton: Institute of Employment Studies.

Stuart, R. (1984) Towards re-establishing naturalism in management training and development, *Industrial and Commercial Training*, July/August: 19–21.

Sun, P. and Anderson, M. (2010) An examination of the relationship between absorptive capacity and organizational learning, and a proposed integration. *International Journal of Management Reviews*, **12**(2): 130–50.

Sydow, J., Lindkvist, L. and DeFillippi, R. (2004) Project-based organizations, embeddedness and repositories of knowledge. *Organization Studies*, **25**(9): 1475–89.

Taylor, H. (1991) The systematic training model: corn circles in search of a spaceship? *Management Education and Development*, **22**(4): 258–78.

Teece, D., Pisano, G. and Shuen, A. (1997) Dynamic capabilities and strategic management. *Strategic Management Journal*, **18**(7): 509–33.

Tsoukas, H. (2000) Knowledge as action, organization as theory. *Emergence*, **2**(4): 104–12.

Van Ruysseveldt, J. and Van Dijke, M. (2011) When are workload and workplace learning opportunities related in a curvilinear manner? The moderating role of autonomy. *Journal of Vocational Behavior*, **79**(2): 470–83.

Victor, B. and Boynton, A. (1998) *Invented Here: Maximizing your Organization's Internal Growth and Profitability*. Boston: Harvard Business School Press.

Von Krogh, G. (2003) Knowledge sharing and the communal resources. In M. Easterby-Smith and M.A. Lyles (eds) *The Blackwell Handbook of Organizational Learning and Knowledge Management*. Oxford: Blackwell.

Von Krogh, G., Nonaka, I. and Rechsteiner, L. (2012) Leadership in organizational knowledge creation: a review and framework. *Journal of Management Studies*, **49**(1): 240–77.

Vygotsky, L. (1978) *Mind and Society: The Development of Higher Mental Processes*. Cambridge, MA: Harvard University Press.

Wang, C.L. and Ahmed, P.K. (2007) Dynamic capabilities: a review and research agenda. *International Journal of Management Reviews*, **9**: 31–51.

Watkins, K.E. and Marsick, V.J. (1993) *Sculpting the Learning Organization: Lessons in the Art and Science of Systemic Change*. San Francisco: Jossey-Bass.

Weick, K. and Westley, F. (1996) Organizational learning: affirming an oxymoron. In S. Clegg, C. Hardy and W. Nord (eds) *Handbook of Organization Studies*. Thousand Oaks, CA: Sage.

Wenger, E.C. and Snyder, W.M. (2000) Communities of practice: the organizational frontier. *Harvard Business Review*, **78**(1): 139–45.

Yang, K. (2012) Further understanding accountability in public organizations: actionable knowledge and the structure–agency duality. *Administration & Society*, **44**(3): 255–84.

Yang, B., Watkins, K.E. and Marsick, V.J. (2004) The construct of the learning organization: dimensions, measurement, and validation. *Human Resource Development Quarterly*, **15**(1): 31–55.

Yanow, D. (2000) Seeing organizational learning: a 'cultural' view. *Organization*, **7**(2): 247–68.

Yanow, D. (2004) Translating local knowledge at organizational peripheries. *British Journal of Management*, **15**(S1): 9–25.

Leadership and Management Development

Julia Claxton and Jeff Gold

Chapter learning outcomes

After studying this chapter, you should be able to:

- Understand the meanings of and approaches to leadership and management
- Understand what is meant by leadership and management development
- Appreciate the strategic approach to leadership and management development
- Explain and critique models of leadership and management development
- Assess key approaches to implementing leadership and management development

Chapter outline

Introduction
Meanings of LMD, leadership and management
A strategic approach to leadership and management development
Models for leadership and management development
Implementing leadership and management development
Summary

Introduction

Both before, during and after the 2007 credit crunch, managers, and especially those called leaders, have had their overall effectiveness questioned. For example, research in the US by Leslie (2009) from 2006 to 2008 in 15 organizations suggested concern for the lack of leadership skills, which were insufficient for current and future needs. In the UK, McBain et al. (2012), drawing on a survey of 4,496 people, including 302 chief executives, found that 43 per cent of managers considered their line manager to be ineffective or highly ineffective. Since there was also a good relationship between high-performing organisations and higher ratings of manager effectiveness, the authors concluded that organisations could improve performances if they could improve managers and leadership. In England, the Chartered Institute of Personnel and Development's survey (CIPD, 2012) found that nearly 60 per cent of organisations reported a lack of management and leadership skills among senior managers, with 85 per cent reporting that line managers lacked these skills. It is assumed that effective leadership and management is key to organisational, national and global progression in all areas of business and society. In all walks of life we need to manage and lead people, systems, processes and resources so it is clear that the more we provide resources for leadership and management development (LMD), the more we will achieve. Does this stand to reason? If you consider for a moment what you and your colleagues mean by effective leadership or management, you might find some interesting differences. You will also be aware that resources for LMD, especially funding for training programmes, are not always available in a recession, but in many organisations, such as small and medium-sized enterprises (SMEs), whatever passes for LMD is mostly about learning at work by solving problems and dealing with staff and customers. Such learning can be made more explicit and recognizable but this would require time, which is not always possible. So, LMD can be visible and recognized, and potentially measurable in terms of impact, but it can also be hidden within the work of those called managers and leaders. As we consider below, this presents both problems and opportunities for making more effective both the practice of leadership and management and the work of those who seek to promote LMD.

Meanings of LMD, leadership and management

Burgoyne et al. (2004) suggested that it is difficult to generalize about developing leaders and managers because of the variations in context and situations faced. Further, given our comments above about visibility, recognition and hiddenness within work, it becomes rather difficult to present a generalized definition of LMD. Gold et al. (2010) suggest instead that LMD can best be understood as a dimension between more planned approaches based on visibility and more emergent approaches based on hiddenness. Firstly LMD is:

> A planned and deliberate process to help leaders and managers become more effective. (p.19)

Planning and deliberation is based on the existence of specified ideas, models and theories which leaders and managers put into practice. This definition underpins many LMD courses and programmes including accredited ones, as we consider below.

In contrast, the second definition of LMD is:

> A process of learning for leaders and managers through recognised opportunities. (p.19)

At an extreme, LMD is completely hidden and can occur informally and experientially without planning and deliberation. A key issue is how leaders and managers come to recognize learning opportunities as part of their work. They need to acknowledge the importance of reflection to capture learning from work and events, and make changes to practice (Vince & Reynolds, 2010). Such a process can also become more public, allowing learning to be shared with others.

In practice, these two definitions could be experienced as contrasting poles of a dimension with variations in between. For example, leaders could attend a very expensive strategic management programme, full of the latest models and ideas about strategy but find that mostly they enjoyed talking with leaders from other companies, some of whom become part of their LinkedIn network. The formal, planned part is soon forgotten but the network thrives and becomes a source of problem sharing. What started as investment in an individual leader, or human capital development, could become more valuable as a way for leaders to network, or social capital development (Powell, 2012).

reflective question

Consider how these two definitions of LMD could be used in:

a A large multi-national
b A local government office
c A small web design company

It would not take too much imagination to discern that the planning and deliberation definition tends to find favour in organisations that have a reasonably clear idea of what their leaders and managers are meant to do, how they need to behave and therefore what they ought to learn through LMD. In other words, there is likely to be an agreed model of leadership and management and such a model will, to varying degrees, reflect theories and ideas of what leaders and managers do or are supposed to do.

Leadership and management differences

An initial question to consider is whether there is a difference between leadership and management and, if so, the nature of such difference? This is an ongoing debate and generally relates to the type of organisation you work in. In many contexts the terms are used interchangeably and the roles are often combined.

The purpose of the organisation is often covered by leadership questions concerning 'why are we doing this?', or 'why are we here?', or 'why are we making this product?'. The 'how are we going to do this?', 'how long will it take?', 'how will it get transported?' questions tend to relate to management aspects, the process, the implementation and the resources needed. So leadership is about direction and pulling together towards a common goal and management is about implementing those plans and managing the resources to execute them effectively and efficiently. Effectiveness and efficiency are, of course, very different things. A manager who minimizes staff resources will be very efficient but if this means the jobs are not completed then he/she is completely ineffective. A manager who gains new contracts may be very effective but if they are giving away free products to gain these contracts then they would be inefficient as they are wasting resources.

Such images relate to a key idea you will find in the literature on whether leadership is different to management (see Bennis and Nanus, 1985, for example). We would argue that in practice, rather than a clear separation, especially in terms of roles, aspects of both are found together. However, there is a tendency, in uncertain and difficult times, for leaders to be given prominence in the expectation that they will provide direction and maintain engagement (Holbeche, 2008a). This can mean that there is a desire to identify leaders from managers in order to focus resources, but if leadership is more about activities relating to processes of influence and mutual working then leadership is found at all levels of the organisation, not just within one or two key individuals (Alimo-Metcalfe & Alban-Metcalfe, 2005). Leadership becomes distributed throughout the organisation and resides within teams, groups and individuals without a position of power or a title (Thorpe et al., 2011). Whether we see leaders and managers as separate or together does have implications for developing them, as does the variety of contexts in which they work. In larger organisations, roles are often more clearly defined, but most people in the UK work in SMEs, many of which are family businesses. In many of these, the term leadership seems to have little meaning or value (Kempster & Cope, 2010). We need to remember that there are also differences between leading and managing in the public sector, the professions and the third sector. In the third sector (voluntary and community organisations), Claxton et al. (2009) found that the main barrier to leadership development was that leaders did not want to be leaders in the first place. Given the variety of purposes in organisations, there are sure to be different values and perspectives on the ethical and moral considerations of decision-making (Robinson, 2010) and the impact of decisions on the environment (Western, 2008).

activity

Go to www.management-standards.org/standards/full-list-2008-national-occupational-standards and choose an area you are interested in developing. What skills and knowledge does the Standard suggest you need and how could you develop these?

Theories of leadership and management

While it is important to see the connection between leadership and management, for many years researchers have developed different theories and ideas under each heading. Under the heading of management during the first part of the twentieth century the American F.W. Taylor (1911) completed an analysis of work tasks so that managers could find the 'one best way' to control work and eliminate waste. In France, Henri Fayol (1949) identified five basic managerial functions – planning, organising, co-ordinating, commanding and controlling, or POC³ – which have provided the basis for management textbooks and LMD programmes ever since. If you add in ideas on bureaucracy based on the work of the German sociologist, Max Weber (Watson, 1980), you have the key elements of a classic description of managerial work.

Already, during the 1930s, the classic view was challenged by findings from the famous Hawthorne investigations which resulted in what became referred to as the Human Relations School. This led to the introduction of psychology into LMD in such aspects as group and team behaviour, motivation, the influence of work conditions and managing conflict at work. The influence of human relations ideas was significant during and after the Second World War in a move towards understanding and emphasising the role of leadership as distinct from that of management.

Interestingly, when researchers began to consider the reality of leadership and management work, in terms of how people actually carry out their work, they found some important differences between theory and practice. Rosemary Stewart (1975), for example, considered the work of hundreds of managers in the UK. She found that most:

- worked at a brisk pace with little free time
- spent a lot of time interacting with people
- based a lot of their work on personal choice
- did not work according to neat, well-organized models.

In the US, John Kotter (1982) found that managers spent a lot time dealing with issues through conversations. Managers seldom had formal plans but worked with an informal agenda and built networks to achieve objectives. Henry Mintzberg (1973) found senior managers worked in a fragmented and varied way with an emphasis on verbal communication and networks. Mintzberg suggested that managerial roles are interpersonal, informational and decisional. He suggested that a leader was just one role within management, which relates back to our question of whether leadership and management are different. One outcome of this research on leaders and managers is that the fragmentation, variety and lack of formal plans suggest that the hidden and informal definition of LMD needs to be taken more seriously.

reflective question   How can informal learning by leaders and managers become more recognized and seen as valuable?

Against the findings of what leaders and managers actually do, in recent years there has been a strong interest in the idea and theory of leadership. Many organisations now attempt to incorporate a particular emphasis on leadership as part of their LMD and talent programmes (CIPD, 2012). Storey (2004) pointed to the enormous growth of literature on leadership, while there has been a slower rate of growth in the LD literature. He also noted high-profile initiatives on leadership in the UK public sector (for example the National College for School Leadership, a leadership centre for the NHS, new leadership initiatives in the police service and the Ministry of Defence), along with the publication of a variety of reports (for example Horne & Stedman-Jones, 2001). One example is in the higher education sector, where the Leadership Foundation for Higher Education was founded in 2003. Improved/enhanced organizational leadership is seen as the appropriate response in all sectors. The search has been on for a model for developing leaders, although there remains a difficulty in specifying a precise meaning of the term leadership, as a search for a definition will reveal (try this on a good search engine).

Explicitly or implicitly, definitions can be connected to various theories of leadership, which can in turn inform LMD. However, much of the early work on leadership was around linking leaders with particular personalities or traits and the idea of developing leaders was not really considered. It was more a case of identifying which type was needed, finding them and hiring them.

It was during and after the Second World War that attention turned to what leaders and managers needed to be able to display through their work. This led to a focus on behaviours that contributed to particular styles of leadership and how style needed to vary according to circumstances such as the situation and the behaviour and capabilities of others, usually referred to as followers. This dual feature of leadership behaviour resulted in the development of diagnostic tools to increase awareness of styles and, importantly, LMD programmes to allow learning to use appropriate styles. For example, leaders have to have followers and each follower is different from the next. This led to the theories around situational leadership and the readiness, or maturity, of followers to be led in a task. This readiness or maturity is a mixture of confidence/enthusiasm and competence/ability in the task requirements (Hersey & Blanchard, 1977). In the 1970s, the move towards transformational leadership (Burns, 1978; Bass, 1985; Salovey & Mayer, 1990) as a new way of seeing leadership as an interaction that affected, as in transformed, both the leader and the follower. It was not something that happened outside of the person but to the person. The Multifactor Leadership Questionnaire (MLQ) by Bass and Avolio (1990) allows the assessment of leaders and managers as transformational and/or transactional.

There is now a vast range of models and ideas relating to leadership which can be used in LMD. However, it does seem that in any design, a contingency approach is needed to take account of strategy, sector, values and goals (Clarke & Higgs, 2010). In addition, there are variations in understanding leadership as a 'property of an individual, a relationship or set of relationships, or indeed part of a much wider system' (p.36). We will consider how such variations can be accommodated below.

activity

Go to www.mlq.com.au for more information about the MLQ. Find how this instrument of assessment for leadership can be used by individuals and teams, linking appraisal with development and cultural change. Find out what is meant by authentic leadership and the Full Range Leadership.

Go to **www.leader-values.com/self_assessment.php** for an online assessment of leadership values.

Find out about Servant Leadership at **https://www.greenleaf.org/what-is-servant-leadership/**.

A strategic approach to leadership and management development

According to Garavan et al. (1999) seeking a causal link between strategy, LMD and performance is based on a 'functional performance rationale' (p.193) involving the following stages:

1   Setting organisation strategy in response to an assessment of changes in the environment

2   Agreeing the response with various stakeholders and interested parties

3   Determining a strategy providing guidance on the requirements for leaders and managers in terms of numbers, skills and performance

4   Developing LMD policy to translate the requirements to provide LMD activities

5   Assessing the outcomes to provide feedback to organisation strategy.

Included in any policy for LMD are responses to identified weaknesses and improvements for performance, succession planning and talent management, values to be promoted (e.g. diversity, ecology, social responsibility), new services or products to be pursued and requirements for new leaders and managers.

The CIPD (2002) suggest two purposes for LMD:

a   To sustain the business by developing leaders and managers with the skills to carry out determined roles

b   To advance the business by developing new models in fast-moving sectors and turbulent environments.

The second purpose suggests that LMD plays a role in *making* strategy as well as *responding* to strategy. This relates to a growing interest in talent management, where a number of organisations develop a talent pipeline for senior positions by strategically identifying staff of high potential and performance for development as leaders and managers (Tansley et al., 2007). In this way LMD influences strategy formation. What leaders and managers learn directs future activities of the organization. This requires a change in how the organisation determines its strategy. Since most approaches to strategy are based on a *prescription* of how strategy should be carried out and aligning the skills of leaders and managers to this (Mintzberg et al., 1998), the second approach goes beyond the alignment of LMD to strategic aims. It gives consideration to how leaders and managers are learning from ongoing actions and reflection, 'what they have done' (p.195). In this way, unplanned learning feeds an *emerging* strategy.

A strategic approach to LMD can stimulate strategic change enhancing capability in strategic management (Brown, 2005). In addition, if consistency at different levels of leadership and management during a strategic initiative can be maintained, a significant improvement in performance can occur (O'Reilly et al., 2010). However, evidence of a strategic approach to LMD is hard to find. LMD providers tend to focus on short-term issues and general business skills rather than future-oriented and strategic skills (Clarke et al., 2004). There has also been a lack of representation of LMD at board level and a view that it is something to cut in a recession, although investment is the better strategy for survival (Holbeche, 2008b). In the face of change and turbulence, such as increasing globalization, technological advances and economic instability, LMD could be seen as a deliberate attempt to implement a strategic response (Brown, 2007).

activity

Go to **www.delni.gov.uk/leading-to-success** to examine the Management and Leadership Strategy for the Department of Employment and Learning in Northern Ireland. Consider to what extent the ideas are concerned with short-term skills or longer-term and future-oriented issues.

Evidence of a link between LMD and performance

Is there evidence that LMD has an impact on an organization's outcomes in terms of profit or customer satisfaction? Recent reports attempt to summarize the evidence of such a link (see BIS, 2012), but there have been difficulties in demonstrating how LMD affects the performance of leaders and managers, and the overall performance of organisations (Holmes, 1995a). Mabey and Thomson (2000) found different views on the impact of LMD between HR managers who provided LMD and managers who did LMD. A model developed by Tamkin and Denvir (2006), shown as Figure 11.1, shows how different factors contribute to the impact of the LMD. The impact and outcomes of LMD come from the management capability and this capability relates to the organisational context.

Leskew and Singh (2007) suggest that best practice LMD has a thorough needs assessment, the selection of a suitable audience, the design of an appropriate infrastructure, the design and implementation of an entire learning system, an evaluation system and corresponding actions to reward success and improve on deficiencies. Also needed is support for the LMD, including a positive HR context that includes career planning, succession planning and fast-tracking, all linked to the LMD processes and with LMD as a priority. Mabey (2002) suggested that such factors indicate that a long-term view is being taken. Perhaps the most crucial factor is the support given to informal learning and development, often seen by managers as effective. In further work by Mabey (2005), the crucial links between LMD and organisation measures such as commitment, performance and productivity are made, as shown in Figure 11.2, where line thickness indicates the strength of the link.

More recently, the connection between LMD and employee engagement has been reinforced in a survey completed by 4,496 people across all levels of management (McBain et al., 2012). Where managers also had career

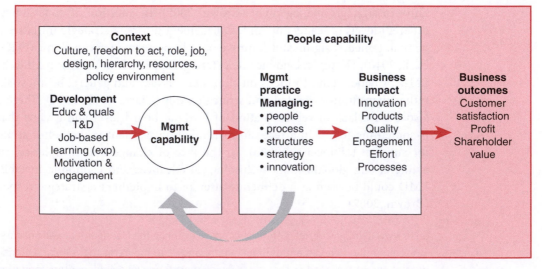

Figure 11.1 A model of impact on organization performance

Source: Tamkin and Denvir (2006, p.12)

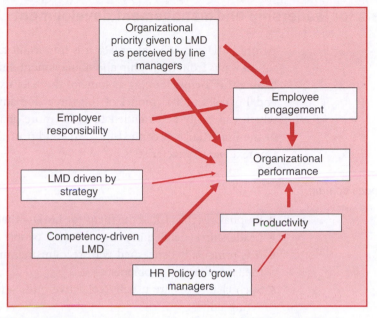

Figure 11.2 How leadership and management development (LMD) links to organization performance (OP)

Source: Mabey (2005)

development opportunities, they were perceived as effective in terms of their management skills and this improved employee engagement. In higher-performance organizations, there was also higher spending on LMD and this could also be affected by senior management commitment to LMD and HR practices such as performance management, succession planning and competency frameworks that reinforce LMD.

Positive perceptions play a crucial part in the evidence for LMD as engagement and therefore performance will be enhanced if the manager perceives that their senior is supporting the LMD. Such evidence-based approaches require, according to Hamlin (2010):

- systematic feedback of opinions and preferences of managers/leaders and organizations
- good critically reflective evaluation data
- relevant, good quality empirical research of all kinds
- the consensus of recognized professional experts in the field of management, leadership
- affirmed professional experience that substantiates practice.

Organisations should gather evidence, reflect on the findings, demonstrate the links of LMD to performance and consider how improvements can be made for future LMD.

reflective question   Is there a strategic case for LMD?

Models for leadership and management development

Before LMD activities take place it is important to understand what the organisation wants from leadership and management. Frameworks are helpful in establishing this. Before looking at some of these let us take note of Pedler, Burgoyne and Boydell's (2004) model of the three domains for leadership development which can easily be extended to LMD more generally. The model reminds us of the importance of context for LMD and portrays three domains: Challenges, Context and Characteristics:

Challenges domain

- Emphasizes the task as the focus for LMD – that is, its raison d'être
- Leadership is defined in action, by what people do
- It is principally concerned with recognising, mobilising and taking action in the face of critical problems
- Such challenges are usually collective ones – few are tackled by one person acting alone.

Context domain

- This is generally neglected in most LMD programmes – yet, effective leadership is always situational
- Action is always local and contextual – done here, with these particular people, for instance
- What works here and now may not work in another place and time
- Emphasizes the collective aspect of leadership and management, working with others in a concerted endeavour.

Characteristics domain

- Most LMD programmes focus on and over-emphasize this domain. This is partly a legacy of leadership being the province of outstanding individuals with rare personal qualities, and partly a training tradition that focuses on individual knowledge and skills.

Frameworks for qualities and competences

In many organisations, models of leadership and management are expressed as frameworks of competences, which are descriptions of behaviours, attributes and skills that people need to perform work effectively, or the outputs to be achieved from such work which can be assessed against performance criteria. A distinction can be made between *generic* models that can be applied to all leaders and managers in all situations, and *organization-specific* models that are developed in specific organizations.

One of the first generic models was presented in the US by Boyatzis (1982), which consisted of five clusters: competences, goal and action, leadership, human resource, directing subordinates and focus on others. In clustering competences Boyatzis made it clear that environment and context would also affect performance. Perren and Burgoyne (2002) presented a framework of abilities for generic leaders and managers, as part of their work for the Council for Excellence in Management and Leadership, shown as Figure 11.3

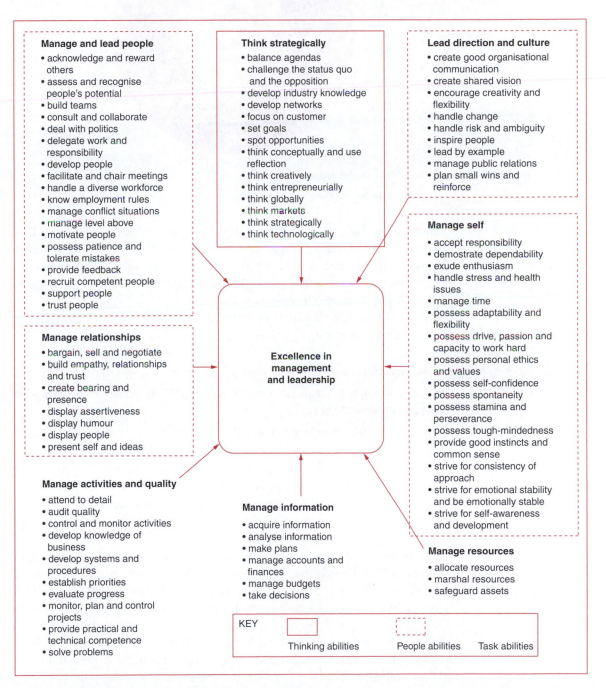

Manage and lead people
- acknowledge and reward others
- assess and recognise people's potential
- build teams
- consult and collaborate
- deal with politics
- delegate work and responsibility
- develop people
- facilitate and chair meetings
- handle a diverse workforce
- know employment rules
- manage conflict situations
- manage level above
- motivate people
- possess patience and tolerate mistakes
- provide feedback
- recruit competent people
- support people
- trust people

Think strategically
- balance agendas
- challenge the status quo and the opposition
- develop industry knowledge
- develop networks
- focus on customer
- set goals
- spot opportunities
- think conceptually and use reflection
- think creatively
- think entrepreneurially
- think globally
- think markets
- think strategically
- think technologically

Lead direction and culture
- create good organisational communication
- create shared vision
- encourage creativity and flexibility
- handle change
- handle risk and ambiguity
- inspire people
- lead by example
- manage public relations
- plan small wins and reinforce

Manage relationships
- bargain, sell and negotiate
- build empathy, relationships and trust
- create bearing and presence
- display assertiveness
- display humour
- display people
- present self and ideas

Excellence in management and leadership

Manage self
- accept responsibility
- demostrate dependability
- exude enthusiasm
- handle stress and health issues
- manage time
- possess adaptability and flexibility
- possess drive, passion and capacity to work hard
- possess personal ethics and values
- possess self-confidence
- possess spontaneity
- possess stamina and perseverance
- possess tough-mindedness
- provide good instincts and common sense
- strive for consistency of approach
- strive for emotional stability and be emotionally stable
- strive for self-awareness and development

Manage activities and quality
- attend to detail
- audit quality
- control and monitor activities
- develop knowledge of business
- develop systems and procedures
- establish priorities
- evaluate progress
- monitor, plan and control projects
- provide practical and technical competence
- solve problems

Manage information
- acquire information
- analyse information
- make plans
- manage accounts and finances
- manage budgets
- take decisions

Manage resources
- allocate resources
- marshal resources
- safeguard assets

KEY

Thinking abilities   People abilities   Task abilities

Figure 11.3 A framework of leadership and management abilities

Source: Perren and Burgoyne (2002)

Figure 11.4 Standards for management and leadership

Source: The Management Standards Centre (http://www.management-standards.org)

Another generic model is Management Standards (2008), see Figure 11.4, which is designed to reflect best practice. The model starts with stating that a key purpose of management and leadership is 'to provide direction, gain commitment, facilitate change and achieve results through the efficient, creative and responsible deployment of people and other resources.'

Each of the six functional areas is broken down into units of competence, elements of competence and performance criteria for each element.

activity

Go to Management Standards at www.management-standards.org/standards/standards

Also see the Institute for Leadership and Management (ILM) website **http://www.i-l-m. com/learn-with-ilm/370.aspx**

How do these models relate to one another?

While generic models can be used by all leaders and managers in any context, or can cover a group of professionals who might work in different contexts, organisation-specific models are expressed in terms of what is understood to be meaningful in one particular context. They provide clarity for leaders and managers, aligned with business requirements.

Both generic and organization-specific models of competences are popular and represent well-supported views of what leaders and managers need to learn. They are therefore the most common approach to assessing and developing leaders and managers, becoming, in the words of Bolden and Gosling (2006, p.147), almost 'ubiquitous'. One area of particular interest in recent years is emotional competences. Salovey and Mayer (1990) first wrote about the concept of emotional intelligence in their famous article in 1990 and it was later developed by Goleman in his book in 1998, particularly on providing competences .

Go to Goleman's website www.eiconsortium.org and to **www.eiconsortium.org/reports/ emotional_competence_framework.html** to look at the 25 areas of emotional compe-tence. Which of these skills do you think are most important for effective management and leadership?

Check out the Emotional and Social Competency Quiz at **www.haygroup.com/ leadershipandtalentondemand/demos/ei_quiz.aspx**

Ever since competences for leaders and managers appeared, they have met with critical comments. There is the danger that the presentation of a frame-work of competences can easily become confused with the reality of leading and managing. Some of the criticism relates to the use of language and vague terms that people find difficult to understand, along with a proliferation of paperwork, which can shift attention away from the purpose of LMD (Gold et al., 2010). Perhaps of more concern is the way competences can falsely bring order to what is a complex activity. As Lawler (2005) suggests, competences can minimize the fluid and objective experience of leaders and managers. However, those who control the competence frameworks gain a degree of power over such experiences, which can also result in pressure to control performance. As argued by Holmes (1995b), competences can become the legitimate way to talk about performance, and this can force out alternative ways of talking. Indeed, it is argued that competences can be use to define leadership and management performance, requiring leaders and managers to align themselves with a particu-lar way of behaving (Salaman & Taylor, 2002).

Making use of the models and frameworks

Models and frameworks of leadership and management can be used to identify skill development needs against desirable competencies. Feedback on perfor-mance is an important part of this process and people respond to feedback differently. Judge et al. (1997) pointed to the importance of key psychological factors, such as self-esteem, self-efficacy, locus of control, self-image and neuroti-cism, which affect responses. For example, as Jordan and Audia (2012) argue, based on the view that people do like to see themselves positively as winners, their response to low performance feedback might be to distort such assessment in order to preserve their self-image. In such cases, the feedback might not be used to identify learning needs to make improvements. Of course, some leaders and managers thrive on feedback, and actively seek it, which can play a role in improving performance. VandeWalle et al. (2000), for example, show the impor-tance of a manager's learning-goal orientation in seeking feedback which is used to develop new skills, although contextual factors such as the behaviour of senior managers of the organisation will play a role too.

How might you respond to feedback which highlights poor performance? Would or do you use it to identify learning needs or do you distort the feedback in some way? For example, do you retrospectively change the goals of your performance to match the poor performance?

Assessment and development centres, different levels of appraisal and multi-source feedback (MSF) can be used to assess performance and determine LMD needs but these are demanding approaches. They need to be supported (Brutus & Derayah, 2002) with results used to set goals for action that are in turn supported by coaching (Luthans & Peterson, 2003). Self-appraisal is always useful but easily distorted, but upward appraisal can be viewed positively if it is anonymous and provides constructive feedback (Antonioni, 1994). Also, where leaders and managers rate themselves more highly than staff, this is unlikely to lead to changes in behaviour, although some might reduce their own ratings in response to lower staff ratings (Dierendonck et al., 2007). Peer appraisal is more likely to lead to LMD if negative evaluation can be avoided. Leaders and managers are less inclined to give formal feedback on performance but might do so informally (Peiperl, 2001). Peer appraisal is also likely to be accepted in professional environments such as schools and hospitals (Dupee et al., 2011) where relationships between fellow professionals are likely to be highly valued.

360-degree appraisal provides a more rounded view of performance but requires confidence and trust in leaders and managers, since the barrage of feedback received could potentially make the process deeply negative and demoralising (Gold et al., 2010). For such reasons, 360-degree appraisal schemes can become unworkable (Fletcher, 1998). Whatever emerges from the process, goals need to be set, LMD undertaken and support provided if performance improvement is to be achieved (Smither et al., 2008). As with any approach to LMD, personal development plans which are meaningful to leaders and managers can be motivating and effective in creating a virtuous process of performance, review and learning (see McCall, 2010).

Setting clear goals and providing immediate feedback are features of how managers can perform best by concentrating on what they are doing against the challenges they are facing. They can achieve a sense of what Csikszentmihalyi (1997) calls flow, which is what happens when the person's skills are fully involved in overcoming a challenge that is just manageable, so that the individual feels they could stretch themselves further and increase the challenge. However, if the challenge is too hard, or the skills not sufficient, the manager will move out of flow and become demotivated. Also, if the challenge is not strong enough or skills are left unused then boredom or disappointment will also demotivate. It is important that LMD opportunities are staged and paralleled with skill development and support before levels of responsibility are increased to ensure the employee remains in the state of flow.

Trust is also an important aspect of this process and therefore must be considered in any LMD. In recent CIPD-sponsored research (Hope-Hailey et al., 2010) the behaviours of 'ability + benevolence + integrity + predictability = trustworthiness' and five types of trust were identified:

Type 1: trust in each other

Type 2: trust in leaders

Type 3: trust in the organisation

Type 4: trust in external relations

Type 5: trust in the direct line manager.

Other factors in building trustworthiness were the 'importance' of the relationship between employees and their line managers and 'open communication'. They found that employees' trust in organisations is generated and sustained when they themselves feel trusted by their managers. Conversely, the results of the survey showed that poor communication, high levels of conflict and limited opportunities for staff to develop and progress were key factors in reducing trust. Leaders and managers need to be especially aware of this and this may come through their LMD.

A manager's communication style is the most reliable predictor of trust in them (Dirks & Ferrin, 2002). However, this covers a broad range of skills. Listening has been singled out as a key factor (Bijlsma & van de Bunt, 2003), as has participating in decision-making (Gillespie & Mann, 2004) and delegation (Duffy & Ferrier, 2003). Duffy and Ferrier also found that excessive monitoring produced less trust. If there is interpersonal trust in a manager then an employee will feel more empowered (Moye & Henkin, 2006).

Developing leaders and managers to empower their staff is important. To empower means to invest, equip or supply with power. Many senior leaders say they want to but they use the term glibly – what they want is control. However, the best way to gain power is to give it away and we have to bend down to lift someone else up – these are the things that really empower people and build trust. Fairness is a foundation of trust and is evidenced in four ways, how the manager: shares out rewards (distributive justice); ensures that everyone has to follow the same processes for whatever outcomes they need (procedural justice); converses with everyone in the same manner so that all receive the same quality of attention (interactional justice); and that information is shared equally and some are not favoured over others (informational justice) (Colquitt, 2001). McKenna and Maister (2002) say it is the leader who is responsible for developing the behaviours of trust in the team.

activity

Go to **http://webarchive.nationalarchives.gov.uk/20120823131012/www.businesslink. gov.uk/bdotg/action/pdp** for an online tool to develop a personal development plan (PDP). It is designed for managers to enable them to assess their skills and form a plan for learning and development.

Implementing LMD

Learning processes which are effective for leaders and managers are one of three aspects that need to be considered for effectiveness in LMD (Gold et al., 2010). The other two are identification of the meaning of effective behaviour for leaders and managers and the development of processes that will help leaders and managers become effective. If the managers and leaders are not able to choose their own learning it can result in problems of transferral of that learning to their own context (Gilpin-Jackson & Bushe, 2007). Also leaders and managers may see little value in undertaking LMD activities. This is referred to as vicious learning (Gold et al., 2010, p.115). Malcom Knowles (1998) provides a helpful reminder that adult learners are self-directed (but also having a conditioned expectation to wanting to be taught), arrive with experience, are a rich resource for each other's learning, learn with a purpose and are more motivated intrinsically than extrinsically.

Experiential learning, especially the learning cycle model presented by Kolb (1984) and learning styles questionnaires from Honey and Mumford (1996) in the UK, have been very influential in LMD (see also Chapter 5). However, these types of questionnaires have been criticized (Coffield et al., 2004; Reynolds, 1997) and as instruments they lack validation. They can also be accused of categorising people in the same way as the left brain/right brain concept does and this can have a detrimental effect on learning (Claxton, 2005). However, experiential learning at work is still relevant if social and political features of organisational life can be incorporated (Reynolds, 2009).

Providing activities for LMD

There is a wide array of activities on the market for LMD but the provision has been 'mixed on quality' and 'confusing' (CEML, 2002, p.4). Bolden (2005) points out that there tends to be an overemphasis on individual development rather than the development of leadership and management capacity. There can be a choice between focusing on the development of individuals or the development of networks, relationships and idea-sharing platforms (Day, 2001). This considers leadership as collective and distributed rather than as the purview of the individual (Gronn, 2008) and appointed leaders may find distributed leadership power and influence a troublesome concept (Harris, 2008).

So the focus of LMD can vary as can the approach. Figure 11.5 shows a typology of LMD activities.

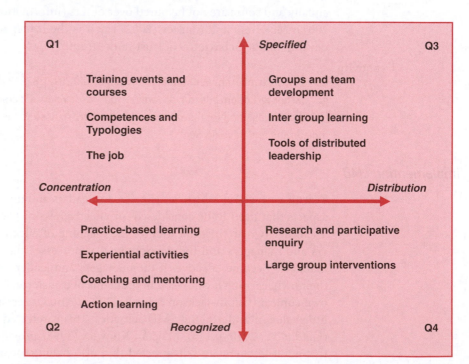

Figure 11.5 A typology of LMD activities

Q1:

Training events and courses make up what most of what people understand as LMD (Suutari & Viitala, 2008), based on theories, models and ideas that are presented as best practice. Objectives or desirable outcomes are predetermined and this can create a gap between what individual leaders and managers *need* and what is *provided* (Antonacopoulou, 1999). Formal qualifications such as MBAs might be considered too focused on analysis skills at the expense of implementation skills (Mintzberg, 2004). However, as recent research has shown (McBain et al., 2012), leaders and managers value qualifications which also have the most impact on abilities, such as the MBA.

Competencies and typologies are used to provide models of behaviours and skills. Models such as Belbin's team role inventory (Belbin, 1981) are used to develop management teams.

The job can be formally used for LMD, through plans to learn about roles or changes in job content. Other planned approaches can include secondment as part of a succession plan (Kur & Bunning, 2002).

Q2:

Practice-based learning from work is now considered a crucial source of LMD, and recognition of the possibilities for this is seen as a way of questioning assumptions that underpin actions, allowing new thoughts and ideas to emerge (Raelin, 2007). Projects relating to specific tasks or problems are a way of making learning explicit, benefiting both participants and the organisation and, if accreditation can be gained, allowing rigour and theoretical contribution to be considered (Rounce et al., 2007). Reflection and subsequent analysis of events which reveals underlying assumptions can be threatening but is also a way by which leaders and managers can become more critical of their practice and find new ways of taking action (Mezirow, 1990). Practice-based learning is connected to Lave and Wenger's (1991) situated learning theory. Situated learning provides a theory to explain these processes by showing how learning occurs within a community of practice where newcomers learn to participate in the community through legitimate peripheral participation by learning from more experienced members . Such newcomers remain on the periphery of the community but learn to move from this position by observing others and copying them (Fox, 1997). The key idea is that learning occurs through practice at work, often informally and incidentally. There are also links between practice-based learning and leaders and managers taking responsibility for their own development, usually referred to as self-development (Pedler et al., 2006), and action learning (see below).

Coaching and mentoring (see also Chapter 13) help leaders and managers make the most of their experiences at work. Coaching involves identifying task-focused learning opportunities and provides support. Coaches are sounding boards for learners to come to their own conclusions about the actions they should take, thereby retaining the responsibility and decision-making. Coaching has seen significant growth in the UK, often in the form of *executive coaching*, where someone outside the organisation provides the service. Research suggests this leads to the formation of more specific goals, more effort to make improvements and better ratings from staff (Smither et al., 2003). Gender seems irrelevant, in that male managers can be coached by females and vice versa (Gray & Goregaokar, 2010). Mentors have been viewed as providing a long-term process more related to personal and career grown job tasks than more personal involvement (Mumford, 1993) and has been shown to be successful in medicine (Sambunjak et al., 2006). There can be problems (see Simon & Eby, 2003) but as long as care is taken in agreeing parameters and both parties are willing to learn then it can be very rewarding (Megginson et al., 2006).

Action learning involves leaders, managers and others who form a small group (called a set) of five to eight participants who agree to help each other work on *individually owned* problems, through *rich* questions and discussion, in a *challenging* yet *supportive* way in order to make decisions concerning the problem that will be reported on back to the set (Revans, 1982). Pedler (2008) suggests the process of action learning can help individuals, teams and organisations deal with change and innovation and Claxton et al. (2009) have shown that this is the case. By taking action and reporting learning, leaders and managers can advance their identities (Anderson & Gold, 2009). Action has to be taken beyond the set, requiring interaction between the participant and the situation he/she is trying to influence. Action learning can also help an organization solve complex problems and ensure an improved return on investment from learning activities, as shown in HRD in Practice 11.1. A more critical approach to action learning makes more explicit the tensions and power dynamics which arise from such interactions (Trehan & Pedler, 2009).

HRD in Practice 11.1

Action learning in Mauritius

Jerome Fabre, Group HR Coordinator DRH at Food and Allied Group Of Companies

Following a learning survey carried out for the first time in a multi-national Mauritian family-based business in 2010, it was estimated that less than 8 per cent of the knowledge is applied in practice, thus bringing unsatisfactory results on ROI for learning and development. Moreover, according to a trend analysis produced by the HR department, the percentage of formal external training events represented 65 per cent of the total number of formal learning hours in 2007–2008, 66 per cent in 2008–2009, 50 per cent in 2009–2010 until the world economic recession when the training budget was cut by two-thirds. Was this the end of training? The answer is no! Training is now limited to generic courses, applied when the company's legal responsibilities are involved and when specialized skills are not possessed by the organization. However, the economic crisis has become an opportunity to develop a cost effective learning strategy with no budget required since knowledge sharing forums are applied, aimed at a maximum number of people. Managers have been trained to enhance their coaching skills. OJT are formalized. In-house development programmes were set up in 2010 called Back to Basic on Technical Skills delivered by managers themselves which represented 21 per cent of formal learning hours. In 2010–2011 and in 2011–2012 external training events represented 21 per cent. Action learningsets (ALS) were successfully introduced in 2010 and represented 7 per cent of formal learning hours in 2010–2011 and 14 per cent in 2011–2012. It became clear that action learning was become a more popular approach to working on difficult issues at work.

We were very happy with this development in that it met our company's aspirations to 'value people's potential'. Further it matches our values of 'team work, trust and strong interpersonal links like a family'.

Participants appreciated that through ALS 'knowledge is immediately applied in a work situation in our own words' and 'we communicate better and learn from each other in whatever language is required,

even in our Mauritian Creole ... ALS helps to develop EQ as criticisms must not be taken personally but as a way to learn especially since here ... maybe due to our insularity, we mix up professional and private roles at work'.

A double digit ROI is expected on learning. The company is very proud of this initiative. Since then ALS has been developed throughout the group of companies.

Q3:

Group, team and community development supports people working together in some form of grouping and LMD needs to involve working on the alignment of all of these (Leithwood et al., 2008). There are well-known, long-used models of group and team development such as in Tuckman and Jensen (1977) and initiatives that support team development such as coaching (Clutterbuck, 2007).

Inter-group learning enables collaborating across boundaries, both within and between organisations. Hejnova (2010) provides a new typology of inter-group networks and stresses how important it is to have an understanding of these and the organisational context in which they operate. Since each group or team can be seen as a configuration of shared leadership, working across boundaries becomes an example of 'co-configuration' (Victor & Boynton, 1998, p.195), requiring joint training in the skills of debate and dialogue to bring to the surface differing values, cultures and disciplines (Tomlinson, 2003).

Tools of distributed leadership provide a means of implementing an approach to leadership that is still not very well understood. There is an emphasis on aligning work practices with performance improvement (Heck & Hallinger, 2010).

Q4:

Research and participative enquiry includes approaches such as Appreciative Enquiry (Reed, 2007) which can be used across whole organisations. It is used to draw out and build on good practice rather than the traditional method of looking at issues as problems and addressing them. Mishra and Bhatnagar (2012) look at the way different models of Appreciative Enquiry have been applied to three organisations including the BBC, where the positive approach to addressing issues improved morale and created knowledge sharing and openness in learning.

Large group interventions can be used by leaders and managers to create a momentum for whole systems change. One approach is to use 'open space technology' (Owen, 2008), which came from Owen noticing that the really good decisions were always made in the coffee breaks in between formal meetings. An open space technology event is a collection of coffee breaks and becomes a creative conference where interested parties gather together in groups, setting their own agendas and recording and disseminating the subsequent outcomes of their discussions in whatever format they find helpful. Anyone can lead a session since they do not profess to be an expert but a facilitator for a group.

activity

For Harrison Owen's website and guidelines on his open space technology go to **www.openspaceworld.com/users_guide.htm**

Have a look at World Café on **www.theworldcafe.com/**

Gender and diversity in LMD initiatives

Many organisations find they have a low proportion of women as senior leaders. For example Aviva has a female staff of 50 per cent yet only 24 per cent of them are senior (Ainley, 2012).

The need for more women leaders was highlighted by David Cameron, UK Prime Minister in a speech at the Northern Future Forum in Stockholm, Feb 9, 2012, when he said:

> The evidence is that there is a positive link between women in leadership and business performance, so if we fail to unlock the potential of women in the labour market, we're not only failing those individuals, we're failing our whole economy.

In the UK, a recent report by Mervyn Davies (2011) recommended increasing the number of women on boards. Progress is being made with women making up 15 per cent of directors of companies in the benchmark FTSE 100 Index in 2012, up from 12.5 per cent in 2011; in 2012 there were ten all-male boards in the FTSE, down from 21 in 2011. In the 2012 *Return on Diversity Inspire Survey Findings Report* (Rosati, 2012), 92 per cent of the survey respondents agreed that women bring a different perspective to the boardroom. The different perspectives they offer ranged from taking a different approach to risk and being more customercentric to offering expanded creativity and more pragmatism. However, it is not about appointing women at board level – recruitment practices can be changed for that – it is about the lack of the talent pool to draw them from which must be addressed through LMD. As Rosati suggests, '... if you want a diverse Board, start by building a diverse pool of managers and business leaders at all levels across all functions in an organisation' (p.14).

activity

Go to **www.harveynash.com/inspire/documents/FinalReturnonDeiversity2012report.pdf** and read this report. What strikes you as important about it?

Also search for and read the policies on women on boards at **https://www.gov.uk/government/policies**

Can LMD activities add value?

In order to convince organisations to invest in LMD they need some confidence that value has been added (Kim & Cervero, 2007). Evaluation of HRD is

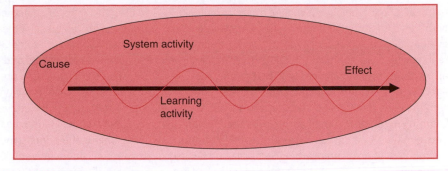

Figure 11.6 Holistic evaluation

Source: Thorpe et al. (2009)

discussed in some detail in Chapter 8. In the specific context of LMD the idea of evaluation is straightforward – find what works and what doesn't, learn the lessons and apply them (Thorpe et al., 2009). However as was noted in Chapter 8 this process is not easy if you have to show a return on investment (ROI) (Russ-Eft & Preskill, 2005).

Mechanistic evaluation has a strong appeal in LMD but as Gold et al. (2010) point out the purpose of evaluation would mean including the broadest array of LMD formal and informal activities, interventions and changes in behaviour in different contexts. Easterby-Smith (1994) suggests that there are four purposes of evaluation for LMD – proving, improving, learning and controlling – where the choice of purpose is decided on grounds of expediency such as the interests of stakeholders. Anderson (2007) gives prominence to the needs of decision-makers in evaluation so 'they' can assess whether investment in learning is contributing to organisational performance.

It is important that a holistic approach is taken to the evaluation of LMD (Thorpe et al., 2009). LMD can only be effective if wider systems and processes support what it is trying to achieve. Figure 11.6 shows that an evaluation must take account of the range of LMD learning activities alongside the supporting or blocking system activity.

An evaluation of their own self-efficacy, the belief that you can achieve behaviours to gain aspired outcomes, can also help leaders and managers (Bandura, 1977). People's ability to believe in themselves relates to their past experiences and feedback from others (Tams, 2008).

HRD in Practice 11.2 shows a strategic approach to the evaluation of LMD at Skipton Building Society.

Evaluation Strategy at Skipton Building Society

HRD in Practice 11.2

Tim Spackman, Head of Organisation Development, Skipton Building Society

At Skipton Building Society, after a number of difficult years following the credit crunch and subsequent recession, renewed investment is now being made in our people in the shape of a number of high profile strategic leadership and talent development programmes. These are significant investments in terms of time, energy and financial resources and in the current economic environment, demonstrating clear benefits is important not only to the Executive, but to all of our employees who are aware of multiple priorities competing for limited funds. Our strategy for evaluation is based on individual and organisational results which are defined at the outset. For instance, all individuals on our Modern Leaders Programme agree clear goals and objectives with success criteria with their line manager and facilitator in a Three-way Learning Agreement meeting. These are then reviewed between the three parties at the end of the programme ten months later. Action Learning Sets are used flexibly to support individual diverse learning agendas and are evaluated against agreed outcomes in the here and now on every occasion. Individual components of our programmes are designed and aligned to our strategic goals in the areas of customers, processes, people and profit and are led by senior leaders from these areas. Our talent programmes and 360 feedback processes are aligned to our Values and Behaviours and overall 360 scores are compared pre- and post-programmes. An assessment of learning progress for all leaders is conducted by our Executive three months post-completion of the Modern Leaders Programme and this complements the primary method of assessment – performance management. Key indicators from our Employee Engagement Survey such as those relating to engagement and coaching are identified and targets are set to improve over the long-term as a result of the programme.

summary

○ There are differing meanings of leadership and management, both in theory and practice. It is suggested that in practice both leadership and management occurs but in uncertain and difficult times leaders tend to be given prominence.

○ Leadership and management development can defined as a planned and deliberate process but also as a process of learning which emerges and has to be recognized.

○ There have been concerns in the UK about the quality and quantity of leaders and managers with recent efforts to show the link between good practice and performance.

○ There are different purposes for leadership and management development strategies including sustaining the business by developing leaders and managers with the right skills, or advancing business by developing new models based on what leaders and managers learn.

○ There is evidence that leadership and management development works best when support is given to informal learning and there are perceptions by leaders and managers that learning and development is given priority.

○ There are both generic and organisation-specific models of leadership and management, expressed as skills, attributes or competences. Models of leadership and management, especially competences, have been subjected to critical comment.

○ Models and frameworks of leadership and management can be used to help leaders and managers determine their needs for learning and development but this is not a straightforward process since it requires an assessment of behaviour and/or performance. Many leaders and managers face Multi-Source Feedback.

○ Leadership and management learning needs to be considered an adult process which is largely self-directed. Experiential learning is a frequent approach to leadership and management development but natural learning in a situation of practice is also important.

○ There are many leadership and management development activities which focus on individuals and more collective units. Activities can also be specified and pre-set or recognized and emergent, requiring reflection and review. Generic or generalized skills or knowledge can result in problems of transfer of learning.

○ Evaluation of leadership and management development is often an act of faith. Evaluation needs to consider wider system impacts as well as the collection of data to show evidence of value-added.

discussion questions

1 How does an understanding of the different approaches to leadership help us to understand what LMD needs to include?
2 What are the domains of leadership development?
3 How useful are competency frameworks in providing assessment of leadership and management abilities? What are their limitations?

4 What part does trust play in LMD? How can we develop trustworthiness?
5 How can LMD help to get more women and other diverse groupings into leadership?

further reading

Adair, J. (2005) *Effective Leadership Development*. London: Chartered Institute of Personnel and Development.
Ford, J. and Harding, N. (2007) Move over management: We are all leaders now. *Management Learning,* **38**(5): 475–93.
Mabey, C. (2012) Leadership Development in Organizations: Multiple Discourses and Diverse Practice. *International Journal of Management Reviews.* http://onlinelibrary. wiley.com/doi/10.1111/j.1468-2370.2012.00344.x/ abstract
Sadler-Smith, E. (2006) *Learning and Development for Managers*. Oxford: Blackwell.

references

Ainley, J. (2012) Report by Tim Smedly 'On My Agenda' reporting on and quoting John Ainley, Group HR Director of Aviva. *People Management*, March, 50–53.
Alimo-Metcalfe, B. and Alban-Metcalfe, J. (2005) Leadership: time for a new direction. *Leadership* **1**(1): 51–71.
Anderson, V. (2007) *The Value of Learning a New model of Value and Evaluation.* London: Chartered Institute of Personnel and Development.
Anderson, L. and Gold, J. (2009) Conversations outside the comfort zone: identity formation in SME manager action learning. *Action Learning: Research and Practice*, **6**(3): 229–42.
Antonacopoulou, E.P. (1999) Training does not imply learning: the individual perspective. *International Journal of Training and Development*, **3**(1): 14–23.
Antonioni, D. (1994) The effects of feedback accountability on upward appraisal ratings. *Personnel Psychology, 47*: 349–56.
Bandura, A. (1977) *Social Learning Theory*. New Jersey: Prentice-Hall.
Bass B.M. (1985) *Leadership and Performance beyond Expectations*. New York, NY: The Free Press.
Bass, B.M. and Avolio, B.J. (1990) *Multifactor Leadership Questionnaire*. Palo Alto, CA: Consulting Psychologists Press.
Belbin, M. (1981) *Management Teams*. London: Heinemann.
Bennis, W. and Nanus, B. (1985) *Leaders*. New York: Harper Row.
Bijlsma, K.M. and van de Bunt, G.G. (2003) Antecedents of trust in managers: a bottom-up approach. *Personnel Review, 32*(5): 638–64.
BIS (2012) *Leadership and Management in the UK – The Key to Sustainable Growth*. London: Department of Business, Innovation and Skills.

Bolden, R. (2005) *What Is Leadership Development?* Exeter: Leadership South West.

Bolden, R. and Gosling, J. (2006) Leadership competencies: time to change the tune? *Leadership,* **2**(2): 147–63.

Boyatzis, R. (1982) *The Competent Manager: A Model for Effective Performance*. New York: John Wiley & Sons.

Brown, P. (2005) The evolving role of strategic management development. *Journal of Management Development,* **24**(3): 209–22.

Brown, P. (2007) Strategic management development (pp.40–59). In R. Hill and J. Stewart (eds) *Management Development, Perspectives from Research and Practice*. London: Routledge.

Brutus, S. and Derayeh, M. (2002) Multi-source assessment programs in organizations: an insider's perspective. *Human Resource Development Quarterly,* **13**: 187–201.

Burgoyne, J., Hirsh, W. and Williams, S. (2004) *The Development of Leadership and Management Capability and its Contribution to Performance: The Evidence, The Prospects and The Research Need*. London: Department for Education and Skills.

Burgoyne, J., Boydell, T. and Pedler, M. (2003) *A Manager's Guide to Leadership*. Maidenhead: McGraw Hill.

Burns J.M. (1978) *Leadership*. New York, NY: Harper & Row.

CEML (2002) *Leaders and Managers: Raising Our Game*. London: Council for Excellence in Management and Leadership.

CIPD (2002) *Developing Managers for Business Performance*. London: Chartered Institute of Personnel and Development.

CIPD (2012) *Learning and Talent Development*. London: Chartered Institute of Personnel and Development.

Clarke, M., Butcher, D. and Bailey, C. (2004) Strategically aligned leadership development (pp.271–92). In J. Storey (ed) *Leadership in Organizations*. London: Routledge.

Clarke, N. and Higgs, M.J. (2010) *Leadership Training Across Business Sectors*. Lancaster: University Forum for Human Resource Development.

Claxton, J. (2005) *A Step Too Far? Are We Abusing the Concept of Left Brain/Right Brain in Learning and Development*. Selected papers from the 16th International Conference on College Teaching and Learning, Jacksonville, Florida.

Claxton, J., Gold, J., Edwards, C. and Coope, G. (2009) Relevant and timely learning for busy leaders. *Action Learning Research and Practice,* **6**(1): 63–70.

Clutterbuck, D. (2007) *Coaching the Team at Work*. London: Nicholas Brealey.

Coffield, F., Moseley, D., Hall, E. and Ecclestone, K. (2004) *Learning Styles and Pedagogy in Post-16 Learning: A Systematic and Critical Review*. London: Learning and Skills Research Centre.

Colquitt, J.A. (2001) On the dimensionality of organisational justice: A construct Validation of a measure. *Journal of Applied Psychology,* **86**(3): 386–400.

Csikszentmihalyi, M. (1997) *Finding Flow: The Psychology of Engagement with Everyday Life*. New York: Basic Books.

Day, D. (2001) Leadership development: a review in context. *Leadership Quarterly,* **11**(4): 581–613.

Davies, M. (2011) *Women on Boards*. Bedfordshire: Cranfield University.

Dierendonck, D., Haynes, C., Borrill, C. and Stride, C. (2007) Effects of upward feedback on leadership behaviour toward subordinates. *Journal of Management Development,* **26**(3): 228–38.

Dirks K.T. and Ferrin, D.L. (2002) Trust in leadership: meta-analytic findings and implications for research and practice. *Journal of Applied Psychology,* **87**(4); 611–28.

Duffy, M.K. and Ferrier, W.J. (2003) Birds of a Feather … ? How supervisor–subordinate dissimilarity moderates the influence of supervisor behaviours on workplace attitudes. *Group and Organisation Management,* **28**(2): 217–48.

Dupee, J.M., Ernst, N.P. and Caslin, K.E. (2011) Does multisource feedback influence performance appraisal satisfaction? *Nursing Management,* **42**(3): 12–16.

Easterby-Smith, M. (1994) *Evaluating Management Development, Training and Education,* 2nd edn. Aldershot: Gower.

Fayol, H. (1949) *General and Industrial Management*. London: Pitman Publishing.

Fletcher, C. (1998) Circular argument. *People Management,* 1 October: 46–9.

Fox, S. (1997) From management education and development to the study of management learning (pp.21–37). In J. Burgoyne and M. Reynolds (eds) *Management Learning*. London: Sage.

Garavan, T., Barnicle, B. and O'Suulleabhain, F. (1999) Management development: contemporary trends, issues and strategies. *Journal of European Industrial Training,* **23**(4/5): 191–207.

Gillespie, N.A. and Mann, L. (2004) Tranformational leadership and shared values: the building blocks of trust. *Journal of Managerial Psychology,* **19**(6): 588–607.

Gilpin-Jackson, Y. and Bushe, G.R. (2007) Leadership development training transfer: a case study of post-training determinants. *Journal of Management Development,* **26**(10): 980–1004.

Gold, J., Thorpe, R. and Mumford, A. (2010) *Leadership and Management Development*. London: Chartered Institute of Personnel and Development.

Goleman, D. (1998) *Working With Emotional Intelligence*. London: Bloomsbury.

Gray, D.E. and Goregaokar, H. (2010) Choosing an executive coach: The influence of gender on the coach-coachee matching process. *Management Learning,* **41**(5): 525–44.

Gronn, P. (2008) The future of distributed leadership. *Journal of Educational Administration,* **46**(2): 141–58.

Hamlin, B. (2010) Evidence-Based Leadership and management Development. In J. Gold, R. Thorpe and A. Mumford (eds) *Gower Handbook of Leadership and Management Development.* Aldershot: Gower.

Harris, A. (2008) Distributed leadership: according to the evidence. *Journal of Educational Administration,* **46**(2): 172–88.

Heck, R. and Hallinger, P. (2010) Testing a longitudinal model of distributed leadership effects on school improvement. *The Leadership Quarterly,* **21**(5): 867–85.

Hejnova, P. (2010) Beyond dark and bright: towards a more holistic understanding of inter-group networks. *Public Administration,* **88**(3): 741–63.

Hersey, P.K. and Blanchard, K. (1997) *Management of Organizational Behavior: Utilizing Human ReSources.* Englewood Cliffs, NJ: Prentice Hall.

Holbeche, L. (2008a) Developing leaders for uncertain times. *Impact,* **23**: 6–9.

Holbeche, L. (2008b) The leadership paradox. *Futures,* **1**: 2–4.

Holmes, L. (1995a) The making of real managers: ideology, identity and management development, available at http://www.re-skill.org.uk/relskill/realmgr. htm – accessed 14 April 2011.

Holmes, L. (1995b) HRM and the irresistible rise of the discourse of competence. *Personnel Review,* **24**(4): 34–49.

Honey, P. and Mumford, A. (1996) *Manual of Learning Styles,* 3rd edn. Maidenhead: Honey Publications.

Hope-Hailey, V., Searle, R. and Dietz, G. (2010) Organisational effectiveness: how trust helps. *People Management,* 30–35.

Horne, M. and Steadman Jones, D. (2001). *Leadership: The Challenge for All?* London: Chartered Management Institute.

Jordan, A.H. and Audia, P. (2012) Self-enhancement and learning from performance feedback. *Academy of Management Review,* **37**(2): 211–31.

Judge, T.A., Locke, E.A. and Durham, C.C. (1997) The dispositional causes of job satisfaction: a core evaluation approach. *Research in Organizational Behaviour,* **19**: 151–88.

Kempster, S. and Cope, J. (2010) Learning to lead in the entrepreneurial context. *International Journal of Entrepreneurial Behaviour & Research,* **16**(1): 5–34.

Kim, H. and Cervero, R.M. (2007) How power relations structure the evaluation process for HRD programmes. *Human Resource Development International,* **10**(1): 5–20.

Knowles, M. (1998) *The Adult Learner,* 5th edn. Houston: Gulf Publishing.

Kolb, D. (1984) *Experiential Learning.* Englewood Cliffs: Prentice Hall.

Kotter, J.P. (1982) *The General Managers.* New York: Free Press.

Kur, E. and Bunning, R. (2002) Assuring corporate leadership for the future. *Journal of Management Development,* **21**(9/10): 761–79.

Lave, J. and Wenger, E. (1991) *Situated Learning: Legitimate peripheral participation.* Cambridge: Cambridge University Press.

Lawler, J. (2005) The essence of leadership? Existentialism and leadership. *Leadership,* **1**(2): 215–31.

Leithwood, K., Mascall, B. and Strauss, T. (eds) (2008) *Distributed Leadership According to the Evidence.* London: Routledge.

Leskew, S. and Singh, P. (2007) Leadership development: learning from best practices. *Leadership & Organization Development Journal,* **28**(5): 444–64.

Leslie, J.B. (2009) *The Leadership Gap.* Greensboro, NC: Center for Creative Leadership.

Luthans, F. and Peterson, S.J. (2003) 360-degree feedback with systematic coaching: empirical analysis suggests a winning combination. *Human Resource Management,* **42**: 243–56.

Mabey, C. (2002) Mapping management development practice, *Journal of Management Studies.* **39**(8): 1139–60.

Mabey, C. (2005) *Management Development That Works: The Evidence.* London: Chartered Management Institute.

Mabey, C. and Thomson, A. (2000) The determinants of management development. *British Journal of Management,* **11**: 3–16.

Management Standards (2008) *Management Standards Centre,* available at http://www.management-standards. org/standards/standards

McBain, R., Ghobadian, A., Switzer, J., Wilton, P., Woodman, P. and Pearson, G. (2012) *The Business Benefits of Management and Leadership Development.* London: Chartered Management Institute.

McCall, M. (2010) Recasting leadership development. *Industrial and Organizational Psychology,* **3**(1): 3–19.

McKenna P.J. and Maister, D.H. (2002) Building team trust. *Consulting to Management,* **13**(4): 51–3.

Megginson, D., Clutterbuck, D., Garvey, B., Stokes, P. and Garrett-Harris, R. (2006) *Mentoring In Action,* 2nd edn. London: Kogan Page.

Mezirow, J. (1990) *Fostering Critical Reflection in Adulthood.* San Francisco: Jossey-Bass.

Mintzberg, H. (1973) *The Nature of Managerial Work.* New York: Harper & Row.

Mintzberg, H. (2004), *Managers Not MBA's: A Hard Look At The Soft Practices Of Managing And Management Development.* San Francisco, CA: Berrett-Koehler.

Mintzberg, H., Ahlstrand, B. and Lampel, J. (1998) *Strategy Safari.* London: Prentice-Hall.

Mishra, P. and Bhatnagar, J. (2012) Appreciative Inquiry: Models & Applications. *The Indian Journal of Industrial Relations,* **47**(3): 543–48.

Moye, M.J. and Henkin, A.B. (2006) Exploring associations between employee empowerment and interpersonal trust in managers. *Journal of Management Development,* **25**(2), 101–17.

Mumford, A. (1993) *How Managers Can Develop Managers.* Aldershot: Gower.

O'Reilly, C., Caldwell, D.F., Chatman, J.A., Lapiz, M. and Self, W. (2010) How leadership matters: The effects of leaders' alignment on strategy implementation. *The Leadership Quarterly,* **21**(1): 104–13.

Owen, H. (2008) *Open Space Technology: A User's Guide,* 3rd edn. San Francisco, CA: Berrett-Koehler.

Pedler, M. (2008) *Action Learning for Managers.* Aldershot: Gower.

Pedler, M., Burgoyne, J. and Boydell, T. (2006) *A Manager's Guide to Self-Development,* 5th edn. Maidenhead: McGraw-Hill.

Pedler, M., Burgoyne, J. and Boydell, T. (2004) *A Manager's Guide to Leadership.* Maidenhead: McGraw-Hill.

Peiperl, M.A. (2001) Getting 360-degree feedback right. *Harvard Business Review,* January, **79**(1): 142–47.

Perren, L. and Burgoyne, J. (2002) *Management and Leadership Abilities: An Analysis of Texts, Testimony and Practice.* London: Council for Excellence in Management and Leadership.

Powell, J. (2012) *33 Million People in the Room.* London: Pearson.

Raelin, J. (2007) Toward an epistemology of practice. *Academy of Management Learning & Education,* **6**(4): 495–519.

Reed, J. (2007) *Appreciative Inquiry.* London: Sage.

Revans, R. (1982) *The Origins and Growth of Action Learning.* Bromley and Lund: Chartwell-Bratt.

Reynolds, M. (1997) Learning styles: a critique. *Management Learning,* **28**(2): 115–33.

Reynolds, M. (2009) Wild frontiers – Reflections on experiential learning. *Management Learning,* **40**(4): 387–92.

Robinson, S. (2010) Leadership ethics (pp.175–96). In J. Gold, R. Thorpe and A. Mumford (eds) *Handbook of Leadership and Management Development.* Aldershot: Gower.

Rosati, C., (2012) *Return on Diversity: A Study of Diversity In the Boardroom.* London: Harvey Nash.

Rounce, K., Scarfe, A. and Garnett, J. (2007) A work-based learning approach to developing leadership for senior health and social care professionals. *Education & Training,* **49**(3): 218–26.

Russ-Eft, D. and Preskill, H. (2005) In search of the holy grail: return on investment evaluation in human resource development. *Advances in Developing Human Resources,* **7**(1): 71–85.

Salaman, G. and Taylor, S. (2002) *Competency's Consequences: Changing the Character of Managerial Work,* paper presented at ESRC Workshop on Managerial Work, Critical Management Studies Seminar, Cambridge, June.

Sambunjak, D., Straus, S. and Marušić, A. (2006) Mentoring in academic medicine. *Journal of American Medical Association,* **296**(6): 1103–15.

Salovey, P. and Mayer, J.D. (1990) Emotional intelligence. *Imagination, Creativity and Personality,* **9**: 185–211.

Simon, S. and Eby, L. (2003) A typology of negative mentoring experiences: a multidimensional scaling study. *Human Relations,* **56**(9): 1083–106.

Smither, J., London, M., Flautt, R., Vargas, Y. and Kucine, I. (2003) Can working with an executive coach improve multi-source feedback ratings over time? A quasi-experimental field study. *Personnel Psychology,* **56**(1): 23–44.

Smither, J.W., Brett J.F. and Atwater, L.E. (2008) What do leaders recall about their multi-source feedback? *Journal of Leadership & Organizational Studies,* **14**(3): 202–18.

Stewart, R. (1975) *Contrasts in Management.* Maidenhead: McGraw-Hill.

Storey, J. (ed.) (2004) *Leadership in Organizations.* London: Routledge.

Suutari, V. and Viitala, R. (2008) Management development of senior executives: methods and their effectiveness. *Personnel Review,* **37**(4): 375–92.

Tamkin, P. and Denvir, A. (2006) *Strengthening the UK Evidence Base on Leadership and Management Capability.* London: Department of Trade and Industry.

Tams, S. (2008) Constructing self-efficacy at work: a person-centered perspective. *Personnel Review,* **37**(2): 165–83.

Tansley, C., Turner, P., Foster, C., Harris, L., Stewart, J. and Sempik, A. (2007) *Talent Strategy, Management and Measurement.* London: CIPD.

Taylor, F.W. (1911) *The principles of Scientific Management.* Harper, freely available at http://www.myvsp.cn/technology/Ma%20ebooks25/The%20Principles%20of%20Scientific%20Management.pdf

Thorpe, R., Gold, J., Anderson, L., Burgoyne, J., Wilkinson, D. and Malby, R. (2009) *Towards Leaderful Communities in the North of England,* 2nd edn. Cork: Oaktree Press.

Thorpe, R., Gold, J. and Lawler, J. (2011) Locating distributed leadership. *International Journal of Management Reviews,* **13**(3): 239–50.

Tomlinson, K. (2003) *Effective Interagency Working: a Review of the Literature and Examples from Practice, (LGA Research Report 40).* Slough: NFER.

Trehan, K. and Pedler, M. (2009) Animating critical action learning: process-based leadership and management development. *Action Learning: Research and Practice,* **6**(1): 35–49.

Tuckman, B.W. and Jensen, M.C. (1977) Stages of small groups development revised. *Group and Organisational Studies,* **2**(3): 419–27.

VandeWalle, D., Ganesan, S., Challagalla, G.N. and Brown, S.P. (2000) An integrated model of feedback-seeking behavior: disposition, context and cognition. *Journal of Applied Psychology*, **85**(6): 96–103.

Victor, B. and Boynton, A. (1998) *Invented Here: Maximizing Your Organization's Internal Growth And Profitability*. Boston: Harvard Business School Press.

Vince, R. and Reynolds, M. (2010) Leading reflection: Developing the relationship between leadership and reflection (pp.331–46). In J. Gold, R. Thorpe and A. Mumford (eds) *The Gower Handbook Of Leadership And Management Development*. Aldershot: Gower Press.

Watson, T.J. (1980) *Sociology, Work and Industry*. Boston: Routledge & Kegan Paul.

Western, S. (2008) *Leadership: A Critical Text*. London: Sage.

chapter 12

Teams and Team Development

Chitra Meade and Paul Iles

Chapter learning outcomes

After studying this chapter, you should be able to:

- Appreciate the importance of teams and team working
- Assess the benefits to individuals, society, teams and the organization of introducing teamwork in organizations
- Assess the impact of diversity on team processes and team performance
- Analyse the nature of team building and team development and the methods used to facilitate it
- Assess the importance of intergroup team building

Chapter outline

Introduction
Teams and groups
Team working
Team building and team development
Intergroup team building
Summary

Introduction

Teams have been in existence in organizations for many years. Here, we will first distinguish between groups and teams before exploring team working, seen here in terms of a team's arrangements, process, behaviour and organization. We will then look at team development: creating new teams (team building), or reviewing and improving the performance of existing ones (team development). We will discuss and evaluate methodologies such as the Team Climate Inventory, task-oriented team development/ GRPI, Belbin's team roles, the Team Role Inventory, Bales' Interaction Process Analysis, team coaching and outdoor development, before assessing the importance of intergroup team building in HRD.

Teams and groups

reflective question

1 How would you define a group?
2 How would you define a team, as distinct from a group?

Interestingly, while group is a neutral term, team is value laden, and is usually used positively – groups of workers are often called teams and their bosses team leaders for this reason (in contrast, words like gang, mob and ringleader are often used pejoratively).

For some, a key characteristic of a team is a common fate, for others, it is an explicit or implicit social structure (for example roles, status, norms). For some, face-to-face interaction is key (but what of virtual teams who never meet?). For most, a group, rather than a category, comes into being when two or more individuals perceive themselves to be members of the same social category, and when they define themselves as members. Group membership has social and psychological consequences, especially for social identity, affecting members' behaviour even when others are not present. Formal groups are established with relatively clear, official roles, rules and goals; informal groups emerge without prescribed goals and relationships.

Stewart (1999, p.325) defines a team as: 'a group of people working in an interdependent manner to achieve a commonly understood goal', whereas Katzenbach and Smith (2004, p.5), discussing 'real teams' rather than groups or so-called teams, introduce mutual accountability and shared commitment, defining a team as:

> a small number of people with complementary skills who are committed to a common purpose, performance goals, and approach for which they hold themselves mutually accountable.

Thus, teams are both different from, and more than, groups; they are now often seen as the key building blocks of organizational life. A group of people therefore becomes a team when team members know they have a common goal, commitment towards those objectives, and how these objectives/goals are to be met, with mutual accountability (Stewart, 1999). According to Levy (2004, p.142), a team 'needs to have the power to control how it operates'. An example of 'good teams going wrong' is provided by the largely autonomous 'dream team' at the Nut Island sewage works in the 1990s. It was performing difficult, dangerous work without complaint, putting in unpaid overtime, handling its own staffing and training decisions, and acting with great esprit de corps and commitment to the mission; yet it contributed to the catastrophic failure of the mission (Levy, 2001).

Team working

Team working can be a means of shifting power and authority from higher levels to employees. Ingram et al. (1997, p.118) point out that 'the most effective linkages between business activities are forged by people and the way in which they work together in groups'. In order to enable successful implementation of teams, organizations need to heavily invest in team building and team development, which makes HRD central to effective team performance.

Teamwork in organizations

The increasing need for flatter organizational structures in knowledge-based economies has given rise to more responsibility, authority, autonomy and flexibility being expected from individuals. The idea of delegating responsibility to groups has often been promoted within HRM (for example innovative work practices or high-performance work systems), as well as in lean manufacturing and business process re-engineering. Task design and supervisory behaviours have been invoked to explain the enhanced performance held to result from teamwork, resulting in higher effort, engagement, commitment and motivation through participation and discretion.

Teamwork usually involves delegation of responsibilities and decentralization of decision-making. This may impact on attitudinal outcomes like job satisfaction, involvement, commitment and trust, which may then affect behavioural outcomes such as turnover and absenteeism, and extra-role behaviours such as organizational citizenship. These may then impact on operational outcomes such as productivity, quality, innovation and flexibility (see Figure 12.1). These impacts may also be enhanced by structural changes brought about by teamwork, such as less complexity, reduction of throughput time and reduction of losses. Operational outcomes may then lead to enhanced financial outcomes such as added value, profitability and costs in a 'performance chain' (Delarue et al., 2008).

Survey-based research on the links between teamwork and organizational performance (often measured operationally, such as productivity, quality, customer satisfaction; or financially, such as value-added or return on capital employed; or attitudinally/behaviourally, such as job satisfaction or absenteeism) is largely supportive. Teamwork can further enhance performance if combined with structural changes such as decentralization and delayering (Delarue et al., 2008). Team working is often introduced alongside other HRM changes, such as training or reward changes, for example profit sharing, or team-based reward systems.

Different types of team working

Many different types of teams are used within organizations, such as top management teams, cross-functional teams, problem-solving teams, project teams, virtual teams, self-managed work teams (SMWT), task force teams, quality circle teams, sales teams and self-directed teams (SDT).

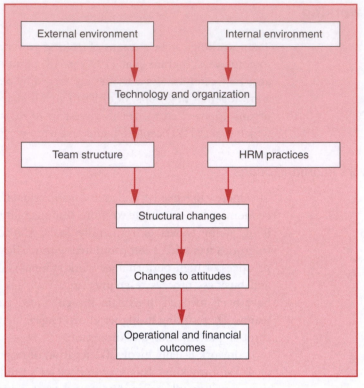

Figure 12.1 Teamwork and organizational performance

Source: Adapted from Delarue et al. (2008, p.144)

Cross-functional teams have become more popular alongside matrix organizations; individuals from different functions come together for a particular project or task. Organizational performance can be improved through adoption of a successful cross-functional team (for example Proehl, 1996; Dufrene et al., 1999). Teams can also be problem-solving teams, individuals coming together to solve identified problems, dissolving when the problem is solved (Torrington et al., 2005; Robbins, 2005). Another is the virtual team: geographically dispersed members may have little or no face-to-face contact, instead keeping in touch through modern communications technologies, for example emails and videoconferencing (Kreitner et al., 2002), working across space, time and organizational boundaries. Virtual teams can also show elements of cross-functional teams/problem-solving teams, bringing together people from different specialist or geographical areas to resolve a problem.

Others make different distinctions. Katzenbach and Smith (2004) distinguish between task forces/project teams, that is, teams that recommend things, working groups that make or do things, and supervising teams that oversee things.

Delarue et al. (2008) suggest some dimensions on which team design may differ:

● degree of self-management
● nature of team membership

- team structure and size, breadth of job definition, degree of autonomy
- team composition
- type of tasks performed
- technology and equipment in use.

Consequently, different types of teamwork may be associated with different organizational outcomes. We can see teams as lying on an autonomy–interdependence dimension, from a self-directed team to a group of workers, as shown in Figure 12.2. The four quadrants are:

- *Quadrant A:* some types, for example professional service teams, could be situated here, with high levels of autonomy but low interdependence between team members
- *Quadrant B:* here a group would show both low interdependence and low autonomy.
- *Quadrant C:* SMWTs usually experience high interdependence, but may still have low autonomy, due to decision-making powers resting with managers or leaders
- *Quadrant D:* SDTs may lie here, showing both high autonomy and high interdependence.

Thus, many organizations may use team development methodologies to prepare teams to move to quadrant D.

Although autonomy and flexibility often seem essential in team working, a study of team working in the UK Inland Revenue identified target-based team working, where these played little part (Procter & Currie, 2004), and interdependence, especially outcome interdependence, was driven by work targets.

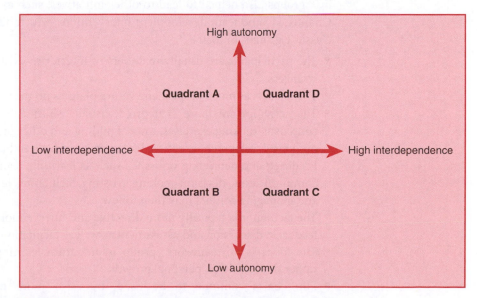

Figure 12.2 Autonomy–interdependence matrix for teams

Source: Adapted from Delarue et al. (2008)

Team building and team development

The terms team building and team development are often used synonymously in HRD, but sometimes distinctions are made between putting a new team together (team building) and working with an existing team (team development). Interest arose out of the early OD work of Lewin, in particular on training groups (T groups) at the National Training Laboratories in the USA after 1945. Changing attitudes and behaviour, such as racial prejudice, was more effective through a team's direct experience of the issues in a group setting or T group rather than lectures or other input (Burke, 2003).

T groups and team building

T groups typically consist of groups of people undergoing training and development as strangers who had never worked together before; an unstructured agenda, with emphasis on direct experience of the here and now, and a focus on personal change, growth and development were key features. Classic T groups had no formal leader or instructor, instead a facilitator intervened at appropriate moments to ask questions and give feedback. Flip charts were used to record the group experience for later feedback and analysis.

However, two main issues emerged around the use of T groups:

- *Psychological damage:* Some participants seemed psychologically damaged by the feedback received on behaviour and attitudes, but as the session ended after one or two days, little in the way of counselling was provided.
- *Transfer of training:* Participants may have learned something powerful about themselves or others in the T group, but this learning was difficult to transfer to the workplace (not just an issue with T groups).

T groups also helped to lead to other initiatives, such as action learning (see Chapter 11) and team development interventions, which differs somewhat from classic T groups, in that:

- The participants are usually members of intact, pre-existing work teams, not strangers.
- The focus is as much on past and future plans as on the present.
- The activities are more structured, usually short activities such as group consensus/ranking exercises, tower building and other practical activities, and outdoor development exercises like treasure hunts, raft building and abseiling. Feedback and debriefing on issues such as learning, team working, listening, communicating, decision-making, trusting, facilitating, leadership, supporting and managing conflict may then follow.
- The facilitator is typically more directive and interventionist, providing input, feedback, discussion and assessment as well as facilitation.
- The focus is on teamwork, group issues, team learning and development, rather than solely on personal growth.
- Flip charts continue to be used, but also more modern technology: camcorders, computers and projectors capture what happens, which is used

later for analysis of performance and to encourage reflection on learning and what the team could do differently next time.

Team building has continued to be popular, in part because issues raised can be worked on back in the office (and any damage is more likely to be addressed, given the continuous nature of many team-building initiatives).

Assessing team development needs

Just as individual training needs assessment is often recommended before training and development interventions are implemented, the HRD needs of teams are often assessed through training needs analysis: questionnaires, focus groups, observation and interviews identify issues such as skill levels, skill mix, team interaction and task achievement. One instrument, amongst many, is the Team Climate Inventory (TCI) (Anderson & West, 1994) which seeks to assess the shared perceptions of policies, practices and procedures in teams, including:

- *Communication:* how members interact, and the structure and style of team meetings
- *Participation:* in decision making and other activities
- *Safety:* how safe people feel, and how much interpersonal trust there is
- *Cohesiveness:* how cohesive the team perceives itself to be, and is perceived by others
- *Task style:* how the team approaches tasks and pursues objectives
- *Vision:* the team's vision or mission, and objectives and targets
- *Innovativeness:* how creative the team is.

The TCI can be used to assess team dynamics and climate.

Team development interventions

Reacting to the frequent emphasis in much team building on improving interpersonal relationships, Beckhard (1972, p.24) listed four purposes for team building, pointing out that:

> unless one purpose is defined as the primary purpose ... people then operate from their own hierarchy of purposes and, predictably, these are not always the same for all members.

The purposes of team building are to:

- *set goals or priorities* – we might now also add mission, vision or purpose
- *analyse or allocate the way work is performed* – according to team members' roles and responsibilities
- *examine the way the team is working* – its processes, such as norms, decision making, or communications
- *examine interpersonal relationships* among members.

In their work on healthcare systems, Rubin et al. (1978) introduced the concept of 'task-oriented team development' (the GRPI model) – any team-building intervention needs to address issues of goals, roles, procedures and interpersonal relationships, in that order. Many team problems, seen as relationship problems or a lack of chemistry, are often addressed through interpersonal training involving attention to communication issues, for example 'the issue is a lack of communication'. In practice, these are often caused by goal or role problems – either members disagree over goals, think they are pursuing the same goals when they have not been discussed, or they have changed without everyone being aware of the changes; or there is lack of role or procedural clarity. Interpersonal relationship issues may then be a symptom of the failure to agree goals, or clarify roles and procedures, not the cause of the team problems. Team builders need to address goal (or mission, vision or purpose) issues first, role issues second, procedural issues third, and only then interpersonal issues.

Goal issues

As Katzenbach and Smith (2004, p.7) point out:

> The best teams invest a tremendous amount of time and effort exploring, shaping and agreeing on a purpose that belongs to them both collectively and individually. This 'purposing' activity continues throughout the life of the team.

Poor teams fail to coalesce around a common mission, purpose or aspiration, translated into specific (for example SMART) performance goals (here, we see the A as *agreed*, as well as the more common *achievable*). Indeed, 'when purposes and goals build on one another and are combined with team commitment, they become a powerful engine of performance' (p.7). Specific goals help to define distinctive work products, facilitate clear communication, maintain focus, build team identity, achieve small wins, and motivate and energize the team to pursue attainable but challenging goals.

Teams may come together for various purposes:

- to develop a new product
- to develop an improved service
- to organize an event such as a conference, launch or farewell party
- to raise money for charity.

The goal or purpose provides a reference point and helps in decisions about what information is necessary, as well as providing a basis on which to measure performance and progress.

reflective question

Think of a team you have worked in, whether in full or part-time work, at college or university, or in a community/voluntary context.

1 How clear were you about what was required of you, or the team as a whole?
2 What did the team sponsor or leader want you to do, for what reason, and by when?
3 What was the big picture? Where did the team's work fit in to what was happening elsewhere, inside or outside the organization?
4 Were objectives SMART – specific, measurable, agreed/achievable, realistic, timed?
5 Was success judged in concrete, recognizable terms? What did success look like?
6 What resources were available to the team? Were they realistic?
7 Were there any things the team was not able to do, or was not told?

Source: Adapted from Fleming (2004, p.26)

Teams are often brought together because members are thought to possess distinctive, necessary and complementary skills, not possessed by any one individual. Requirements include technical or functional expertise, problem-solving and decision-making skills, and interpersonal skills. Teams are also often powerful vehicles for developing skills.

Team members can approach team tasks and roles with different levels of energy and attitude, or commitment, towards the role and/or task. One way of looking at this is to develop an energy investment model, with attitude (or commitment) on one axis and energy on the other, as in Figure 12.3. It is then possible to map, across time, the contributions of team members. Teams do not want contributors who are *walking dead* – low energy levels combined with negative attitudes. But do all teams want everyone to be *players* – members with high energy and high, positive attitudes? *Spectators* – positive in attitude but low in energy – may be shy, undervalued, or feel any contributions will be marginalized, put down or ignored. They may be thinkers rather than doers (reflectors or theorists rather than activists, in the language of Chapter 5). Teams may want to give them the option to play more, as long as the team values their efforts.

Cynics – high in energy but with apparently negative attitudes – may also have valid perspectives: they may be unsure about the direction in which the team is heading, feel it is 'throwing the baby out with the bath water' or themselves to be defenders of the 'true identity' of the team, or think things have not been fully thought through. *Cynics* may turn into the *walking dead*, spreading apathy or suspicion, but may also be converted, if listened to or included, into *players*, using their energy for positive ends – not putting a brake on anything ('seen it all before', 'it can't work here') but ensuring that actions taken are well considered, with objections raised in constructive rather than overly critical ways.

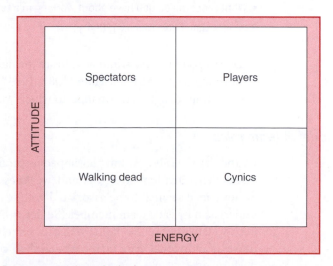

Figure 12.3 Roles team members play in change processes

Source: Adapted from Miller (2008, p.10)

The roles played by team members should be clear, overlapping, but not conflicting, and teams should employ a mix of roles and skills sufficient for the tasks before them. Stewart (1999, p.28) supports this by acknowledging that:

> whatever the form of team-working being introduced, the team members need to be clear about what the team is set up to achieve and understand their role within the team.

Role conflict or role ambiguity might be explored through role analysis – role requirements are defined and analysed through focal role occupiers initiating an analysis of the role, its rationale, and its associated duties. Tasks and behaviours can be added or subtracted until the incumbent and the team as a whole are satisfied with the role description, allowing role profiles to be developed, and other roles to be analysed and clarified in turn (Dayal & Thomas, 1968).

Role negotiation may then be used to enable each role holder to change some of their duties, responsibilities or behaviours in return for changes in others' behaviours, duties or responsibilities. Such changes can be written up in the form of a contract, with further meetings to determine if such contracts have been honoured and to evaluate their effectiveness (Harrison, 1972; Iles & Auluck, 1993).

activity

Form groups of three. Each person answers the following questions. Share your findings with the other two.

- What skills do you think you have developed, at work, college/university, or in the wider community?
- What are your achievements?
- What have you learned from working in teams?
- How do you prefer to operate in a team?
- What do you value in the way other team members operate?
- What do you think you can contribute to a team?
- What are your interests? What do you see as a worthwhile challenge?
- What concerns do you have about working in a team?

Source: Adapted from Fleming (2004, p.30)

Questions like these stimulated more formal work into what made for a high-performing team, leading Belbin (1981, 1993) to the identification of team roles contributing to high performance, to which we now turn.

Belbin's model of team roles

In the early 1980s, Belbin developed a profile, the Team Role Inventory, to assess the individual strengths and weaknesses of team members; high team performance seemed to be associated with teams balanced in terms of the roles undertaken by each team member (Senior, 1997). Belbin's (1981, 1993) work has been widely used in the past two decades in elucidating the strengths and weaknesses of individual team members and their contribution to team dynamics and performance.

Theoretically, Belbin's work can be traced to bureaucratic (the need for specialization to match job competencies) and human relations theories (good interpersonal relationships are important to organizational functioning). The distinction between task-oriented and relationship-oriented or social-emotional/maintenance-oriented roles in groups has also been influential (Bales, 1950). Belbin (1981, 1993) argues that if team members all have similar weaknesses, the team as a whole may tend to have a similar weakness. In contrast, if team members have similar strengths, they may compete for tasks and responsibilities. A team role (not to be confused with a functional role) is defined by personality, ability, current values and motivation, field constraints, work experience and role learning.

More specifically, Belbin tries to:

- Define an individual's current preferences (a moment in time or a snapshot of the person here and now)
- Identify their typical team behaviour against the Team Role Inventory
- Assess their suitability to a team role, chosen from one of nine (originally eight) types: plant, resource investigator, coordinator, shaper, monitor evaluator, teamworker, implementer, completer finisher and a specialist.

Assessments are not strictly psychometric personality tests, because they measure preferred behaviour, not personality factors or dispositions. Up until 2001, analysis was based on findings from the Team Role Inventory, a simple questionnaire completed by the individual, a Self Perception Inventory (SPI), and then by the peer group for the purpose of assessing preferred behaviours and characteristics that are either beneficial or detrimental to a team. Seven sections, comprising ten descriptive statements, each section having ten points allocated by the respondent between the ten sentences, assess:

1 Potential contribution to the team
2 Shortcomings relating to teamwork
3 Personal influence towards group tasks
4 Relationships with other team members
5 Personal job satisfaction in teamwork
6 Leadership style within stressful constraints
7 Personal problems experienced when working in groups.

This SPI typically consists of about 80 questions, determining the profile that an individual may show when taking a role.

Nine clusters of behaviour are assessed, called team roles (see Table 12.1).

Certain types of combination could potentially result in tensions and conflicts; pairing a shaper (SH) with a monitor evaluator (ME), a resource investigator (RI) with a specialist (SP), or a plant (PL) with an implementer (IM) without facilitator intervention may well result in conflict.

The profiling questionnaire has now been replaced by the Belbin e-interplace software package to more reliably:

- improve self-awareness and personal effectiveness
- foster mutual trust and understanding between work colleagues
- match people to jobs for the purpose of selection and career planning
- enhance team building and team development.

Table 12.1 Belbin's team roles

Team role		Contribution	Allowable weaknesses
Plant		Creative, imaginative, free-thinking. Generates ideas and solves difficult problems.	Ignores incidentals. Too preoccupied to communicate effectively.
Resource investigator		Outgoing, enthusiastic, communicative. Explores opportunities and develops contacts.	Over-optimistic. Loses interest once initial enthusiasm has passed
Co-ordinator		Mature, confident, identifies talent. Clarifies goals. Delegates effectively.	Can be seen as manipulative. Offloads own share of the work.
Shaper		Challenging, dynamic, thrives on pressure. Has the drive and courage to overcome obstacles.	Prone to provocation. Offends peoples feelings.
Monitor evaluator		Sober, strategic and discerning. Sees all options and judges accurately.	Lacks drive and ability to inspire others. Can be overly critical.
Teamworker		Co-operative, perceptive and diplomatic. Listens and averts friction	Indecisive in crunch situations. Avoids confrontation.
Implementer		Practical, reliable, efficient. Turns ideas into actions and organises work that needs to be done.	Somewhat inflexible. Slow to respond to new possibilities.
Completer finisher		Painstaking, conscientious, anxious. Searches out errors. Polishes and perfects.	Inclined to worry unduly. Reluctant to delegate.
Specialist		Single-minded, self-starting, dedicated. Provides knowledge and skills in rare supply.	Contributes only on a narrow front. Dwells on technicalities.

Source: http://www.belbin.com/rte.asp?id=3, accessed 5 September 2012.

Reproduced by kind permission of Belbin Associates: www.belbin.com.

Observer assessment has been added to the e-interplace system to provide feedback on how others see the person undertaking the self-assessment and provide a more robust profile than assessment based purely on self-reporting.

Belbin uses the nine team roles to create four work roles, defined as a mix of tasks and responsibilities undertaken by individuals or within a team. A colour classification system to clearly differentiate between the four categories of work is used to avoid ambiguities and misunderstandings and enable managers to assign a type of work to a subordinate most suited to that particular category of work role. It is a simple way of allocating resources to tasks that can be delegated to a team member.

It is now usually recognized as dysfunctional that membership of any given team should remain static. Further perspectives within the team need to be widened, and facilitating career moves within the organization offers one means of achieving this aim, while also offering the advantage of growing a bigger person. Another way is to arrange periodic swaps of members within existing teams in order to deepen understanding of the broader field.

One issue is that of the stages of a team's development, discussed later, linked to the need for different team roles at different stages:

- identifying needs
- finding ideas (needs plants, shapers and coordinators)
- formulating plans
- making ideas
- establishing organization
- following through (needs completer finishers and implementers).

Emotional intelligence seems to be linked to the coordinator and resource investigator roles, but not to the shaper or completer roles (Davies & Kanaki, 2006; Aritzeta et al., 2007).

Just as there are 'horses for courses', there are 'teams for pitches'; Belbin distinguishes negotiators (resource investigators and team workers) from manager/workers (implementers and completer finishers), and intellectuals (monitor evaluators and plants) to team leaders (coordinators and shapers) (Morgeson, DeRue and Karam, 2010). High-performing teams need to have a balanced representation of all team roles.

Belbin's model of team roles has remained popular in HRD practice, with nearly 50 per cent of organizations making use of it, according to CIPD (2012). However, doubts remain as to the psychometric properties of the Belbin inventory. Davies and Kanaki (2006) showed that personality dimensions associated with the SYMLOG Interpersonal Effectiveness Profile based on the Interaction Process Analysis (IPA) of groupwork developed by Bales (1950) were clearly and strongly related to team roles. The dominance (upward) dimension was associated with the roles of implementer, coordinator and resource investigator, while the accepting authority (forward) dimension was associated with the roles of monitor evaluator and completer finisher, and negatively associated with plant and shaper. The friendly (positive) dimension was positively associated with teamworker and plant.

Aritzeta et al. (2007) have shown that the evidence for the construct validity of Belbin is mixed, but that the model and the inventory show adequate convergent validity. However, there were strong associations between some team roles, indicating weak discriminant validity among some scales. Much research to measure the relationship between Belbin's team roles and organizational performance has shown generally positive results (Senior, 1997; Blenkinsop & Maddison, 2007; van de Water et al., 2008).

Using Belbin's Team Role Inventory in a PR/advertising top team

One example of how Belbin's Team Role Inventory might be used in team building is given by a PR/advertising company (cited in Swart et al., 2005). The company used it to improve the performance of its senior management team, and to identify individual team styles and interactions. The data were combined with observations of problem-solving activities to analyse team role behaviours, team contributions and miscommunications and misunderstandings between team members. Members could identify how to change behaviour to improve team performance and identify not just individual training needs but also organizational issues.

While Belbin's model remains popular, there are other diagnostic approaches to roles that have better psychometric properties. For example, the Occupational Personality Questionnaire assesses a person's perception of preferred styles of behaviour against job competences. It is based on what are referred to as the Big Five framework of personality traits of

- Openness (inventive/curious vs. consistent/cautious)
- Conscientiousness (efficient/organized vs. easy-going/careless)
- Extraversion (outgoing/energetic vs. solitary/reserved)
- Agreeableness (friendly/compassionate vs. cold/unkind)
- Neuroticism (sensitive/nervous vs. secure/confident)

activity

An online version of the Big Five personality test can be found at **www.outofservice.com/bigfive**

Your results will be used for research but you will get feedback. How could you use the results in working with others in a group or team?

An alternative to Belbin is the Team Management System. Go to **www.tmsdi.com/profiles/team-management-profile** for more details.

Procedural issues

Within teams, there will be many members with experiences of things going wrong and teams adopting faulty procedures, such as meetings that overrun their allotted time, or teams that postpone decisions.

Teams need to ensure that they are open to new ideas and constantly look at what they are doing, and how, in order to make improvements (Fleming, 2004), including asking:

- Why are we meeting?
- How often do we need to meet?
- Who will chair meetings?
- How do we solve problems and make decisions – by consensus, voting, the leader?
- How will decisions be communicated?

- How will success be judged?
- How will we monitor progress against goals and objectives?
- How are we functioning in terms of openness, cooperation, communication, conflict, use of talents, dealing with issues and problems, lessons learned?

One example of the importance of considering team procedures is given by the study of US cardiac surgery teams by Edmondson et al. (2004). Implementing new processes and adopting new technologies required a focus on the active management of learning by team leaders. The best team leaders were *partners* – accessible, asking for input and admitting their errors. Effective teams were designed for real-time learning, leaders framed motivating learning challenges, and an environment of psychological safety that fostered communication and innovation was developed (similar to the TCI of Anderson & West, 1994). The authors recommended that leaders should be chosen not just for technical expertise, but also for their ability to create learning environments. Knowledge sharing and learning are particularly evident in 'communities of practice' (Wenger & Snyder, 2004), informal self-organizing groups bound together by shared expertise and a passion to drive strategy, generate new business lines, promote best practice, develop skills and recruit and retain talent. Managers need to bring the appropriate people together, provide a facilitating infrastructure, such as time, sponsors, links with HRD and support teams, and measure value in innovative ways.

Meyer (2004) argues that traditional, results-oriented performance measurement systems fail to support multifunctional teams, and may indeed undermine them; the system should help the team, not top managers, monitor progress, and the team itself must play a lead role in designing its own measurement system, creating new, relatively few, process measures to track delivery, within the context of strategic goals and understandings.

Interpersonal issues

An influential way of looking at interpersonal processes in groups and teams is Bales' Interaction Process Analysis (IPA), a method for analysing the 'systems of human interaction' (Bales, 1950, p.257) in, originally, small face-to-face groups. Bales' contribution to the analysis of small groups was in distinguishing team process, how the group went about its business, from team task or content, what the group's goals were, with a primary focus on process. The IPA consists of 12 complementary–paired group processes, further subdivided into four major functions two associated with task behaviour and two with social- emotional behaviour, describing interaction/communications issues or problems (Table 12.2).

How the team addresses issues of task and social-emotional process reveals important data about its interpersonal workings, structures, and priorities as a microscopic social system. The model uses a 'unit of speech or process' (p.259) as the unit for coding and analysis: sentences or utterances, noted either with the

Table 12.2 System of process categories in the IPA, related psychosocial group functions and common communications problems

General category A: positive (and mixed) actions	
1	Seems friendly
2	Dramatizes
3	Agrees
General category B: attempted answers	
4	Gives suggestions
5	Gives opinions
6	Gives information
General category C: questions	
7	Asks for information
8	Asks for opinions
9	Asks for suggestions
General category D: negative (and mixed) actions	
10	Disagrees
11	Shows tension
12	Seems unfriendly

observer/coder present, or from audio recordings. IPA analysis generates three descriptions of team interaction processes:

1 positive or negative social-emotional reactions, and task focus on questions or answers
2 relative amounts of orientation, evaluation, control, decision, tension management, and integration behaviours
3 relative frequencies of the 12 category types, reflecting the communications strategies commonly employed by the team.

The mutually exclusive categories of the IPA have been criticized because single codes require that one judgement be made about what may be a subtle and complex statement. On the other hand, the method has also been recognized as innovative, because it identifies the presence and importance in group interaction of both task and relational functions as demonstrated by actual verbal behaviour.

One way IPA can be used in team building is in a fishbowl activity. Here a group is split into two teams, one seated in an inner circle and one acting as observers in an outer circle. While the inner team performs a task (for example a consensus activity of the 'lost on the moon/at sea/in the desert' kind, or a strategy discussion activity), the outer observers each take one team member and analyse their performance in the team task according to the IPA profile (for example, does the team member ask questions, give opinions, manage tensions and so on). At the end of the activity, each observer gives feedback on the performance of one team member; roles are then reversed and the observer group now takes the inner circle, to be observed by the new, outer circle group. The whole exercise could also be recorded and analysed later with reference to, for example, how well the team performed its task (content, for example, decision-making) as well as how it performed in terms of its process (for example, managing tension or conflicts, communicating).

Although the concept of emotional intelligence is usually applied to individuals such as leaders and managers, it can be applied to teams (Druskat & Wolff, 2004), as effective teams seek to build relationships inside and outside the team, with mutual trust, team identity and a sense of team efficacy providing a strong basis for cooperation and collaboration. Teams that allow emotions to surface, perhaps through posters and storyboards, and understand how they can affect the team's work are more likely to be effective. Teams must pay attention to the emotional issues involved on three levels: team to individual, team to itself and team to external actors. From the perspective of the individual, there is a need for interpersonal understanding, perspective taking, confronting and caring. From the perspective of the team, there is a need for self-evaluation, seeking feedback, creating resources such as time, and procedures to manage emotions, creating a positive, optimistic environment, and a proactive problem-solving style. From an external perspective, there is a need for organizational understanding and the building of external relationships and networking.

Team building in a community drug team

HRD in Practice

12.2

A community drug team in East Dorset, consisting of members drawn from five professions and three different employing agencies, used task-oriented team development and the GRPI model to resolve issues of mistrust and poor teamwork (for example not passing information on training courses on to other members). A particular focus was dealing with goals. Should the team focus on research, training, direct services to clients, service development, support and advice or liaison, service coordination and evaluation? Line manager pressure, member interest and desire for credibility with colleagues may push the team to more direct user contact, but at the expense of other goals and priorities. Initially, ill-defined goals and mission were clarified and specific objectives set and agreed with senior managers, such as setting up specific user groups and a family support service.

In order to clarify roles, the team defined generic and profession-specific skills; some members had specific professional requirements (for example, appearing at court for probation workers). It also attempted to resolve role conflicts (given that each member was also a member of other teams) through role analysis and role negotiation, adopting a coordinated team structure, where the team leader, a clinical psychologist, obtained agreed authority and accountability.

In order to clarify procedures, the team agreed to record new referrals in a common book, and allocate cases by workload and case characteristics through a key worker system. All cases, and case closures, were reviewed at clinical meetings, with minuted weekly meetings. All team correspondence, and one set of notes, were accessible to all members.

In order to improve relationships, the team attempted to meet frequently, share projects, include everyone at monthly lunches, train together and identify joint training needs, including using outside facilitators. In addition, the team spent a first week at an event to generate a common identity and knowledge base, developed further through corporate PR and articles in professional journals. Given staff changes and the formation of specific subgroups such as a women's group, periodic team maintenance was felt to be necessary.

Team building through outdoor development

Team development interventions in the UK have commonly used outdoor development, or ropes and slopes, involving physical challenges of some sort, for example in mountain or marine environments (Lewis, 2010). Some common questions for team building generally, and outdoor development in particular, include:

- What does it offer in terms of a learning experience?
- For what purposes can it be used?
- What issues need to be taken into account in running an event and ensuring transfer to the workplace?

Outdoor development involves:

- Use of outdoor activities to provide a problem or a challenge
- Individual/group attempts to solve a problem or face up to a challenge
- Competitive or non-competitive tasks (individual or group)
- Review of task through feedback, analysis and reflection
- Use for personal development, team building and leadership skills.

Its characteristics may have some or all of the following:

- A powerful experiential learning
- An unfamiliar environment
- A real environment
- An open-ended design
- Emotional intensity
- Psychological safety
- Physical safety.

However, there is little evidence that comprehensive evaluation happens; a survey in 1997 found that only 3 per cent of organizations using outdoor development used pre/post-test comparisons. However, 95 per cent claimed that learning transferred to the workplace, 47 per cent claimed a contribution to corporate objectives, and 79 per cent claimed increased effectiveness in the workplace (Badger et al., 1997). A rigorous evidence base on this issue is still lacking, however.

HRD in Practice 12.3

Team building at Marks & Spencers

In the early 2000s the head office merchandising team at Marks & Spencer was party to a significant re-organization. They were required to change their ways of working to deliver clothing products to 130 franchise international stores within 12 weeks compared to a norm of 7 months. This necessitated significant change and demanded a genuine team culture. Marks & Spencer commissioned Outdoor Development (an organization operating in conjunction with the University of Brighton) to engage a forty strong team to deliver this business transformation. The team development programme was instrumental in motivating the team to enable them to understand how they needed to work together and to deliver to the new supply timescales. The approach related outdoor challenges (e.g. getting team members across a barrier) to the Marks & Spencer change programme. Analysis and feedback were used to identify patterns also shown in the workplace (for example not listening, not cooperating, not taking the initiative, failing to take responsibility).

Team development stages

A popular topic in team building has been the notion that teams go through a series of stages as they develop. Tuckman (1965) identified five stages of team development (originally proposed as stages of group development) (see Figure 12.4):

- *forming*: characterized by dependence on the leader
- *storming*: independence/counter-dependence
- *norming*: interdependence
- *performing*: interdependence
- *adjourning (mourning)*: exit, break-up, moving on, for example rituals are often used to address emotional issues of loss and grief in project teams, for example reunions, parties, gifts.

Effective leaders will aspire to bring fully fledged teams to the performing stage as quickly as possible to attain high performance.

Tuckman's stages have been widely used and accepted in academic and practitioner worlds, although some have questioned their linear nature (do all teams have to go through all stages in the same order? Can teams slip back/regress to an earlier stage?), as well as the applicability of a model derived from the study of experimental/training groups to real-world teams.

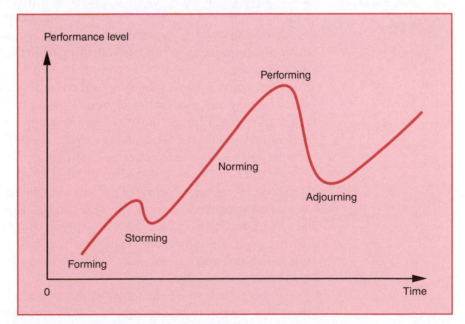

Figure 12.4 Tuckman's group development stages

Source: Adapted from Tuckman (1965)

The stages are as follows:

- *Forming*: At the first stage of team development, people are only just coming together to form a team. This stage is characterized by anxiety about the composition of the team, and people are concerned with what the team is for and who fits where. Thus, team members focus their attention on the leader/chair/sponsor, and tend to assess whether to trust them or not, while having to depend on them for their roles and responsibilities. Members are often polite and guarded. This may cause the leader to focus more on individual tasks, while providing links among the team members to encourage interaction. In this scenario, decision making is fragmented, with individuals often focusing only on their own performance. Team leaders need to think about preparation, including what they want out of it, who will be coming, what they will expect, and what experience/skills/knowledge they bring, as well as how to break the ice, perhaps by getting members to share experiences and ideas.

- *Storming*: Tuckman (1965) suggests that groups (teams) go to storming when members reach a level of familiarity and are comfortable interacting with each other (Levi, 2001). As members become more familiar with each other, they test each other and role boundaries through challenges and may jockey for position, which can lead to confusion, demotivation, emotional resistance or rebellion. Team members are still experimenting at this stage and are concerned with 'how we work together'. Levy (2001, p.41) asserts that in this instance the team members start to realize that the project might be more difficult than they had anticipated, and 'may become anxious, defensive, and blameful'. These issues will need to be worked through; the team leader may try to resolve conflicts by interacting with team members either individually or as a team, inviting questions and opinions while noting verbal and nonverbal reactions. The decision-making process can be adversarial, with challenges and threats to the leader, raising concerns for the sponsor, and frequent rumours, scapegoating and splits within the team into us and them. The storming stage is important, bringing to the fore different perspectives on issues.

- *Norming*: Once a certain level of understanding is reached, the group starts trusting the processes and begins to organize itself around tasks, rules, systems and procedures. As there is group cohesion, views may be exchanged openly and new ideas actively sought. Team members may interact and facilitate team processes, enhancing mutual support and cooperation and establishing a shared group identity and purpose (Levy, 2001). Decision making becomes part of the process, while team rules/norms, such as punctuality, positively impact on performance. However, there might still be some difficulties, and a danger of slipping back to storming, especially if newcomers are introduced. This may be handled through constructive discussion and negotiation, since levels of communication between team members are much higher.

- *Performing*: This is where the team has matured and is able to operate effectively as a team, with higher degrees of trust among team members, mutual support and dynamic interaction. The team focuses fully on problem solving, information sharing, tolerance, energy and collective decision making and cooperation (Tuckman, 1965; Senior, 1997; Levy, 2001). There are constructive attempts to complete tasks when roles allow for flexible and effective work. Not all teams manage to reach this stage successfully, as they may get stuck in earlier, more conflicting stages, or slip back. Many team leaders will try to get through all the previous stages as quickly as possible to achieve goals, but this may be a mistake, masking unresolved issues and conflicts. The team leader may even take on more of a coaching role to help team members identify their team development needs.

- *Adjourning:* Tuckman later identified a fifth stage (perhaps accompanied by *mourning*), whereby the team is psychologically prepared beforehand for break-up or dissolution. Some teams may have planned endings, such as problem-solving or project teams. When team goals or objectives are achieved, members disperse. Guzzo and Dickson (1996) argue that after a few years of working together, a team's prolonged existence can be harmful for performance, increasing the need for the adjourning stage to bring freshness to the team. Too much cohesion can harm team creativity by reducing conflict and challenge, encouraging complacency, and enhancing the likelihood of *groupthink*. Here, as we saw earlier, (in particular, the Nut Island case), teams may ignore crucial information and distort reality, partly in the interests of maintaining group cohesion, so that discussion of threats is avoided, silence is interpreted as consent, and self-censorship prevails. Members voicing dissent may be seen as disloyal, traitors or 'not one of us'.

One way of avoiding groupthink is through greater team diversity, as the more diverse range of capabilities team members bring to a team, the more flexible that team will be in meeting changing demands. Teams that allow for varied and differing perspectives while enabling members to work towards common problems can enhance their performance through organizational learning. Archival studies in the US financial sector have shown positive relationships between top team heterogeneity and strategic change, especially the adoption of innovative strategies. Although Northcraft et al. (1995) argue that diversity in the team impacts on the amount of time it takes for a team to move through the first three stages, diverse teams may be more creative in the long run.

Other teams may be unsuccessful in reaching the performing stage because they have failed to work through issues arising in earlier stages. Levy (2001) points out that a team's life is often a roller coaster of successes and failures; teams may go through different levels of performance during low or high periods when members are trying to resolve issues.

After Tuckman, there have been many different models of team development put forward (McGrath, 1990; Ancona & Caldwell, 1990; McIntyre & Salas, 1995), but Tuckman (1965) is still widely used and consulted when developing a team because of the clarity and simplicity of stage definition.

activity

If you are introducing teamwork in your current workplace or doing a team-based project in your college/university, would you use Tuckman's team development stages, outdoor development, Belbin's roles, all three or something else? Explain your decision.

Team coaching

Coaching is usually seen as a one-to-one intervention, but Clutterbuck (2007, p.77) argues it can also be applied to:

> Helping the team improve performance, and the processes by which performance is achieved, through reflection and dialogue.

This is similar to individual coaching, but is more complex, and has some extra dimensions:

- confidentiality
- scope of the relationship
- speed of decision making.

Team coaching has been less studied, but similar models to individual coaching apply, ranging from directive (for example GROW model) to non-directive (for example process consultation). Unlike a facilitator, the team coach is more engaged and inside the team. Unlike team building, dialogue is more frequent and more intensive (Clutterbuck, 2007).

reflective question Thinking of an organization you are familiar with or you currently work for, what learning would you need to make an effective team coach?

Intergroup team building

Most team building focuses on developing internal relationships in the team. However, some methodologies have been developed to focus on intergroup or inter-team relationships, especially in terms of managing intergroup/inter-team conflict. One such technique, organizational mirroring, involves a host group (for example a unit, team, or department, or a function, like educational psychologists) receiving feedback from other groups (for example other teams, units, departments, or functions, like head teachers) about how it is perceived. A study of social workers and nurses in Bradford, for example, showed how negative perceptions of each other affected referral rates of, in particular, Asian women (Iles & Auluck, 1988). Another development, three-dimensional mirroring, involves two separate groups building and sharing two or three lists. One concerns perceptions of how the group sees itself, another how it perceives the other group. A third might involve predictions of how the other group will perceive it. The two groups then meet separately to discuss the implications of the two lists, and then meet together to resolve priority issues between the two groups, and action plans are then devised (Blake et al., 1965).

An alternative, devised by Fordyce and Weil (1971), gets each group to devise three lists:

- *a positive feedback list:* attributes or behaviours that the group likes and values about the other group and wishes it to keep or continue doing
- *a bug list:* things the group dislikes about the other group and wishes it to stop doing

- *an empathy list:* what it thinks the other group is saying about it, or what it wants the other group to start doing.

The two groups share their lists and the total group builds a key list of unresolved issues and priorities. Subgroups are then formed to work on each item and report back to the whole group for action planning and evaluation. Such techniques can be used to address diversity issues, such as facilitating successful joint work by male and female or black and white colleagues (Iles & Auluck, 1988).

summary

There are several types of team now being commonly used in organizations, for example cross-functional teams, project teams, virtual teams and self-managed work teams. However, this list is not exhaustive.

T groups have been in use to build teams since the 1950s. The classic T groups used mainly strangers and focused on issues in the here and now and the personal growth of the trainee. The use of T groups has grown in the UK but the problems of training transferability became a common issue. This has been overcome by the use of team development and outdoor training activities.

Team development needs may be assessed through such instruments as the Team Climate Inventory.

Another example is task-oriented team development or GRPI, focusing on team goals, roles, procedures and interpersonal relationships. Bales' Interaction Process Analysis may be used to develop interpersonal skills in a team.

Belbin's team role profiling is widely used to analyse preferred team roles, despite continuing doubts about its psychometric properties.

Tuckman's team development stages are still widely used in organizations to train teams at different levels of development. Tuckman (1965) came up with five stages – forming, storming, norming, performing and adjourning.

Relations between teams may be explored and improved through a variety of techniques of intergroup team building.

discussion questions

1 Why would you wish to introduce team working?
2 When do you think team building would be useful?
3 Do you see any problems arising from a cohesive, conflict-free team?

4 How autonomous should self-directed teams be?
5 If a team seems to be experiencing conflict, would you send it on an outdoor development course?

further reading

Braun, F.C., Avital, M. and Martz, B. (2012) Action-centered team leadership influences more than performance. *Team Performance Management,* **18**(3/4): 176–95.

Lewis, S. (2010) Outdoor programmes and the training needs of industry in the UK. *5th International Mountain and Outdoor Sports Conference Outdoor Activities in Educational and Recreational Programmes.* 18th–21st November 2010. Czech Republic.

Lencion, P.M. (2012) *The Five Dysfunctions of a Team: Intact Teams Participant Workbook.* New York: John Wiley and Sons.

Jong, A., de Ruyter, J. and Lemmink, J. (2005) Service climate in self-managing teams: mapping the team member perceptions and service performance outcomes in a business-to-business setting. *Journal of Management Studies,* **42**(8): 1593–620.

references

Ancona, D. and Caldwell, D. (1990) Beyond boundary spanning: managing external dependence in product development teams. *Journal of High-Technology Management Research*, **1**(1): 119–35.

Anderson, N. and West, M. (1994) *Team Climate Inventory*. Windsor: NFER Nelson.

Aritzeta, A., Swailes, S. and Senior, B. (2007) Belbin's team role model: development, validity and applications for team-building. *Journal of Management Studies*, **44**(1): 96–118.

Badger, B., Sadler-Smith, E. and Michie, E. (1997) Outdoor management development: use and evaluation. *Journal of European Industrial Training*, **21**(9): 318–25.

Bales, R.F. (1950) *Interaction Process Analysis: A Method for the Study of Small Groups*. Reading, MA: Addison-Wesley.

Beckhard, R. (1972) Optimizing teambuilding efforts. *Journal of Contemporary Business*, **1**(3): 23–32.

Belbin, M. (1981) *Management Teams: Why they Succeed or Fail*. London: Heinemann.

Belbin, M. (1993) *Team Roles at Work*. Oxford: Butterworth Heinemann.

Blake, R.R., Shepherd, H.A. and Mouton, J.S. (1965) *Managing Intergroup Conflict in Industry*. Ann Arbor, MI: Foundation for Research on Human Behavior.

Blenkinsop, N. and Maddison, A. (2007) Team roles and performance in defence acquisition. *Journal of Management Development,* **26**(7): 667–82.

Burke, W. Warner (2003) *Organization Change: Theory and Practice.* Thousand Oaks, CA: Sage.

CIPD (2012) *Learning and Talent Development*. London: Chartered Institute of Personnel and Development.

Clutterbuck, D. (2007) *Coaching the Team at Work*. London: Nicholas Brealey.

Davies, M.F. and Kanaki, E. (2006) Interpersonal characteristics associated with different team roles in work groups. *Journal of Managerial Psychology*, **21**(7): 638–50.

Dayal, I. and Thomas, J. (1968) Operation KPE: developing a new organization. *Journal of Applied Behavioral Science*, **4**(4): 473–506.

Delarue, A., van Hootegem, G., Procter, S. and Burridge, M. (2008) Teamworking and organizational performance: a review of survey-based research. *International Journal of Management Reviews*, **10**(2): 127–48.

Druskat, V.U. and Wolff, S.B. (2004) Building the emotional intelligence of groups, in *Harvard Business Review on Teams that Succeed*. Boston, MA: Harvard Business School Press.

Dufrene, D., Sharbrough, W., Clipson, T. and McCall, M. (1999) Bringing outdoor challenge education inside the business communication classroom. *Business Communication Quarterly*, **62**(3): 24–36.

Edmondson, A., Bohmer, R. and Pisano, G. (2004) Speeding up team learning, in *Harvard Business Review on Teams that Succeed*. Boston, MA: Harvard Business School Press.

Fleming, I. (2004) *Teamworking Pocketbook*, 2nd edn. Arlesford: Management Pocketbooks.

Fordyce, J.K. and Weil, R. (1971) *Managing with People: A Manager's Handbook of Organization Development Methods*. Reading, MA: Addison-Wesley.

Guzzo, R.A. and Dickson, M.W. (1996) Teams in organizations: recent research on performance and effectiveness. *Annual Review of Psychology*, **48**: 307–38.

Harrison, R.C. (1972) When power conflicts trigger team spirit. *European Business*, Spring: 27–65.

Iles, P.A. and Auluck, R.K. (1988) Managing equal opportunity through strategic organization development. *Leadership and Organization Development Journal*, **4**(3): 3–10.

Iles, P.A. and Auluck, R.K. (1993) Inter-agency team development. In C. Mabey and B. Mayon-White (eds) *Managing Change*, 2nd edn. Milton Keynes: Open University Press.

Ingram, H., Teare, R., Scheving, E. and Armistead, C. (1997) A systems model of effective teamwork. *The TQM Magazine*, **9**(2): 118–27.

Katzenbach, J.R. and Smith, D.K. (2004) The discipline of teams, in *Harvard Business Review on Teams that Succeed*. Boston, MA: Harvard Business School Press.

Kreitner, R., Kinicki, A. and Buelens, M. (2002) *Organizational Behavior*, 2nd edn. Maidenhead: McGraw-Hill.

Levi, D. (2001) *Group Dynamics for Teams*. Thousand Oaks, CA: Sage.

Levy, P.F. (2004) The Nut Island effect: when good teams go wrong, in *Harvard Business Review on Teams that Succeed*. Boston, MA: Harvard Business School Press.

Lewis, S. (2010) Outdoor programmes and the training needs of industry in the UK. *5th International Mountain and Outdoor Sports Conference Outdoor Activities in Educational and Recreational Programmes*. 18th–21st November 2010. Czech Republic.

McGrath, J. (1990) Time matters in groups. In J. Gallegher, R. Kraut and C. Egido (eds) *Intellectual Teamwork: Social and Technological Foundations of Cooperative Work*. Hillsdale, NJ: Lawrence Erlbaum.

McIntyre, R.M. and Salas, E. (1995). Measuring and managing for team performance: emerging principles from complex environments. In R.A. Guzzo and E. Salas (eds) *Team Effectiveness and Decision Making in Organizations*. San Francisco: Jossey-Bass.

Meyer, C. (2004) How the right measures help teams excel, in *Harvard Business Review on Teams that Succeed*. Boston, MA: Harvard Business School Press.

Miller, D. (2008) *Brilliant Teams: What to Know, Do and Say to Make a Brilliant Team*. Harlow: Prentice Hall.

Morgeson, F.P., De Rue, D.S., and Karam, E.P. (2010) Leadership in teams: a functional approach to understanding leadership structures and processes. *Journal of Management*, **36**(1): 5–39.

Northcraft, G.B., Polzer, J.T., Neale, M.A. and Kramer, R. (1995) Productivity in cross-functional teams: diversity, social identity, and performance. In S.E. Jackson (ed.) *Diversity in Work Teams: Research Paradigms for a Changing World*. Washington DC: APA Publications.

Procter, S. and Currie, G. (2004) Target-based teamworking: groups, work and interdependence. *Human Relations Journal*, **57**(12): 1547–72.

Proehl, R.A. (1996) Enhancing the effectiveness of cross-functional teams. *Leadership and Organization Development Journal*, **17**: 3–10.

Robbins, S.P. (2005) *Organizational Behaviour*, 11th edn. Upper Saddle River, NJ: Pearson Education.

Rubin, I.M., Plovnick, M.S. and Fry, R.F. (1978) *Task-oriented Team Development*. New York: McGraw-Hill.

Senior, B. (1997) Team roles and team performance: is there really a link? *Journal of Occupational and Organizational Psychology*, **70**(3): 241–58.

Stewart, R. (ed.) (1999) *Gower Handbook of Teamworking*. Aldershot: Gower.

Swart, J., Mann, C., Brown, S. and Price, A. (2005) *Human Resource Development: Strategy and Tactics*. Oxford: Elsevier Butterworth Heinemann.

Torrington, D., Hall, L. and Taylor, S. (2005) *Human Resource Management*, 6th edn. London: Pearson Education.

Tuckman, B. (1965) Developmental sequence in small groups. *Psychological Bulletin*, **63**(6): 384–99.

Van de Water, H., Ahaus, K. and Rozier, R. (2008) Team roles, team balance and performance. *Journal of Management Development*, **27**(5): 499–512.

Wenger, E. and Snyder, W. (2004) Communities of practice: the organizational frontier, in *Harvard Business Review on Teams that Succeed*. Boston, MA: Harvard Business School Press.

chapter 13

Talent and Career Development

Michelle Blackburn, Jim Stewart and Jeff Gold

Chapter learning outcomes

After studying this chapter, you should be able to:

- Explain the meanings of talent, talent management and career development
- Evaluate approaches to and methods of talent and career development
- Critically assess debates on connections between talent management and career development
- Analyse the contribution of career development to talent management

Chapter Outline

Introduction
A strategy for talent development
Coaching
Career management and development
Mentoring
Summary

Introduction

It was only a few years ago, during the late 1990s and early 2000s, that many organizations were engaged in a 'war for talent' (Michaels et al., 2001). This was based on the view that high potential staff were needed for high performance at work and that there was a shortage of such staff and hence competition between organizations to attract, develop and retain them. One consequence of this view has been the growth of Talent Management (TM) as a policy with Talent Development (TD) as a key feature of that policy (Novations, 2009). With the arrival of a recession, the ideas of TM and TD seemed to be more concerned with developing talent in-house and increasing the focus on retention of talent (CIPD, 2009). In recent years, surveys suggest a slight reduction in the number of organizations that undertake TM and TD activities (CIPD, 2012) but among those that do, activities such as coaching, mentoring and career planning are common processes. For example, at BT a Talent Deal sets out commitments to those considered part of its talent pool, consisting of career planning, networking opportunities and mentoring. Focusing activities on those considered as talented can also enhance motivation and the obligation to develop and apply skills (Höglund, 2012). This raises key questions concerning the meaning of talent in organizations, how talented staff are identified and then considered for development, including a connection to such issues as succession planning and career development. We will consider such questions in this chapter.

reflective question   What is your understanding of talent? How would this help identify talent for development in organizations? Who would be in your talent pool?

A strategy for talent development

Talent Development is a crucial component of any TM strategy, which itself is linked to an organization's strategy (Cook & Macaulay, 2009). TM is concerned with the integraton of processes to attract, develop, manage and evaluate talent so that organization priorities can be achieved (Tansley et al., 2007; Sistonen 2005). One obvious impression here is that TM represents a repackaging of traditional HRM processes such as selection, assessment, development and reward and so could be seen as 'old wine in new bottles' (Chuai et al., 2008). This does raise the question of whether there is anything different about TM generally and TD in particular? One view is that TM and TD provide HRM specialists with a chance to focus on helping leaders and managers make better decisions about people and performance based on talent data and analysis (Boudreau & Ramstad, 2007). However, there remains the problem about the meaning of the term talent in organizations and Tansley (2011) argues that a clear meaning is needed so as to distinguish the idea from other terms like skill or competences. She suggests that whatever definition is adopted, it needs to be organization-specific based on the type of industry and nature of the work, with group level implications. She also found in her research that most meanings focused on individuals, but there are other possibilities as shown in Figure 13.1

In Figure 13.1, there are two dimensions:

a. exclusivity/inclusivity

b. people/position
    These provide four possible patterns:

1   The exclusive/people pattern considers that talent resides with individuals or 'stars' (Groysberg, 2010), probably considered as high potential and/or high performing. CIPD (2012) surveys suggest this remains the prominent view of talent.

2   The exclusive/position pattern considers that key positions are needed to meet the organization's strategy. For example, Huselid et al. (2005) consider how strategically critical jobs are, with 'A' positions needing 'A' players whose performance will have a more than proportionate effect on organization outcomes. Other jobs, 'B' or 'C' positions, are less significant and can be outsourced or eliminated.

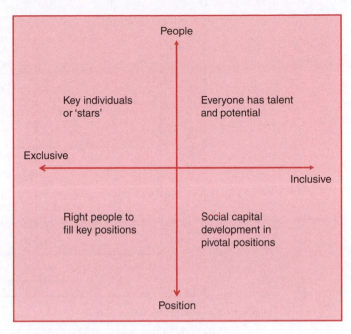

Figure 13.1 Approaches to talent management and development

3 The inclusive/people pattern is a recognition that talent can be found more widely in an organization, so every employee has talent and potential. The restaurant chain Nando's, for example, takes the view that all staff can 'grow and develop' and that recruitment based on 'pride, passion, courage, integrity and family – is key' (Evans, 2007, p.16).

4 The inclusive/position pattern points to a more collective understanding of talent, based on relationships, networks and team membership, all aspects of social capital shared between people. Collings and Mellahi (2009) argue for the importance of this position perspective in developing a TM and TD strategy.

activity

Go to **http://annualreport.marksandspencer.com/** and find a copy of the latest M&S annual report. Search through the report and consider how this company uses the word 'talent'. Consider the approach taken against Figure 13.1.

Succession Planning

As we have already indicated, TM involves identifying members of a talent pool from which present and future work positions can be filled. This process links TM to succession planning, although the obvious connection is not always recognized (Tansley et al., 2007). Membership of a talent pool involves selection through, for example, interviews, 360-degree assessments and performance reviews. There can be different pools for different levels such as entry-level, emerging talent, rising stars and executives (Tansley et al., 2007) or for different functions, such as in Google, which has talent pools for IT specialists and customer service staff. Each pool can be connected by a talent pipeline and this

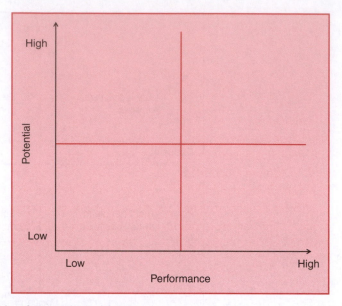

Figure 13.2 A performance/potential chart

allows flexibility in succession with a flow of the right people at the right time in what Ready and Conger (2007) refer to as a talent factory. Filling the pools and ensuring the flow requires identifying and developing the right people and Figure 13.2 shows a typical approach.

The chart provides combinations of performance and potential and is used to identify staff for talent pools. For example, the top left corner identifies staff with high potential but low performance and this may reveal staff not ready for a talent pool, until their performance is improved. There is more differentiation between the boxes if a middle position on each dimension is added, resulting in nine boxes. The value of this grid is the debate and discussion that can develop about talent, but there is also the problem of how decisions are made about placing particular people in particular positions on the grid (e.g. high performance, low or middle potential). Such decisions can be made on simple or inadequate information and not linked to strategy or organization culture (Vaiman et al., 2012). They could also be potentially discriminatory. In some organizations, where large numbers of staff might be involved, data on the global talent pool requires software to allow tracking for TD, succession planning and identifying blockages as part of a TM system (see Pollitt, 2007; Ensley et al., 2011).

reflective question What TD approach would you adopt for someone in the top left corner of the chart (low performance, high potential)?

One outcome of TM decisions and allocation to a talent pool is the focus on TD. As defined by Garavan et al. (2012), TD is concerned with

planning, selection and implementation of development strategies for the entire talent pool to ensure that the organisation has both the current and future supply of talent to meet strategic objectives and that development activities are aligned with organisational talent management processes (p.6).

Once again, we might argue that TD does not look very different from the ideas of strategic HRD (see Chapter 2). It is not surprising to find that TD is easily combined with HRD in organizations, with recent surveys indicating that development programmes and coaching are common TD practices (CIPD, 2012). Further, given the focus on high potential staff, TD can be accommodated with leadership and management development programmes (see Chapter 11). However, with different talent pools, there can be varied development routes or pathways and a blend of development strategies to form what Gandz (2006) calls a TD pipeline architecture. This is likely to include performance management processes such as coaching and career development, including mentoring.

Coaching

In a large number of organizations, coaching is seen as a key feature of HRD generally and TD in particular. Traditionally viewed as a relatively directive way of improving performance of a work-related task, survey evidence suggests that in the UK around 77 per cent of organizations use coaching, with rising or stable expenditure on this activity during a recession (CIPD, 2011). Coaching by line managers is now rated as the second most effective learning and development practice (topped only by in-house development programmes) (CIPD, 2012).

From an organizational perspective coaching can be introduced to achieve a wide range of objectives. In a survey of coaching practice amongst 45 employers, Wolf (2012) comments that improving employee performance and developing leadership skills were the most popular reasons for using coaching, closely followed by helping employees with their careers and tackling poor performance. Other reasons include assistance with development, culture change, communication and diversity goals. In addition the CIPD (2012) highlight the role of coaching in talent management and international development.

Over the last ten years, coaching has become a significant TD activity as shown in HRD in Practice 13.1

HRD in Practice

13.1

Ernst and Young launch maternity coaching scheme to retain talented staff

Ernst and Young has launched a maternity coaching scheme for its staff. The scheme, which has been taken up by over 240 employees, is part of the firm's commitment to retain talented women and invest in their career development. Participants in the scheme receive four tailored coaching sessions, which take place before, during and after their maternity leave.

The coaching covers issues such as managing relationships with clients and colleagues, exploring alternative work patterns, and reintegrating into the workplace. Line managers with team members going on maternity leave also attend a dedicated coaching session on how to provide the right level of contact and support.

Liz Bingham, partner sponsor of the programme at Ernst and Young, said: 'Maternity coaching is not about informing staff about our corporate policies. It is about giving our employees the confidence to have conversations about their working arrangements, keeping them informed while on leave, and helping them transition and reintegrate back into the workplace.'

'The scheme was initially aimed at women and their line managers but the anecdotal feedback has been so positive that we are planning to open it out to new fathers. Becoming a parent is a life changing event and we recognize that fathers, as well as mothers, need help as they seek to adjust and balance their personal and professional commitments.'

Adapted from **www.employeebenefits.co.uk/item/13020/23/5/3**

Of course, the image of coaching is most closely connected with improving performance in sport (Evered and Selman, 1989). This image has been transferred to organizations where coaching is concerned with performance and development issues, based on a relationship between a line manager and staff (Gray, 2010). In organizations, as in sport, this relationship is not without tensions and as a result, staff responses to being coached can vary since it might indicate the need for fixing performance through remedial work (Western, 2008, p.99). Coaching as an activity can also be found in a variety of other forms in different locations. For example, business support for SMEs can be based on coaching, as can work with students in higher education. Another variation is peer and team coaching (Parker et al., 2008).

Coaching Cultures

Focusing on TD, coaching seeks to develop and enhance the performance and potential of those identified for the talent pool. Of course, depending on the stance of the organization towards talent, such a pool might be more or less inclusive. In some organizations, such as Morrisons, coaching is seen as an inclusive process, to be undertaken throughout the organization (Devins & Clark, 2011). Such an approach can be seen as an attempt to create a coaching culture or coaching organization (Garvey et al., 2009) where coaching becomes embedded as a valued activity. Knights and Poppleton (2008) completed a study of 20 organizations and found three approaches to creating coaching cultures:

- *Centralized and structured* – senior managers provide high support and formal structures to ensure consistency, as found in London's Metropolitan Police.
- *Organic and emergent* – based on informality and networks, coaching evolves slowly according to the context of practice, as in the international emergency assistance organization, the Cega Group.
- *Tailored middle ground* – a blend of the previous two approaches, with some degree of direction for consistency but also a response to the particulars of the context.

The BBC provides an example of the third approach. Coaching began with a small of group of committed and interested coaches requiring a response from the organization for more structure and direction. The build-up of momentum in creating a coaching culture leads to what Knights and Poppleton called the 'tipping point' where coaching becomes mainstream with evidence of adding value. Coaching can become part of the competency framework for leaders and managers (see also Chapter 10) and there may even be the development of coaching supervisors, or master-coaches (Garvey et al., 2009, p.62), who provide guidance and support for other coaches but who also continue to learn about the coaching process, models of coaching and how coaching can support culture change (Stober & Grant, 2006). In this way, an organization can develop its own understanding of coaching as a contributor to TD.

It should be clear that leaders and managers are central to creating a coaching culture. Gold et al. (2010a) suggest that there are two key features: first, leaders and managers who are coached are more likely to improve performance; and second, leaders and managers who coach are more likely to learn about their staff and improve their performance. Leaders and managers must therefore be motivated as coaches (McComb, 2012). However, there are also reasons why leaders and managers may not be willing to coach or even be coached. For example, they may find it difficult to develop staff when there is a need to meet performance targets, with the latter usually taking precedence. Or there may be negative or adverse aspects in the relationship between leaders and managers and their staff (Ellinger et al., 2008)

reflective question   Can coaching be both performance- and development-focused?
Will the focus affect the approach of the coach and methods used?

One way of motivating leaders and managers in favour coaching, especially those in senior positions, might be to provide them with someone from outside the organization as an executive coach (EC). It is argued that senior managers often have to work in lonely and isolated contexts (Carter, 2001), so need help from someone who, according to Feldman and Lankau (2005):

- does not provide answers on specific business issues – that is the role of consultants
- helps improve the performance and skills of the manager
- does not act as a mentor from within the organization but is an outsider usually contracted for six to 18 months
- does not act as a therapist but is more focused on performance.

Emerging research suggests that EC is valued by leaders and managers where the EC builds a good relationship based on empathy, with a shift from specific behaviours and change towards a helpful process composed of 'support, encouragement, listening and understanding' (de Haan et al., 2011). This kind of role is similar to that which has long been termed a critical friend in educational contexts (Costa & Kallick, 1993).

Coaching Models

While there are several models of coaching, the most well-known is Whitmore's (2002) GROW model:

- *Goal* – establish a clear objective to be achieved
- *Reality* – establish the current performance and situation
- *Options* – finding ideas and alternatives
- *Will or Way Forward* – commitment to action.

This model is especially useful for introducing coaching, although it lacks a theoretical base. As argued by Barner and Higgins (2007), all coaching practice is implicitly based on a theoretical model and these models need to be more clearly understood and articulated. The theoretical models identified are:

the clinical model – concerned with helping coachees understand themselves better through self-disclosure and an exploration of personal history to assess impact on current issues faced

the behaviour model – concerned with helping coachees understand the impact of their behaviour on others, possibly by using feedback data (360-degree appraisals) before guiding changes in behaviour

the systems model – concerned with helping coachees understand the context and system in which they work so that any change is set against the possible constraints and the enabling conditions needed, such as support from others

the social constructionist model – concerned with helping coachees understand the meaning of language used by themselves and otherswhere it is used to construct current realities and possibly change them.

activity

Read the article by Barner and Higgins (2007), then go to **http://www.mentoring-forchange.co.uk/classic/index.php** for information about 14 models of coaching. What theories, if any, underpin the models?

Whatever model is employed, a coach needs to show skill within the relationship. Anderson et al. (2009) identified the following coaching behaviours for managers:

- Shared decision-making
- Listening
- Making action plans
- Questioning
- Giving feedback
- Developing staff personally and professionally.

Models and skills provide a degree of clarity and help in the design of HRD programmes. There is also a growing list of qualifications and accreditation frameworks for coaching, and emerging bodies seeking to provide quality assurance for coaches and an element of professional regulation (for example see www.emccouncil.org).

activity

Go to www.emccouncil.org for information about the European Mentoring and Coaching Council. Check how quality and standards are being used. Go to www.emccouncil.org/eu/en/accreditation and consider the code of ethics.

Are coaches (and mentors) becoming professionalized? Go to www.i-l-m.com/learn-with-ilm/850.aspx and consider the awards for coaching. Is this a route to professionalization?

Peer coaching

While coaching is mainly concerned with the relationship between line manager and staff, it is also recognized that relationships between staff at the same level of work can also play a role in TD. Referred to as peer coaching (Parker et al., 2008), relationships between staff can provide a more equal framework for TD by removing differences based on power, salary and staff. As trust is established, peer coaching provides for a supportive and challenging environment, similar to action learning.

Peer coaching can be especially important in the way feedback from formal processes, such as 360-degree assessment, is utilized. Working with a respected partner, feedback can be presented more meaningfully. An example of this process, based on work with head-teachers, is shown in Figure 13.3

Formed into partnerships, the participants met every two weeks to review learning, provide feedback and share ideas. This became a learning conversation which, after repeated cycles, established the basis for trust and creative responses to new demands.

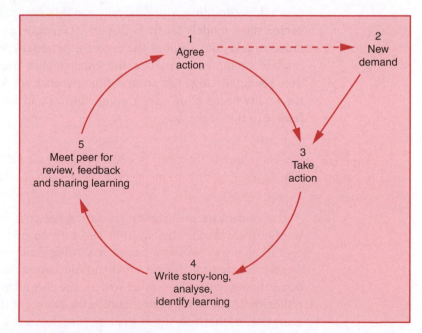

Figure 13.3 A peer coaching process

Peer coaching can also be extended beyond partners to larger groups who can collaborate around identified issues. Often this involves the use of social network technologies such as Facebook, to provide a home for the community of learners (Li et al., 2011).

Career management and development

TD incorporates a focus on the retention of identified staff with potential, who in turn expect their career development to be addressed (Scott & Revis, 2008). If we also accept that talented staff are also likely to be highly-employable staff, they will be able to find new jobs more easily based on their flexibility and access to labour market opportunities (Nauta et al., 2009). The idea of a career, therefore, is likely to be valued by talented staff.

So what is a career? Superficially it seems a fairly simply question, however the answer (like many studied in the academic world!) is much more complex, changing as a consequence of research, the evolving nature of work and, perhaps unsurprisingly, the expectations of the workforce.

Traditional careers are probably what most of us think of when we attempt to define the term career, as Wilensky (1961, p.523) suggested: 'A career is a succession of related jobs arranged in a hierarchy of prestige, through which persons move in an ordered, (more or less predictable) sequence.' This definition implied that careers were organized in a step by step approach, a notion that is often referred to as the career ladder, where success is seen as moving through an organizationally-defined hierarchy towards a pre-determined goal which represents success (Townsend, 1970). There were even models that suggested each step within the career ladder was achieved within a pre-determined age range. Many of these so-called career stage models (such as Super, 1957; Schein, 1978; Greenhaus, 1987) failed to take into account the career experiences of women. However, later models attempted to redress the balance (like Super, 1980) and included non-gendered language around home-maker roles but failed to represent the reality of the child-care responsibilities and career opportunities of the female in the workplace.

reflective question   How do you think the changes in UK legislation around age discrimination and the phasing out of the default retirement age challenge career life-stage models?

Traditional careers therefore reflect the paternal and power paradigms that were in place during the late 19th and early to mid 20th centuries where the organization was seen as a parent rewarding good behaviour with appropriate career advancement. Kanter (1989) would have defined this as a bureaucratic career, however, like many other writers, she goes on to suggest that this model is rather limited in aiding understanding the careers of the late 20th and early 21st centuries and therefore this is what we consider next.

The changing nature of careers

Baruch (2006) suggests that there are both macro and micro reasons behind changes in the nature of careers. At a macro level he suggests that global economic influences (and their instability), more diversity (though with discrimination still in existence) and organizational restructuring all have an impact. At a micro level he suggests the nature of careers is influenced by changing attitudes to life and work. For example Holbeche (2009) suggests that Generation Y (those born in the 1970s to mid 1990s) is characterized by workers who 'have never expected loyalty from a company, nor have they expected to give it' (p.180). This is quite a stark statement for organizations seeking to create career opportunities in order to retain staff in their talent pools.

However, it would be mistaken to assume that the concept of the career ladder and formal routes for career progression have ceased to exist. In the UK there are still formal routes in the NHS and the Civil Service despite significant restructuring. The same can be said of the Australian public sector (McDonald et al., 2005). It is perhaps then the private sector that has experienced the most significant shift in career opportunities and expectations.

Adamson et al. (1998) suggested that there have been three changes in organizational career philosophy:

- an end to the long-term view of the employer–employee relationship
- an end to movement through the hierarchy being seen as career progression
- an end to logical, ordered and sequential careers.

All of this suggests that there has been a change in the nature of careers and therefore there has been the need for both workers and organizations to adjust their psychological contracts. The emerging contract is perhaps more transactional but dynamic in nature (Lee et al., 2011), particularly where newer generations have different ideas of what a career might look like. These alternative career models will be outlined below.

Modern careers

Kanter (1989) offered two alternatives to the *bureaucratic* career. She identified the *professional* career, which suggested a more flexible employment relationship based upon challenging assignments that offered an opportunity for enhanced 'knowledge and reputation' (p.515). She also identified the *entrepreneurial* career, where individuals seek to add value to an organization and success is measured by 'progress when the territory grows BELOW them [thereby creating] freedom, independence, and control' (Kanter, 1989, p.516).

A related view is that of the boundaryless career, a concept introduced by DeFillippi and Arthur (1994) based simply on the notion that careers no longer have formal boundaries. Organizational walls across departments, functions and role responsibilities are seen as no longer limiting progression. Indeed the walls that exist around the organization, that separate it from competitors, are no longer seen as a barrier to individuals seeking career development. Careers are progressed then within any number of organizations and roles and changes are driven by an individual's world view and external notions of success. How realistic this is needs to be questioned. Even if the individual sees freedom from career boundaries, are organizations willing and able to accommodate these aspirations? At what point will the CV with a larger variety of roles and organizations be seen as characteristic of someone unable to settle or perform appropriately in a given role?

The protean career is a concept often seen as closely linked to that of the boundaryless career. It is characterized as 'a process which the person, not the organization, is managing… The protean person's own personal career choices and search for self-fulfilment are the unifying or integrative elements in his or her life' (Hall, 1976, p.201). The key here is the driver of self-fulfilment rather than simply moving across boundaries for advancement (as is characterized by the boundaryless career). The search for psychological fulfilment, characterized by Hall (1996, p.1) as a search for meaning, purpose, identity and learning, is at the heart of this approach. More recently, Khapova et al. (2007, p.115) have presented a similar idea as the subjective career based on an 'individual's interpretation of his or her career situation at any given time'.

reflective question   What are the individual and organizational benefits of these different career models?

Activities and processes

As the previous discussion highlights, the concept of career can be examined through two lenses. One that suggests that responsibility lies with the organization, which is perhaps a more traditional perspective (or one more focused on talent management). The other perspective suggests that individuals now have the desire and opportunity to manage their own careers. Both of these notions suggest career development, defined by Greenhaus et al. (2010, p.13) as 'an ongoing process by which individuals progress through a series of stages, each of which is characterized by a relatively unique set of issues, themes, and tasks'. This section will begin by discussing this progress from an individual perspective before considering the organization's viewpoint and then finishing with a hybrid approach.

As we can see from the above, the idea of individuals actively managing and developing their own careers began in the 1970s with Hall (1976) but evidence of individuals actively engaged in this process only emerged in the 1990s (Hall & Moss, 1998). If individuals are actively engaged in their own career development, then there is perhaps the need for a defined set of capabilities that they need to possess to be effective in this endeavour. DeFillippi and Arthur (1995) developed the concept of the intelligent career, and within that listed three career competencies: know why, know how, and know whom. These competencies were later extended by Jones and DeFillippi (1996) writing about the US film industry to also include know what, know where and, perhaps unsurprisingly, know when! Table 13.1 illustrates a framework based on that of Jones and DeFillippi (1996) incorporating their know… concepts with current challenges and practical career management strategies.

Table 13.1 A career competencies framework

Competencies	Challenges	Strategies
Knowing what: A SWOT (Strengths, Weaknesses, Opportunities, Threats) analysis of the industry/sector	• Less stability in income • Balance income needs • Resilience during gaps in work	• Select opportunities that enhance personal brand • Know the industry and how to benchmark personal capabilities against industry success measures • Personal brand management to gain reputation for quick, high quality work
Knowing why: Personal values that underpin motives and meaning	• Work life balance • Sustaining long-term enjoyment in the work	• Consciously acknowledge and balance all of life's values – work and life • Follow and commit to the dream
Knowing where: How to begin, develop and achieve within the sector	• Accessing entry-level opportunities • Remaining and advancing in the industry	• Supplementing qualifications with work experience • Active management of personal brand/profile • Take opportunities that advance, avoid those that offer a step backwards
Knowing how: Technical competence, relationship management and personal brand	• Being unique • Sustaining technical capability in the face of increasingly rapid change • Maintaining effective working relationships	• Develop a personal brand statement • Seek breadth and depth in skill base • Demonstrate value and nurture relationships
Knowing when: Timing of career choices, development activities and roles accepted	• Avoiding labelling through status or long-term commitment to a particular role • Finding opportunities to expand or utilize new skill base • Timing and availability of appropriate opportunities	• Become known for something different – challenge stereotypes • Control timing of opportunities • Develop own opportunities
Knowing whom: Membership and acceptance within key networks/social groups	• Establishing a sound reputation and relationships with key influencers/decision makers	• Ensure reciprocity in networks • Establish long-term relationships based on friendship as well as leverage • Active self marketing – more than relying on work history and online profiles

Source: Adapted from Jones and DeFillippi (1996)

Greenhaus et al. (2010, p.58) produce a much more simplified list of approaches to effective career management and development. They suggest that it requires:

• a deep knowledge of oneself and an accurate picture of the environment
• development of realistic conceptual and operational goals
• development and implementation of appropriate career strategies
• continual feedback.

They also provide seven major career strategies:

1 Attaining competence in current job
2 Putting in extended hours
3 Developing new skills
4 Developing new work opportunities
5 Attaining a mentor
6 Building one's image and reputation
7 Engaging in organizational politics.

Baruch (2004, p.90) suggested these approaches are US biased and 'in other countries different strategies will have different relevance or impact'. While acknowledging this bias, they are included as they provide a useful comparator to the Jones and DeFillippini (1996) model, which was based on an analysis of a fairly unique industry sector.

We have seen that careers have changed, often in response to external drivers such as the introduction of technology. Individual career development has had to respond in much the same way; this means that new technology, like social networking sites (SNS) have had an impact upon career development activities. Strehlke (2010) examines the advice career development practitioners provide to those engaged in role acquisition activities. She provides a useful framework for analysing the impact of SNS on career development, suggesting that individuals need to consider their visibility, presentation and network connections. As part of this she has produced some interesting questions for SNS users to consider (Strehlke, 2010):

Table 13.2 The impact of Social Networking Sites on Career Development

User visibility
Are you an active user of social networking websites? Have you used them in the past?
What SNSs do you currently use? How often do you log on?
Do you use privacy settings on your account? Why or why not?
Have you heard of employers in your industry checking out applicants on SNSs?
If a prospective employer were to take a look at your SNS profile, how would you feel? Do you think it would help or hinder your chances of being hired?
Is there anything on your profile that you would prefer to keep private? Why or why not?
How do you stay up to date on the features and tools of your SNS?
Self presentation
How often do you update your profile?
Does your profile already include information about your skills, education, work experience, or career goals? Is the information consistent with your other job search tools (i.e. résumé)?
What are the benefits of professionalizing your portfolio? What are the disadvantages?
What skills and accomplishments would you like to highlight in your profile? How can you present them effectively online?
Is there anything in your profile, or in your communication with others, that could be misinterpreted by an employer? Do you see a way to minimize that risk?
Network connections
How many contacts do you have on your SNS?
How many do you consider to be close contacts? What makes them close?
Which contacts have information on or connections to your occupation or industry?
How would you categorize the people in your network? What social groups or interests do they represent?
Which contacts would be most useful in connecting you to employers in your field? Why?
Do you use your SNS to meet new people? How?

Source: Strehlke (2010)

It all sounds fairly simple then, individuals should just engage in the management and development of their careers, in person or online. But, is it really that simple?

reflective question Is everyone equally placed to realize the benefits of adopting these career development strategies? Try and rationalize your answer with some examples from your own life and reading before you move on.

Hopefully you have considered some of the areas of potential discrimination highlighted in an ILO (2011) report which explains that equality of access to jobs has been compromized recently because of the economic downturn. In addition, it suggests that while workers in more stable employment relationships have suffered less in the economic downturn, 'the risk is especially acute for the low-skilled, older and migrant workers, as well as those workers – including university graduates – who are looking for their first job' (p.ix). The report goes on to list a wide variety of dimensions of discrimination, including those covered by the UK Equality Act 2010, as well as areas such as political opinion, HIV status, genetics and lifestyle (namely obesity and smoking). Rooth (2007) undertook a study in Sweden and found that applications with photographs of obese people had 20 per cent fewer invitations for interview compared to those of 'normal' weight. Both of these examples serve to illustrate that dimensions of diversity can have a significant impact upon job (and by implication career) opportunities.

You may also have been prompted by the social networking discussion to consider access to broadband facilities and the internet, for example: 'In 2009 ... around 1.5 million households, often clustered in rural areas, still have little or no broadband availability for technical reasons. Of the 10.2 million adults in the UK who have never even used the internet, 4 million (9 per cent of the population) are also considered socially excluded. Digital divides are in danger of opening again.' (Parliament UK, 2012).

Overall, you have probably listed a range of responses. Was personality one of them? Research suggests that personality has an impact upon networking capability. Consider the fact that networking, whether online, external or internal seems to underpin many of the strategies advocated thus far. Wolff and Kim (2012) considered the relationship between networking behaviours and the Big Five personality traits of openness, conscientiousness, extraversion, agreeableness and neuroticism. They found that, perhaps unsurprisingly, extraversion is positively related to networking, particularly when it comes to establishing relationships (they may have to work harder on maintaining them). Agreeableness was positively related to internal (i.e. within the company) but not external networking – the authors suggest that more research is needed to understand this outcome. Their results also suggested that openness to new experiences also supports networking behaviours. Conscientious workers were not associated with networking – the authors speculated that this could be because they were focused on their job roles and less on relationship management. Emotional stability (neuroticism) the final dimension was also found not to be associated with networking. So, what does this all mean? Well, that an individual's career successes are not only influenced to some extent by the strategies they adopt but also by a range of internal and external factors, some of which are beyond their control.

activity

You can try a Big Five personality test at www.outofservice.com/bigfive
How do the results relate to your networking capability?

An organizational perspective

Why should organizations involve themselves in career management and development, particularly when it appears that employees are less likely to accept organizational boundaries to career development? One response is that the retention and management of talent is seen as essential for global competitiveness (Schuler et al., 2011). King (2004) answers the question thus:

> By developing able and motivated employees and giving them an environment in which they can excel, effective career management should, in conjunction with other factors, enable the business to achieve superior performance in terms of labour productivity, cost-effective investment in HR, quality, innovation and customer satisfaction (p.11).

Sturges et al. (2002) suggest affective commitment is also a desired organizational career management outcome. Affective commitment is seen as 'emotional attachment to, identification with and involvement in the organization' (Meyer & Allen, 1997, p.11). Many of these objectives are now captured under the term employee engagement, an ill-defined concept that 'is all about the willingness and ability of employees to give sustained discretionary effort to help their organization succeed' (Cook, 2008, p.3). King's (2004) definition includes cost effective, so how do we measure career development investment to see if it is cost effective? According to Tymon and MacKay (2010) it involves calculating the return on investment against the speed at which expected career trajectories are achieved. Basically, did people get into more senior roles, with greater speed, and did the company realize an appropriate financial return as a consequence of this speedy development? This return on investment question is at the heart of many talent management programmes.

So what career development initiatives is it appropriate for an organization to use? As with all HRD initiatives it comes down to questions of such as HRD strategy, cost, industry sector, all of which will have an impact upon which initiatives are selected. Many of them will require the involvement of effective line management, others will be company-led general training initiatives, others still part of an organization's talent management strategy. All of them will be influenced by the psychological contract. King (2004, p.9) suggests that effective career management should be guided by four principles: consistency, proactivity, collaboration and dynamism. Table 13.2 provides some of the options that organizations may consider alongside King's (2004) recommendations:

Yarnall (2008) produced a useful checklist to evaluate these initiatives, particularly when they are considered for high potential staff, (pp.184–185):

- What experiences do our talent pool demand?
- Where in the organization can we source these experiences?

Table 13.3 Career development options

Mentoring/coaching:	Networks:
• internal support via line manager, HR or trained internal provision • external support – more likely at senior levels	• formal, informal, online, female only • work outside of existing or previous teams • attendance at conferences/events • visits/trips to external organizations • membership of panels, committees, working parties
Funding:	Opportunities for work experience:
• development regardless of subject matter • development linked to company objectives • development supported by a business case	• secondments internal or external • temporary promotions • projects/change management initiatives • lateral moves • job rotation • career break schemes
Development initiatives:	Supporting career moves:
• development centres or career action centres • personal development plans for all • defined career paths/maps • dual career ladders • succession planning • 360-degree analysis and feedback • learning sets	• internal vacancy notification • career workshops, e-learning tools, workbooks etc. • out- or in-placement assistance • career counselling • access to diagnostic career-inventory instruments

All of the above should be underpinned by a focus on diversity:

- equity across all development provisions
- organizational role models to highlight achievements of under-represented workers
- cross-cultural/international team working
- diversity awareness training
- supporting flexible working practices
- culturally-sensitive development assessment tools
- monitoring access to development provision by under-represented groups

- Where are the gaps between the opportunities we can provide and the experiences needed?
- Are the purposes of developmental opportunities clear to individuals?
- Are the expected learning outcomes from such opportunities tracked?
- How proactive is your company in seeking opportunities for development in your wider supplier and customer networks?
- Are people aware of how secondments and developmental assignments can be achieved?
- Are managers encouraged to consider a broad spectrum of developmental approaches?
- Is it clear to individuals what opportunities are open to them?
- What are the possible barriers to success for each opportunity?
- What support will the organization need to give, particularly with induction?
- What will the knock-on effects be on the people around them?
- How will the outcomes from the organization and individual be measured?

Having considered the individual and the organizational approach to career management and development, it is appropriate now to consider the reality, which is probably a hybrid of the two.

What do you think is currently the balance for you?

Is your career development individually driven or is your career managed by an organization?

Looking forward ten years what would you like the balance to be and why?

It seems unlikely that an individual or an organization will be solely responsible for career development. It is likely to manifest itself somewhere between the two (e.g. Kamoche et al., 2011). HRD in Practice 13.2 helps illustrate this.

HRD in Practice 13.2

Shell has invested heavily in an online global career management system called Open Resourcing. This system contains internal vacancies (roles and projects), it enables individuals to upload searchable personal profiles and to set up automatic vacancy alerts. The system is designed to enable a greater range of individuals to explore the opportunities that are available to them within global Shell operations and at the same time it enables Shell to obtain a richer picture of its people. This system is not unique, Smedley (2012), in an article about organizations attempting to capitalize on employee engagement with social networking, outlines the fact that The Big Lottery Fund have created Big Connect (a system modelled on social networking sites) where individuals can create groups, perhaps around a project, where people can be tagged or even express a desire for involvement. An additional benefit to this sort of system is the ability for an organization to search for skill sets amongst the details that employees have loaded, a sort of self-created competency list. Something particularly valuable when competencies acquired in previous external roles are not recorded on internal systems.

What benefit and issues can you see with an organization adopting this approach?

In some way the above begins to model a kind of mutuality of exchange. The organization providing the interface and the opportunities, the individuals engaged in active self-marketing. This could be seen, perhaps, as a more open and honest way of generating internal applicants but, it should be remembered, not all employees are great at blowing their own trumpets and it may be that the organization needs to invest in supporting individuals in the development of these self-marketing capabilities.

Mentoring

If coaching is mainly concerned with improving immediate or short-term performance, in contrast, mentoring focuses more on the medium- to long-term. In terms of TD, mentoring considers current performance less and potential for future performance more. Mentoring can be informal, concerned with careers and personal growth, and research suggests it is successful in these aspects of TD in such contexts as medicine (Sambunjak et al., 2006) and teaching (Roehrig et al., 2008). Mentoring does not always work and can result in problems, such as the mentor taking more credit than is due for the achievements of a mentee (Simon & Eby, 2003). Therefore, it is important for expectations to be clear and for there to be a willingness to learn by both parties (Megginson et al., 2006).

Mentoring can mean different activities in different contexts but one definition by Megginson and Clutterbuck (1995) captures the main thrust, mentoring is: 'off-line help by one person to another in making significant transitions in knowledge, work or thinking' (p.13). This definition highlights the importance of a degree of distance between mentor and mentee so that a clearer view of issues can be taken. The focus is on how the mentee can move forward in some way. Eby (2010) also makes this clear by referring to mentoring as a 'developmentally oriented interpersonal relationship' (p.505). Kram (1983) made a useful distinction between the career function of mentoring and the psychosocial function. The former includes sponsorship, coaching, protection, exposure-and-visibility and challenging work. The latter includes role modelling, counselling and friendship. We can see here how a relationship might focus on career mentoring in the short term but move in the direction of psychosocial support over time. This might be a typical approach to graduate development and employees identified to have talent. Recent research by Bozionelos et al. (2011) of over 190 MBA students in employment suggested that mentoring was most closely connected with career success. Further, managers who received mentoring were more likely to become mentors and this also enhanced careers, suggesting a double benefit for TD.

reflective question   Who has been your mentor?

What have been the benefits?

Mentoring has often been understood as an informal process for TD and not without criticism in the way the process might discriminate against women and ethnic minority groups, or might reinforce the values of dominant groups in an organization (Townley, 1994). During the 1990s, there were growing efforts to make mentoring more formal and systematic, making use of an organization's competency framework or typologies of skills. In some respects, formality can give precedence to meeting requirements pre-set from outside the mentoring relationship, at the expense of the development of learning within the relationship (Gibb, 2003). As mentoring has grown, there have been increasing efforts to improve the quality and competence of mentors, and provide more effective matching between mentors and mentees. Training courses for mentors can make use of a range of tools and instruments (Gilbreath et al., 2008).

The practice of mentoring

We need to recognize that mentoring can have a negative impact in practice, as Simon and Eby (2003) found in their exploration of mentoring experiences among MBA students. Among such experiences were sexual harassment, neglect through lack of interest and direction, and abuse of power by the mentor over the mentee through intimidation and put downs. However, there is ample evidence of benefit too. Mentoring is probably a preferred mode of TD among professional groups. For example in academic medicine, mentoring has been shown to be important for personal development and careers, although there may not always be enough mentors, and women particularly may have difficulty in finding a mentor (Sambunjak et al., 2006). Various large-scale surveys and reviews of evidence on mentoring in organizations point to satisfaction and improvement of careers outcomes with informal mentoring more highly favoured (Ragins et al., 2000; Underhill, 2006). Clutterbuck (2004) showed how benefits are gained by mentees in terms of skills and confidence, mentors gain through the satisfaction of passing on knowledge and the organization gains because of the impact on recruitment, retention, commitment and engagement.

Lester et al. (2011) completed a six-month study of military cadets at West Point in the US, seeking to explore the impact of mentoring on leadership efficacy and performance. Leadership efficacy refers to a leader's belief in their perceived capabilities in relation to particular leadership situations. It was found that the mentoring programme had a positive impact on leadership efficacy and overall performance as a leader through the establishment of trust and the willingness of mentees to learn from feedback. Other studies of leaders, such as Rosser (2005), showed how mentoring was considered key to development and indispensable to achievement.

One interesting feature of mentoring is that informality may hide what is happening. In practice, mentoring may not be recognized as the activity they are engaged in; it may simply be part of the job and part of the relationship, for good or ill. Research in an international management consultancy (Welsh et al., 2012) found that because mentoring was informal, mentors and mentees did not always recognize each other as part of a mentoring relationship. For example, mentees recognized that they had a mentor less than 50 per cent of the time. This is important, since mutual recognition was also related to satisfaction. A clear finding from Megginson et al.'s (2006) case studies was the need to ensure both mentors and mentees have an idea of what they want from the relationship and this requires a recognition of the relationship as mentoring.

As with coaching, the idea of mentoring has moved beyond dyad towards groups. Mitchell (1999) showed the value of group mentoring within a women's network, which allowed each person in the group to become a mentor or mentee. The value of support and reducing feelings of loneliness were revealed. In other cases, group mentoring is a way of replacing traditional HRD programmes by allowing groups of learners, often considered as high potential staff, to set learning topics. Each group facilitates its own programme with leaders as advisors (see Emelo, 2011).

Another development is the use of ICT and Web 2.0 technologies for e-mentoring, which can result in less emphasis on factors such as age, gender or ethnic background. It also allows a recording of interactions (Ensher et al., 2003). Headlam-Wells et al. (2005) showed how e-mentoring for pairs of women helped in career development but that other methods of communication were needed to support relationships between participants. This is important because part of the case for e-mentoring could be to reduce the costs of TD by reducing the need for meeting face to face in non-virtual locations. However, the very presence of participants in the same space may be crucial to the development of relationships. Simmonds and Lupi (2010) argue that this problem can be reduced in e-mentoring if mentees are more involved in selecting mentors on the basis of factors such as professional skills, interests and hobbies and socio-economic background.

summary

○ There exists a variety of interpretations of talent manage-ment and talent development, both in the academic literature and in organizational practice.

○ Talent pools are used as a pipeline for future appointments. They can exist at different levels of potential/capability and for different functions.

○ Care needs to be taken when selecting staff for talent pools to ensure the right individuals are selected and that discrimination is avoided.

○ Organizations seeking to embed a coaching culture to foster talent development embrace a variety of approaches, from organic/emerging where internal advocates encourage its adoption, to centralized and structured where coaching skills are embedded in competency frameworks and are a regular feature of management/leader development programmes.

○ There can be a reluctance to embrace coaching by those who see it is a remedial rather than a developmental tool and by managers who may see it as getting in the way of the day job or existing relationships with staff.

○ There are a number of coaching models and approaches – which have yet to be tested empirically – but the industry is striving, through emerging professional bodies and accreditation, to regulate practice.

○ Careers have changed over time from traditional careers and the idea of career ladders (managed by the organization) to the notions of boundaryless and protean careers (managed by the individual). The reality may lie somewhere between the two.

○ There are a range of strategies recommended for individuals and organizations engaged in career development activities. Many of them embrace a Western notion of career and career development, their cross-cultural applicability has not been evaluated.

○ Career development and management is not a level playing field – a number of internal and external factors can have an impact upon the career opportunities available to individuals.

○ Mentoring can be both formal (as part of a talent development initiative) and informal. It is seen as particularly useful in the long-term career development of professional groups. It is not however without its challenges, particularly for women mentees.

discussion questions

1 What approaches could be used to ensure selection for talent pools avoids discrimination *and* selects for the best long-term performance potential?

2 What are the challenges presented by a line manager acting as coach for his/her own staff? How could these challenges be overcome?

3 Should organizations seek to control the career development activities of all, some or none of their staff? Why?

4 What problems/challenges do you think would need to be overcome for the HRD professional managing careers of staff operating across a range of cultures?

5 What initiatives should be put in place to ensure that the mentoring relationship benefits all parties involved?

further
reading

references

Allen, T.D., Eby, L.T., O'Brien, K.E. and Lentz, E. (2007) The state of mentoring research: a qualitative review of current research methods and future research implications. *Journal of Vocational Behaviour,* **73**(3): 343–57.

Briscoe, J.P., Hall, D.T. and Mayrhofer, W. (2012) *Careers Around the World: Individual and Contextual Perspectives.* London: Routledge.

Garvey, B., Stokes, P. and Megginson, D. (2009) *Coaching and Mentoring: Theory and Practice.* London: Sage.

Stewart, J. and Rigg, C. (2010) *Learning and Talent Development.* London: CIPD.

Adamson, S., Doherty, N. and Viney, C. (1998) The meaning of career revisited: implications for theory and practice. British Journal of Management, **9**(4): 251–59.

Anderson, V., Rayner, C. and Schyns, B. (2009) *Coaching at the Sharp End: The Role of Line Managers in Coaching at Work.* London: Chartered Institute of Personnel and Development.

Barner, R. and Higgens, J. (2007) Understanding implicit models that guide the coaching process. *Journal of Management Development,* **26**(2): 148–58.

Baruch, Y. (2004) *Managing Careers Theory And Practice.* Harlow: FT Prentice Hall.

Baruch, Y. (2006) Career development in organizations and beyond: balancing traditional and contemporary viewpoints. *Human Resource Management Review,* **16**(2): 125–38.

Boudreau, J.W. and Ramstad, P.M. (2007*) Beyond HR: The New Science of Human Capital.* Boston, MA: Harvard Business School Press.

Bozionelos, N., Bozionelos, G., Kostopoulos, K. and Polychroniou, P. (2011) How providing mentoring relates to career success and organizational commitment: a study in the general managerial population. *Career Development International,* **16**(5): 446–68.

Carter, A. (2001) *Executive Coaching: Inspiring Performance at Work.* Report 379. Sussex: Institute of Employment Studies.

Chuai, X., Preece, D. and Iles, P. (2008) Is talent management just 'old wine in new bottles'? *Management Research News,* **31**(12): 901–11.

CIPD (2009) *Fighting Back Through Talent Innovation.* London: Chartered Institute of Personnel and Development.

CIPD (2011) *The Coaching Climate.* London: Chartered Institute of Personnel and Development.

CIPD (2012) *Learning and Talent Development.* London: Chartered Institute of Personnel and Development.

Clutterbuck, D. (2004) *Everyone Needs a Mentor.* London: Chartered Institute of Personnel and Development.

Collings, D. and Mellahi, K. (2009) Strategic talent management: a review and research agenda. *Human Resource Management Review,* **19**(4): 304–13.

Cook, S. (2008) *The Essential Guide To Employee Engagement: Better Business Performance Through Staff Satisfaction.* London: Kogan Page.

Cook S. and Macaulay S. (2009) Talent management: key questions for learning and development. *Training Journal,* July: 37–41.

Costa, A.L. and Kallick, B. (1993) Through the lens of a critical friend. *Educational Leadership,* **51**(2): 46–51.

DeFillippi, R.J. and Arthur, M.B. (1994) The boundaryless career: a competency-based perspective. *Journal of Organizational Behaviour,* **15**(4): 307–24.

de Haan, E., Culpin, V. and Curd, J. (2011) Executive coaching in practice: what determines helpfulness for clients of coaching? *Personnel Review,* **40**(1): 24–44.

Devins, D. and Clark, J. (2011) *Evaluation of the Coaching for Performance Programme at Morrisons: Survey Results.* Leeds Metropolitan University: Policy Research Institute, available at www.leedsmet.ac.uk/lbs/Morrison_Report_HiRes.pdf, accessed 6 June 2012.

Eby, L.T. (2010) Mentorship (pp.505–25). In S. Zedack (ed.) *APA Handbook Of Industrial And Organizational Psychology.* Washington, D.C.: American Psychological Association.

Ellinger, A., Hamlin, R. and Beattie, R. (2008) Behavioural indicators of ineffective managerial coaching. *Journal of European Industrial Training,* **32**(4): 240–57.

Emelo, R. (2011) Group mentoring best practices. *Industrial And Commercial Training,* **43**(4): 221–27.

Ensher, E.A., Heun, C., and Blanchard, A. (2003) Online mentoring and computer-mediated communication: New directions and research. *Journal of Vocational Behaviour,* **63**: 264–88.

Ensley, M., Carland, J., Ensley, R. and Carland, J.C. (2011) The theoretical basis and dimensionality of the talent management system. *Academy of Strategic Management Journal,* **10**(1): 81–114.

Evans, J. (2007) Talent strategy feeds growth at Nando's. *People Management,* **3** May: 16.

Evered, R.D. and Selmen, J.C. (1989) Coaching and the art of management. *Organizational Dynamics,* Autumn: 16–32.

Feldman, D.C. and Lankau, M.J. (2005) Executive coaching: a review and agenda for future research. *Journal of Management,* **31**(6): 829–48.

Gandz, J. (2006) Talent development: the architecture of a talent pipeline that works. *Ivey Business Journal Online,* January/February, available at www.iveybusinessjournal.com/topics/innovation/talent-development-the-architecture-of-a-talent-pipeline-that-works, accessed 2 June 2012.

Garavan, T., Carbery, R. and Rock, A. (2012) Mapping talent development: definition, scope and architecture. *European Journal of Training and Development,* **36**(1): 5–24.

Gibb, S. (2003) What do we talk about when we talk about mentoring? Blooms and thorns. *British Journal of Counselling and Guidance,* **31**(1): 39–49.

Gilbreath, B., Rose, G. and Dietrich, K. (2008) Assessing mentoring in organizations: an evaluation of commercial mentoring instruments. *Mentoring & Tutoring: Partnership in Learning,* **16**(4): 379–93.

Garvey, B., Stokes, P. and Megginson, D. (2009) *Coaching and Mentoring: Theory and Practice.* London: Sage.

Gold, J., Thorpe, R. and Mumford, A. (2010a) *Leadership and Management Development.* London: Chartered Institute of Personnel and Development.

Gray, D.E. (2010) *Business Coaching for Managers and Organizations: Working with Coaches Who Make the Difference.* Amherst, MA: HRD Press.

Greenhaus, J.H. (1987) *Career Management.* Fort Worth: Dryden Press.

Greenhaus, J.H., Callanan, G.A. and Godshalk, V.M. (2010) *Career Management,* 4th edn. London: Sage Publications.

Groysberg, B. (2010) *Chasing Stars: The Myth of Talent and the Portability of Performance.* Princeton, NJ: Princeton University Press.

Hall, D.T. (1976) *Careers in organizations.* Glenview, IL: Scott, Foresman.

Hall, D.T. and associates (1996) *The Career Is Dead, Long Live The Career: A Relational Approach To Careers.* San Francisco: Jossey-Bass.

Hall, D.T. and Moss, J.E. (1998) The new protean career contract: helping organizations and employees adapt, *Organizational Dynamics,* **26**(3): 22–37.

Headlam-Wells, J., Gosland, J. and Craig, J. (2005) 'There's magic in the web': e-mentoring for women's career development. *Career Development International,* **10**(6/7): 444–59.

Höglund, M. (2012) Quid pro quo? Examining talent management through the lens of psychological contracts. *Personnel Review,* **41**(2): 126–42.

Holbeche, L. (2009) *Aligning Human Resources and Business Strategy,* 2nd edn. Oxford: Butterworth-Heinemann.

Huselid, M., Beatty, R.W. and Becker, B.E (2005), A Players or A Positions? The strategic logic of workforce management. *Harvard Business Review,* December: 110–17.

ILO (International Labour Organisation) (2011) *Equality at Work: The Continuing Challenge,* available from: http://www.ilo.org/wcmsp5/groups/public/-ed_norm/-relconf/documents/meetingdocument/wcms_154779.pdf, accessed 11 April 2012.

Jones, C. and DeFillippi, R.J. (1996) Back to the future in film: Combining industry and self-knowledge to meet career challenges of the 21st century. *Academy of Management Executive,* **10**(4): 89–103.

Kamoche, K., Pang, M. and Wong A.L.Y. (2011) Career development and knowledge appropriation: a genealogical critique. *Organization Studies,* **32**(12): 1665–79.

Kanter, R.M. (1989) Careers and the wealth of nations: a macro perspective on the structure and implications of career forms (pp.506–22). In M.B. Arthur, D.T. Hall and B.S. Lawrence (eds) *The Handbook of Career Theory.* Cambridge, MA: Cambridge University Press.

Khapova, S.N. Arthur, M.B. and Wilderom, C.P.M (2007) The subjective career in the knowledge economy (pp.114–30). In H. Gunz and M. Peiperl (eds) *Handbook of Career Studies*. Thousand Oaks, CA: Sage Publications.

King, Z. (2004) *Career Management: A CIPD Guide*, available from < http://www.cipd.co.uk/binaries/2994-guidecareermgmnt.pdf> Downloaded 13 December 2012.

Knights, A. and Poppleton, A. (2008) *Developing Coaching Capability in Organisations*. London: Chartered Institute of Personnel and Development.

Kram, K.E. (1983) Phases of the mentor relationship. *Academy of Management Journal,* **26**(4): 608–25.

Lee, C., Liu, J., Rousseau, D.M., Hui, C. and Chen, Z.X. (2011) Inducements, contributions, and fulfillment in new employee psychological contracts. *Human Resource Management*, **50**(2): 201–26.

Lester, P., Hannah, S., Harms, P., Vogelgesang, G. and Avolio, B.J. (2011) Mentoring impact on leader efficacy development: A field experiment. *Academy of Management Learning and Education*, **10**(3): 409–29.

Li, S., Sun, H. and Zheng, X. (2011) *A Case Study on Design of Teacher Peer-Coaching Activities Supported by a Web 2.0 Community*. Proceedings on the International Conference Hybrid Learning, pp.40–50.

McComb, C. (2012) Developing coaching culture: are your managers motivated coaches? (Part 1). *Industrial and Commercial Training*, **44**(2): 90–93.

McDonald, P., Brown, K., and Bradley, L. (2005) Have traditional career paths given way to protean ones? evidence from senior managers in the Australian public sector. *Career Development International*, **10**(2): 109–29.

Megginson, D. and Clutterbuck, D. (1995) *Mentoring In Action*. London: Kogan Page.

Megginson, D., Clutterbuck, D., Garvey, B., Stokes, P. and Garrett-Harris, R. (2006) *Mentoring In Action,* 2nd edn. London: Kogan Page.

Meyer, J. and Allen, N. (1997) *Commitment in the Workplace: Theory, Research and Application*. Thousand Oaks: Sage.

Michaels, E., Handfield-Jones, H. and Beth, A. (2001) *The War For Talent*. Boston: Harvard Business School.

Mitchell, H. (1999) Group mentoring, does it work? *Mentoring and Tutoring*, **7**(2): 113–20.

Nauta, A., Van Vianen, A., Van der Heijden, B., Van Dam, K., and Willemsen, M. (2009) Understanding the factors that promote employability orientation: The impact of employability culture, career satisfaction, and role breadth self-efficacy. *Journal of Occupational and Organizational Psychology*, **82**(2): 233–51.

Novations (2009) *Talent Development Issues Study*. Long Island, New York:Novations Group.

Parliament.uk (2012) Broadband access, available from www.parliament.uk/business/publications/research/key-issues-for-the-new-parliament/social-reform/broadband-access Downloaded: 12 April 2012.

Parker, P., Hall, D.T. and Kram, K.E. (2008) Peer coaching: a relational process for accelerating career learning. *Academy of Management Learning & Education,* **7**(4): 487–503.

Pollitt, D. (2007) Software solves problem of global succession planning at Friesland Foods. *Human Resource Management International Digest*, **15**(6): 21–23.

Ragins, B.R., Cotton, J.L. and Miller, J.S. (2000) Marginal mentoring: the effects of type of mentor, quality of relationship and program design on work and career attitudes. *Academy of Management Journal*, **43**(6): 1177–94.

Ready, D. and Conger, J. (2007) Make your company a talent factory. *Harvard Business Review,* **85**(6): 68–77.

Roehrig, A., Bohn, C., Turner, J. and Pressley, M. (2008) Mentoring beginning primary teachers for exemplary teaching practices. *Teaching and Teacher Education*, **24**(3): 684–702.

Rooth, D-O (2007) *Evidence of unequal treatment in hiring against obese applicants: a field experiment*, IZA Discussion Papers, No. 2775, available from http://hdl.handle.net/10419/34672, accessed 12 April 2012.

Rosser, M.H. (2005) Mentoring from the top: CEO perspectives. *Advances in Developing Human Resources,* **7**(4): 527–39.

Sambunjak, D., Straus, S. and Maruši ̂ c, A. (2006) Mentoring in academic medicine. *Journal of American Medical Association,* **296**(9): 1103–15.

Schein, E.H. (1978) *Career Dynamics: Matching Individual and Organizational Needs.* Reading, MA: Addison-Wesley.

Schuler, R.S., Jackson, S.E. and Tarique, I. (2011) Global talent management and global talent challenges: Strategic opportunities for IHRM. *Journal of World Business,* **46**(4): 506–16.

Scott, B. and Revis, S. (2008) Talent management in hospitality: graduate career success and strategies. *International Journal of Contemporary Hospitality Management*, **20**(7): 781–91.

Simmonds, D. and Lupi, A. (2010) The matching process in e-mentoring: a case study in luxury hotels. *Journal of European Industrial Training*, **34**(4): 300–16.

Simon, S.A. and Eby, L.T. (2003) A multidimensional scaling study of negative mentoring experiences. *Human Relations,* **56**: 1083–106.

Sistonen, S. (2005) *Talent Management*. New York: Deloitte & Touche Oy.

Strehlke, C. (2010) Social network sites: a starting point for career development practitioners. *Journal of Employment Counseling,* **47**(45): 38–48.

Smedley, T. (2012) Net worth. *People Management,* April: 40–42.

Stober, D. and Grant, A.M. (2006) *Evidence-Based Coaching Handbook.* New York: John Wiley.

Sturges, J., Guest, D., Conway, N. and Mackenzie Davey, K. (2002) A longitudinal study of the relationship between career management and organizational commitment among graduates in the first ten years at work. *Journal of Organizational Behavior,* **23**(6): 731–48.

Super, D.E. (1957) *The Psychology of Careers.* NY: Harper and Row.

Super, D.E. (1980) A life-span, life space approach to career development. *Journal of Vocational Behaviour,* **16**(3): 282–98.

Tansley, C., Turner, P. and Foster, C. (2007) *Talent: Strategy, Management, Measurement: Research into Practice.* London: Chartered Institute of Personnel and Development.

Tansley, C. (2011) What do we mean by the term 'talent' in talent management? *Industrial and Commercial Training,* **43**(5): 266–74.

Townley, B. (1994) *Reframing Human Resource Management: Power, Ethics and the Subject at Work.* London: Sage.

Townsend, R. (1970) *Up the Organization.* London: Coronet Books.

Tymon, A. and MacKay, M. (2010) Developing employees. In G. Rees and R. French (eds) *Leading, Managing and Developing People.* London: CIPD.

Underhill, C. (2006) The effectiveness of mentoring programs in corporate settings: A meta-analytical review of the literature. *Journal of Vocational Behavior,* **68**(2): 292–307.

Vaiman, V., Scullion, H. and Collings, D. (2012) Talent management decision making. *Management Decision,* **50**(5): 925–41.

Welsh, E., Bhave, D. and Kim, K. (2012) Are you my mentor? Informal mentoring mutual identification. *Career Development International,* **17**(2): 137–48.

Wester, S. (2008) *Leadership: A Critical Text.* London: Sage.

Whitmore, J. (2002) *Coaching for Performance: Growing People, Performance and Purpose.* 3rd edn. London: Nicholas Brealey.

Wilensky, H.L. (1961) Careers, lifestyles, and social integration. *International Social Science Journal,* **12**: 553–58.

Wolf, C. (2012) How to make a success of employee coaching: the 2012 Xpert HR Survey. *IRS Employment Review.*

Wolff, H-G. and Kim, S. (2012) The relationship between networking behaviors and the Big Five personality dimension. *Career Development International,* **17**(1): 43–66.

Yarnall, J. (2008) *Strategic Career Management – Developing Your Talent.* Oxford: Butterworth-Heinemann.

chapter 14

HRD and Diversity

Victoria Harte, Jim Stewart and Helen Rodgers

Chapter learning outcomes

After studying this chapter, you should be able to:
- Identify and examine the complex debates emerging in the literature about diversity in organizations
- Critically evaluate the varying views of the meaning of diversity in relation to managing and valuing diversity
- Describe and assess the role of HRD in facilitating diversity in organizations
- Explore cases of diversity in relation to key themes arising from the literature
- Reflect on individual diversity awareness and sensitivity

Chapter outline

Introduction

This chapter is concerned with the notion of diversity and its connections with HRD. Diversity is a relatively new term and concept, which has come into common usage only in the past 15 years or so. Its origins lie in attempts to create more interest and commitment in work organizations to the principles and aspirations associated with the earlier term and concept of equal opportunities in relation to the treatment of people at work (Kandola & Fullerton, 1998). A simple distinction can be drawn between the terms on the basis that equal opportunities is based on the moral argument of social justice, translated in some countries, including the UK, the USA and all members of the EU, into legal requirements governing the way employers treat actual and potential employees. In contrast, diversity refers to an argument in favour of similar principles and aspirations based not specifically on moral grounds but on the grounds of business need and other benefits that can be achieved by treating actual and potential employees fairly and with dignity (Kandola & Fullerton, 1998). This is not to say that applying the notion of equal opportunities cannot and does not bring organizational benefits, or that the case for diversity does not have a moral dimension. It is simply a matter of emphasis and context. However, there are also differences in understanding of the idea of fairness in relation to the two concepts, which we will explore later.

reflective question

1 What do the words fair and fairness mean to you?
2 Where and how do you think you came to have your understanding of these words?

Diversity and HRD

Organizations face a number of challenges with regard to diversity because a central legal principle is that all employees will be treated with fairness, dignity and respect. This requires that all employees also operate and behave in accordance with that legal principle. In practice, this requires a workplace culture that acknowledges and responds positively to the different needs of individuals and a work environment where difference and potential are nurtured and valued. These requirements for particular organizational cultures, workplace environments and individual behaviour show an immediate and significant connection with an role for HRD. According to Stewart (2007), the purpose of HRD is to change behaviour at both individual and organizational levels. As Figure 14.1 shows, organizational-level behaviour is a function of what is referred to as core competence and culture.

Stewart argues that, at an individual level, behaviour is a function in part of knowledge, skills and values. The distinction between the two levels is primarily analytical, since it is only individuals who actually behave, separately and collectively. But the collective behaviour we call organization culture influences the separate behaviour of individuals, and the same is true in reverse. This means that if organizations wish to create workplace cultures and environments that are supportive of treating all employees with fairness, dignity and respect, HRD will have a critical role in bringing about the necessary changes in individual and collective behaviour. We will explore how that might be done in practice later in the chapter. We will now examine the meaning of the notion of diversity in more detail.

Conceptual and theoretical meanings of diversity

The debates outlined in this section suggest that the conceptual shift from equality to diversity is wrought with complexity. Many theoretical debates acknowledge the historical evolution of the terms equality and diversity and

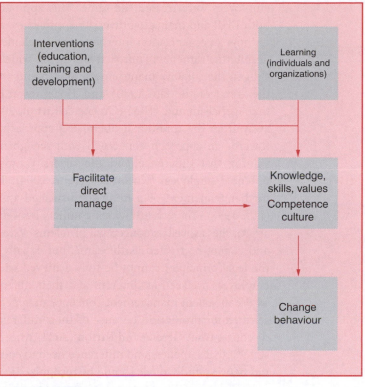

Figure 14.1 A model of HRD

register their incongruity (Bentley & Clayton, 1998; Winstanley & Woodall, 2000). In the late 1990s, there was a shift from an equal opportunities (EO) focus to a diversity focus, argued on the basis that the EO approach was insufficiently holistic in its attempts to eradicate discrimination. In addition, the case for diversity emerges out of this critique of the EO approach and its inability to deliver demonstrable organizational results, despite 30 years of legislation (Rodgers et al., 2004; EOC, 2007). The changing social, demographic and geographic drivers impacting on 21st-century organizations have also shifted the need towards increased representation of diverse social groups in the workforce. Thus, raising the profile of diversity a level higher due to getting the right people in the job, out of which the term talent management was born (See Chapter 13). This presents a number of conceptual challenges for those with an interest in managing and developing people.

The issue of equality management has existed since the 1970s and 1980s when employers and trade unions had their own policy approaches (Greene & Kirton, 2004), albeit somewhat simplistic compared to today's approach to equality and human rights (EHR). However, in the late 1980s, Jewson and Mason (1986) brought about a shift to, in what was considered at the time, a more refined approach to dealing with equality. This shift was known as the sameness approach, which became embedded as part of the traditional liberal EO agenda. The theoretical underpinning of the sameness approach was that employees were treated the same. This approach is still widely used today in both EHR and managing diversity approaches, although the latter is dependent on how an organization interprets and implements a diversity policy. However, despite the sameness approach still being widely used, there has been another shift in the equality management movement, which happened in tandem with the trend of the late 1980s and 1990s towards deregulation, flexibility, new managerialism and HRM (Greene & Kirton, 2004). This shift involved a move away from the traditional liberal EO approach, that is, the sameness agenda, towards an approach concerned with recognizing employees as different and valuing that difference and the diversity among individual employees and potential employees (Kirton & Greene, 2004). This shift could be considered a further refinement or a more sophisticated approach to dealing with equality (Liff, 1997). There are obvious conflicts between the sameness and difference approaches as well as conceptual problems. Paradoxically, employees should not and cannot be treated as the same, but equally social justice and equality (i.e. the legal principle) cannot be fully achieved with the diversity approach where employees are seen as different and their differences valued. It is at this point where the talent management concept can appear, resulting in individuals being selected for promotion because of their differences. This has provoked further discourse from Greene and Kirton (2004) who, from a trade union perspective, suggest that sameness and difference need to coexist, reflecting that the common ties between individuals should be recognized.

Furthermore, the coexistence of sameness and difference strengthens a more collectivist and moral framework of diversity management as opposed to an individualist, utilitarian framework for managing diversity. The principles of Western management are dominated by a focus on the individual from recruitment and selection through to development and progression, while also recognizing the benefits of performance and employee engagement through teams.

These conceptual differences create challenges for organizations, mainly in the drive to acknowledge the different needs of individuals and to create environments where the differences and potential of individuals can be nurtured and valued, whilst acknowledging the legal principle. Adopting a diversity approach in organizations is an attempt to eradicate discrimination on a number of levels. For example, individual personal characteristics are often used for job segregation. Individual perceptions and prejudice can often affect the effectiveness of recruitment and development practices in organizations, which may result in a number of detrimental consequences, including various forms of bullying, harassment and discrimination.

In organizations, diversity may take many forms and mean different things, from the need to attend to changes in an organization's environment, through changes in labour market profiles, to the changing expectations of people engaged in the work process. Thus, while the foundation for diversity is rigorously embedded within the multicultural nature of 21st-century organizations, understanding what it is to practice, or do, diversity is often unclear and this is the key challenge for those involved in developing organizations and individuals. This challenge can be clearly seen in what is referred to as talent management, where a fundamental question facing those who engage in the process is whether to adopt an exclusive approach – which defines and treats only some employees as talented, an employees as different approach –, or an inclusive approach – which defines and treats all employees as talented, an employees as the same approach (see Tansley et al., 2007 for a discussion of this issue).

Reflecting these conceptual developments in the UK, on October 1, 2007, the three commissions concerned with the rights of different social groups were combined under one umbrella. What were previously known as the Commission for Racial Equality (CRE), the Disability Rights Commission (DRC) and the Equal Opportunities Commission (EOC) merged to become the Commission for Equality and Human Rights (CEHR), formed to protect the rights of individuals across a diverse mix of interests. They then became known as the Equality and Human Rights Commission (EHRC).

Issues and concerns in diversity

So far we have discussed the theoretical underpinnings of diversity and how it might be applied in practice in society, the economy and organizations. We have also discussed the drivers of diversity in those same contexts. But to what extent does actual practice match the theory, in other words, as with HRM/HRD more widely (McGoldrick & Stewart, 1996; Legge, 2004), is there a gap between the rhetoric and reality? Clearly, the potential existence of such a gap is a major issue and concern for those involved in managing diversity.

What is diversity?

Since the EHRC'S merging in 2007, they have made a number of changes to their vision and focus, one in particular being the updating of equality legislation. A new Equality Act (2010) came into force on 1 October 2010 and brings together over 116 separate pieces of legislation into one single Act. Combined, they provide a legal framework to protect the rights of individuals and advance equality of opportunity for all.

The Act simplifies, strengthens and harmonises the current legislation to provide Britain with a new discrimination law which protects individuals from unfair treatment and promotes a fair and more equal society.

The nine main pieces of legislation that were merged are:

the Equal Pay Act 1970

the Sex Discrimination Act 1975

the Race Relations Act 1976

the Disability Discrimination Act 1995

the Employment Equality (Religion or Belief) Regulations 2003

the Employment Equality (Sexual Orientation) Regulations 2003

the Employment Equality (Age) Regulations 2006

the Equality Act 2006, Part 2

the Equality Act (Sexual Orientation) Regulations 2007

activity

To view the full Equality Act 2010 go to www.equalityhumanrights.com/legal-and-policy/equality-act/what-is-the-equality-act

For the training video and details of the changes go to www.equalityhumanrights.com/advice-and-guidance/new-equality-act-guidance/equality-act-starter-kit/video-understanding-the-equality-act-2010

Despite this recent change the remit of the EHRC remains largely unchanged for what it considers central to equality and human rights. However, there have been three significant inclusions in the new Equality Act 2010 relating to:

- Carers – people caring for a disabled child or relative will be protected from discrimination at work.
- Disabled people – in most cases employers will no longer be allowed to ask job applicants about their health to limit employers from screening out disabled people during the recruitment process.
- For mothers – mothers can breastfeed their children in places like cafés and shops and not be asked to leave.

There are other schools of thought that extend and go beyond the Equality Act (2010) to include numerous other elements that are believed or considered to be important to the issue of diversity (Mavin & Girling, 2000; CIPD, 2005). These include economic status, family/marital status, nationality, spent convictions, part-time working, political/opinion affiliation, educational qualifications, languages and work experience. These are clearly outside the remit of the CEHR – what might be termed as the standard, or established, scope of EO – or even what might be justifiably subject to legislation.

Rhetoric versus reality

In relation to EHR and the EHRC, is there a gap between the rhetoric of the commission and what happens in reality? Can legislation really protect everyone in the workplace from discriminatory practices from peers or senior colleagues? Policies pursued by the former EOC that purport to reduce gaps in gender salaries and other forms of discrimination offer some indication through assessing whether their targets were met. Rodgers et al. (2004) suggest that while many organizations claim to operate EO policies, a detailed assessment of the effectiveness of such policies (aside from statistical monitoring) is often neglected and in many instances this perpetuates inequality and a lack of diverse representation at senior levels in organizations.

The most recent publication from the EOC (2007) on gender outlines how a revolution that began in the 1970s remains unfinished with regard to the roles that men and women undertake in society in relation to the workplace and family and home life. This accords with the judgement of the CIPD on progress with diversity policies more generally (Line, 2008). A lot of work is still to be done, as the most recent statistics on gender from 2005 and beyond (EOC, 2006; EHRC, 2010 and 2011) might illustrate (see Table 14.1).

Table 14.1 Progress in achieving gender equality

Employment		
	2005	**Beyond 2005**
Part-time employment	42% of working women aged 16–59 in 2005 worked part time, as opposed to 9% of working men. Part-time work is the most common alternative working arrangement for women	26% of working women aged 16–59 in 2008 worked part time, as opposed to 6% of working men aged 16–64. Part-time work is the most common alternative working arrangement for women
Employment by age	60% and 40% of working women aged 25–44 in 2005 worked full time and part time, as opposed to 96% and 4% of working men respectively	39% and 26% of working women aged 16–59 in 2008 worked full time and part time, as opposed to 59% and 6% of working men aged 16–64 respectively
Employment by disability	54% and 46% of working women aged 16–59 in 2005 were disabled working full time and part time, as opposed to 87% and 13% of working men respectively	78.6% of non-disabled working people aged between 16–64 were in employment as opposed to 50% of disabled working people aged between 16–64 in 2008
Employment by ethnic group	57% and 43% of white working women aged 16–59 in 2005 worked full time and part time, as opposed to 91% and 9% of white working men respectively	39% and 28% of white working women aged 16–59 in 2008 worked full time and part time, as opposed to 60% and 5% of white working men aged 16–64 respectively
	68% and 32% of Indian working women aged 16–64 in 2005 worked full time and part time, as opposed to 91% and 9% of Indian working men respectively	39% and 18% of Indian working women aged 16–59 in 2008 worked full time and part time, as opposed to 58% and 7% of Indian working men aged 16–64 respectively
	73% and 27% of black Caribbean working women aged 16–64 in 2005 worked full time and part time, as opposed to 87% and 13% of black Caribbean working men respectively	46% and 18% of black Caribbean working women aged 16–59 in 2008 worked full time and part time, as opposed to 48% and 7% of black Caribbean working men aged 16–64 respectively
Pay and income		
	2005	**2011**
Full-time and part-time weekly earnings	There is a 17.1% gender pay gap between women and men who work full time and a 38.4% gender pay gap between women and men who work part time	There is a 21.5% gender pay gap between women and men who work full time and a 70.2% gender pay gap between women and men who work part time
Annual full-time earnings	There is a 27.1% gender pay gap between women and men	There is a 26.1% gender pay gap between women and men

Source: Adapted from EOC (2006), EHRC (2011) and EHRC (2010)

It is clear from the above snapshot data that there are still inequalities in gender in relation to salaries and employment.

There are numerous strategies to enable the EHRC to tackle the issue of inequality but the pay gap appears to be their biggest challenge. The Commission's strategic approach to equal pay involves a mix of legislative and non-legislative interventions. The Commission's work is focused not only on the equal pay legislation of the Equality Act 2010, but also on interventions such as promotional activity, provision of practical guidance and the promulgation of best practice in dealing with pay gaps on several grounds, including gender, ethnicity and disability, particularly around pay audits and the active management of pay systems.

The rationale for action by the Commission is that while equal pay legislation has been in place for thirty years, there is still a significant gender pay gap; it will take another 20 years to close the gap without further corrective action.

Committing to addressing issues of inequality, particularly the pay gap, is easily done when written in a strategy but is very different in reality. An example of this is in a report from the Financial Times in June 2012 that highlights that the gap between men's and women's retirement incomes has narrowed over the past few years but not as a result of a rise in female incomes but due to a decrease in male incomes (See http://www.ft.com/cms/s/0/1634a192-b0cf-11e1-a2a6-00144feabdc0.html#axzz2MlvkymK6). Therefore, the pay gap in pension income for females will not improve given this decrease in male pension income.

Furthermore, prior to 2012 the Commission were open about not being able to 'give direct legal assistance to everyone' but could offer advice through its helpline and online resources. However, due to the Government's austerity measures the EHRC was effectively downsized and the helpline closed. The Commission's response was that they will always be ready to tackle issues across the seven protected areas of equality, despite the loss of valuable resources. The opportunities to push the boundaries of the law, create legal precedents or clarify and improve the law in relation to inequalities in society appear even fewer now.

In relation to diversity rather than EO, and more particularly managing diversity, what is rhetoric and what is reality? This is a question that still remains largely unanswered, mostly due to a lack of critical evaluative research, the misinterpretation of managing diversity, the misuse of the term managing diversity, the use of the term by senior management within organizations for the wrong reasons, and the sheer number of definitions of diversity that are almost as diverse as the subject itself (CIPD, 2005). Were things simpler when the term EO was the only term in use? Is the sophistication in the use of the terms diversity, difference and managing diversity muddying the waters? Some say 'yes' (Greene & Kirton, 2004) and some say 'no' (CIPD, 2005). The views of Greene and Kirton and the CIPD are at opposite ends of the continuum. A gap between rhetoric and reality still seems to exist, but it appears to be more than that for some, there is the view that managing diversity is still a rhetorical concept (Mavin and Girling, 2000).

It is argued that there are distinct differences between the concepts of EHR and managing diversity (Mavin & Girling, 2000; Greene & Kirton, 2004; CIPD, 2005). That said, it is suggested that this also may be a rhetorical claim (Mavin & Girling, 2000). EHR is about human rights for individuals in respect of their age, disability, gender, gender reassignment, race, religion or belief, and sexual orientation and ensures equality, ethics and social justice, protected by legislation, holistically. But the approach to EHR within the workplace in organizations is about individuals within homogeneous categories or social groups – groups of women, black and ethnic minorities, people with disabilities and so on – that is, people with an assumed sameness that are ensured of a voice, a fair hearing. In addition to this is the strengthening of these collective groups in organizations where there is trade union representation. Managing diversity is somewhat more complex. As discussed earlier, it has many guises. Much of the existing literature suggests that it can be broadly categorized as 'doing little more than reiterating the traditional arena of EO' (Cooper & White, 1995; Ellis & Sonnerfield, 1995; Copeland, 1998). This would suggest EO in managing diversity's coat. A research report from Greene and Kirton (2004) suggests that managing diversity is something that could only happen once basic levels of

EO had been achieved. The following comment from a trade union officer from the GPMU particularly resonates with Greene and Kirton's (2004, p.17) view of managing diversity:

> It's about valuing the people you've already got in the company and giving them opportunities...We're still at the level of talking about equality...overcoming barriers as opposed to that kind of diversity view of managing people to fulfil their potential.

Furthermore, Rodgers et al. (2004) remark that leading and managing with a diversity agenda presupposes that equality, or the treatment of like as like on the basis of characteristics such as gender, age, race, disability, sexual orientation, religion and employment status already exist, or are implicit within an organization's norms, therefore allowing diversity through difference to be nurtured, valued and celebrated.

Another view of managing diversity goes far beyond the conventional approach to EO, such as compliance to legislation and targeted homogeneous group initiatives, and views it as an explicit strategic approach to managing the difference of individuals, as opposed to their sameness (Mavin & Girling, 2000). One notion would be to enable sameness and difference to coexist and recognize both these in individuals throughout an organization. However, this would be an extremely challenging pursuit. This is also recognized by Greene and Kirton (2004). They suggest that the sameness and difference approaches are seen as appropriate strategies, albeit within different contexts. While recognition of the heterogeneity of social groups is important, as well as the diversity of interests within social groups, the collective aspects of group membership are also seen as significant. Finding a harmony between individuals and groups in one single approach seems almost impossible. Viewing women as homogeneous single interest groups does not recognize their differences. Can they be viewed as heterogeneous on a collective basis, particularly when an issue of inequality relates to equal pay? Furthermore, this particular debate is not new and fears of throwing good after bad have led to calls for approaches that build on existing EHR interventions (Liff, 1997; Dickens, 1999; Cornelius, 2002).

HRD in Practice 14.1

The BBC, the UK national public service broadcast organization, uses both terms, equal opportunities and diversity, in its policy statements, as detailed below.

The BBC's commitment

Diversity for the BBC is a creative opportunity to engage the totality of the UK audience. That includes diverse communities of interest, as well as gender, age, ethnicity, religion and faith, social background, sexual orientation, political affiliation and so on.

Delivering on our commitment to equal opportunities and diversity is important to the BBC for a number of reasons. For example, the audiences that we serve are increasingly diverse. The BBC is also a public service broadcaster funded by a licence fee paid by all sections of UK society.

- The BBC is committed to reflecting the diversity of the UK audience in its workforce, as well as in its output on TV, on radio and online.
- The BBC also has a number of legal obligations to comply with current legislation, for example around the Disability Discrimination Act (DDA).
- The BBC has set itself diversity workforce targets.

The BBC is a member of the major industry networks on disability and ethnicity, as well as of the main UK employer forums which bring together organizations committed to driving progress on diversity.

Our equal opportunities statement

The BBC is committed to promoting equal opportunities for all, irrespective of colour, race, religion or belief, ethnic or national origins, gender, marital/civil partnership status, sexuality, disability or age.

The BBC is committed to reflecting the diversity of the UK and to making its services accessible to all. This applies both to our output and to the people who work here.

The BBC aims to create and sustain an inclusive work environment which provides equality of opportunity for everyone.

Find out more about the BBC's approach to diversity by visiting www.bbc.co.uk/diversity/

reflective question

1 What do you think of the practice of framing a commitment using the language of diversity and a policy statement in the language of equal opportunities?

2 Does the content of the BBC document suggest a difference between diversity and EO or are they essentially the same? Why?

Costs and benefits of diversity policies

While a plethora of legislation underpins employment contracts, many theorists suggest that commitment to a diversity agenda has other benefits, but why should an employer want to push the boundaries set by law? Equal opportunity is often seen as treating everyone in exactly the same way. But to provide real equality of opportunity, people often need to be treated differently in ways that are fair and tailored to their needs. Currently, employer attention to pushing the boundaries and the management of diversity is based on an economic argument; it makes sound business sense to use the talents of many diverse social groupings and individuals in order to achieve the economic outcomes required to sustain an organization's effectiveness. In their ground-breaking book *Diversity in Action: Managing the Mosiac*, Kandola and Fullerton (1998) make a distinction between proven benefits, debatable benefits and indirect benefits.

Proven benefits include:

- the recruitment of scarce labour and skills
- reduction in employee turnover
- reduction in absenteeism
- enhanced organizational flexibility.

Proven benefits can be explicitly quantified and tracked by the organization. *Debatable benefits* include:

- enhanced team creativity and problem solving
- improved decision making
- improved customer service and responsiveness
- improved quality.

Debatable benefits are less quantifiable but are generally thought to add to the organization's capacity and effectiveness.

Indirect benefits include:

- improved morale
- increased job satisfaction
- better public image
- increased competitive edge.

Indirect benefits enhance the work experience and add to the organizational ethos and general sense of employee engagement. Other authors take up the idea of a wider set of advantages offered by a diversity approach as representing social justice, attending to the fulfilment and satisfaction of employee needs and expectations, and extending the organization's corporate reputation.

This social justice argument is based on the belief that everyone should have a right to equal access to employment and, when employed, they should have a right to equal pay and equal access to training and development, as well as being free of any direct or indirect discrimination, harassment or bullying. This is often described as the right to be treated fairly. In addition to this, the employee needs and expectations argument asserts that people aspire to work for employers with good and fair employment practices and to feel valued at work. To be competitive, organizations need to derive the best contributions from everyone. Skill shortages and difficulties in filling vacancies are forcing more organizations to recruit from more diverse talent pools and to offer different employment packages and working arrangements. Creating an open and inclusive workplace culture is integral to achieving this type of employment model. The links between diversity and corporate reputation present a compelling argument for employers. Healthy businesses flourish in healthy societies and the needs of people, communities and businesses are interrelated. Social exclusion and low economic activity rates limit business markets and their growth. Thus, businesses need to consider corporate social responsibility (CSR) in the context of diversity. CSR is often thought of as being linked to environmental issues, but an increasing number of employers take a wider view, seeing the overall image of an organization as important in attracting and retaining both customers and employees. Indeed, it can be argued that CSR is part of the new psychological contract emerging between a firm and the community, or communities, in which it operates.

Building on these arguments, many organizations and employers in the UK and Europe have implemented what we might term as diversity policies. Most diversity policies are voluntary initiatives by employers to recruit, retain and develop employees from diverse social groups. Such employers range across business organizations, national governments, equality agencies, trade unions and nongovernmental organizations. There are a number of basic fundamentals that any organization needs to consider before embarking on the implementation of a diversity policy. First, the identification of what the policy is intended to achieve. Not all organizations set out to achieve the same goals when addressing diversity. This is a key consideration because benefits for individuals, groups and the organization will be dependent on goals being achievable and realistic and not the rhetorical form that may be used to express them. Second, costs are another significant consideration associated with, for example, the implementation of large-scale HRD programmes to change internal cultures as part of diversity policy goals. Other costs linked with complying with the laws on discrimination and opportunity, costs associated with the diverting of management time in executing the policy and change programmes also need careful consideration. These costs are a mixture of explicit and implicit and care needs to be taken to ensure that costs are, as far as possible, identified and managed.

reflective question

1 What do you think are the goals being pursued at Pearson?
2 How realistic and achievable are these goals?

Assessing benefits

In 2003, the European Commission (EC, 2003) commissioned a report to examine the measurement of costs and benefits of workforce diversity policies against a background of the implementation of new anti-discrimination directives throughout the EU and increased investment in workforce diversity policies by businesses. Its findings provide extremely informative evidence on diversity policies, their measurement, the type of measurement and outcomes from the implementation of such policies. Two principal benefits that organizations seek from their investment in diversity policies were identified and these are linked to economic gains. This has a direct connection with the business case for diversity.

The two economics benefits are (EC, 2003):

- *Strengthening long-term value-drivers:* tangible and intangible assets that allow companies to be competitive, generate stable cash flows, and satisfy their shareholders. These include building a differentiated reputation with key stakeholders and customers, and improving the quality of human capital within a company.
- *Generating short- and medium-term opportunities to improve cash flows:* for example by reducing costs, resolving labour shortages, opening up new markets, and improving performance in existing markets. These are also known as return on investment benefits.

One point to note is that the research was qualitative in design and so these benefits are reported rather than actually measured. So far, there is little evidence of quantitative assessment or systematic measurement of benefits and outcomes. Additional benefits of having strategic, achievable and operational diversity policies that foster inclusivity and respect for the dignity of the individual are that organizations free themselves of costly lawsuits, hostile environments and divisive conflict-ridden cultures (Iles & Hayers, 1997).

Assessing costs

Organizations face four types of additional cost when they invest in workforce diversity policies. These are (EC, 2003):

- *Costs of legal compliance:* potential costs include record-keeping systems, training of staff and communication of new policies.
- *Cash costs of diversity:* the main cash costs are specialist staff, education and training, facilities and support, working conditions and benefits, communication, employment policies, and monitoring and reporting processes. Some of these are one-off and short-term but most are long-term, recurring expenses.
- *Opportunity costs of diversity:* opportunity costs represent the loss of benefits because a scarce resource cannot be used in other productive activities. These include diversion of top management time, diversion of functional management time and productivity shortfalls.
- *Business risks of diversity:* many programmes designed to change corporate cultures take longer than planned to implement or fail completely. This execution risk is widely understood among companies. Sustainable diversity policies are an outcome of a successful change in corporate culture.

It will be clear from the EU research and the points made here that measuring the costs and benefits of diversity policies is highly complex and probably impossible to achieve in practice in any exact form.

Do we value diversity?

The relationship between costs and benefits raises the question of whether we, as a society in the UK, value diversity in its own right. It is fair to say that there are differences within our society, illustrated by contentious political parties in regional areas of the UK and conflict-ridden cultures displaying a disregard and lack of respect for individuals and groups in society. The former Labour Government demonstrated its commitment to diversity when it published a new equality Bill entitled *Framework for a Fairer Future* on 26 June 2008, which set out its approach to addressing inequalities in society, social mobility being one. The Commons address by Harriet Harman outlined the then Government's view of those inequalities and described what it believed they were:

> addressing those inequalities and creating a fairer society is important for three reasons. First, fairness is important for the individual. Secondly, fairness is important for our society – a society that is equal and fair is one that is more at ease with itself. Thirdly, fairness is important for our economy – diversity makes us outward facing and helps us to compete in the global economy.

It appears that the former Government's rationale represented basic approaches to tackling the issues of a diverse and inclusive society and the current Government's position has not produced any radical interventions. Considering that migration to the UK is not a new phenomenon – it started at the end of the Mesolithic times (4000 BC) – it seems that fostering an inclusive society is not, and has never been, easy. Even though society is more civilized today than it was in 4000 BC, there are still many hurdles to overcome, perhaps best illustrated currently in relation to race and religion. These points relate to the government's focus on individuals and society as a whole. The government considers its focus on the economy to be equally important. The UK organizations that support the UK economy are charged with competing in the global economy from a diverse perspective. An approach that many organizations take to adopting this perspective involves strategic input from their HRM/HRD departments. Stewart and Beaver (2003) suggest that an increasing number of organizations are recognizing that effectively managing their HR necessitates recognition and incorporation of the global context.

As a consequence of globalization and the changing nature of the labour market, partly due to an increase in migration to the UK, organizations can no longer settle for culturally and ethnically homogeneous workforces, thus transferring the onus to employers to adopt a different approach to managing increasingly diverse workforces, which is argued to be good for organizations and their ongoing survival (Stewart & Beaver, 2003). This approach encompasses the business case for diversity, linking the effective and efficient management of a diverse workforce to the direct success of an organization and the economic benefits associated with this. This focus on managing a diverse workforce has clear implications for HRM and HRD. HRM policies and activities are mainly associated with recruitment and selection, rewards and the development of specific diversity policies, while HRD is mainly focused on learning interventions to support the implementation of these policies and the achievement of associated objectives. We now move onto delivering diversity through the use of HRD interventions.

Delivering diversity through HRD

From the late 1990s onwards diversity management became a necessity for all successful organizations. In 1995 Littlefield identified training as a key intervention to solve diversity problems across 50 countries. Since then, globalization and workforce mobility have heightened the need for interventions relating to diversity and for HRD to manage that responsibility (Hite & McDonald, 2010).

Given the opposing debates discussed earlier, two key questions for managers and leaders are:

- What are the problems we face in relation to EHR and diversity?
- What initiatives can be put in place to help us move in the right direction?

While the development of an HRD agenda for diversity has grown substantially over the past few years, identifying the right development areas for organizations and understanding the needs of individuals in embracing diversity presents a number of challenges.

Training: what type/s and who gets it?

Previous research (Harris, 1991) suggests that the number of organizations providing diversity training has increased significantly over the years, and that two-thirds of companies conducted diversity training for managers and almost 40 per cent provided training for all employees. Yet the current statistical evidence, presented in Table 14.1 above, suggests that segregation, an unequal distribution of roles and discrimination still prevail in organizations.

The definition of diversity training varies from organization to organization and depends on how the concept of diversity is understood by those championing the diversity agenda. Most organizations that provide training offer awareness and/or skill-based training in an attempt to sensitize employees to the issues presented by diversity in the workplace, yet the nature and outcome of diversity training is rarely scrutinized.

Pendry, Driscoll and Field (2007) suggest that diversity training is defined as a distinct set of programmes aimed at:

- facilitating positive intergroup interactions
- reducing prejudice and discrimination
- enhancing the skills, knowledge and motivation of people to interact with diverse other.

Diversity training differs from other types of training because it seeks to challenge the way one views the world and deals with issues that may seem emotional or subjective (Hanover & Cellar, 1998). Behaviour and attitudes towards diverse others are formed in individuals before training, which is why diversity training may be more emotionally and politically charged than other types of training (Alderfer, 1992; Paluck, 2006; Paluck & Green, 2009).

The role of HRD

HRD interventions can take many forms, from diversity policies to training. A number of HRD interventions will be necessary, sometimes as part of major change programmes, such as achieving the successful implementation of diversity policies. With diversity training, whose objectives are borne out of the diversity policies, many of the goals include compliance, harmony, inclusion, justice and transformation (Rossett & Bickham, 1994); goals which can ultimately contribute to the welfare of all involved in the interaction. Such goals are said to achieve the following in individuals:

- individuals become more satisfied due to positive work or social climates (Combs & Luthans, 2007);
- diverse groups can be more effective and generate more new ideas for innovation (cf. Williams & O'Reilly, 1998)
- organizations can also obtain a competitive advantage due to less turnover, better coordination of information and more client relations (Naff & Kellough, 2003)

Programmes and training such as those described above are called for by the CIPD (Line, 2008) and already feature in many organizations' approach to managing diversity (Michielsens et al., 2008). The civil service approach featured in HRD in Practice 14.4 is a good example. However, not all organizations can or choose to adopt major cultural change through diversity policy but instead rely on and select from a range of different HRD interventions. Before detailing some of these, it is worth making the point that some or all may be included in cultural change programmes. The key difference is that in those programmes HRD activities form part of an integrated strategy.

Considerations for Diversity Training

Following a recent critical review of the literature on diversity training, Bezrukova et al. (2010) suggest that there are certain factors that need consideration when designing diversity training and they have categorized these as training inputs and training outputs.

Training inputs

The training inputs include the training context (such as diversity policy, training design and trainee characteristics), the last two both being to a greater or lesser extent determined by the training context. They also extend inputs to include the training approach, for instance stand-alone vs. integrated with other organizational practices and training attendance, whether this be mandatory or voluntary.

Further aspects are group-specific vs. inclusive focus and awareness vs. skills-based training. From their review it appears that characteristics such as the design of diversity training have been tackled independently but never brought together with other important aspects of diversity training like training context. They see this as an important relationship and one that requires consideration, in particular for the effective design, delivery and success of diversity training.

Training outputs

Training outputs include trainee reactions and affective or attitudinal, cognitive, and behavioural learning outcomes. Bezrukova et al. (2010) highlight that recent research on diversity training has been largely informative in summarising the outcomes of diversity training programmes but has not yet paid much attention to its short- and long-term consequences. As discussed above in types of training, it is difficult to measure and see the effectiveness of diversity interventions and the effects of training. However, considering an evaluation or measurement of diversity training is important and something that should be considered at the input stage, in particular when designing training.

We would urge anyone responsible for, or involved in, the design of diversity training to read the work of Bezrukova et al. as their review comprehensively highlights many of the issues significant in diversity training.

Here though, we include an at a glance précis of their framework of things to consider when tackling this issue.

Table 14.2 Significant issues in diversity training

Diversity Training Context	• Training setting 　■ Campuses (educational setting) 　■ Organization workplace 　■ Other i.e. hotel, conference venue
	• Training approach 　■ Stand-alone 　■ Integrated
	• Training attendance 　■ Mandatory 　■ Voluntary
Diversity Training Design	• Training focus 　■ Group-specific 　■ Inclusive
	• Training type 　■ Awareness 　■ Behaviour-based
	• Training instruction 　■ Many methods 　■ One method
Trainee Characteristics	• Demographic attributes – race, gender, age etc. • Personality and cultural attributes
Training Outcomes	• Reactions 　■ Short-term 　■ Long-term
	• Cognitive learning 　■ Short-term 　■ Long-term
	• Affective/attitudinal learning 　■ Short-term 　■ Long-term
	• Behavioural learning (including results) 　■ Short-term 　■ Long-term

Source: Adapted from Bezrukova et al. (2010)

We now discuss some examples of diversity training.

Attitudes and behaviour

Probably the most common HRD intervention is some form of awareness training aimed at all or most employees. Diversity awareness training has grown out of attempts to implement EO policies related to particular categories and groups, for example race awareness and sexism awareness training. The intellectual rationale for this intervention is that individual behaviour needs to change and this in turn requires individual attitudes to change through raising awareness of the existence of an (illogical) rationale for and negative effects of, for example, sexist beliefs and attitudes (Stewart, 1996). The success of this type of intervention is essential but sadly one that is hard to measure. The attempts that have been made suggest mixed results and there is some evidence that they can reinforce and deepen the very attitudes they are supposed to change (Stewart, 1996; Home Office, 2002). Bezrukova (2010) suggests that behaviour-based training is rarely used alone and is usually conducted in conjunction with awareness-based training. However, a strong behavioural component can be harmful in behavioural change-oriented diversity training. As with Stewart (1996), Bezrukova found that to challenge someone's existing belief system can have detrimental consequences; unnecessary feelings of discrimination against one's beliefs should be avoided.

A further argument against awareness training is that it shifts responsibility from the organization to individual employees. In any case, the assumed causal relationship between individual attitudes and individual behaviour has yet to be established (Stewart, 1996).

Awareness raising training

Alban-Metcalfe and Alban-Metcalfe (2005) make the distinction between awareness raising and the building of skills when operating within a diverse workforce. Distinctions are made in the mode of delivery and the outcome from the different HRD interventions. Awareness training is usually a classroom-based activity and may be useful to impart knowledge, provide wider perspectives and offer new ways of thinking and seeing. More specifically, it can be used to correct the myths and stereotypes that permeate an organization and increase employee sensitivity to diversity issues (Nagamootoo et al., 2005).

Advantages of the awareness training approach are that it can be focused on particular workplace contexts, planned and delivered across organizations relatively easily and cover large numbers of people at a reasonable cost. However, the classroom-based approach has been criticized for its generalized nature in not being able to meet the needs of individuals, particularly its inability to impart skills and influence the types of behavioural change to enable the cultural shifts towards truly embracing diversity in the workplace.

Behaviour changing training

Skills-based training builds on awareness training by attending to the behavioural aspects of the individual and providing new tools and techniques to promote more effective interactions between different individuals, the aim being to promote behavioural change. The underlying rationale for skills-based training comes from Bandura's (1986) social learning theory, which proposes that participants will learn more through behaviour role modelling. In terms of developing skills based on diversity sensitivity, participating in role play encourages rehearsal and practice of managing diversity-related issues. Here individuals are offered a safe and supportive environment in which to develop their skill sets and receive one-to-one feedback or reinforcement about their behaviour development from an experienced coach.

The claims made of the skills-based approach are that it assists learning and development on an individual basis and promotes deep, long-term learning and behavioural change. It can be tailored to consider specific workplace contexts and is more interactive than the class-based exchanges often used in awareness training. However, it is time-consuming and costly and for these reasons tends to be targeted at senior members of the organization.

While the two approaches offer a different set of advantages and outcomes, most studies (Bezrukova et al., 2010; Nagamootoo et al., 2005) suggest that a mix of both awareness training and skills-based training is suitable for organizations, where the balance should be guided by organizational context. Using both awareness training and skills development assists organizations to answer the why, what and how of embracing a diversity culture.

However, as Stewart (1996) suggests in the light of plausible evidence for a causal relationship between individual attitude and individual behaviour, the shift of responsibility to the individual needs to be matched with an organizational commitment to a sustainable momentum for change. Awareness training should not be seen as a one-off, quick fix intervention and should change to reflect the ever-changing demands of the organization and its strategy. In addition, skills-based training should be supported by effective coaching and development long after the initial intervention.

E-learning Diversity Training

A common group-based HRD intervention is a programme to inform, communicate and educate employees on the organization's diversity policy and the rights and responsibilities of all employees arising from the policy. This is likely to be the minimum HRD intervention used by any organization adopting a diversity policy. Delivery of these programmes does not have to be face-to-face and methods utilizing e-learning (see also Chapter 9), for example, may be used by large employers Additional programmes are also usually developed and delivered for those with particular responsibilities within a diversity policy, for example those involved with recruitment and selection. Many of these will be managers.

While it is important for organizations to consider meaningful diversity training throughout the organization, so that individuals can keep ahead of the game, there is a large body of evidence (Schein, 1985; Bass & Avolio, 1993; Alban-Metcalfe & Alban-Metcalfe, 2005) to suggest that senior managers, leaders and those promoting the public face of the organization are key to creating the right environment and developing appropriate strategies to enable the delivery of a diversity agenda. It is also important to recognize the important role played by line managers in offering support and promoting opportunity for their staff with fairness, dignity and respect and in deciding what is of merit in the process of appraising staff. However, diversity tends to feature separately from the development of leaders and managers and so programmes on recruitment and selection are often designed and delivered by HR staff and departments rather than HRD staff and departments. Both these interventions were well-established before the term diversity came into common usage and were standard interventions associated with EO policies.

More recent HRD interventions have focused on both individuals and groups associated with diversity policies. Individual interventions include coaching and mentoring, for example for women to support their development as managers. While coaching and mentoring programmes may be aimed at groups such as women or members of black and minority ethnic groups, the methods themselves are one-to-one and so the HRD activities support individuals. Group-based HRD interventions include use of action learning sets as well as support networks. These methods were also utilized as part of implementing EO policies but have become more common as part of approaches to managing diversity. So too have what are known as positive action programmes, as used by the civil service for example (see HRD in Practice 14.4). These are HRD interventions aimed at underrepresented groups to help overcome barriers to particular careers. Again, although such programmes were originally developed under the banner of EO, they have been taken up to a greater extent under the banner of managing diversity.

We would argue that there has been little progress in designing and developing new HRD interventions to support diversity since those developed to support the achievement of EO and this is echoed in the work of Bezrukova et al. (2010). Perhaps one significant development is that of diversity leadership programmes for senior managers, although there has arguably been little progress here, as pointed out by Line (2008). So, our conclusion is that HRD theory and practice has yet to initiate any meaningful response to managing diversity.

Diversity in the bureaucratic and post-bureaucratic organization

We have mentioned that fairness, dignity and respect are at the heart of social justice within organizations. We have also mentioned talent management and intimated what that might mean for the organization and its employees in connection with the sameness and difference agendas.

An example here is the notion of the bureaucratic and post-bureaucratic organization. The bureaucratic organization is more likely to uphold the legal principle of treating all employees the same, this is because of the structures, procedures and processes that the organization upholds in relation to the legal principle. Take the promotion of an individual from assistant to officer, for example; all qualified and experienced employees that meet the job criteria will be eligible to apply, resulting in the most successful applicant being offered the job via the selection process.

However, in the post-bureaucratic or organic organization, the same structures, procedures and processes may not apply and/or will certainly be more informal. So, whereas in the bureaucratic organization, all qualified and experienced employees are offered an opportunity for promotion, it may not necessarily be the same in the post-bureaucratic organization. This is because structures in the formal sense may not exist. In the post-bureaucratic organization a manager may view one employee as more talented than another and promote that person informally and give them more responsibility, thus resulting in other employees not being given the opportunity to try for promotion. This will probably leave them feeling that they have not been treated fairly, that they have been discriminated against and that the legal principle has not been upheld. Similar processes may apply to rewards, with employees in the same or similar jobs having varying salaries. Situations such as these remain a challenge for HRM/HRD and it is clear that creating an effective organization through the nurturing of a diverse workforce is not without its problems.

Diversity policy in the UK civil service

HRD in Practice 14.3

The UK civil service has launched a new diversity policy which replaces the former ten-point plan. The new policy titled 'Promoting Equality, Valuing Diversity: A Strategy for the Civil Service' (**http://www.civilservice.gov.uk/recruitment/working/diversity**) covers employment issues with a view to meeting the new single Equality Duty, which is covered overall by the new Equality Act 2010, as discussed above.

This new strategy focuses on four key themes that will build on the progress made by departments and agencies as they implemented the former diversity ten-point plan.

The four themes: changing behaviours; strong leadership; talent management systems and a diverse workforce at all levels reaching targets for females, ethnicity and disability are linked and designed to drive the mainstreaming of equality and diversity further into every aspect of their business. Taken together, these themes and supporting actions provide a framework for delivering equality and diversity in the Civil Service for the coming years.

The full report can be found at **http://resources.civilservice.gov.uk/wp-content/uploads/2011/07/diversity-strategy.pdf3**.

activity

Access the website above to consider the following questions:

1 What is the role of HRD to the effective implementation of the first three themes described within the new policy?
2 Is this use and contribution of HRD appropriate and realistic?
3 Does HRD have a visible presence in the strategic aims of the themes of this new strategy?
4 What other contributions might have been sought from HRD interventions in securing the aims and objectives of this new strategy?

Use your responses to these questions to produce a short statement describing the role of HRD in achieving effective diversity policy in organizations. Compare and contrast your statement with those produced by fellow students or colleagues.

summary

○ The notion of diversity had clear links with, and grew out of, earlier notions associated with equal opportunities. There are no clear distinctions or agreed differences between the two concepts and some argue that there is in fact no difference.

○ Partly because of the above, diversity and managing diversity are complex concepts and activities.

○ Central to this complexity is the range of different and sometimes competing arguments in favour of achieving effective diversity management in work organizations. These include moral imperatives, achieving business benefits, compliance with legislation, contributing to achieving social justice and applying the principles of corporate social responsibility.

○ An added feature of the complexity is specifying the groups covered by diversity, whether it is in fact useful to apply the term to particular and specified groups, and the challenge of achieving respect, fairness and dignity in the treatment of all individual current and potential employees.

⬤ Arising from the former point on groups versus individuals is the problem of deciding whether to treat individuals the same or each individual differently or, perhaps more accurately, the problem of doing both at the same time.

⬤ Two additional and related significant issues with managing diversity are first separating rhetoric from reality or principles from practice and second assessing the impact of attempts to apply principles in practice. A particular and important example of the second difficulty is establishing, specifying and measuring the costs and benefits of investing in managing diversity.

⬤ HRD is clearly a significant and important component of any attempt to achieve effective diversity management policy and practice in work organizations. This is most clearly the case because of the link between individual and collective behaviour and effective diversity management.

⬤ HRD practice has a number of contributions to make with perhaps the central one being achieving cultural change to facilitate effective diversity management.

⬤ Additional HRD interventions include the communication of organizational policies, awareness training, skills development and positive action programmes.

⬤ A range of standard activities within HRD professional practice will be relevant to these contributions, including the design and delivery of HRD interventions and the provision of management and team development programmes. Leadership Development may, however, be the most significant and important HRD contribution to achieving effective diversity management in work organizations.

⬤ **discussion questions**

1 In 2004, *Business Week* revealed that US research showed:
on average, companies with the highest percentage of women among their top officers had a return on equity 35 per cent higher than those with the fewest high-level women. Total return to shareholders was 34 per cent higher for the companies with the most executive women vs those with the fewest. (Alimo-Metcalfe & Brutsche, 2005)

So why are so few women at the top?

2 There is considerable evidence to suggest that black and minority ethnic employees are rated lower in performance evaluations than white employees (Friedman et al., 1998), especially when the raters themselves are white (Alban-Metcalfe, 2005).

What assumptions and norms do you suggest are influencing the management and evaluation processes underway here? What policies and practices might an HRD professional consider implementing in order to change this situation?

3 What role and contribution can team development play in achieving effective diversity management?
4 Which target groups in organizations will be most likely to benefit from diversity skills development programmes and why?
5 What features and components would you include in a leadership development programme designed to increase the effectiveness of diversity management?

⬤ **further reading**

Bierema, L. (2009) Critiquing human resource development's dominant masculine rationality and evaluating its impact. *Human Resource Development Review*, **8**: 68–96.

CEHR (Commission for Equality and Human Rights) (2008) *Talent not Tokenism: The Business Benefits of Workforce Diversity*. London: CBI Human Resources Policy Directorate.

Foster, C. and Harris, L. (2005) Easy to say, difficult to do: diversity management in retail. *Human Resource Management Journal*, **15**(3): 4–17.

Home Office (2002) *Training in Racism Awareness and Cultural Diversity*. London: Research, Development and Statistics Directorate.

Lorbiecki, A. and Jack, G. (2000) Critical turns in the evolution of diversity management. *British Academy of Management*, **11**, S17–S31.

Perfect, D. (2011) Gender Pay Gaps. London: Equality and Human Rights Commission, http://www. equalityhumanrights.com/uploaded_files/research/ gender_pay_gap_briefing_paper2.pdf

references

Alban-Metcalfe, J. (2005) *Perceptions and Prospects: Diversity Issues Among Managers in Local Government,* paper presented at HRD Conference, Leeds: Leeds University Press.

Alban-Metcalfe, J. and Alban-Metcalfe, J. (2005) *A 3600 Approach to Diversity and the Development of Skills-Based Training,* paper presented at HRD Conference, Leeds.

Alderfer, C. P. (1992) Changing race relations embedded in organizations: Report on a long-term project with the XYZ corporation (pp.138–66). In S. E. Jackson (ed.) *Diversity in the Workplace: Human Resource Initiatives.* New York: Guilford Publications.

Alimo-Metcalfe, B. and Brutsche, M. (2005) *Gender and Leadership: Does It Really Matter?* paper presented at HRD conference, Leeds.

Bandura, A. (1986) *Social Foundations of Thought and Action: A Social Cognitive Theory.* Englewood Cliffs, NJ: Prentice Hall.

Bass, B.M. and Avolio, B.J. (1993) Transformational leadership and organizational culture. *Public Administration Quarterly,* **17**(1): 112–21.

Bentley, T. and Clayton, S. (1998) *Profiting from Diversity.* Aldershot: Gower.

Bezrukova, K., Jehn, K. and Spell, C. (2012) Reviewing diversity training: where we have been and where we should go. *Academy of Management Learning & Education,* **11**(2): 207–27.

CIPD (2005) *Change Agenda: Managing Diversity; Linking Theory and Practice to Business Performance.* London: Chartered Institute of Professional Development.

Cooper, M. and White, B. (1995) Organisational behaviour. In S. Tyson (ed.) *Strategic Prospects for HRM.* London: Institute of Personnel and Development.

Combs, G. M. And Luthans, F. (2007) Diversity training: Analysis of the impact of self-efficacy. *Human Resource Development Quarterly,* **18**: 91–120.

Copeland, L. (1988) Valuing diversity, part 2, pioneers and champions of change. *Personnel,* July: 44–9.

Cornelius, N. (ed.) (2002) *Building Workplace Equality: Ethics, Diversity and Inclusion.* London: Thomson.

Dickens, L. (1999) Beyond the business case: a three-pronged approach to equality action. *Human Resource Management Journal,* **9**(1): 9–19.

EC (2003) *The Costs and Benefits of Diversity: A Study on Methods and Indicators to Measure the Cost-effectiveness of Diversity Policy in Enterprises.* Brussels: European Commission.

EHRC (2010) *How fair is Britain? Equality, Human Rights and Good Relations in 2010: The First Triennial Review.* London: Equality and Human Rights Commission.

EHRC (2011) *Annual Report and Account.* London: Equality and Human Rights Commission.

Ellis, C. and. Sonnerfield, J.A. (1995) Diverse approaches to managing diversity. *Human Resource Management,* **33**(1): 79–109.

EOC (2006) *Facts about Men and Women in Great Britain.* Manchester: Equal Opportunities Commission.

EOC (2007) *The Gender Agenda.* Manchester: Equal Opportunities Commission.

Friedman, R.A., Kane, M. and Cornfield, D.B. (1998) Social support and career optimism: examining the effectiveness of network groups among black managers. *Human Relations,* **51**(9): 1155–77.

Hanover, J. and Cellar, D. (1998) Environmental factors and the effectiveness of workforce diversity training. *Human Resource Development Quarterly,* **9**: 105–24.

Harris, P. (1991) *Managing Cultural Differences.* Houston, TX: Gulf.

Home Office (2002) *Training in Racism Awareness and Cultural Diversity.* London: Research, Development and Statistics Directorate.

Hite, L.M. and McDonald, K.S. (2010) Perspectives on HRD and diversity education. *Advances in Developing Human Resources,* **12**(3) 283–94.

Iles, P. and Hayers, P.K. (1997) Managing diversity in transnational project teams: a tentative model and case study. *Journal of Managerial Psychology,* **12**(2): 95–117.

Jewson, N. and Mason, D. (1986) The theory and practice of equal opportunities policies: liberal and radical approaches. *Sociological Review,* **34**(2): 307–34.

Kandola, R.S. and Fullerton, J. (1998) *Diversity in Action: Managing the Mosaic.* London: CIPD.

Kirton, G. and Greene, A.M. (2004) *Views from Another Stakeholder: Trade Union Perspectives on the Rhetoric of 'Managing Diversity.* Warwick Papers in Industrial Relations, Number 74. Warwick University: Industrial Relations Unit.

Legge, K. (2004) *Human Resource Management: Rhetorics and Realities.* Basingstoke: Palgrave Macmillan.

Liff, S. (1997) Two routes to managing diversity: individual differences or social group characteristics. *Employee Relations,* **19**(1): 11–26.

Line, F. (2008) *Diversity: Done and Dusted?* paper presented at CIPD conference, Developing the Profession, University of Nottingham, 26–27 June.

Littlefield, D (1995) Managing diversity seen as core economic value. *People Management*, **1**(12): 15.

Mavin, S. and Girling, G. (2000) What is managing diversity and why does it matter? *Human Resource Development International*, **3**(4): 419–33.

McGoldrick, J. and Stewart, J. (1996) The HRM-HRD nexus. In J. Stewart and J. McGoldrick (eds) *HRD: Perspectives, Strategies and Practice*. London: Pitman.

Michielsens, E., Urwin, P. and Tyson, S. (2008) *Implementing Diversity Employment Policies: Examples from Large London Companies*, paper presented at CIPD conference, Developing the Profession, University of Nottingham, 26–27 June.

Naff, K. and Kellough, E. (2003) Ensuring employment equity: Are federal diversity programs making a difference? *International Journal of Public Administration*, **26**: 1307–36.

Nagamootoo, N., Birdi, K. and Adams, M. (2005) *Diversity Training: How Can We Make It More Effective?* Paper presented at HRD conference, Leeds.

Paluck, E.L. (2006) Diversity training and intergroup contact: a call to action research. *Journal of Social Issues*, **62**(3): 577–95.

Paluck, E.L. and Green, D.P. (2009) Prejudice reduction: What works? A review and assessment of research and practice. *Annual Review of Psychology*, **60**: 339–67.

Pendry, L.F., Driscoll, D.M. and Field, C.T. (2007) Diversity training: Putting theory into practice. *Journal of Occupational and Organizational Psychology*, **80**: 227–50.

Perfect, D. (2011) *Gender Pay Gaps*. London: Equality and Human Rights Commission.

Rodgers, H., Frearson, M., Holden, R. and Gold, J. (2004) *Equality, Diversity and Leadership: Different Journeys, Variegated Landscapes,* paper presented at the HRD conference, Limerick University.

Rossett, A. and Bickham, T. (1994) Diversity training: hope, faith and cynicism. *Training*, **31**: 40–46.

Schein, E.H. (1985) *Organizational Culture and Leadership*. San Francisco, CA: Jossey-Bass.

Stewart, J. (1996) *Managing Change through Training and Development*, 2nd edn. London: Kogan Page.

Stewart, J. (2007) The ethics of HRD. In C. Rigg, J. Stewart and K. Trehan (eds) *Critical Human Resource Development: Beyond Orthodoxy*. Harlow: FT/Prentice Hall.

Stewart, J. and Beaver, G. (2003) *Human Resource Development in Small Organisations*. London: Routledge.

Tansley, C., Turner, P.A., Foster, C., Harris, L.M., Stewart, J., Sempik, A. and Williams, H (2007) *Talent: Strategy, Management, Measurement*. London: CIPD.

Williams, K. and O'Reilly, C.A. (1998) Demography and diversity: a review of 40 years of research (pp.77–140). In B.M. Staw and L.L. Cummings (eds) *Research in Organizational Behavior*. Greenwich, CT: JAI Press.

Winstanley, D. and Woodall, J. (2000) *Ethical Issues in Contemporary Human Resource Management*. Basingstoke: Palgrave Macmillan.

Lifelong Learning and Continuing Professional Development

Jeff Gold

Chapter learning outcomes

After studying this chapter, you should be able to:

- Explain the meaning of lifelong learning (LL) and continuing professional development (CPD)
- Understand the rationale for LL and CPD
- Assess the benefits to individuals, society and groups and to the economy
- Assess the importance of LL and its practice
- Explain the nature of professional work and the various methods of CPD

Chapter outline

Introduction
Why lifelong learning and CPD?
Lifelong learning
Professional work and CPD
Summary

Introduction

Even if there hadn't been a recession which created worry for those in formal learning at school and college, it would still have been the case that everyone would need to give serious attention to becoming a lifelong learner. In the UK and the rest of Europe, the population is becoming older and more diverse and people face increasing unpredictability before, during and beyond their working lives (McNair, 2009). Therefore, it is important for everyone to become a lifelong learner, even though recession seems to have led to a decline in funding and opportunities for learning and therefore expectations (Tuckett & Aldridge, 2011). In many of the arguments for LL, much is made of the developments in knowledge-intensive work as part of the knowledge economy and knowledge society (Rohrbach, 2007). For growing numbers of workers, knowledge is vital to the process of work and also the main constituent of the output of work, whether as a tangible product or an intangible service. Increasingly, work occurs in knowledge-based organizations employing knowledge workers (Newell et al., 2009) using knowledge-based technology (Cipriano, 2012). Professional workers especially are able to make claims for their expertise in particular fields of knowledge work and such workers are usually members of a professional body that protects and enhances their professional status, for example solicitors belonging to the Law Society. As we will explain below, a key characteristic of professional work is the command of an underpinning body of knowledge. Therefore, in response to rapid changes in knowledge that is vital for claiming expert status, it has become increasingly recognized that all professionals need to undertake continuing professional development (CPD). Professional bodies, such as the Law Society and the Chartered Institute of Personnel and Development (CIPD), seek to engender LL for their members in CPD as a representation of good professional practice (Roscoe, 2002). As a consequence, there are now various policies, approaches and methods that enable, support and sometimes pressurize professionals to build on their qualifications by undertaking CPD. In this chapter, we will consider how this occurs.

Why lifelong learning and CPD?

As with all arguments presented, those made in favour of LL and CPD, as well as providing facts, are also attempts to persuade people to do something about their learning. If we have entered the 'risk society' (Beck, 1992), and events of the last few years have done nothing to change this view, we apparently must do something about our learning. Such arguments therefore have a rhetorical quality (Edwards, 2001). Nevertheless, few can doubt that there are significant and interconnected technological, economic and social changes that underpin the arguments. Change was the principal reason presented in the Fryer report (NAGCELL, 1997) in the late 1990s that sought to broaden the idea of LL, although it is also interesting to note that the report was cautious about learning being seen as the only response to change. It was, however, crucial to the development of government policy on LL in the UK. Of course, throughout history, people have learned to cope with change and, even today, many people are able to deal with change without reference to policies for LL or CPD. Such informal learning still represents the most common form of learning in all forms of work practice, although it is quite possible to use informal learning more deliberately and consciously (see Gold et al., 2007).

reflective question

1 What is your response to the idea of the 'risk society'?
2 How do you feel about the prospect that you must consider learning for the rest of your life?

There are a number of key dimensions of change that impact all areas of work requiring the need for LL and CPD.

a Globalization

Changes in the global economy such as the growth of world trade and market liberalization accompanied by highly mobile capital, labour and information (Scase, 1999) are consistently invoked as a rationale for LL. The emerging BRIC economies (Brazil, Russia, India and China), and others, are seen as a reason for Western nations such as the UK to invest more in higher level or world class skills (Leitch, 2006; UKCES, 2011a) in order to compete, innovate and grow. There is continuing hope for an export-led recovery based on high-value work (CBI, 2011).

b Competition and deregulation

This is strongly connected to globalization, where many jobs have been exposed to low-cost competition. However, even among professionals, who traditionally enjoyed a degree of protection from competitive forces, there is now recognition that a response must be made. For example, under the recent Legal Services Act 2011, lawyers have been able to work in Alternative Business Structures (ABS) providing a range of legal and financial services. The key idea, sometimes called 'Tesco Law' is that competition between providers will promote innovation and value for customers. It also has raised concerns about the quality of such services (Leighton, 2011).

c Technology

There has always been a link between learning and changes in technology. Castells (1996) highlighted how ICT enabled knowledge generation combined with processing and communication devices, with a feedback loop that enables accumulation and production of further innovations. The move to online availability has allowed a massive expansion of digital opportunities for learning but there are also concerns about exclusion from such opportunities (Enyon & Helsper, 2011).

d Knowledge

The focus on knowledge gives more emphasis to the skills of workers who can be recognized as knowledge workers working in knowledge-intensive firms (Newell et al., 2009), a key source of any organization's intellectual capital (Stewart, 1997). Knowledge provides the basis for expertise, and it becomes more possible to reconfigure work around different combinations of expert knowledge. Increasingly, experts work across disciplinary boundaries though dialogue and negotiation using open source web-based platforms (Raptis et al., 2012). In addition, since the solutions to many problems are now available online, experts and professionals will need to learn from customers and clients about how to provide value-added services that cannot be found elsewhere. In organizations, there has been a switch to e-learning during recession as a replacement for external training (CIPD, 2010).

reflective question

1 Why do we need doctors if we can access **www.nhsdirect.nhs.uk?**
2 Do you need lecturers if you can download a podcast?
3 Do you need a lawyer if you can find out about employment law decisions at **www. danielbarnett.co.uk?**

e Social

Throughout the 20th century, it was expected that children would be able to find better work than their parents, referred to as intergenerational social mobility. However, there are now concerns that this process has ceased or slowed down (Eriksen & Goldthorpe, 2010), particularly affecting children from socially disadvantaged backgrounds (Blanden & Machin, 2008). It is suggested that the UK is less socially mobile than other countries (Cabinet Office, 2011). Another obvious social trend relates to the growing number of people who are aged over 65 years, estimated to be over 15.5 million in 2030 and 19 million in 2050 (Cracknell, 2010). Even in the face of funding pressures, this trend is bound to have implications for healthcare requirement and planning services (Caley & Sidhu, 2011). It also means that lifelong learning ideas need to be extended to include people living for many years beyond their working life.

f Political

The dimensions noted above have forced governments, and bodies such as professional associations, to take a more strategic view of LL and CPD. Throughout the Western world they have responded with reforms to education systems and qualifications as well as HRD (Eurydice, 2001). In the UK, and especially following the Fryer reports (NAGCELL, 1997, 1998), there were a range of initiatives to engender a culture of LL so that everyone is oriented towards skill development in order to respond to, and take advantage of, change. However, the recession since 2007 has created a degree of uncertainty for many in considering learning for the future. While forecasts suggest that there will be employment growth in high-skilled work, especially among managers and skilled professionals, and low-skilled work such as caring and personal occupations, there will be a decline in skilled and semi-skilled manual roles (UKCES, 2011b). It remains important for learners to gain qualifications and continue learning.

activity

Find out about the latest developments in LL policy in England at **www.excellencegateway. org.uk/node/57** and **www.lifelonglearningnetworks.org.uk**

For the Scottish strategy on lifelong learning, go to **www.scotland.gov.uk/Publications/ 2003/02/16308/17750**

For Wales, go to **http://cymru.gov.uk/topics/educationandskills/publications/circulars /learnerinvolvementstrategy/?lang=en**

For Northern Ireland, go to **www.delni.gov.uk/index/publications/pubs-sectoral/ skills-strategy-ni.htm**

Lifelong learning

Lifelong learning (LL) is a simple idea, even a tautology, that everyone learns throughout their lives. In some respects, the idea of LL is broad and all-encompassing, stretching to any aspect of life where we learn to do something different; understand ideas and learn facts, skills and so on. As Field (2006, p.2) states, LL 'covers pretty much everything – and rightly so'. Nevertheless, for the reasons we outlined earlier, LL has increasingly been seen as a requirement for participation in the knowledge society (Rohrbach, 2007) and as a contribution to social and economic well-being at home, in the community and at work.

The idea of learning throughout life has a long pedigree, especially among liberal-minded educationists, and during the last quarter of the 20th century and into the 21st, LL became a 'dominant and organizing discourse in education and training policy' (Green, 2002, p.611). One reason for this is what is referred to as the 'speed of change' argument (Tamkin, 1997), where LL is a way of responding to significant changes in the way work is practised, requiring new skills and knowledge. Beyond individuals, other terms such as 'learning companies', 'learning regions' and 'learning societies' (Coffield, 2000a), signalled the importance of learning as a way of coping with rapid change. Allied to this is the recognition that for economic success there is a need for people to reskill in line with the requirements of work or to aspire to move into more highly skilled work. Even those with basic skills seem to recognize the need for more learning rather than none (McQuaid et al., 2012). The importance of skills for productivity was recognized by the Leitch review (2006) that, crucially, argued that gaps in learning and skills were a principal reason for failure not only by organizations to compete in global markets but also for individuals to participate in economic activity. Even in recession, some employers continue to experience skills deficiencies which affect how they can function (UKCES, 2011c).

activity

Go to **http://employersurveys.ukces.org.uk** for the latest survey results on skills and employer perspectives on skills.

We can see how the LL movement embraces an economic imperative to compete globally as well as to enhance and widen participation and inclusion of greater numbers in the workforce. The latter is part of the social cohesion argument for LL where, through the acquisition of skills, individuals become more employable and are able to find work to match their talents, thereby contributing to and benefiting from social and economic prosperity. Further, they have the ability to manage their lives from the cradle to the grave – referred to as the life cycle argument for LL. As the UK population, in line with other populations throughout the world, becomes older, with many people living for many years beyond retirement, it is suggested that LL becomes even more necessary to prevent a waste of talent through economic and social exclusion (Schuller & Watson, 2009). However, and crucially, LL is mostly linked to opportunities within work for learning, and as has often been found, organizations may be more oriented towards profit and even cost reduction than learning and development (Riddell et al., 2009).

Models of lifelong learning

The broad view of LL finds much favour with writers and practitioners who have for many years taken a more humanist approach to learning and development. It is a model of LL that seeks to help people to participate in a free democracy, especially those who lack privileges in general education opportunities and other spheres of life. It is a model of emancipation and social justice (Schuetze & Casey, 2006), which can appear idealistic and utopian, although there are some clear influences of this model in policies that seek to support learning for disadvantaged communities. Schuetze and Casey identify two other models of LL that seek to enhance access and participation. These are a cultural model that aims to support individuals to seek fulfilment in life and self-realization and an open society model in which LL is concerned with the development of a learning system for those who want, and are able, to participate. As a contrast to each of these models, most policies relating to LL, while recognizing the wider meanings, tend to emphasize the importance of human capital development as part of an economic imperative for learning in the face of rapid technological advances and globalization of markets (Preston & Dyer, 2003). In reality, this narrows the focus and connects LL to NHRD agendas and models (see Chapter 1). This tends to see LL as an aspect of the VET system that is necessary to provide sufficient skills for a country to gain competitive advantage. The narrowness, as well as the prominence, given to the vocational slant often underlies some of the key debates around LL.

reflective question   To which of these models would you give prominence?

Skills and LL

The human capital model of LL underpins recent attempts in the UK to raise skill levels. For example, the Leitch review (2006) set 2020 as a target to achieve world leader status, benchmarked by the upper quartile of OECD figures. This would be indicated by:

- 95 per cent of working age adults achieving functional literacy and numeracy
- more than 90 per cent of workforce adults qualified to at least level 2 where feasible
- shifting the balance of intermediate skills from level 2 to level 3 and improving the esteem, quantity and quality of intermediate skills
- more than 40 per cent of the adult population qualified to level 4 and above.

Recent indicators suggest that the UK will have difficulty meeting the desire to move from low to intermediate skills but there is more likelihood of achieving high-level skills aspirations (UKCES, 2010). However, there are ongoing concerns about the ambitions of employers to pursue high-performance working based on a strategy to compete on high-valued-added products and services.

In Chapter 1, we set out the key principles of the National Qualifications Framework (NQF) and the Qualifications and Credit Framework (QCF) based on vocational qualifications (VQs). Vital to the acceptance of the frameworks is the use of qualifications as a measurement by proxy of skills in an economy, a process referred to as credentialism. An obvious criticism of using qualifications as a measurement tool is that it drives the system, in the sense that only qualifications count as learning. As Coffield (2000b, p.5) argued, learners become 'intent on increasing their credentials rather than their understanding'. In most cases, informal learning is more likely, especially for adults in the work context, and this is not always amenable to certification (see below). This divide is a product of the UK's cultural and historical tradition, which has valued thinking over doing. However, there is a growing move to remove this divide and create a more unified pathway for learners to progress in paths of their choice. For example, in 2004, the NQF was extended to include academic qualifications up to doctorate level, providing some clarity for those seeking to move from vocational education into higher education. This is seen as part of an agenda to widen participation in higher education and a contributor to social justice as well as economic competitiveness. However, there is still a need for universities and colleges to consider how they can develop the curriculum to make their programmes more relevant to those seeking a vocational education.

In the UK, Lifelong Learning Networks were established in 2005 to enhance progression opportunities for vocational learners, providing a bridge from vocational education to higher education, covering nearly all universities and colleges. A key activity of the network has been to set up progression agreements between institutions to allow recognition of credit for learning and transfer. It has also helped in the development of foundation degrees, which have been developed with employers and allow the combination of academic study and workplace learning, making them relevant to performance at work. These are mainly delivered in further education colleges but are validated by universities. Shaw et al. (2011) provide a range of examples of the work of Lifelong Learning Networks from 2005 to 2010, including mentoring non-traditional learners, enabling women to undertake engineering and widening participation.

Loking more widely in terms of lifelong learning across Europe, whilst each EU member state is responsible for its own education and training systems, Union- level policies are designed to support national actions and help address common challenges such as: ageing societies, skills deficits among the workforce, and global competition. These areas demand joint responses and countries can benefit from sharing experiences. One such response is the EU's policy and programme framework for lifelong learning (HRD in Practice 15.1). This approach recognizes that high-quality pre-primary, primary, secondary, higher and vocational education and training are fundamental to Europe's success. However, in a rapidly changing world, lifelong learning needs to be a priority; it is the key to employment, economic success and allowing people to participate fully in society.

<table>
<tr><td>

HRD in Practice

15.1

</td></tr>
</table>

The EC Lifelong Learning Programme: education and training opportunities for all

The European Commission's Lifelong Learning Programme enables people at all stages of their lives to take part in stimulating learning experiences, as well as helping to develop the education and training sector across Europe.

With a budget of nearly €7 billion for 2007 to 2013, the programme funds a range of actions, including exchanges, study visits and networking activities. Projects are intended not only for individual students and learners, but also for teachers, trainers and all others involved in education and training.

There are four sub-programmes which fund projects at different levels of education and training. Each have been set targets:

- Comenius for schools – should involve at least 3 million pupils in joint educational activities, over the period of the programme
- Erasmus for higher education – should reach a total of 3 million individual participants in student mobility actions since the programme began
- Leonardo da Vinci for vocational education and training – should increase placements in enterprises to 80,000 a year by the end of the programme
- Grundtvig for adult education – should support the mobility of 7,000 individuals a year involved in adult education by 2013.

For further information see http://ec.europa.eu/education/lifelong-learning-programme/index_en.htm

activity   Explore the EU's Grundtvig programme. What are its objectives? How does it aspire to meet these?

Human capital development, whether accredited or not, has been associated with a growth in average labour productivity (Mason et al., 2012). In the UK however, it is the supply of intermediate skills that has for several years been identified as a source of weakness. It is a weakness that successive governments do not seem to have addressed and one that prevents young people especially from entering the labour market (Unwin, 2010). Often, the focus has been on the mismatch in technical and craft jobs and the number of qualified adults when compared to France and Germany (National Skills Task Force, 2000). In the next few years, as public sector cuts result in fewer jobs, this mismatch takes on a spatial feature, where knowledge-based service jobs that require higher skills, may not be located where jobs are needed (Wright et al., 2010).

Intermediate skills are usually classified at level 3 in the NQF and include skills such as communications, innovation and problem solving, in addition to technical skills and personal attributes such as motivation, judgement, leadership and initiative. However, the precise meaning of intermediate skills will vary between occupations and sectors. This means that a term such as craft in one sector might be more or less complex compared to other sectors and be categorized at different levels in the NQF (Smeaton & Hughes, 2003). A crucial element in learning intermediate skills seems to be their development at work in a programme of structured learning. This immediately creates difficulties for those who do not have access to work contexts due to low educational attainment, a lack of basic skills and/or opportunities.

Of course, most learning and development is undertaken in a work context, although much of it is not accredited. In the UK, various surveys of employers' skills (NESS, 2006 and 2008) suggest that more than 60 per cent of the workforce receive training, mostly on-the-job. Most of it is concerned with improving skills or knowledge and there will be some connection to organization performance. This is most people's experience of LL and gives rise to Boshier's (1998) comment that LL is 'human resource development in drag'. However, this is not always the case and during the 1990s, some organizations began to provide employee-led development (ELD) schemes, which allowed employees to choose learning programmes that were not necessarily work related. Such attempts to stimulate adults to undertake learning have a long history in the UK (Corner, 1990). For example, Cadbury's provided support for non-work-related learning in the early 20th century. Perhaps the most well-known recent scheme is the Ford Motor Company's Employee Development and Assistance Programme (EDAP), developed in collaboration with trade unions in 1988, first in the US and then in the UK. Under the scheme, all employees are entitled to £200 a year for non-work-related learning and health/fitness sessions. The apparent success of this scheme, and growing enthusiasm for ideas like the learning company in the 1990s, saw a growth of such schemes in the UK and elsewhere (Lee & Cassell, 2009). Holden and Hamblett (1998) point to the assumption that ELD is a good thing based on a mutuality of interests between employers and employees, allowing the establishment of a learning culture at work. However, the idea that ELD can eventually link to organization success and competitive advantage is seen as problematic and avoids difficult considerations of how skills are formed and products and services specified and designed (Hamblett & Holden, 2000).

reflective question Suppose your employer offers you £200 for any non-work-related learning. What would be your reaction? To what extent might it increase your desire to learn at work?

While not all ELD schemes are collaboratively developed with trade unions, there is evidence that recognition of unions can lead to more effective HRD strategies (Green et al., 1999). Under the provisions of the Employment Act 2002, organizations can grant recognition to union learning representatives (ULRs), who can promote training and learning to union members and consult with employers on issues concerning training and learning. They can also establish learning agreements with employers to provide joint mechanisms for coordinating and monitoring learning activities. ULRs can also draw funding from a union learning fund (www.unionlearningfund.org.uk) provided by the government for projects to promote workplace learning. Wood and Moore (2005) completed a survey of union learning and found positive outcomes for unions and employers, although this mainly occurred where there were already cooperative relations between unions and management. Stuart et al., (2010) show how the Union Learning Fund helps unions set up training and learning committees with employers, which improves trust and relations during a recession. In recent years, partnerships between unions and employers have used learning activities to enhance employee engagement. For example, Merseytravel has a network of 28 ULRs who promote a learning agenda worked out with the company.

activity

Go to www.unionlearningfund.org.uk for details of the Union Learning Fund.

For more about the employee engagement initiative at Merseytravel, go to www.unionlearningfund.org.uk/case-studies/Merseylearnemployerengagement.cfm

Informal or non-formal learning

Most LL is recognized in formal terms; employees undertake training, students attend courses, apprentices complete qualifications and so on. However, a moment's reflection will soon reveal how much informal learning occurs, mainly through interactions with others on an everyday basis. Even on formal programmes, there is likely to be a great deal of interaction that is not strictly in line with the formal requirements but probably vital to it (Field, 2006). Personal learning acquired informally through practice, surprises and ambiguity in work are all part of the accumulation of experience. Such processes are also vital to LL more generally and this is becoming increasingly recognized. For example, in SMEs, informal learning – by exploring, experimenting, problem solving and mistakes – is now understood as a key feature of the world of entrepreneurs (CEML, 2002). Marsick and Watkins (1990, p.12) point to the need for informal learning to 'deliberately encourage' in order to make it more effective through processes such as mentoring, team working, providing feedback and trial and error working. They also highlight how much incidental learning occurs every day, although this is usually unconscious.

Eraut (2000, p.12) sees the term informal learning as too much of a catch-all label that covers all learning that is not formal, but the term is also confused with aspects of dress and ways of talking. He prefers the term non-formal learning to contrast with formal learning. He sets out three types of non-formal learning:

1 *Implicit learning*: learning that occurs without intention and awareness at the time it has taken place but becomes part of experience, used unconsciously in future events.

2 *Reactive learning*: learning occurs spontaneously in response to events, there might be awareness that learning has occurred but there is little time to consider this except through reflection.

3 *Deliberative learning*: learning from events is recognized through reviewing and reflecting on actions, and time is provided to allow this to happen.

These views of learning are seen as a source of tacit knowledge, which has a particular value for organizations in the process of creating knowledge (see Chapter 10). For example, Nonaka and Takeuchi's (1995) knowledge-creating model begins with tacit knowledge by individuals that is then expressed to others, although there are doubts about the degree to which tacit knowledge can be expressed (Beckett & Hager, 2002). Nevertheless, in many organizations where knowledge is essential to the production and provision of services, proactive efforts are being made to reveal knowledge from non-formal learning to provide new ways of doing things (Garvey & Williamson, 2002). Essential to this is knowledge sharing through reviewing and reflecting on experiences.

Review and reflection on experiences are often seen as key features of self-directed learning by adults who take responsibility for their own learning. Mezirow (1990), for example, sees critical reflection as a route to new ideas and transformative learning. This requires a challenge to assumptions so that new possibilities can be identified. Self-directed learning is mainly characterized by projects where the learning is owned and controlled by the learner. The individual chooses what to learn, when to learn and how, and for many people such choices are available both formally and non-formally, according to preferences. Increasingly, individuals gain access to learning programmes through online sources and e-learning packages (see also Chapter 9).

Professional work and CPD

Although relatively unknown until the 1960s, most professional associations now have a CPD policy on the basis that the knowledge professionals use, the tasks performed and the roles completed become dated (Gear et al., 1994). Some professional associations, such as the Law Society, have a mandatory policy on CPD which is a requirement of the Solicitors Regulation Authority. Solicitors registered as European Lawyers are required to complete a minimum of 16 hours a year on activities recognized as CPD. This approach is referred to as a sanctions model of CPD (Rapkins, 1995). Other associations, such as the Institute of Logistics and Transport, have a voluntary policy where the association suggests that members complete CPD but does not invoke sanctions against those who do not – referred to as a benefits model. As we show below, the model adopted is a reflection of the status of a profession and the degree of guardianship provided by the professional association. While there does appear to be some confusion around policies, implementation and how CPD is undertaken (Woodall & Gourlay, 2004), there is considerable pressure on professionals to undertake CPD.

In Western societies, professional life and status are key attractors and in the UK it is estimated that around 20 per cent of the workforce either hold or seek a professional qualification. Professionals have been considered vital to support growth, not only in services but also in manufacturing where professionals are considered necessary for achieving technological and productivity gains. While professionals can be found in all advanced societies performing similar work (Brecher, 1999), in the UK many professions have been a feature of life for over two centuries and some can trace their roots to pre-Enlightenment days. For example, law, medicine and the ministry have been termed the status professions, with their origins in medieval times as university disciplines to be studied by the sons of the aristocracy (Elliott, 1972). Since then, many areas of life have been professionalized and it is argued that this process has been a key contributor to the view of Britain as a meritocratic society (Perkin, 1989). Non-professionals who feel ignorant when faced with complex decisions in many aspects of their life seek out the services of those recognized as experts, this provides the economic basis for professionalism (Dietrich & Roberts, 1997). To arrive at fully-fledged professionalism this recognition of expertise can be followed by organization and institutionalization into professional associations (Witz, 1992). Over time, recognition of the need for particular kinds of expertise becomes more solid and grants power to those who have the credentials and command of the required knowledge to act and practise as professionals (Boreham, 1983).

reflective question

1 Is this explanation of professionalism one that matches the common understanding of those called professionals in modern life?
2 What would be meant by someone acting unprofessionally?

Freidson (2001) has presented an ideal type of professionalism composed of five interdependent elements:

1 specialized work that is grounded in a body of theoretically-based discretionary knowledge and skill, which is given special status
2 an exclusive jurisdiction created and controlled by occupational negotiation
3 a sheltered position within labour markets based on the qualifying credentials of the occupation
4 a formal training programme to provide qualifying credentials
5 an ideology that asserts a commitment to quality and doing good.

You can use these elements to assess various claims for professionalism. For example, Gold et al. (2003) examined the status of HRD professionals and showed that HRD had partial claims for professionalism; there was an emerging body of theoretical knowledge that underpinned practice, with a growing number of dedicated journals and a growing importance attached to learning at work, which assisted HRD professionals in establishing an occupational division from others. However, it still remained possible for anyone to claim the ability to practise HRD, that is, membership of the relevant professional association, the CIPD, did not grant a licence to practise.

In some respects, various professions, such as teaching and even HRD and HRM, have faced constraints and restrictions on how they practise as professionals. This may be due to limits in their authority, not only in relation to other professions or various control systems but also the shaping of the techniques of practice by outsiders who control the design of those techniques (Evans, 2008). In contests between experts, professional knowledge needs to provide a source of moral authority and CPD becomes essential (Bailey, 2011).

Professional knowledge

It should be clear from the above that knowledge plays a central role in professional work. Here it is customary to distinguish between what Eraut (2000) refers to as public knowledge versus personal knowledge. The former is knowledge that is explicit, communicable and provides the content of formal learning programmes that lead to certification and professional accreditation. It can also be formally stated as codified knowledge in abstract terms and abstraction distinguishes the professions from other groups (Abbott, 1988). Novices are accepted into the realm of a profession by proving their understanding of theories and models and their application within a range of practical situations. However, to progress from novice to expert requires learning within situations through practice and this is mostly achieved informally (Cheetham & Chivers, 2001) through building networks of contacts and finding support for ongoing knowledge development. As Durning et al. (2010) argue, for many years those in professional practice have often been faced with flux and challenge to their practice and this requires a spiral of knowledge development to sustain and enhance their expertise. As professionals add to their personal knowledge, it is accumulated as tacit knowledge which is highly situated, difficult to copy and, like all tacit knowledge, might even be difficult to talk about (Gourlay, 2006). As Eraut (2000, p.128) suggests, it 'cannot be accomplished by procedural knowledge alone or by following a manual'. Schön (1983) highlighted tacit knowledge as an aspect of reflection-in-action, which is the ability of professionals to respond spontaneously to surprise through improvisation, without thought. He contrasted such knowing with technical rationality, composed of formulable propositions within a distinct product of a body of knowledge aimed at problem solving, predictability and control.

These distinctions between codified and tacit knowledge do provide something of a complication for professionals and professional associations seeking to develop policies and requirements for CPD. Clearly, because abstract knowledge can be presented in codified form, through books, journal articles, websites and so on, it forms the basis of educational programmes for professional qualification and CPD. However, tacit knowledge is gained through practice, informally within various contexts, usually through interaction with others, such as clients and fellow professionals. The difficulty here is recognizing or articulating that learning has occurred. However, for most professionals, it is the most common form of learning. As we shall see below, CPD presents professional associations and their members with a number of dilemmas and paradoxes (Megginson & Whitaker, 2007).

CPD policies and practices

In order to protect and advance the claims for expert status, most professional bodies have developed CPD policies for their members to undertake following the completion of the initial qualification that allows entry to the profession. Madden and Mitchell (1993, p.12) have defined CPD as:

> The maintenance and enhancement of the knowledge, expertise and competence of professionals throughout their careers, according to a plan formulated with regard to the needs of the professional, the employer and society.

As we can see from this definition, there are two key features of CPD. First, it is a planned and formulated process, and second, the focus is almost entirely on individual professionals. As we will see, on both counts these features have been subjected to some criticisms in recent years.

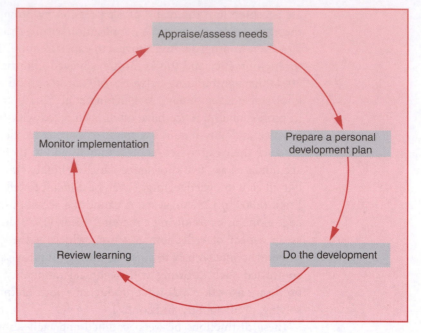

Figure 15.1 A CPD model

Most professional associations seek to help their members manage their CPD by providing guidance on planning, implementing and monitoring. In this way, CPD models are similar to the systematic approaches to training based on a series of steps (Grant et al., 1999). Figure 15.1 provides a CPD model showing a typical series of steps.

Although shown as a cycle, the usual starting point is an appraisal and assessment of needs. Because much professional work occurs in relationships with clients, it is difficult for those outside the relationship to make judgements about needs. Where performance is difficult to observe and is knowledge-based, it is difficult to impose performance management processes such as appraisal and assessment from the outside (Reilly, 2005). It is therefore suggested that professionals should take responsibility to appraise and assess themselves. Of course, this also provides the potential for distortion in judgements. Also, many professionals work in organizations where, as part of a performance management system, they may be appraised and assessed by line managers for a variety of purposes including development. For example, Redman et al. (2000) examined appraisal in an NHS hospital and found strengths in personal development planning along with setting objectives, although there was some inconsistency in implementing the appraisal process. Nevertheless, professional associations are likely to focus on their members as individuals and make them responsible for their CPD. For example, the Institute of Chartered Accountants in England and Wales (ICAEW) requires its members to make a yearly CPD declaration which members can complete online. Members have to choose from two statements:

1 Confirming that they have reviewed training and development needs and have acted to address requirements or

2 Claiming exemption from CPD if retired or on a career break.

It is left to members to work out what needs should be met, but the ICAEW suggests various ways to stay up to date such as:

- Reading the ICAEW email alert –containing updates and news
- Attending a workshop, conference, seminar or webinar
- Reading a book or journal, such as a faculty publication
- Participating in the ICAEW community
- Arrange an informal training session with a colleague

It is also left to members to identify how the needs are met by identifying particular inputs; we refer to this as the input approach to CPD. The ICAEW offers the following suggestions, which are not untypical for CPD:

- Technical reading
- Learning at work
- Meetings with experts
- Conferences
- Courses and seminars
- Online learning
- Workshops with peers
- Reading magazines, newspapers and journals
- Registering for updates and email alerts.

Attending courses and seminars would also be typical for CPD, although the ICAEW does not specify the achievement of a certain number of hours or points, nor a requirement to attend a certain number of courses or seminars. However, other professional associations are more prescriptive. Depending on the power of the professional association, members may be required to complete a record of what inputs they identify and complete as part of their CPD. For example, the Law Society operates on an annual cycle and each solicitor returns a completed training record, an example of which is shown in Table 15.1. Notice the way the record requires the specifying of particular inputs and conforms to a standard view of professional learning, where CPD is seen as a way of topping up the initial period of compulsory education in qualifying as a professional. The record becomes a demonstration that CPD is being taken seriously (du Boulay, 2000).

This approach to managing CPD through the recording of inputs undertaken can be seen as a feature of control by professional associations. Taylor (1996), for example, suggests that monitoring is a feature of most CPD schemes and can become a pointless exercise, where the end becomes the recording, rather than the use, of inputs by professionals in their work. This also raises a crucial issue for any HRD activity, the extent to which it is transferred to work practice. Research by Muijs and Lindsay (2008), which sought to consider the evaluation of CPD, found that most evaluation focused on participant satisfaction with a programme with less attention given to the use of new skills or value for money.

Various studies of CPD point to the difficulties of transfer in CPD which limits impact. For example, Bolton (2002, p.322) studied chiropractors' views of CPD and found little impact on practice. CPD was not seen as 'instrumental in improving the care of patients', even though they had positive views on what they

Table 15.1   Example of a CPD training record

Date	Training activity (for course attendance, indicate course title, provider name and reference otherwise state how activity was undertaken)	Comments	Number of hours credit
10.11.03	Attendance at update on Revenue Law (inhouse) 123/ABCD video and discussion	Provided a review of the provisions in the budget which need to be taken into account when advising on personal investments and will planning	2 hours and 10 minutes
12.12.03	Time spent on building portfolio of evidence for NVQ in management	Prepared and gathered evidence in respect of units on budgeting and recruitment interviews	3 hours
06.01.04	Attended course run by Institute of Taxation on legal aspects of taxation practice	Of great value to see the legal issues from a non-lawyer's point of view. This will help in preparing a new approach to putting across some of these issues	4 hours
29.01.04	Delivery of course on case management at inhouse accredited course	Formal presentation, leading of dicussions, feedback on case studies worked through by delegates	2 hours and 15 minutes

Source: Solicitors Regulation Authority, available at www.sra.org.uk/solicitors/cpd/solicitors.page, accessed 6 May 2012.

did in CPD. Allery et al. (1997) studied 100 GPs and consultants and found that organized education only accounted for one-third of changes to practice and that most of these occurred through a combination of organizational and social factors. In a review of impact evidence in dentistry, Eaton et al. (2011) found very few robust studies and so there were significant difficulties in making an assessment of CPD outcomes.

HRD in Practice 15.2 shows an example of how one professional, a leading solicitor in Leeds, took control of his own CPD.

HRD in Practice 15.2

CPD in the legal profession

I am a Leeds-based lawyer with a long interest in and involvement with management. Like most lawyers, I am probably intelligent enough to know when I need external input or knowledge and arrogant enough to either ignore it or persuade myself that I can manage without it. Against that background, the hardest part of engaging in the CPD process leading to a Masters was acknowledging my need for such education and the considerable value it would add.

I have been delighted with the value that has been added both to my firm and to me personally by every stage of the programme; not only has the process been stimulating and thought-provoking, it has generated clear and tangible results in my firm in the form of real differences of approach and insights, which have informed and improved management processes.

An example of the direct application of the learning gained would be the impact of my investigation of leadership as a concept and the development of the theories surrounding it. Before beginning my exploration of this field, I would have put myself very much towards the 'command' style of leadership, although not quite at the extreme of that model. I am now a convert to and advocate of 'distributed leadership', and have already rolled out my first open space technology session and am exploring further ways of mining the pool of talent available within my firm.

Source: Richard Marshall, Managing Director, Lupton Fawcett, Leeds (personal communication)

A criticism of input-driven approaches to CPD is that they pay insufficient attention to the context of practice and the ability and motivation of professionals to make attempts to change their practice. Eraut (2001, p.8) considered many models of CPD to be one-dimensional because of the difficulty in considering their application and continued learning. A further difficulty occurs for professionals who work in organizations that prioritize organizational needs against those of individual professionals and learners more generally (Jones & Fear, 1994).

Because there are restrictions with an input-driven approach to CPD, some models have also incorporated the outcomes of learning. This allows professionals to justify that learning has taken place through an impact on practice. This also allows CPD to be widened to include different forms of learning and how such learning might be shared with others as well as enhancing performance (Grant, 1999). E-learning is now recognized as a key aspect of CPD (Pawlyn, 2012) and one interesting development by a number of professional associations is to support CPD by the creation of online communities.

activity

The CIPD has created a number of professional communities as well as providing downloads of tools and podcasts at **www.cipd.co.uk/community**

The ICAEW has created a Community area containing blogs, forum areas and a private network at **www.ion.icaew.com**

The shift towards outcomes does seem to have widened the scope of CPD and also recognizes that professional learning can occur within and from practice, including informal events and in collaboration with others (Cordingley et al., 2003). Thus, working with a mentor or coach and developing learning contracts can all be included. The onus is now on proving that learning has occurred. There is more attention to reflection, perhaps in learning logs or diaries as part of a process of continuous review as well as recording (Gibbons, 1995). We can see here the important influence of Kolb's (1984) learning cycle and Schön's (1983) notion of reflection-on-action and even critical reflection (Gold et al., 2002).

Nevertheless, despite the extension towards outcomes, there still remain problems, given the complexity of professional work. For example, many professionals achieve outcomes by working with others, so it becomes impossible to attribute outcomes achieved to a single professional, although CPD schemes focus on individual professionals as the learners. A further difficulty arises in who judges what counts as CPD. Professional associations are the main arbiters of the meaning of CPD for their members and this can create restrictions. For example, in a study of professional learning in context, Thorpe et al. (2004, p.12) found that surprise, contradiction and ambiguity were not uncommon in informal learning at work. One recently qualified professional learned that, in contrast to her training, the work was more hands-on. with work piling up and little time to reflect. The importance of such features is that they are all part of the personal learning that we identified earlier as being crucial to working as a professional, which goes beyond the theories and procedures (Eraut, 2000), although it might not be recognized by professional associations as CPD. Gold et al. (2007) explored what they called the missing perspective in CPD, how professional learning occurs in the course of practice. Their study of solicitors in a law firm highlighted the significant and powerful ways in which professionals learned in their practice, which not only added to their knowledge and understanding, both explicitly and tacitly, but also generated new ideas and new understandings that provided an immediate and relevant form of CPD. The study chimes with what Webster-Wright (2009) refers to as authentic professional learning, based on how the lived experience of professionals requires learning to occur in practice and this has to take into account the support and constraints of a working context. This also has the potential to widen the consideration of CPD beyond the traditional focus on individual professionals to consider how CPD needs to be viewed as a collective endeavour, as shown by Gold and Thorpe (2009). Hardy and Rönnerman (2011) also suggest a move towards professional learning that considers a focus on situated and specific practice. Professionals need to understand how their actions are enabled and constrained by the conditions of their work and that this can be achieved by completing learning projects with others.

summary

○ LL has become a key idea in education and training policy, stimulated by the speed of change in knowledge-intensive work and technology. Professionals need to undertake CPD to preserve and advance their status as professionals.

○ There are significant and interconnected technological, economic and social changes that underpin the arguments for LL and CPD.

○ LL has increasingly been seen as a requirement for participation in the knowledge society as well as a contribution to social and economic well being where learning stretches to any aspect of life.

○ LL underpins attempts to raise skill levels through credentialism, measured by qualifications gained at different levels.

○ In the UK, there are difficulties of a vocational/academic divide in skills and qualifications, which policies are seeking to address.

○ In the workplace, most LL is connected to improving skills or knowledge for organization performance but there are schemes that allow employees to undertake non-work-related learning.

○ Informal and tacit learning are now recognized as vital features of LL.

○ Professionals are considered vital in advanced societies and are recognized for their expertise because of the complexity of decisions faced by clients and consumers.

○ Professional knowledge is composed of codified and abstracted knowledge and its application, which results in tacit knowledge.

○ Most professional bodies have developed policies for CPD for their members in order to protect and advance claims for professional status.

○ CPD is generally understood as a planned and formulated process of learning with an individual focus but there is growing interest in practice-based learning and collective learning.

discussion questions

1 Why should we all become lifelong learners?
2 Should LL be work related?
3 Who should be responsible for LL?

4 Can informal learning be recognized more fully?
5 Can we compel professionals to complete CPD?
6 How can professionals demonstrate that they are up to date in their knowledge and skills?

further reading

Coffield, F. (1999) Breaking the consensus: lifelong learning as social control. *British Educational Research Journal*, **25**(4): 479–99.

Kennedy, A. (2005) Models of continuing professional development: a framework for analysis. *Journal of In-service Education*, **31**(2): 235–50.

Su, Y-H (2011), Life-long learning as Being: the Heideggerian perspective. *Adult Education Quarterly*, **61**(1): 57–72.

Yeo, R.K. (2008) How does learning (not) take place in problem-based learning activities in workplace contexts? *Human Resource Development International*, **11**(3): 317–30.

references

Abbott, A. (1988) *The System of Professions*. Chicago: University of Chicago Press.

Allery, L.A., Owen, P.A and Robling, M.R. (1997) Why general practitioners and consultants change their clinical practice: a critical incident study. *British Medical Journal*, **314**: 870–74.

Bailey, M. (2011) Policy, professionalism, professionality and the development of HR practitioners in the UK. *Journal of European Industrial Training*, **35**(5): 487–501.

Beck, U. (1992) *Risk Society: Towards A New Modernity*. London: Sage.

Beckett, D. and Hager, P. (2002) *Life, Work and Learning*. London: Routledge.

Blanden, J. and Machin, S. (2008) Up and down the generational income ladder in Britain: past changes and future prospects. *National Institute Economic Review*, **205**: 101–17.

Bolton, J. (2002) Chiropractors' attitudes to, and perceptions of, the impact of continuing professional education on clinical practice. *Medical Education*, **36**: 317–24.

Boreham, P. (1983) Indetermination: professional knowledge, organization and control. *Sociological Review*, **31**: 693–718.

Boshier, R. (1998) Edgar faure after 25 years (pp.3–20). In J. Holford, P. Jarvis and C. Griffin (eds) *International Perspectives on Lifelong Learning*. London: Routledge.

Brecher, T. (1999) *Professional Practices: Commitment and Capability in a Changing Environment*. London: Transaction.

Cabinet Office (2011) *Open Doors, Breaking Barriers: A Strategy for Social Mobility*. London: Cabinet Office.

Caley, M. and Sidhu, K. (2011) Estimating the future healthcare costs of an aging population in the UK: expansion of morbidity and the need for preventative care. *Journal of Public Health*, **33**(1): 117–22.

Castells, M. (1996) *The Rise of the Network Society*. Oxford: Blackwell.

CBI (2011) *Winning Overseas: Boosting Business Export performance*. London: Confederation of British Industry.

CEML (Council for Excellence in Management and Leadership) (2002) *Joining Entrepreneurs in their World*. London: CEML.

Cheetham, G. and Chivers, G. (2001) How professionals learn in practice. *Journal of European Industrial Training*, **24**(7): 247–92.

CIPD (2010) *Learning and Talent Development*. London: Chartered Institute of Personnel and Development.

Cipriano, P. (2012) The importance of knowledge-based technology. *Nursing Administration Quarterly,* **36**(2): 136–46.

Coffield, F. (2000a) Introduction: a critical analysis of the concept of a learning society (pp.1–38). In F. Coffield (ed.) *Different Visions of a Learning Society*. Bristol: Policy Press.

Coffield, F. (2000b) The structure below the surface: reassessing the significance of informal learning (pp.1–11). In F. Coffield (ed.) *The Necessity of Informal Learning*. Bristol: Policy Press.

Cordingley, P., Bell, M., Rundell, B. et al. (2003) *The Impact of Collaborative CPD on Classroom Teaching and Learning: How Does Collaborative Continuing Professional Development (CPD) For Teachers of the 5–16 Age Range Affect Teaching and Learning?* London: EPPI-Centre.

Corner, T.E. (1990) *Learning Opportunities for Adults*. London: Routledge & Kegan Paul.

Cracknell, R. (2010) *The Ageing Population.* London: House of Commons Library Research.

Dietrich, M. and Roberts, J. (1997) Beyond the economics of professionalism (pp.14–33). In J. Broadbent, M. Dietrich and J. Roberts (eds) *The End of the Professions?* London: Routledge.

du Boulay, C. (2000) From CME to CPD: getting better at getting better? *British Medical Journal,* **320**: 393–94.

Durning, B., Carpenter, J., Glasson, J. and Watson, G.B. (2010) The spiral of knowledge development: professional knowledge development in planning. *Planning Practice & Research,* **25**(4): 497–516.

Eaton, K., Brooks, J., Patel, R., Batchelor, P., Merali, P. and Narain, A. (2011) *The Impact of Continuing Professional Development in Dentistry: A Literature Review*. London: The General Dental Council.

EC (European Commission) (1995) *Teaching and Learning: Towards the Learning Society*. Brussels: European Commission.

EC (European Commission) (2001) *A Memorandum on Lifelong Learning*. Brussels: European Commission.

Edwards, R. (2001) Researching the rhetoric of lifelong learning, *Journal of Education Policy,* **16**(2): 103–12.

Elliott, P. (1972) *The Sociology of the Professions*. Basingstoke: Macmillan.

Enyon, R. and Helsper, E. (2011) Adults learning online: Digital choice and/or digital exclusion? *New Media & Society,* **13**(4): 534–51.

Eraut, M. (2000) Non-formal learning and tacit knowledge in professional work. *British Journal of Educational Psychology,* **70**: 113–36.

Eraut, M. (2001) Do continuing professional development models promote one-dimensional learning? *Medical Education,* **35**: 8–11.

Erikson, R. and Goldthorpe, R. (2010) Has social mobility in Britain decreased? Reconciling divergent findings on income and class mobility. *The British Journal of Sociology,* **61**(2): 211–23.

Eurydice (2001) *National Actions to Implement Lifelong Learning in Europe*. Brussels: Eurydice.

Evans, L. (2008) Professionalism, professionality and the development of education professionals. *British Journal of Educational Studies,* **56**(1): 20–38.

Field, J. (2006) *Lifelong Learning and the New Educational Order*. Stoke on Trent: Trentham Books.

Freidson, E. (2001) *Professionalism*. Cambridge: Polity Press.

Garvey, R. and Williamson, B. (2002) *Beyond Knowledge Management*. Harlow: Pearson.

Gear, J., McIntosh, A. and Squires, G. (1994) *Informal Learning in the Professions*. University of Hull: Department of Adult Education.

Gibbons, A. (1995) A personal approach to CPD. In S. Clyne (ed.) *Continuing Professional Development*. London: Kogan Page.

Gold, J., Holman, D. and Thorpe, R. (2002) The role of argument analysis and story-telling in facilitating critical thinking. *Management Learning,* **33**: 371–88.

Gold, J., Rodgers, H. and Smith, V. (2003) What is the future for the human resource development professional? A UK perspective. *Human Resource Development International,* **6**(4): 437–56.

Gold, J., Thorpe, R., Woodall, J. and Sadler-Smith, E. (2007) Continuing professional development in the legal profession: a practice-based learning perspective. *Management Learning,* **38**(2): 235–50.

Gold, J. and Thorpe, R. (2009) Collective CPD, professional learning in a law firm (pp.30–46). In D. Jemielniak and J. Kociatkiewicz (eds) *Handbook of Research on Knowledge-Intensive Organizations*. Hershey PA: IGI Global.

Gourlay, S. (2006) Towards conceptual clarity for 'tacit knowledge': a review of empirical studies. *Knowledge Management Research and Practice,* **4**: 60–9.

Grant, J. (1999) Measurement of learning outcome in continuing professional development. *Journal of Continuing Education in the Health Professions,* **19**: 214–21.

Grant, J., Chambers, E. and Jackson, G. (eds) (1999) *The Good CPD Guide: A Practical Guide to Managed CPD*. Sutton, London: Reed Business Information.

Green, A. (2002) The many faces of lifelong learning: recent education policy trends in Europe. *Journal of Education Policy,* **17**(6): 611–26.

Green, F., Machin, S. and Wilkinson, D. (1999) Trade unions and training practices in British workplaces. *Industrial and Labor Relations Review*, **52**(2): 179–95.

Hamblett, J. and Holden, R. (2000) Employee-led development: another piece of left luggage? *Personnel Review*, **29**(4): 509–20.

Hardy, I. and Rönnerman, K. (2011) The value and valuing of continuing professional development: current dilemmas, future directions and the case for action research. *Cambridge Journal of Education*, **41**(4): 461–72.

Holden, R. and Hamblett, J. (1998) Learning lessons from non-work related learning *Journal of Workplace Learning*, **10**(5): 241–50.

Jones, N. and Fear, N. (1994) Continuing professional development: perspectives from human resource professionals. *Personnel Review*, **23**(8): 49–60.

Kolb, D. (1984) *Experiential Learning*. Englewood Cliffs, NJ: Prentice Hall.

Lee, B. and Cassell, C. (2009) Learning organizations, employee development and learning representative schemes in the UK and New Zealand. *Journal of Workplace Learning*, **21**(1): 5–22.

Leighton, P. (2011) The Legal Education and Training Review (LETR), 2011–2012. *The Law Teacher*, **45**(3): 361–64.

Leitch, S. (2006) *Prosperity for All in the Global Economy: World Class Skills*. London: HM Treasury.

Madden, C.A. and Mitchell, V.A. (1993) *Professions, Standards and Competence: A Survey of Continuing Education for the Profession*. University of Bristol: Department of Continuing Education.

Marsick, V. and Watkins, K.E. (1990) (eds) *Informal and Incidental Learning in the Workplace*. London: Routledge.

Mason, G., O'Leary, B. and Vecchi, M. (2012) Certified and uncertified skills and productivity growth performance: Cross-country evidence at industry level. *Labour Economics*, **19**(3): 351–60.

McNair, S. (2009) *Demography and Lifelong Learning*. London: NIACE.

McQuaid, R., Raeside, R., Canduela, J., Egdell, V. and Berry, C. (2012) *Engaging Low Skilled Employees In Workplace Learning*. London: UKCES.

Megginson, D. and Whitaker, V. (2007) *Continuing Professional Development*. London: CIPD.

Mezirow, J. (1990) *Fostering Critical Reflection*. San Francisco: Jossey-Bass.

Muijs, D. and Lindsay, G. (2008) Where are we at? An empirical study of levels and methods of evaluating continuing professional development. *British Educational Research Journal*, **34**(2):195–211.

NAGCELL (1997) *Learning for the 21st Century*, available from www.lifelonglearning.co.uk/nagcell, accessed 26 July 2012.

NAGCELL (1998) *Creating Learning Cultures: Next Steps in Achieving the Learning Age,* available from www. lifelonglearning.co.uk/nagcell2, accessed 26 July 2012.

National Skills Task Force (2000) *Skills for All: Research Report from the National Skills Task Force*. London: DfEE.

NESS (National Employers' Skills Survey) (2006) *National Employers' Skills Survey 2005*. Coventry: Learning and Skills Council.

NESS (National Employers' Skills Survey) (2008) *National Employers' Skills Survey 2007*. Coventry: Learning and Skills Council.

Newell, S., Scarbrough, H. and Swan, J. (2009) *Managing Knowledge Work,* 2nd edn.. Basingstoke: Palgrave.

Nonaka, I. and Takeuchi, H. (1995) *The Knowledge-creating Company*. New York: Oxford University Press.

OECD (Organization for Economic Co-operation and Development) (1996a) *Lifelong Learning for All*. Paris: OECD.

OECD (Organization for Economic Co-operation and Development) (1996b) *The Knowledge-based Economy*. Paris: OECD.

Pawlyn, J. (2012) The use of e-learning in continuing professional development. *Learning Disability Practice*, **15**(1): 33–37.

Perkin, H. (1989) *The Rise of the Professional Society: England Since 1880*. London: Routledge.

Preston, R. and Dyer, C. (2003) Human capital, social capital and lifelong learning: an editorial introduction. *Compare*, **33**(4): 429–36.

Rapkins, C. (1995) Professional bodies and continuing professional development. In S. Clyne (ed.) *Continuing Professional Development*. London: Kogan Page.

Raptis, D., Mettler, T., Tzanas, K. and Graf, R. (2012) A novel open-source web-based platform promoting collaboration of healthcare professionals and biostatisticians: A design science approach. *Informatics for Health and Social Care*, **37**(1): 22–36.

Redman, T., Snape, E., Thompson, D. and Ka-Ching Yan, F. (2000) Performance appraisal in an NHS hospital. *Human Resource Management Journal*, **10**(1): 48–62.

Reilly, P. (2005) Get the best from knowledge workers, *People Management*, **29** September: 52–3.

Riddell, S., Ahlgren, L. and Weedon, E. (2009) Equity and lifelong learning: lessons from workplace learning in Scottish SMEs. *International Journal of Lifelong Education*, **28**(6): 777–95.

Rohrbach, D. (2007) The development of knowledge societies in 19 OECD countries between 1970 and 2002. *Social Science Information*, **46**(4): 655–89.

Roscoe, J. (2002) Continuing professional development in higher education. *Human Resource Development International*, **5**: 3–10.

Scase, R. (1999) *Britain Towards 2010: The Changing Business Environment*. London: ESRC.

Schön, D.A. (1983) *The Reflective Practitioner: How Professionals Think in Action*. London: Maurice Temple Smith.

Schuetze, H. and Casey, C. (2006) Models and meanings of lifelong learning: progress and barriers on the road to a learning society. *Compare*, **36**(3): 279–87.

Schuller, T. and Watson, D. (2009), *Learning Through Life*. London: NIACE.

Shaw, J., Wise, J. and Rout, A. (2011) *Research in the Lifelong Learning Networks*. York: Lifelong Learning Networks National Forum.

Smeaton, B. and Hughes, M. (2003) *A Basis for Skills: Investigating Intermediate Skills*. London: Learning and Skills Development Agency.

Stewart, T.A. (1997) *Intellectual Capital: The New Wealth of Organizations*. New York: Doubleday.

Stuart, M., Cook, H., Cutter, J., and Winterton, J. (2010) *Assessing The Impact Of Union Learning And The Union Learning Fund: Union And Employer Perspectives*. Leeds: Leeds University Business School.

Tamkin, P. (1997) Lifelong learning: a question of privilege? *Industrial and Commercial Training*, **29**(6): 184–86.

Taylor, N. (1996) Professionalism and monitoring CPD: Kafka revisited. *Planning Practice and Research*, **11**(4): 379–89.

Thorpe, R., Woodall, J., Sadler-Smith, E. and Gold, J. (2004) Studying CPD in professional life. *British Journal of Occupational Learning*, **2**(2): 3–20.

Tuckett, A. and Aldridge, F. (2011) Tough time for adult learners. *Adults Learning*, **22**(9), 9–11.

UKCES (2010) *Ambition 2020: World Class Skills and Jobs for the UK*. London: UK Commission for Employment and Skills.

UKCES (2011a) *Towards Ambition 2020: Skills, Jobs, Growth*. London: UK Commission for Employment and Skills.

UKCES (2011b) *Working Futures 2010–2020*. London: UK Commission for Employment and Skills.

UKCES (2011c) *UK Employer Skills Survey 2011*. London: UK Commission for Employment and Skills.

Unwin, L. (2010) Learning and working from the MSC to New Labour: young people, skills and employment. *National Institute Economic Review*, **212**(1): R49-R60.

Webster-Wright, A. (2009) Reframing professional development through understanding authentic professional learning. *Review of Educational Research*, **79**(2): 702–39.

Witz, A. (1992) *Professions and Patriarchy*. London: Routledge.

Wright, J., Brinkley, I. and Clayton, N. (2010) *Employability and Skills in the UK: Redefining the Debate*. London: The Work Foundation.

Wood, H. and Moore, S. (2005) *An Evaluation of the UK Union Learning Fund: Its Impact on Unions and Employers*. London Metropolitan University: Working Lives Research Institute.

Woodall, J. and Gourlay, S.N. (2004) The relationship between professional learning and continuing professional development in the UK: a critical review of the literature (pp.98–111). In J. Woodall, M. Lee and J. Steward (eds) *New Frontiers in HRD*. London: Routledge.

Graduates and Graduate Employment

Rick Holden, Shakiya Nisa, Crystal Ling Zhang and Niki Kyriakidou

Chapter learning outcomes

After reading this chapter, you should be able to:

- Identify significant trends in the UK graduate labour market
- Understand certain tensions in terms of the supply of and demand for graduates
- Assess claims that graduates may increasingly be under-utilized
- View the transition from university to work as problematic
- Locate interest in graduates and graduate jobs within ideas about the knowledge economy, human and social capital

Chapter outline

Introduction
The graduate labour market
The utilization of graduate labour
Graduate employability
Graduates and the knowledge economy
Summary

Introduction

When discussing the contents of this chapter we asked ourselves if we knew of any country in the world where the number of graduates as a proportion of the working population was declining. We could think of none. Indeed, all the evidence, empirical and anecdotal, suggests considerable growth, leading to a key question: are graduates the new vanguard of HRD? The number of students around the globe enrolled in higher education is forecast to more than double to 262 million by 2025 (Maslen, 2012). In Finland, 70 per cent of young people enter higher education (HE) and in several other OECD countries (e.g. New Zealand, Poland) the figure exceeds 50 per cent. The current Europe 2020 strategy has a target for 40 per cent of Europe's young people to have a higher education qualification by the end of this decade (European Commission, 2011).

All this is powerful testimony to the prevailing assumption that graduates are a desirable societal asset. Indeed, we would go a step further and suggest that the dominant view held by governments internationally is that more graduates equals greater economic prosperity. European social and economic policy, for example, is predicated on the assumption that increased skill levels as a result of education and training hold the key to success of Europe in terms of global competition (European Commission, 2011). However such a virtuous scenario is not without its critics. There is an important body of research and argument which questions some of the assumptions that underpin policies of higher education expansion. Some of the main questions include:

- Is the continued expansion of HE justifiable on principally economic grounds?
- Is there increasing evidence of graduate unemployment and under-employment?
- What evidence is there of inequalities within graduate labour, perpetuating traditional class or ethnic divisions?
- Might the transition into employment be increasingly troublesome for a large number of graduates year on year?
- What implications are there for the very notions of graduateness and graduate jobs if the expectations and aspirations inculcated in the process of HE turn out to be at odds with reality?

Subsequent sections of this chapter pick up these issues. A clearer picture of the graduate labour market and developing trends is a useful starting point.

The graduate labour market

In the mid-1950s in most European countries, including the UK, the proportion of graduates was less than 5 per cent. However, expansion of the university sector has seen this proportion rise significantly. In the UK throughout the 1990s and 2000s, the overall numbers of students in HE rose sharply, driven by a mixture of aggressive recruitment by some institutions and, in the mid 2000s, by public policy seeking to widen and expand university entry. In 1999 there were 334,594 accepted applicants. Ten years later in 2009 there were 481,854, an increase of 44 per cent (Figure 16.1).

Interestingly, while Figure 16.1 indicates a substantial increase in the numbers of students within HE in the UK, OECD (2011) data show Britain slipping down the league table in terms of its production of graduates; from third highest to fifteenth among top industrialized nations for the proportion of young people graduating. The UK now trails higher education systems in, amongst others, Australia, Denmark, Iceland, Italy, and Slovakia.

Alongside the substantial increase in the number of new graduates available to recruiters, year on year, their composition has also changed radically. This relates to government policies for widening participation in HE.

activity

Conduct a straw poll among colleagues on your course. How many are new entrants into HE, in the sense that none of their immediate family have a degree? Note the social characteristics, that is, family background, ethnicity, age and so on, of any new entrants.

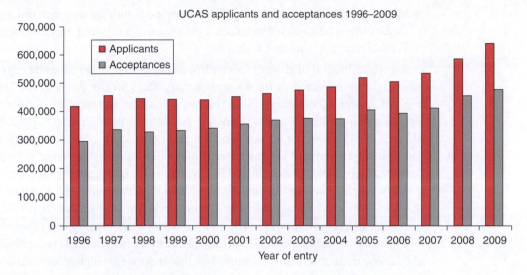

Figure 16.1 A decade of applicants and acceptances

Source: UCAS (2011)

The following points highlight the changed, and changing, profile of graduates in the UK:

- Although considerable inequities persist (see also Chowdry et al., 2010) young people from all socio-economic backgrounds are much more likely to gain a degree today as compared to 15 or 20 years ago. HESA statistics indicate that 30 per cent of today's graduates are students from socio-economic groups 4, 5, 6 and 7 (HESA, 2012).

- HE is a major success story for ethnic minorities. They represent a higher proportion of graduate output relative to their share of the population. Research suggests that British Indians were the largest ethnic minority group in UK universities in 2007–08 at 3.3 per cent. This compares to 2.7 per cent of the total population of 18–24-year-olds. They were followed by black or black British Africans (3.2 per cent) who have almost tripled their university presence in the last 12 years. British Bangladeshi and British Pakistani students continue to be the most under-represented groups within UK universities (HESA, 2012).

- Historically, women have been under-represented in Higher Education. However, in 2011, 57 per cent of graduates were women (HESA, 2012) It is projected that this proportional increase in participation on behalf of women will strengthen further.

- Graduation in the UK is no longer the almost exclusive preserve of the under-25s. One in five of new graduates are now over 25 years of age (HESA, 2012), many of whom study part-time. While the number of full-time students has increased substantially, the number of part-time students (at undergraduate level) has more than doubled (HESA, 2012).

- Increasingly, graduates emerge from new universities (formerly Polytechnics) which deliver more vocationally oriented courses such as accountancy, graphic design, information technology and nursing.

● Whilst this provides a glimpse of the changing profile of students and graduates it cannot be assumed that such a profile carries forward into employment. We will return to this theme shortly.

Any introduction of student fees and/or increase in charges made by universities might be expected to have a dampening effect on the demand for HE. In the UK, where such changes have recently been introduced, statistics for 2012 do indicate a decline of approximately 5 per cent in young person applications (UCAS, 2012). However, establishing the main reason for such a decline is difficult. Employer demand for graduates is likely to be as much a factor as levels of fees. Also, it remains unclear if the UK Government's new funding regime (which penalises high-charging universities who cannot recruit sufficient numbers with AAB 'A' level grades) may result in further reductions of intake. This said, the overall evidence from both the UK and elsewhere is of a strong *underlying* trend of increased participation in HE. What may be more questionable is the ability of the labour market to fully accommodate this increase in higher level skills. It is to the theme of graduate employment that we turn now.

Graduate employment

In February 2012, the Daily Mail ran this headline:

Shocking truth about graduate unemployment: They have the same chance of being out of work as a school leaver with one GCSE

(http://www.dailymail.co.uk/news/article-2104986/Shocking-truth-graduate-unemployment-chance-work-school-leaver-GCSE.html#ixzz1xs8WPYjO)

However such reports need to be treated with some caution. It is important, firstly, to make a distinction between unemployment and under-employment. We will explore the latter in more detail shortly. Secondly, the evidence over the years does not support a picture of large-scale graduate unemployment.

HESA first destination statistics suggest graduate unemployment (at the time surveyed) has averaged at around 8 per cent over the last six years (HESA, 2012). Figure 16.2 illustrates first destination statistics for two contrasting disciplines: a traditional degree subject (history) and a more vocationally oriented course of study (business and management).

A flaw with the data presented above is that it is drawn from survey data six months after graduation. Increasingly there is evidence to suggest that graduate career paths may take some years to unfold. A period of one or two years in temporary employment or travelling is increasingly common. Important research funded by the ESRC takes this into account by assessing graduate employment some years after graduation. The evidence suggests a high percentage of graduates in full-time career related employment (Purcell et al., 2005).

Looking at graduate employment from the perspective of demand for graduates a similar, generally positive, picture emerges. Whilst the Association of Graduate Recruiters (AGR, 2009) reported a recessionary impact upon graduate recruitment (most notably in banking and finance) other organizations openly state that its demand for graduates has been unaffected by any economic downturn.

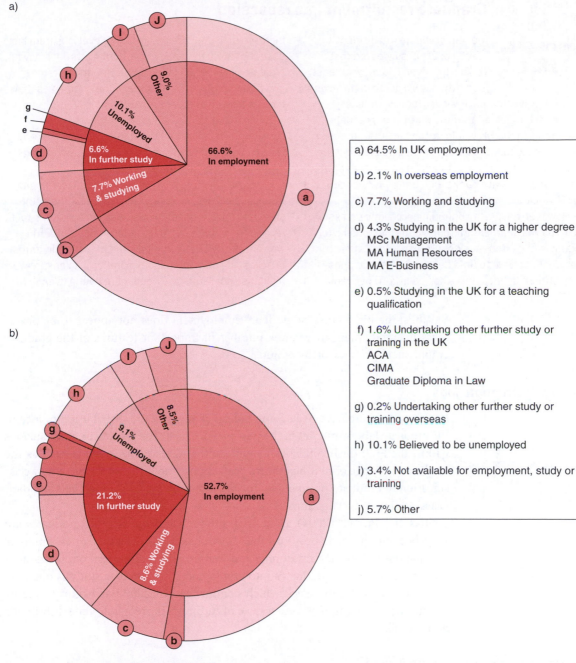

a) 64.5% In UK employment

b) 2.1% In overseas employment

c) 7.7% Working and studying

d) 4.3% Studying in the UK for a higher degree
MSc Management
MA Human Resources
MA E-Business

e) 0.5% Studying in the UK for a teaching qualification

f) 1.6% Undertaking other further study or training in the UK
ACA
CIMA
Graduate Diploma in Law

g) 0.2% Undertaking other further study or training overseas

h) 10.1% Believed to be unemployed

i) 3.4% Not available for employment, study or training

j) 5.7% Other

Figure 16.1 a) Business and Management Studies Graduates 2011
b) History Graduates from 2011

Source: What do Graduates do? 2012

Graduate recruitment in a recession

HRD in Practice 16.1

The AGR graduate recruitment survey in 2009 suggested that 'the party's over ... for now at least' (see http://www.onrec.com/news/news-archive/the-partys-over-for-now-at-least).
The report indicated that the number of graduate vacancies in the UK would decline in 2009, the first time since 2003, with most employers blaming the economic downturn. The financial sector appeared to be hardest hit, with banks expecting a 28 per cent cut in vacancies.

However, despite a continuing economic recession, 2012 paints a rather different picture. Regionally, for example, data from the West Midlands indicates an upturn. According to Grad Central, a West Midlands recruitment agency, there has been 'a 10 per cent increase in the number of graduate-level jobs from last year, with more than half these coming through newly created roles'. Yell, Coca-Cola Enterprises, Marston's and National Express are some of the companies that have increased graduate recruitment.

Importantly also, some large recruiters have consistently bucked any trend to reduce numbers. At the start of 2012 BP indicated that it was increasing its graduate recruitment by 50 per cent, thereby creating nearly 250 vacancies annually. According to Emma Judge, BP's head of graduate recruitment, the significant rise is down to business units wanting to recruit 'the brightest young minds in the UK ... 2011 was one of the strongest years in our history in terms of accessing new areas for exploration ... to ensure we maximise our return, we need more young talent.'

Whilst the big picture of graduate employment does not appear to be one of mass unemployment there are a number of important features of the graduate employment profile worthy of note.

Changing graduate jobs

Importantly, there have been some radical changes in the distribution of jobs in the graduate labour market in the past two decades. The growth in graduate jobs within the IT industry has been significant, and also within fields such as the media and a range of new healthcare professions. Table 16.1 describes a new classification of graduate occupations (occupations are based on the 1990 Standard Classification of Occupations).

Elias and Purcell (2004) argue that although the majority of graduates are absorbed into graduate positions the growth has happened among new graduate occupations rather than traditional and well-established modern ones. Research into the transition of graduates into employment and further study is ongoing. A project called Future track which commenced in 2006 has begun to report its findings. See http://www.hecsu.ac.uk/futuretrack_research_reports.htm for more details.

An uneven employment landscape?

Three other features of the graduate employment landscape are worthy of note:

Graduate jobs and gender

Even though more women are going to university than ever before it is men who fare better in terms of employment, rising to higher levels of seniority and earning more than their female counterparts (see also Purcell & Elias, 2006; Allen, 2011).

Table 16.1 Classification of graduate jobs

Type of occupation	Description	Examples
Traditional graduate occupations	The established professions, for which, historically, the normal route has been via an undergraduate degree programme	Solicitors Medical practitioners HE, FE and secondary education teachers Biological scientists/biochemists
Modern graduate occupations	The newer professions, particularly in management, IT and creative vocational areas, which graduates have been entering increasingly since educational expansion in the 1960s	Chartered and certified accountants Software engineers, computer programmers Primary school and nursery teachers Authors/writers/journalists
New graduate occupations	Areas of employment to which graduates have increasingly been recruited in large numbers; mainly new administrative, technical and caring occupations	Marketing and sales, advertising managers Physiotherapists, occupational hygienists Social workers, probation and welfare officers
Niche graduate occupations	Occupations where the majority of incumbents are not graduates, but within which there are stable or growing specialist niches which require HE skills and knowledge	Entertainment and sports managers Hotel and accommodation managers Midwives, nurses Buyers (non-retail)
Non-graduate occupations	Graduates are also found in jobs that are likely to constitute under-utilization of their HE skills and knowledge	Sales assistants Filing and record clerks Routine laboratory testers Debt, rent and cash collectors

Source: Elias and Purcell (2004)

Ethnicity

Minority ethnic degree graduates also fare worse in the labour market than their white counterparts (HEA, 2008). Initial unemployment is higher and for some groups much higher (e.g. male Pakistani and Chinese). In part this is a reflection of poorer performance at university. Fewer minority ethnic students gain first or upper second class degrees than white students. In particular black students are more likely to get a third or lower class degree. Such graduates may face a double whammy. Edwards (2011) argues that some employers are failing to recognize diversity, favouring white, middle class characteristics. Important differences are also evident within BME groups. Although having a degree dramatically reduces Bangladeshi and Pakistani women's unemployment rates, they are much less likely than Indian or white women to obtain professional or managerial employment (Bagguley & Hussain, 2007). Explanatory factors relate to a range of cultural factors including perceptions of what is appropriate employment post-graduation and close family ties impacting mobility.

Old vs. new universities

There is some evidence that the type of university can influence labour market prospects. As with ethnicity there is a higher incidence of initial unemployment amongst graduates of new universities and who subsequently perform less well in the labour market. The explanatory factors are not straightforward. Unsurprisingly, given different entry requirements, the traditional university sector recruits the more able students. This has an impact on the quality of degree attained. Some employers still regard a degree from an old university as preferable to that from a new university, despite the latter's more vocational ethos. Furthermore, students from BME communities and lower socio-economic groups are more likely to attend lower status institutions (David et al., 2008).

Finally in this section we note the new flavour of the month in terms of graduate employment: starting a business. In 2004, the government established the National Council for Graduate Entrepreneurship, with a key policy objective to encourage more graduates to consider starting their own business. Start-Up Britain, launched in 2012, provides start-up loans for young people aged 18–24. Many universities have created units to encourage and support start-ups and entrepreneurship features increasingly in the curriculum. Whilst considerable activity is evident, available data suggests the numbers remain relatively small, about 4 per cent of the graduate labour market (see also Nabi et al., 2010).

activity

Employment prospects from your university

Aston University have one of the highest graduate employment rates in the UK. At over 80 per cent it is well above the national average. Data from Leeds Met University indicates the top five graduate jobs are primary teachers, nurses, advertising and marketing executives, sales reps and agents and secondary teachers.

Compare and contrast the employment prospects data from your university/course with that illustrated above.

In sum, the graduate labour market contains many contrasts and some apparent contradictions for understanding supply and demand. What is clear is that for those involved in it – graduates and recruiters – it has been something of a roller coaster ride during the 1990s and 2000s. The radical expansion in supply has triggered a heightened level of debate about its impact on the labour market. On the face of it the increased supply of graduates appears to have been successfully absorbed into the labour market. However, this requires rather closer scrutiny and it is to the theme of graduate utilization that we now turn.

The utilization of graduate labour

We begin this section with another extract from the press:

> One in three graduates is in a job that does not require a degree (Financial Times, 24.11.2006)

On the face of it this does not sit comfortably with the research evidence noted above from the likes of HESA and Prospects. It raises a question about the size of Elias and Purcell's fifth category and about the nature of work in the category reflecting most growth (new graduate jobs). More fundamentally it raises questions about the nature of what constitutes a graduate job and a graduate career.

The blue-chip corporate milk round still flourishes, albeit with notable changes in the use of web-based technology to attract and engage graduate recruits. The promise is much as it has been: exciting, challenging, stretching jobs that build fully on HE. Some years ago a report for the Centre for Research in Employment and Technology argued that employers wanted graduates to 'hit the ground running' (Rajan et al., 1998), implying a virtuous circle of existing capability, utilization and opportunity for further development. Little has changed. HRD in Practice 16.2 illustrates the recruitment of graduates at Hallmark Cards plc.

Hallmark Cards plc

HRD in Practice 16.2

Hallmark are the UK's leading greeting cards publisher, representing 60 per cent of the Hallmark International business. Since 2007 Hallmark have recruited a small number of newly-qualified graduates each year. The scheme operates over two years; each graduate spending approximately eight months in three distinct parts of the business. This is seen as fundamental in terms of ensuring that graduates develop a thorough understanding of the commercial and product sides of the business. The emphasis is on stretching the graduate from day one. Departmental managers have to apply to host a placement and produce clear plans as to how the graduate will be deployed to ensure contribution and ongoing development. According to Melanie Colwill (Learning & Development Manager) graduate recruits are seen as the 'succession pipeline for the future'. Whilst small in numbers there is 'massive commitment and support from the company'. It is not unusual for the most senior managers in the company to be involved in recruitment and to act as mentors for the graduate recruits.

Three recent graduates highlight aspects of the work and challenges they have faced:

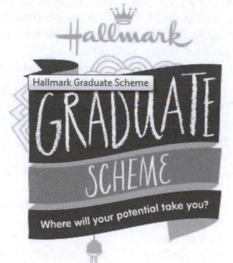

Sarah, referring to her first placement as an Assistant Product Manager (APM), notes that: 'as graduates we do have to try and accomplish more in a short space of time. As an APM I wanted to complete the placement "owning" some of new product development processes ... more normally this might take 12 months or so.'

Sophie, 2 weeks into her placement as an E Commerce Product Manager, points to the upcoming launch of a new series of online products: 'I have a key role in that ... on my first day it sounded quite daunting ... but I'm starting to see how it will all join up.'

Ray, now into his third placement notes: 'for my second placement they put me in charge of a team of 130 people ... and I thought how on earth do I do this! ... but this is Hallmark saying "we'll give you the opportunity, you can say you can rise to it, figure out how you can do it and go for it".'

Source: Hallmark, 2012

Research lends some testimony to such scenarios. Holden and Hamblett (2007), for example, report that graduates are clearly drawing considerably on their degree and being stretched well beyond it in their first year of working. One graduate, an engineer, notes in interview:

> By the second week there were new jobs coming in and I was soon onto new jobs and starting from scratch and with quite a bit of responsibility ... thinking about it now [six months after joining the firm] I certainly didn't expect to be doing anything like this within the first year of starting ... I am being asked to try and achieve a very stiff challenge.

On the basis of research conducted in 22 different organizations, Hesketh (2009) identifies how graduates bring added value in a number of ways including, for example, a capacity to articulate innovations and the ability to cope with the changes this brings about. Additionally, Hesketh highlights a general consensus among employers that graduates contribute in the region of three times their salaries.

Nationally, the Knowledge Transfer Partnerships programme (each partnership employs one or more recent graduates to work on a project, which is core to the strategic development of the business) annually reports a significant bottom line impact as a result of the recruitment of graduates (www.ktponline.org.uk). Further supporting data is evident from studies of graduate placements and internships. For example, Atfield et al. (2009) indicate that when these tasks utilize the skills of the person on placement effectively, the placements contributed to the development of skills both of the person on placement and within the organization generally.

Herein, though, lies the key issue of effective utilization. There is evidence that sits less comfortably with the sort of scenarios and evidence noted above. If we first consider HRD in Practice 16.3.

Waiting on tables

HRD in Practice 16.3

In a study of the utilization of hospitality graduates, Holden and Jameson (1999) note the experience of one organization that has recruited one or two graduates into its growing vegetarian restaurant business. One of the partner's discusses Lucy, the most recent graduate recruit: 'She's one of the few people who actually works across all the restaurants ... she's also the best person I've ever employed. She's quite stunning really, she has a real understanding of what we're about as a company.'

This is a glowing testimony for Lucy, in many ways the star of recent graduate recruits. But the same partner is acutely aware that, for all that, Lucy actually spends 70 per cent of her time waiting on tables.

He comments: 'My problem is this ... this is a fairly small company, growing but still small. How much can you afford to have people doing, you know, project-type stuff ... They've got a certain level of intelligence, they've reached a certain maturity and they've got a bit of background knowledge ... what worries me with graduates is how much of that knowledge they ever get to apply in something like this.'

Of course, the context here is clearly that of a small business and there is some evidence to suggest that such problems may be more acute within this sector than within large organizations (see also Chapter 3). In a large research project Mason (2002) explored the impact of higher education on high-skills utilization in the retailing, computer services, and transport and communications industries. In all three industries graduates had been taken on in increasing numbers in recent years, partly in order to meet growing demands for analytical ability, generic skills and technical knowledge, and partly as a result of larger numbers of graduates applying for relatively low-paid, undemanding jobs. Mason found evidence of graduate substitution for non-graduates.

Similarly, research undertaken by the LSE's Centre for Economic Performance (Green and Zhu, 2010) indicated that the proportion of graduates in non-graduate jobs had risen sharply since 1992. The research only covered graduates over the age of 25 to allow those surveyed time to settle into their careers, but nevertheless it showed that for male and female graduates, the proportion in non-graduate jobs was approximately one-third. The authors conclude that the evidence provides a sharp counter to the government's arguments to increase the supply of graduates. More recently, research into the Australian labour market (Carroll & Tani, 2011) suggests that a substantial proportion of the tertiary-educated labour force is under-utilized relative to their level of education. The authors define graduate under-utilization as a job for which a sub-degree qualification would suffice. They found that 26 per cent of graduates were under-utilized immediately after course completion and 15 per cent were under-utilized three years later, although this varied considerably between subgroups.

Research such as that illustrated above provides an important critical perspective on the graduate utilization debate but without necessarily providing any insight into reasons. An interesting study into the experience of graduates working as call centre operators found that they themselves had made active choices to engage in non-graduate work following graduation for reasons related to lifestyle and other choices (Blenkinsopp & Scurry, 2007). The same study also found that such choices can lead to changes in career aspirations and also a situation where graduates become stuck in non-graduate jobs because of their initial decisions on graduation.

Clearly we have a somewhat ambiguous picture. The evidence from the work of Green and Zhu, for example, seems to be at odds with that from Elias and Purcell where, even in the categories of new and niche graduate jobs, over 80 per cent are reported to be using their skills. Part of the ambiguity might be explained by what is meant by using one's degree as compared to using one's skills (see below). Further conceptual ambiguity is reflected in an ongoing failure to pin down just what a graduate job is. We conclude that there are sufficient empirical data to at least question the prevailing orthodoxy of justifying an expansion of HE on the basis that the knowledge economy is a reality; a reality requiring an ever-increasing supply of graduates. We turn now to a closely related theme, that of the employability of graduates in the context of their capabilities on completion of their HE.

Graduate employability

A fundamental question within any exploration of the graduate labour market is whether it is the role of HE to create 'oven ready' graduates (Brown & Hesketh, 2004). Influenced by the voice of the employer, a set of issues has emerged that refer to matters under a banner of the skills agenda. What skills do new graduates need as they leave behind their three or four years within HE and begin to take a significant step down a career pathway? This question has occupied the thoughts of successive governments (firmly wedded to the notion of the knowledge economy absorbing an increasing supply of graduates) and vice chancellors up and down the land (seeking to indicate how their particular institution will best add value). In other words, successful absorption into the labour market is simply about matching skills acquired through their degree programme with those required and demanded by employers.

It is important to make a clear distinction between graduate employment and graduate employability. According to the Paul Redmond – President of theAssociation of Graduate Careers Advisory Services, 'Employability is a highly dynamic concept. It denotes a progression and a certain amount of self-sufficiency' (Papadatou, 2011). The CBI (2009) defines employability skills as: 'a set of attributes, skills and knowledge that all labour market participants should possess to ensure they have the capability of being effective in the workplace – to the benefit of themselves, their employer and the wider economy.'

Analysis of several years of employer surveys (see, for example, CBI, 2009) suggests the desired employability skills for graduates fall into four broad areas:

- Self reliance skills (proactive, willingness to learn)
- People skills (team working, interpersonal skills, customer orientation)
- General employment skills (problem solving, business acumen, IT literacy)
- Specialist skills (languages, technical skills)

Figure 16.3 illustrates what Hallmark are looking for in their graduates.

Importantly also, research (see for example, Hogarth et al., 2007; Gallup, 2010) increasingly highlights that many employers prefer graduates from sandwich degrees or who have done work placements, because they have gained practical experience and have a better idea about what the world of work has in store for them.

The 2000s saw a decade of initiatives to encourage HE institutions to do more by way of enhancing graduate employability. For example:

- Centres of Excellence in Teaching and Learning (CETLs): Higher Education Funding Council CETLs commenced in 2004. Their purpose was 'to reward excellent teaching practice and to invest in that practice further in order to increase and deepen its impact across a wider teaching and learning community' (HEFCE, 2004/5, para.21). Sheffield Hallam's CETL, for example, was 'Embedding, Enhancing and Integrating Employability' and sought to embed and integrate a coherent range of employability features in its degree programmes to benefit all students. (For a review of the CETL initiative see Butcher et al., 2011).

Figure 16.3 What Hallmark look for in their graduates

Source: Hallmark, 2012

● Personal effectiveness skills: few undergraduate degree programme are now without some sort of complementary curriculum which engages with personal, professional, work-related skills and development. Higson and Bullivant (2006) provide an interesting account of an Aston University initiative to encourage students to reflect on their employment experience, while Major (2006) describes the provision of career information to enhance the employability of undergraduate travel and tourism management students at Northumbria University.

Higher education graduates recruited in the last 3–5 years have the skills required to work in respondent's companies

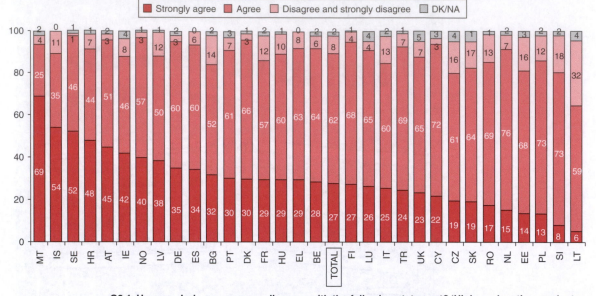

Q3.1. **How much do you agree or disagree with the following statement? 'Higher education graduates recruited in the last three to five years have the skills required to work in my company'.**
Base: companies that have recruited higher education graduates, % by country

Figure 16.4 Do graduates have the skills companies require?

Source: FlashEurobarometer/Gallup (2010)

The UK Government Higher Education White Paper - Students at the Heart of the System (BIS 2011) reinforces its commitment to preparing students for the job market.

Employer dissatisfaction?

Despite an ongoing debate that graduates are not ready for the world of work, recent research evidence in fact suggests that large-scale employer dissatisfaction with the employability of graduates may be something of a myth. For example, research for the EC by Gallup in 2010 indicated that a large majority (89 per cent) of employers who had recruited graduates in the past five years agreed that these graduates had the skills required to work in their company (Figure 16.4).

Of course, one interpretation may be that the decade of employability initiatives is clearly having an impact. Interestingly, graduates themselves seem rather more critical than their employers! Research within the engineering sector in the UK suggests that only 43 per cent of graduates believe their university course had equipped them with the skills they needed for work. Concerns identified were a lack of real world applications and, as noted above, the importance of placements/internships to fill the gaps identified in the degree programme (The Engineer, 2012). Interestingly, Brennan (2008), summarizing the REFLEX (Flexible Professional in the Knowledge Society) project, notes that UK graduates were much less likely to believe they were well prepared to perform their first destination graduate jobs than their European counterparts.

One further question is worthy of note at this point. Against a background of a process of harmonization of European HE systems since the 1999 Bologna Declaration (see also European Commission, 2011), some research suggests there is a change in how employers perceive the value of a first degree as an entry qualification into the labour market. Little (2008), for example, cites studies that report German employers' concerns that those with only a bachelor's degree will need more in-house training. This would shift responsibility for such work-related training from universities to the employers themselves. Some support for a shift in emphasis is evident from the Gallup research (above) which indicates that a substantial minority of employers (35 per cent) consider a masters degree would provide 'a better fit' (p.9). In the context of the UK, however, Little questions if continuing international pressures towards the master's degree could in fact lead to a 'devaluing of the bachelor's degree' within the UK (p.209). She concludes that such shifts are less likely, or at least will be slower, in the UK. This is because of a stronger influence from the professions within the UK; a first degree in the UK is more likely to be followed by relevant employment and continuing development aligned to professional bodies. This said, Little acknowledges the likelihood of a heightening tension in the perceived responsibilities between HE and employers in terms of initial work readiness.

Questioning the skills agenda

Whilst graduate employability has become an influential discourse it is important to note the concerns of those who see fundamental flaws in this skills agenda. Critically it appears to lack any explanatory purchase in terms of employment outcomes (see Mason et al., 2006). Specifically in terms of particular demographics, Wilton (2011) suggests that labour market disadvantage still appears evident 'regardless of the extent to which graduates develop employability skills during their undergraduate studies' (p.85).

Holmes (2001, 2006, 2011) identifies conceptual and practical problems with the dominant orthodoxy evident in much of current HE practice; what he calls the 'employment as possession approach' (2011, p.14). For the employer, and indeed the student/graduate, the plethora of lists and frameworks creates uncertainty and ambiguity:

> How can any employer make sense of the multitude of lists of skills in order to make a decision between candidates who come from different institutions? How is any graduate to know whether the skills they 'possess' are the 'right' ones? (p.9)

Of greater value, Holmes maintains, is the notion of identity and how and in what ways a student/graduate on their journey into post-HE employment, might acquire a sense of graduate identity. How does a graduate 'get into and get on within an organization' (Holmes, 2006, p.2)? In this 'graduate employability as process' approach the message is 'develop ways of presenting your claim on the identity (of being a graduate worthy of employment) in such a way that it stands a good chance of being affirmed by those who make the selection decisions on job applications you make' (Holmes, 2011, p.14). Such arguments resonate with the views of Angot et al. (2008) who, on the basis of research with graduates within French companies, question orthodox notions of the construction of 'professional identity'. Some of these identities, the authors suggest, are 'born of cynicism and disillusion' engendered by their experience. Similarly, Holden and Hamblett (2007), on the basis of their research with graduates at various points over their first year in employment, maintain that the situational context of learning about self for new graduates in employment renders much of the well-meaning personal and career development-type programmes within degree programmes of questionable relevance (see also Transition below).

Transition

Much of the literature relating to graduate employment has tended to focus on initial entry into the labour market (recruitment and employability). However, Jenner (2008) argues that there has been little focus on the evolving nature of the relationship or the systems that support it. Shaw and Fairhurst (2008) argue that graduate development managers need to re-examine their development schemes to ensure that they meet not only the needs and expectations of the organization but also of the individuals for whom they are designed. The context for this suggestion is the notion that graduates in the latter half of the 2000s and the early 2010s might be regarded as a new generation of graduates: Generation Y, or millennials (see also ILM, 2011). Shaw and Fairhurst discuss and illustrate how McDonald's has adjusted and tuned its graduate development programme to meet the perceived needs and attributes of these Generation Y graduates; and will Generation Z – children born post-2002 and labelled the virtual, or the silent, generation on the account of how much time they will spend online – require further adjustments and changes (see also Chapter 17)?

Clearly tensions exist in terms of the employability, development and utilization of graduates. These are poorly understood for one very obvious reason. There has been insufficient research looking closely at the real experience of graduates in supposedly graduate jobs across different sectors and over a sufficiently long period of time to enable meaningful insight. The transition from HE to work is difficult and complicated. Of course, we are not the first to make such an observation. Arnold and McKenzie Davey (1992) and Connor and Pollard (1996) have previously suggested a transition characterized by expectation mismatch with respect to the nature of work, line manager support, training and development and career management. Jenner (2008) suggests that transition models highlight the pivotal role of good support on joining an organization and the need for new graduates to be 'socialized' to their new surroundings. HRD in Practice 16.4 provides an indication of how one major graduate recruiter endeavours to manage what it acknowledges as difficult.

Kentz Engineers and Constructors

HRD in Practice 16.4

Kentz Engineers and Constructors is an international company with approximately 7,000 staff in Europe, Africa, the Middle East and Asia. The company provides a range of engineering and construction services. The oil and gas markets are prominent in the work of the company. According to its website (**http://www.kentz.com/careers/who-we-hire.aspx**) the company places considerable value on its graduate recruits, wanting them to succeed and achieve their career goals.

In an article describing Kentz's approach to graduate deployment, O'Donnell et al. (2008) note

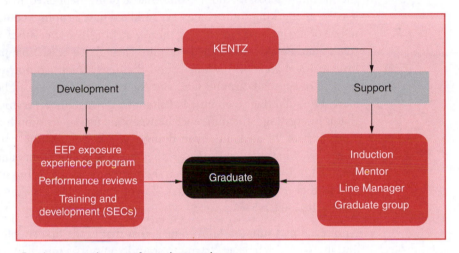

Development and support for graduate engineers

Source: O'Donnell et al. (2008).

the following model used to plan and guide graduate development.

The authors argue that the Kentz model enables the company to help engineering graduates rapidly 'perform as junior engineers' and be ready to 'step up into design engineer, field engineer or project engineer'. For example, the provision of mentoring is critical as regards socialization but also in respect of 'agreeing objectives and standards with the mentee' and more broadly 'monitoring progress through work rotations'.

The case of Kentz reflects what might be considered the prevailing orthodoxy in terms of how the transition from HE to work might best be managed. The award-winning NHS Graduate scheme adopts a largely similar model. Specialist training is at the heart of the scheme, both work-based and via formal quailfications. The trainee's primary relationships in the workplace are with their Placement Managers and Programme Manager, together with their Mentor (see also www.institute.nhs.uk/images//documents/Graduate/Graduate_Scheme_Handbook/2010%20intake%20Handbook%20April%2011.pdf).

However, research by Fineman and Gabriel (1996), Holden and Hamblett (2007) and Jenner (2008) suggests that, even within the likes of Kentz and the NHS, the reality may be somewhat different to the rhetoric. Jenner highlights the contested nature of organizational life. In a case of graduate development within British Aerospace, she shows how graduate training, development and career management are best understood as discursive practice; shared understandings about the nature of work are constructed through a communication nexus of key stakeholders. Holden and Hamblett (2007) rely on the testimony of five graduates in different employment settings to tell their stories of the ups and downs of the transition process over their first year of employment. Two extracts are presented below; one from a graduate working in the hospitality industry and one from a graduate engineer:

> I'm starting to develop my manager voice as well, which is quite good, it gets the meaning across…Another one that actually happened just three days ago, I was checking some rooms. As I walked past a room, I couldn't believe it, one of my guys was just sitting there watching TV. Everybody knows that that's unacceptable and I made it quite clear that I wasn't happy, and that little incident went all the way round the department, so now everyone is on a bit of eggshells around me…But the porters…they are all Polish…had started to build their own little Polish mafia downstairs, so trying to control that is interesting…the difference between me five or six months ago where I was sort of 'hi guys, how you doing?', you know, shaking hands and all that, now 'what are you doing?' if they are not on the floors and all that I want to know why, why I have seen them in the smoking room fifteen times and all that in the last ten minutes, do you know what I mean? (Holden & Hamblett, 2007, p.536)

> And certainly I suppose I did come across that in the first couple of months and it was just people are trying to sound you out as much as you're trying to sound them out…I had one engineer and he tried to put some simple filing in my tray even though we've got a filing clerk. I'd handed something to him to sign as checker and he knows for a fact that it just needed to be put in the tray for the filing clerk to file it away and he purposely came and sat it on my in-tray, so I picked it up, walked back to his desk and put it in his in-tray and said, 'I'm not the f*****g file clerk.' And walked off and you could see he was like, 'well actually yeah this lad does stand his ground as well, we won't bother him'…But he was just doing it to test the waters and see…after that happened, another engineer said 'My, that took some guts doing that.' I said, 'Why, I'm not his filing clerk.' He said, 'I know but if you hadn't done it he'd have kept doing it. You're obviously learning quick!' (Holden & Hamblett, 2007, p.552)

reflective question   Contrast the lived experience of these two graduates with your exposure to personal and career development. Do they sit together comfortably?

Holden and Hamblett (2007) use the terms fragmentation and cohesion to help explain the lived reality of the transition into work over a period of a year. They note that from time to time such activities generate problems, moments of fragmentation are experienced as mistakes or misunderstandings occur. New experiences are encountered and as a result the role, and the ways to perform effectively in role, are assimilated and they move towards cohesion. The words of Joanna, another one of the graduate respondents, provide the authors with an insightful way of thinking about transition:

> She talks about learning 'from the inside'. We find this a particularly pregnant phrase. It suggests that 'things' look different 'from the inside'; that an 'outsider' might never really be made privy to the heart of the matter. We would sum the point thus: 'Conventions' are much bigger inside than they appear from the outside. (p.574)

From current research with a group of graduates from Hallmark (Holden, 2012), respondents talked about learning 'local understandings' in relation to their different teams in different placements. Particularly important was the need to 'tune into' how their team viewed them as 'the graduate' and manage this appropriately vis à vis their own graduate identity. There is no simple solution to such practice although all referred to the value of the regular 'catch-up' (review) sessions with HR and their buddies (graduates from the year before) to help them cope with and address the fragmentation and discomfort experienced from time to time.

In sum, and reflecting back to the influential graduate employability agenda, the research highlighted above suggests we should be somewhat sceptical about HE's role in equipping students with employability skills, or that neatly packaged induction programmes within the workplace can really address issues of power, identity and a sense of feeling at home. The reality of learning about the job and learning about self are such that the HE curriculum and managers with responsibility for new graduates need a more nuanced, less mechanistic approach to assisting the HRD process for their graduate recruits.

Graduates and the knowledge economy

reflective question

Consider these two quotes:
- 'Graduates are the generators of business in five or ten years time' (head of global HR consulting, PricewaterhouseCoopers, *Financial Times*, 8.8.08)
- 'We need to reform higher education … too many graduates struggle to find jobs or quality work.' (Androulla Vassiliou, European Commissioner for Education, Culture, Multilingualism and Youth, 2011)

Is the seemingly inexorable rise of a graduate labour force a driver of economic growth or simply a response to such growth?

The questions posed above take us to the heart of a debate about the supply of, and demand for, graduate labour. We have noted the significance of ideas and policies around graduate employability. These are underpinned by an even more significant set of assumptions relating to the idea of the rise of a knowledge economy; assumptions influencing the policies of advanced economies in terms of the expansion of higher education and accompanying rhetoric around competitiveness, opportunity, mobility and equality. Briefly, the orthodox argument unfolds as follows. A knowledge economy is developed around a more professional (and thus educated) workforce. It has witnessed a fundamental shift away from a set of traditional industries dominated by unskilled and semi-skilled work to one where most work is knowledge work. The growth in jobs within the knowledge economy is for jobs requiring high levels of education and skill. Knowledge has replaced capital as a key element in production and thus graduates, with their high levels of knowledge and skill, are in considerable demand.

Governments bolster the economy needs more graduates perspective with powerful human capital arguments (investment in skills through education and training; see, for example, Becker, 1964), noting the evidence of a graduate earnings premium. Thus, in terms of HRD and the knowledge economy, graduates are indeed at the vanguard; they are a critical resource to enable the knowledge economy to grow and flourish. National policies are clearly influenced by such assumptions. For example, the influential Browne Report (2010) for the UK Government, whilst proposing important changes to the funding of HE, maintains that

> Higher education matters because it drives innovation and economic transformation. Higher education helps to produce economic growth, which in turn contributes to national prosperity...Employing graduates creates innovation, enabling firms to identify and make more effective use of knowledge, ideas and technologies. (p.14)

However, a closer look at this whole thesis suggests that reality may fall some way short of the hype. And, in terms of the focus of this chapter, as soon as one begins to question the pervasiveness of the knowledge economy, a whole bundle of questions appears in relation to the graduate labour market and graduate employment. Where better to see the knowledge economy emerging in its full glory than in the USA, the most advanced industrial economy in the world? Yet this claim sits uneasily with the data. In relation to the USA and drawing on US Bureau of Labour Statistics, Brown and Hesketh (2004, p.47) note that no more than 30 per cent of all Americans are in occupations requiring a bachelor's degree: 'For every job requiring a degree there are two that do not.' They also note an extract from one of George Bush's government initiatives to develop the workforce:

> Most new jobs will arise in occupations requiring only work-related training (on-the-job training or work experience) even though these occupations are projected to grow more slowly. This reflects the fact that these occupations accounted for about 7 out of 10 jobs in 2000. (Brown and Hesketh, 2004, p.47)

Others raise similar concerns and questions. In their searching examination of the nature of modern day work Bolton and Houlihan (2009) talk of the 'persistent growth of routinised work' (p.1). They acknowledge that in advanced economies, whilst some jobs have moved from advanced to developing economies, a vast number of routine jobs remain. Grugulis (2007), exploring the myths and realities of the knowledge economy, acknowledges that we can see a rise in knowledge-intensive workplaces (R&D, consultancies, advertising and marketing agencies). However, she distinguishes between such knowledge-intensive firms and 'knowledgability in work', where customer service staff, clerks and call centre workers know a great deal about the work they do but tasks are constrained and discretion limited.

Specifically in the context of the UK, and in some contrast to official government predictions noted above, the Leitch report (2006) on UK skills argues that most of the skills gaps are at an intermediate level and not at degree level. (Intermediate skills are specific occupational skills needed in jobs ranging from the trades to associate professional occupations. They constitute a meaningful skill segment identifiable in most countries as craft or technician level skills.) Keep (2009) is more critical, arguing that Taylorism is alive and well. Substantial numbers of organizations in certain sectors of the UK economy compete on costs and not skill levels. The pressure, if anything, is to deskill. This is an entirely rational response, he argues, to the economic environment in which such organizations find themselves. HRD managers face a dilemma; they are under pressure from the rhetoric of good practice to upskill – perhaps recruit a graduate – yet under an equal but countervailing pressure from the reality of survival in a low-skills equilibrium marketplace (see also Chapter 1). Lauder et al. (2012) go a step further referring to 'Digital Taylorism' which 'enables innovation to be translated into routines that might require some degree of education but not the kind of creativity and independence of judgment associated with the knowledge economy' (p.46).

In the face of such questions, the pervasiveness of the knowledge economy thesis begins to crumble somewhat. If large sections of the economy do not sit comfortably with knowledge economy characteristics and if sections of the knowledge economy in fact require relatively minimal levels of skill, this is of critical importance in the context of the rapidly increasing graduate population discussed earlier in the chapter.

Perhaps we should begin to question the relationship between graduates, graduate capability and human capital. Consider this extract from a speech by Bill Gates (of Microsoft fame) when addressing a group of new Harvard graduates.

> Be activists. Take on big inequities…You have an awareness of global inequity, which we did not have. And with that awareness you likely have an informed conscience that will torment you if you abandon those people whose lives you could change with very little effort. (www.networkworld. com/news/2007/060807-gates-commencement.html)

Gates is referring to the potential for graduates to contribute to social capital. The notion of social capital refers to the value that social networks and relationships have within a society. It has its roots in debate and discussion about democracy (see, for example, de Tocqueville, 1998), and the value of education (Dewey, 1899). The publication of Robert Putnam's *Bowling Alone* in 2000, which warned that our stock of social capital – 'the very fabric of our connections with each other' – has renewed interest in how best to build and sustain social structures and networks.

Increasingly a consensus is emerging that HE has a particularly important role to play in engendering and fostering social capital. Societies with higher proportions of graduates demonstrate higher proportions of volunteering, take more action on environmental issues and hold more positive attitudes towards race and gender equality (OECD, 2011, 2012). In Scotland, for example, the 2007 HE spending review argued that the societal impact of higher education is not purely economic (Scottish Government, 2007). The report cites the *Wellbeing Scotland* report, which indicates that graduates are healthier, less obese, have longer life expectancy, commit less crime and participate more fully in civic society (Universities Scotland, 2007). Graduates, it argues, play a major part in nurturing effective citizenship.

We might conclude, therefore, that the contribution of graduates to social capital may go beyond the direct labour market and macroeconomic effects. Thus, graduates who next year and the year after find themselves unemployed or, more likely, underemployed can sleep easily, confident in the knowledge that they are a valuable asset to society simply by virtue of being a graduate!

As we draw this chapter to a close we note the argument in Chapter 1 that higher education is a site and context of HRD practice. The issues addressed in this chapter provide clear support for this position. Increasingly, the workforce of tomorrow, globally, will hold degree level qualifications. In this sense graduates are indeed the vanguard of HRD; it is graduates who are equipped with the highest levels of knowledge and associated skills that societies can provide. However, the relationship with work is far from straightforward. As we understand more about this relationship we may be forced to revisit what we have come to understand as a graduate job and a graduate career, or at very least that the availability of such is unproblematic.

summary

○ Globally, the number of graduates as a proportion of the working population is rising. The European Union's target is for 40 per cent of young people to participate in HE.

○ The high level of skills and capabilities associated with graduate labour raises the prospect that graduates might be regarded as the new vanguard of HRD.

○ A key rationale for the expansion of HE is based on the demands of the knowledge economy. In reality, such arguments require a critical assessment.

○ A picture of a complex graduate labour market emerges, raising issues about:

○ the changing profile of graduate jobs

○ whether a substantial minority of graduates may be overqualified and under-utilized in the work they do after qualifying

○ graduate identity and the very notion of what is graduateness.

○ Current trends are for HE to emphasize the importance of employability. However, research suggests the transition process is often fragmented, uneven and difficult to manage, raising doubts as to the real value of the whole employability agenda within HE.

○ While graduates may conventionally be considered as human capital, recent research suggests that their contribution to social capital may actually outweigh any direct labour market effect.

discussion questions

1 Why might graduates be regarded as the vanguard of HRD?

2 In the context of recent rises in the numbers of graduates explore the unevenness of the profile of graduates (e.g. gender, ethnicity).

3 How would you define a graduate job?

4 How does your degree course purport to enhance employability? How does research on the transition from HE into work shed light on this process?

5 What is the relationship between graduates and what is commonly understood as the knowledge economy?

further
reading

references

Allen, J. and van der Velden, R. (2011) *The Flexible Professional in the Knowledge Society. New Challenges for Higher Education*. Springer.com.

Brown, P. and Hesketh, A. (2004) *The Mismanagement of Talent: Employability and Jobs in the Knowledge Economy*. Oxford: Oxford University Press.

Cranmer, C. (2006) Enhancing graduate employability: best intentions and mixed outcomes. *Studies in Higher Education*, **31**(2): 169–84.

Prospects UK, *What Do Graduates Do?* Higher Education Careers Services Unit, available at www.prospects.ac.uk/assets/assets/documents/wdgd_2010.pdf

Allen, A. (2011) *Girls, Graduate Jobs and the Gender Chasm, Gender and Education Association*, available at www.genderandeducation.com/issues/girls-graduate-jobs-and-the-gender-chasm, accessed 11 October 2012.

Angot, J., Malloch, H. and Kleymann, B. (2008) The formation of professional identity in French apprentice managers. *Education and Training*, **50**(5): 406–22.

Arnold, J. and McKenzie Davey, K. (1992) Beyond unmet expectations: a detailed analysis of graduate experiences during the first three years of their careers. *Personnel Review*, **21**(2): 45–68.

Atfield, G., Purcell, K. and Hogarth, T. (2009) *The Impact of Graduate Placements on Businesses in the South West of England*. Warwick: Institute for Employment Research.

Bagguley, P. and Hussain, Y. (2007) *The Role of Higher Education in Providing Opportunities for South Asian Women*. York: The Joseph Rowntree Foundation.

Becker, G.S. (1964) *Human Capital: A Theoretical Analysis with Special Reference to Education*. New York: Columbia University Press.

BIS (2011) *Students at the Heart of the System*. London: Department of Business, Innovation and Skills.

Blenkinsopp, J. and Scurry, T. (2007) Hey gringo!: the HR challenge of graduates in non-graduate occupations. *Personnel Review*, **36**(4): 623–37.

Bolton, S.C., and Houlihan, M. (2009) *Work Matters: Critical Reflections On Contemporary Work*. Basingstoke: Palgrave.

Brennan, J. (2008) *The Flexible Professional in the Knowledge Society (REFLEX): Overview Report*. Open University: Centre for Higher Education Research and Information.

Brown, P. and Hesketh, A. (2004) *The Mismanagement of Talent: Employability and Jobs in the Knowledge Economy*. Oxford: Oxford University Press.

Browne, J. (2010) *Securing a Sustainable Future for Higher Education: An Independent Review of Higher Education Funding and Finance*, available at http://www.bis.gov.uk/assets/BISCore/corporate/docs/S/10−1208-securing-sustainable-higher-education-browne-report.pdf

Butcher, V., Smith, J., Kettle, J. and Burton, L. (2011) *Review of Good Practice in Employability and Enterprise Development by Centres for Excellence in Teaching and Learning*. York: Higher Education Academy.

Carrol, D. and Tani, M. (2011) *Labour Market Under-Utilisation of Recent Higher Education Graduates: New Australian Panel Evidence*. Econstor Discussion Paper 6047, Leibniz Information Centre for Economics.

CBI (2009) *Future Fit: Preparing Graduates For The World Of Work*. London: CBI.

Chowdry, H., Crawford, C., Deardon, L., Goodman, A. and Vignoles, A. (2010) *Widening Participation in Higher Education*. London: Institute for Fiscal Studies.

Connor, H. and Pollard, E. (1996) *What Do Graduates Really Do?* Report No. 308. Brighton: Institute of Employment Studies.

David, M., Parry, G., Vignoles, A., Hayward, G., Williams, J., Crozier, G., Hockings, C. and Fuller, A. (2008) *Widening Participation in Higher Education: A Commentary by the Teaching and Learning Research Programme*. London: Economic and Social Research Council.

De Tocqueville, A. (1998) *Democracy in America*. Ware: Wordsworth.

Dewey, J. (1899) *The School and Society*. Chicago: University of Chicago Press.

Edwards, M.R. and Kelan, E.K. (2011) Employer branding and diversity: foes or friends? In Brannan, M.J., Parsons, E.and Priola, V. (eds) *Branded Lives - The Production and Consumption of Meaning at Work*. Cheltenham: Edward Elgar, pp. 168–81.

The Engineer (2012) *More Than Half of Graduates Feel 'Unprepared' for Work*. Available at http://www.theengineer.co.uk/skills-and-careers/more-than-half-of-graduates-feel-unprepared-for-work/1012488.article, accessed 5 March 2013.

Elias, P. and Purcell, K. (2004) *Researching Graduate Careers Seven Years On,* Research Paper No. 3. Warwick: Institute for Employment Research.

European Commission (2011) *Recent Developments in European Higher Education Systems*. Brussels: European Commission.

Fineman, S. and Gabriel, Y. (1996) *Experiencing Organizations*. London: Sage.

Gallup (2010) *Employers' Perception Of Graduate Employability,* Flash EB Series 304. London: The Gallup Organisation.

Green, F. and Zhu, Y. (2010) Overqualification, job dissatisfaction, and increasing dispersion in the returns to graduate education. *Oxford Economic Papers,* **62**(4): 740–63.

Grugulis, I. (2007) *Skills, Training and Human Resource Development*. Basingstoke, Palgrave Macmillan.

HEA (2008) *Ethnicity, Gender and Degree Attainment Project: Final Report*. New York: Higher Education Academy.

HECSU (2012) *What Do Graduates Do?* Manchester: Higher Education Careers Service.

HEFCE (2004) *Centres for Excellence in Teaching and Learning: Invitation To Bid For Funds.* Bristol: Higher Education Funding Council for England.

HESA (2012) *Performance Indicators in Higher Education in the UK*. Available from http://www.hesa.ac.uk/content/view/2072/141/, accessed 4 March 2013.

Hesketh, A.J. (2009) *Adding Value Beyond Measure*. London: Association of Graduate Recruiters.

Higson, H. and Bullivant, N. (2006) Preparing Aston Business School students to reflect on their employment experience. In N. Becket and P. Kemp (eds) *Enhancing Graduate Employability in Business and Management, Hospitality, Leisure, Sport and Tourism*. York: Higher Education Academy.

Hogarth, T., Winterbotham, M., Hasluck, C., Carter, K., Daniel, W.W., Green, A.E and Morrison, J. (2007) *Employer and University Engagement in the Use And Development of Graduate Level Skills*, Research Report 835. London: Department for Education and Skills.

Holden, R.J. (2012) *Graduate Employment at Hallmark*. Leeds Metropolitan University.

Holden, R.J. and Hamblett, J. (2007) The transition from higher education into work: tales of cohesion and fragmentation. *Education and Training*, **49**(7): 516–88.

Holden, R.J. and Jameson, S.M. (1999) A preliminary investigation into the transition and utilisation of hospitality graduates in SMEs. *Tourism and Hospitality Research*, **1**(3): 231–42.

Holmes, L. (2001) Reconsidering graduate employability: the graduate identity approach. *Quality in Higher Education*, **7**(2): 111–19.

Holmes, L. (2006) *Reconsidering Graduate Employability: Beyond Possessive Instrumentalism*. Seventh International Conference on HRD Research and Practice Across Europe, University of Tilburg, 22–24 May.

Holmes, L. (2011) Competing perspectives on graduate employability: possession, position or process? *Studies in Higher Education*, DOI:10.1080/03075079.2011.587140.

Jenner, S. (2008) Graduate development, discursive resources and the employment relationship at BAE Systems. *Education and Training*, **50**(5): 423–38.

Keep, E. (2009) Labour market structures and trends, the future of work and the implications for initial E&T, available from www.beyondcurrenthorizons.org.uk/labour-market-structures-and-trends-the-future-of-work-and-the-implications-for-initial-et, accessed 10 October 2012.

Lauder, H., Brown, P. and Tholen, G. (2012) The global auction model, skill bias theory and graduate incomes: reflections on methodology (pp.43–65). In H. Lauder, M. Young, H.Daniels, M. Balarin and J.Lowe (eds) *Educating for Knowledge Economy*. Abingdon: Routledge.

Leitch, S. (2006) *Prosperity for all in the Global Economy: World Class Skills*. London: HM Treasury.

Little, B. (2008) Graduate developments in European employment: issues and contradictions. *Education and Training*, **50**(5): 379–90.

Major, B. (2006) Enhancing travel, tourism and hospitality management graduates employability. In N. Becket and P. Kemp (eds) *Enhancing Graduate Employability in*

Business and Management, Hospitality, Leisure, Sport and Tourism. York: Higher Education Academy.

Maslen, G. (2012) Worldwide student numbers forecast to double by 2025. *University World News*, Issue No: 209, 19 February.

Mason, G., (2002) High skills utilisation under mass higher education: graduate employment in service industries in Britain. *Journal of Education and Work*, **15**: 427–56.

Mason, G., Williams, G. and Cranmer, S. (2006) *Employability Skills Initiatives in Higher Education: What Effects Do They Have On Graduate Labour Market Outcomes?* London: NIESR.

Nabi, G., Holden, R.J., and Walmsley, A. (2010) Entrepreneurial intentions among students: towards a re-focused research agenda. *Journal of Small Business and Enterprise Development*, **17**(4): 537–51.

O'Donnell, H., Karallis, T., Sandelands, E. et al. (2008) Corporate case study: developing graduate engineers at Kentz Engineers and Constructors. *Education and Training*, **50**(6): 439–52.

OECD (2011) *Education at a Glance 2011: OECD Indicators*. Paris: OECD Publishing.

OECD (2012) *Better Life Index: Education*, available at www.oecdbetterlifeindex.org/topics/education, accessed 10 October 2012.

Papadatou, A. (2011) The future of graduate employability: looking forward to 2012. *Guardian Professional*, Monday 24 October.

Purcell, K., Elias, P., Davies, R. and Wilton, N. (2005) *The Class of '99: A Study of the Early Labour Market Experience of Recent Graduates*. Warwick: Institute for Employment Research.

Purcell, K and Elias, P. (2006) *Achieving Equality in the Knowledge Economy*. GeNet Working Paper, Employment Studies Research Unit, University of the West of England.

Putnam, R. (2000) *Bowling Alone: The Collapse and Revival of American Community*. New York: Simon & Schuster.

Rajan, A., Chapple, K. and Battersby, L. (1998) *Graduates in Growing Companies: The Rhetoric of Core Skills and Reality of Globalisation*. Tunbridge Wells: Centre for Research in Employment and Technology in Europe.

Scottish Government (2007) *Scottish Budget Spending Review 2007*. Edinburgh: Scottish Government.

Shaw, S. and Fairhurst, D. (2008) Engaging a new generation of graduates. *Education and Training*, **50**(5): 366–78.

UCAS (2012).*How Have Applications for Full-Time Undergraduate Higher Education in the UK Changed in 2012?* Available from http://www.ucas.ac.uk/about_us/media_enquiries/media_releases/2012/2012applications analysis, accessed 4 March 2013.

Universities Scotland (2007) *Wellbeing Scotland: The Contribution of Higher Education to Scotland's Wellbeing*. Edinburgh: Universities Scotland.

Wilton, N., (2011) Do employability skills really matter in the UK: the case of business and management graduates *Work, Employment and Society*, **25**(1): 85–100.

Creative Comforts (UK)

Introduction and background

Creative Comforts (UK) is a US-owned furniture and home design and production company. Based in the Midlands, the company employs around 3,000 staff, many with design skills. CC's main customers in the UK and now in Europe are large department stores and supermarkets where customers can work with designers for home and office fittings, including bespoke production of furniture. While there is little knowledge of CC by the customer, the association with well-known brands of supermarket and department stores has for many years ensured success. However, there are problems facing the business as key leaders and managers move towards retirement.

The problem of succession

Tom Kane is the Learning and Development Manager for CC (UK). He is highly respected and is very keen to ensure that the company has a robust succession plan for critical positions. Over the last two years, he has tried to do this by asking senior managers to identify talented staff with the potential for leadership positions. In each year, 15 staff were presented and attended the company's Leadership and Talent programme, consisting of an assessment of leadership style involving 360-degree feedback, workshops relating to company values and, if possible, coaching from line managers. The programme lasts eight months and Tom tries to evaluate throughout but his main indicator of success is how many of the 15 staff are promoted within 18 months. However, to date this has shown a disappointing return with only 15 per cent of the programme participants moving into more senior positions. A further 10 per cent left the company.

One difficulty, which becomes apparent once participants finish the programme, is that while there is talk of a talent pool, this does not seem to be recognised by the company when promotions become available. Tom is not a member of the Executive Team and relies on an HR Director to represent his concerns, but there seems to be little enthusiasm for action to link succession to the talent strategy, based on the programme.

Another difficulty seems to be a reticent response from line managers to act as Talent Champions. There are some wonderful examples of good coaching and career support and these represent key reasons for participant progress, but most line managers do not respond to requests from Tom to take on such roles, citing pressure of work as the reason. One consequence is a low transfer of learning from the Leadership and Talent programme, which is now being questioned as a value-adding process (and causing Tom to fear for his job).

Perhaps most significantly, there does seem to be a clear business strategy and a consideration of how particular positions are critical to fulfilling the strategy. The linkages between strategy, talent, career development, succession and leadership are just not made explicit or considered in an integrated way.

Questions

1 How can succession and talent strategies be aligned with each other and then business strategy?
2 What are the requirements for the successful working of a talent pool in an organization?
3 How can line managers learn to support talented staff?
4 What does Tom Kane need to do to ensure more value-added from the Leadership and Talent programme and thus preserve his job?

the **future**

chapter 17

The Future of Human Resource Development

Jeff Gold, Rick Holden, Paul Iles, Jim Stewart and Julie Beardwell

Chapter learning outcomes

After studying this chapter, you should be able to:

- Appraise the status of HRD
- Understand the use of various tools to consider the future
- Consider some possibilities for the future of HRD

Chapter outline

Introduction
HRD and the future
Futures tools and HRD
Possibilities for the future
Summary

Introduction

In 2007 and then into 2008, many organizations were surprised by the speed and depth of what was then the credit crunch which turned into a recession, double-dip in some places, along with a global financial crisis, an ongoing Eurozone crisis and various other disturbances. If we consider that the word crisis is derived from the Greek *krinein*, meaning a moment in time which brings about a change in the way we understand the world, then the process of learning has to be central. Alternatively, as Revans (1982) once warned, if learning is not at least equal to or greater than the rate of change in the environment, failure would follow. It is clear, that this warning has not been heeded. Certainly, while leaders and managers in organizations have now become familiar with the uncertainty, they seem powerless to respond or, importantly, learn how adapt to future surprises (Randell, 2009). What we can say is that we all face a future, which, to some degree, can be predicted by considering various trends and indicators. Nevertheless, the consideration of these will always be in the present and based on the past; more challenging is the prospect that much of the future cannot be known – it is to a great degree unknowable (Stacey, 1992). Perhaps the best we can do is to work intelligently with trends and indicators to reduce uncertainty, and work creatively and speculatively where prediction is too difficult or impossible. As Stacey (2002) pointed out, there is a difference between an uncertain future and a complex future, where the latter is characterized by a large number of factors interacting dynamically, making it impossible to determine logical patterns for understanding. Perhaps too much reliance on the certainty of trends and indicators resulted in the credit crunch and what followed. How many organizations were ready for this by using creative thinking around different future possibilities? In this final chapter, we plan to consider briefly how HRD can participate in this endeavour. We will also examine various tools for creative thinking about the future before we report the results of one process in which we considered the future of HRD.

HRD and the future

It has been suggested that analytical and creative thinking are required to work on the future (PIU, 2001). Figure 17.1 shows a dimension of possibilities. Analytical thinking is concerned with using patterns of information that form trends and underpin predictions and forecasts. However, a degree of challenge and critical thinking is needed to use such information (Gordon, 2009). Creative thinking is concerned with complexity and multiple future possibilities. Complexity occurs when there are large numbers of interacting elements, which behave in a very difficult to predict and non-linear fashion and are likely to be subjected to ongoing flux and movement (Cilliers, 1998). Learning is essential to both modes of thinking but creativity particularly requires imagination, the willingness to think new thoughts, make unmade connections, to be ridiculed but also be open to laughter. Such skills, recognized as skills of futurists and foresighters (Dator, 2003), need to become part of the repertoire of HRD practitioners.

For a number of years, the status of HRD, as a domain of practice and a field of study, has been seen as contentious and ambiguous (Mankin, 2001). As we have indicated, HRD has its origin in a limited view of training and has close links with HRM and OD. These historical roots tend to both help and hinder

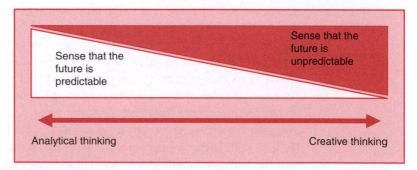

Figure 17.1 Analytical and creative approaches to the future

Source: PIU (2001, p. 15)

the progress of HRD. There is help in the form of the infusion of ideas and theories from different directions, as we have seen throughout this book. In addition, for those who practise HRD, there is a means of claiming enhanced professional status through membership, in the UK, of the CIPD. For one of the fastest-growing professions in recent years, the CIPD offers a qualification process and a certain degree of control over who can enter the profession, although the control is not yet exclusive. Thus it is still possible to practise HRD (and HRM) without membership of the Chartered Institute of Personnel and Development (CIPD). HRD could also be hindered by the CIPD through a loss of its independence and claims for a unique identity centred around knowledge, skills and learning (Gold et al., 2003). However, there are signs and opportunities for HRD professionals to enhance their status over the next few years. For example, recent survey evidence from CIPD (2012) points to a shift in the direction towards in-house development and the importance of coaching and on-the-job training. More generally, the evidence shows that there is still a lot of attention given to developing high-potential employees (Iles et al., 2010). However, if such practices improve attitudes towards learning, this will improve Organizational Learning Capability (OLC) which has been shown to play a key role in the link between high-performance work and overall organization performance (Camps & Luna-Arocas, 2012). At the very least, such evidence must be used to ensure that HRD becomes part of any strategic discussion to advance organization outcomes, through the use of high-level skills. Further, it becomes crucial that the outcome of such discussions is incorporated into the practice of managers. It is here that practices such as coaching can have a greater role, but it requires considerable persuasive powers to ensure that managers, especially line managers, become accountable (Burke & Saks, 2009). Such opportunities, if grasped, will allow HRD as a profession to move from a restricted position based on external experts and prescriptive knowledge, towards an approach which requires a commitment to an 'iterative developmental process' (Evans, 2008, p.27) of professional practice.

We also argue that part of this process is a more rigorous engagement with theory or, better, theory making. One of the difficulties in the past was that HRD did not seem to have its own body of theory, which is often seen as the basis for calling an area of practice professional (Freidson, 2001). Over the last 20 years, there have been growing efforts to develop a theoretical base in HRD, with the development of journals, conferences, books and so on, but there has been no clear agreement on the boundaries of HRD as a body of theory or how theory should be constructed. In the 1990s, McGoldrick and Stewart (1996) examined the relationship between HRD and HRM. Part of their purpose was to argue the space for HRD within academic practices of teaching and research. Later research and writing by the editors of this book have focused on the connections between HRD and other related areas, including the learning organization (LO) (Tjepkema et al., 2002) and Knowledge Management (KM) (Stewart & Tansley, 2002). These two concepts have an obvious relationship with the notion of Organization Learning (OL). Stewart (2005) argued a connection between LO, OL and OD and mentioned the long-accepted connection between OD and HRD.

In the preceding paragraph, we used six different abbreviations to denote a focus of academic teaching and research that claims a distinctive, if not a truly unique, academic space. Yet every one of these spaces draws on the same core disciplines and, to a varying extent, which is a matter of degree rather than substance, focuses on the same social and organizational practices in its research. Stewart (2005) developed the idea of a battle of the acronyms, a theme which has three arguments:

1   HRD is indeed engaged in a battle for academic space.
2   The internal debate on the meaning and theory of HRD has weaknesses as well as strengths (Poell, 2007). One of those weaknesses is to reduce the effectiveness of HRD in the battle of the acronyms.
3   The battle itself, because of internal preoccupations with academic space, threatens the potential benefits to the material conditions of humanity brought about by the work of each of the acronyms.

What follows from these arguments is that there may be little point or benefit in attempts to settle the debates on meaning and theory in relation to HRD. Indeed, some would argue against a specification of HRD if that would mean closing off new and emerging areas of study (Lee, 2001). One such idea that has emerged more recently is how the making of theory, or theorizing, can provide a way of bridging the gap between academics and practitioners (Stewart & Gold, 2011). This follows recent concerns about the relevance of management and organization research more widely but including HRD research. It is argued that, in the pursuit of rigour, researchers in HRD attempt to privilege scientific theorising but this also means that relevance to practice can be less important. For example, Lynham (2002) argues that HRD research needs to conform to the rigour of scientific theory-building but this can also result in a relevance gap between theories and practice (Starkey & Madan, 2001). In order to reduce the gap and 'span the HRD academic-practitioner divide' (Gray et al., 2011), it is argued that HRD scholars and practitioners engage with the making of theory in the context of its application, referred to by Gibbons et al. (1994) as Mode 2 research. Such an approach begins by considering the problems that are inherent in practice and the generation of questions to which there is no obvious response. Gold et al. (2011) argue that when practitioners seek possible solutions to difficult problems that begins a process of reasoning that is called abductive reasoning, whose outcomes can lead to propositions or ideas which can then be tested. Such ideas, referred to as hypotheses on probation, based on the work of Peirce (1903), represent the first moves in making a theory for practice and the production of practitioner knowledge which is relevant in the particular context. If HRD scholars can engage at this level, it becomes possible to build relevant and rigorous theories through the co-creation of knowledge (Antonacopoulou, 2010).

In times when many HRD practitioners are required to reduce costs and show the value-added of their work (CIPD, 2012), there are many possibilities for joint working with academics and other practitioners. One example might be how to increase the return on investment from HRD activities such as leadership development and team building. In such areas of HRD work, learners often find it difficult to apply new skills and knowledge, which leads to a waste of 'time, money and resources' (Latham, 2007, p.3) and this hardly advances HRD's case in difficult times. However, the transfer of learning problem has been a thorn in the side of HRD for many years but through collaboration it becomes possible to show some improvements and attend to the factors that are most likely to enable transfer, such as the role of line managers in preparing learners for participation in HRD and then making changes to work behaviour based on their participation (see Colwill et al., 2012). Crucially, such issues can be considered in a collective atmosphere and be framed as a joint endeavour between HRD practitioners and academics.

Of course, difficult issues in HRD sometimes means challenging deeply embedded assumptions and this requires help with critical thinking. In recent years, there has been a growing interest in what is referred to as critical HRD (CHRD) (see Elliott & Turnbull, 2005; Rigg et al., 2007). A major focus and purpose of CHRD is to identify and highlight the social and cultural dimensions, purposes and impact of HRD as well as the narrow economic dimensions that traditionally characterize theory and practice. The ideas around CHRD have featured only marginally in this book but they have potential for greater relevance and utility not only in relation to key issues in HRD but also to wider issues within and beyond organizations.

So, as we consider the future of HRD, it would seem that theory and practice are at a crossroads. Perhaps this book is part of a trend pushing HRD towards growth and increasing influence along with some of the ideas for reducing the gaps between theory and practice that we have just referred to. This would match options presented by Torraco (2008), which point to an increasing acceptance of HRD research and practice throughout work organizations, communities, schools and colleges. Further, HRD will play a leading role in trends such as diversity, cross-cultural understanding and ethical competence as well as economic growth and/or sustainability. Of course, these options were seen as trends before 2007/2008. Nevertheless, if HRD is accepted as a path for learning and development, its influence will grow during and after the crises. Of course, there is Torraco's contrasting option, which sees a decline in influence and a reduced role or even elimination of HRD. This does become a possibility if economic recession results in cost cutting, a problem that traditionally beset training in the past. In this option, HRD researchers become disconnected from the problems facing organizations and are seen as irrelevant.

The crises and flux will clearly create the need for learning and change. The question is, will HRD be able to keep up, cope and respond? In one of the findings from a survey by Ruona et al. (2003), HRD professionals were criticized for not changing fast enough in responding to global and organization requirements. Although it was recognized that HRD had grown quickly, there were doubts that this would continue in the future. However, we would argue that HRD practitioners and researchers can play a leading role in responding to change and difficulties. Along with Ulrich (2007), we argue that the HRD community can create and add value with and to the people, organizations, institutions, nations and indeed the whole world. This can be done by working analytically with trends and creatively with future unknowns, as indicated in Figure 17.1. Such work draws on ideas and theories from futures and foresight, a field concerned with the study of the future and the use of knowledge to enable the identification of choices and options (Slaughter, 1999). Futurists need imagination, the ability to test out thoughts and ideas in practice and learn from failure.

Futures tools and HRD

While trends imply a degree of predictability, much of the future is more difficult, if not impossible, to predict. We can talk about the future, but this is, by necessity, speculative. However, futures research and futures ideas are less concerned with the accuracy of predictions and more oriented towards assisting decisions. Learning about the future provides possible options on how the future will proceed. Futures writers such as Bell (1997) suggest that the purpose of futures work is concerned with heightening awareness about the future to help other disciplines, such as HRD, make better decisions. There are a variety of possible outcomes in the future, but action can only occur in the present and such actions can be part of an argument for how the future will be enacted. This would seem particularly important for those involved in HRD, given the options for HRD presented above by Torraco (2008).

Scenarios

Futurists believe that there is great value in considering the variety of possible futures, both positive and negative, orthodox and unconventional. To support learning about the future, a range of tools and methods has been developed. For example, one approach is to develop a scenario where participants with a variety of views create different stories for future possibilities. De Geus (1988, p.70) argued that scenarios 'are the scenery into which actors walk' through the creation of a number of 'internally consistent stories of possible futures'. Scenarios are not forecasts but should be considered as future possibilities providing participants with the chance to develop a joint conversation about the future (Ringland, 1998). An example of this approach is provided by Gold et al. (2003), where four scenarios were developed concerning the future of the HRD profession in the UK to the year 2020:

1 a highly positive scenario where the learning society has been achieved and learning is highly valued throughout society.
2 a scenario of mixed fortunes for HRD, where learning is accepted as the norm but not for everyone; instead a selective approach is adopted.
3 another scenario of mixed fortunes, where learning opportunities are available for a wide group of people but these opportunities are constrained and narrowed by the particular requirements of organizations, which are specified in an HRD plan and delivered top-down against targets.
4 a pessimistic scenario, where a low status is given to learning and HRD activities are limited to a select few with little room for creativity and new ideas.

Futures writers Rogers and Tough (1996, p.495) once stated that 'facing the future is definitely not for wimps', and if we reflect on these scenarios ten years after they were written, we can see that HRD still remains at a point where elements of all four scenarios seem to apply.

Future search conferences

Another futures method is to hold a future search conference (FSC). This seeks to bring together a large range of stakeholders who have a joint interest in an issue so that they can share intentions and create plans. According to Weisbord and Janoff (2000), the basic principles of an FSC are:

- getting a cross-section of the whole system in one room
- exploring the whole before seeking to act on any part
- focusing on common ground and desired futures
- treating problems and conflicts as information, not action
- letting participants self-manage and take responsibility for action.

Dewey and Carter (2003) report the results of an FSC held in Florida in 2001 entitled Shaping the Future: Leading Workplace Learning and Performance. The event lasted three days and was attended by 64 participants. Working in groups, the participants considered past and present trends, analysis of present reality leading to common ground themes that could be developed into agreed ideas for plans. Through discussion and dialogue the final area of common ground included:

- creating synergy between research and practice
- leveraging available technology without losing the human touch and social component of learning
- striking a healthy balance between work life and personal life
- striving to create humane workplaces
- acknowledging intellectual capital as the life blood of the organization – the true bottom line
- developing a sense of social responsibility
- embracing globalization
- embracing multiculturalism
- partnering in the fundamentally changing role for education
- managing knowledge and learning effectively
- developing partnerships and collaboration internal and external to the organization
- fostering lifelong learning.

Based on the beliefs and values of the participants, this list is broadly expressed in positive terms and is inevitably constrained by their understanding in 2001. We do not know if there was any follow-up activity or review. Certainly, most of the ideas were and are part of what people in HRD often talk about now and have done over the past decade. But they do seem to lack a critical or alternative stance. To bring current understanding into this process, and as a way of involving HRD practitioners in this book, an FSC to consider the future of HRD to 2020 and beyond was held in Leeds in November 2011. In the next section, we report some of the findings from the participants who attended, and who have helped write up what they developed.

Possibilities for the future

The FSC sought to consider the future of HRD to 2020 and beyond. It was attended by 39 participants from a variety of organizations as well as several universities. Five self-managed groups were formed to explore three areas,

1 The past – for individuals to map and share their learning journey from two perspectives, personal and professional
2 The present – to develop a rich picture of what is currently working and what is not
3 The future – to plan scenarios for 2020 and beyond.

Findings were shared at each stage and during the final review the participants agreed to work on a joint paper which would report the findings of each group. Here we provide some of the key features from each group's presentation.

From past to present

Viewing HRD from the past to the present enabled participants to share their own journeys and also see how a number of continuities could be considered as trends. Firstly, it seemed that HRD, both in theory and practice, seemed to be guilty of ongoing efforts to reduce complexity and difficulty into simple models, such as the systematic training model with its roots in a military context and technological understanding (Eckstrand, 1964). While serving as a solution to times when HRD was characterized by unstructured and poorly designed events, such models were valued for their logic and sequence in planning action (Buckley & Caple, 2007) despite many criticisms of such models. We could see how such a linear view of training could easily remain blind to key contextual features that impact on the training and learning at work that relies on the possibility of management support, but more likely a failure to support, as well the vagaries of culture and history (Chiaburu & Tekleab, 2005). However, one key trend, and obviously related to the recent, and still current, economic crisis in Europe and elsewhere, is that there is less funding available to support HRD activities. When HRD budgets require low-cost solutions, we could see a continued use of models from the past. For example, recent surveys suggest that new ideas on learning and development from neuroscience, economics and social psychology were hardly ever used in HRD and there were continuing preferences for older models, such as Belbin Team Roles and the Honey and Mumford Learning Styles Questionnaire (LSQ) (CIPD, 2012). Competency models were another reduction of complex behaviour into simplicity (Bolden & Gosling, 2006).

A long-standing difficulty for HRD has been the failure to demonstrate a return on investment (ROI) on activities. Models of evaluation have a tendency to follow a similar linear logic to the systematic view of training we referred to above, with Kirkpatrick's (1983) stages or levels model setting a framework.

However, as many have found, the in-built linearity of the model has proven difficult to implement beyond 'reactionnaires' (Rae, 2002) following learning activities. For many HRD activities, such as leadership development and interpersonal skills, the act of learning alone is not sufficient for training to be considered efficient (Grossman & Salas, 2011).

We identified a rising demand from both employers and individuals for learning to be certified. This may be associated with the notion of employability and a corresponding interest in qualifications. It is also though thought to be associated with credentialism and the way that is emphasised in national VET and HRD policies; for instance, the rise of the NVQ system in the UK. Governments utilize qualifications as a proxy measure to assess the skill base of national economies and changes/improvements in that base. So, they too support the demand for certification. We noted the long-standing doubts about the value of NVQs and their effectiveness in HRD (see, for example, Grugulis, 2003) and recent criticism that low level NVQs have little use or value in the labour market, even though they are undertaken by large numbers of 16/17 year olds (Wolf, 2011).

This trend was linked to the fall and rise of apprenticeships as a means of engagement and progression for young people. In the post-war period, apprenticeships offered a sheltered and extended period in which the young person was able to grow up and become job ready (Vickerstaffe, 2007). However, over time the status of apprenticeships eroded as industrial restructuring took place, the manufacturing industry in the UK declined, and the influence of trades unions waned. As a result there was a significant decline in apprentice numbers from 171,000 in 1968 to just 34,500 in 1990. However, we noted that during the 1990s apprenticeship became confused with various schemes (YOPS, YTS, etc.) which often became associated with wider economic, social and political ends including cheap labour, social engineering, low educational value and the massaging of employment statistics (Ryan & Unwin, 2001). We could not help noticing that we seemed to be back in a similar place. The UK Government's Strategy Document Skills for Sustainable Growth placed apprenticeships at the heart of the system and announced additional funding to expand the number of adult Apprenticeships available (to 200,000 p.a.) and to develop clear progression routes into level 3 Apprenticeships, and routes from level 3 Apprenticeships to higher level skills, including level 4 Apprenticeships or Higher Education (BIS, 2011). However, with unemployment rising, especially among 16–24 year olds, apprenticeships as a route to employment, along with various other schemes such as the Work Experience Programme and the Work Programme, become confused with policies to reduce the impact of young people on unemployment figures.

Of course, training and qualifications do not mean employment. Young people want work to match their skills and provide opportunities for advance. With a shortage of suitable work, the bar is being raised for specific jobs and occupations. Further, with more young people with degrees and qualifications, in the market for jobs the bar for requirements is raised even further, a trend that may change as the market for higher education is disturbed by fee charges. However, a persistent trend seems to be a mismatch of skills and the experience graduates get from work as they suffer under-employment (Scurry & Blenkinsopp, 2011). Those who are graduating now, along with young people more generally, are considered to be more aware of the possibilities they are not getting. Variously termed as Generations Y or Z, or the Me generation (Twenge et al., 2008), all are able to make use of technology to provide choices for all aspects of their lives. Vilemetter (2011) sees this as feeding the trend of individualism, considered to involve the freedom to making of choices about work and life in congruence with personal values. If work does not provide satisfaction, many will find other means to do so and remain optimistic (SIRC, 2009), creatively or destructively.

A familiar feature of any gathering, including formal lectures, is that tweets will soon be on the move, a reminder that for some time now, the 'The Networked Society' (Castells, 2010) has been with us and all that this implies about connectivity across space and time. Technology is now part of society, business and social interaction and includes anything from computers, to mobile phones, to satellite navigation (Hopper & Rice, 2008). Each of these aspects are ingrained into society to the point where the majority of the developed world is reliant upon this technology to function efficiently and effectively. Technology mediates learning, allowing advantages such as access to resources and completion of programmes at the convenience of the learners (CIPD, 2006). However, e-learning also allows lower cost, lower payment, more control of delivery and perhaps lower quality.

Back to the future

Based on what were seen as continuing trends, the FSC then turned towards the future to consider HRD to 2020 and beyond. Groups were asked to produce a number of scenarios and, as we have already indicated, as possible stories of the future, scenarios are not predictions. To stimulate the development of scenarios, a number of questions were posed, including:

- Is there a future for HRD?
- Is HRD valued?
- Will technology provide emancipation or demumanization in HRD?
- Will HRD service individual well-being or organization performance?
- Is virtual emotional intelligence a key talent differentiator?
- What is the role of the HRD function if greater individualism is seen as a reality that organizations will need to confront?

Based on such questions, a range of different answers are possible, such as:

- HRD seen as fundamental to organizations and society
- Technology dehumanizes the human in HRD
- ICT equalises and democratises access to learning
- HRD is overtaken by changes in society and technology
- HRD is intrinsically and extrinsically valued

Based on such responses, and others, a range of scenarios were produced. Here we can only give a brief overview of some of these. However, they do give a flavour of much that was held in common between the different voices in the conference.

Scenario 1

One scenario is based on optimism for HRD and the role that HRD professionals play in the organization. HRD is accepted as a key role alongside other professional areas such as Finance and Production Management. HRD makes a clear and obvious strategic contribution to business success in the ways envisaged by Garavan (2007), where they:

> negotiate appropriate HRD solutions that meet their professional requirements, address the needs of stakeholders, contribute to the process of change, sustain continuity and at the same time, facilitate the necessary flexibility to adjust and change where necessary (p.27).

In short, in the optimistic scenario for HRD, the value of learning and development is valued by everyone and is seen to provide a link between corporate objectives, individual activities and learning and development needs. Even in the absence of hard data to demonstrate the impact of HRD on the bottom line, HRD is seen as a foundation for business, and as a necessary and positive solution.

Allied to this view is the use of technology in HRD. Access is not dependent on wealth or position in society or in an organization. The price of technology is such that it can be afforded by all and technology provides the primary access to learning. There is also almost infinite flexibility in delivery modes and methods to make the choices even greater and available to all on an equal basis.

The different approaches to learning of the different generations are accommodated. For example, Generations 'Y', 'Z' and beyond with their 'hypertext mindset' are able to interact simultaneously across different platforms and with different people (Oblinger & Oblinger, 2005). In addition Generations 'Y', 'Z' and Me get extensive feedback, to fulfil their narcissistic need for external sources of affirmation.

Scenario 2

This scenario is more pessimistic, where HRD is only valued where it makes a direct and measurable contribution to social and organizational problems. It is dispersed. HRD happens informally in workplaces according to need more than through established professional HRD services and because such services are no longer valued. Part of the reason for the profession's decline is that the availability of HRD knowledge, which can be so easily and instantly obtained, becomes ubiquitous (Collins & Evans, 2007). HRD's decline in society has also meant a reversal for those involved in supporting the advance of the profession.

People can satisfy their learning needs from a variety of open sources but what is available is of uniform quality. The free market determines what is popular and in demand and so that process limits choice. Further, because competition and piracy have become embedded and intellectual property cannot be defended, quality is compromised in order to hold down prices. The effect is that learning becomes homogenous.

One the key features of technology is that within organization contexts, and perhaps also within education, the surveillance functions of ICT become as important as their learning support functions. This is partly associated with the trend of metrics, where ICT is used to monitor, measure and control learning.

Scenario 3

This scenario offers something different to both optimism and pessimism. While a distinct HRD profession may be in decline, learning and development are widely valued but the value is dispersed into communities and virtual worlds created online and in the clouds, which are seen as safer ways of communicating and socialising with others (Brown, 2011). Learning itself takes place through the interchange of ideas via a variety of online media including forums, discussion groups and Skype. As knowledge workers, sharing learning with others through information media becomes an important element of personal identity and the creation of their individual brand. So we can now talk about a knowledge worker's e-social reputation. Where HRD roles do survive it is because they have adapted to the growth in technology, into a role not characterized as experts of learning and development but what is termed as 'work solution partners' (Yoon & Lim, 2010, p.715) and which also play a key part in the transformation of organizations.

One difficulty, however, is that virtual environments can make it more difficult to identify and nurture talent and informal learning can be hidden or become less visible (Spreitzer, 2008). On the upside is the creativity and learning that is evident from the growth of networks, whether social or virtual, and the interweaving of the social as well as the world of work. Networks rely on self-management, self and peer learning, and are focused on developing a portfolio and reputation rather than gaining credentials and qualifications. Learning is gained through experience and practices, through the sharing of knowledge and opportunities through 'thick' networks (Broadbent, 2003), information networks, co-working spaces and ideas. Some of these networks will be closed to HRD professionals but with the right skills HRD can play a new role of creative brokerage between networks (Burt, 2004). As they play such roles HRD professionals can also set up new relationships with emerging areas of expertise which lead to the creation of hybrid roles such Techno-HRD or Bio-HRD.

Summary

As we have identified in this chapter, scenarios are not predictions. However, they can be the source of strategic and creative conversations (van der Heijden, 2004). Crucially, in such a process, they also become the source of learning for the present and the future. We must remind ourselves, especially at a time of difficulty for many people in the UK, Europe and everywhere else, that while trends can set the direction of the future, there is still so much that can be made through joint action. We have to see HRD as a vital part of this process and, while we cannot be precious about names and titles, we know that in whatever form, HRD will continue to make progress. Throughout this book, HRD as a field of research and practice has come a long way in a relatively short period of time. There are some clear trends emerging that provide good opportunities for creating and adding value to a broad range of stakeholders at all levels of activity. We firmly believe that this can be achieved and we very much hope that we have enrolled you in this process. In the midst of a great deal of uncertainty, difficulty and change in the world, what better response can there be but an exploration of learning and a critical examination of our assumptions for our future lives together.

Good luck to you all.

references

Antonacopoulou, E.P. (2010) Making the business school more 'critical': reflexive critique based on phronesis as a foundation for impact. *British Journal of Management,* **21**(s1): s6–s25.

Bell, Wendell (1997) *Foundations Of Future Studies* (Volume 1). New Brunswick, NJ: Transaction Publishers.

BIS (2011) *Skills for Sustainable Growth*, available at https://www.gov.uk/government/uploads/system/uploads/attachment_data/file/32368/10–1274-skills-for-sustainable-growth-strategy.pdf, accessed 1 April 2012.

Bolden, R. and Gosling, J. (2006) Leadership competencies: time to change the tune? *Leadership,* **2**(2): 147–63.

Broadbent, J. (2003) Movement in context: Thick networks and Japanese environmental protest (pp.204–229). In M. Diani and D. McAdam (eds) *Social Movements and Networks*. Oxford: Oxford University Press.

Brown, A. (2011) Relationships, community, and identity in the new virtual society. *Futurist,* **45**(2): 29–34.

Buckley, R. and Caple, J. (2007) *The Theory and Practice of Training*. London: Kogan Page.

Burke, L.A. and Saks, A.M. (2009) Accountability in training transfer: adapting Schlenker's model of responsibility to a persistent but solvable problem. *Human Resource Development Review,* **8**(3): 382–402.

Burt, R. S. (2004) Structural holes and good ideas. *American Journal of Sociology,* **110**: 349–99.

Camps, J. and Luna-Arocas, R. (2012) A matter of learning: how human resources affect organizational performance. *British Journal of Management,* **23**(1): 1–21.

Castells, M. (2010) *The Information Age: Economy, Society and Culture, Volume 1: The Rise of the Network Society*, 2nd edn. London: Blackwell.

CIPD (2006) *HR and Technology: Beyond Delivery*. London: Chartered Institute of Personnel and Development.

CIPD (2012) *Learning and Talent Development Survey*. London: Chartered Institute of Personnel and Development.

Chiaburu, D. and Tekleab, A. (2005) Individual and contextual influences on multiple dimensions of training effectiveness. *Journal of European Industrial Training,* **29**(8):604–26.

Cilliers, P. (1998) *Complexity and Postmodernism*. London: Routledge.

Collins, H. M. and Evans, R. (2007) *Rethinking Expertise*. Chicago: University of Chicago Press.

Colwill, M., Johnson, N., Kelsey, S., Shire, J., Clegg, J., Jones, O., Rix, M. and Gold, J. (2012) *Working Towards Increasing ROI from Learning: A Transfer of Learning Project*. Paper presented at the European HRD Conference, May, Portugal.

Dator, J. (2003) *Future Studies and Sustainable Community Development*, available at http://www.futures.hawaii.edu/publications/futures-studies/FSAndFuturistAttributes1993.pdf, accessed 12 June 2012.

De Geus, A. (1988) Planning as learning. *Harvard Business Review,* **66**(2): 70–4.

Dewey, J. and Carter, T. (2003) Exploring the future of HRD: the first future search conference for a profession. *Advances in Developing Human Resources,* **5**(3): 245–56.

Eckstrand, G. A. (1964) *Current Status of the Technology of Training*. Ohio: Aerospace Medical Research Labs.

Elliott, C. and Turnbull, S. (eds) (2005) *Critical Thinking in HRD*. Routledge, London.

Evans, L. (2008) Professionalism, professionality and the development of education professionals. *British Journal of Educational Studies,* **56**(1): 20–38.

Freidson, E. (2001) *Professionalism*. Cambridge: Polity Press.

Garavan, T. (2007) A strategic perspective on human resource development. *Advances in Developing Human Resources*, **9**(1): 11–30.

Gibbons, M., Limoges, C., Nowotny, H., Schwartzman, S., Scott, P. and Trow, M. (1994) *The New Production of Knowledge*. London: Sage.

Gold, J. Rodgers, H. and Smith, V. (2003) What is the future for human resource development professionals? A UK perspective. *Human Resource Development International*, **6**(4): 437–56.

Gold, J., Walton, J., Cureton, P. and Anderson, L. (2011) Theorising and practitioners in HRD: the role of abductive reasoning. *Journal of European Industrial Training*, **35**(3): 230–46.

Gordon, A. (2009) *Future Savvy*. New York: AMACOM.

Gray, D., Iles, P. and Watson, S. (2011) Spanning the HRD academic-practitioner divide: bridging the gap through mode 2 research. *Journal of European Industrial Training*, **35**(3): 247–63.

Grossman, R. and Salas, E. (2011) The transfer of training: what really matters *International Journal of Training and Development*, **15**(2): 103–20.

Grugulis, I. (2003) The contribution of national vocational qualifications to the growth of skills in the UK. *British Journal of Industrial Relations*, **41**(3): 457–75.

Hopper, A. and Rice, A. (2008) Computing for the future of the planet. In *Philosophical Transactions Of the Royal Society: Mathematical, Physical & Engineering Sciences*, **366**(1881): 3685–97.

Iles, P., Chuai, X. and Preece, D. (2010) Talent management in multinational companies in Beijing: definitions, differences and drivers *Journal of World Business*, **45**(2): 179–89.

Kirkpatrick, D. L. (1983) Four steps to measuring training effectiveness. *Personnel Administrator*, **28**(11): 19–25.

Latham, G. P. (2007) *Work Motivation: History, Theory, Research And Practice*. Thousand Oaks, CA: Sage.

Lee, M. (2001) HRD: a refusal to define HRD. *Human Resource Development International*, **4**(3): 327–41.

Lynham, S. (2002) The general method of applied theory building research. *Advances in Developing Human Resources*, **4**(3): 221–41.

McGoldrick, J. and Stewart, J. (1996) The HRM–HRD nexus. In J. Stewart and J. McGoldrick (eds) *HRD: Perspectives, Strategies and Practice*. London: Pitman.

Mankin, D.P. (2001) A model for human resource development. *Human Resource Development International*, **4**(1): 65–85.

Oblinger, D. and Oblinger, J. (eds) (2005) *Educating the Net Generation*. Educause, available at: www.educause.edu/Resources/EducatingtheNetGeneration/IsItAgeorIT FirstStepsTowardUnd/6058, accessed 18 March 2012.

Peirce, C.S. (1903) *Harvard Lectures on Pragmatism*, CP 5:171–72.

PIU (Performance and Innovation Unit) (2001) *Benchmarking UK Strategic Futures Work*. London: PIU.

Poell, R.F. (2007) W(h)ither HRD? Towards a self-conscious, self-critical, and open-minded discipline. *Human Resource Development International*, **10**(4): 361–63.

Rae, L. (2002) *Assessing The Value Of Your Training*. Burlington, VT: Gower.

Randell, D. (2009) Exploring and learning from the future: five steps for avoiding strategic surprises. *Strategy & Leadership*, **37**(2): 27–31.

Revans, R. (1982) *The Origins and Growth of Action Learning*. Bromley: Chartwell-Bratt.

Rigg, C., Stewart, J. and Trehan, K. (eds) (2007) *Critical Human Resource Development*. Harlow: FT/Prentice Hall.

Ringland, G. (1998) *Scenario Planning*. Chichester: Wiley.

Rogers, M. and Tough, A. (1996) Facing the future is not for wimps. *Futures*, **28**(5): 491–96.

Ruona, W., Lynham, S. and Chermack, T. (2003) Insights on emerging trends and the future of human resource development. *Advances in Developing Human Resources*, **5**(3): 272–82.

Ryan, P. and Unwin, L. (2001) Apprenticeship in the British 'Training Market'. *National Institute Economic Review*, **178**: 99–114.

Scurry, T. and Blenkinsopp, J. (2011) Under-employment among recent graduates: a review of the literature. *Personnel Review*, **40**(5): 643–59.

SIRC (2009) *Generation Recession*. Oxford: Social Issues Research Centre.

Slaughter, R. (1999) Professional standards in futures work. *Futures*, **31**: 835–51.

Spreitzer, G.M. (2008) Leadership development in the virtual workplace (pp.71–86). In Murphy, S.E and Riggio, R.E (eds) *The Future of Leadership Development*. New Jersey: Lawrence Erlbaum Associates, Inc.

Stacey, R.D. (1992) *Managing the Unknowable: Strategic Boundaries between Order and Chaos in Organizations*. San Francisco, CA: Jossey-Bass.

Stacey, R.D. (2002) *Strategic Management and Organizational Dynamics: The Challenge of Complexity*. London: FT/Prentice Hall.

Starkey, K. and Madan, P. (2001) Bridging the relevance gap: Aligning stakeholders in the future of management research. *British Journal of Management*, **12**(1): 3–26.

Stewart, J. (2005) The current state and status of HRD research. *The Learning Organization*, **12**(1): 90–5.

Stewart, J. and Gold, J. (2011) Guest editorial. *Journal of European Industrial Training*, **35**(3): 196–98.

Stewart, J. and Tansley, C. (2002) *Training in the Knowledge-based Economy*. London: CIPD.

Tjepkema, S., Stewart, J., Sambrook, S. et al. (2002) *HRD and Learning Organisations in Europe*. London: Routledge.

Torraco, R.J. (2008) The future of human resource development. *Human Resource Development Review*, **7**(4): 371–73.

Twenge, J.M., Konrath, S., Foster, J.D., Campbell, W.K. and Bushman, B.J. (2008) Egos inflating over time: A cross-temporal meta-analysis of the Narcissistic Personality Inventory. *Journal of Personality,* **76:** 875–901.

Ulrich, D. (2007) Dreams: where human resource development is headed to deliver value. *Human Resource Development Quarterly,* **18**(1): 1–8.

van der Heijden, K. (2004) *Scenarios: The Art of Strategic Conversation.* London: Wiley.

Vickerstaffe, S (2007) I was just a boy around the place: What made apprenticeships successful? *Journal of Vocational Education and Training,* **59**(3): 31–347.

Vilemetter (2011) *Talent Forward Series*. London: Chartered Institute of Personnel and Development.

Weisbord, M. and Janoff, S. (2000) *Future Search*, 2nd edn. San Francisco: Berrett-Koehler.

Wolf, A. (2011) *Review of Vocational Education.* London: Department of Education.

Yoon, W.S. and Lim, H.D. (2010) Systemizing virtual learning and technologies by managing organizational competency and talents. *Advances in Developing Human Resources,* **12**(6): 715–27.

Index